Contemporary Project Management

ORGANIZE / PLAN / PERFORM

SECOND EDITION

TIMOTHY J. KLOPPENBORG

Xavier University

SOUTH-WESTERN
CENGAGE Learning

Australia • Brazil • Japan • Korea • Mexico • Singapore • Spain • United Kingdom • United States

SOUTH-WESTERN
CENGAGE Learning

**Contemporary Project Management:
Organize / Plan / Perform,
Second Edition**
Timothy J. Kloppenborg

Vice President/Editorial Director:
Jack W. Calhoun

Senior Acquisition Editor:
Charles McCormick Jr.

Developmental Editor: Elizabeth Lowry

Marketing Manager: Adam MarshSenior

Marketing Communications Manager:
Libby Shipp

Production Manager: Jean Buttrom

Senior Rights Acquisitions
Specialist-Text/Image: John Hill

Manufacturing Buyer: Miranda Klapper

Senior Art Director: Stacy Shirley

Content Project Management:
PreMediaGlobal

Production House/Compositor:
PreMediaGlobal

Cover Designer: Lou Ann Thesing

Cover Image: © Shutterstock LLC/Mariola
Kraczowska

For product information and technology assistance, contact us at
Cengage Learning Customer & Sales Support, 1-800-354-9706

For permission to use material from this text or product,
submit all requests online at **cengage.com/permissions**
Further permissions questions can be emailed to
permissionrequest@cengage.com.

Library of Congress Control Number: 2010936992

ISBN-13: 978-0-538-47702-4

ISBN-10: 0-538-47702-4

South-Western
5191 Natorp Blvd
Mason, OH 45040
USA

Cengage Learning is a leading provider of customized learning solutions with office locations around the globe, including Singapore, the United Kingdom, Australia, Mexico, Brazil, and Japan. Locate your local office at **www.cengage.com/global.**

Cengage Learning products are represented in Canada by Nelson Education, Ltd.

For your course and learning solutions, visit **www.cengage.com.**

Purchase any of our products at your local college store or at our preferred online store **www.cengagebrain.com.**

Printed in the United States of America
1 2 3 4 5 6 7 15 14 13 12 11

To my wife Bet and our children Kate and Nick

Brief Contents

Preface   xv
About the Author   xxi

PART **1**	**Organizing Projects**
1	Introduction to Project Management 2
2	Project Selection and Prioritization 26
3	Organizational Capability: Structure, Culture, and Roles 52
4	Chartering Projects 82

PART **2**	**Planning Projects**
5	Stakeholder Analysis and Communication Planning 112
6	Scope Planning 140
7	Scheduling Projects 168
8	Resourcing Projects 206
9	Budgeting Projects 242
10	Project Risk Planning 266
11	Project Quality Planning and Project Kick-off 290

PART **3**	**Performing Projects**
12	Project Supply Chain Management 324
13	Leading and Managing Project Teams 350
14	Determining Project Progress and Results 384
15	Finishing the Project and Realizing the Benefits 422

Appendix A   *PMBOK® Guide* Area   439
Appendix B   Strengths Themes as Used in Project Management   441
Glossary Terms from the *PMBOK® Guide*   443
Index   451

Contents

Preface xv
About the Author xxi

PART 1   Organizing Projects

CHAPTER **1**
Introduction to Project Management 2

1.1 What Is a Project?   4

1.2 History of Project Management   4

1.3 How Can Project Work Be Described?   5
    Projects versus Operations 5 / Soft Skills and Hard Skills 5 / Authority and
        Responsibility 6 / Project Life Cycle 6

1.4 Understanding Projects   7
    Project Management Institute 7 / Project Management Body of Knowledge (PMBOK®) 8 /
        Selecting and Prioritizing Projects 9 / Project Goals and Constraints 9 / Defining
        Project Success and Failure 10 / Using Microsoft Project to Help Plan and Measure
        Projects 11 / Types of Projects 11 / Scalability of Project Tools 13

1.5 Project Roles   14
    Project Executive–Level Roles 14 / Project Management–Level Roles 14 / Project
        Associate–Level Roles 15

1.6 Overview of the Book   15
    Part 1—Organizing Projects 15 / Part 2—Planning Projects 16 / Part 3—Performing
        Projects 18

    Summary   19

    Chapter Review Questions   20

    Discussion Questions   21

    PMBOK® Guide **Questions**   21

    Example Project   22

    Project Management *in Action*: Selecting a Training Project at Skyline Chili   24

CHAPTER **2**
Project Selection and Prioritization 26

2.1 Strategic Planning Process   28
    Strategic Analysis 28 / Guiding Principles 28 / Strategic Objectives 31 / Flow-Down
        Objectives 31

2.2 Portfolio Alignment   31
    Portfolios 32 / Programs 32 / Projects and Subprojects 33 / Assessing an
        Organization's Ability to Perform Projects 35 / Identifying Potential Projects 35 /
        Methods for Selecting Projects 36 / Using a Financial Model to Select Projects 37 /
        Using a Scoring Model to Select Projects 38 / Prioritizing Projects 40

2.3 Securing Projects   42
    Identify Potential Project Opportunities 42 / Determine Which Opportunities to
        Pursue 42 / Prepare and Submit a Project Proposal 43 / Negotiate to Secure the
        Project 43

Summary 43

Chapter Review Questions 44

Discussion Questions 45

PMBOK® Guide **Questions** 45

Exercises 45

Example Project 46

Project Management *in Action:* Prioritizing Projects at D. D. Williamson 48

CHAPTER **3**

Organizational Capability: Structure, Culture, and Roles 52

3.1 Types of Organizational Structures 54
Functional 54 / Projectized 55 / Matrix 56

3.2 Organizational Culture and Its Impact on Projects 59
Culture of the Parent Organization 60 / Culture of the Project 61

3.3 Project Life Cycles 62
Define-Measure-Analyze-Improve-Control (DMAIC) Model 63 / Research and
Development (R&D) Project Life Cycle Model 63 / Construction Project Life Cycle
Model 63 / Information Systems (IS) Project Life Cycle Model 64 / Agile Project Life
Cycle Model 64

3.4 Project Executive Roles 65
Steering Team 65 / Sponsor 66 / Chief Projects Officer/Project Management Office 67

3.5 Project Management Roles 68
Functional Manager 68 / Project Manager 68 / Facilitator 71 / Customer 72

3.6 Project Team Roles 74
Core Team Members 74 / Subject Matter Experts 75 / Fitting People into Project
Roles 75

Summary 75

Chapter Review Questions 76

Discussion Questions 77

PMBOK® Guide **Questions** 77

Exercises 77

Example Project 77

Project Management *in Action:* Project Leadership Roles at TriHealth 80

CHAPTER **4**

Chartering Projects 82

4.1 What Is a Project Charter? 84

4.2 Why Is a Project Charter Used? 84

4.3 When Is a Charter Needed? 85

4.4 Typical Elements in a Project Charter 85
Title 87 / Scope Overview 87 / Business Case 88 / Background 88 / Milestone
Schedule with Acceptance Criteria 88 / Risks, Assumptions, and Constraints 89 /
Spending Approvals or Budget Estimates 90 / Stakeholder List 90 / Team Operating
Principles 90 / Lessons Learned 90 / Signatures and Commitment 91

4.5 Constructing a Project Charter 91
Scope Overview and Business Case Instructions 91 / Background Instructions 91 /
Milestone Schedule with Acceptance Criteria Instructions 91 / Risks, Assumptions, and
Constraints Instructions 94 / Spending Approvals or Budget Estimates Instructions 96 /

Stakeholder List Instructions   97 / Team Operating Principles Instructions   97 /
Lessons Learned Instructions   98 / Signatures and Commitment Instructions   98

4.6 Ratifying the Project Charter   99

4.7 Starting a Project using Microsoft Project   99
MS Project 2010 Introduction   99 / Initialize Microsoft Project for General Use   101 /
Initialize a Project   101 / Construct a Milestone Schedule   103

Summary   104

Chapter Review Questions   105

Discussion Questions   105

***PMBOK® Guide* Questions**   105

Exercises   106

Example Project   106

Project Management *in Action*: Information Systems Enhancement Project Charter   107

PART **2**   Planning Projects

CHAPTER **5**
Stakeholder Analysis and Communication Planning 112

5.1 Develop the Project Management Plan   114

5.2 Understand Stakeholders   116
Identify Stakeholders   116 / Prioritize Stakeholders   117

5.3 Build Relationships   120
Relationship Building within the Core Team   121 / Relationship Building with All Other
Stakeholders   122

5.4 Plan Communications   122
Purposes of a Project Communications Plan   122 / Communications Plan
Considerations   123 / Communications Matrix   124 / Knowledge Management   125

5.5 Project Meeting Management   126
Improving Project Meetings   126 / Issues Management   127

5.6 Communications Needs of Global and Virtual Project Teams   130
Virtual Teams   130 / Cultural Differences   130 / Countries and Project Communication
Preferences   131

5.7 Communications Technologies   131
Current Technology Types   132

Summary   134

Chapter Review Questions   135

Discussion Questions   136

***PMBOK® Guide* Questions**   136

Example Project   136

Project Management *in Action*: Using Appreciative Inquiry to Understand Stakeholders   138

CHAPTER **6**
Scope Planning 140

6.1 Introduction to Scope Planning   142

6.2 Collect Requirements   143
Gather Stakeholder Input   143

6.3 Define Scope   145
Reasons to Define Scope   145   /   How to Define Scope   145

6.4 Work Breakdown Structure (WBS)   146
What Is the WBS? 146   /   Why Use a WBS?   147   /   WBS Formats   148   /   Work Packages   150   /   How to Construct a WBS   151

6.5 Establish Change Control   154

6.6 Using MS Project for Work Breakdown Structures (WBS)   158
Set Up the WBS   158

Summary   162

Chapter Review Questions   163

Discussion Questions   163

Exercises   163

***PMBOK® Guide* Questions**   163

Example Project   164

Project Management *in Action*: Development of Inventory System Project   166

CHAPTER **7**
Scheduling Projects   168

7.1 Introduction to Project Time Management   170

7.2 Purposes of a Project Schedule   171

7.3 Historical Development of Project Schedules   171

7.4 How Project Schedules Are Limited and Created   173

7.5 Define Activities   174

7.6 Sequence Activities   176
Leads and Lags   178   /   Alternative Dependencies   179

7.7 Estimate Activity Duration   180
Problems and Remedies in Duration Estimating   181   /   Learning Curves   181

7.8 Develop Project Schedules   183
Two-Pass Method   184   /   Enumeration Method   187

7.9 Uncertainty in Project Schedules   188
Program Evaluation and Review Technique   188
Monte Carlo Simulation   190

7.10 Show the Project Schedule on a Gantt Chart   192

7.11 Using Microsoft Project for Critical Path Schedules   193
Set Up The Project Schedule   193   /   Build the Logical Network Diagram   197   /   Understand the Critical Path   199   /   Display and Print Schedules with MS Project   199

Summary   200

Chapter Review Questions   201

Discussion Questions   201

Exercises   201

***PMBOK® Guide* Questions**   202

Example Project   203

Project Management *in Action*: Project Schedule Emphasizing Critical Path Activities   205

CHAPTER **8**
Resourcing Projects   206

8.1 Abilities Needed when Resourcing Projects   208

The Science and Art of Resourcing Projects 208 / Considerations when Resourcing Projects 209 / Activity- versus Resource-Dominated Schedules 209

8.2 Estimate Resource Needs 210

8.3 Create a Staffing Management Plan 210

Identify Potential Resources 210 / Determine Resource Availability 211 / Decide Timing Issues when Resourcing Projects 212

8.4 Project Team Composition Issues 213

Cross-Functional Teams 213 / Co-Located Teams 214 / Virtual Teams 214 / Outsourcing 214

8.5 Assign a Resource to Each Activity 214

Show Resource Responsibilities on RACI Chart 215 / Show Resource Assignments on Gantt Chart 216 / Summarize Resource Responsibilities by Time Period with Histogram 216

8.6 Dealing with Resource Overloads 217

Methods of Resolving Resource Overloads 218

8.7 Compress the Project Schedule 220

Actions to Reduce the Critical Path 220 / Crashing 221 / Fast Tracking 224

8.8 Alternative Scheduling Methods 225

Critical Chain Project Management (CCPM) 226 / Reverse Phase Schedules 227 / Agile Project Planning 227 / Auto/Manual Scheduling 227 / Rolling Wave Planning 228

8.9 Using MS Project for Resource Allocation 228

Step 1: Defining Resources 228 / Step 2: Assigning Resources 229 / Step 3: Finding Overallocated Resources 232 / Step 4: Dealing with Overallocations 233

Summary 235

Chapter Review Questions 235

Discussion Questions 236

Exercises 236

PMBOK® Guide **Questions** 237

Example Project 237

Project Management *in Action*: Managing Software Development with Agile Methods and Scrum 239

CHAPTER **9**

Budgeting Projects 242

9.1 Introduction to Project Budgeting 244

9.2 Estimate Cost 244

Types of Cost 245 / Accuracy and Timing of Cost Estimates 248 / Methods of Estimating Costs 249 / Project Cost Estimating Issues 251

9.3 Determine Budget 254

Aggregating Costs 255 / Analyzing Reserve Needs 256 / Determining Cash Flow 257

9.4 Establishing Cost Control 257

9.5 Using MS Project for Project Budgets 258

Develop Bottom-Up Project Budget 258 / Develop Summary Project Budget 259

Summary 260

Chapter Review Questions 261

Discussion Questions 261

Exercises 262

PMBOK® Guide **Questions** 262

Example Project 262

Project Management *in Action*: The Value of Budget Optimization 264

CHAPTER **10**

Project Risk Planning 266

10.1 Plan Risk Management   268
Roles and Responsibilities   270 / Categories and Definitions   270

10.2 Identify Risks   272
Information Gathering   272 / Reviews   274 / Understanding Relationships   275 / Risk Register   275

10.3 Risk Analysis   276
Perform Qualitative Risk Analysis   276 / Perform Quantitative Risk Analysis   279 / Risk Register Updates   279

10.4 Plan Risk Responses   279
Strategies for Responding to Risks   280 / Risk Register Updates   283

Summary   283

Chapter Review Questions   283

Discussion Questions   284

Exercises   284

PMBOK® Guide **Questions**   285

Example Project   285

Project Management *in Action*: Risk Management on a Satellite Development Project   288

CHAPTER **11**

Project Quality Planning and Project Kick-off 290

11.1 Development of Contemporary Quality Concepts   293
Quality Gurus   293 / Total Quality Management/Malcolm Baldrige   293 / ISO 9001:2008   295 / Six Sigma   295

11.2 Core Project Quality Concepts   296
Stakeholder Satisfaction   298 / Process Management   299 / Fact-Based Management   302 / Empowered Performance   303 / Summary of Core Concepts   305

11.3 Project Quality Management Plan   306
Quality Policy   306 / Quality Baseline   307 / Quality Assurance   308 / Quality Control   309

11.4 Project Quality Tools   309

11.5 Complete Project Management Plan   309
Resolve Conflicts   309 / Establish Configuration Management   311 / Apply Sanity Tests to All Project Plans   312

11.6 Kick Off Project   312
Preconditions to Meeting Success   312 / Meeting Activities   313

11.7 Baseline and Communicate Project Management Plan   314

11.8 Using MS Project for Project Baselines   314
Baseline the Project Plan   314 / First Time Baseline   315 / Subsequent Baselines   315

Summary   316

Chapter Review Questions   317

Discussion Questions   317

Exercises   318

PMBOK® Guide **Questions**   318

Example Project   319

Project Management *in Action*: Affinity and Relationship Diagrams for Project Kick-off   321

PART **3**   Performing Projects

CHAPTER **12**

Project Supply Chain Management 324

12.1 Introduction to Project Supply Chain Management   326
SCM Components   328 / SCM Factors   328 / SCM Decisions   328 / Project
Procurement Management Processes   329

12.2 Plan Procurements   329
Outputs of Planning   329 / Make or Buy Decisions   330

12.3 Conduct Procurements   331
Sources for Potential Suppliers   332 / Information for Potential Suppliers   332 /
Approaches Used When Evaluating Prospective Suppliers   332 / Supplier Selection   334

12.4 Contract Types   336
Fixed-Price Contracts   336 / Cost-Reimbursable Contracts   337 / Time and Material
(T&M) Contracts   337

12.5 Administer Procurements   338

12.6 Improving Project Supply Chains   338
Project Partnering and Collaboration   338 / Third Parties   342 / Lean Purchasing   343 /
Sourcing   343 / Logistics   343 / Information   343

Summary   344

Chapter Review Questions   344

Discussion Questions   345

PMBOK® Guide Questions   345

Exercises   346

Example Project   346

**Project Management *in Action*: Implications for Project Management
in a Networked Organization Model**   348

CHAPTER **13**

Leading and Managing Project Teams 350

13.1 Acquiring the Project Team   353
Preassignment of Project Team Members   353 / Negotiation for Project Team
Members   353 / On-Boarding Project Team Members   354

13.2 Developing the Project Team   355
Stages of Project Team Development   355 / Characteristics of High-Performing Project
Teams   357 / Assessing Individual Member Capability   359 / Assessing Project Team
Capability   360 / Building Individual and Project Team Capability   362 / Establishing
Project Team Ground Rules   364

13.3 Managing and Leading the Project Team   368
Project Manager Power and Leadership   368 / Assessing Performance of Individuals and
Project Teams   370 / Project Team Leadership and Management Outcomes   370

13.4 Managing Stakeholder Expectations   371

13.5 Managing Project Conflicts   373
Sources of Project Conflict   373 / Conflict Resolution Process and Styles   374 /
Negotiation   375

Summary   377

Chapter Review Questions 377

Discussion Questions 378

PMBOK® Guide **Questions** 379

Example Project 379

Project Management *in Action*: Centralizing Planning and Control in a Large Company After many Acquisitions 382

CHAPTER **14**

Determining Project Progress and Results 384

14.1 Project Balanced Scorecard Approach 386

14.2 Internal Project Issues 387
Direct and Manage Project Execution 387 / Monitor and Control Project Work 389 / Monitoring and Controlling Project Risk 391 / Distribute Information 392

14.3 Customer Issues 395
Perform Quality Assurance 395 / Perform Quality Control 396

14.4 Financial Issues 403
Control Scope 404 / Control Schedule and Costs 404 / Earned Value Management for Controlling Schedule and Costs 404

14.5 Using MS Project to Monitor and Control Projects 408
What Makes a Schedule Useful? 409 / How MS Project Recalculates the Schedule Based on Reported Actuals 409 / Current and Future Impacts of Time and Cost Variance 409 / Define the Performance Update Process 409 / Steps to Update the Project Schedule 410

14.6 Replanning if Necessary 414

Summary 415

Chapter Review Questions 416

Discussion Questions 416

PMBOK® Guide **Questions** 417

Exercises 417

Example Project 418

Project Management *in Action*: D. D. Williamson's Rules for Project Control 420

CHAPTER **15**

Finishing the Project and Realizing the Benefits 422

15.1 Verify Scope 424

15.2 Close Procurements 425
Terminate Projects Early 425

15.3 Close Project 427
Write Transition Plan 427 / Knowledge Management 428 / Create the Closeout Report 432

15.4 Post Project Activities 432
Reassign Workers 432 / Celebrate Success and Reward Participants 433 / Provide Ongoing Support 433 / Ensure Project Benefits Are Realized 433

15.5 Using MS Project for Project Closure 434

Summary 434

Chapter Review Questions 434

Discussion Questions 435

PMBOK® Guide Questions   435

Exercises   436

Example Project   436

Project Management *in Action*: Transition Plan for Beech Acres Knowledge
Management Project   438

Appendix A *PMBOK® Guide* Area 439
Appendix B Strengths Themes as Used in Project Management 441
Glossary Terms from the *PMBOK® Guide* 443
Index 451

Preface

While project managers today still need to use many techniques that have stood the test of twenty to fifty years of time, they increasingly also need to understand the business need for a project, sort through multiple conflicting stakeholder demands, and know how to deal with rapid change, a myriad of communication issues, global and virtual project teams, modern approaches to quality improvement, and many other issues that are more challenging than in those of previous times.

Contemporary project management utilizes the tried-and-true project management techniques along with modern improvements such as the most current versions of Microsoft® Project Professional 2010 and the fourth edition of the *Guide to the Project Management Body of Knowledge (PMBOK® Guide)*. Contemporary project management also uses many tools and understandings that come from modern approaches to quality and communications, expanded role definitions, leadership principles, human strenghts, and many other sources. Contemporary project management is scalable, using simple versions of important techniques on small projects and more involved versions on more complex projects.

Organization of Topics

The book is divided into three major parts.

Part 1, Organizing and Initiating Projects, deals with both the environment in which projects are conducted and getting a project officially approved.

- *Chapter 1 introduces contemporary project management by first tracing the history of project management, then discussing what makes a project different from an ongoing operation. Various frameworks that help one understand projects—such as the PMBOK® Guide—are introduced, as well as the executive-, managerial-, and associate-level roles.*
- *Chapter 2 discusses how projects support and are an outgrowth of strategic planning, how a portfolio of projects is selected and prioritized, how a client company selects a contractor company to conduct a project, and how a contractor company secures project opportunities from client companies.*
- *Chapter 3 deals with organizational capability issues of structure, life cycle, culture, and roles. The choices parent organizations make in each of these provide both opportunities and limitations to how projects can be conducted.*
- *Chapter 4 presents project charters in a step-by-step fashion. Short, powerful charters help all key participants to develop a common understanding of all key project issues and components at a high level and then to formally commit to the project. Charters have become nearly universal in initiating projects in recent years. Microsoft® Project Professional 2010 is used to show milestone schedules within charters.*

Part 2, Planning Projects, deals with all aspects of project planning as defined in the *PMBOK® Guide*.

- *Chapter 5 introduces methods for understanding and prioritizing various stakeholder demands and for building constructive relationships with stakeholders. Since many projects are less successful than desired due to poor communications, detailed communication planning techniques are introduced along with meeting management.*

- *Chapter 6 helps students understand how to determine the amount of work the project entails. Specifically covered are methods for determining the scope of both the project work and outputs, the work breakdown structure (WBS) that is used to ensure nothing is left out, and how the WBS is portrayed using Microsoft® Project Professional 2010.*
- *Chapter 7 is the first scheduling chapter. It shows how to schedule activities by identifying, sequencing, and estimating the durations for each activity. Then critical-path project schedules are developed, methods are shown for dealing with uncertainty in time estimates, Gantt charts are introduced for easier communications, and Microsoft® Project Professional 2010 is used to automate the schedule development and communications.*
- *Chapter 8 is the second scheduling chapter. Once the critical path schedule is determined, staff management plans are developed, project team composition issues are considered, resources are assigned to activities, and resource overloads are identified and handled. Schedule compression techniques of crashing and fast tracking are demonstrated and multiple alternative scheduling techniques are introduced. Resource scheduling is demonstrated with Microsoft® Project Professional 2010.*
- *Chapter 9 deals with project budgeting. Estimating cost, budgeting cost, and establishing cost controls are demonstrated. Microsoft® Project Professional 2010 is used for developing both bottom-up and summary project budgets.*
- *Chapter 10 demonstrates project risk planning. It includes risk management planning, methods for identifying risks, establishing a risk register, analyzing risks for probability and impact, and deciding how to respond to each risk with contingency plans for major risks and awareness for minor risks.*
- *Chapter 11 starts by covering project quality planning. This includes explaining the development of modern quality concepts and how they distill into core project quality demands. Then the chapter covers how to develop a project quality plan and how to utilize the simple project quality tools. It then ties all of the planning chapters together with discussions of a project kick-off meeting, a baselined project plan, and the ways Microsoft® Project Professional 2010 can be used to establish and maintain the baseline.*

Part 3, Performing Projects, discusses the various aspects that must be managed simultaneously while the project is being conducted.

- *Chapter 12 deals with project supply chain management issues. Some of these issues, such as developing the procurement management plan and qualifying and selecting vendors, are planning issues, but for simplicity they are covered in one chapter with administer procurements and to improve the project supply chain.*
- *Chapter 13 deals with leading and managing both the project team and stakeholders. It includes acquiring and developing the project team, assessing both potential and performance of team members and the team as a whole, various types of power a project manager can use, and how to deal productively with project conflict.*
- *Chapter 14 is concerned with determining project results. This chapter starts with a balanced scorecard approach to controlling projects. Internal project issues covered include risk, change, and information. Quality is the customer issue. Financial issues are scope, cost and schedule, including how to use Microsoft® Project Professional 2010 for control.*
- *Chapter 15 deals with how to end a project—either early or on time. Included are verifying to ensure all scope is complete, formally closing procurements and the project, knowledge management, and ensuring the project participants are rewarded and the clients have the support they need to realize intended benefits when using the project deliverables.*

Distinctive Features

- *Student oriented, measurable learning objectives*—*Each chapter begins with a listing of the most important points students should learn and identifies the PMBOK® topics covered in the chapter. The chapter material, end-of-chapter questions and problems, PowerPoint® slides, and test questions have all been updated to correlate to specific objectives.*

- *PMBOK® Guide approach*—*All fourth edition PMBOK® Guide knowledge areas and processes are specifically included. All glossary definitions are from the PMBOK® Guide. The end of each chapter contains several PMBOK® Guide–type questions typical of what would be seen on PMP® and CAPM® exams. This consistency with the established standard gives students a significant leg up if they decide to become certified Project Management Professionals (PMPs®) or Certified Associates in Project Management (CAPMs®).*

- *Microsoft® Project Professional 2010 fully integrated into the fabric of eight chapters*—*In each case, the chapter material is introduced in a simple, practical manner. Then the techniques are demonstrated in a by-hand fashion. Finally, a demonstration of how to automate the techniques using Microsoft® Project Professional 2010 is shown in a step-by-step manner with numerous screen captures. On all screen captures, critical path activities are shown in contrasting color for emphasis.*

- *Actual project as learning vehicle*—*One section at the end of each chapter lists deliverables for students to create (in teams or individually) for a real project. These assignments have been refined over the last decade while working with the local PMI® chapter, which provides a panel of PMP® judges to evaluate projects from a practical point of view. Students are encouraged to keep clean copies of all deliverables so they can demonstrate their project skills in job interviews.*

- *Blend of classical and modern methods*—*Proven methods developed over the past half century are combined with exciting new methods that are emerging from both industry and research.*

- *Executive, managerial, and associate roles*—*This book covers the responsibilities of many individuals who can have an impact on projects so aspiring project managers can understand not only their own role, but also those of people with whom they need to deal.*

- *Balanced scorecard approach*—*Many factors are included in how project success is measured and how project results are determined. An adaptation of the balanced scorecard helps students understand how these fit together.*

- *Integrated example project*—*An example project has been developed to demonstrate many of the techniques throughout the book. That way students can see how the various project planning and control tools develop and work together.*

- *Templates*—*Electronic templates for many of the techniques are available at the CPM® website. These Microsoft Word and Excel documents can be downloaded and filled in for ease of student learning and for consistency of instructor grading.*

- *Human strengths*—*This book includes as Appendix B a list of human strengths as applied to project management. These strengths, derived from positive psychology and developed by Gallup, help a person understand how each individual naturally thinks, feels, and behaves. This knowledge is used in the "soft side" of project management.*

Distinctive Approach

This book covers the topics of contemporary project management. It was also developed using contemporary project management methods. For example, when considering the topic of dealing with multiple stakeholders, every chapter was reviewed by students, practitioners, and academics. This allowed student learning, practitioner realism, and academic research and teaching perspectives to be simultaneously considered.

The practical examples and practitioner reviewers came from many industries and from many sizes and types of projects to promote the scalability and universality of contemporary project management techniques.

Instructor and Student Support Materials

Instructor's Manual with Solutions

Prepared by Tim Kloppenborg and based on his years of experience facilitating the student learning experience in his own project management classes, the Instructor's Manual includes for each chapter an overview of learning objectives, detailed chapter outlines, teaching recommendations, and many detailed suggestions for implementing community-based projects into your project management class. Solutions are also provided for all of the end-of-chapter content. The Instructor's Manual is available on the Instructor's Resource CD-ROM and online.

Test Bank

Prepared for the second edition by Joyce D. Brown, PMP and Thomas F. McCabe, PMP of University of Connecticut, this comprehensive test bank builds upon the original test bank created by Kevin Grant of the University of Texas at San Antonio. The test bank is organized around each chapter's learning objectives. All test questions are consistent with the PMBOK. Every test item is labeled according to its difficulty level and the major topical heading within the textbook that it relates to, allowing instructors to quickly construct effective tests that emphasize the concepts most significant for their course. The Test Bank includes true/false, multiple choice, essay, and quantitative problems for each chapter. The Test Bank is available on the Instructor's Resource CD-ROM and online.

PowerPoint® Presentation

Prepared by Deborah Tesch of Xavier University, the PowerPoint® Presentation provides comprehensive coverage of each chapter's essential concepts in a clean, concise format. Key exhibits from the textbook are also included to enhance in-class illustration and discussion of important concepts. Instructors can easily customize the PowerPoint® Presentation to better fit the needs of their classroom. It is accessible on the Instructor's Resource CD-ROM and online.

Instructor's Resource CD-ROM

This CD-ROM includes the key instructor support materials—Instructor's Manual with Solutions, Test Bank, ExamView®, Data Set solutions, PowerPoint® Presentation, and key exhibits from the textbook in jpg format—providing instructors with a comprehensive capability for customizing their classroom experience. Microsoft® Project Professional 2010

Microsoft® Project Professional 2010 Student CD-ROM

New copies of *Contemporary Project Management* include a trial version of Microsoft® Project 2010 at no additional cost. The practical use of this key project management application is fully integrated into eight chapters of the textbook.

Website: www.cengage.com/decisionsciences/kloppenborg

This book's website contains all the materials included in the IRCD. Students can find the Student Data Sets CD-ROM containing Microsoft Excel® data used in the completion of select end-of-chapter problems and templates in Word and Excel for completing various project planning and control tools.

Acknowledgments

A book-writing project depends on many people. Through the last three decades of project work I have been privileged to learn from thousands of people including students, faculty members, co-trainers, co-consultants, co-judges, clients, research partners, and others. Hundreds of individuals who have provided help in research and developing teaching methods are members of the Southwest Ohio and Miami Valley chapters of the Project Management Institute and of the Cincinnati and Louisville sections of the Center for Quality of Management. Many individuals have provided wonderful examples. Those who wish to be acknowledged are named with their contributions.

I also want to acknowledge the wonderful help of various professionals at Cengage Learning. The two individuals there who have provided extensive help are Charles McCormick, Jr., Senior Acquisitions Editor, and Elizabeth Lowry, Developmental Editor.

Other individuals who have provided significant content are Lynn Frock, PMP®, of Lynn Frock and Company, who provided the Microsoft® Project material, Lifang Wu of Xavier University, who provided the supply chain management material, Debbie Tesch of Xavier University, who provided the PowerPoint® slides, Joyce D. Brown, PMP® and Thomas F. McCabe, PMP of University of Connecticut,who provided the test bank, Chris Bridges and Patrick Coffey of Xavier University who provided the Alternate Breaks integrated project example, and Kate Noel Kloppenborg of Saluda Schools who provided the PMBOK type questions

Reviewers include:

Carol Abbott
Fusion Alliance, Inc.

Vittal Anantatmula
Western Carolina University

Shari Bleure
Skyline Chili

John Cain
Viox Services

Steve Creason
Metropolitan State University

Jacob J. Dell
University of Texas at San Antonio

Scott Dellana
East Carolina University

Maling Ebrahimpour
Roger Williams University

Jeff Flynn
ILSCO Corporation

Jim Ford
University of Delaware

Lynn Frock
Lynn Frock & Company

Lei Fu
Hefei University of Technology

Kathleen Gallon
Christ Hospital

Kevin P. Grant
University of Texas San Antonio

Raye Guye
ILSCO Corporation

Sarai Hedges
University of Cincinnati

Marco Hernandez
Dantes Canadian

David L. Keeney
Stevens Institute of Technology

Anil B. Jambekar
Michigan Technological University

Dana M. Johnson, Ph.D
Michigan Technological University

Naomi Kinney
MultiLingual Learning Services

Paul Kling
Duke Energy

Kate Noel Kloppenborg
Saluda Schools

Matthew Korpusik
Six Sigma Black Belt

Young Hoon Kwak
George Washington University

Laurence J. Laning
Procter & Gamble

Dick Larkin
Central Washington University

Lydia Lavigne
Ball Aerospace

Claudia Levi
Edmonds Community College

John S. Loucks
St. Edward's University

Diane Lucas
Penn State University, DuBois Campus

Daniel S. Marrone
SUNY Farmingdale State College

Chris McCale
Regis University

Abe Meilich
Walden University

Bruce Miller
Xavier Leadership Center

William Moylan
Eastern Michigan University

Warren Opfer
Life Science Services International

Peerasit Patanakul
Stevens Institute of Technology

Joseph Petrick
Wright State University

Kenneth R. Pflieger
Potomac College

Chris Rawlings
Bob Jones University

Natalee Regal
Procter & Gamble

Pedro Reyes
Baylor University

Linda Ridlon
*Center for Quality of Management,
Division of GOAL/QPC*

Sheyrl R. Schoenacher
SUNY Farmingdale State College

Jan Sepate
Kimberly Clark

Patrick Sepate
Summitqwest Inc.

William R. Sherrard
San Diego State University

Kimberlee D. Snyder, Ph.D
Winona State University

Rachana Thariani
Atos-Origin

Guy Turner
Castellini Company

Jayashree Venkatraman
Microsoft Corporation

Timothy J. Kloppenborg

About the Author

Timothy J. Kloppenborg

Timothy J. Kloppenborg is Castellini Distinguished Professor of Management at Williams College of Business, Xavier University. He previously held faculty positions at the University of North Carolina at Charlotte and the Air Force Institute of Technology and as visiting professor at Southern Cross University. He has over eighty publications with over fifty different co-authors during his more than twenty-five years as a college professor. Previous books include *Project Leadership* and *Managing Project Quality*. His articles have appeared in *Project Management Journal, Journal of Management Education, Journal of General Management, SAM Advanced Management Journal, Information Systems Education Journal, Journal of Managerial Issues, Quality Progress, Management Research News, Journal of Small Business Strategy,* and others. Tim has been active with the Project Management Institute for over twenty-five years and has been a certified Project Management Professional (PMP®) since 1991. Dr. Kloppenborg is a retired U.S. Air Force Reserve officer, having served in numerous transportation, procurement, and quality assurance positions in his twenty-one-year military career. Dr. Kloppenborg has worked with well over 100 volunteer organizations, many directly and others through supervising student projects. He has hands-on and consulting project management experience in construction, information systems, research and development, and quality improvement projects in various industries. Tim is certified as both a Level 1 and Level 2 Strength Coach by Gallup Faith Division. He is currently president of Colleagues in Jesuit Business Education (CJBE) and serves on the board of International Association of Jesuit Business Schools (IAJBS). Dr. Kloppenborg has also developed and delivered various innovative corporate training, undergraduate, MBA, and executive MBA classes in project management, leadership, teamwork, and quality improvement, and he routinely teaches PMP® prep classes. He holds a BS in business administration from Benedictine College, an MBA from Western Illinois University, and a Ph.D in operations management from the University of Cincinnati.

Some of his clients include Atos-Origin, Center for Quality of Management, Cincinnati Children's Hospital Medical Center, D. D. Williamson, David J. Joseph Co., Duke Energy, Ernst and Young LLP, Executive Jet Management, Greater Cincinnati Water Works, Hillenbrand Industries, Honey Baked Ham, J & B Steel Erectors, The Kroger Company, Management Concepts, National Underground Railroad Freedom Center, New Zealand Qualifications Authority, Procter & Gamble, Robin Imaging Systems, Shepherd Color, Standard Textile, St. Elizabeth's Medical Center, Texas Children's Hospital, The Weather Channel, TriHealth, and U.S. Army 101st Airborne Division.

PART **1**

ORGANIZING PROJECTS

organize / plan / perform

Chapter 1
Introduction to Project Management

Chapter 2
Project Selection and Prioritization

Chapter 3
Organizational Capability: Structure, Culture, and Roles

Chapter 4
Chartering Projects

Introduction to Project Management

CHAPTER OBJECTIVES

After completing this chapter, you should be able to:

- Define a project in your own words using characteristics that are common to most projects and describe reasons why more organizations are using project management.

- Describe major activities and deliverables at each project life cycle stage.

- List and define the nine knowledge areas and five process groups of the project management body of knowledge (*PMBOK*®).

- Delineate measures of project success and failure and reasons for both.

- Identify project roles and distinguish key responsibilities for each.

Phil Boorman/Cultura/Jupiter Images

I have returned from a successful climb of Mt. Aconcagua in Argentina; at 22,841 feet, it is the highest peak in the world outside of the Himalayas. While there, seven other climbers died; we not only survived, but our experience was so positive that we have partnered to climb together again.

During the three decades that I've been climbing mountains, I've also been managing projects. An element has emerged as essential for success in both of these activities: the element of discipline. By discipline, I am referring to doing what I already know needs to be done. Without this attribute, even the most knowledgeable and experienced will have difficulty avoiding failure.

The deaths on Aconcagua are an extreme example of the consequences associated with a lack of discipline. The unfortunate climbers, who knew that the predicted storms would produce very hazardous conditions,

PMBOK®
GUIDE TOPICS

- Project management framework introduction
- Project life cycle
- Stakeholders
- Project management processes

decided to attempt the summit instead of waiting. They did not have the discipline that we demonstrated to act on our earlier decision to curtail summit attempts after the agreed-to turn-around time or in severe weather.

I've experienced similar circumstances in project management. Often I have found myself under pressure to cast aside or shortcut project management practices that I have come to rely on. For me, these practices have become the pillars of my own project management discipline. One of these pillars, planning, seems to be particularly susceptible to challenge. Managing projects at the Central Intelligence Agency for three decades, I adjusted to the annual cycle for obtaining funding. This cycle occasionally involved being given relatively short notice near the end of the year that funds unspent by some other department were up for grabs to whoever could quickly make a convincing business case. While some may interpret this as a circumstance requiring shortcutting the necessary amount of planning in order to capture some of the briefly available funds, I understood that my discipline required me to find a way to do the needed planning and to act quickly. I understood that to do otherwise would likely propel me toward becoming one of the two-thirds of the projects identified by the Standish Group in their 2009 CHAOS report as not successful. I understood that the top 2 percent of project managers, referred to as Alpha Project Managers in a 2006 book of the same name, spend twice as much time planning as the other 98 percent of project managers. The approach that I took allowed me to maintain the discipline for my planning pillar. I preplanned a couple of projects and had them ready at the end of the year to be submitted should a momentary funding opportunity arise.

A key to success in project management, as well as in mountain climbing, is to identify the pillars that will be practiced with discipline. This book offers an excellent set of project management methods from which we can identify those pillars that we will decide to practice with the required levels of discipline. I believe that project management is about applying common sense with uncommon discipline.

Michael O'Brochta, PMP, founder of Zozer Inc. and previously senior project manager
at the Central Intelligence Agency

1.1 What Is a Project?

Frequently, a business is faced with making a change, such as improving an existing work process, constructing a building, installing a new computer system, merging with another company, moving to a new location, developing a new product, entering a new market, and so on. These changes are best planned and managed as projects. So, what is a project?

A **project** is "a temporary endeavor undertaken to create a unique product, service, or result."[1] A project requires an organized set of work efforts that are planned in a level of detail that is progressively elaborated upon as more information is discovered. Projects are subject to limitations of time and resources such as money and people. Projects should follow a planned and organized approach with a defined beginning and ending. Project plans and goals become more specific as early work is completed. The output often is a collection of a primary deliverable along with supporting deliverables such as a house as the primary deliverable and warrantees and instructions for use as supporting deliverables. Each project typically has a unique combination of **stakeholders**—"persons or organizations … that are actively involved in the project, or whose interests may be positively or negatively affected by execution or completion of the project. A stakeholder may also exert influence over the project and its deliverables."[2] Projects often require a variety of people to work together for a limited time and each needs to understand that completing the project will require effort in addition to their other assigned work.

Project management is "the application of knowledge, skills, tools and techniques to project activities to meet project requirements."[3] This includes work processes that initiate, plan, execute, control, and close work. During these processes, tradeoffs must be made among the following factors:

- Scope (size)
- Quality (acceptability of the results)
- Cost
- Schedule

When project managers successfully make these tradeoffs, the project results meet the agreed upon requirements, are useful to the customers, and promote the organization. Project management includes both administrative tasks for planning, documenting, and controlling work and leadership tasks for visioning, motivating, and promoting work associates. Project management knowledge, skills, and methods can be applied and modified for most projects regardless of size or application.

1.2 History of Project Management

Projects of all sizes have been undertaken throughout history. Early construction projects included the ancient pyramids, medieval cathedrals, and Indian cities and pueblos. Other large early projects involved waging wars and building empires. In the development of the United States, projects included laying railroads, developing farms, and building cities. Many smaller projects have consisted of building houses and starting businesses. Throughout most of history, projects were conducted, but there was very little systematic planning and control. Some early projects were accomplished at great human and financial cost. Others took exceedingly long periods of time to complete.

Project management eventually emerged as a formal discipline to be studied and practiced. In the 1950s and 1960s, techniques for planning and controlling schedules and costs were developed, primarily on huge aerospace and construction projects. During this time, project management primarily involved determining project schedules based on understanding the order in which work activities must be completed. Many large manufacturing, research and development, government, and construction projects used and refined management techniques. In the 1980s and 1990s, several software companies offered ever more powerful and easier ways to plan and control project costs and schedules. Risk management techniques that were originally developed on complex projects have increasingly been applied in a simplified form to less complex projects.

In the last few years, people have realized more and more that communication and leadership play major roles in project success. Rapid growth and changes in the information technology and telecommunications industries especially have fueled massive growth in the use of project management in the 1990s and early 2000s. People engaged in banking, insurance, retailing, hospital administration, and many other service industries are now turning to project management to help them plan and manage efforts to meet their unique demands. Project planning and management techniques that were originally developed for large, complex projects can be modified and used to better plan and manage smaller projects. Now project management is commonly used on projects of many sizes and types in a wide variety of manufacturing, government, service, and nonprofit organizations.

The use of project management has grown quite rapidly and is likely to continue growing. With increased international competition, customers demand to have their products and services developed and delivered better, faster, and cheaper. Because project management techniques are designed to manage scope, quality, cost, and schedule, they are ideally suited to this purpose.

1.3 How Can Project Work Be Described?

Project work can be described in the following ways:

- Projects are temporary and unique while other work, commonly called operations, is more continuous.
- Project managers need certain "soft skills" and "hard skills" to be effective.
- Project managers frequently have more responsibility than authority.
- Projects go through predictable stages called a life cycle.

Projects versus Operations

All work can be described as fitting into one of two types: projects or operations. Projects as stated above are temporary, and no two are identical. Some projects may be extremely different from any other work an organization has performed up to that time, such as planning a merger with another company. Other projects may have both routine and unique aspects such as building a house. Operations, on the other hand, consist of the ongoing work needed to ensure that an organization continues to function effectively. Operations managers can often use checklists to guide much of their work. Project managers can use project management methods to help determine what to do, but they rarely have checklists that identify all of the activities they need to accomplish. Some work may be difficult to classify as totally project or totally operations. However, if project management methods and concepts help one to better plan and manage work, it does not really matter how the work is classified.

Soft Skills and Hard Skills

To effectively manage and lead in a project environment, a person needs to develop both "soft" and "hard" skills. Soft skills include communication and leadership activities. Hard skills can include risk analysis, quality control, scheduling, budgeting work, and so forth. Soft and hard skills go hand in hand. Some people have a stronger natural ability and a better comfort level in one or the other, but to be successful as a project manager a person needs to develop both along with the judgment of when each is more necessary. A wise project manager may purposefully recruit an assistant that excels in his area of weakness. Training, experience, and mentoring can also be instrumental in developing necessary skills.

Authority and Responsibility

A project manager will frequently be held accountable for work that she cannot order people to perform. Projects are most effectively managed with one person being assigned accountability. However, that person often needs to negotiate with a **functional manager**, who is "someone with management authority over an organizational unit ... the manager of any group that actually makes a product or performs a service."[4] Functional managers negotiate for workers to perform the project work in a timely fashion. Since the workers know their regular manager often has other tasks for them and will be their primary rater, they are tempted to concentrate first on the work that will earn rewards. Hence, a project manager needs to develop strong communication and leadership skills in order to persuade subordinates to focus on the project when other work also beckons.

Project Life Cycle

All projects go through predictable stages called a project life cycle. A **project life cycle** is "a collection of generally sequential project phases whose name and number are determined by the control needs of the organization or organizations involved in the project."[5] An organization's control needs are to be assured that the work of the project is proceeding in a satisfactory manner and that the results are likely to serve its customer's intended purpose. The project customer is the person or organization that will use the project's product, service, or result. Customers can be internal to the organization (that is, part of the company that is performing the project) or external to the organization (they do not work for the same company). Many different project life cycle models are used for different types of projects, such as information systems, improvement, research and development, and construction. The variations these pose will be explored in Chapter 3. In this book we will use the following project stages (as seen in the chapter opener Project Life Cycle diagram for all of the following chapters.):

- **Selecting and initiating**—starts when an idea for a project first emerges and the project is selected and planned at a high level, and ends when key participants commit to it in broad terms.
- **Planning**—starts after the initial commitment, includes detailed planning, and ends when all stakeholders accept the entire detailed plan.
- **Executing**—starts when the plan is accepted, and includes authorizing, executing, monitoring, and controlling work until the customer accepts the project deliverables.
- **Closing and realizing**—includes all activities after customer acceptance to ensure project is completed, lessons are learned, resources are reassigned, contributions are recognized, and benefits are realized.

The pace of work and amount of money spent may vary considerably from one life cycle stage to another. Often, the selecting is performed periodically for all projects at a division or corporate level and then initiating is rather quick—just enough to ensure that a project makes sense and key participants will commit to it. The planning stage can become rather detailed and will normally require quite a bit more work. The execution stage or stages is the time when the majority of the "hands-on" project tasks are

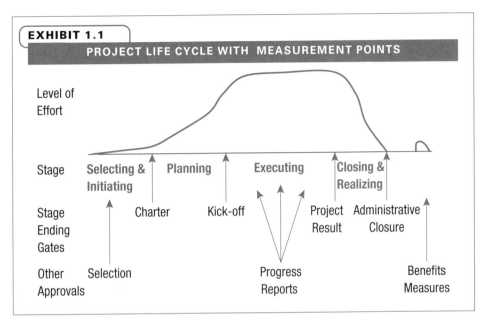

EXHIBIT 1.1

PROJECT LIFE CYCLE WITH MEASUREMENT POINTS

accomplished. This tends to be a time of considerable work. Closing is a time when loose ends are tied up and the work level decreases significantly, but realizing benefits from the project occurs over time, may be measured months after project completion, and may be done by people other than those who performed the project. See Exhibit 1.1 for a simple project life cycle.

Three other points should be made concerning the project life cycle. First, most companies with well-developed project management systems insist that a project must pass an approval of some kind to move from one stage to the next.[6] In Exhibit 1.1, the approval to move from selecting and initiating to planning, for instance, is the approval of a charter. Second, in many industries, the project life cycle is highly formalized and very specific. For example, in information systems, the executing stage is often described as two stages: writing code and testing code. In the construction industry, the executing stage is often described as the three stages of design, erection, and finishing. Many companies even have their own project life cycle model, such as the one Midland Insurance Company has developed for quality improvement projects as shown in Exhibit 1.2. This book will present examples of company-specific life cycle models, but for clarity will use the simple, generic model shown in Exhibit 1.1 when describing concepts. Third, in addition to stage-ending approvals, frequently projects are measured at additional points such as selection, progress reporting, and benefits realization, as shown in Exhibit 1.1.

1.4 Understanding Projects

Several frameworks that can help a person better understand project management are described below: the Project Management Institute (PMI); the *Project Management Body of Knowledge (PMBOK® Guide)*; methods of selecting and prioritizing projects, project goals and constraints; project success and failure; use of Microsoft Project to help plan and measure projects, and various ways to classify projects.

Project Management Institute

Project management has professional organizations just as do many other professions and industry groups. The biggest of these by far is the Project Management Institute.

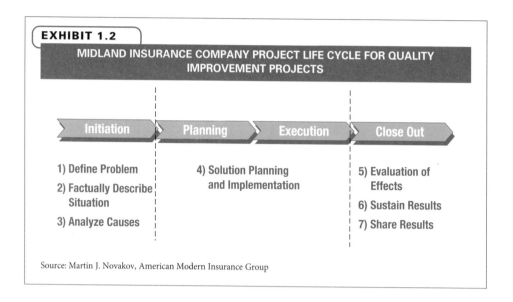

EXHIBIT 1.2

MIDLAND INSURANCE COMPANY PROJECT LIFE CYCLE FOR QUALITY IMPROVEMENT PROJECTS

| Initiation | Planning | Execution | Close Out |

1) Define Problem
2) Factually Describe Situation
3) Analyze Causes

4) Solution Planning and Implementation

5) Evaluation of Effects
6) Sustain Results
7) Share Results

Source: Martin J. Novakov, American Modern Insurance Group

It was founded in 1969, grew at a modest pace until the early 1990s, and has grown quite rapidly since. As of January 2010, PMI had well over 300,000 members worldwide. PMI publishes and regularly updates *A Guide to the Project Management Body of Knowledge (PMBOK® Guide)*. PMI has established a professional certification entitled Project Management Professional (PMP). To be certified as a PMP, a person needs to have the required experience and education, pass an examination on the *PMBOK® Guide*, and sign and be bound by a code of professional conduct. PMI has also established a second certification—Certified Associate in Project Management (CAPM)—that is geared toward junior people working on projects before they are eligible to become PMPs. All of the definitions in this book come from the *PMBOK® Guide*.[7]

Project Management Body of Knowledge (PMBOK®)

The Project Management Body of Knowledge consists of a project life cycle (see earlier "Project Life Cycle" section), five process groups, and nine knowledge areas. A **project management process group** is "a logical grouping of the project management inputs, tools and techniques, and outputs."[8] The five process groups, paraphrased from the *PMBOK® Guide*, are as follows:

- **Initiating**—"defines and authorizes a project or a project phase"
- **Planning**—"defines and refines objectives and plans actions to achieve objectives"
- **Executing**—"directs and manages people and other resources to accomplish project work"
- **Monitoring and controlling**—"collects data and checks progress to determine any needed corrective actions"
- **Closing**—"formalized acceptance of project outcomes and ending the project"[9]

The nine knowledge areas, paraphrased from the *PMBOK® Guide*, are as follows:

- **Integration management**—"processes and activities needed to define, combine, unify, and coordinate the various processes and project management activities"[10]
- **Scope management**—"processes required to ensure that the project includes all the work required, and only the work required, to complete the project successfully"[11]

- **Time management**—"processes required to manage timely completion of the project"[12]
- **Cost management**—"processes involved in estimating, budgeting, and controlling costs so that the project can be completed within the approved budget"[13]
- **Quality management**—"processes and activities of the performing organization that determine quality policies, objectives, and responsibilities so that the project will satisfy the needs for which it was undertaken"[14]
- **Human resources management**—"processes that organize, manage, and lead the project team"[15]
- **Communications management**—"processes required to ensure timely and appropriate generation, collection, distribution, storage, retrieval, and ultimate disposition of project information"[16]
- **Risk management**—"processes of conducting risk management planning, response planning, and monitoring and control … to increase the probability and impact of positive events and decrease the probability and impact of negative events in the project"[17]
- **Procurement management**—"processes necessary to purchase or acquire products, services, or results from outside the project team"[18]

Selecting and Prioritizing Projects

During the selecting and initiating stage of a project, one of the first tasks leaders must do is to identify potential projects. Ideally, this is accomplished in a systematic manner—not just by chance. Some opportunities will present themselves. Other good opportunities need to be discovered. All parts of the organization should be involved. For example, salespeople can uncover many opportunities through open discussions with existing and potential customers. Operations staff members may identify potential productivity enhancing projects. Everyone in the firm should be aware of industry trends and use this knowledge to identify potential projects.

Once identified, organizations need to prioritize among the potential projects. The best way to do this is to determine which projects align best with the major goals of the firm. The executives in charge of selecting projects need to ensure overall organizational priorities are understood, communicated, and accepted. Once this common understanding is in place, it is much easier to prioritize among the potential projects. The degree of formality used in selecting projects varies widely. In a small company, it may be straightforward. Regardless of the company's size and the level of formality used, the prioritization efforts should include asking the following questions:

- What value does each potential project bring to the organization?
- Are the demands of performing each project understood?
- Are the resources needed to perform the project available?
- Is there enthusiastic support both from the external customers and from one or more internal champions?
- Which projects will best help the organization achieve its goals?

Project Goals and Constraints

All projects should be undertaken to accomplish specific goals. Those goals can be described both by **scope**—"the sum of the products, services, and results to be provided as a project"[19] and by **quality**—"the degree to which a set of inherent characteristics fulfills requirements."[20] Taken together, scope and quality are often called performance and should result in outputs that customers can be satisfied with as they use them to effectively do their job. Projects generally have time and cost constraints. Thus, a project

---

EXHIBIT 1.3

PROJECT CUSTOMER TRADEOFF MATRIX

	ENHANCE	MEET	SACRIFICE
Cost			Pay up to $5,000 extra if it saves 10 days
Schedule	Save up to 10 days		
Quality		Must meet	
Scope		Must meet	

Source: Adapted from Timothy J. Kloppenborg and Joseph A. Petrick, *Managing Project Qualify* (Vienna, VA: Management Concepts, 2002): 46.

---

manager needs to be concerned with achieving desired scope and quality subject to constraints of time and cost. If the project were to proceed exactly according to plan, it would be on time, on budget, with the agreed upon scope and the agreed upon quality.

However, many things can happen as a project is conducted. Obstacles or challenges that may limit the ability to perform often arise, as well as opportunities to exceed original expectations. A project manager needs to understand which of these four goals and constraints should take precedence and which can be sacrificed. The project manager needs to help the customer articulate how much he wants to enhance achievement of one of these four dimensions. The customer must also state which dimension he is willing to sacrifice, by how much, and under what circumstances to receive better achievement of the other one. For example, on a research and development project, a customer may be willing to pay an extra $5,000 to finish the project 10 days early. On a church construction project, a customer may be willing to give up five extra light switches in exchange for greater confidence that the light system will work properly. Understanding the customer's desires in this manner enables a project manager to make good project decisions. A project manager can use a project customer tradeoff matrix such as the one in Exhibit 1.3 to reflect the research and development project tradeoffs discussed above.

Defining Project Success and Failure

Project success is creating deliverables that include all of the agreed upon features (meet scope goals). The outputs should satisfy all specifications and please the project's customers. The customers need to be able to use the outputs effectively as they do their work (meet quality goals). The project should be completed on schedule and on budget (meet time and cost constraints).

Project success also includes other considerations. A successful project is one that is completed without heroics—that is, people should not burn themselves out to complete the project. Those people who work on the project should either learn new skills and/or refine existing skills. Organizational learning should take place and be captured for future projects. Finally, the performing organization should reap business-level benefits such as development of new products, increased market share, increased profitability, decreased cost, and so on. A contemporary and complete view of project success is shown in Exhibit 1.4.

Project failure can be described as not meeting the success criteria listed in Exhibit 1.4. In reality, many projects are fully successful in some ways but less successful in others. The goal of excellent project management is to reach high levels of success on all measures on all projects. Serious project failure—when some of the success criteria are

---

EXHIBIT 1.4

PROJECT SUCCESS

- **Meeting Agreements**
  - Cost, schedule, and specifications met
- **Customer' Success**
  - Needs met, deliverables used, customer satisfied
- **Performing Organization's Success**
  - Market share, new products, new technology
- **Project Team's Success**
  - Loyalty, development, satisfaction

Source: Timothy J. Kloppenborg, Debbie Tesch, and Ravi Chinta, "Demographic Determinants of Project Success," *Proceedings, PMI Research and Education Conference 2010* (Washington, DC, July 2010).

---

missed by a large amount and/or when several of the success criteria are missed by even a small margin—can be attributed to numerous causes. In each chapter of this text, more specific possible failure causes will be covered, along with how to avoid them, but a few of the basic causes of failure are as follows:

- Not enough resources are available for project completion.
- Not enough time has been given to the project.
- Project expectations are unclear.
- Changes in the scope are not understood or agreed upon by all parties involved.
- Stakeholders disagree regarding expectations for the project.
- Adequate project planning is not used.

Using Microsoft Project to Help Plan and Measure Projects

A useful tool to capture and conveniently display a variety of important project data is Microsoft® (MS) Project. A fully functional, 60-day demonstration copy of MS Project is included with this text. MS Project is demonstrated in a step-by-step fashion using screen shots from a single integrated project throughout the book.

Types of Projects

Four ways to classify projects that help people understand the unique needs of each are by industry, size, understanding of project scope, and application.

CLASSIFYING BY INDUSTRY Projects can be classified in a variety of ways. One method is by industry, which is useful in that projects in different industries often have unique requirements. Several industry-specific project life cycle models are in use, and various trade groups and special interest groups can provide guidance. For example, PMI had 32 specific interest groups, colleges, and communities of practice as of May 12, 2010, as shown in Exhibit 1.5. All of these groups are in the process of becoming communities of practice that will allow project managers worldwide to share and learn together. Many of those groups are devoted to specific challenges faced by project managers in a particular industry.

CLASSIFYING BY SIZE Another method of classifying projects is by size. Large projects often require more detailed planning and control. However, even the smallest projects still need to use planning and control—just in a more simplified manner. For example,

---

EXHIBIT 1.5

PMI COMMUNITIES OF PRACTICE

Aerospace and Defense

Agile

Automation Systems
Consulting

Design-Procurement-Construction

Diversity

E-Business

Financial Services

Global Sustainability

Government

Healthcare

Human Resource

Information Systems

Innovation and New Product Development

International Development

Learning, Education and Development

Manufacturing

Marketing and Sales

Oil, Gas, Petrochemical

Organizational

Performance Management

Pharmaceutical

Program Management Office

Quality

Retail

Risk Management

Scheduling

Service and Outsourcing

Students of PM

Troubled Projects

Utility

Women in PM

Source: http://www.pmi.org/GetInvolved/Pages/PMI-Specific-Interest-Groups.aspx, accessed May 12, 2010.

---

construction of a multistory building in China would require a highly detailed construction schedule, but a much simpler construction project of building a one-car garage would also need to follow a schedule.

CLASSIFYING BY TIMING OF PROJECT SCOPE CLARITY A third method of classifying projects deals with how early in the project the project manager and team are likely to be able to determine with a high degree of certainty what the project scope will be.

A large construction project, like this multistory building in China, requires a highly detailed construction schedule.

For example, it may be rather simple to calculate the cubic feet of concrete that are required to pour a parking lot and, therefore, how much work is involved. At the opposite end of the spectrum, when developing a new pharmaceutical, very little may be determined in the project until the results of some early experiments are reported. Only at that time is it possible to begin estimating cost and determining the schedule with confidence. The planning becomes iterative, with more detail as it becomes available. In the first case, project techniques that deal with detailed planning and control of work activities may work well. In the second case, methods to help determine the scope and plan for risks may be more important.

CLASSIFYING BY APPLICATION For the purpose of this book, we will discuss many types of projects, such as those dealing with organizational change, quality and productivity improvement, research and development (R&D), information systems (IS), and construction. Many of these projects include extensive cross-functional work, which adds to the challenge. These various types of projects will demonstrate differences in level of detail in planning, industry-specific control issues, and different approaches that make sense depending on whether or not a project's scope can be determined quickly. Remember, all projects require planning and control. Part of the art of project management is determining when to use certain techniques, how much detail to use, and how to tailor the techniques to the needs of a specific project.

Scalability of Project Tools

Projects range tremendously in size and complexity. If one were to consider construction projects, think of the range from building a simple carport to building an office tower. In both cases, one would need to determine the wants and needs of the customer(s), understand the amount of work involved, determine a budget and schedule, decide what workers are available and who will do which tasks, and then manage the construction until the owner accepts the project results. It should be easy to see that while both projects require planning and control, the level of detail for the carport is a tiny fraction of that for the office tower. In this book, we first demonstrate concepts and techniques at a middle level and then use a variety of project examples to demonstrate how to scale up or down the complexity of the techniques.

1.5 Project Roles

To successfully initiate, plan, and execute projects, a variety of executive, management, and associate roles must be accomplished, as shown in Exhibit 1.6. In a large organization, a person often fills only one of these roles; sometimes, more than one person fills a particular role. In small organizations, the same person fills more than one role. The names of the roles also vary by organization. The work of each role must be accomplished by someone. Project managers tend to be more successful when they build strong working relationships with the individuals who execute each of these roles.

Project Executive–Level Roles

The three project executive–level roles are the steering team, the chief projects officer, and the sponsor. A steering or leadership team for an organization is often the top leader (CEO or other officer) and his or her direct reports. From a project standpoint, the important role for this team is to select, prioritize, and resource projects in accordance with the organization's strategic planning and to ensure that accurate progress is reported and necessary adjustments are made.

The chief projects officer's role is sometimes called a **project management office (PMO)**, which is defined as "an organizational body or entity assigned various responsibilities related to the centralized and coordinated management of those projects within its domain. The responsibilities of the PMO can range from providing project management support functions to actually being responsible for the direct management of a project."[21]

The third executive-level project role is that of sponsor. PMI's official definition of a **sponsor** is "the person or group that provides the financial resources, in cash or in kind, for the project."[22] For this textbook, the sponsor's role is elaborated further. The sponsor takes an active role in chartering the project and reviewing progress reports, as well as a behind-the-scenes role in mentoring and assisting the project manager throughout the project life.

Project Management–Level Roles

The most obvious management-level role is the project manager. The **project manager** is "the person assigned by the performing organization to achieve the project objectives."[23] The project manager is normally directly accountable for the project results, schedule, and budget. This person is the main communicator, is responsible for the planning and execution of the project, and works on the project from start to finish. The project manager often must get things done through the power of influence since his or her formal power may be limited.

Another key management role is the functional manager. Functional managers are the department heads—the ongoing managers of the organization. They normally determine how the work of the project is to be accomplished, often supervise that work, and likely negotiate with the project manager regarding which workers are assigned to the project.

The third managerial role is that of facilitator. If the project is complex and/or controversial, it sometimes makes sense to have another person help the project manager with the process of running meetings and making decisions.

The final managerial-level project role is that of the senior customer representative. This person ensures that the needs and wants of the various constituents in the customer's organization are identified and prioritized and that project progress and decisions continually support the customer's desires.

EXHIBIT 1.6	PROJECT ROLES		
EXECUTIVE ROLES	MANAGERIAL ROLES	ASSOCIATE ROLES
Steering team	Project manager	Core team member
Chief projects officer	Functional manager	Subject matter expert
Sponsor	Facilitator	
	Senior customer representative	

Project Associate–Level Roles

The **project management team** is composed of "members who are directly involved in project management activities."[24] In this book, these individuals are called core team members. The core team, with the project manager, does most of the planning and makes most of the project-level decisions.

The temporary members that are brought on board are called subject matter experts. These people are used on an as-needed basis.

1.6 Overview of the Book

When a person conceptualing contemporary project management, it is important to remember that it is integrative, iterative, and collaborative. Project management is integrative since it consists of the nine knowledge areas and the five process groups described in the *PMBOK® Guide*, and one must integrate all of them into one coherent whole. Project management is iterative in that one starts by planning at a high level and then repeats the planning in greater detail as more information becomes available and the date for the work performance approaches. Project management is collaborative since there are many stakeholders to be satisfied and a team of workers with various skills and ideas who need to work together to plan and complete the project. With these thoughts of integration, iteration, and collaboration in mind, this book has three major parts: Organizing and Initiating Projects, Planning Projects, and Performing Projects.

Part 1—Organizing Projects

Part 1 consists of four chapters. The first deals with project management basics, the second with selecting projects, the third with organization, and the fourth with getting a project initiated—that is, taking it from an idea to a formally accepted project.

CHAPTER 2 Chapter 2 covers project selection and prioritization. This includes both internal projects, which should be selected in a manner consistent with the strategic planning of the organization, and external projects. It also explains how to respond to requests for proposals.

CHAPTER 3 Chapter 3 focuses on organizational structure, organizational culture, project life cycle, and project management roles of the parent organization. The organizational structure section outlines the various manners in which an organization can be configured and the advantages and disadvantages of each approach in regard to managing projects. Next covered is the culture of the parent organization and the impact it has on the ability to effectively plan and manage projects. The industry and type of project

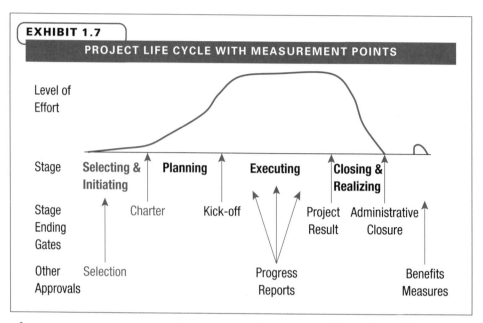

EXHIBIT 1.7

PROJECT LIFE CYCLE WITH MEASUREMENT POINTS

often encourage managers to select or customize a project life cycle model. The roles covered include executive-, managerial-, and associate-level responsibilities that must be performed. The demands of each role are explained, along with suggestions for how to select and develop people to effectively fill each role, considering both the role and the unique abilities and interests of each person.

CHAPTER 4 Chapter 4 discusses chartering projects. The **project charter** is "a document issued by the project initiator or sponsor that formally authorizes the existence of a project, and provides the project manager with the authority to apply organizational resources to project activities."[25] The charter can further be considered an agreement by which the project sponsor and project manager (and often the project core team) agree at a high level what the project is, why it is important, key milestone points in the schedule, major risks, and possibly a few other items. It allows the project manager and core team to understand and agree to what is expected of them. Finally, Microsoft Project, a tool that facilitates effective project planning, controlling, and communicating, is introduced. Microsoft Project is utilized in eight chapters to demonstrate how to automate various project planning and control techniques. The examples and illustrations in this book use Microsoft Project 2010. If a person is using an earlier version of Microsoft Project, there are slight differences. If a person is using a competing project scheduling package, the intent remains the same, but the mechanics of how to create certain documents may differ.

Part 2—Planning Projects

Part 2 includes seven chapters dealing with various aspects of project planning. The first two planning chapters deal with the project stakeholders and the actual project work. Once members of a project team understand those, they can plan the schedule, necessary workers, budget, risk, and quality. Finally, all components of the project plan are unified and approved as a baseline.

CHAPTER 5 Chapter 5 begins by identifying the various project stakeholders, their wants and needs, and how to prioritize decisions among them. Chapter 5 also includes communications planning for the project because poor communication can doom an otherwise well-planned and well-managed project. The information needs of each stakeholder group should be included in the communications plan.

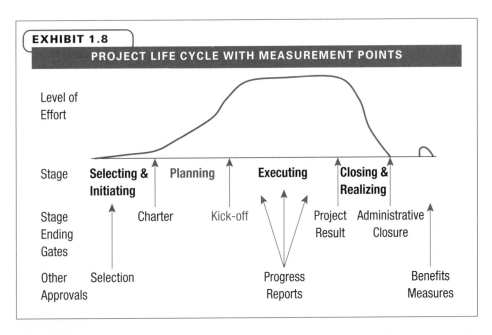

EXHIBIT 1.8

PROJECT LIFE CYCLE WITH MEASUREMENT POINTS

Level of Effort

| Stage | **Selecting & Initiating** | **Planning** | **Executing** | **Closing & Realizing** |

| Stage Ending Gates | | Charter | Kick-off | Project Result | Administrative Closure |

| Other Approvals | Selection | | | Progress Reports | | Benefits Measures |

CHAPTER 6 Chapter 6 shows how to determine the project scope and outline it in the **work breakdown structure (WBS)**. The WBS is "a deliverable-oriented hierarchical decomposition of the work to be executed by the project team to accomplish the project objectives and create the required deliverables. It organizes and defines the total scope of the project."[26] The WBS is a document that progressively breaks the project down into its components so that each piece can be described as a work activity for which one person can plan, estimate the costs, estimate the time, assign resources to, manage, and be held accountable for the results. This is a critical document since it is the foundation for most of the other planning and control. The chapter ends with instructions on putting a WBS into Microsoft Project.

CHAPTER 7 Chapter 7 deals with scheduling projects. The **project schedule** includes "the planned dates for performing schedule activities and the planned dates for meeting schedule milestones."[27] This chapter starts with a background on project scheduling and then covers construction of schedules by defining activities, determining the order in which they need to be accomplished, estimating the duration for each, and then calculating the schedule. Chapter 7 also includes instructions on how to interpret a project schedule; clearly communicate it using a bar chart called a Gantt chart; and use Microsoft Project to construct, interpret, and communicate project schedules.

CHAPTER 8 Chapter 8 demonstrates how to schedule resources on projects: determining the need for workers, understanding who is available, and assigning people. All of the techniques of resourcing projects are integrated with the behavioral aspects of how to deal effectively and ethically with the people involved. Resource needs are shown on a Gantt chart developed in Chapter 7, the responsibilities are shown as they change over time, conflicts and overloads are identified, and methods for resolving the conflicts are introduced. Alternative approaches for creating and compressing schedules are shown. Many of the techniques in this chapter are also shown with MS Project.

CHAPTER 9 A project budget, the subject of Chapter 9, is dependent on both the schedule and the resource needs developed in the previous two chapters. The **budget** is "the approved estimate for the project or any work breakdown structure component or any schedule activity."[28] Cost planning, estimating, budgeting, establishing cost control, and using MS Project for project budgets are all included.

CHAPTER 10   Chapter 10, Project Risk Planning, starts with establishing a risk management plan. It covers methods for identifying potential risks and for determining which risks are big enough to justify specific plans for either preventing the risk event from happening or dealing effectively with risk events that do happen. Finally, in risk response planning, strategies for dealing with both positive risks (opportunities) and negative risks (threats) are discussed.

CHAPTER 11   Chapter 11 begins with a discussion of how modern project quality concepts have evolved. Then it deals with core project quality demands of stakeholder satisfaction, empowered performance, fact-based management, and process management. The third chapter topic is developing the project quality plan. Next, the chapter describes various quality improvement tools for projects.

Since this is the last planning chapter, it concludes with a method of integrating the various sections developed in the previous chapters into a single, coherent project plan. Conflicts that are discovered should be resolved, judgment needs to be applied to ensure that the overall plan really makes sense, and one or more kickoff meetings are normally held to inform all of the project stakeholders and to solicit their enthusiastic acceptance of the plan. At this point, the project schedule and budget can be baselined in MS Project. While bits of the project that might have caused delays if they were not started early may already be in progress, the formal kick-off is the signal that the project is under way!

Part 3—Performing Projects

Part 3 deals with performing the project. Project managers need to ensure that contractors perform per the project plan. Project managers need to utilize both leadership and management when ensuring that people assigned to the project jell and perform as a team and that all stakeholders are satisfied. Project managers also need to control the more technical issues of cost, schedule, scope, and quality. Finally, project managers strive to conclude on a high note.

CHAPTER 12   Chapter 12 begins by introducing relevant supply chain concepts such as a supply chain view of projects, the components that form a supply chain, factors to consider when dealing with a supply chain, and methods of improving the performance

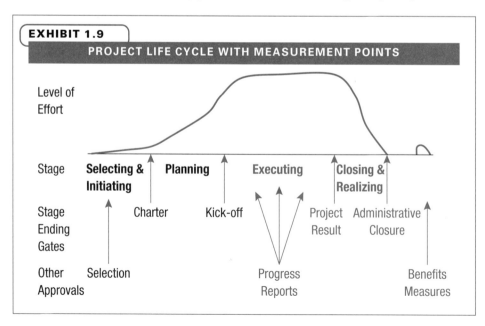

EXHIBIT 1.9

PROJECT LIFE CYCLE WITH MEASUREMENT POINTS

of a supply chain. Make-or-buy analysis and contract types lead the reader through procurement planning. Identifying and selecting sellers lead into managing contracts to assure receipt of promised supplies and services according to contractual terms. The chapter ends with advantages and requirements of effective project partnering.

CHAPTER 13 Chapter 13, Leading and Managing Project Teams, describes how to carry out the project work in order to accomplish the project objectives. The material leading up to this chapter has laid the groundwork for establishing project plans and requirements; this chapter deals with accomplishing the requirements by performing according to plan. The project manager needs to simultaneously champion the needs of the project, the team, and the parent organization. This includes the task side, in which the project manager authorizes work to be accomplished, manages tradeoffs, and assures stakeholders that both the amount and quality of the project work are progressing as planned. The project manager also must manage the people side of the project by effectively using the stages of project team development, assessing and building the team members' capability, supervising their work, managing and improving their decision making, and helping them maintain enthusiasm and effective time management. Gathering and distributing project information according to the communication plan helps to keep the project running smoothly.

CHAPTER 14 While the project work is being performed, the project manager needs to determine that the desired results are achieved—the subject of Chapter 14. **Monitor and control project work** is defined as "the process of tracking, reviewing, and regulating the progress to meet the performance objectives defined in the project plan."[29] This starts with gathering performance data already identified during project initiating and planning. The actual performance data are then compared to the desired performance data so that both corrective and preventive actions can be used to ensure that the amount and quality of the project work meet expectations. MS Project can be used for this progress reporting and for making adjustments. Earned value analysis is used to determine exactly how actual cost and schedule progress is compared with planned progress. Overcoming obstacles, managing changes, resolving conflicts, reprioritizing work, and creating a transition plan all lead up to customer acceptance of the project deliverables.

CHAPTER 15 Chapter 15 deals with finishing projects and realizing benefits. **Close project** is defined as "the process of finalizing all activities across all of the project process groups to formally close a project or phase."[30] This chapter includes a section on terminating projects early in case either the project is not doing well or conditions have changed and the project results are no longer needed, and a section on timely termination of successful projects. Topics include how to secure customer feedback and use it along with the team's experiences to create lessons learned for the organization; reassign workers and reward those participants who deserve recognition; celebrate success; perform a variety of closure activities; and provide ongoing support for the organization that is using the results of the project. Finally, after the project deliverables have been used for some time, an assessment should determine if the promised benefits are being realized.

Summary

A project is an organized set of work efforts undertaken to produce a unique output subject to limitations of time and resources such as money and people. Since the world is changing more rapidly than in the past, many people spend an increasing amount of their working time on projects. Project management includes work processes that initiate, plan, execute, monitor and control, and close project work. During these processes, tradeoffs must be made among the scope, quality, cost, and schedule so the project results meet the agreed upon requirements, are useful to the customers, and promote the organization.

All projects, regardless of size, complexity, or application, need to be planned and managed. While the level of detail and specific methods vary widely, all need to follow generally accepted methods. PMI is a large professional organization devoted to promoting and standardizing project management understanding and methods. One of PMI's standards, *A Guide to the Project Management Body of Knowledge (PMBOK® Guide)*, is composed of five process groups: initiating, planning, executing, monitoring and controlling, and closing; along with nine knowledge areas: cost, time, scope, quality, risk, communications, human resources, procurement, and integration.

To successfully initiate, plan, and execute projects, two more things are needed. One is to understand what project success is and what drives it, along with what project failure is and its major causes. The other is an understanding of the various executive-, managerial-, and associate-level roles in project management. This book is organized to be useful to students who will enter a variety of industries and be assigned to projects of all sizes and levels of complexity. Students will learn how to understand and effectively manage each of these process groups and knowledge areas. Microsoft Project is used in eight chapters to illustrate how to automate various planning, scheduling, resourcing, budgeting, and controlling activities. All definitions used are from the *PMBOK® Guide*, 4th edition. This book follows a chronological approach throughout a project's life cycle, emphasizing knowledge and skills that lead to project success.

Key Terms from the *PMBOK® Guide*

The glossary in this book exclusively uses terms as defined in *A Guide to the Project Management Body of Knowledge (PMBOK® Guide)*

project, 4
stakeholders, 4
project management, 4
functional manager, 6
project life cycle, 6
project management process group, 8
initiating processes, 8
planning processes, 8
executing processes, 8
monitoring and controlling processes, 8
closing processes, 8
integration management, 8
scope management, 8
time management, 9
cost management, 9
quality management, 9

human resources management, 9
communications management, 9
risk management, 9
procurement management, 9
scope, 9
quality, 9
project management office (PMO), 14
sponsor, 14
project manager, 14
project management team, 15
project charter, 16
work breakdown structure (WBS), 17
project schedule, 17
budget, 17
monitor and control project work, 19
close project, 19

Chapter Review Questions

1. What is a project?
2. How are projects different from ongoing operations?
3. What is project management?
4. What tradeoffs need to be made when managing a project?
5. Why are more people spending more of their work time on projects?

6. How do you define project success?
7. How do you define project failure?
8. What are the nine project management knowledge areas?
9. What forces contribute to the importance of project management?
10. At what stage of a project life cycle are the majority of the "hands-on" tasks completed?

11. At what stage of a project life cycle does the project become officially sanctioned?
12. What two project dimensions are components of project performance?
13. What types of constraints are common to most projects?
14. List at least four common causes of project failure.
15. What are three common means of classifying projects?

16. List and describe each of the project executive, managerial, and associate roles.
17. What is a challenge in managing subject matter experts?
18. What document is critical because most other planning is based upon it?
19. What needs must a project manager simultaneously champion?
20. What makes a person or group a project stakeholder?

Discussion Questions

1. Using an example, describe a project in terms that are common to most projects.
2. Describe the general project life cycle model including each stage.
3. List and describe several issues that pertain to each stage of the project life cycle.
4. Name and describe each of the nine project management knowledge areas.
5. Name and describe the five project management process groups.
6. List and describe several issues that pertain to each of the nine project knowledge areas.
7. Explain how to scale up or down the complexity of project planning and management tools with examples.

8. List and describe "soft skills" needed in managing projects. Why is each skill important?
9. List and describe "hard skills" needed in managing projects. Why is each skill important?
10. What is the best way for an organization to prioritize among potential projects?
11. Define program and portfolio and explain how they are different.
12. Describe a subproject and tell why it might be useful.
13. Contrast project managers from functional managers.
14. Contrast core team members from subject matter experts.

PMBOK ® Guide Questions

The purpose of these questions is to help visualize the type of questions on PMP and CAPM exams.

1. Each project management process can be described to include all of the following *except:*
   a. inputs
   b. knowledge areas
   c. outputs
   d. tools and techniques
2. Which role describes someone as having authority over a group that actually makes a product or performs a service?
   a. functional manager
   b. project manager
   c. project team member
   d. sponsor
3. Work activities aimed to ensure that the project includes all the work required, and only the work required, are part of which knowledge area?

   a. cost management
   b. quality management
   c. risk management
   d. scope management
4. A logical grouping of the project management inputs, tools and techniques, and outputs is a project:
   a. governance system
   b. life cycle
   c. knowledge area
   d. process group
5. The process that defines and authorizes a project or a project phase is:
   a. budgeting
   b. closing
   c. executing
   d. initiating

Example Project

This book is designed to give your professors the option to have you practice the concepts and techniques from each chapter on a real project. Often, the project chosen will be for a nonprofit group of some kind such as a United Way agency, a church, or a school. The project could, however, be for a company or a part of the university. For traditional classes, the example project can often be one that several students will be assigned to work on as a team. For online classes, it may be more practical to have each student work on a separate project at their place of employment.

Each chapter provides suggested assignments to practice project management skills on the real or potential project you are using. Depending on the emphasis your professor chooses, you may need to perform some, most, or all of these assignments. At a minimum, your professor will probably assign the charter, work breakdown structure, and schedule.

In any case, each chapter after this prompts you to perform various activities to plan and execute the project. At some point in the first couple of weeks, your professor will probably invite at least one representative from each organization to your class to introduce their project and to meet you. We will call this person the sponsor and define their role more fully in Chapter 3. Since this first chapter is a broad introduction to project management, your task for Chapter 1's sample project is to familiarize yourself with your new student team, your sponsor, your sponsor's organization, and the overall direction of your project. Your professor may ask you to answer certain specific and/or open-ended questions concerning your newly assigned project.

Subsequent chapters give you more in-depth tools to acclimate you to your project, the organization you will be working for, and the various stakeholders who have an interest in the project. For example, in the next chapter, you learn how project selection flows from an organization's strategic planning, and you should seek to learn why this project was chosen and how it supports the strategic goals of the organization.

References

A Guide to the Project Management Body of Knowledge (PMBOK® Guide), 4th ed. (Newtown Square, PA: Project Management Institute, 2008).

Cioffi, Dennis, *Managing Project Integration* (Vienna, VA: Management Concepts, Inc., 2002).

Cooper, Robert G., "Winning at New Products: Pathways to Profitable Innovation," *Proceedings, PMI Research Conference 2006* (Montreal, July 2006).

Crowe, Andy, *Alpha Project Managers: What the Top 2% Know That Everyone Else Does Not* (Atlanta: Velociteach, 2006).

Dobson, Michael S., *The Triple Constraints in Project Management* (Vienna, VA: Management Concepts, 2004).

Kloppenborg, Timothy J. and Warren A. Opfer, "The Current State of Project Management Research: Trends, Interpretations, and Predictions," *Project Management Journal* 33 (2) (June 2002).

Kloppenborg, Timothy J., Debbie Tesch, and Ravi Chinta, "Demographic Determinants of Project Success," *Proceedings, PMI Research and Education Conference 2010* (Washington, DC, July 2010).

Mesihovic, Samir, John Malmqvist, and Peter Pikosz, "Product Data Management System-Based Support for Engineering Project Management," *Journal of Engineering Design* 15 (4) (August 2004): 389–403.

Muller, R. and Turner, R., "The Influence of Project Managers on Project Success Criteria by Type of Project," *European Management Journal,* 25 (4) (2007): 298–309.

PMI Community of Practice Listing, http://www.pmi.org/GetInvolved/Pages/Communities-of-Practice.aspx, accessed May 12, 2010.

Shenhar, A. J. and D. Dvir, *Reinventing Project Management* (Boston: Harvard Business School Press, 2007).

http://www1.standishgroup.com/newsroom/chaos_2009.php, accessed May 12, 2010.

Endnotes

1. *PMBOK® Guide* 442.
2. *PMBOK® Guide* 450.
3. *PMBOK® Guide* 443.
4. *PMBOK® Guide* 436.
5. *PMBOK® Guide* 443.
6. Robert G. Cooper, "Winning at New Products: Pathways to Profitable Innovation," *Proceedings, PMI Research Conference 2006* (Montreal, July 2006).
7. Project Management Institute, *A Guide to the Project Management Body of Knowledge (PMBOK® Guide)*, 4th ed. (Newtown Square, PA: Project Management Institute, 2008). Copyright and all rights reserved. Material from this publication has been reproduced with permission of PMI.
8. *PMBOK® Guide* 443.
9. *PMBOK® Guide* 39.
10. *PMBOK® Guide* 71.
11. *PMBOK® Guide* 103.
12. *PMBOK® Guide* 129.
13. *PMBOK® Guide* 165.
14. *PMBOK® Guide* 189.
15. *PMBOK® Guide* 215.
16. *PMBOK® Guide* 243.
17. *PMBOK® Guide* 273.
18. *PMBOK® Guide* 313.
19. *PMBOK® Guide* 448.
20. *PMBOK® Guide* 445.
21. *PMBOK® Guide* 443.
22. *PMBOK® Guide* 449.
23. *PMBOK® Guide* 444.
24. *PMBOK® Guide* 444.
25. *PMBOK® Guide* 442.
26. *PMBOK® Guide* 452.
27. *PMBOK® Guide* 444.
28. *PMBOK® Guide* 428.
29. *PMBOK® Guide* 438.
30. *PMBOK® Guide* 428.

PROJECT MANAGEMENT *IN ACTION*

Selecting a Training Project at Skyline Chili

This section of each chapter will include one example project to illustrate some of the material covered.

Skyline Chili, Inc., includes 34 corporately owned restaurants, five partnerships, and over 125 franchised restaurants with a menu specializing in high-quality chili-related food products served in a table-service or cafeteria-style format. Consumers consistently rank Skyline Chili higher overall than all our quick service competitors, many of whom are national chains with vast resources. The foundation of our strong position is the Skyline team. Our unparalleled hospitality is what our customers truly value.

Skyline management wanted to ensure Skyline's training program remains in alignment with Skyline's strategic business plan of providing unparalleled hospitality. The following explains a bit of the project chartered for that purpose:

The Project Team consisted of District Managers, Franchise Consultants, and Human Resources. The Project Sponsors were the Sr. VP Restaurant Operations and Sr. VP Franchise Operations.

The required outcome is to have high-performing, execution-ready, hospitable employees.

The initial meeting included brainstorming and prioritizing training projects that the project team identified as critical. The project team committed time and allocated resources against the determined priorities.

Each participant was instructed to silently write one idea per Post-it® Note. They were asked to complete a total of three Post-it Notes in response to the question stated in the theme. The participants were instructed to write down problems, not solutions.

With the entire project group participating, the Post-it Notes were read aloud, openly discussed to clarify the meaning, and placed on a white board.

Then everyone on the team arranged the Post-it Notes based on similarity of meaning.

Similar themes or groups were then titled using a sentence that conveyed the common meaning of the Post-it Note grouping.

The project team then voted on the most important groups to focus action steps against. Each project team member was given three colored dots: Red was the most important (3 points), blue dot (2 points), and green dot (1 point). The results are shown in Exhibit 1.7.

Points were totaled. The top priority identified was to establish a centralized training department with a point contact person. This outcome was unexpected, and the organization was not initially prepared to address it. The expense for a training department and contact person was not planned or budgeted. The project team took the recommendation to the team sponsors. Over the next month, a business case and job analysis were built. As a result, a director of training was put into place.

EXHIBIT 1.7

SKYLINE TRAINING PROJECT

What training objectives (projects) need to be completed in order to ensure alignment with Skyline's Strategic Business Plan?

○ 3 points
◐ 2 points
● 1 point

Titles

19 points — Need fo Centralized Training Department

18 points — Develop a Train the Trainer Program

15 points — Certify Training Stores

14 points — Management Development Program

Post-it® Notes with one idea per note card

◀ Groups of Ideas

Source: Shari Bleuer, Skyline Chili, Inc.

CHAPTER 2

Project Selection and Prioritization

CHAPTER OBJECTIVES

After completing this chapter, you should be able to:

- Describe the strategic planning and portfolio alignment processes.

- Itemize strengths and weaknesses of using financial and scoring models to select projects.

- Describe how to select and prioritize projects as an outgrowth of strategic planning.

- Given organizational priorities and several projects, demonstrate how to select and prioritize projects using a scoring model.

- From a contractor's viewpoint, describe how to secure projects.

Robert Llewellyn/Image State/Alamy

How does a truly global company with fewer than 200 associates achieve noteworthy results and market leadership? Certainly strong and talented people are a key part of the answer. A good set of leadership and management tools and processes, and the discipline to use them, is another key. A small, privately held company in Louisville, Kentucky has been fortunate to use both talent and process to achieve success by any measure. That company is D. D. Williamson.

D. D. Williamson was founded in 1865 and today is a global leader in non-artificial colors. Operating nine facilities in six countries and supplying many of the best-known food and beverage companies around the world, D. D. Williamson has more complexity to manage than most companies, regardless of their size.

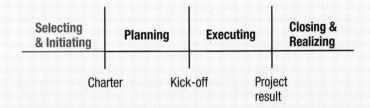

Selecting & Initiating	Planning	Executing	Closing & Realizing

Charter   Kick-off   Project result

**PMBOK®
GUIDE TOPICS**

- Portfolio management
- Program management
- Projects and strategic planning
- Source selection criteria
- Project statement of work
- Business case

Late in 2004, the company was embarking on a new vision to double growth and profitability in five years and identified the need to improve project management as a key strategy to achieve the vision. Our weakness was twofold—we had too many projects that were championed as important, and the projects that were active were sometimes late, over budget, and not achieving the predicted results. We began with prioritization, creating a prioritization matrix to select 16 "critical projects" that would have senior leadership sponsors and be assigned trained and capable project managers to improve our execution.

The prioritization matrix was a great initial step to narrow our focus and improve our results—overall project completion improved. However, 16 projects meant that the scope and impact of projects still had wide variation. Smaller, more simple projects were likely to be executed brilliantly and improve our total percentage of "on time and on target" projects, but if the project that was late or over budget was very high impact, we were still leaving opportunities for growth and profitability "on the table."

In 2009, we made more changes to our prioritization process, selecting no more than five "Vision Impact Projects" (VIPs) that would get high-level focus and attention—monitoring and asking for corrective measures in weekly senior management meetings, tracking online in our project management system for our Continuous Improvement Manager, and funneling time and resources to help when projects get off course.

The results are dramatic—large and complicated projects are getting the attention and resources and are hitting our strategic target of "on time, on budget and on target" regularly. Our successes have positioned D. D. Williamson to continue to do what we do best—serve customers effectively, grow our business, and return strong financial results to ensure a solid future for the business.

Elaine Gravatte, Chief People Officer and North American President, D. D. Williamson

27

2.1 Strategic Planning Process

One of the tasks of a company's senior leadership is to set the firm's strategic direction. Some of this direction setting occurs when an organization is young or is being re-vamped, but some needs to occur repeatedly. Exhibit 2.1 depicts the steps in strategic planning and how portfolio management should be an integral part.

Strategic Analysis

The first part of setting strategic direction is to analyze both the external and internal environments and determine how they will enhance or limit the organization's ability to perform. This strategic analysis is often called strengths, weaknesses, opportunities, and threats (SWOT). The internal analysis (elements within the project team's control) consists of asking what strengths and weaknesses the organization possesses in itself. The external analysis (elements over which the project team has little or no control) consists of asking what opportunities and threats are posed by competitors, suppliers, customers, regulatory agencies, technologies, and so on. The leaders of an organization often need to be humble and open to ideas that are unpleasant when conducting this analysis. Performed correctly, a strategic analysis can be very illuminating and can suggest direction for an organization. An example of SWOT analysis for the Built Green Home at Suncadia is shown in Exhibit 2.2. (The Built Green Home at Suncadia, Washington, was developed using advanced sustainability concepts and a large degree of stakeholder involvement. A more detailed description of this house appears in Chapter 5.)

Guiding Principles

Once the SWOT analysis is complete, the organization's leadership should establish guiding principles such as the vision and mission. Some organizations break this step into more parts by adding separate statements concerning purpose and/or values. Often,

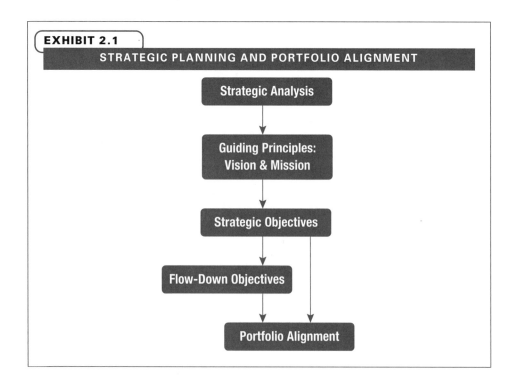

EXHIBIT 2.1

STRATEGIC PLANNING AND PORTFOLIO ALIGNMENT

Strategic Analysis

↓

Guiding Principles:
Vision & Mission

↓

Strategic Objectives

↓

Flow-Down Objectives

↓

Portfolio Alignment

EXHIBIT 2.2

SWOT ANALYSIS FOR THE BUILT GREEN HOME AT SUNCADIA

STRENGTHS	WEAKNESSES
Green building has a buzz	Green building has not reached mainstream
Seattle has a strong green building community support	Limited project resources community
Strong community support	Distance away from Seattle
Growth in green building projects that demonstrate value	Green building is perceived to be costly
Need to provide numbers on green building value	High cost of green projects
Committed developer and builder	
OPPORTUNITIES	THREATS
Uniqueness of product	Existing thinking on green building and its niche focus
Location	Building schedule
Community surrounding house	Community (location)
Lack of data on green building (wealth) value	Rumors

Source: Brenda Nunes, developer, BuiltGreen Home at Suncadia.

these sections are included in the mission. For simplicity's sake, they will be treated as part of the mission in this book. It is more important to understand the intent of each portion and achieve it rather than worry about the exact format or names of individual portions.

VISION   The vision should present a "vivid description of a preferred future."[1] It should be both inspiring and guiding, describing the organization as it can be in the future, but stated in the present tense. A clear and compelling vision will help all members and all stakeholders of an organization understand and desire to achieve it. Visions often require extra effort to achieve but are considered to be worth the effort. Visions are often multi-year goals that, once achieved, suggest the need for a new vision.

One of the visions most often cited, because it was so clear and compelling, was President John F. Kennedy's goal of placing a man on the moon before the end of the 1960s. Kennedy set this goal after Russia launched Sputnik and the United States found itself behind in the space race. His vision was very effective in mobilizing people to achieve it.

A more recent example was in 2009 when hundreds of community leaders in Cleveland, Ohio, decided to use a systems approach to guide many interrelated social and economic efforts in their region. The vision they stated is to become the "green city on the blue lake."[2] They use this vision to guide regional leaders as they choose where to invest their time and resources in bettering the region and life for its residents.

Increasingly companies are incorporating the triple bottom line into their vision statements. This approach emphasizes the social, environmental, and economic health of all of the company's stakeholders rather than a narrow emphasis only on the economic return for shareholders. This stated desire to be a good corporate citizen with a long-term view of the world can motivate efforts that achieve both economic return for shareholders and other positive benefits for many other stakeholders.

MISSION STATEMENT The vision should lead into the mission statement, which is a way to achieve the vision. The mission statement includes the "organization's core purpose, core values,"[3] beliefs, culture, primary business, and primary customers. Several of these sections may flow together in the mission statement and, sometimes, an overall statement is formed with expanded definitions of portions for illustration. The rationale for including each section (either as one unified statement or as separate statements) is as follows:

- By including the organization's purpose, the mission statement communicates why the organization exists.
- By including the organization's core values, a mission statement communicates how decisions will be made and the way people will be treated. True organizational values describe deeply held views concerning how everyone should act—especially when adhering to those values is difficult.
- By including beliefs, a mission statement communicates the ideals for which its leaders and members are expected to stand. Beliefs are deeply held and slow to change, so it is quite useful to recognize them as they can either help or hinder an organization's attempt to achieve its vision.
- By including the organization's culture, the mission statement instructs members to act in the desired manner.
- By including the primary business areas, everyone will know in what business the organization wishes to engage.
- By identifying the primary customers, everyone will understand which groups of people need to be satisfied and who is counting on the organization. The mission needs to be specific enough in describing the business areas and customers to set direction, but not so specific that the organization lacks imagination. An example of a vision and mission statement from Cincinnati Children's Hospital Medical Center is shown in Exhibit 2.3.

EXHIBIT 2.3

CINCINNATI CHILDREN'S HOSPITAL MEDICAL CENTER VISION AND MISSION

Vision

Cincinnati Children's Hospital Medical Center will be the leader in improving child health.

Mission Statement

Cincinnati Children's will improve child health and transform delivery of care through fully integrated, globally recognized research, education and innovation. For patients from our community, the nation and the world, the care we provide will achieve the best:

- Medical and quality of life **outcomes**
- Patient and family **experiences** and
- **Value**

today and in the future.

Source: Cincinnati Children's Hospital Medical Center, http://www.cincinnatichildrens.org/about/corporate/mission.htm, accessed June 28, 2007.

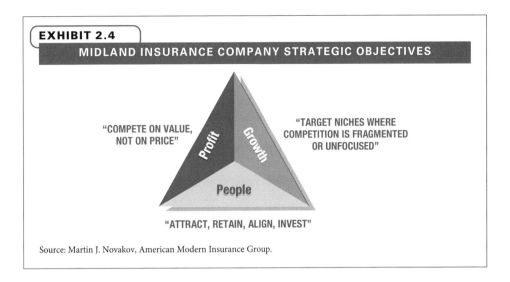

EXHIBIT 2.4

MIDLAND INSURANCE COMPANY STRATEGIC OBJECTIVES

"COMPETE ON VALUE, NOT ON PRICE"

Profit

Growth

"TARGET NICHES WHERE COMPETITION IS FRAGMENTED OR UNFOCUSED"

People

"ATTRACT, RETAIN, ALIGN, INVEST"

Source: Martin J. Novakov, American Modern Insurance Group.

Strategic Objectives

With the strategic analysis, mission, and vision in place, leaders turn to setting strategic objectives, which should be means of achieving the mission and vision. For most organizations, this strategic alignment of objective setting occurs annually, but some organizations may review objectives and make minor revisions at three- or six-month intervals. While the planning is normally performed annually, many of the strategic objectives identified will take well over one year to achieve. The objectives describe both short- and long-term results that are desired along with measures to determine achievement. Organizations that embrace a triple bottom line in their guiding values will have objectives promoting each bottom line, and projects that are selected will contribute toward each. These objectives should provide focus on decisions regarding which projects to select and how to prioritize them since they are an expression of the organizational focus. Many writers have stated that for objectives to be effective, they should be "SMART—that is specific, measurable, achievable, results-based, and time-specific."[4] An example of strategic objectives from Midland Insurance Company is shown in Exhibit 2.4.

Flow-Down Objectives

Once an organization's strategic objectives are identified, they must be enforced. Some objectives may be implemented by work in ongoing operations. However, projects tend to be the primary method for implementing many objectives. If the organization is relatively small, the leaders may proceed directly to selecting projects at this point. Larger organizations may elect a different route. If the organization is so large that it is impractical for the overall leaders to make all project selection decisions, they might delegate those decisions to various divisions or functions with the stipulation that the decisions should be aligned with all of the organization's strategic planning that has taken place to this point. Regardless of whether the organization is small and the top leaders make all project selection decisions or whether the organization is large and some of the decisions are cascaded one or more levels down, several methods of project selection may be used.

2.2 Portfolio Alignment

Companies that use a strategic project selection process to carefully align projects with their organizational goals will find they tend to be more successful at completing their projects and deriving the expected benefits from them. Project success at these companies is measured by how much the project contributes to the organization's objectives (business needs) as well as the traditional measures of staying within budget and schedule and achieving the specific technical goals promised at the start of the project so as to obtain a desired return on investment.

This project portfolio alignment is very similar to financial portfolio alignment from a company's perspective. In a financial portfolio, efforts are made to diversify investments as a means of limiting risk. However, every investment is selected with the hope that it will yield a positive return. The returns on each investment are evaluated individually, and the entire portfolio is evaluated as a whole.

For ease of understanding how various work is related, many organizations utilize an approach of classifying portfolios, programs, projects, and subprojects. Not all companies use all four classifications, but understanding how they are related helps one see where any particular portion of work fits in the organization.

Portfolios

Organizations require many work activities to be performed, including both ongoing operational work and temporary project work. Large organizations often have many projects underway at the same time. A **portfolio** is "a collection of projects or programs and other work that are grouped together to facilitate effective management of that work to meet strategic business objectives. The projects or programs of the portfolio may not necessarily be interdependent or directly related."[5] Each project in the portfolio should have a direct impact on the organization. Put another way, an organization's leaders should identify the organization's future direction through strategic planning. Then multiple possible initiatives (or projects) can be identified that might help further the organization's goals. The leaders need to sort through the various possible projects and prioritize them. Projects with the highest priority should be undertaken first. Organizations typically try to have a sense of balance in their portfolios. That is, an organization includes in its portfolio:

- Some large and some small projects
- Some high-risk, high-reward projects and some low-risk projects
- Some projects that can be completed quickly and some that take substantial time to finish

Programs

A **program** is "a group of related projects managed in a coordinated way to obtain benefits and control not available from managing them individually. Programs may include elements of work outside of the scope of discrete projects in the program."[6] Programs often last as long as the organization lasts, even though specific projects within a program are of limited duration. For example, the U.S. Air Force has an engine procurement program. As long as the Air Force intends to fly aircraft, it will need to acquire engines. Within the engine program are many individual projects. Some of these projects are for basic research, some are for development of engines, and others are for purchasing engines. Each project has a project manager, and the entire program has a program manager. While the project managers are primarily concerned with the tradeoffs of cost, schedule, scope, and quality on their individual projects, the program manager is concerned with making tradeoffs between projects for the maximum benefit of the entire program. To avoid confusion, programs deal with a specific group of related projects, while a portfolio deals with all of an organization's projects. A portfolio can include multiple programs as well as multiple projects.

While the leadership group of a company may make portfolio decisions and delegate the program management decisions to a program manager, both portfolios and programs are managed at a level above the typical project manager. For practical purposes, project managers should attempt to understand how both portfolio and program decisions impact their projects and then spend most of their efforts focused on their project.

Projects and Subprojects

Just as a program is made up of multiple projects, a large project may be composed of multiple subprojects. A **subproject** is "a smaller portion of the overall project created when a project is subdivided into more manageable components or pieces."[7] If the project is quite large, individuals may be assigned as subproject managers and asked to manage their subproject as a project. Some of those subproject managers may even work for another company. The project manager needs to coordinate the various subprojects and make decisions that are best for the overall project. Sometimes this may require that a particular subproject be sacrificed for the greater project good. The relationships among a portfolio, programs, projects, and subprojects are illustrated in Exhibit 2.5.

Because projects are frequently performed in a fast-paced environment, it is helpful if they can be guided by organizational priorities. Some of the most typical reasons for project failure are:

- Not enough resources
- Not enough time
- Unclear expectations
- Changes to the project
- Disagreement about expectations

The first step in overcoming these problems is to carefully align potential projects with the parent organization's goals. While many companies are motivated to align projects with organizational goals for these benefits, an additional reason for companies that sell to the government is that the U.S. Federal Office of Management and Budget in 2003 mandated that "federal agencies show that IT projects align with top-level goals for

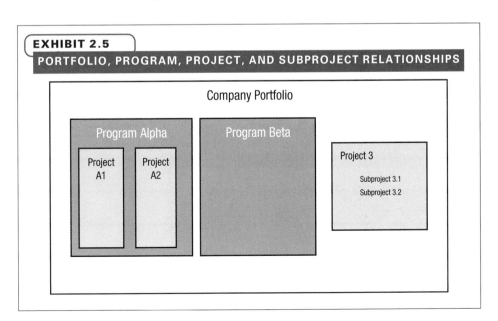

EXHIBIT 2.5

PORTFOLIO, PROGRAM, PROJECT, AND SUBPROJECT RELATIONSHIPS

Company Portfolio

Program Alpha

Program Beta

Project 3

Project A1

Project A2

Subproject 3.1

Subproject 3.2

government efficiency and service."[8] This was the introduction of the Sarbanes-Oxley requirements. All publicly traded companies must now follow certain guidelines that require some sort of financial decision model to be made in deciding to do a project.

A project portfolio is a collection of projects grouped so they can be collectively managed. A project portfolio is similar to the set of classes a student takes in a given term. Each class contributes toward degree requirements. Most students will choose to take a mix of some easy and some hard classes rather than all hard classes at the same time. In the same way, all projects in a portfolio are selected to contribute toward the organization's goals, and a mix of some high-risk, high-reward projects and some easy projects is normal.

When managers assess the organization's ability to perform projects and then identify, select, and prioritize a portfolio of projects and other work that they believe will help the organization achieve its strategic goals, they are performing portfolio alignment. Portfolio alignment helps an organization achieve its goals by "removing duplicated project efforts, ironing out inconsistencies between project scopes, and improving the mix and scheduling of projects."[9] While the majority of the portfolio alignment activities may be conducted by a team of senior executives, project managers should understand how their specific projects are aligned with the organization's objectives since they will need to either make or provide input on many decisions.

When companies consider their entire portfolio of work, they sometimes envision projects as means of developing knowledge that can be capitalized upon in ongoing work processes to provide profit, as shown in Exhibit 2.6.

In times when the economy is poor, many companies straggle to get enough business. In such an environment, some firms might accept almost any work they can get. Even during bleak economic times, however, one should be careful how internal projects are selected since selecting one project limits resources (money, people, etc.) available to

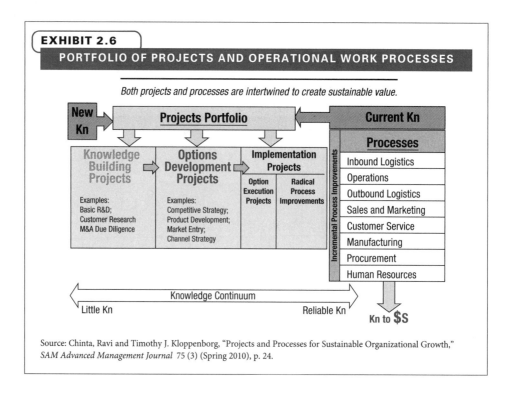

EXHIBIT 2.6

PORTFOLIO OF PROJECTS AND OPERATIONAL WORK PROCESSES

Both projects and processes are intertwined to create sustainable value.

Source: Chinta, Ravi and Timothy J. Kloppenborg, "Projects and Processes for Sustainable Organizational Growth," *SAM Advanced Management Journal* 75 (3) (Spring 2010), p. 24.

other projects. During good or bad economic times, people should take the same care with external projects—ensure that they are consistent with the organization's goals.

Assessing an Organization's Ability to Perform Projects

Assessing an organization's strengths and weaknesses is an essential part of aligning projects with the organization; if an organization does not have the right capabilities, a project that may otherwise support organizational goals may be too difficult to successfully complete. Some questions to ask regarding a firm's ability to support projects are as follows:

- Do we have a teamwork attitude, free and open communication, creativity, and empowered decision making?
- Do we have a clearly defined project management process?
- Do our associates have the right attitudes, skills, and competencies to use the project management process?
- Are our leaders at each level willing to take appropriate personal risk?
- Does senior leadership establish a strong leadership foundation?
- Do individuals and teams exhibit leadership at their respective levels?
- Do we monitor and understand our external environment?

Identifying Potential Projects

The second part of aligning projects with the firm's goals is to identify potential projects. These potential projects can be in response to a market demand, business need, customer request, legal requirement, or technological advance.[10] Ideally, this is accomplished in a systematic manner—not just by chance. Some opportunities will present themselves to the organization. Other good opportunities will need to be discovered. All parts of the organization should be involved. This means people at all levels, from front-line workers to senior executives, and people from all functional areas need to help identify potential projects. For example, salespeople can uncover many opportunities by maintaining open discussions with existing and potential customers, and operations staff may identify potential productivity-enhancing projects. Everyone in the firm should be aware of industry trends. Many industries have trade journals such as *Elevator World* or *Aviation Week and Space Technology* that can be read regularly for potential project ideas. One reasonable goal is to identify approximately twice as many potential projects as the organization has time and resources to perform. Under close examination, some potential projects may not be a good fit. Any company that accepts practically every potential project will probably waste some of its resources on projects that do not support its organizational goals.

Once potential projects are identified, the next step is to develop a brief description of each. The leadership team that will select and prioritize projects needs to understand the nature of the projects they are considering. While the level of documentation different firms require varies greatly, a bare minimum can be called the elevator pitch. This is when a person meets another waiting for an elevator and asks "I hear you are on XYZ Project. What is it all about?" The responder may have only a brief time to give a reply before the elevator arrives and must be prepared to answer quickly with simple statements about the project work and why it is important to the organization. The work is often summarized in a brief **statement of work**, which is a "narrative description of products or services to be provided by the project."[11] Why the project is important is often summarized as a **business case**, which "provides the information needed from a business standpoint to determine if the project is worth the investment."[12] The business case generally includes both why the project is needed and, if the firm uses financial justification as part of project selection, an estimate of costs and benefits. Armed with this "elevator pitch," the series of processes that collectively are used to select, prioritize, and initiate projects begins as shown in Exhibit 2.7. The rectangles represent work processes and the documents represent inputs into and deliverables out of the work processes. Some of this work will be described in Chapters 4 and 5.

Methods for Selecting Projects

The people in charge of selecting projects need to ensure overall organizational priorities are understood, agreed upon, and communicated. Once this common understanding is in place, it is much easier to prioritize potential projects. The degree of formality used in selecting projects varies widely. In a small company, it can be straightforward. The prioritization should include asking questions such as these:

- What value does each potential project bring to the organization?
- Are the demands of performing each project understood?
- Are the resources needed to perform the project available?
- Is there enthusiastic support both from external customers and from one or more internal champions?
- Which projects will best help the organization achieve its goals?

There are several different methods of systematically selecting projects. The methods include both financial and scoring models. The primary reason for including financial analysis—either to make the project selection decisions directly or to at least assist in the decision making—is that, from management's perspective, projects are investments. Therefore, proper selection should yield a portfolio of projects that collectively contribute to organizational success.

Three different approaches are commonly used to ensure both financial and nonfinancial factors are considered when selecting projects. First, some organizations use financial analysis as the primary means of determining which projects are selected, and management merely tempers this with informal inclusion of nonfinancial factors. Second, some organizations use financial models as screening devices to qualify projects or even just to offer perspective; qualified projects then go through a selection process using a scoring model. Third, at still other organizations, financial justification is one factor used in a multifactor scoring model. The common thread in all three of these approaches

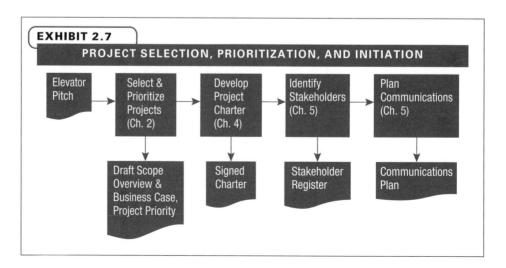

EXHIBIT 2.7

PROJECT SELECTION, PRIORITIZATION, AND INITIATION

Elevator Pitch → Select & Prioritize Projects (Ch. 2) → Develop Project Charter (Ch. 4) → Identify Stakeholders (Ch. 5) → Plan Communications (Ch. 5)

Select & Prioritize Projects (Ch. 2) ↓ Draft Scope Overview & Business Case, Project Priority

Develop Project Charter (Ch. 4) ↓ Signed Charter

Identify Stakeholders (Ch. 5) ↓ Stakeholder Register

Plan Communications (Ch. 5) ↓ Communications Plan

is that both financial and nonfinancial factors are considered when selecting projects. Let us consider both financial and scoring models. Financial models will be covered in concept, but the calculations will not be shown since they are explained in depth in most required finance courses. Scoring models will be covered in both concept and calculation since many students might not have them in another course.

Using a Financial Model to Select Projects

Financial models generally compare expected project costs to expected project benefits. Several financial models can be used in making project selection decisions.

NET PRESENT VALUE (NPV) Net present value (NPV) is the most widely accepted model and will be covered first. When using net present value, the analyst first discounts the expected future value of both the project costs and benefits, recognizing that a dollar in the future is worth less than a dollar today. Then the analyst subtracts the stream of discounted project costs from the stream of discounted project benefits. The result is the net present value of the potential project. If the net present value is positive, then the organization can expect to make money from the project. Higher net present values predict higher profits. See the summary in Exhibit 2.8.

BENEFIT-COST RATIO (BCR) A second financial model sometimes used is benefit-cost ratio (BCR). The ratio is obtained by dividing the cash flow by the initial cash outlay. A ratio above 1.0 means the project expects to make a profit, and a higher ratio than 1.0 is better.

INTERNAL RATE OF RETURN (IRR) The third financial model is internal rate of return (IRR). In this model, the analyst calculates the percentage return expected on the project investment. A ratio above the current cost of capital is considered positive, and a higher expected return is more favorable.

PAYBACK PERIOD (PP) The fourth financial model that is sometimes used is the payback period (PP). In this analysis, a person calculates how many years would be required to pay back the initial project investment. The organization would normally have a stated period that projects should be paid back within, and shorter payback periods are more desirable.

EXHIBIT 2.8

FINANCIAL MODELS FOR PROJECT SELECTION

	NET PRESENT VALUE (NPV)	BENEFIT-COST RATIO (BCR)	INTERNAL RATE OF RETURN (IRR)	PAYBACK PERIOD (PP)
Calculation	PV revenue − PV cost	Cash flow/Project investment	Percentage return on project investment	Project costs/ Annual cash flows
Neutral Result	NPV = $0	Ratio = 1.0	IRR = Cost of capital	Payback period = Accepted length
If used to screen projects or to select projects outright	NPV > Acceptable amount	Ratio > Acceptable amount	IRR > Acceptable amount	Payback period < Acceptable length
If used to compare projects	Higher NPV better	Higher ratio better	Higher IRR better	Shorter payback period better

ADVANTAGES AND DISADVANTAGES OF EACH METHOD Financial models are useful in ensuring that selected projects make sense from a cost and return perspective. Several models have weaknesses that need to be understood before they are used. For example, payback period models do not consider the amount of profit that may be generated after the costs are paid. Thus, two projects with a similar payback period could look equal, but if one has substantially higher revenue after the payback period, it would clearly be superior. BCR would not be acceptable unless all costs and benefits were calculated in present dollars (in which case it is similar to NPV except it is a ratio of benefits to cost instead of the difference between revenue and cost). IRR and BCRs have problems if used for choosing between mutually exclusive projects because they can favor smaller projects that create less total value for the firm but have high percentage returns. For example, a huge project with a medium rate of return would create a lot of value for a firm but might not be picked over a smaller project with a higher return if only one can be chosen. Additionally, it is sometimes quite difficult to calculate an IRR if a project has nonconventional cash flows. For the most part, the finance field recommends using net present value. The other measures can be calculated to provide perspective on whether a project passes a minimum financial return threshold or to communicate with people who might not understand NPV.

However, none of the financial models ensure alignment with an organization's strategic goals. Therefore, financial analysis, while very useful, is normally not enough. Decision makers need to also consider how well a project fits according to additional factors. They will often use a scoring model for this purpose. Sometimes, a scoring model used in this fashion is called a project selection and prioritization matrix.

Using a Scoring Model to Select Projects

In addition to ensuring that selected projects make sense financially, other criteria often need to be considered. A tool called a scoring model helps to select and prioritize potential projects. It is useful whenever there are multiple projects and several criteria to be considered.

IDENTIFYING POTENTIAL CRITERIA These criteria should include how well each potential project fits with the organization's strategic planning. The criteria may also include such items as risk, timing, resources needed, etc. A normal practice is for the company's leadership team to jointly determine what criteria will be used to select projects. Midland Insurance Company uses the three objectives of profit, growth, and people as shown in Exhibit 2.4. A list of questions executives may use to develop their list of criteria is shown in Exhibit 2.9.

DETERMINING MANDATORY CRITERIA Once the leadership team agrees on a list of criteria that are important, the next step is to determine whether any of the criteria are mandatory. That is, are there any situations that dictate a project must be chosen regardless of any other considerations? Examples of this include government mandates and clear safety or security situations. This list of "must do" projects should be kept as small as possible since these projects automatically get selected and can crowd out other worthwhile projects.

WEIGHTING CRITERIA Next, the leadership team determines the relative importance or weight of each decision criteria. While more complex methods of determining criteria weights and project evaluations have been used in the past, many firms now use the simple methods described here for determining criteria weights. See Exhibit 2.10 for an example of project evaluations. First, executives determine which criterion is most

---

EXAMPLES OF PROJECT SELECTION CRITERIA

How well does this project fit with at least one organizational objective?
How many customers are there for the expected results?
How competitively can the company price the project results?
What unique advantages will this project provide?
Does the company have the resources needed?
What is the probability of success?
Are the data needed to perform the project available or easily collected?
Do the key stakeholders agree that the project is needed?
What is the expected return on investment?
How sustainable will the project results be?
How does this project promote (or hinder) our corporate social responsibility?
What risks are there if we do not perform this project?

---

important and give that a weight of 10. Then they ask how important in comparison each of the other criteria is. For example, if the executives in a consumer products company thought development of new products was most important, it would be assigned a weight of 10. If the customer relations factor was deemed almost as important as new product development, maybe it would be assigned 8. If the factors of supplier relations and probability of project success were each deemed to be half as important as new product development, each would be assigned 5. Perhaps other criteria such as cost reduction, safety, and so forth were also considered but determined to not be as important. The resulting criteria with weights are shown in Exhibit 2.10 in the top row of the selection and prioritization matrix. Most organizations will decide to use about three to five criteria. Lesser-rated criteria can be used as tie breakers if needed.

EVALUATING PROJECTS BASED ON CRITERIA Now the leadership team evaluates each project on each criterion. The most efficient and accurate method is to concentrate on one criterion at a time, going down each column in turn. An easy method for this is to rate each project on that particular criterion with scores ranging from 1 (potential

---

PROJECT SELECTION AND PRIORITIZATION MATRIX

Project\Criteria & Weight	New Products 10	Customer Relations 8	Supplier Relations 5	Success Probability 5	Weighted Total Score
Project A					
Project B					
Project C					
Project D					

project has very little or even negative impact on this criterion) to 5 (project has excellent impact on this criterion). The upper left portion of each cell in the matrix can display the rating, representing how well that project satisfies that criterion.

Once a project has been rated on a particular criterion, that rating should be multiplied by the weight assigned to that criterion and displayed as the weighted score in the main body of each cell. The total for each project should be added across the row. The highest-scoring projects would ordinarily be selected. If several projects have close scores (virtual ties), either other criteria or discussion can be used to break the tie. For example, in Exhibit 2.11, there is a virtual tie between Projects A and B.

SENSITIVITY ANALYSES Scoring models allow leadership teams to perform sensitivity analyses—that is, to examine what would happen to the decision if factors affecting it were to change. Selection criteria may be added or altered. Participants may decide that some criteria are more important than others and weight them accordingly. Missing criteria or new alternatives can be added and the decision revisited. For example, if the executive team evaluating the projects in Exhibit 2.11 had a bad experience with an unsuccessful project and decided to reevaluate their decisions with success probability now weighted a 9 for very important, the new project selection and priority matrix would be calculated as shown in Exhibit 2.12.

Decision makers can ensure that they use very solid ratings for each potential project. For example, if one criterion was the number of customers, the marketing department could interview some potential customers to gauge their level of interest.

A company might want to select several projects. If so, the scores from the selection matrix could serve as one method of prioritizing the projects.

Prioritizing Projects

Once all projects have been selected, they will need to be prioritized—that is, the decision makers will need to determine which ones will get assigned resources and be scheduled to begin first. If a company selects a number of projects for a year (or even for a fiscal quarter), it cannot possibly expect to start all of them at the same time. The scoring models are very useful in providing input into the starting order of projects. Most leadership teams will consider the weighted scores of each project as a starting point in

---

EXHIBIT 2.11

COMPLETED PROJECT SELECTION AND PRIORITIZATION MATRIX

Project\Criteria & Weight	New Products 10		Customer Relations 8		Supplier Relations 5		Success Probability 5		Weighted Total Score
Project A	5	50	3	24	4	20	5	25	119
Project B	4	40	3	24	5	25	5	25	114
Project C	1	10	5	40	3	15	3	15	80
Project D	2	20	4	32	1	5	2	10	67

EXHIBIT 2.12

REVISED PROJECT SELECTION AND PRIORITIZATION MATRIX

Project\Criteria & Weight	New Products 10		Customer Relations 8		Supplier Relations 5		Success Probability 9		Weighted Total Score
Project A	5	50	3	24	4	20	5	45	139
Project B	4	40	3	24	5	25	5	45	134
Project C	1	10	5	40	3	15	3	27	92
Project D	2	20	4	32	1	5	2	18	75

Source: Chris Bridges.

---

assigning resources to projects and determining their start dates. The leadership team members, however, also generally discuss other issues such as:

- The urgency of each project
- The cost of delaying the expected benefits from various projects
- Practical details concerning the timing

For example, an important process improvement project may be far less disruptive to perform when the factory is shut down for routine maintenance. One more discussion frequently occurs in the prioritizing process—if there is a conflict between resource needs for two projects, which one gets the needed resources first? Often, this is left to the project sponsors to iron out; for especially important projects, it may be formally decided by the leadership team. In that way, the probability of the critical project being held up by a misunderstanding is greatly decreased.

Exhibit 2.13 shows how the Alternative Breaks (AB) planning committee at a university ranked spring break projects. This exhibit shows four of the twenty-six projects that were selected for trips. This book will include multiple examples of the AB project to illustrate how various project planning tools work together. Each trip is a small project while the combination of all twenty-six trips form the overall project.

EXHIBIT 2.13

ALTERNATIVE BREAKS PROJECT SELECTION AND PRIORITIZATION MATRIX

PROJECT/SELECTION CRITERIA	ACTIVE SERVICE OPPORTUNITY 9		ISSUE ITSELF 10		ORGANIZATION TO WORK WITH 6		COST 5		Total
New York Vegan Farm	5	45	4	40	3	18	4	20	123
West Virginia Sustainability	4	36	3	30	4	24	5	25	115
Chicago Halfway House	2	18	4	40	4	24	4	20	102
El Salvador Cultural Immersion	1	9	5	50	5	30	1	5	94

2.3 Securing Projects

The discussion above pertains to projects that are internal to an organization. This section deals with projects a company (called the client) wants performed, but for which it may hire external resources (called contractors) to execute significant parts or all of the work. External projects can be viewed either from the perspective of the client company that wants the project to be executed or from the perspective of the contractor company that wants to perform the work. Client companies may first put prospective external projects through a selection and prioritization process as described above and, if selected, then decide whether to perform the work internally (make) or hire the project to be performed by others (buy). If the decision is to buy, then the client company needs to plan and conduct the procurement.

Contractor companies need to identify potential project opportunities, determine which they will pursue, submit proposals, and be prepared to either bid or negotiate to secure the work. We consider the client company's perspective in Chapter 12, Project Supply Chain Management. We consider the contractor's perspective next.

Identify Potential Project Opportunities

Contractors seeking external projects to perform should pursue this in a fashion similar to that of any company considering internal projects, as described in the portfolio alignment section on identifying potential projects earlier in this chapter. Additionally, since they need to look externally, contractor companies should have representatives at trade shows, professional conferences, and anywhere information on the intentions of potential customers and competitors may surface. Contractor companies should also actively practice customer relationship management by establishing and nurturing personal contacts at various levels and functions. Contractor companies can also practice customer relationship management by linking information systems to the extent practical so as to identify any useful information concerning potential future projects and improve management of current projects.

Determine Which Opportunities to Pursue

Many companies find that targeting their opportunities is a better use of their time and resources than bidding on every potential project.

Just as all companies should decide which internal projects to select, as previously described in the methods for selecting projects, most contractor companies are best served by targeting the projects they wish to pursue. Some companies have a policy that they will bid on every potential project, knowing that if they do not bid, they will not be awarded the project. More companies find that if they target their opportunities, their "hit rate" or probability of securing the work on any given proposal increases. It takes time and resources to put together a good proposal, so it makes sense to increase the acceptance rate by developing a bid/no-bid decision strategy.

Each company has strengths and weaknesses compared to its competitors. Hence, a quick SWOT analysis could be used to decide whether to pursue a potential project, just as a more involved version of SWOT analysis was described earlier and depicted in Exhibit 2.2. Decision makers can also ask how well a potential project will help achieve their objectives. If they determine a project will help achieve their objectives, the next considerations are the cost to pursue the work and the probability of successfully

> ## EXHIBIT 2.14
>
> ### TYPICAL SOURCE SELECTION CRITERIA
>
> | TECHNICAL | MANAGEMENT | FINANCIAL | OPERATIONAL |
> | --- | --- | --- | --- |
> | Technical experience | Management experience | Financial capacity | Production capacity |
> | Needs understanding | Project charter | Life cycle cost | Business size and type |
> | Technical approach | Planning and scheduling | Cost basis and assumptions | Past performance |
> | Risk mitigation | Project control | Warranties | References |

securing the project given the likely competition. A company frequently considers risks both of pursuing and not pursuing a potential project. Finally, does the company have the capability to perform the work if it is awarded?

Prepare and Submit a Project Proposal

When a firm prepares to submit a proposal, it is really conducting a small project with the primary deliverable of the project being an accurate and complete proposal. The contractor should understand the source selection criteria the client will use to decide to whom they will award the project. While criteria will vary extensively from one project to another, generally four main areas will be considered—technical, management, financial, and operational factors. In other words, a client will likely want to be convinced that the potential contractor is technically, managerially, financially, and operationally competent. Successful project managers try very hard to convince potential clients that they are capable on all three dimensions. A short list of these factors is shown in Exhibit 2.14.

Negotiate to Secure the Project

Once all proposals have been delivered and evaluated, the client company may elect to either award the project or enter into negotiations with one or more potential contractors. On more routine projects, the contract may be awarded at this point. Further clarifications and negotiations may follow for complex projects.

A client company and a contractor company may negotiate the amount of money to be paid for a project. They may also negotiate the contractual terms, schedule, specific personnel to be assigned to work on the contract, quality standards, reporting mechanisms, and various other items. A project manager may need to make arrangements with potential suppliers to secure the products and services needed to perform the project. All of these considerations will be covered in subsequent chapters.

Successful project managers understand that they need to prepare well for negotiations. This starts with a clear understanding of what is most important to their management. Often, it includes fact-finding with the client company to understand its needs and abilities. Armed with understanding of both perspectives, a project manager attempts to find a solution that allows the organization to secure the project work with enough profit potential and with the start of a good working relationship with the client. In the end, the client company will select the contractor(s) and award the contract(s).

Summary

Project selection does not occur in isolation. Ideally, it begins with the organization's strategic planning. This planning begins with a strategic analysis of the organization's internal strengths and weaknesses as well as the external threats and opportunities it faces. The organization should then develop its guiding principles such as mission and vision statements. Most companies will have an annual planning session in which strategic objectives are developed. Larger organizations will continue this effort with one or more levels of planning in which the overall objectives are flowed down to determine objectives that are appropriate for each organizational level.

Once the strategic planning is accomplished, the organization's leadership team engages in portfolio alignment. The first part of the organizational alignment is an open and honest assessment of the organization's ability to perform projects. The decision makers need to understand how many resources are available, the organization's overall capabilities, and the capabilities of the individuals who will be assigned to projects. An ongoing portfolio alignment activity is for everyone in the firm to identify possible opportunities that they feel might help the organization achieve its goals. Each potential project should be described at least by stating in a sentence or two what work is involved and how it would help the organization achieve one or more of its goals.

Once potential projects are identified and briefly described with statements of work and business cases,

they should be put through a process to determine which will be selected and what their relative priorities are. Both financial and scoring models are frequently used to evaluate potential projects. Net present value is the preferred financial method, although others are sometimes used. Financial analysis tells the leadership team how much each potential project is worth from a benefits-versus-cost comparison, but does not tell how each potential project may help to achieve the organization's goals. Scoring models can incorporate various goals and should also be used. Once a project list is selected, the projects need to be prioritized so some can start right away and others can start later.

Contractor companies need to be constantly on the lookout for potential project opportunities. Once potential projects are identified, companies need to decide which ones they pursue. Just as for internal projects, some external projects will be better at helping an organization reach its goals because they are a better fit. The contractor needs to prepare and submit proposals for desired projects and be prepared to follow up and often negotiate in order to secure them.

Key Terms from the *PMBOK® Guide*

statement of work, 35

business case, 35

Chapter Review Questions

1. List and describe each step in the strategic planning process.
2. Why are multiple-criteria project selection models preferred?
3. What happens to a project proposal that does not meet a "must" objective in a project selection system?
4. What does the strategic analysis acronym SWOT stand for?
5. Which parts of SWOT are internal? Which parts are external?
6. What are some examples of guiding principles an organization's leaders might develop after they have completed strategic analysis?
7. In what tense should a vision be written?
8. Name at least four things a mission statement should include.
9. Why should a mission statement be neither too specific nor not specific enough?
10. In addition to short- and long-term results, what should strategic objectives include?
11. What does the acronym SMART mean with regard to goals?
12. What is the primary method of implementing organizational objectives?
13. What is the first step in avoiding common reasons for project failure?
14. Who should be involved in the second part of aligning projects with the firm's goals, which is identifying potential projects?
15. How many potential projects should be identified in comparison to how many the organization plans to actually implement? Why?
16. What is the most common financial analysis technique used in project selection? Why?
17. Which type of financial model would you normally use in project selection? Why?

Discussion Questions

1. Describe how to prioritize projects to ensure top management involvement.
2. Describe all of the issues management must consider when determining priorities of projects.
3. Tell why gaining top management support is vital to project success.
4. List and describe the steps in strategic direction setting.
5. Describe how to conduct each portion of a SWOT analysis.
6. Describe what knowledge is gained from each portion of a SWOT analysis and how it helps project managers.
7. Describe the interaction between vision and mission statements.
8. List and describe the steps in prioritizing projects with a scoring model. Why are they performed in this order?
9. Describe advantages and disadvantages of financial and scoring models in project selection.
10. Describe three different ways decision makers might select projects while considering both financial and nonfinancial factors.

PMBOK® Guide Questions

1. Work that is grouped together to facilitate effective management of that work to meet strategic business objectives is called a:
   a. portfolio
   b. program
   c. project
   d. subproject
2. Projects may be undertaken as a result of any of the following strategic reasons **except:**
   a. business need
   b. customer request
   c. executive preference
   d. technological advance
3. Program management includes all of the following **except:**
   a. aligning organizational and strategic direction
   b. managing shared client relationships
   c. resolving issues and change management
   d. resolving resource constraints
4. Typical source selection criteria for projects include all of the following capabilities **except:**
   a. financial
   b. management
   c. marketing
   d. technical
5. A narrative description of products or services to be provided by the project is a:
   a. business case
   b. project proposal
   c. project statement of work
   d. subproject

Exercises

1. Complete the following scoring model. Show all your work. Tell which project you would pick first, second, third, and last. How confident are you with each choice? If you lack confidence regarding any of your choices, what would you prefer to do about it?

Project\ Criteria & Weight	Criteria 1 10	Criteria 2 6	Criteria 3 4	Weighted Total Score
Project A	4	3	5	
Project B	3	2	3	
Project C	2	4	3	
Project D	1	3	4	

2. Complete the following scoring model. Show all your work. Tell which project you would pick first, second, third, and last. How confident are you with each choice? If you lack confidence regarding any of your choices, what would you prefer to do about it?

Project\ Criteria & Weight	Criteria 1 10	Criteria 2 7	Criteria 3 3	Weighted Total Score
Project A	1	3	4	
Project B	3	5	3	
Project C	5	4	3	
Project D	2	3	1	

3. Pretend you are on the leadership team for a pharmaceutical company that is in a difficult financial situation due to patents that have died on two of your most profitable drugs. Brainstorm a list of criteria by which you would select and prioritize projects. Weight the criteria.

4. Pretend you are on the leadership team of a manufacturing company that is currently challenged by low-cost competition. Brainstorm a list of criteria by which you would select and prioritize projects. Weight the criteria.

Example Project

Your instructor will probably bring example projects to class and facilitate the assignment of students to the various project teams. Therefore, you will probably not be involved in the project selection. However, one of the first things you should do when assigned to a project is to learn about the company or other organization that wants the project to be completed. Why did they select this project? Is it a "must do" project or did it get picked over other competing projects? By understanding what makes the project so important, you will make better decisions and will be more motivated through the term. If your project is a "must do" project, explain why. If it is not a "must do" project, explain how it was selected. Explain where it fits in priority with other work of the organization.

References

A Guide to the Project Management Body of Knowledge (PMBOK® Guide) 4th ed. (Newtown Square, PA: Project Management Institute, 2008).

Aldag, Ramon J. and Loren W. Kuzuhara, *Mastering Management Skills: A Manager's Toolkit* (Mason, OH: Thomson South-Western, 2005).

Barclay, Colane and Kweku-Muata Osei-Bryson, "Toward a More Practical Approach to Evaluating Programs: The Multi-Objective Realization Approach," *Project Management Journal* 40 (4) (December 2009): 74–93.

Brache, Alan P. and Sam Bodley-Scott, "Which Imperatives Should You Implement?" *Harvard Management Update*, Article reprint no. U0904B (2009).

Cannella, Cara, "Sustainability: A Green Formula," *2008 Leadership in Project Management* 4: 34–40.

Caron, Franco, Mauro Fumagalli, and Alvaro Rigamonti, "Engineering and Contracting Projects: A Value at Risk Based Approach to Portfolio Balancing," *International Journal of Project Management* 25 (2007): 569–578.

Chinta, Ravi and Timothy J. Kloppenborg, "Projects and Processes for Sustainable Organizational Growth," *SAM Advanced Management Journal* 75: 2 (Spring 2010): 22–28.

Cooper, Robert G., "Winning at New Products: Pathways to Profitable Innovation," *Proceedings of PMI Research Conference 2006* (Newtown Square, PA: Project Management Institute, 2006).

Daft, Richard L., *Management*, 9th ed. (Mason, OH: South-Western Cengage Learning, 2010).

Eager, Amanda, "Designing a Best-in-Class Innovation Scoreboard," *Technology Management* (January–February 2010): 11–13.

Essex, David E., "In Search of ROI," *PMNetwork* 19 (10) (October 2005): 46–52.

Evans, R. James and William M. Lindsay, *Managing for Quality and Performance Excellence*, 8th ed. (Mason, OH: South-Western Cengage Learning, 2011).

Fretty, Peter, "Find the Right Mix," *PMNetwork* 19(9) (September 2005): 26–32.

Kenny, John, "Effective Project Management for Strategic Innovation and Change in an Organizational Context," *Project Management Journal* 34 (1) (March 2003): 43–53.

Kloppenborg, Timothy J., Arthur Shriberg, and Jayashree Venkatraman, *Project Leadership* (Vienna, VA: Management Concepts, 2003).

Labuschagne, Les and Carl Marnewick, "A Structured Approach to Derive Projects from the Organizational Vision," *Proceedings of PMI Research Conference 2006* (Newtown Square, PA: Project Management Institute, 2006).

Mais, Andy and Sam Retna, "Decision Time," *PMNetwork* 20 (3) (March 2006): 58–62.

Milosevic, Dragan Z. and Sabin Srivinnaboon, "A Theoretical Framework for Aligning Project Management with Business Strategy," *Project Management Journal* 37 (3) (August 2006): 98–110.

Organizational Project Management Maturity Model Knowledge Foundation, 2nd ed. (Newtown Square, PA: Project Management Institute, 2008).

Reginato, Justin and C. William Ibbs, "Employing Business Models for Making Project Go/No Go Decisions," *Proceedings of PMI Research Conference 2006* (Newtown Square, PA: Project Management Institute, 2006).

Senge, Peter, Bryan Smith, Nina Kruschwitz, Joe Laur, and Sara Schley, *The Necessary Revolution: How Individuals and Organizations Are Working Together to Create a Sustainable World* (New York: Broadway Books, 2008).

Smallwood, Deb and Karen Furtado, "Strategy Meets the Right Projects at the Right Time," *Bank Systems & Technolgy* 46 (4) (June–July 2009): 34.

Thamhain, Hans J., "Developing Winning Proposals," *Field Guide to Project Management*, 2nd ed., edited by David I. Cleland (Hoboken, NJ: John Wiley & Sons, Inc., 2004): 180–201.

The Standard for Portfolio Management, 2nd ed. (Newtown Square, PA: Project Management Institute, 2008).

Wheatley, Malcolm, "Beyond the Numbers" *PMNetwork* 23 (8) (August 2009): 38–43.

Zhang, Weiyong, Arthur V. Hill, Roger G. Schroeder, and Kevin W. Linderman, "Project Management Infrastructure: The Key to Operational Performance Improvement," *Operations Management Research* 1 (1) (September 2008): 40–52.

http://en.wikipedia.org/wiki/Triple_bottom_line, accessed February 2, 2010.

http://www.gcbl.org/

Endnotes

1. Aldag, Ramon J. and Loren W. Kuzuhara, *Mastering Management Skills: A Manager's Toolkit* (Mason, OH: Thomson South-Western, 2005): A10.

2. http://www.gcbl.org, accessed March 3, 2010.

3. Lussier, Robert N. and Christopher F. Achua, *Leadership: Theory, Application, Skill Development*, 4th ed. (Mason, OH: Thomson South-Western, 2010): 425.

4. Lussier, Robert N. and Christopher F. Achua, *Leadership: Theory, Application, Skill Development*, 4th ed. (Mason, OH: Thomson South-Western, 2010): 426.

5. *PMBOK® Guide* 441.

6. *PMBOK® Guide* 442.

7. *PMBOK® Guide* 450.

8. Essex, David E., "In Search of ROI," *PMNetwork* 19 (10) (October 2005): 49.

9. Mais, Andy and Sam Retna, "Decision Time," *PMNetwork* 20(3) (March 2006): 60.

10. *PMBOK® Guide* 10.

11. *PMBOK® Guide* 75.

12. *PMBOK® Guide* 75.

PROJECT MANAGEMENT *IN ACTION*

Prioritizing Projects at D. D. Williamson

One of the most difficult, yet most important, lessons we have learned at D. D. Williamson surrounds project prioritization. We took three years and two iterations of our prioritization process to finally settle on an approach that dramatically increased our success rate on critical projects (now called VIPs, or "Vision Impact Projects").

Knowing that one of the keys to project management success is key management support, our first approach at prioritization was a process where our entire senior management team worked through a set of criteria and resource estimations to select a maximum of two projects per senior management sponsor—16 projects in total. Additionally, we hired a continuous improvement manager to serve as both our project office and a key resource for project facilitation. This was a great move forward (the year before we had been attempting to monitor well over 60 continuous improvement projects of varying importance). Our success rate improved to over 60 percent of projects finishing close to the expected dates, financial investment, and results.

What was the problem? The projects that were *not* moving forward tended to be the most critical—the heavy-investment "game changing" projects. A review of our results the next year determined we left significant money in opportunity "on the table" with projects that were behind and over budget!

This diagnosis led us to seek an additional process change. While the criteria rating was sound, the number of projects for a company our size was still too many to track robustly at a senior level and have resources to push for completion. Hence, we elevated a subset of projects to highest status—our "VIPs." We simplified the criteria ratings—rating projects on the level of expected impact on corporate objectives, the cross-functional nature of the team, and the perceived likelihood that the project would encounter barriers which required senior level support to overcome.

The results? Much better success rates on the big projects, such as design and implementation of new equipment and expansion plans into new markets. But why?

The Global Operating Team (GOT) now has laser focus on the five VIPs, reviewing the project plans progress and next steps with our continuous improvement manager in every weekly meeting. If a project is going off plan, we see it quickly and can move to reallocate resources, provide negotiation help, or change priorities within and outside the organization to manage it back on track. Certainly, the unanticipated barriers still occur, but we can put the strength of the entire team toward removing them as soon as they happen.

A couple of fun side benefits—it is now a development opportunity for project managers to take on a VIP. With only four to six projects on the docket, they come with tremendous senior management interaction and focus. Additionally, we have moved our prioritization process into our functional groups, using matrices with criteria and resource estimations to prioritize customer and R&D projects with our sales, marketing, and science and innovation teams, as well as IT projects throughout the company. The prioritization process has become a foundation of our cross-functional success!

Following are excerpts from the spreadsheet D. D. Williamson used to select and prioritize our VIP projects last year. Exhibit 2.15 shows the five criteria used to prioritize the projects. Exhibit 2.16 shows how associate time when assigned to a project is not available for other projects. Projects can also be limited by the amount of funds. Finally, Exhibit 2.17 defines terms used in project selection.

EXHIBIT 2.15

PROJECT PRIORITIZATION FOR D. D. WILLIAMSON

PROJECTS (REDUCED FOR EXAMPLE)

Qtr to start project	Project number	Project list — continuous improvement and innovation	Level of difficulty	Achieve sales revenue of $XXX, XXX, XXX	Weight	Weighted criteria—sales	Drive additional sales in natural colors of $X, XXX, XXX	Weight	Weighted criteria—natural colors	Achieve return on capital employed of XX%	Weight	Weighted criteria—ROCE	Repeatability of project—other locations	Weight	Weighted criteria—repeatability	Risk of project barriers to completion	Weight	Weighted criteria—barriers	Total rating
1		Powder packaging equipment installation		8	5	40	1	5	5	9	4	36	5	3	15	5	3	15	111
1		Design and install "new processing equipment" in China operation		8	5	40	1	5	5	10	4	40	9	3	27	9	3	27	139
2		Implement expansion plans for new products (X)		9	5	45	10	5	50	8	4	32	8	3	24	8	3	24	175
2		Install "new environmental scrubber"		4	5	20	3	5	15	10	4	40	10	3	30	10	3	30	135

EXHIBIT 2.16

ASSOCIATE TIME ASSIGNED TO PROJECTS

PROJECT LIST—CONTINUOUS IMPROVEMENT AND INNOVATION	TOTAL ASSOCIATE AVAILABLE HOURS FOR PROJECTS	TED	MARGARET	ELAINE	BRIAN	ANN	GRAHAM	EDIE	CAMPBELL
Associate "improvement" hrs for quarter:		120	120	120	120	120	120	120	120
Total associate hrs committed:		**80**	**120**	**60**	**180**	**0**	**60**	**40**	**60**
Total hours exceeding available quarter		**−40**	**0**	**−60**	**60**	**−120**	**−60**	**−80**	**−60**
Powder packaging equipment installation				60	60				
Design and install "new processing equipment" in China operation					60			40	
Implement expansion plans for new products (X)		80	120				60		60
Install "new environmental scrubber"					60				

EXHIBIT 2.17

	TERMS USED IN PROJECT SELECTION
DEFINITIONS OF KEY TERMS	
Project Ownership	Defines the functional area with primary responsibility for the project
Global vs. Local	Global projects will be implemented or impact on more than one location in the year defined; otherwise projects are defined as local
Prioritization	The five weighted criteria on worksheet one were used to put projects in rank order—used to assign resources and identify the cut off
CI Project	An improvement effort which is not part of an associate's daily work requirements
Team Charter	The plan for completing CI projects, often in seven-step format for problem resolution, though formats vary according to project type and complexity. Includes the plan for communicating progress and results
Project Roles	The defined roles on an improvement team—not all teams will have all roles, but each project will have at least a project manager and sponsor
Project Manager (PM)	*The owner of a project—will be expected to charter the team, ensure the forward movement of the project, and report on progress, completion of the project, and closure/celebration of successes and learnings. Also responsible for the communication plan within the charter. Must be a leadership program graduate, and typically a functional manager, either global or local*
Sponsor (S)	*Typically a senior manager/GOT member—responsible for ensuring assignment of appropriate resources, clearing any barriers, and otherwise championing the project*
Team Member (TM)	*An associate who has a significant contribution to make to the improvement effort, often a representative of an involved function. Attends all team meetings and shares responsibility for completion of the project*
Subject Matter Expert (SME)	*An associate with needed knowledge for project outcome—may not be significantly affected by changes. Attends only when knowledge is required, but commits to sharing knowledge when it is needed.*
Level of Difficulty	*The estimated human resource effort that will be required to complete a project (**estimated on a per quarter basis**)*
Level 1	*Low investment of hours required (may require capital); solution is known and implementation of solution is predictable; likely only 2–3 people involved* ***Level 1 projects—estimated hours for resource allocation: PM: 10 hours; S: 2 hours; SME: 5 hours***
Level 2	*Medium investment of hours required; may require upfront measurement and multiple solutions, but solutions and implementation are still expected to be simple. Probably requires 3–5 team members* ***Level 2 projects—estimated hours for resource allocation: PM: 60 hours; S: 15 hours; TM: 30 hours; SME 15 hours***
Level 3	*High investment of hours required; trying to solve complex and/or ongoing problems. Likely to involve a behavior change in others—solutions or implementation outcomes may be unknown or less simple. Likely a team of 4–8 people, perhaps cross-functional/cross location* ***Level 3 projects—estimated hours for resource allocation: PM: 120 hours; S: 30 hours; TM: 60 hours; SME: 30 hours***

Source: Elaine Gravatte, Chief People Officer and North American President, D. D. Williamson

CHAPTER 3

Organizational Capability: Structure, Culture, and Roles

CHAPTER OBJECTIVES

After completing this chapter, you should be able to:

- Compare and contrast the advantages and disadvantages of the functional, project, strong matrix, balanced matrix, and weak matrix methods of organization; describe how each operates and when to use each.

- Describe organizational culture elements that are helpful in planning and managing projects and describe how to overcome organizational culture elements that hinder project success.

- Describe different project life cycle models and tell when each is appropriate.

- Describe the duties, motivations, and challenges of each of the executive, managerial, and team roles in projects and list important attributes for selecting each.

Jon Feingersh/Iconica/Getty Images

Over the last 15 years, my company (Atos Origin) has been through three significant mergers/acquisitions and has seen good growth. As new lines of businesses and employees have been added, we have become truly a global company, where people from many countries where our businesses operate come together to present the best solution to our clients. An excellent example is the work we do for the Olympics games (Atos Origin has been the worldwide IT partner for the Olympics for several years).

The overall project life cycle for most of the projects in the company follows the typical IT project management approach. What has evolved over time is the use of employees from different regions of the world to service a client need. For instance, we have onsite operations for a client in the United States and in Europe. The development and testing work is done offshore in India. The onsite team members are primarily the program manager, project managers (who deal with the client), business analysts, and technical

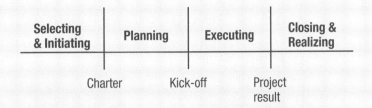

Selecting & Initiating	Planning	Executing	Closing & Realizing

Charter   Kick-off   Project result

PMBOK® GUIDE TOPICS

- Organizational culture
- Organizational structure
- Stakeholders
- Role of project manager
- Develop human resource plan
- Project management office
- Project life cycle

architects. The offshore team members include designers, developers, and testers. There are also project managers who lead the team in India and interact with their onsite counterpart on a regular basis.

The entire operation is managed through a program management office (PMO) that is responsible for identifying, prioritizing, and ensuring delivery of all the projects. It is a matrix structure where the team members report into the PMO as well as their functional heads in their countries. The PMO has its own culture of hard work, striving toward goals in a step-by-step manner, and promoting team spirit. It fits right into our overall organization culture of getting things done for the client, promoting innovation and conviviality, and never compromising on ethical behavior.

I have observed that adaptability and empathy are helpful strengths for project managers in this environment. Adaptability because the different locations bring with them a set of challenges, including the ability to hold the global team together. Empathy is extremely useful as well. Although the project manager may not agree with the choices made by team members, he or she must respect them.

Recently we had a team member from India absent from work for over two weeks because his father was seriously ill. Typically in the United States that would not be the case. Most people live away from their parents here and are not able to take so much time off for their illness. In India, parents often live with and are cared for by their children. The project manager from the United States understood the Indian culture well enough to know that until the team member's father was well enough, he would have to arrange for a different resource to perform on the project. Fortunately, because of his traits of adaptability and empathy, he had recognized this up front and was able to achieve his project timeline.

It is important for you, as a student of project management, to understand and appreciate that organizations are different and are continuously evolving. Entities in an organization in different parts of the world are different. Team members have different strengths and weaknesses. Clients have different expectations from a global company. As a project manager, you will need to use your strengths to ensure that all your stakeholders are happy before, during, and after project delivery.

Rachana Sampat (Thariani), Atos Origin

3.1 Types of Organizational Structures

Contemporary companies choose among various methods for establishing their organizational structure. Organizational structure can be considered to include work assignments, reporting relationships, and decision-making responsibility. Each method of structuring organizations has strengths and weaknesses. In this section, we will investigate various organizational methods and the impact of each on managing projects. The advantages and disadvantages of each organizational form are discussed in the following sections and then summarized in Exhibit 3.5.

Functional

A **functional organization** is "a hierarchical organization where each employee has one clear superior, staff are grouped by areas of specialization, and managed by a person with expertise in that area."[1] This is the traditional approach when there are clear lines of authority according to type of work. For example, all accountants might report to a head of accounting, all marketers report to a head of marketing, and so on. An organizational chart for a functional organization is shown in Exhibit 3.1. Note that everyone in the organization reports up through one and only one supervisor. That supervisor is the head of a discipline or function (such as marketing).

The functional manager generally controls the project budget, makes most project decisions, and is the primary person who coordinates project communications outside of the functional areas by contacting his or her peer functional managers.

ADVANTAGES One advantage of the functional form of organization is called unity of command—all workers understand clearly what they need to do because only one "boss" is giving them instructions. Another advantage is that since all workers in a discipline report to the same supervisor, they can learn readily from each other and keep their technical skills sharp. A third advantage is that workers know that when they finish work on a project they will still have a job because they will continue to report to the

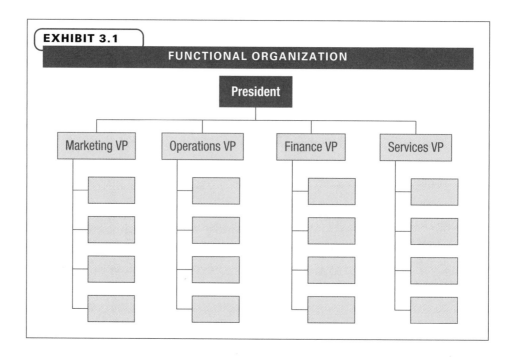

EXHIBIT 3.1

FUNCTIONAL ORGANIZATION

same functional manager. For small projects that require most of the work from one department, the functional organization often works well both because of the advantages already stated and because the functional manager can share resources among various small projects and centrally control the work.

DISADVANTAGES However, the functional form of organization can make for slow communications when multiple functions need to have input. It also can be challenging from a technical standpoint if input is required from multiple disciplines. The functional manager is probably quite good within his or her domain, but may have less understanding of other disciplines. In small organizations where most people have been forced to understand multiple areas, this may be less of an issue. Coordination between departments is frequently conducted at the manager level as the functional managers have a great deal of decision-making authority. This often means communication needs to first travel up from worker to manager, then across from one functional manager to another manager, then down from manager to worker. These long communication channels often make for slow decision making and slow response to change. For these reasons, some organizations choose other forms of organization.

Projectized

The exact opposite form of organization is the **projectized organization,** which is defined as "any organizational structure in which the project manager has full authority to assign projects, apply resources, and direct work of persons assigned to the project."[2] In this organizational form, sometimes called a divisional approach, the larger organization is broken down into self-contained units that support large projects, geographies, or customers. Most people in the organization are assigned to a project and report upward through the project manager, as can be seen in Exhibit 3.2. While the structure of the two organizational charts appears similar, the reporting manager is a project manager instead of a functional manager. The project manager has extensive authority for budgets, personnel, and other decision making in this organizational structure.

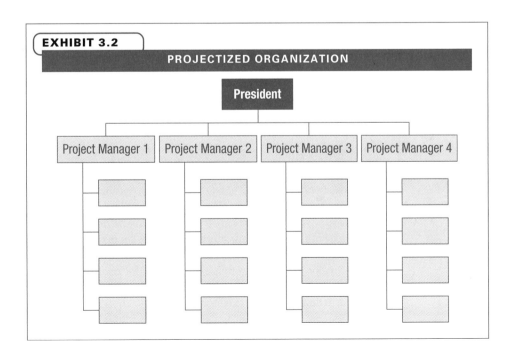

EXHIBIT 3.2

PROJECTIZED ORGANIZATION

ADVANTAGES The advantages of the projectized organizational form are very different from the advantages of the functional form. Because people from different functions now report to the same project manager, traditional department barriers are reduced. Since the project manager is responsible for communications, response times and decision making tend to be swift. All workers understand clearly what they need to do because only one "boss"—the project manager—is giving them instructions.

Projectized organizational structures often utilize the technique of **co-location,** which is "an organizational placement strategy where the project team members are physically located close to one another to improve communication, working relationships, and productivity."[3] This co-location often results in enhanced project team identity, strong customer focus, and effective integration of effort on the project.

DISADVANTAGES However, this organizational form also has disadvantages. Team members are often assigned to just one project, even if the project only needs part of their time. This can be costly. Since the project manager is in charge and the team may be physically located onsite rather than with the rest of the organization, some projects tend to develop their own work methods and disregard those of the parent organization. While some of the new methods may be quite useful, project teams not watched closely can fail to practice important organizational norms and sometimes do not pass the lessons they learn on to other project teams. Team members who are co-located, while learning more about the broader project issues, often do not keep up their discipline-specific competence as well. Team members sometimes worry about what they will do when the project is completed.

Matrix

Each of the extreme strategies already described (extreme in the sense that either the functional manager or the project manager has a great deal of authority) has great advantages, yet significant weaknesses. In an attempt to capture many of the advantages of both, and to hopefully not have too many of the weaknesses of either, many organizations use an intermediate organizational strategy in which both the project manager and the functional manager have some authority and share other authority.

This intermediate strategy is the **matrix organization,** which is "any organizational structure in which the project manager shares responsibility with the functional managers for assigning priorities and directing work of persons assigned to the project."[4] A matrix organization is shown in Exhibit 3.3. Note that project team members report to both functional and project managers. This is a clear violation of the unity-of-command principle; however, it is necessary to enjoy the benefits of a matrix organization. In short, the hoped-for benefit of a matrix structure is a combination of the task focus of the projectized organizational structure with the technical capability of the functional structure.

ADVANTAGES Matrix organizations have many advantages, which is why an increasing number of companies are using some variation of them today. One advantage is that because both project and functional managers are involved, there is good visibility into who is working where, and resources can be shared between departments and projects. This reduces possible duplication—a major advantage in this age of lean thinking in business. Since both types of managers are involved, cooperation between departments can be quite good. There is more input, so decisions tend to be high quality and are better accepted. This is a major issue since enthusiastic support for controversial decisions often helps a project team work through challenges. Since people still report to their functional manager, they are able to develop and retain discipline-specific knowledge. Since the various disciplines report to the same project manager, effective integration is still possible. Because people report to both the project manager, who is responsible for capturing lessons learned, and to the

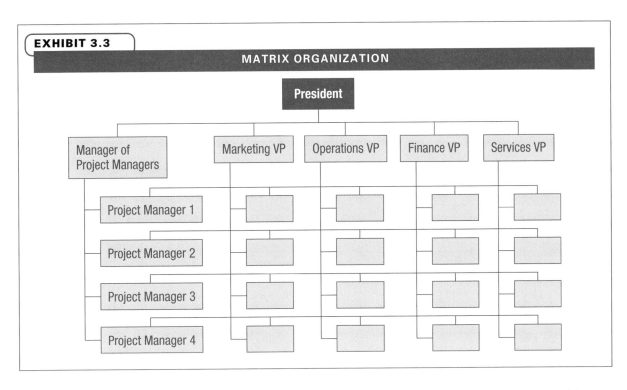

EXHIBIT 3.3

MATRIX ORGANIZATION

functional manager, who is responsible for how the work in a function is performed, lessons learned can be shared effectively between projects.

Yet another advantage of the matrix form is its flexibility. The amount of decision-making authority can be shared equally in whatever manner is desired. When the functional managers have relatively more power, it is almost like a functional organization. This is how many organizations start evolving—by giving project managers a bit more decision-making authority. This is called a weak matrix since the project managers have less authority than functional managers. The next step in the progression is a balanced matrix in which project managers and functional managers have about equal power. Finally, a strong matrix is one where the project managers have more power than functional managers. This is more similar to a projectized organizational form. The progression of forms is shown in Exhibit 3.4.

DISADVANTAGES The matrix organizational form has drawbacks as well. Some people claim that having two bosses (both a functional manager and a project manager) is a disadvantage. This problem certainly needs to be managed because the two managers may each try to do what they think is best for their project or department and may give conflicting advice. However, this is common territory for most people. Most students take multiple classes per term. Most companies have multiple customers. Having

EXHIBIT 3.4

PROGRESSION OF ORGANIZATIONAL FORMS

ORGANIZATIONAL FORM	FUNCTIONAL	WEAK MATRIX	BALANCED MATRIX	STRONG MATRIX	PROJECTIZED
Who has power?	FM almost all	FM more	Equally shared	PM more	PM almost all

EXHIBIT 3.5

ORGANIZATIONAL STRUCTURE COMPARISON

	FUNCTIONAL	MATRIX	PROJECTIZED
Who makes most project decisions?	Functional manager	Shared	Project manager
Advantages	• Good discipline-specific knowledge • Easy for central control • Effective for shared resources • One "boss" • Clear career path for professionals	• Flexible • Easy to share resources • Good cooperation between departments • More input for decisions • Wide acceptance of decisions • Good discipline-specific knowledge • Effective integration on project • Increased knowledge transfer between projects	• Break down department barriers • Shorter response time • Quicker decisions • One "boss" • Enhanced project team identity • Customer focus • Effective integration on project
Disadvantages	• Slow communication between departments • Slow response to change • Slow decision making	• Two "bosses" • Many sources of conflict • More meetings • Slow reaction time • Hard to monitor and control	• Duplication of resources • Rules not always respected • Potential lessons learned can be lost • Discipline-specific knowledge can slip • Less career continuity for project team members

Source: Adapted from Richard L. Daft, *Management,* 9th ed. (Mason, OH: South-Western Cengage Learning, 2010): 250–255; and *PMBOK® Guide,* 28–32.

to balance competing demands can be difficult, but it is very normal for most people. Since more people are providing the necessary input, there are more sources of conflict, more meetings, and more challenges to control. Decisions may not get made as fast.

Firms need to consider which organizational structure is best for them in the sense that they can capitalize on its advantages and mitigate its disadvantages. These decisions can change over time. Exhibit 3.5 summarizes a comparison of organizational structures.

Note that in a matrix organization a new role is inserted in the organizational chart—that of manager of project managers. Sometimes this person leads an office called the project management office (PMO). In some organizations, an additional manager will be in the reporting chain between the project managers and the person in charge (shown as the president). In other matrix organizations, the project managers report directly to the person in charge. For simplicity, this chart shows each function with four workers and each project with four team members. In actuality, some functions may have more workers than others and some projects may have more team members than others. In fact, some people may only report to a functional manager since they are not currently assigned to a project, and others may report to more than one project manager since they are assigned on a part-time basis to multiple projects. Those people will have more than two supervisors.

EXHIBIT 3.6

360-DEGREE PERFORMANCE REVIEWS

In some organizations, the functional manager performs a 360-degree evaluation. This appraisal style requires that the functional manager seek feedback from a representative sample of the staff that have worked with that project team member to provide feedback on a 360-degree form. Being appraised by your peers or team members on a given project is considered best practice because they've observed the individual in action "in the trenches." Many large organizations use this appraisal technique since in large and/or complex organizations some staff rarely see their direct supervisor or manager, depending upon their function in that organization.

Source: Naomi J. Kinney, CPLP, principle consultant, MultiLingual Learning Services.

While both project managers and functional managers have certain authority in any matrix organization, the extent of this authority can vary substantially. Often, the project manager has authority to determine what work needs to be accomplished and by when. The functional manager often retains authority to determine how the work is accomplished. Sometimes, the two managers will negotiate to determine which workers will be assigned to the project. While both hopefully want the best for the overall organization, each has specific responsibilities. For example, the functional manager with several workers reporting to her wants each employee to have enough work but not be overloaded. She also wants all workers to grow in expertise. The project manager, on the other hand, wants the best workers for the project so she can be more assured of delivering good results. In a case like this, when they negotiate, the project manager may want the best resource (who is already busy) and the functional manager may offer the least experienced resource (who is available).

One other source of potential conflict between the project and functional managers deals with performance reviews. Often, the functional manager is tasked with writing performance reviews, yet some workers may spend a great deal of their time on projects. If the project managers are not allowed to provide input into the performance reviews, some project team members will work harder to please their functional managers and the projects can suffer. One project manager offers ideas regarding performance reviews in Exhibit 3.6.

Closely related to the organizational structure is another organizational decision that needs to be made—that of organizational culture. Project managers are not often part of the executive group that decides on organizational structure or organizational culture, but they certainly need to understand how these decisions impact reporting relationships, decision-making methods, and commitment for their projects.

3.2 Organizational Culture and Its Impact on Projects

Just as project managers need to understand the structure of the parent organization, they also need to understand the culture of the parent organization if they are to communicate effectively. Organizational culture is comprised of the formal and informal practices and the values that are shared among members of the organization and are taught to new members. "Values are deep seated, personal standards that influence our moral judgments, responses to others, and commitment to personal and organizational goals."[5] Through shared values, organizational cultures can informally:

- Motivate the ethical actions and communications of managers and subordinates;
- Determine how people are treated, controlled, and rewarded;

- Establish how cooperation, competition, conflict, and decision making are handled; and
- Encourage personal commitment to the organization and justification for its behavior[6]

Once a project manager understands the culture of the parent organization, he can determine how to best develop the culture within his project. Many projects are completed cooperatively between two or more parent organizations, or one organization (a contractor) will perform the project for the other organization (a client). Whenever more than one parent organization is involved, the project manager needs to understand the culture of each well enough to facilitate effective project communications and decision making.

Culture of the Parent Organization

When a project manager studies the culture of the parent organization, she needs to ask the following questions:

- What is the orientation of the corporate culture in general?
- What are the ascribed values?
- How is the organization viewed by others in terms of living the values?
- How does the organization like to communicate internally and externally?
- How well does the organization support project management specifically?

TYPES OF POWER One framework that is helpful in understanding a corporate culture distinguishes the following four types of power according to what is the most powerful motivator:

1. Power culture
2. Role culture
3. Task culture
4. Personal culture

Power cultures exist when the supervisor exerts a great deal of economic and political power and everyone tries to please the boss. Those in formal authority control competition, conflict resolution, and communication.

Role cultures motivate everyone to understand and closely follow their appointed roles. Reliable workers follow formal designations of responsibility with utmost respect for regulations and laws.

In task cultures, it is more important to get the job done than to worry about who does the work or who gets credit. Hallmarks of task cultures are skill-based assignments, self-motivated workers, and more deference paid to knowledge than to formal authority.

In personal cultures, people show genuine interest in the needs of workers, consider worker development as critical to the organization's success, and display an attitude that collaboration is satisfying and stimulating.[7]

Many organizations will have one dominant culture modified by at least one of the other types. An astute person will look not only for what people say when trying to understand the culture, but also actions, decisions, symbols, and stories that guide behavior.

A variety of organizational culture characteristics make project success more likely. These characteristics include support for cross-functional teams, stakeholder involvement, integrity, innovation, open communication, continuous improvement, respect for individuals, project management competencies, and a common project management language.[8]

MIDLAND INSURANCE COMPANY Midland Insurance Company espouses its values by giving every employee the "One Pager" that lists the organization's mission, strategic imperatives, and core values. The CEO, John Hayden, will often pull his "One Pager" out at meetings and expects everyone else to do likewise. In talk and in action, Midland tries to live out the core values that comprise its organizational culture. Exhibit 3.7 shows Midland's culture.

EXHIBIT 3.7

MIDLAND INSURANCE COMPANY VALUES

- Integrity
- Win/Win
- Team
- Humility
- Strong Work Ethic
- Creativity
- Propriety
- Sharing/Caring
- Personal Growth

Source: Martin J. Novakov, American Modern Insurance Group.

HIXSON ARCHITECTURE AND ENGINEERING A second example of organizational values comes from Hixson Architecture and Engineering. The firm's values guide its employees' practice, as can be seen in Exhibit 3.8.

Culture of the Project

While some of the project's culture is dictated by that of the parent organization, effective sponsors and project managers can do many things to promote a good working culture within the project. Many times, participants on a project have not worked together previously and may even come from parts of the organization (or outside organizations) that have historically been rivals. The sponsor and project manager need to understand organizational politics and work to develop cooperation both within the core project team and among the various groups of project stakeholders.

When the project sponsor and manager are determining how to create the project culture, ethics should be an important consideration. One aspect of an ethical project culture is to determine how people should act. Project sponsors and managers learn that they need to

---

EXHIBIT 3.8

HIXSON ARCHITECTURE AND ENGINEERING VALUES

WELCOME TO HIXSON

Insight, Advocacy and Intelligent Project Execution

Well-designed, cost-effective projects that meet your needs today and prepare you for the changing environment of tomorrow don't just happen by chance. At Hixson, our **insight** will demonstrate our knowledge and experience to help you consider all the issues. Through our **advocacy**, you will have the confidence that we are working—unbiased—on your behalf. In addition, the practical ways we stay with projects to effective conclusions are at the heart of everything we do. That's **intelligent project execution**.

Standing firmly behind each of these goals are Hixson's values: to be the employer of choice for our associates, build impenetrable client loyalty and creatively contribute to our communities. These are the principles that guide our actions and enable our employees, our clients and the communities where we work and live to benefit from our involvement.

Put your projects on the right path... right from the beginning. Discover Hixson today!

Source: Hixson Architecture Engineering Interiors.

act in the best interests of three constituencies: the project itself—attempting to deliver what is promised; the project team—encouraging and developing all team members; and the other project stakeholders—satisfying their needs and wants. Ethical project managers make decisions so that one of the three constituencies does not suffer unfairly when satisfying the other two. One list of behaviors adapted from the *PMI Code of Ethics and Professional Conduct* tells project managers to exhibit the following:

- Responsibility—take ownership for decisions.
- Respect—show high regard for ourselves, others, and resources.
- Fairness—make decisions and act impartially.
- Honesty—understand the truth and act in a truthful manner.[9]

The other aspect of an ethical culture is how people actually act. Every project has difficult periods, and the measure of project ethics is how people act at those times. The project manager needs to show courage both in personally making the right decisions and in creating an atmosphere in which others are encouraged to make the right decisions. An ethical project culture in which people know how to act and have the courage to do so yields better ideas; when a spirit of mutual trust prevails, everyone participates with their ideas and effective partnering relationships within and beyond the project team.

3.3 Project Life Cycles

All projects go through a predictable pattern of activity, or project life cycle. Project planning teams use project life cycle models because various types of projects have differing demands. A research and development project may require a certain test to be performed before management approves the expenditure of large amounts of cash, while the manager of a quality improvement project may need to document how the work is currently performed before it makes sense to experiment with a new method. The major types of project life cycle models, while differing in details, have some things in common.

- They all have definite starting and ending points.
- They involve a series of phases that need to be completed and approved before proceeding to the next phase.
- The phases generally include at least one initiating, one planning, one closing, and one or more executing phases.
- The various life cycle models are all frequently adapted by the companies where they are used to better fit with the organizational culture and language.

We will now look at several generic models that represent the variety used in improvement, research, construction, and information systems projects. In the remainder of the book, we will deal with a generic model that includes selecting and initiating, planning, executing, and closing and realizing benefits, as shown in Exhibit 3.9.

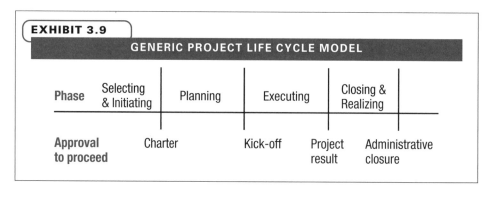

EXHIBIT 3.9

GENERIC PROJECT LIFE CYCLE MODEL

Phase	Selecting & Initiating	Planning	Executing	Closing & Realizing	
Approval to proceed	Charter		Kick-off	Project result	Administrative closure

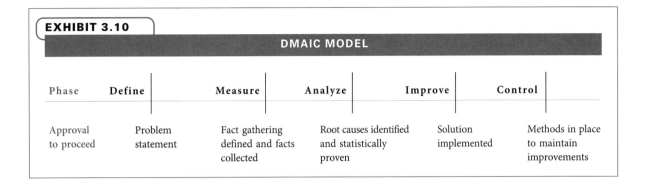

EXHIBIT 3.10

DMAIC MODEL

Phase	Define	Measure	Analyze	Improve	Control
Approval to proceed	Problem statement	Fact gathering defined and facts collected	Root causes identified and statistically proven	Solution implemented	Methods in place to maintain improvements

Define-Measure-Analyze-Improve-Control (DMAIC) Model

Many firms use projects to plan and manage quality and productivity improvement efforts. Various models are used for these improvement efforts. While these models appear to be somewhat different, they all strive to use facts to make logical decisions and to ensure that the results are as desired. The Six Sigma approach to quality improvement (a popular current approach explained in Chapter 11) uses the DMAIC model. A simple version of this model is shown in Exhibit 3.10.

Research and Development (R&D) Project Life Cycle Model

Many organizations use project management techniques to organize, plan, and manage research and development efforts. These can vary in length from as much as a decade for taking a new pharmaceutical from idea to successful market introduction to as little as a few weeks to reformat an existing food product and deliver it to a client. Some R&D project models are complex and have many phases because of huge risks and demanding oversight, yet some are much simpler. One simple R&D model adapted from defense development projects is shown in Exhibit 3.11.

Construction Project Life Cycle Model

Just as in other project applications, since construction projects differ greatly in size and complexity, a variety of project life cycle models are in use. A generic construction project life cycle model is shown in Exhibit 3.12.

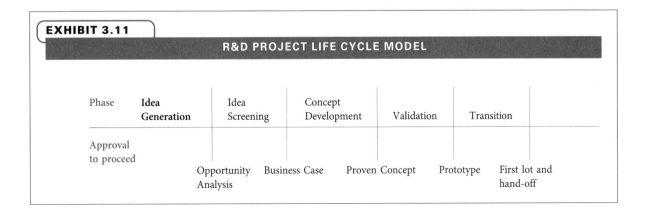

EXHIBIT 3.11

R&D PROJECT LIFE CYCLE MODEL

Phase	Idea Generation	Idea Screening	Concept Development	Validation	Transition	
Approval to proceed		Opportunity Analysis	Business Case	Proven Concept	Prototype	First lot and hand-off

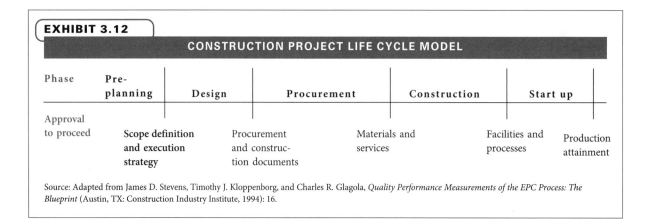

EXHIBIT 3.12

CONSTRUCTION PROJECT LIFE CYCLE MODEL

Phase	Pre-planning	Design	Procurement	Construction	Start up	
Approval to proceed	Scope definition and execution strategy	Procurement and construction documents	Materials and services	Facilities and processes	Production attainment	

Source: Adapted from James D. Stevens, Timothy J. Kloppenborg, and Charles R. Glagola, *Quality Performance Measurements of the EPC Process: The Blueprint* (Austin, TX: Construction Industry Institute, 1994): 16.

Information Systems (IS) Project Life Cycle Model

Many life cycle models are applied to information systems projects. Some variations may exist because:

- Time pressures encourage rapid development.
- Multiple versions of hardware and software may cause some features to be postponed.
- Some systems may be much more complex than others.

Nevertheless, most IS project life cycle models have some features in common. They all include requirements gathering and testing. Often, the testing overlaps with writing code. A generic IS project life cycle model is shown in Exhibit 3.13.

Agile Project Life Cycle Model

One type of model sometimes used in information systems and research projects allows for incremental plans and benefits. While *agile* is the umbrella name, some of the specific approaches are called *SCRUM, XP, Crystal, EVO, phased delivery, rapid prototyping,* and *evolutionary*. While these models may start like other project life cycle models, they provide short bursts of planning and delivery of benefits in multiple increments during project execution. A generic agile project life cycle model is shown in Exhibit 3.14.

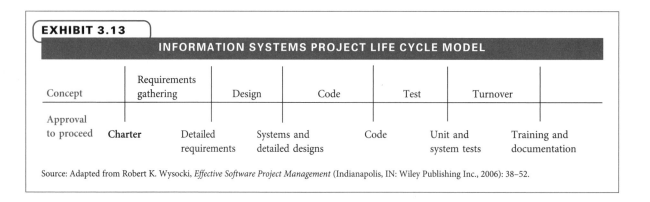

EXHIBIT 3.13

INFORMATION SYSTEMS PROJECT LIFE CYCLE MODEL

Concept	Requirements gathering	Design	Code	Test	Turnover	
Approval to proceed Charter	Detailed requirements	Systems and detailed designs	Code	Unit and system tests	Training and documentation	

Source: Adapted from Robert K. Wysocki, *Effective Software Project Management* (Indianapolis, IN: Wiley Publishing Inc., 2006): 38–52.

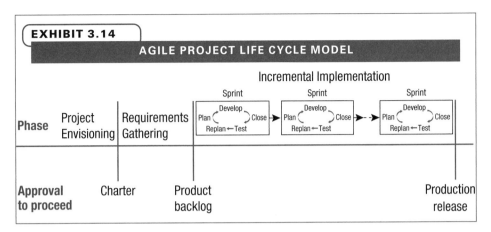

EXHIBIT 3.14

AGILE PROJECT LIFE CYCLE MODEL

3.4 Project Executive Roles

Projects do not exist in a vacuum. They exist in organizations where they require resources and executive attention. Projects are the primary method that organizations use to reach their strategic goals. As such, a variety of players need to be involved at the executive, managerial, and associate levels, as shown in Exhibit 3.15. Especially in small organizations, one person may perform more than one role. For example, a sponsor may perform some or all of the activities normally expected from the customer. The three project executive roles are the steering team (ST), the sponsor, and the chief projects officer (CPO).

Steering Team

In small to medium-sized organizations, the steering team (sometimes known as the executive team, management team, leadership team, operating team, or other titles) often consists of the top person in the organization and his or her direct reports. They should collectively represent all of the major functions of the organization. In larger organizations, there may be steering teams at more than one level. When that occurs, the steering teams at lower levels are directed and constrained by decisions the top-level steering team makes. Some organizations divide the duties of the steering team by creating project review committees and delegating tasks to them. In any event, the duties of the steering team revolve around the following five activities:

1. Overall priority setting
2. Project selection and prioritization
3. Sponsor selection
4. General guidance
5. Encouragement

EXHIBIT 3.15

PROJECT EXECUTIVE, MANAGERIAL, AND ASSOCIATE ROLES

EXECUTIVE LEVEL	MANAGERIAL LEVEL	ASSOCIATE LEVEL
Steering team (ST)	Functional manager (FM)	Core team member
Sponsor	Project manager (PM)	Subject matter expert (SME)
Chief projects officer (CPO)	Facilitator	
	Customer	

The steering team generally sets overall organizational priorities with the CEO. This is a normal part of strategic planning, as described in Chapter 2. Once the overall organizational goals have been set, the steering team agrees on the criteria for selecting projects and then selects the projects the organization plans to execute during the year. Once the overall project list is complete, they determine the relative priorities of the projects to determine which will start first.

Simultaneously, the steering team often helps the CEO decide who will sponsor potential upcoming projects. In turn, the steering team often helps the sponsor select the project leader. In some cases, the steering team even gets involved in deciding which critical team members will be on the project. This is especially true if very few people in the organization have highly demanded skills. The steering team can decide which project these people will work on as part of the prioritizing effort.

Guidance from the steering team includes feedback during formal reviews as well as informal suggestions at other times. Since steering teams understand how important project success is in achieving organizational objectives, they normally demand to have formal project reviews. These can occur either at set calendar times or at a project **milestone,** which is "a significant point or event in the project."[10] At these formal reviews, the steering team can tell the project team to continue as is, to redirect their efforts in a specific manner, or to stop the project altogether.

In terms of informal suggestions, it is very empowering to project participants if the steering team members ask how the project is going and offer encouragement when they run into each other in the normal course of work. It shows project participants that their work is important and has high visibility in the organization.

Sponsor

PMI defines a **sponsor** as "the person or group that provides financial resources, in cash or in kind, for the project."[11] In this sense, the sponsor is normally an individual who has a major stake in the project outcome. Sponsors often perform a variety of different tasks that help a project, both in public and behind the scenes. Major sponsor responsibilities are shown by project stage in Exhibit 3.16. The sponsor for major projects is often a member of the steering team. On smaller projects, the sponsor may hold a lower position in the organization.

EXHIBIT 3.16

PROJECT SPONSOR RESPONSIBILITIES BY PROJECT STAGE

Selecting & Initiating Stage
- Align project
- Prioritize project
- Define performance/success
- Mentor project manager
- Start project team

Planning Stage
- Start stakeholder relations
- Ensure planning
- Ensure project management

Executing Stage
- Build stakeholder relations
- Provide resources
- Ensure risk and quality
- Ensure communications
- Ensure progress

Closing and Realizing Stage
- Ensure goals and satisfaction
- Ensure closure
- Ensure knowledge management
- Ensure benefits are realized

Source: Adapted from Kloppenborg, Timothy J., Chris Manolis and Debbie Tesch, "Investigation of the Sponsor's Role in Project Planning," *Journal of Managerial Issues*, in press; and Kloppenborg, Timothy J., Chris Manolis and Debbie Tesch, "Successful Project Sponsor Behavior During Project Initiation: An Empirical Investigation," *Journal of Managerial Issues* (Spring 2009).

As a member of the steering team, the sponsor should understand the corporate strategy and be prepared to help with project selection and prioritization. Sponsors should pick the project manager and core team (sometimes with help from the project manager and/or others). Sponsors should mentor the project manager to ensure that person understands his role and has the skills, information, and desire to successfully manage the project.

In the next chapter, we discuss chartering. Sponsors ideally take an active role in chartering the project by creating a first draft of the business case and scope overview statements for the project. If a sponsor does not take time for this, the project manager needs to ask questions to elicit this business case and scope overview information. Then the sponsor should insist that a milestone schedule, preliminary budget, risk identification, assessment criteria, communication plan, and lessons learned be developed by the project manager and team. The sponsor then either personally approves the charter or takes the charter to the steering team for approval.

As the project progresses, the sponsor helps behind the scenes by obtaining resources, removing roadblocks, making high-level decisions, and interfacing between the project core team and the executive team. Sponsors often share their vision for the project with various stakeholders. When providing staff, sponsors ensure they are adequate in number and skill. This may include training. It may also include negotiating for staff. Sponsors often let their project managers arrange this training and negotiate for resources. However, the sponsor needs to make sure that both are satisfactorily completed.

Once again, sponsors with experienced project managers may merely need to ensure their project managers have the means in place to monitor and control their projects. Large projects with many stakeholders should have formal kick-off meetings. The sponsor's presence demonstrates corporate commitment. Sponsors represent the customer to the project team. The sponsor must ensure that several important customer-related tasks are performed as follows:

- All customers (stakeholders) have been identified.
- Their desires have been uncovered and prioritized.
- The project delivers what the customers need.
- The customers accept the project deliverables.

Again, the project manager should do much of this, but the sponsor is also responsible for its completion. While sponsors represent their projects, they also represent the larger organization. As such, they often should be one of the first persons to determine the need to stop a project that is no longer needed or is not performing adequately.

Chief Projects Officer/Project Management Office

Organizations need to have one person who "owns" their project management system and is responsible for all the people who work on projects. While different companies use different titles for this position (such as project director or manager of project managers), we will use the title chief projects officer (CPO). Just as companies' size and complexity vary greatly, so does the role of CPO. Large companies frequently have a project management office (PMO). The PMO performs the CPO role. At small companies, the CPO role may be performed informally by the CEO, who also juggles many other time demands. Companies in the medium-size range may find it useful to appoint an executive who already has other responsibilities as the CPO. Ensuring projects are planned and managed well is so central to the success of most companies that a highly capable individual is normally assigned this responsibility.

So, what are the responsibilities of the chief projects officer? They include ensuring that the company's steering team:

- Identifies potential projects during strategic planning
- Selects a manageable set of projects to be implemented
- Prioritizes effectively within that set
- Ensures enough resources (people, money, and other resources) are available to perform the projects
- Selects appropriate project sponsors and teams
- Charters the project teams
- Monitors and controls the implementation of the projects
- Rewards the participants
- Enjoys the results of successful projects!

If that is not enough, the CPO also ensures that each individual serving on a project:

- Receives the training he or she needs
- Captures lessons learned from completed projects
- Uses lessons learned from previous projects on new projects
- Uses templates and standards when appropriate

3.5 Project Management Roles

The manager-level roles in projects include the functional manager, project manager, facilitator, and customer.

Functional Manager

Functional managers are often department heads. Projects come and go, but departments generally remain. Functional managers have a large role in deciding how the project work in their functional area is done. Functional managers and project managers may negotiate who will be assigned to work on the project.

Generally, top management in an organization needs to decide how the relative decision-making power in the organization is divided between project managers and functional managers. Organizations that are new to formalized project management often start with functional managers having more power. Often, this changes over time until project managers for big projects have relatively more power.

Project Manager

The project manager is the focal point of the project. He or she spends a large amount of time communicating with everyone who is interested in the project. The project manager leads the planning, execution, and closing of the project. This person ideally should be a flexible, facilitating leader. Since project managers are responsible for the project schedule, they have a large role in deciding when project activities need to be accomplished. Project managers are trusted with delivering project results needed by their parent organizations. As such, project managers need to be worthy of that trust by possessing both integrity and necessary skills. "Skills and knowledge can be acquired through learning and practice."[12]

DESIRED BEHAVIORS Exhibit 3.17 shows a few of the behaviors project managers can develop first in regard to integrity and then in regard to each of the nine project management knowledge areas needed to successfully plan and manage projects. This book

EXHIBIT 3.17

DESIRED PROJECT MANAGER BEHAVIORS

INTEGRITY:

A great project manager demonstrates integrity by making honest decisions, caring for and protecting people, defending core values, leading major change, believing in self and team, honoring trust, showing respect, establishing a project culture of honesty, and displaying total commitment to both project and people.

COMMUNICATIONS:

An effective project manager displays good communications by listening well, communicating well orally, advocating the project vision, maintaining enthusiasm, focusing attention on key issues, establishing order in situations of ambiguity, working through conflict appropriately, seeking senior management support, and openly sharing information.

HUMAN RESOURCES:

A people-oriented project manager effectively handles human resource issues by leading in a facilitating manner when possible and forcefully when needed, using various forms of credibility, developing an effective project team, inspiring confidence, attracting and retaining workers for projects, creating a sense of urgency when needed, making decisions cooperatively when possible, and empowering team members.

INTEGRATION:

A great project manager is an effective integrator by leading the chartering process, coordinating assembly of a detailed and unified project plan, balancing the needs of all stakeholders, making sensible tradeoff decisions, monitoring earned value, keeping all efforts focused on the primary objectives, and clearly understanding how the project supports organizational goals.

SCHEDULE:

A time-sensitive project manager is an effective scheduler by leading schedule development, understanding resource and logic limitations, understanding the project life cycle, focusing on achieving key milestones, and making schedule decisions while continuing to be aware of cost and scope issues.

SCOPE:

A perceptive project manager deftly handles project scope by obtaining a deep understanding of stakeholder wants and needs, determining true requirements, learning whether a proposed change is essential or merely useful, utilizing effective change control to stop unnecessary scope creep, demonstrating flexibility when change is needed, while continuing to be aware of cost and schedule issues.

QUALITY:

A quality-focused project manager achieves the right project quality by learning customer expectations and how they relate to organizational objectives, insisting project decisions are made based upon facts, utilizing lessons learned from previous projects, ensuring effective work processes are used, leading testing, changing what does not work, questioning work processes, and continually demonstrating quality to stakeholders.

RISK:

A secure project manager effectively deals with project risk by openly identifying risks and opportunities, honestly evaluating each, developing avoidance strategies when practical, cooperatively establishing mitigation strategies when necessary, courageously recommending actions up to and including project cancellation if necessary, monitoring all risks and opportunities, and ensuring risk learning is used in the organization.

EXHIBIT 3.17

DESIRED PROJECT MANAGER BEHAVIORS (CONTINUED)

PROCUREMENT:

A supply-minded project manager effectively procures necessary project goods and services by fearlessly making honest decisions on whether to make or buy items, accurately documenting all requirements, identifying and fairly considering all potential sellers, selecting sellers based upon project and organizational needs, proactively managing contracts and relationships, and ensuring delivery of useful products and services.

COST:

A cost-effective project manager maintains cost control by developing an accurate understanding of the project scope, learning various means of cost estimating and when each is appropriate, determining reliable cost estimates, assigning costs equitably to cost centers, controlling all project costs, calculating and honestly reporting cost variances in a timely manner, and making appropriate decisions while being aware of scope and schedule issues.

---

describes some of the factual knowledge project managers need to acquire to become proficient. Project managers also need to acquire experiential knowledge by practicing these behaviors on projects. Not all project managers will become equally adept at each behavior, but an understanding of the behaviors exhibited by excellent project managers is a great way to start. Remaining chapters in this book elaborate on these behaviors. Collectively, all of these skills make for a great, well-rounded project manager.

COMMUNICATION CHANNELS Envision a bicycle wheel, as shown in Exhibit 3.18. The project manager is like the hub, and the spokes are like the many communication channels the project manager needs to establish and use with project stakeholders. While there are many project manager requirements, some of the technical needs can probably be delegated, but every project manager needs integrity, leadership, and communications skills.

CHALLENGES Project managers deal with several challenges. One is that they often have more responsibility than authority. This means they need to persuade people to accomplish some tasks rather than order them to do so. Project managers can create

---

EXHIBIT 3.18

PROJECT MANAGER COMMUNICATION CHANNELS

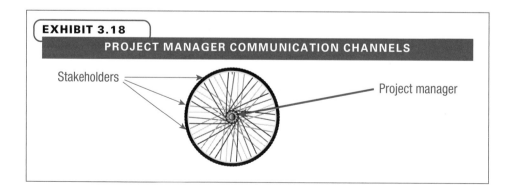

interesting and challenging work assignments for their team members. Many people find this stimulating. Project managers can more effectively attract followers when they display high integrity and the ability to get the job done. This includes both technical ability and communications ability. Project managers primarily deal with networks of people both within and outside their parent company. An effective project manager knows how to get to the source of the networks. A challenge for project managers is determining how networks function within certain organizational cultures. This is why organizational culture is so important. What are the networks within the organization? How do people work, communicate, and problem solve beneath the function of their job titles?

A rookie project sponsor and rookie project manager should not be assigned to the same project. While the sponsor normally mentors the project manager, when a sponsor is new, some of the mentoring may go the other way—just as a master sergeant may help a new lieutenant learn about leading troops.

JUDGMENT CALLS Due to the very nature of projects—each one having a unique set of stakeholders, output, and project team—project managers cannot always follow a cookbook approach in how they manage. They must develop judgment. Exhibit 3.19 lists some judgment calls that project managers need to be prepared to make on a frequent basis.

COMPETENCIES BY PROJECT STAGE Just as sponsor demands vary by project life cycle stage, so do those of project managers, as shown in Exhibit 3.20.

Facilitator

Many situations in project management require facilitation because the situation is so complex and/or because the opinions are so varied. Sometimes, the workers on a project need to expand their thinking by considering the many possibilities (possible projects, approaches, risks, personnel, and other issues). Other times, the workers on the project

---

EXHIBIT 3.19

PROJECT MANAGER JUDGMENT CALLS

A few general questions that project managers need to ask themselves to develop judgment are as follows:

- When to change expectations vs. when to accept them
- When to lead vs. when to follow
- When to act vs. when to analyze
- When to promote order (control) vs. when to promote innovation (freedom)
- When to repeat vs. when to change
- When is project conflict is constructive vs. when is it destructive
- When to focus on the big picture vs. when to focus on details
- When to take over vs. when to let the team perform
- When to demonstrate optimism vs. when to demonstrate pessimism
- When to lead vs. when to administer
- When to focus on technical vs. when to focus on behavioral
- When to concentrate on the short term vs. when to focus on the long term
- When to focus communications inside the project vs. when to focus them outside
- When to advocate for the project vs. when to accept termination
- When to focus on organizational goals, project goals, personal career goals, and team member career goals
- When to enhance, maintain, or accept changes in scope, quality, cost, and schedule

---

EXHIBIT 3.20

PROJECT MANAGER COMPETENCIES BY PROJECT LIFE CYCLE STAGE

STAGE	COMPETENCY
Initiation	Effective questioning/generating feedback
	Persuasiveness/marketing/selling
	Listening skills
	Vision oriented/articulate the business problem
	Consensus building
Planning	Project management skills and knowledge
	Consensus building
	Technical skills/theoretical knowledge
Implementation	Ability to get along/team player
	Results oriented
	Truthful/honest
Close	Writing skills
	Share information and credit
	Pride in workmanship/quality
	Truthful/honest

Source: Skulmoski, Gregory J. and Francis T. Hartman, "Information Systems Project Manager Soft Competencies: A Project-Phase Investigation," *Project Management Journal* (March 2010): 61–77.

---

need to focus their thinking by selecting from many options (a project, an approach, a contractor, or a mitigation strategy). Some project managers and sponsors can and do facilitate many of the meetings. However, the project manager may prefer to focus on the content of a meeting and enlist a facilitator to help focus on the process of the meeting. In these situations, an outside facilitator may be useful. Often, a disinterested sponsor or project manager (one who works on other projects, but not on this one) is used when a facilitator is needed. Sometimes, the chief projects officer or an outside consultant is used to facilitate.

Customer

While the specific demands of the customer role are spelled out here, understand that some or all of this role may be carried out by the sponsor—particularly for projects internal to a company. When a busy customer buys something, it may be tempting to just place an order and have it delivered. That process is fine for an off-the-shelf item or for a transactional service. Often, when it is a one-of-a-kind project, hands-off ordering does not work. The question then becomes: What does a customer need to do to ensure the desired results? Exhibit 3.21 shows a list of seven tasks a customer can do before and during a project to enhance the probability of success. The customer performs three of these tasks independently and the other four jointly with the project contractor. The three customer-only project tasks are prioritizing the project need, carefully selecting a good contractor, and killing the project if necessary. The four joint tasks are writing and signing the project charter, developing clear and detailed requirements, setting up and using project control systems, and conducting a great project kick-off meeting.

EXHIBIT 3.21

CUSTOMER TASKS ON PROJECTS

INDEPENDENT TASKS	JOINT TASKS WITH CONTRACTOR
1. Prioritize project.	1. Write and sign charter.
2. Select good contractor.	2. Develop clear requirements.
3. Kill project if needed.	3. Use control system.
	4. Conduct kick-off meeting

INDEPENDENT TASKS The first requirement is to prioritize each project. The knowledge that one particular project is the highest priority for a company should be communicated, and that project should be tackled by the "A team." A related prioritization question is: Do we need this project so badly right now that we are willing to start it even without the skilled personnel, resources, or technology on hand that would improve the probability of successful completion? If so, ensure this particular project gets top billing. If not, consider delaying it. Some accrediting bodies now require customers to prioritize projects as shown in Exhibit 3.22.

The second customer task is to carefully select a competent and honest contractor to perform the project. All of the important joint tasks are much easier with the right contractor, the probability of success goes up, and everyone's stress level goes down.

The third customer task is to determine whether to pull the plug on a troubled project. This could happen right at the start if the project appears to be impractical. It could happen during detailed planning when the requirements, schedule, budget, risks, or other aspects indicate trouble. More often, it occurs during project execution when the project

---

EXHIBIT 3.22

JOINT COMMISSION REQUIRES PROJECT PRIORITIZATION

In a hospital environment, the Joint Commission on Accreditation for Healthcare Organizations (JCAHO) requires that hospitals prioritize improvement projects from a quality standpoint, demonstrating gradual improvement in patient care. When JCAHO comes for their unannounced accreditation visits, they will ask how leadership prioritizes their improvement projects. It is usually done by an improvement coordinating committee of individuals or it could be an entire quality management department (in larger organizations). They will be looking at (and approving) *all* requests for hospital-wide improvement projects to see which project will give the hospital the "best bang for it's buck." From a quality lens, it is optimum to receive suggestions from the employee's themselves.

The coordinating committee (or quality department) will consider some of the following criteria when approving improvement projects:

1.   Will it help the hospital remain fiscally and financially sound?
2.   Will the project be an improvement for patients and families?
3.   Will the project improve the level of customer service we're providing our patients, guests and visitors?
4.   Will the project help mitigate a high-risk situation for the hospital?

Source: Naomi J. Kinney, CPLP, principle consultant, MultiLingual Learning Services.

progress does not live up to the plan. A customer needs to decide when to stop throwing good money after bad.

JOINT TASKS WITH CONTRACTOR   The first joint task for customers to get involved in is creating and ratifying the project charter. The charter (as explained more fully in Chapter 4) is a broad agreement concerning the project goals, rationale, risks, timeline, budget, approach, and roles—even though all of the details have yet to be determined. The charter should help to identify projects that appear risky or otherwise impractical from the outset. These projects should either be scrapped or a different approach should be used. If the project looks promising, both the contractor and the customer normally sign the charter and feel morally bound to its spirit.

Once the key players sign a charter, the contractor and customer need to develop the detailed requirements. One of the challenges many customer companies have is that different members have different expectations from the project. Somehow the conflicting desires of these multiple people in the customer's organization need to be combined into one set of requirements and provided to the people who will perform the project work. A senior customer representative and the project manager frequently work together to determine the requirements.

The customer and the contractor often work together to set up and use several project control systems. One of these is a communications plan (which is explained in Chapter 5). Since the customer is often the recipient of communications, he needs to tell the contractor what he needs to know, when he needs to know it, and what format will be most convenient. This should include regular progress reports. Second is a change control system (also explained in Chapter 5). Most projects will have multiple changes. A method must be created to approve potential changes, document their impact, and ensure that they are carried out as agreed. Third is a risk management system (explained in Chapter 10). Customers should work with developers to brainstorm possible risks, consider how likely each risk is to occur, measure a risk's impact should it happen, and develop contingency plans. The customer needs to ensure that effective communications, change management, and risk management systems are used.

Customers must help plan and participate in a project kick-off meeting. This meeting should be widely attended, give everyone involved in the project a chance to ask questions, and be used to build excitement for the project.

Customers get what they pay for on projects, but only when actively involved in key activities. Customers have the sole responsibility of prioritizing their own needs, selecting a contractor to perform their project, and terminating a project that is not working. Customers share with their contractor responsibility for crafting and agreeing to a project charter, articulating requirements, developing and using project control systems, and conducting an informative and energetic project kick-off.

3.6 Project Team Roles

The team- or associate-level roles in projects are core team members and subject matter experts.

Core Team Members

Core team members are the small group of people who are on the project from start to finish and who jointly with the project manager make many decisions and carry out many project activities. If the project work expands for a period of time, the core team members may supervise the work of subject matter experts who are brought in on an as-needed basis. Ideally, the core team is as small as practical. It collectively represents and

Image Source/Jupiter Images

understands the entire range of project stake-holders and the technologies the project will use. It is generally neither necessary nor useful to have every single function represented on the core team since that would make communication and scheduling meetings more difficult. Also, if every function is represented directly, team members tend to fight for turf.

The most ideal type of core team member is one who is more concerned with completing the project (on time, with good quality, and on budget if possible) than with either personal glory or with only doing work in his or her own discipline. He or she does what it takes to get the project done.

Core team members understand all aspects of the project and stay with the project through completion.

Subject Matter Experts

While core team members are typically assigned to the project from start to finish, many projects also have a specific and temporary need for additional help. The necessary help may be an expert who can help make a decision. It may be extra workers who are needed at a busy time during the life of the project. Some extra help may be needed for as little as one meeting; other extra help may be needed for weeks or months. These extra helpers are often called subject matter experts (SMEs) since they are usually needed for their specific expertise.

Subject matter experts are sometimes called extended team members. They are brought in for meetings and for performing specific project activities when necessary. A project could have almost any number of SMEs depending on its size and complexity.

SMEs are not on the core team but still are essential to the project. SMEs may be on a project for a long time and thus be almost indistinguishable from core team members.

However, SMEs may spend only a little time on a particular project and, therefore, may not relate strongly to it. At times, it is a struggle to get them scheduled and committed. Typically, a project manager would have a newly assigned SME read the project charter and the minutes from the last couple of meetings before discussing the project with him. It is a balancing act to ensure that the SME understands what she needs to do and how important it is, without spending a great deal of time in the process.

Fitting People into Project Roles

Considering the many responsibilities of each project role, careful selection of individuals to fill the various roles is ideal. In many organizations, however, there are limited choices of who will serve in each role. Leaders can use assessments such as StrengthsFinder to understand the unique strengths (natural thinking patterns) of people so they can help them develop in their respective roles. This developmental process will be discussed more in Chapter 13, and profiles of each strength with respect to how it may be used in project management roles are shown in Appendix B.

Summary

Projects are accomplished either within an organization or between multiple organizations when different firms work together. Project managers are more effective if they understand the impact the organization has on the project. In contemporary society, different organizations choose different organizational structures because they feel there is an advantage in their unique circumstances. While many are still officially organized in a traditional functional manner, an increasing number of organizations have at least informal matrix relationships. The days of having only one boss are gone for many workers—and especially for many project managers. Each form of organization has strengths and challenges with respect to projects.

Organizations also have a culture—the formal and informal manner in which people relate to each other and decisions are made. The hierarchical approach with the boss having supreme authority has long vanished in many places. Many organizations today use a more collaborative approach—some much more than others. Whatever the approach, project managers need to understand it and the impact it creates on their project. Project managers and sponsors need to create a culture in their project that is consistent with, or at least can

work effectively with, that of the parent organization. Both organizational structure and culture can become more complicated if more than one organization is involved in the project and if they differ in these respects.

Projects follow a predictable pattern or project life cycle. Many industries have typical project life cycles, but they vary greatly. A project manager needs to at least understand what project life cycle model is used at her organization and often needs to select or modify the project life cycle to the specific demands of the project.

Multiple executive-, managerial-, and associate-level roles need to be performed in projects. The project manager is a central role and the subject of this book. Project managers need to understand the other roles and relate effectively to them.

Key Terms from the *PMBOK® Guide*

functional organization, 54
projectized organization, 55
co-location, 56

matrix organization, 56
milestone, 66
sponsor, 66

Chapter Review Questions

1. Describe project management responsibilities.
2. Indicate how project managers can ensure their project work is accomplished even though they may lack formal authority.
3. Review characteristics that should be considered when selecting team members.
4. Describe how a strong (project) matrix is different from a weak (functional) matrix.
5. List advantages and disadvantages of functional, projectized, and matrix forms of organization.
6. Describe the responsibilities of each of the following: sponsor, steering team, CPO, functional manager, project manager, facilitator, customer, core team member, and subject matter expert.
7. Are work assignments, reporting relationships, and decision-making responsibility all components of (1) organizational culture, (2) organizational structure, or (3) co-location?
8. In a functional organizational structure, everyone in the organization has one supervisor, also known as chain of command. True or false?
9. Which organizational structure is often used for small projects that require most of their work from a single department?

10. Which organizational structure has no formal departments?
11. What is co-location, and why is it used?
12. In a matrix organizational structure, to whom do project team members report?
13. Name some possible consequences to a project if the project manager does not provide input into team member performance reviews.
14. List each of the four organizational culture types with respect to power and briefly describe what is the strongest motivator for each type.
15. For what five activities is the project steering team responsible?
16. What additional role may a steering team member sometimes play?
17. Who should select the project manager and the core team?
18. Who is responsible for ensuring that the steering team completes its tasks?
19. What types of control systems should a customer and contractor work together to set up and utilize?

Discussion Questions

1. List and defend three advantages and three disadvantages of the matrix form of organization.
2. Describe how organizational structures and cultures may change with project management experience.
3. Review the primary organizational culture characteristics and disclose why each is important in managing projects.
4. Describe multiple methods project leaders can employ in leading by example.
5. Define your project code of ethics.
6. Utilize qualities of effective project leaders to resolve ethical conflicts on projects.

7. List and describe at least four organizational culture characteristics that increase the likelihood of project success and tell why each is helpful.
8. List and briefly describe each of the project executive roles.
9. Describe a possible imbalance between a project manager's authority and responsibility and the impact it may have on a project.
10. Compare and contrast the two associate-level project roles.
11. Is it important to choose a member from every impacted function of a project for the core team? What is the impact of your decision?

PMBOK® *Guide* Questions

1. All of the following are advantages of a projectized organization **except:**
   a. quicker decisions
   b. good discipline-specific knowledge
   c. break down of department barriers
   d. customer focus
2. Sponsor selection, general guidance, and overall priority setting are some of the chief duties of:
   a. the steering team
   b. the facilitator
   c. the project manager
   d. core team members
3. A culture in which workers have specifically appointed jobs and do not overstep their boundaries is an example of a:
   a. power culture
   b. role culture

   c. task culture
   d. person culture
4. Project sponsors and managers need to act in the best interest of which three constituencies?
   a. themselves, stockholders, and the project team
   b. themselves, stakeholders, and the project team
   c. the project itself, stockholders, and the project team
   d. the project itself, stakeholders, and the project team
5. The actual construction of a new building represents which stage of a project life cycle?
   a. initiating
   b. planning
   c. executing
   d. closing

Exercises

1. Given a scenario, select a preferred organizational structure and justify your selection.
2. Describe, with examples, how your project manager did or did not exhibit desirable project manager behaviors as described in Exhibit 3.17.

3. Briefly describe how the sponsor of your project is or is not displaying appropriate offensive and defensive strategies as described in Exhibit 3.16.

Example Project

For your example project, describe the organizational structure of the agency or company for which you are

planning the project. Describe as many of the organizational culture attributes as you can. List, by name, as many of the project executive, management, and team roles as you can identify. Be sure to assign roles to yourself. How do you anticipate that the organizational structure, culture, and role assignments help or hurt your ability to successfully plan this project? Describe the project life cycle model that is used in the organization—and if one is not currently used, describe the life cycle model you plan to use and tell why it is appropriate.

References

A Guide to the Project Management Body of Knowledge, (PMBOK® Guide), 4th ed. (Newtown Square, PA: Project Management Institute, 2008).

Aldag, Ramon J. and Loren W. Kuzuhara, *Mastering Management Skills* (Mason, OH: Thomson South-Western, 2005).

Andersen, Erling S., "Understand Your Project's Character," *Project Management Journal* (December 2003): 4–11.

Blomquist, Tomas and Ralph Muller, "Practices, Roles and Responsibilities of Middle Managers in Program and Portfolio Management," *Project Management Journal* (March 2006): 52–66.

Crawford, Lynn, "Developing Organizational Project Management Capability: Theory and Practice," *Project Management Journal* (August 2006): 74–86.

Daft, Richard L., *Management*, 9th ed. (Mason, OH: South-Western Cengage Learning, 2010).

Evans, James R. and William M. Lindsay, *An Introduction to Six Sigma & Process Improvement* (Mason, OH: Thomson South-Western, Mason, 2005): 488–191.

Herrenkohl, Roy C, *Becoming a Team: Achieving a Goal* (Mason, OH: Thomson South-Western, 2004).

Hixson Architecture Engineering Interiors, http://www.hixson-inc.com/about/history.asp, accessed May 15, 2007.

Jiang, James J., Gary Klein, and Houn-Gee Chen, "The Relative Influence of IS Project Implementation Policies and Project Leadership on Eventual Outcomes," *Project Management Journal* (September 2001): 49–55.

Johnson, Craig E., *Meeting the Ethical Challenges of Leadership: Casting Light or Shadow*, 3rd ed. (Thousand Oaks, CA: Sage Publications, Inc., 2009).

Kendra, Korin and Laura J. Taplin, "Project Success: A Cultural Framework," *Project Management Journal* (April 2004): 30–15.

Kloppenborg, Timothy J., Chris Manolis and Debbie Tesch, "Investigation of the Sponsor's Role in Project Planning," *Journal of Managerial Issues*, in press.

Kloppenborg, Timothy J., Chris Manolis and Debbie Tesch, "Successful Project Sponsor Behavior During Project Initiation: An Empirical Investigation," *Journal of Managerial Issues* (Spring 2009).

Kloppenborg, Timothy J., Deborah Tesch, Chris Manolis, and Mark Heitkamp, "An Empirical Investigation of the Sponsor's Role in Project Initiation," *Project Management Journal* (August 2006): 16–25.

Laufer, Alexander, Todd Post, and Edward J. Hoffman, *Shared Voyage: Learning and Unlearning from Remarkable Projects* (Washington, DC: National Aeronautics and Space Administration, 2005).

Lussier, Robert N. and Christopher F. Achua, *Leadership: Theory, Application, and Skill Development*, 4th ed. (Mason, OH: South-Western Cengage Learning, 2010).

Mullaly, Mark, "Longitudinal Analysis of Project Management Maturity," *Project Management Journal* (August 2006): 62–73.

Pennypacker, James S. and Kevin P. Grant, "Project Management Maturity: An Industry Benchmark," *Project Management Journal* (March 2003): 4–11.

Project Management Institute Code of Ethics and Professional Conduct, http://www.pmi.org/PDF/ap_pmicodeofethics.pdf accessed August 9, 2010.

Rath, Tom and Barry Conchie, *Strengths Based Leadership: Great Leaders, Teams, and Why People Follow* (New York: Gallup Press, 2008).

Salwin, Peter, "Fostering Innovation and Entrepreneurship in a Value Driven Organization," *Leadership and Management in Engineering* (July 2003): 153–158.

Skulmoski, Gregory J. and Francis T. Hartman, "Information Systems Project Manager Soft Competencies: A Project-Phase Investigation," *Project Management Journal* (March 2010): 61–77.

Sotiriou, Dean and Dennis Wittmer, "Influence Methods of Project Managers: Perceptions of Team Members and Project Managers," *Project Management Journal* (September 2001): 12–20.

Stevens, James D., Kloppenborg, Timothy J. and Charles R. Glagola, *Quality Performance*

Measurements of the EPC Process: The Blueprint (Austin, Texas: Construction Industry Institute, 1994): 16.

Ward, J. Leroy, "Project Management Techniques for Adaptive Action," *Chief Learning Officer* (December 2005): 20–23.

Wikipedia, http://en.wikipedia.org/wiki/New_product_development, accessed May 28, 2010.

Wysocki, Robert K, *Effective Software Project Management* (Indianapolis, IN: Wiley Publishing Inc., 2006): 38–52.

http://www.pmi.org/PDF/ap_pmicodeofethics.pdf, accessed March 25, 2010.

Endnotes

1. *PMBOK® Guide* 436.
2. *PMBOK® Guide* 445.
3. *PMBOK® Guide* 429.
4. *PMBOK® Guide* 438.
5. Aldag, Ramon J. and Loren W. Kuzuhara, *Mastering Management Skills* (Mason, OH: Thomson South-Western, 2005).
6. Adapted from Andersen, Erling S., "Understand Your Project's Character," *Project Management Journal* (December 2003): 4–11; and Aldag, Ramon J. and Loren W. Kuzuhara, *Mastering Management Skills* (Mason, OH: Thomson South-Western, 2005).
7. Adapted from Andersen, Erling S., "Understand Your Project's Character," *Project Management Journal* (December 2003): 4–11.
8. Adapted from Kendra, Korin and Laura J. Taplin, "Project Success: A Cultural Framework," *Project Management Journal* (April 2004): 30–45.
9. *PM1 Code of Ethics and Professional Conduct*, http://www.pmi.org/PDF/ap_pmicodeofethics.pdf, accessed March 25, 2010. (Newtown Square, PA: Project Management Institute, 2006): 12–13.
10. *PMBOK® Guide* 438.
11. *PMBOK® Guide* 449.
12. Winseman, A. L., D. O. Clifton, and C. Liesveld. *Living Your Strengths Catholic Edition: Discover Your God-Given Talents and Inspire Your Community*, 2nd ed. (New York: Gallup Press, 2008).

PROJECT MANAGEMENT *IN ACTION*

Project Leadership Roles at TriHealth

TriHealth is a company that manages several large hospitals and a variety of other health organizations, such as physical fitness facilities and nursing services. Due to the company's increasing size and complexity, TriHealth leadership decided they needed to formally define roles of project executive sponsor, project leader, performance improvement consultant, core team member, and subject matter expert. These roles are shown below.

Project Executive Sponsor

Initiating Stage

- Empower project leader with well-defined charter, which is the overarching guide
- Clearly define expected outcomes
- Demonstrate commitment to and prioritization of project
- Define decision-making methods and responsibility—sponsor/project leader/team
- Partner with project leader to identify obstacles, barriers, and silos to overcome

Planning Stage

- Ensure Project Leader understands business context for organization
- Ensure Project Leader develops overall project plan
- Assist Project leader in developing vertical and horizontal communication plan
- Demonstrate personal interest in project by investing time and energy needed
- Secure necessary resources and organizational support

Executing Stage

- Communicate and manage organizational politics
- Visibly empower and support Project Leader vertically and horizontally
- Build relationships with key stakeholders
- Actively listen to and promote team and project to Stakeholders
- Remove obstacles and ensure progress of project
- Ensure goals are met and Stakeholders are satisfied

Closing Stage

- Ensure closure; planned completion or termination

- Ensure results and lessons learned are captured and shared
- Ensure assessment of related applications or opportunities
- Ensure any necessary next steps are assigned and resourced
- Recognize contributions and celebrate completion
- Negotiate follow-up date(s) to assess project status

Project Leader

All of the roles listed are the ultimate responsibility of the project leader. However, in the development of the charter, the Sponsor and the Project Leader will have a discussion about the Project Leader role. At that time, the individuals will determine if the Project Leader needs additional assistance or skills to facilitate the project success and which of these responsibilities need to be delegated to others with expertise in those areas.

- Leads negotiation with Sponsor for charter definition.
- Collaborates with Sponsor to clarify expectations.
- Provides direction to the team with integrity, leadership, and communication skills.
- Facilitates productive meetings and supports the team's decisions.
- Prepares the high-level work plan and timeline.
- Champions the project on the management level and with the staff.
- Leads the implementation of the project.
- Manages project flow, including agenda setting, meeting documentation, and coordination of team assignments.
- Develops implementation, education, and communication plans for the project.
- Responsible for the team and project progress and proactively intervenes to promote team and project success.
- Identifies, communicates, and facilitates the removal of barriers to enable successful project completion.
- Supports the team with tools and methodologies to accomplish goals.

- Facilitates collection and analysis of data.
- Leads the team in developing a plan to sustain the change and monitor effectiveness.
- Leads team in developing recommended next steps.
- Closes project with Sponsor and assure lessons learned are captured.
- Establish with Sponsor the dates for post-project check-up and overall measurable effectiveness of project.

Performance Improvement Consultant

If the Sponsor and the Project Leader determine additional support/expertise is needed, a Performance Improvement Consultant can provide the following expertise:

- Provides direction to the Project Leader in establishing targets and a measurement and monitoring system.
- Mentors the Project Leader on leading the team through the project management process.
- Collaborates with the Project Leader to prepare a work plan and timeline for the project.
- Proactively intervenes to promote team and project success based on teamwork and interactions.
- Assists the Project Leader in identifying, communicating, and removing barriers to enable successful project completion.
- Assists in the researching of research, best practices, and benchmarking.
- Coaches the Project Leader on the development and implementation of a comprehensive communication, education, and change management plan.
- Provides the Project Leader support in assuring regular communication with the Sponsor and Stakeholders.
- Offers expertise to the team with tools and methodologies to accomplish goals.
- Collaborates with the Project Leader on the collection and analysis of data.
- Assures a system-wide perspective is considered and downstream effects analyzed.

- Provides change management education and assists the Project Leader in developing key strategies for successful change management
- Provides coaching to the Project Leader on key strategies for successful planning, implementation, and sustainability of the project.

Core Team Member

- Takes responsibility for the success of the team.
- Attends meetings for duration of the project.
- Actively participates in team meetings.
- Understands the entire range of the project.
- Actively participates in the decision-making process.
- Supports the team's decisions.
- Completes outside assignments.
- Carries out many of the project activities; produces deliverables on time.
- Provides testing or validation of decisions being made by the team.
- Provides data collection and reporting.
- Participates in the communication, education, implementation, and evaluation of the project.
- Gathers input from the areas they represent, if appropriate.
- Shares team decisions and plans throughout the project.
- May work directly with Stakeholders or Subject Matter Experts.

Subject Matter Expert

- Not a core team member of the team.
- Participates in demonstrations/presentations and/or team meetings, as needed.
- Carries out project activities as assigned; produces deliverables.
- Responsible for supplying requirements.
- Provides input to the team or complete activities based on a specific expertise he or she possesses that is essential to the project.

Source: TriHealth

Chartering Projects

After completing this chapter, you should be able to:

- Describe what a project charter is and why it is critical to project success.

- List the various elements of a charter and tell why each is used.

- Create each section of a charter for a small sample project using given project information.

- Work with a team to create a complete charter for a real project.

- Initialize a project in Microsoft Project and set up a milestone schedule.

Comstock/Jupiter Images

Planning a project is similar to putting together a large puzzle. If you were to dump a 1000-piece puzzle on a table, you would probably not start the detailed "planning" right away by comparing two pieces randomly to see if they fit. You would likely take several preliminary steps. Some of these steps might include turning the pieces so the picture side was visible on each, sorting outside pieces so you could form the boundaries, studying the picture on the box, and sorting by color so you could match pieces more easily. These preliminary steps make the detailed planning of the puzzle much easier and more efficient. If completing projects is analogous to putting puzzles together, then project charters are the initial steps. Initiating a project requires some preliminary actions, including understanding the needs and concerns of stakeholders, most critically the project sponsor.

Ball Aerospace & Technologies Corp., Systems Engineering Solutions provides a wide range of air, space, and counterspace engineering and

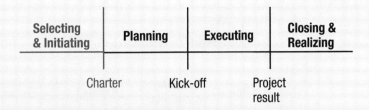

Selecting & Initiating	Planning	Executing	Closing & Realizing

Charter   Kick-off   Project result

PMBOK® GUIDE TOPICS

- Develop project charter
- Develop schedule
- Identify risks
- Perform qualitative risk analysis
- Plan risk responses
- Identify stakeholders

professional analytic services. At Ball, we increase stakeholder buy-in by addressing and thinking about things up front; with an agreed upon charter, this gives the project team some guidance to effectively plan and execute the effort. In addition, by going through the chartering process, stakeholders take ownership in the project.

At Ball, our project sponsors are typically U.S. government customers, and we provide work for them on a contractual basis. They provide funding and broad direction for our efforts, and we go through a formal proposal process for all our projects. Project sponsors provide initial statements of work or objectives defining their goals for the task and then select among several proposals from interested companies such as Ball to fulfill their requirements. The chosen company is then under an official formal contract to complete the project. This is in effect a pre-chartering process.

Typically, after an effort is under contract, a kickoff meeting is scheduled to review the objectives of the project between the project sponsor and the chosen company. This is part of the initiating stage, where stakeholders review and approve the following as part of the project's charter:

- Overall project objectives
- Contrast between technical approach as written in the company's proposal for execution and sponsor expectations
- Milestones, checkpoints, and potential payment plans
- Success criteria and schedule
- Identification of key stakeholders and risks
- Processes for executing, monitoring, controlling, and overall management of the project

There are a number of things to consider when initiating a project and generating a project charter. These serve as pieces of the overall puzzle of managing and executing a project. A little pre-work in initiating the project goes a long way, with increased goodwill and understanding from the project sponsor, clear tasks and goals for the project team, and a single way forward towards achieving the products and services of the project.

This chapter describes what a project sponsor, manager, and team need to understand to quickly initiate a project. The project then proceeds into planning, and the elements of a charter are planned in as much detail as needed. Chapters 5 through 11 describe project planning.

Lydia Lavigne, Ball Aerospace

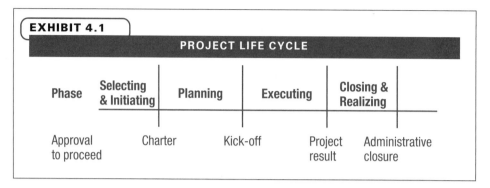

EXHIBIT 4.1

PROJECT LIFE CYCLE

Phase	Selecting & Initiating	Planning	Executing	Closing & Realizing
	Approval to proceed	Charter	Kick-off	Project result Administrative closure

4.1 What Is a Project Charter?

For a project manager, team member, or project sponsor, one of the first and most important project management concerns is a project charter. This short document (usually about three pages) serves as an informal contract between the project team and the sponsor (who represents both senior management of the organization and the outside customer, if there is one). Since a charter is like a contract, it is helpful to remember what a contract is. First, it is an agreement entered into freely by two or more parties. Second, one party cannot arbitrarily change it. Third, there is something of value in it for each party. Finally, it is a living document that can evolve with changing conditions if both parties agree and receive something of value for making the change. The charter signing represents the transition from the high-level project initiation stage into the more detailed project planning stage. See Exhibit 4.1 for a review of the project life cycle.

The project charter is the deliverable that grants a project team (that is, the project manager and the core team) the right to continue into the more detailed planning stage of a project. This may include *only* permission to plan the project, permission to make decisions that would slow the project if delayed (such as ordering long-lead materials or hiring special workers), or permission to plan and perform the entire project in the case of a small, simple project. While either party (the sponsor or the project team) can write the rough draft, more often than not the team writes the draft charter. Ideally, then, the project team and the sponsor candidly discuss each part of the charter. Like a contract, the people who sign a charter are wise to ensure that they understand and agree to every detail within it. Unlike a contract, however, both parties feel obligated to the spirit (as opposed to the letter) of the charter since the project details have not yet been worked out and specifics will certainly change.

Thinking of a charter like a contract means that both the team and the sponsor sign the charter willingly and strive to make the project successful. If the team feels bullied into making a change, it is not a free choice. However, the sponsor may legitimately need to insist on receiving the project results more quickly or make some other change to the project. In the spirit that one party cannot arbitrarily change a contract, the sponsor would not just tell the project team, "I need the project a month sooner and you get no more resources and no relief from any other work responsibilities." Rather, if the project must change, the sponsor needs to consider herself or himself to be a partner with the project team in determining how to accomplish the change.

4.2 Why Is a Project Charter Used?

The four major purposes for a charter are to:

1. Authorize the project manager to proceed
2. Help the project team and sponsor develop a common understanding

3. Help the project team and sponsor commit
4. Quickly screen out obviously poor projects

First, a project charter "formally authorizes the project … documents initial requirements that satisfy the stakeholders' needs and expectations … and provides the project manager the authority to apply resources to project activities."[1] Many project managers do not have the authority to commit resources without a charter. This gives the project and the project manager official status within the parent organization.

Second, everyone involved in the upcoming project needs to develop a common understanding of what the project entails. This includes at least the broad justification for the project, including how it aligns with goals of the parent organization, determination of what is included and excluded, major risks, rough schedule, rough estimate of resource needs, and success measures. On larger and more complex projects, additional understanding may be required at this point. Once everyone has a common understanding of clear project goals, several additional benefits occur:

- Teamwork develops.
- Agreement, trust, communication, and commitment between the sponsor, project manager, and project team develop.
- The project team does not worry if management will accept a decision.
- The sponsor is less likely to unilaterally change the original agreement.[2]

Third, each person needs to personally and formally commit to doing their level best to achieve the agreed upon project results—even when things do not go as planned. It is a moral duty of project team members to commit to the shared goals articulated in the charter. This formal commitment often helps a person decide to keep working hard on a project when things are not going well.

Fourth, a charter is used to quickly screen potential projects to determine which appear to be poor choices. A charter is much quicker to put together than a full, detailed project plan and schedule. If by constructing a charter it is determined that the project is likely to fail, much planning time (and therefore money) will be saved.

Remember, the charter helps all project stakeholders. Charters are often publicly shown to many individuals beyond the project team and sponsor for communication. The culture of some companies is more trusting, competitive, focused on time, preoccupied with details, and so on than at other companies. Therefore, charters used in different industries and companies have somewhat different elements and formats.

4.3 When Is a Charter Needed?

Project methods can be scaled from very simple to very detailed. A project manager wants to use just enough detail. TriHealth has developed both full and mini charters, for large and small projects respectively. They have also developed the decision matrix shown in Exhibit 4.2 to help people determine if a full charter, mini charter, or no charter is needed.

4.4 Typical Elements in a Project Charter

The following sections list some of the typical key elements in a project charter. While the intent of most of these sections is included in many charters, some project teams combine sections or leave out one or two of them. Furthermore, while the term *charter* is a widely used standard, some organizations use other names such as *project request, project submission form,* or *project preplanning form.* As long as the four purposes of a charter (authorization, understanding, commitment, and screening) are accomplished,

EXHIBIT 4.2

PROJECT CHARTER DECISION MATRIX

PROJECT CHARTER DECISION MATRIX

Project Name
Date

When an improvement, change, or new program is going to be implemented, it is important to first determine whether or not it is a project. If it is a project, TriHealth has specific tools that should be used to guide the planning and implementation.

In general, a project is "a temporary endeavor undertaken to create a unique product, service, or result." If your project impacts more than one department, requires expertise or resources beyond your own department, or could affect the operations in another area, the standardized templates should be used. Answering the questions below with a check will help you determine what types of tools are needed for your project. Evaluate where the majority of your checks lie and use the tools best indicated.

Resources	☐	Little or no monies, supplies, or change in resources	☐	Requires moderate resources	☐	Requires significant and/or additional FTEs
Multidisciplinary	☐	1 discipline involved/impacted	☐	2–3 disciplines involved/impacted or more than one site	☐	More than 3 disciplines involved/impacted
Complexity	☐	Little complexity	☐	Moderate complexity; affects care delivery	☐	Very complex
Technology Involvement	☐	No technology changes	☐	IS consult needed	☐	IS resources assigned
Approvals	☐	None needed	☐	Approval by immediate supervisor	☐	Executive level approval
Potential Risk Level	☐	Minimal impact on customer	☐	Moderate impact on customer	☐	Significant impact on customer
Staff Commitment	☐	Involvement of 2–3 people for solution	☐	Small team needed to generate solutions	☐	Requires large team of multiple departments for improvement
Communication and Education	☐	Simple communication plan or unit based education only	☐	Moderate communication plan; requires education across departments	☐	Complex communication/education plan with various media
Metrics	☐	Requires at least a one-time follow up check	☐	Improvement will be tracked	☐	Baseline and ongoing tracking of data
If the majority of your checks lie in this area:		⇩		⇩		⇩
		No charter needed		Complete a Mini Charter		Complete a Full Project Charter

Source: TriHealth.

EXHIBIT 4.3

CHARTER ELEMENTS AND QUESTIONS ANSWERED

CHARTER ELEMENT	ANSWERS THE QUESTION
Scope overview	What?
Business case	Why?
Background	Why?
Milestone schedule	When?
Success criteria	What?
Risks, assumptions, and constraints	Whoa!
Budget estimate or spending approval	How much?
Stakeholders	Who?
Team operating principles	How?
Lessons learned	How?
Signatures and commitment	Who?

---

the exact format and title are negotiable. Typical charter elements and the question each answers are shown in Exhibit 4.3.

The charter should be short enough so the project team and sponsor (and any other interested stakeholder) can examine it carefully to ensure they understand and agree. Two to four pages in total is generally about the right length.

Title

The existence of a meaningful project title is critical. In an organization with a number of projects, the title can be used to quickly identify which project is being referenced.

Scope Overview

The scope overview and business case sections are the high-level "what and why" of the project. They are sometimes considered to be the "elevator speech" that a person would use if given a very short amount of time, such as a one-floor elevator ride, to describe their project. Sometimes an additional background statement is helpful.

The scope overview is the project in a nutshell: a high-level description of what needs to be accomplished and how it will be done. What needs to be accomplished can be described as the **product scope**, the "features and functions that characterize a product, service or result,"[3] or as **requirements**, each of which is a "condition or capability that must be met ... to satisfy ... needs, wants, and expectations of the sponsor, customer, and other stakeholders."[4] How it will be done is the **project scope**, "work that must be performed to deliver a product, service, or result."[5] The scope overview quickly describes the project work and results. The scope overview is used to distinguish between what the project will and will not do. It is used to help prevent **scope creep**, which is "adding features and functionality (project scope) without addressing the effects of time, costs, resources, or without customer approval."[6] The scope overview can be considered to be the project boundaries. It states what is included and what is not—at least at a fairly high level.

Quantifying the scope, such as "15 touch points will be included," helps everyone to better understand the project's size. If a project could be compared to an animal, the scope overview briefly describes both the size and features so one can tell if it is a rabbit or an elephant. By understanding what is included and what is not, the project team is more likely to accurately estimate cost, resource, and schedule needs and to understand and handle project risks.

Business Case

The business case is the project purpose or justification statement. It answers the question "why?" and helps all parties understand the purpose of the project. A business case is used to justify the necessity of the project. It should clearly tie the project to the organization's strategy and explain the benefits the organization hopes to achieve by authorizing the project. Depending on the organization, a business case can either be just the rationale for the project or it can also include high-level estimates of the costs and benefits of the project. In either scenario, a well-written business case should persuade decision makers to support the project and inspire team members to work hard on it. The business case states the problem prompting the project in a simple manner and helps people develop a passion for the project. This passion often proves to be useful in persuading people to work extra hard if the project experiences difficulties.

Background

Many people are quite busy and prefer short statements that can be quickly read. Some project stakeholders will know enough about the project that short scope overview and business case statements will provide all of the information they need. Some other stakeholders may need more detail to understand the background behind these statements. A more detailed background statement may be helpful in these cases. Unlike the first two statements, which should be limited to about two to four sentences each, the background statement can be any length. The background statement is purely optional—only develop one if necessary.

Milestone Schedule with Acceptance Criteria

The **milestone schedule** is "a summary-level schedule that identifies the major schedule milestones or significant points or events in the project."[7] It divides the project into a few (about three to eight) intermediate points or milestones whose completion can be verified. The team estimates a date when they expect to complete each milestone. A milestone schedule should list major milestones and deliverables that the project team especially wants to ensure are completed both on time and to the satisfaction of key decision makers.

A **deliverable** is "any unique and verifiable product, result, or capability to perform a service that must be produced to complete a process, phase, or project. Often ... subject to approval by the project sponsor or customer."[8] Sometimes, milestones occur right before the approval of a large expenditure. At other times, they occur at completion of a critical design. It is helpful to identify the relatively few milestones and key deliverables in the project that the team wishes to check closely.

Adding a column for acceptance criteria factors to the milestone schedule helps the project team understand who will judge the quality of the deliverable associated with each milestone and what criteria will be used for that determination. **Acceptance criteria** are "those criteria, including performance requirements and essential conditions, which must be met before project deliverables are accepted."[9]

Acceptance criteria are like the project's vital signs. A paramedic would check pulse, breathing, maybe skin color, and body temperature immediately when answering a 911 call. Other tests are not as critical and may be performed, just not immediately. It is important to identify the vital signs for the project. Project success is easy to measure after the project is complete. The equally important, but often more challenging, decision is how to measure it while the project is progressing so there is still time to make changes if necessary.

Another way to understand acceptance criteria is to understand how a key stakeholder such as the sponsor or customer is going to determine if the deliverables created are of good enough quality to accept. Since some of the milestones are often preliminary (drafts, proto-types, concepts, outlines, etc.), it is helpful to have the same person who will judge the final project deliverables judge them at the intermediate milestones. By doing this, the decision maker is much less likely to state at the end of the project, "No, that is not what I meant." Including acceptance criteria is extremely useful since the project team will never have to guess whether a decision maker will approve a milestone—they will understand in advance exactly what is required. This advance understanding is similar to the old saying that a trial lawyer never asks a question without knowing how the witness will answer. An astute project manager never turns in a deliverable without knowing how it will be judged.

Risks, Assumptions, and Constraints

A **risk** is "an uncertain event or condition that, if it occurs, has a positive or negative effect on a project's objectives."[10] **Assumptions** are "factors that, for planning purposes, are considered to be true, real, or certain without proof or demonstration."[11] Project teams frequently identify, document, and validate assumptions as part of their planning process. Assumptions generally involve a degree of risk. A **constraint** is "an applicable restriction or limitation, either internal or external to the project, that will affect the performance of the project."[12]

Taken together, risks, assumptions, and constraints are what could cause a project problems. They are included so that all of the key participants—sponsor, project manager, and core team—are aware in advance of what could prevent them from successfully completing the project. While it is unrealistic to believe that the team can think of every single thing that could go wrong, the more comprehensive this section is, the more likely the team is to uncover problems before they occur while there is time to easily deal with them.

If an assumption turns out to be false, it becomes a risk. A constraint that limits the amount of money, time, or resources needed to successfully complete a project is also a risk. Some organizations group all risks, assumptions, and constraints together while others handle each as a separate charter section. The most important point is not how each is handled, but that each *is* handled.

Project managers and teams should look at risks for three reasons. First, any risk that may inhibit successful project completion (to the satisfaction of stakeholders, on time, and on budget) needs to be identified and, if it is a major risk, a plan must be developed to overcome it. Second, a risk that can create a positive effect on a project can be considered an opportunity to complete the project better, faster, and/or at lower cost or to capitalize upon the project in additional ways, and a plan should be developed to capitalize upon it. Third, sometimes there is more risk to the organization if the project is not undertaken—and this provides additional rationale for doing the project.

For each major risk identified, one or more contingency plans are normally developed to either lessen the probability of the risk event from happening in the first place and/or to reduce the impact if the risk event should materialize. The goal is not to eliminate all risk, but to reduce the risk to a level that decision makers deem acceptable. An "owner" is assigned responsibility for each contingency plan.

Spending Approvals or Budget Estimates

Depending on the type of project and the organization's methods of operating, a preliminary project budget may be estimated at this time. Since there is only very general understanding of the project at this point, the budget will also be approximate and should be stated as such by calling it a preliminary budget and including the level of confidence one has in the estimate. This could be expressed in percentage terms (such as plus or minus 50 percent).

On some internal projects, a formal budget is never developed. In these situations, the pay for the associates who work on the project often comprises much of the expense. Frequently, however, at least a few additional expenses are incurred. It is helpful to identify which expenses the project manager can authorize and which the sponsor needs to control. If the project manager has a spending approval, he or she does not have to go to the sponsor for every little detail.

Stakeholder List

Project success is partially dictated by identifying and prioritizing stakeholders, managing robust relationships with them, and making decisions that satisfy stakeholder objectives. Therefore it is good practice to identify and prioritize stakeholders early in a project.

Team Operating Principles

Team operating rules or principles are sometimes established to enhance team functioning. The goal is to increase team effectiveness and ensure that all parties are aware of what is expected. "You can get your team off to a good start by … getting everyone to discuss how they want the team to operate."[13] Team operating principles that are especially useful are those that deal with conducting meetings, making decisions, accomplishing work, and treating each other with respect. Some organizations have established expectations for all teams and do not write this section individually for each project, but rather incorporate it by reference. This section is especially helpful for an unusual project where people who have no history of working together need to establish effective methods.

Nuno Silva/iStockphoto.com

The key players of a project show their commitment to the project by signing the commitment section of the charter.

Lessons Learned

While every project is unique, a great deal can be learned from the successes and failures of previous projects and turned into practical advice. **Lessons learned** are "the learning gained from the process of performing the project."[14] To ensure that lessons learned are used, a sponsor should only sign a charter authorizing the project to begin when at least one or two good, specific lessons from the successes and/or failures of recently completed projects are included. This essentially forces the new project manager and team to look at the organization's lessons learned knowledge base to find applicable learnings. A **lessons learned knowledge base** is "a store of historical information and lessons learned about both the outcomes of previous project selection decisions and previous project performance."[15] These lessons could be stored in a dedicated database, on a shared drive, or in a less formal manner. It is important for new project teams to learn together or risk repeating mistakes from previous projects.

Signatures and Commitment

The commitment section of the charter lists who is involved and sometimes describes the extent to which each person can make decisions and/or the expected time commitment for each person. This is where the project sponsor, project manager, and core team members publicly and personally show their commitment to the project by signing the charter. By formally committing to the project, the key players are more likely to keep working hard during difficult periods and see the project through to a successful conclusion.

4.5 Constructing a Project Charter

It is wonderful if the sponsor can work with the team in constructing the charter. The sponsor, however, as a busy executive, often does not have time to be present for the entire chartering period. In that case, it is very helpful if the sponsor can create the first draft—however crude—of the elevator speech. A sponsor's ability to tell the project manager and core team concisely what the project is and why it is important gets the team off to a good start. If the sponsor wants the team to consider any important constraints, assumptions, risks, or other factors, she can help the team by pointing that out up front.

Sometimes, on an especially important project, the organization's leadership team may draft more than just the business case and scope overview statements. If the leadership team feels something is very important, they can save everyone time by just stating it up front. Likewise, if the sponsor knows he or she will only approve a charter with one of the elements written a particular way, he or she should tell the team that up front. Otherwise, the team most frequently writes much of the rough draft themselves.

Scope Overview and Business Case Instructions

When possible, the first draft of these two sections should be provided by the sponsor or the leadership team. One to four sentences for each is enough—but it needs to be in writing. Many teams find that, because these are the "what and why" of the project, it is easier to work on them at the same time. Teams often brainstorm key ideas and then craft the parts they agree upon into a smooth-flowing statement. If the sponsor provides a first draft of these sections, the project manager and core team carefully dissect it to ensure they both understand and agree. The project manager and team frequently propose refinements on the original draft.

Scope overview and business case examples are depicted in Exhibit 4.4.

Background Instructions

The project manager and team decide whether this optional section is necessary for their project as they construct the scope overview and business case. If the scope overview and business case seem detailed enough for all important stakeholders, an extra background section may not be needed. If necessary, the team probably brainstorms ideas and then combines them into a single smooth statement. An example of a background statement for a project that implemented a Malcolm Baldrige assessment to achieve improvement is shown in Exhibit 4.5.

Milestone Schedule with Acceptance Criteria Instructions

This section of the charter can be developed most effectively by focusing on why you are doing a project before diving into all of the details. A method of depicting all of this information so it is simple to understand is to set up a four-column table with *Milestone, Completion Date, Stakeholder,* and *Acceptance Criteria* heading the columns. An example of a milestone schedule with acceptance criteria for a project converting to a centralized electronic record system for a major research hospital is shown in Exhibit 4.6.

EXHIBIT 4.4

SCOPE OVERVIEW AND BUSINESS CASE EXAMPLES

PHASE II MULTI-CENTER TRIAL SCOPE OVERVIEW

This project will initiate a phase II multi-center clinical trial at Cincinnati Children's Hospital Medical Center (CCHMC). The trial will be conducted at five medical centers in the United States to investigate the safety and efficacy of an investigational drug's ability to improve cognitive functioning and quality of life in pediatric patient with Tuberous Sclerosis Complex. The project is a follow-up study of a Phase I clinical trial conducted at CCHMC.

ONLINE TUITION REIMBURSEMENT PROJECT SCOPE OVERVIEW

This project will design, develop, and implement an online tuition reimbursement system that will provide employees with a self-service tool to submit a request for tuition reimbursement payment. This project will incorporate a workflow process that will:

- Move the request to the appropriate personnel for approval,
- Alert the employee of any additional items necessary for processing the request,
- Upon approval, send the request to payroll for final processing, and
- Notify the employee of payment processing.

DEVELOPMENT OF A BIOLOGICAL RESEARCH SPECIMEN SHIPPING CENTER PROJECT BUSINESS CASE

The purpose of this shipping center is to provide professional shipping services and supplies for CCHMC employees who are responsible for shipping biological specimens as part of research. This shipping center will improve compliance, streamline shipping processes, enhance research productivity, reduce time and money invested in employee training, and reduce potential liability for noncompliance.

ESTABLISHING A SECOND PULMONARY FUNCTION TESTING (PTF) LAB PROJECT BUSINESS CASE

An additional PTF lab will *enhance patient access* by:

- Decreasing wait times and
- Providing a convenient location close to primary care appointments.

It will also *improve patient outcomes* by assisting in:

- Diagnosis,
- Accurate assessment, and
- Chronic management of pediatric lung disease.

In addition, establishing a PFT lab will *increase revenue* by:

- Increasing availability of PTF and
- Increasing community referrals for PFT.

Source: Cincinnati Children's Hospital Medical Center.

SIX STEPS IN CONSTRUCTING A MILESTONE SCHEDULE The most effective way to construct the milestone schedule with acceptance criteria is to use the six-step procedure described below. Identifying the end points first (steps 1 and 2) helps project teams avoid the problem of sinking into too much detail too quickly. Note that dates are the final item to be identified. It is unethical for a project manager to agree to unrealistic dates. Even though the milestone schedule is not very detailed, it is the first time a team thinks through how the project will be performed and how long it will take at each point. This allows a bit of realism in the schedule.

Step 1   The first task is to briefly describe (in three or four words preferably) the current situation that requires the project and place this description in the first row of the milestone column. The current state may be a shortened version of the business case. On a quality or productivity improvement project, it may describe current difficulties. On

---

EXHIBIT 4.5

BACKGROUND SECTION EXAMPLE

Orion Academy is a brand new school, currently enrolling students from kindergarten through the fifth grade. Similar to all schools managed by National Heritage Academies of Grand Rapids, Michigan, Orion encourages and rewards high academic achievement, sound moral values, and responsible citizenship. The Malcolm Baldrige assessment system in education will demand that each individual stakeholder (student, parent, teacher, administrator, etc.) be held accountable for his or her educational progress. In addition, Orion Academy's staff will help assure not only a beneficial education for its students, but the Baldrige criteria will promote performance excellence throughout the school.

Source: Dennis J. McNeal, principal, Orion Academy.

---

the second or subsequent phase of a multiphase project, it may reflect the outcome of an earlier phase. In any event, keep it very short and it will form an effective starting place. In Exhibit 4.6, the problem was paper records that were not centralized.

Step 2   Once the current state is agreed upon by the project manager and team, skip to the desired future state. Describe the project (or phase if there will be future phases) at its successful completion in three or four words. Put this description in the last row of the milestone column. It is hard for many core teams to distill this to the ideal three or four words, but keeping it concise helps the team develop a better understanding of what is truly most important. If the current project is a phase of a larger project, also write briefly what the final successful result of the last future stage will be. In Exhibit 4.6, the desired future state is to have records centralized and available in electronic form, and the ultimate goal is for seamless information flow throughout the organization. More work will need to be completed beyond this project to reach that ultimate goal.

Step 3   Next, describe the acceptance criteria for the final project deliverables (at the future state). What stakeholder(s) will make this determination, and on what basis? Exactly how will they become confident that the project results will work as desired? These stakeholders will almost always demand a demonstration of project results. The project team wants to understand what that demonstration will be at this early point so they can plan to achieve it. Note that there very well could be multiple stakeholders and multiple methods of ensuring the project results are satisfactory. At this point, strive to identify the most important stakeholders and acceptance criteria. Place these in the bottom row of the third and fourth columns. In Exhibit 4.6, the sponsor wants a representative from each department to show they can enter and retrieve pertinent data.

Step 4   Now, go back to the milestone column. Determine the few key points where quality needs to be verified. On most small to medium-sized projects, approximately three to eight intermediate points are satisfactory. Start by identifying the three most important intermediate points and add more if necessary. If you need to identify considerably more major deliverables at this point, you might consider splitting your project into phases and concentrate on the first phase for now. Satisfactory completion of each milestone will be determined by how the sponsor and other stakeholders will judge your performance. They should be in enough detail so stakeholders are comfortable with your progress, yet not so detailed that you feel micromanaged. The project in Exhibit 4.6 is near the top end for milestones with seven.

Step 5   Now for each milestone, determine who the primary stakeholder(s) is and how he or she will judge the resulting deliverable. Remember, these are intermediate deliverables, and often it is not as easy to determine desired performance. One idea to keep in mind—if

EXHIBIT 4.6

MILESTONE SCHEDULE WITH ACCEPTANCE CRITERIA EXAMPLE

MILESTONE	COMPLETION DATE	STAKEHOLDER	ACCEPTANCE CRITERIA
Current state: Paper, non-centralized records			
Needs assessment	28-Feb	Ops management	List of needed features
Hardware selection	15-Apr	Ops management, CIO	Hardware choice with contract
Vendor selection	30-May	Ops management	Vendor choice with contract
Installation and configuration	15-Jul	Application specialist, IS department head	Functional software in test environment
Conversion	31-Aug	Application specialist, IS department head	All files converted
Testing	15-Oct	Application specialist, IS department head	Sign-off on test
Training	30-Nov	Ops management, HR	Sign-off on training
Future state: Electronic, centralized records	30-Nov	Sponsor	Ability to enter and retrieve information from all departments
↓ **Ultimate goal** Seamless information flow throughout organization			

practical, ask the person who will judge the overall project results at the end to judge the intermediate deliverables also to make sure you are on the right track. Quite a few different stakeholders will judge various milestones in the project in Exhibit 4.6.

Step 6 Finally, determine expected completion dates for each milestone. Do not be overly optimistic or pessimistic. You will be at approximately the right level of detail if you have a milestone somewhere between every one and six weeks on many projects. Obviously, there will be exceptions for especially large or small projects. Most of the milestones in the project in Exhibit 4.6 are about six weeks apart.

Some companies that perform many projects use templates to guide their project teams through chartering and other activities. An example of a template for the milestone schedule and acceptance criteria for a Six Sigma project is shown in Exhibit 4.7.

Risks, Assumptions, and Constraints Instructions

First, the project manager and team (and sponsor if the sponsor is available) together should brainstorm all the things that could pose a risk to the project schedule, budget,

EXHIBIT 4.7

SIX SIGMA MILESTONE SCHEDULE AND ACCEPTANCE CRITERIA TEMPLATE			
Milestone	**Completion Date**	**Stakeholder**	**Acceptance Criteria**
Current Situation Define	_____ _____ _____	_____ _____ _____	Problem in operational terms Customers and metrics identified Project schedule and assignments
Measure	_____ _____ _____	_____ _____ _____	Causal relationships defined Data gathering procedures approved Sufficient data gathered
Analyze	_____ _____	_____ _____	Potential variables identified Root causes statistically proven
Improve	_____ _____ _____	_____ _____ _____	Problem resolution ideas gathered Solution evaluated and confirmed Solution implemented
Control Future State	_____	_____	Standards, procedures, training in place

usefulness of any project deliverables, or satisfaction of any project stakeholder. These can be envisioned as constraints on money, resources, or time. Assumptions can also be listed that, if false, might pose a threat to the project. Assumptions are especially important when a cross-functional team is performing the project because some team members may make vastly different assumptions based upon the manner in which work is normally accomplished in their respective departments. The brainstorming often works very well with each team member writing one risk, constraint, or assumption per Post-it Note. On large, complicated projects, risks, assumptions, and constraints may form separate sections of a charter. However, in this book, we deal with them together. From this point forward, all risks, assumptions, and constraints are simply referred to as risks.

Either the project manager or one of the team members can then act as a facilitator and assess one risk at a time. Risks can be assessed on any of several dimensions such as probability of occurring, impact if realized, timing of probable occurrence, ability to detect, and so forth. In this book, the risks are assessed on the two most frequently used dimensions: probability of occurrence and impact if realized. Both dimensions can be shown with a simple continuum of low to high using a flip chart or marker board. The team can agree to assess each risk at any point on the continuum. It works best if one dimension is considered at a time. For example, first ask how likely the risk event is to occur. Only after this is answered, ask how big the impact will be if it happens.

After all risks are assessed, the team needs to decide which of the risks should be considered major risks. That is, which are important enough to require a formal contingency plan with someone assigned responsibility? The other, more minor risks are not formally considered further in the charter, but very well may get more attention in the planning and executing stages. The project team constructs a table depicting each major risk, with its contingency plan and "owner."

Examples of risk assessment and major risk contingency planning for a hardware upgrade project in an Irish factory are shown in Exhibits 4.8 and 4.9, respectively.

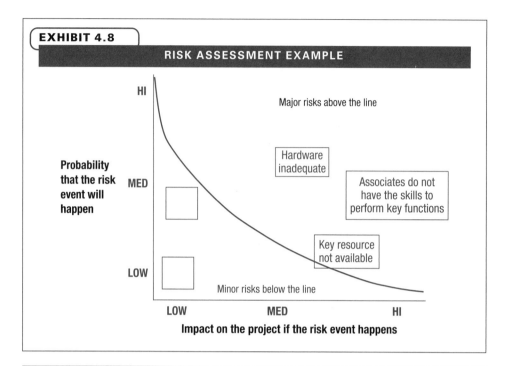

EXHIBIT 4.8

RISK ASSESSMENT EXAMPLE

Major risks above the line

Hardware inadequate

Associates do not have the skills to perform key functions

Key resource not available

Probability that the risk event will happen

Minor risks below the line

Impact on the project if the risk event happens

EXHIBIT 4.9

RISK CONTINGENCY PLAN EXAMPLE

RISK EVENT	CONTINGENCY PLAN	WHO OWNS THE CONTINGENCY PLAN?
Hardware inadequate	1. Techs revise existing hardware 2. Replace hardware	1. Edie 2. Mike
Associates do not have the skills to perform key functions	1. Train existing associates 2. Hire additional people	1. Padraig 2. Ute
Key resource not available	1. Identify external/consultant to fill need	1. Ute

Spending Approvals or Budget Estimates Instructions

Armed with the milestone schedule, the project manager and team may be prepared to make a very crude estimate of the project budget. Alternatively, the sponsor may have given the project manager a rather crude budget that the project manger and team now need to consider for reasonableness. It is imperative to describe how the estimate was developed and the level of confidence the team has in the estimate, such as "this is an order of magnitude estimate only based upon the milestones, and the true project cost could range from 40 percent below this to 100 percent above it." On many projects, especially those without customers internal to the organization, a budget is not established. However, a limit of spending authority for the project manager is often developed. The team needs to understand the sponsor's wishes in this area. An example of a spending approval for a project is shown in Exhibit 4.10.

Stakeholder List Instructions

Stakeholders are all the people who have an interest in a project. They can be internal or external to the organization, be for or against the project, and have an interest in the project process and/or the project results. Project managers need to begin by identifying all stakeholders and determining which are most important. A stakeholder list example for a clinical research project is shown in Exhibit 4.11.

Team Operating Principles Instructions

The project manager and team will need to decide if they can use previously established project team operating principles (and merely reference them here) or if they need to create their own. Essentially, the operating principles establish how meetings will be conducted, how decisions will be made, how work will get done, and how everyone will treat each other with respect. Exhibit 4.12 is an example of team operating principles.

EXHIBIT 4.10

SPENDING APPROVAL EXAMPLE

The overall project is expected to be about $50,000, and the project manager can spend up to $500 per incident, or $2,000 for the entire project with no further approval.

EXHIBIT 4.11

STAKEHOLDER LIST EXAMPLE

STAKEHOLDER	INTEREST IN PROJECT
Institutional Review Board	Unexpected problems, progress
Food and Drug Administration	Serious adverse events, progress
Site Principal Investigators	Protocol, safety reports, changes
Pharmaceutical Company (Customer)	Serious adverse events, progress
Research Subjects (Patients)	Purpose of study, risks and benefits, protocol

---

EXHIBIT 4.12

TEAM OPERATING PRINCIPLES EXAMPLE

ABC Project Team Operating Principles

1. Team members will be prepared with minutes from previous meeting, agenda, and project updates.
2. Meetings will normally last for up to 90 minutes.
3. Team members will rotate the role of recorder.
4. Each team member will be responsible for setting his or her own deadline.
5. In the event that a team member cannot have his or her assignment complete by the expected date, he or she must notify the team leader prior to the due date.
6. The team leader will be responsible for drafting the minutes from the previous meeting and the agenda for the next meeting within 48 hours.
7. Decisions will be made by:
   Team leader on _____ issues.
   Consensus on _____ issues.
   Delegation on _____ issues.

Lessons Learned Instructions

Each project by definition is at least somewhat different from any other project. That said, there are many commonalities in how projects can be planned and managed. A project manager and team need to consider what has worked well and what has worked poorly on previous projects when starting a new one. A sponsor is wise not to sign a project charter authorizing work until the project manager and team show they have learned lessons from recently completed projects. One easy way to accomplish this is to have each project report lessons learned at key reviews and at project completion and to have the lessons available to all in a lessons learned knowledge base (perhaps stored on a shared drive). The project manager and team can then look at the lessons until they find at least a couple that can help them on their project. These lessons are included in the charter. The more specific the lessons, the more likely the team will find them useful. Exhibit 4.13 is an example of project lessons learned.

Signatures and Commitment Instructions

The project sponsor, manager, and team members sign the charter to publicly acknowledge their commitment. Sometimes other key stakeholders also sign. An example of a charter signature section is shown in Exhibit 4.14.

EXHIBIT 4.13

PROJECT LESSONS LEARNED EXAMPLE

- All parties are responsible for defining and following the project scope to avoid scope creep.
- All parties should share good and bad previous experiences.
- Aligning team roles to sponsor expectations is critical.
- Keep sponsor informed so sponsor stays committed.
- Identify any possible changes as soon as possible.
- Use weekly updates on project progress to avoid unpleasant schedule surprises.
- Review previous events for specific lessons.

EXHIBIT 4.14

CHARTER SIGNATURE EXAMPLE

Anne E., Sponsor _____

Signature   *Date*

Karen H., Project Leader _____

Signature   *Date*

Jim B., Team Member _____

Signature   *Date*

Charlie H., Team Member _____

Signature   *Date*

Mitch N., Team Member _____

Signature   *Date*

Katie S., Team Member _____

Signature   *Date*

4.6 Ratifying the Project Charter

The project manager and team formally present the project charter to the sponsor for approval. In some organizations, the leadership team is also present for this meeting. The sponsor (and leadership team members if present) ideally are supportive, but also ready to ask questions regarding any part of the charter. These questions are both for clarification and agreement. Once all questions are satisfactorily answered—including any agreements regarding changes—the sponsor, project manager, and core team all sign the project charter and feel bound by it.

4.7 Starting a Project using Microsoft Project

A useful tool to capture and conveniently display a variety of important project data is Microsoft (MS) Project. A fully functional, 60-day demonstration copy of MS Project 2010 is included in this text. Exhibit 4.15 shows where MS Project is demonstrated in this book. Each process is described in a step-by-step fashion using screen shots from a single integrated project throughout the book.

MS Project 2010 Introduction

This introduction to MS Project 2010 focuses on what is unique to MS Project relative to other Microsoft Office products. That uniqueness is driven in large part by visual and calculation conventions long in use by Project Management Professionals (PMPs). This

---

EXHIBIT 4.15

CHAPTER	CHAPTER TITLE	MS PROCESS
4	Chartering Projects	Introduce MS Project 2010 Initialize the project Create milestone schedule
6	Scope Planning	Set up the work breakdown structure (WBS)
7	Scheduling Projects	Understand MS Project 2010 definitions and displays Build the logical network diagram Understand the critical path Display and print schedules
8	Resourcing Projects	Define resources Assign resources Identify overallocated resources Deal with overallocated resources
9	Budgeting Projects	Develop bottom-up project budget Develop summary project budget
11	Project Quality Planning and Project Kick-off	Baseline the project plan including quality gates
14	Monitoring and Controlling Projects	Report progress Review and adjust time and cost projections as needed
15	Finishing Projects and Realizing Benefits	Capture final project results

introduction to MS Project addresses those features that are visible when MS Project is started, as shown in Exhibit 4.16.

1. Quick Access toolbar—In the top left of the graphical user interface (GUI) is a customizable set of clickable, frequently used commands, such as undo, open, and close.

2. Ribbon—The Microsoft Project ribbon is a command bar made up of six tabs. These tabs contain the controls (or access to controls) that are used to construct, resource, baseline, status, and communicate information about a schedule. On a tab, sets of closely related controls are organized into named groups. For example, the control to create a milestone is found in the Insert group of the Task tab. Also in the Insert group are controls to create a task, a recurring task, and a summary task.

   Some controls are accessed with a drop-down arrow that presents a command menu. There are a few dialog box launchers. To minimize the ribbon, right click in the ribbon and click Minimize the Ribbon. To expand the ribbon, right click on any ribbon tab and then click Minimize the Ribbon.
   There are six ribbon tabs:

   - The File tab opens the Backstage window, with file controls such as Open, Save, Save As, and Help and access to the Options dialog box.
   - The Task, Resource, and Project ribbons provide for task, resource, and project data entry and modification.
   - The View ribbon allows selection of different views (single and combination pane) plus tables, filters, groups, and forms.
   - The Format ribbon selectively displays only the formatting controls that apply to the current active view. The Format tab header identifies the currently active view.

3. Project Schedule Information window—Below the ribbon are (one or optionally two) horizontal panes that display information about the project schedule. If a two-pane display is selected, a horizontal splitter bar divides the two panes. The bar may be dragged up or down to allocate space between the panes. Only one pane is active. A pane is activated by left clicking anywhere in the inactive pane. The active pane is

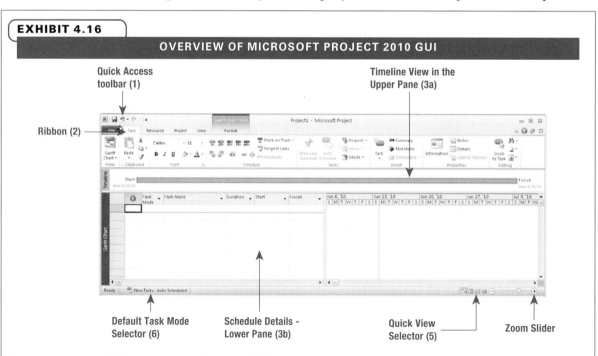

EXHIBIT 4.16

OVERVIEW OF MICROSOFT PROJECT 2010 GUI

Quick Access toolbar (1)

Timeline View in the Upper Pane (3a)

Ribbon (2)

Default Task Mode Selector (6)

Schedule Details - Lower Pane (3b)

Quick View Selector (5)

Zoom Slider

marked by a bolder blue vertical band at the far left of the application window. Either the view name or the type of data is displayed in that blue band.

There are three information formats that can be displayed in a pane:

a. Timeline—This graphic consists of a Gantt chart–like bar, which is a high-level representation of the entire duration of the schedule. Key events along the duration may be marked. Parallel events may be shown stacked or as separate bars. The timeline may be displayed singly or combined with a task or resource view. If combined, it is in the upper pane. The timeline is customizable.

b. Schedule Details—This is a presentation that displays the task, resource, and/or assignment data that helps form a schedule. Data are entered or calculated. Data can be displayed in a table, a graphic, a timescale, or a combination of two of these. A second pane may be added, displaying either the timeline (upper pane) or a form (lower pane). Tables, graphics, and the timescale are customizable. These are further discussed starting in Chapter 7.

c. Forms—These are described starting in Chapter 8.

4. Zoom Slider—Found in the lower right corner on the status bar, the zoom slider is a control to quickly change the zoom level of graphical task views. There are also Zoom In and Zoom Out buttons. The Zoom control in the View tab's Zoom group may be preferred.

5. Quick View selector—Located in the lower right next to the zoom alider, this control provides quick access to four useful views: Gantt chart, task usage, team planner, and resource sheet.

6. Default Task Mode selector—Displayed near the left side of the status bar, this control reports the default scheduling mode (manual or automatic) for each new task. To change the default, right click the control and click the desired default setting from the list. Changing this setting will only apply to the active schedule.

Initialize Microsoft Project for General Use

There are two scheduling modes (task mode) in MS Project 2010: Auto Scheduled and Manually Scheduled. With Auto Scheduled selected, MS Project automatically calculates a schedule as previous versions have, using a set of schedule drivers to calculate the start and finish dates for all tasks and summaries. The new Manually Scheduled mode ignores those drivers (as per option settings), instead using manually entered data. Manually Scheduled is the default for all new projects. We will now override that, making Auto Scheduled the default, but allowing individual tasks to be manually scheduled as needed.

Set Auto Scheduled as the Default Task Mode, as shown in Exhibit 4.17.

1. On the File tab, Options, click Schedule.
2. On the Schedule page, Scheduling options for this project, enter All New Projects.
3. On the Schedule page, New tasks created, click Auto Scheduled.
4. Click OK.

Initialize a Project

Initializing a project has the following three steps:

1. Set the project start date.
2. Enter identifying information.
3. Automatically generate a project summary row.

STEP 1: SET THE PROJECT START DATE Set the project start date as shown in Exhibit 4.18.

1. On the Project tab, Project Information, Start date, enter "Mon 4/11/11."
2. Click OK.

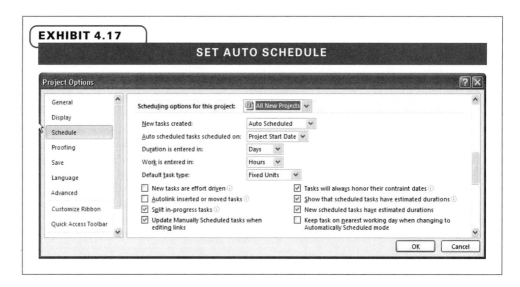

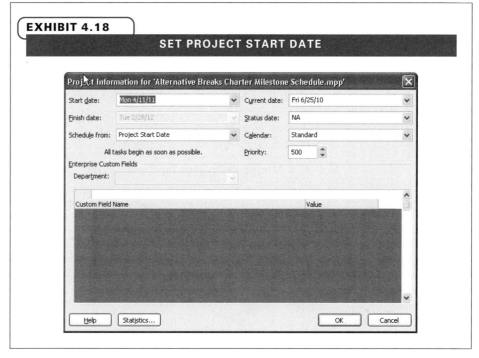

STEP 2: ENTER IDENTIFYING INFORMATION Enter identifying information as shown in Exhibit 4.19.

1. On the File tab, Info, Project Information, click Advanced Properties.
2. On the Summary tab, Title box, enter your project's name.
3. On the Summary tab, enter other information for display on reports.
4. Click OK.

STEP 3: AUTOMATICALLY GENERATE A PROJECT SUMMARY ROW MS Project can automatically generate a project summary row using the contents of the Title field (filled in step 2), as shown in Exhibit 4.20. This row will have an Id column value of zero and represents the entire project.

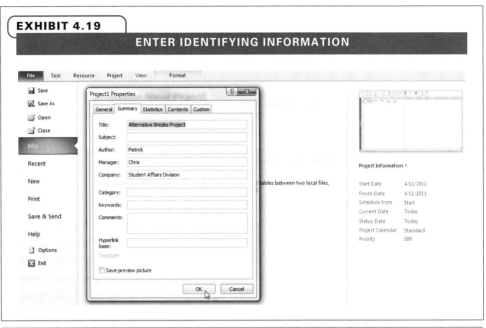

EXHIBIT 4.19

ENTER IDENTIFYING INFORMATION

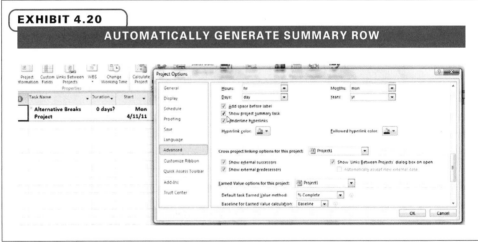

EXHIBIT 4.20

AUTOMATICALLY GENERATE SUMMARY ROW

1. On the File tab, Options, click Advanced.
2. On the Advanced page, click Show project summary task.
3. Click OK.

Construct a Milestone Schedule

After you have set the scheduling mode to Auto Scheduled and initialized a new project, create a milestone schedule as shown in Exhibit 4.21. This will serve to capture significant deliverables as milestones in a schedule format.

1. In the Task Name cells below the Project Summary row, enter the milestone names.
2. In the Duration cells, enter a value of zero for each milestone.
3. For each milestone row:
   a. Double click a field in the row to activate the Task Information dialog.
   b. In the Advanced tab, Constraint Type, enter Must Finish On.
   c. In Constraint date, enter the milestone date.
   d. Click OK.

The resulting milestone schedule appears as the example in Exhibit 4.22.

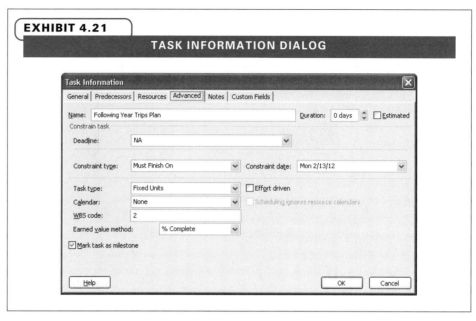

EXHIBIT 4.21

TASK INFORMATION DIALOG

EXHIBIT 4.22

ALTERNATIVE BREAKS MILESTONE SCHEDULE

Summary

The project charter is a vital document since it enables the project sponsor, project manager, and core team to reach mutual understanding and agreement on the project at a high level. All parties can commit to the intent of the charter with confidence. Charters typically include sections such as a scope overview, business case, milestone schedule, acceptance criteria, risks, and signatures. Many charters include additional sections.

The sponsor or leadership team might write the rough draft of the business case and scope overview, but the project manager and core team typically write the rough draft of the majority of the charter.

Once the draft is written, the sponsor meets with the project manager and core team to go over the charter in detail both to ensure understanding and to reach agreement.

The charter, by signaling commitment on the part of the team and authorization on the part of the sponsor, is the document that completes the project initiating stage. Once the charter is complete, the project team can usually turn their attention to planning the details of the project. The first detailed project planning, stakeholder analysis and communication planning, is the subject of the next chapter.

Key Terms from the *PMBOK® Guide*

product scope, 87
requirements, 87
project scope, 87

scope creep, 87
milestone schedule, 88
deliverable, 88

acceptance criteria, 88
risk, 89
assumptions, 89

constraint, 89
lessons learned, 90
lessons learned knowledge base, 90

Chapter Review Questions

1. What is a charter?
2. How is a charter like a contract?
3. How is a charter different from a contract?
4. What are typical elements in a charter? What is the purpose of each element?
5. Describe at least three reasons to use a charter.
6. What are the possible project outcomes that may come from using a charter?
7. How long should a typical charter be?
8. The charter signing marks the transition between which two project stages?
9. The team always writes the charter rough draft. True or false?
10. Charters help secure both formal and informal authority. True or false?
11. List at least three early management activities.
12. List at least three early leadership activities.
13. List at least three important purposes of charters.
14. How does the preliminary scope statement compare to a charter?
15. Each contingency plan should have an "owner" who is responsible for it. True or false?
16. Ideally, who should create the first draft of the "elevator speech"?
17. What are the four columns of the milestone schedule?
18. On most small to medium-sized projects, how many intermediate milestones should be identified in the charter?
19. What are the two most frequently used dimensions of risk?

Discussion Questions

1. Consider a place where you have worked and speculate how a project charter would be accepted.
2. What would be required to successfully use a project charter in this workplace?
3. If you are a project manager with an inexperienced sponsor, what can you do concerning a charter to help the situation?
4. If you are a project manager and have the choice of forming your core team either before or after charter approval, which would you do and why?
5. List and describe at least four lessons you have learned from previous projects. Relate how each is valuable in planning a new project.
6. In your opinion, what are the three most important items on your project charter? How did each help you plan your project better?
7. Contrast a project charter with a preliminary scope statement both in terms of purpose and contents.
8. Describe what an effective charter should accomplish.
9. List and describe what a charter can be used to help understand.

PMBOK® Guide Questions

1. Which of the following is **not** a purpose of a project charter?
   a. authorize project manager to proceed
   b. allocate financial resources
   c. screen out poor projects
   d. firm up commitment from project team and sponsor
2. Adding to the project after it has already begun without changing constraints of time, money, or resources is known as
   a. scope creep
   b. risk
   c. milestones
   d. acceptance criteria
3. "It is inconvenient and time-consuming for employees to walk across campus everyday to eat lunch, which is why we need an employee lunch room in our building," is an example of:
   a. project scope
   b. business case
   c. milestone schedule
   d. constraint

4. Categorize the following statement: "The project *must* be completed by November 10."
   a. risk but not constraint
   b. constraint but not risk
   c. both risk and constraint
   d. neither risk nor constraint

5. The "what and why" of a project that always come at the beginning of a project charter are the:
   a. background and scope overview
   b. milestone schedule and background
   c. business case and milestone schedule
   d. scope overview and business case

Exercises

1. Consider a major team assignment for a class. Write the scope overview and business case sections of a charter.

2. Write the purpose and scope overview sections of a project charter for a project in which your company is considering buying out another company.

3. You are part of a student team that is going to host a picnic style party as a fund raiser event for a deserving local nonprofit. Develop a milestone schedule with acceptance criteria for this event. Include between four and eight milestones.

4. You are part of a student team that has volunteered to host an alumni event at a recently reopened museum in the downtown part of your city for the twin purposes of establishing contacts with long-lost alumni and raising awareness of the newly reopened museum. Brainstorm the potential risks for this, quantify them both according to probability and impact, and create one or more contingency plans for each major risk. Assign responsibility for each contingency plan.

5. You are part of a student team that is hosting a number of inner-city junior high and high school students from several nearby cities at your campus for a weekend. The primary purpose is to encourage them to attend college and secondarily to attend your college. Identify as many stakeholders as possible for this project and create a communications plan.

6. You have started a project working with your peers at your rival college to create a "cross-town help-out." You want to encourage many people in the community to contribute a day's work on a Saturday for various community projects. You have a rather heated rivalry with this other college. Create a comprehensive set of team operating principles to use on this project. Which of these principles is most important and why? Do you expect any of them to be difficult to enforce and why? What do you plan to do if some of them do not work?

7. List at least four deliverables your agency will need to create on the project you are planning. Who will be responsible for each?

Example Project

You have a great deal of involvement with stakeholders in charter writing and approval. First, one member of your student project team needs to be the primary contact with the project sponsor. The manager or executive who came to class on the night when projects were announced serves as the sponsor. This person is also the customer representative. This sponsor was encouraged by your professor to come with a draft of the business case and scope overview sections of the charter, but some sponsors probably did a better job than others. You need to ensure that you understand these statements and how they fit with the organization's goals.

Then your student team needs to draft the remainder of the charter with as much help as you can get from the sponsor and/or other people at the organization. Once the charter is in rough draft form, submit it for comments to your professor. Armed with the professor's suggestions, you can present it to your sponsor and any other people your sponsor chooses. Often, this may involve a leadership team, department heads (functional managers), and/or project team members. One difference on this project is that your student team will likely do most of the planning and only a little of the execution, while members of the company or agency for whom you are planning the project will need to complete the execution. Therefore, you need to consider how you will transition responsibility over to the parent organization near the end of the class.

References

A Guide to the Project Management Body of Knowledge (PMBOK® Guide), 4th ed. (Newtown Square, PA: Project Management Institute, Inc., 2008).

Altwies, Diane and Frank Reynolds, *Achieve CAPM Exam Success: A Concise Study Guide and Desk Reference* (Ft. Lauderdale, FL: J. Ross Publishing, 2010).

Assudani, Rashmi and Timothy J. Kloppenborg, "Managing Stakeholders for Project Management Success: An Emergent Model of Stakeholders," *Journal of General Management* 35:3 (Spring 2010): 67–80.

Christenson, Dale and Derek Walker, "Understanding the Role of Vision in Project Success," *Project Management Journal* (September 2004): 39–49.

Evans, James R. and William M. Lindsay, *The Management and Control of Quality,* 8th ed. (Mason, OH: Cengage, 2011).

Haynes, Diane S., "Evaluation and Application of a Project Charter Template to Improve the Project Planning Process," *Project Management Journal* (March 2000).

Johnson, Craig E. *Meeting the Ethical Challenges of Leadership* (Los Angeles: Sage, 2009).

Kavanaugh, John, "Clear Business Case and User Engagement Are Keys to Project Management Success," *Computer Weekly* (May 17, 2005).

Kloppenborg, Timothy J. and Joseph A. Petrick, *Managing Project Quality* (Vienna, VA: Management Concepts, Inc., 2002).

Knack, Ruth E., "Getting Your Act Together: How Project Management Can Bring in Every Project on Time and Under Budget," *Planning* (October 2004): 20–23.

Senge, Peter M. et al., *The Fifth Discipline Fieldbook: Strategies and Tools for Building a Learning Organization* (New York: Currency Doubleday, 1994).

Skilton, Paul F. and Kevin J. Dooley, "The Effects of Repeat Collaboration on Creative Abrasion," *Academy of Management Review* 35(1) (2010): 118–134.

The Team Memory Jogger™ (Madison, WI: GOAL/QPC and Joiner Associates, Inc., 1995).

Endnotes

1. *PMBOK® Guide* 73, 442.
2. Kloppenborg, Timothy J. and Joseph A. Petrick, *Managing Project Quality* (Vienna, VA: Management Concepts, Inc., 2002): 39.
3. *PMBOK® Guide* 442.
4. *PMBOK® Guide* 445.
5. *PMBOK® Guide* 444.
6. *PMBOK® Guide* 448.
7. *PMBOK® Guide* 438.
8. *PMBOK® Guide* 432.
9. *PMBOK® Guide* 426.
10. *PMBOK® Guide* 446.
11. *PMBOK® Guide* 427.
12. *PMBOK® Guide* 429.
13. The Team Memory Jogger (Madison, WI: GOAL/QPC and Joiner Associates, Inc., 1995): 31.
14. *PMBOK® Guide* 437.
15. *Ibid.*

PROJECT MANAGEMENT *IN ACTION*

Information Systems Enhancement Project Charter

The following charter was used when a nonprofit agency formed a project team to upgrade its information systems. Comments on the left side give advice from a communications perspective regarding how to write a project charter, and comments on the right side offer suggestions regarding the content of each section.

DESIGN PRINCIPLES

Headings: Macro Organizers

Headings facilitate *scanning* by identifying information covered in each section.

Headings allow readers to find information in a message quickly.

Subheadings are useful in highlighting the logic of long sections.

The subject line is the first and most important heading: Highlight it by writing it in all capitals, boldfaced, and centered on the page.

Heading descriptions should accurately indicate the information that follows.

Lists: Micro Organizers

Listing techniques help readers remember key details of a message.

Numbers, bullets, and other ordering devices promote retention and improve visual design.

Lists are best limited to five points so they do not look overwhelming to readers.

Lists are written in parallel structure, with the first word of each item having the same grammatical form, such as all nouns, all verbs, or all *-ing* words.

Indentation:

Indentation indicates the hierarchy of thought. For example, indenting the five subheadings under Communication Plan shows they are specific subelements of the over- all communication plan.

PROJECT CHARTER: INFORMATION SYSTEMS ENHANCEMENT PLAN

Scope Overview

This team will create an interdepartmental proposal based on a needs assessment of personnel of the agency. The plan will (1) detail technological issues, as well as upward, downward, and lateral communications issues within each department and (2) identify issues within the company's infrastructure such as:

- Specific office needs related to information technology and
- Software package options for each program area.

Business Case — Objective

The agency needs to overhaul facilities information systems and technology at its summer camp, increase productivity for staff, and create additional learning opportunities for the participants.

MILESTONE	COMPLE- TION DATE	STAKE- HOLDER	ACCEP- TANCE CRITERIA
Outdated facility, poor productivity	Start		
Staff survey	1/27/11	Sponsor	Discussion with department heads
Final project charter	2/1/11	Sponsor & Core Team	Charter signed
Scope and schedule	2/10/11	Operations Manager	All areas included, schedule appears feasible
Project funded	2/25/11	Board	Realistic, within budget
Vendor selected	3/20/11	Project Manager	Best meets qualifications
Technology in place	4/28/11	Project Manager	System test demonstration
Updated facility, productivity improved	5/15/11	Sponsor	Two-week data reports from department heads

CONTENT PRINCIPLES

Scope Overview: The What

The scope overview describes the project in a nutshell. It defines the major deliverables. It sets project boundaries by clarifying what is included and, sometimes, what is not included.

Business Case: The Why

The business case defines project objectives and why they are important to the parent organization. It should inspire people to think this is an important project.

Milestone Schedule:

The milestone schedule shows the project starting point, about three to eight major milestones and deliverables, and the ending point of the project along with the estimated time of each.

Acceptance Criteria Factors:

These identify which stakeholder will judge the acceptability of each project milestone and what criteria they will use to make the determination.

DESIGN PRINCIPLES

Tables:
Use tables to organize complex information into an easy-to-follow column and row format.

Design tables so they make sense when read independently of the text.

Use table headings that reflect logical groupings of information.

Phrase column language so it is in parallel structure.

Character Formatting:
Use character formatting, including boldface, italics, underlines, and centering to highlight headings.

Use character formatting hierarchically. Boldface, underlines, and all caps are best for major headings. Use fewer or less dramatic techniques for subheadings.

Type Size and Face:
Use 9, 10, 11, or 12 point type for most documents. Near-sighted readers prefer larger type.

Use a conventional typeface, such as Arial, Times Roman, or Palatino.

White Space:
Use white space to separate document sections attractively and to improve readability.

Margins:
Use a 3/4" margin (especially at the top and on the left-hand side) so readers can make notes in that space.

Page Breaks:
When possible, complete entire sections on the same page. Redesign documents where one or two lines of text from a section run onto the next page.

Risks and Assumptions

RISK/ ASSUMPTION	RISK OWNER	CONTINGENCY PLANS
Project scope may extend beyond the timeline of the project (R)	Project Manager	Work with sponsor to define top defect and focus exclusively on it for project.
Implementation cost (R)	Accountant	Identify areas of cost reduction and nonprofit funding.
Lack of sponsor buy-in (R)	Project Manager	Conduct staff survey to identify critical-to-quality characteristics of the project.
Lack of program participant benefit from improved information technology plan (R)	Lead User (core team member)	Understand sponsor requirements. Focusing on improving administrative abilities of the program may reduce program participant benefit.
Improving program administrative abilities is key (A)	Lead User (core team member)	Improve administrative abilities so productivity increases flow to participants.
Lack of buy-in and follow-up will impede SSC achieving long-term goals (A)	Project Manager	Negotiate sponsor buy-in. Develop feasible plan for stepping stones to execute.

Stakeholder List

STAKEHOLDER	INTEREST IN PROJECT
Sponsor	Overall project success, resource needs
Department Heads	Impact on their department, resource needs
Lead user	New work methods, productivity increases
Board	Overall cost and overall project success

CONTENT PRINCIPLES

Project Risks and Assumptions:
Future Issues and Responses

This section identifies major potential issues and allows group to agree in advance on how to identify them in their early stages and how to deal with them if and when they occur. One person is assigned responsibility for each contingency plan.

Stakeholder List: Who Cares

Identifies those individuals and groups who have an interest in either the project process and/or results. These individuals may be for or against the project, but identifying them early helps ensure their desires are used in project planning to follow.

DESIGN PRINCIPLES

Paragraphs:

To help readers understand the logic of your message quickly, organize paragraphs deductively, starting each paragraph with the point that is most important to readers.

Devise a complete argument by following each paragraph's topic sentence with why it is true or important and the data that support your claim.

Compose two- to six-line paragraphs to improve visual appeal.

Sentences:

To express complex ideas effectively and to make ideas easy for readers to understand, compose most sentences to be 15–25 words long.

Break sentences that run over 50 words into two concise sentences.

Simple Language:

So all readers understand your language easily, substitute short, action-oriented, easily understood words for long, unfamiliar, and unpronounceable words.

Positive Positioning:

Use positive phrasing by replacing words such as *not, yet, but,* and *however* with positive phrases such as *and, moreover,* and *significantly.*

Team Operating Principles

- Commitment to timetable. The project management team members will complete their assigned project deliverable as defined by the project timeline.
- Regularly scheduled project team and sponsorship meetings. Project team meetings will be held every Saturday at 4:15 p.m. The team will also communicate via e-mail as required. Sponsorship committee meetings with the agency staff will be held bimonthly or on an as-needed basis.
- Timely communication. The project management team will communicate status, issues, and questions with agency via e-mail or conference call weekly. Project actions will be distributed to the team every Monday.
- Majority rule. The project management team will negotiate and resolve issues on a majority-rule basis.

Lessons Learned

- Agreeing on project scope is a key preliminary project planning activity.
- Maintaining project goals and timeline requires open communication and quick issue resolution.
- Understanding roles and responsibilities facilitates smooth teamwork and timely project completion.

Commitment

C B—Sponsor	B—Project Manager
G L—Lead User	B—Core Team Member
S J—Core Team Member	—Core Team Member

CONTENT PRINCIPLES

Operating Principles:

Operating principles indicates agreement on deadlines, meetings, and decision-making rules, and generally shows how participants will treat each other with respect.

Lessons Learned:

This section highlights specific learnings from previous similar projects that will help the team copy good practices and avoid problems.

Commitment:

Project principals signal agreement in principle to the project, recognizing that some of the specifics will probably change when the detailed planning is complete.

PART 2

PLANNING PROJECTS
organize / plan / perform

Chapter 5
Stakeholder Analysis and Communication Planning

Chapter 6
Scope Planning

Chapter 7
Scheduling Projects

Chapter 8
Resourcing Projects

Chapter 9
Budgeting Projects

Chapter 10
Project Risk Planning

Chapter 11
Project Quality Planning and Project Kick-off

CHAPTER 5
Stakeholder Analysis and Communication Planning

Comstock/Jupiter Images

The Built Green Home, a demonstration project developed by Brenda Nunes, was one of the first homes built in the new resort of Suncadia, located in Kittitas County, Washington, approximately 80 miles east of Seattle. Suncadia is a four-season resort community on 6,300 acres of forest and grassland in rural central Washington. It has been certified as the highest three-star level and largest Built Green-certified community in Washington State. Eighty percent of the property will remain as open space and golf courses, with 40 miles of trails. A 1,200-acre conservation easement along the Cle Elem River is protected as a riparian habitat. The community maintains stringent guidelines for all development within its boundaries that include measures to protect against erosion and pollution.

A large component of Nunes' vision centered on education; she believed that more people would build green if they knew they could do it without sacrificing style or creature comforts, and especially if it meant a healthier indoor environment. Working closely with builder Grey Lundberg of CMI

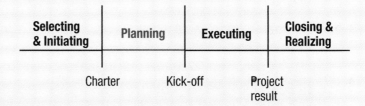
PMBOK® GUIDE TOPICS

- Develop project management plan
- Virtual teams
- Develop project team
- Identify stakeholders
- Plan communications
- Manage stakeholder expectations

Homes of Bellevue, Washington, Nunes studied every aspect of the home for its green potential. Nunes and Lundberg organized a steering committee of local experts who met regularly to help guide the project through the maze of decisions—adherence to its mission, materials choices and costs, installation, functionality, accessibility, and educational focus.

The following list presents some of the many challenges and stakeholders involved in this project that required the careful selection of the right steering committee:

- Although 80 miles did not seem that far, the building site was on the other side of a mountain pass that was closed for days at a time due to multiple rock slides and severe weather.
- The Green Building Program that the house was being built in adherence to had not yet been introduced to either the resort or the central Washington building community.
- The demonstration house had many innovative products that were new to the builder. Many of the suppliers were new to him as well.
- Since this house was one of the first being built in Suncadia, it presented an opportunity to educate many and make a very large impact on future homes.

Careful attention was given to create a steering committee that was large enough to represent the diverse group of stakeholders but small enough to be effective. Key areas of needed expertise included builder and support personnel, developer, architect, green building specialist, energy specialist, energy providers, sponsorship development, resort participants, communications specialist, Central Washington Home Builders Association representative, Master

The Built Green Home at Suncadia in Kittitas County, Washington.

Northwest Property Imaging, Inc.

Builders Association of King and Snohomish Counties/Built Green, material specialist, marketing specialist, air quality expert, and government representative.

The Built Green Home at Suncadia demonstrates the need to identify stakeholders and understand their needs. Once this is accomplished, relationships can be nurtured and effective communications can be established. Project managers who are able to manage stakeholder expectations and communications—the subject of this chapter—dramatically enhance the prospects of completing their projects successfully.

Brenda Nunes, Developer, Built Green Home

5.1 Develop the Project Management Plan

Chapters 2 and 3 of this book discuss organizational issues such as strategic planning, project selection, and roles of key individuals. Chapter 4 details how to initiate a project —usually by composing and ratifying a charter. This chapter bridges initiating and planning. Exhibit 5.1 shows the process flow of getting a project started. Everything through the process "Identify Stakeholders" is part of selecting and initiating projects, while "Plan Communications" is a planning process.

Because each project is unique, a project team needs to plan specifically for each project. While the details of each plan will differ, projects have many issues in common that must be planned. For example, all projects are undertaken to achieve a purpose. This means that a set of stakeholders wants the project results and that the results have scope of work and quality considerations. All projects are subject to cost and scheduling constraints and are accomplished with and through people and other resources. The planning for people includes both determination of who will work on the project and how they will develop effective team and stakeholder relationships.

As stated in Chapter 1, project management is integrative, iterative, and collaborative. Project planning must integrate the nine knowledge areas described in the *PMBOK® Guide* into a single project management plan. Project planning is iterative in that one starts by planning at a high level and then repeats the planning in greater detail as more information becomes available. Project planning is collaborative since there are many stakeholders to be satisfied and a team of workers with various skills and ideas who need to work together. For ease of understanding, in this book planning has been divided into chapters, but a team cannot complete all the planning in a chapter-by-chapter manner. Decisions

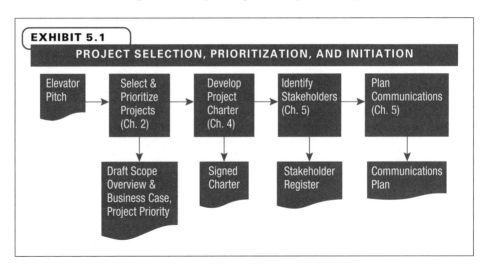

EXHIBIT 5.1

PROJECT SELECTION, PRIORITIZATION, AND INITIATION

Elevator Pitch → Select & Prioritize Projects (Ch. 2) → Develop Project Charter (Ch. 4) → Identify Stakeholders (Ch. 5) → Plan Communications (Ch. 5)

Select & Prioritize Projects (Ch. 2) → Draft Scope Overview & Business Case, Project Priority

Develop Project Charter (Ch. 4) → Signed Charter

Identify Stakeholders (Ch. 5) → Stakeholder Register

Plan Communications (Ch. 5) → Communications Plan

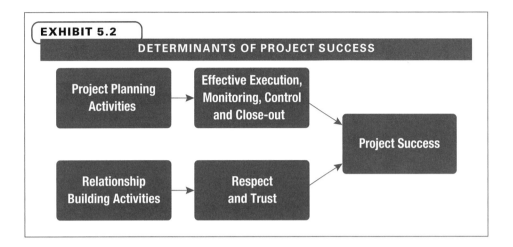

EXHIBIT 5.2

DETERMINANTS OF PROJECT SUCCESS

Project Planning Activities → Effective Execution, Monitoring, Control and Close-out → Project Success

Relationship Building Activities → Respect and Trust → Project Success

made in planning one function will often require revisions in another. For example, if the proposed schedule is too slow, perhaps a client will authorize the use of overtime pay, which will probably increase the budget.

Effective project planning lays the groundwork for effective project execution, monitoring, control, and closeout. Developing effective team and stakeholder relationships leads to a foundation of respect and trust which, in turn, leads to project success, as displayed in Exhibit 5.2. Thus, during project planning, details of the various functions need to be planned and the groundwork needs to be established for effective team and stakeholder relationships.

Projects vary tremendously in size and complexity. Therefore, project management planning can vary from filling out a few simple templates to completing many detailed forms and hosting multiple facilitated meetings. When a project team is trying to decide how detailed the planning needs to be, the team members need to remember that the purpose of the project management plan is to become a basis for executing, monitoring, controlling, and closing all project work. It is wise to spend $100 in planning to save $1,000 in execution, but not the other way around.

A project team develops a variety of plans for communications, schedules, budgets, and so forth. They need to ensure these various plans all fit together into one unified project plan. Typically, a good way to begin planning is to develop the outline of a **project management plan**, which is "a formal, approved document that defines how the project is executed, monitored, and controlled. It may be summary or detailed and may be composed of one or more subsidiary management plans and other planning documents."[1] At this point, whatever documentation was developed in the process of initiating the project can be used.

Since both relationship building and detailed planning of the various project functions need to occur simultaneously, our coverage will start with a type of planning that does both. The PMBOK task **plan communications** is "the process of determining project stakeholder information needs and defining a communications approach."[2]

In this book, project management plans include communications, scope, schedule, budget, resources, risks, and quality. While much of the planning is iterative, we first discuss an understanding of project stakeholders—everyone who has an interest in either the process of performing the project work or in using the project deliverables. Once a team understands who has an interest in or can exert influence over their project, they can develop a **communications management plan**, which is "the document that describes: the communication needs and expectations for the project; how and in what format information will be communicated; when and where each communication will be made; and who is responsible for providing each type of communication."[3] After the communications management plan, the project team will determine the scope. Once the scope is determined, the project team can plan other aspects of the project, such as:

- Schedule
- Budget
- Resources needs
- Risks
- Quality

Some of these issues impact others, so the team develops the project management plan to ensure that all of these subsidiary plans work effectively together. One final and important thing to remember is that the project management plan, once formally approved, can only be updated and revised by formally approved changes. Many projects have changes identified when the project is well underway and require replanning throughout the project life cycle.

5.2 Understand Stakeholders

Projects are undertaken because someone needs the project's output. A project must satisfy its users to be successful. Several things can complicate this. First, there may be multiple users and each may have different wants and needs. Second, often users do not fully understand what they want because they do not know what alternatives may be available. Third, the customer who pays for the project may not be the actual person or group who uses the result, and the customer may not fully understand the users' needs. Fourth, when someone else is paying for the project, some users will ask for many project outcomes that are expensive or time consuming to deliver. Finally, many stakeholders in addition to the users of a project's outcomes have an interest in the project. Project managers need to first understand their stakeholders, build relationships with them, and then develop a communications plan for dealing with them.

Identify Stakeholders

One way to understand who stakeholders are is to ask, "Who will use or be affected by the result of a project?" The answer includes users of the project results and others who may have some changes forced upon them by the project. The PMBOK task **identify stakeholders** is "the process of identifying all people or organizations impacted by the project, and documenting relevant information regarding their interests, involvement, and impact on project success."[4] Stakeholders also include those who are affected by the process of performing the project. This includes people who:

- Work on the project
- Provide people or resources for the project
- Have their routines disrupted by the project

Another way to identify stakeholders is to determine whether they are internal to the organization performing the project or external to it. Examples of project stakeholders based on these categories are shown in Exhibit 5.3. Note that there are potentially more types of stakeholders affected by the process of performing the project than by the project results and more external than internal stakeholders.

Project managers and project core teams (often in consultation with their sponsor) can use the examples in Exhibit 5.3 to identify possible project stakeholders. This stakeholder analysis can be conducted as a brainstorming session. Classic rules of brainstorming apply—initially, the emphasis is on generating a long list of potential stakeholders in the first column of a chart. It may be easiest to construct this chart on a large work

EXHIBIT 5.3		
EXAMPLES OF PROJECT STAKEHOLDERS		
	INTERNAL	EXTERNAL
Affected by Project Process	Owner	Suppliers
	Sponsor	Partners
	Project Manager	Creditors
	Functional Managers	Government Agencies
	Competing Projects	Special Interest Groups
	Financing Source	Neighbors
	Project Core Team	Client
	Subject Matter Experts	Professional Groups
	Employees	Media
	Stockholders	Taxpayers
		Union
		Competitors
Affected by Project Result	Internal Customer	Client
	Sponsor	Public
	Users	Special Interest Groups
		Neighbors
		Potential Customers

surface such as a white board or flip chart. Another suggestion is to be specific; identify stakeholders by name when possible.

For each potential stakeholder, list the various project processes and results in which he or she might have an interest. Consider both financial and emotional interests of potential stakeholders. The project charter can be useful here. Many stakeholders have an interest in multiple aspects of a project. Once the stakeholders and their interests have been listed, they may be combined into like groups with the same interests.

Prioritize Stakeholders

The next step is to prioritize the stakeholders. Prioritization is important because on many projects there are too many stakeholders to spend a great deal of time with each. While it is important not to ignore any stakeholder, it also makes sense to concentrate on those who are most vital. Bourne and Walker developed a method that requires the project core team to determine three aspects in prioritizing stakeholders.[5] All three aspects can be rated on a simple scale of 1 to 3, with 3 representing the highest priority. For the first aspect, *proximity* to the project, a stakeholder who has significant direct contact with the project team would be a 3, while a much more remote stakeholder would be a 1. For the second aspect, *power,* a stakeholder who could order the project shut down or changed in a major way would be a 3, and a stakeholder who could not change the project much would be a 1. For the third aspect, *urgency,* a stakeholder with great time sensitivity would be a 3, and a stakeholder with only routine time needs would be a 1. The scores from the three aspects are added to form a total prioritization score. Exhibit 5.4 shows this stakeholder identification and prioritization.

By determining who the stakeholders are and what each group wants, project managers effectively:

- Set clear direction for further project planning, negotiating, and execution
- Prioritize among competing objectives

EXHIBIT 5.4

STAKEHOLDER IDENTIFICATION AND PRIORITIZATION MATRIX

Stakeholder: Interested in Project Process or Result (Be specific)	PRIORITY OF STAKEHOLDER			
	Proximity	Power	Urgency	Total

- Learn to recognize complex tradeoffs and the consequences of each
- Make and facilitate necessary decisions
- Develop a shared sense of risk
- Build a strong relationship with their customers
- Lead associates, customers, and suppliers with an empowering style
- Serve as good stewards of the resources of both the parent and customer organizations

The project team should next select the top 10 to 15 stakeholders for emphasis in the remainder of their planning. The stakeholders with the highest total scores are often considered to be primary influencers for the project. The project manager and core team should also plan to periodically review this prioritized list of stakeholders, as the relative importance may change as the project progresses, especially if the project goals are not clear at the outset.

One additional consideration is that various stakeholders often have competing interests. For example, the client may want the work done quickly while the accountant is worried about cash flow. Exhibit 5.5 itemizes how different types of stakeholders frequently define project success. Another consideration is that the project was selected to support a specific business purpose and that purpose should help determine the relative importance of various stakeholders. Typically, when a conflict exists, external paying customers and top management are considered to be highly important stakeholders. If the project team developed the stakeholder identification and prioritization matrix without their sponsor, now would be a good time to share it with the sponsor and ask for feedback. Chances are good the sponsor will want to make some adjustments before the team continues. Sponsors are especially useful in helping to sort out conflicting priorities. The project team primarily considers these top stakeholders while they:

- Develop a communications plan (see next section)
- Scope the project (see Chapter 6)
- Identify threats and opportunities (see Chapter 10)

EXHIBIT 5.5

SUCCESS CRITERIA FOR VARIOUS STAKEHOLDERS

STAKEHOLDER/ SUCCESS CRITERIA	ON TIME	ON BUDGET	MEET REQUIR-EMENTS	PARTNER-SHIP	PROFIT REALIZED	FOLLOW-ON WORK	MINIMAL OVERTIME	RECO-GNITION	CHALLENGE	WELL-PAID	QUALITY
Customer	X	X	X	X							X
End user	X		X	X			X				X
Customer management	X	X	X	X			X	X			X
Project manager	X	X	X	X	X	X	X	X		X	X
Contractor management	X	X	X	X	X	X	X				X
Project team member	X		X	X		X	X	X	X	X	X
Subcontractor	X	X		X	X	X	X			X	X

Source: Adapted from Ralph R. Young, Steven M. Brady and Dennis C. Nagle, Jr., *How to Save a Failing Project: Chaos to Control* (Vienna, VA: Management Concepts, 2009): 14. © 2009 by Management Concepts, Inc. All rights reserved. www.managementconcepts.com/pubs.

EXHIBIT 5.6

ALTERNATIVE BREAKS PROJECT STAKEHOLDER MATRIX

STAKEHOLDER	INTEREST IN PROJECT	PRIORITY	SUPPORT/MITIGATION STRATEGIES
Students	Going on trip	1 Key	Support and guide through process
Families	Monetary support, worry about student	3	Help students guide families through process
Community organizations	We support them	2	Constant communication
VP Student Affairs	Success for division	1 Key	Share and publicize "wins"
Executive Director of Faith and Justice	Success for faith and justice	1 Key	Share and publicize "wins," keep informed of progress
Board	Success for board and students	1 Key	Constant improvement
Advisor	Success for board, students, and advisor	2	Constant improvement
Winter break trip	Learn from alternative breaks	3	Remain in contact, share strategies
National Organization Break Away	2 way sharing	2	Continue current relationship

Source: Chris Bridges.

- Determine quality standards (see Chapter 11)
- Prioritize among cost, schedule, scope, and quality objectives (see Chapter 11)

The primary output of the "identify stakeholders" process is a stakeholder register. The stakeholder register is a list of all stakeholders with supporting information such as their interest in the project, the prioritization of how relatively important each is, and strategies to either capitalize upon their support or to mitigate the impact of their resistance. The stakeholder register is a living document that changes as needed. A stakeholder matrix for the alternative breaks example project is shown in Exhibit 5.6. Note that priority 1 stakeholders are listed as key.

5.3 Build Relationships

Project managers and teams seek to develop strong working relationships with important stakeholders. This is an ongoing process throughout the life of the project. In fact, the project manager normally continues to nurture the relationship even after the project is completed to increase the chances of securing future project work. In building relationships both within the project core team and with other stakeholders, project managers need to remember that mutual respect and trust greatly enhance the prospect of project success. Therefore, relationship-building activities that lead to respect and trust should be planned and carried out carefully. Typically, these activities are most effective when they are used in the process of planning a project. Project relationship-building activities that are described more fully below and are especially useful include the following:

- Share individual motives.
- Encourage open communication.
- Jointly establish agendas.
- Use shared learning.

- Regularly celebrate success.
- Share enjoyment of project.
- Use appropriate decision making and problem solving.[6]

Relationship Building within the Core Team

Project sponsors and managers who wish to create highly productive workplaces ensure that core team members understand what is expected of them, have the chance to do work they are well-suited to perform, receive appropriate recognition, have good co-workers, have their opinions considered, and have opportunities to grow and develop.[7] The sponsor and the project manager ideally begin by asking one another about personal expectations from the project. Each may have project goals such as certain specific capabilities in the project deliverables. Both the project manager and sponsor may have *individual motives* also. It is helpful to acknowledge these personal goals to each other. The project manager, in turn, asks each core team member what he or she personally wants from involvement in the project. These conversations not only help the project manager understand priorities, but also motivations. For example, core team members may want to participate in a stimulating experience, gain skill, or earn a promotion. Understanding these motivations will make it easier for the project manager to address them.

The project manager can encourage *open communication* by keeping people informed, showing that everyone's input is valued, personally sharing feelings, and respecting confidentiality. She should set the expectation that all team members also practice these habits.

Joint establishment of project meeting agendas helps with relationship building because all team members feel their concerns are addressed and they develop a greater sense of ownership in meetings. When members get to *share in meaningful project learning,* they feel their judgment is valued. *Frequent celebration of small successes* helps project team members *share the enjoyment* of working on a project, which in turn helps them stay committed to successful project completion.

One other key relationship-building activity that needs to start early and continue throughout the project concerns *appropriate decision making and problem solving.* The project manager and core team need to understand who makes each type of project decision and how each is made. One consideration is that people involved in making decisions tend to better support them. Decisions made by groups tend to take longer, and projects are often pushed for time. Some decisions are best made by a single expert, while others are best made by a group that represents various points of view. Each project team will need to determine who will make which types of decisions. Exhibit 5.7 gives general advice that can be applied in making this determination.

EXHIBIT 5.7	
PROJECT DECISION-MAKING GUIDE	
PERSON/METHOD	WHEN
Sponsor decides	Critical decision, large monetary stake, "big picture" needed
Project manager decides	Time is critical, no need for other input
Functional manager decides	"How" functional work is done
Core team discusses and project manager decides	Team input is useful
Core team consensus	Buy-in is critical
Delegated to one or two team members to recommend	Needs to be investigated, team input useful
Delegated to one or two team members to decide	Needs to be investigated, team input not needed

Relationship Building with All Other Stakeholders

Establishing a positive relationship early on with all key stakeholders is vital for two reasons. First, it helps create a desire on the part of stakeholders to give positive support to the project, or at least refrain from disrupting the project. Second, it serves as the communications foundation for the project. The remainder of the project planning and execution are greatly enhanced by effective communications channels with key project stakeholders.

The sponsor, project manager, and core team can establish powerful relationships with key stakeholders by delivering on all promises, always providing fair treatment, creating a sense of pride by association, and even helping the stakeholder develop a passion for the project.[8] This starts by learning what motivates each stakeholder. The old saying "What is in it for me?" describes what each stakeholder wants, and that is what the project team needs to understand. Stakeholders who feel threatened can disrupt a project during its process and are less likely to perceive that they receive project benefits in the end. Unhappy stakeholders are a sign of project failure. On the other hand, stakeholders can be treated as partners right from the start of planning by the project team speaking their language and providing them opportunity to participate. These stakeholders are more likely to take ownership in the project by educating the project team about their needs and making timely project decisions and, in turn, are more likely to feel their expectations match the project team's plans. They are more likely to go beyond merely inspecting results and writing checks. They may participate early and often when their input is meaningful and they feel that the project is successful. All of the other project relationship-building activities listed previously can be applied in a similar fashion to that described for the core team in the previous section. The important thing for project managers to remember is that developing respect and trust among all project stakeholders is a goal that must be started early and continued throughout the project. This is just as critical to project success as the more technical planning and should also demand attention from project managers.

5.4 Plan Communications

The project team should next create the communications management plan. This plan guides the project communications and needs to be a living document that adapts to changing project needs.

Purposes of a Project Communications Plan

Projects have many challenges, including technical, cost, and schedule difficulties. Failure to manage any of these well can throw off a project. Another very common challenge to project success is communication. Many projects require people to work together who have not done so before. Projects may involve people from various functional areas that all have their own unique challenges. People from multiple companies may end up working together on projects. All projects are unique and therefore have different sets of stakeholders. "Communication leads to cooperation, which leads to coordination, which leads to project harmony, which leads to project success."[9]

A project manager must use effective communications to set and manage expectations from all stakeholders as well as to ensure that project work is completed properly and on time. Communications *from* stakeholders are necessary in determining requirements, uncovering and resolving issues, and receiving feedback on project progress and results. Different stakeholders often have conflicting desires; effective communications are necessary to understand and resolve these differences. Communications *to* stakeholders are necessary to help them make good decisions (by understanding options and risks), to assure them of adequate understanding and progress, and to enable them to more fully commit to the project. Finally, communications plans ensure that at project conclusion, meaningful lessons can be documented to benefit future projects.

Communications Plan Considerations

A myriad of considerations must be kept in mind when creating a communications plan. A project team can develop a workable communications plan, use it, and improve it as the project progresses. Some factors to consider when creating a project communications plan are shown in Exhibit 5.8. These factors apply to all project communications. Therefore, we discuss these factors first and then explain who the project team needs information from and to whom they need to supply information.

PURPOSE COLUMN The first column in Exhibit 5.8 instructs a project team to consider the *purpose* for each communication. If there is no good use for the communication, it makes no sense to develop it. However, if the communication has a legitimate business purpose, the team should work hard to ensure that it is correctly developed. The team can keep the six Cs of project communications in mind:

- Clearly state the subject.
- Concisely make the point.
- Courteously deliver the message.
- Consistently reinforce your point.
- Respect confidentiality at all times.
- Compel the recipient to be receptive.[10]

EXHIBIT 5.8

PROJECT COMMUNICATIONS PLAN CONSIDERATIONS			
PURPOSES	STRUCTURES	METHODS	TIMING
Authorization	Existing organizational forms (reuse)	Push Methods:	Project life cycle
Direction setting		Instant messaging	Charter
Information seeking	Project specific:	E-mail	Project plan
Status Reporting:	Templates (adapt)	Voice mail	Milestones
Schedule	Unique (create)	Fax	Output acceptance
Cost			Project close-out
People		Pull Methods:	
Risk		Shared document repositories	Routine time
Issues		Intranet	Daily—member
Quality		Blog (repository)	Weekly—core team
Change Control		Bulletin boards	Monthly—sponsor
Approval of project outputs		Interactive Methods:	As needed—others
		Telephone-teleconferencing	
		Wikis	
		VOIP/videoconferencing	
		Groupware	

While most of the six Cs of project communications are self-explanatory, confidentiality needs to be clarified. A project manager develops trust with her core team and other stakeholders partly by using open communications to the extent possible. However, she needs to respect all promises of confidentiality and to use good judgment on what is or is not appropriate to share.

STRUCTURES COLUMN Each of the other three columns in Exhibit 5.8 includes important considerations when developing a project communications plan. For example, the second column suggests that if there are existing organizational communication *structures,* use them! There is no need to reinvent every document and, indeed, it would be confusing and costly to do so. Many stakeholders in organizations are accustomed to a particular method of communications, and using that method will make it easier for them to understand you. Remember, no one loves your project as much as you do. Therefore, you need to make communications simple for the receiver so they will pay attention. When no exact organizational model is available to follow for a particular communication, one can be modified. Modification is still easier than the third choice of creating an entirely new type of document, which should obviously be the last resort.

Using any of the three choices, project teams need to maintain version control on all of their communications. Since many documents have contributions from multiple people, some method of version control is essential. One easy method is to end the file name of every document with six numbers representing year, year, month, month, and day, day. For example, an early version of this chapter was saved on May 24, 2010, and the file name given was "Chapter 5 Stakeholder Analysis and Communication Planning 100524." The advantage of a simple system is that the files can still be easily found by their descriptive named titles, but they can also be sorted easily by the last date they were updated.

METHODS COLUMN The third column in Exhibit 5.8 deals with *methods* of communicating. Projects rely on "push" methods in which communications are sent or pushed; "pull" methods where communications are posted either on paper or in electronic form and interested stakeholders need to take the initiative to receive the communication; and interactive methods in which communications flow in multiple directions. A typical project communication plan will utilize a variety of these methods.

TIMING COLUMN The fourth column is a reminder that a project team needs to consider *timing* issues when developing a project communications plan. Communications typically are delivered according to one of three types of timing schedules. First is the project life cycle, with communications typically needed at the end of each major stage in the project and at the end of each major project deliverable. The second timing schedule follows a more formal organizational structure. Project progress is often reported at regularly scheduled meetings. Meetings at the frontline level are usually more frequent than reports to higher levels within the organization. The third timing scheme is an as-needed basis. Many times, a stakeholder wants to know a certain fact about a project and cannot wait until the next formal meeting or report. Project teams need to keep themselves up to date so they can handle the as-needed requests.

Communications Matrix

At this point, project teams will normally assemble a project communications matrix. This matrix lists the following information:

Who	does the project team need to learn from?
What	does the team need to learn from this stakeholder?

Who	does the project team need to share with?
What	does this stakeholder need to know?
When	do they need to know it?
What	is the most effective communications method for this stakeholder to understand?
Who	on the project team is responsible for this communication? (the owner)

An example of a completed project communications matrix is shown in Exhibit 5.9. The communications needs of each project are unique and, therefore, the assignment of communications responsibilities will vary widely from project to project.

Knowledge Management

If a company does extensive project work and uses project management capability as an organizational strength, it is important to keep developing expertise in it. One way to develop and expand expertise is to capture and reuse the knowledge developed. Knowledge is "a conclusion drawn from information after it is linked to other information and compared to what is already known."[11] In order to increase knowledge and the successful use and reapplication of it, organizations often create a lessons learned knowledge base. For this database to be useful, it is important to communicate project successes and failures from all aspects of the project process. Captured throughout the life of the project, recommendations to improve future performance can be based on technical, managerial, and process aspects of the project. In addition, part of the project closeout process should include facilitating a lessons learned session for the entire project, especially on unsuccessful projects.

EXHIBIT 5.9

ALTERNATIVE BREAKS PROJECT COMMUNICATIONS MATRIX

STAKEHOLDER	LEARN FROM	SHARE WITH	TIMING	METHOD	OWNER
Student	Needs	Education, reflection	Bi-weekly and as needed	Meetings, test, email	Board, site coordinators
Families	Concerns	Plan and study info	At start, before, and during trip	Student AB website	Student and advisor
Community organizations	Education, needs	Our plans and needs	At start, before, and during trip	Phone	Site coordinators
VP Student Affairs	Definition of success	"Wins"	At start and at "wins"	E-mail	Advisor
Executive Director of Faith and Justice	Definition of success	"Wins" and progress	At start, at wins, and monthly	E-mail and meetings	Advisor
Advisor	University needs and strategic outlook	Progress, needs	Almost daily	E-mail and meetings	Board
National Organization Break Away	Summer student training, Listserv info	Forms, methods, daily guidelines	At start and monthly	E-mail	Chair and advisor

Source: Chris Bridges.

5.5 Project Meeting Management

Planning and conducting projects requires a variety of meetings, such as meetings to:

- Establish project plans
- Conduct the project activities
- Verify progress
- Accept deliverables
- Close out projects

Meetings are an important process on projects since many important decisions are made at meetings and much time of expensive project personnel is invested in meetings.

Improving Project Meetings

Project meetings should be conducted in as efficient and effective a manner as possible. One way to improve the project meeting process is to apply the simple and effective plan-do-check-act (PDCA) model.

PDCA MODEL The idea behind process improvement with the PDCA is that any process practiced repeatedly, focusing on reusing and adapting things that worked well and avoiding things that did not work well, improves over time. Exhibit 5.10 depicts the PDCA model as it is applied to project meetings.

PROJECT MEETING AGENDA TEMPLATE When applying the PDCA improvement model specifically to improving project meetings, the first step is planning the project meeting in advance. The project manager makes sure that the agenda is prepared and distributed ahead of time. If a project team is meeting often, this advance agenda preparation may be done at the end of one meeting for the next meeting. That way, everyone understands beforehand what will be covered in the upcoming meeting and has the opportunity to be prepared. The agenda also can be helpful in deciding whether to invite

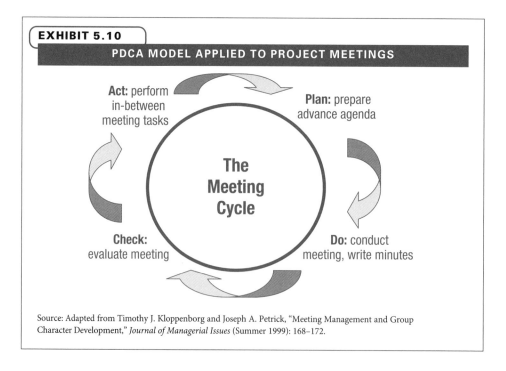

EXHIBIT 5.10

PDCA MODEL APPLIED TO PROJECT MEETINGS

Act: perform in-between meeting tasks

Plan: prepare advance agenda

The Meeting Cycle

Check: evaluate meeting

Do: conduct meeting, write minutes

Source: Adapted from Timothy J. Kloppenborg and Joseph A. Petrick, "Meeting Management and Group Character Development," *Journal of Managerial Issues* (Summer 1999): 168–172.

EXHIBIT 5.11

PROJECT MEETING AGENDA TEMPLATE

Project Team _____ Date _____ Time _____ Place _____

PURPOSE:

Topic	Person	Time
Review agenda	_____	2 min
_____	_____	_____
_____	_____	_____
_____	_____	_____
Summary	_____	5 min
Meeting evaluation	_____	2 min

---

a particular subject matter expert (SME) or other guest to the meeting. A project meeting agenda template is shown in Exhibit 5.11.

The top part of the agenda contains meeting logistics. The second item on the template asks for the meeting purpose. If a project manager cannot state in a sentence or two why he wants to conduct a meeting, perhaps the meeting is not necessary. The main body of the agenda has three columns. First is a list of the topics. This starts with a quick review of the agenda, because projects often move quickly and this provides an opportunity to add or delete an item from the agenda. The major topics of the meeting are listed next in the order in which they will be covered. Often, remaining items from previous meetings or other urgent matters top the list. However, a project manager wants to be sure to cover the most important matters even if they may not have the same sense of urgency. The second-to-the-last item on the standard agenda is the meeting summary. The project manager summarizes major decisions that were made as well as work assignments that were distributed. This helps people remember what they agreed to do. The final item on the agenda is an evaluation of the meeting. This is explained in the check step of the PDCA model.

The second column lists the person responsible for each topic on the agenda. Typically, the project manager takes care of the meeting start and close, but individual project team members may be assigned specific action items. When people know in advance that they are responsible for an action item, they are more likely to be prepared. Additionally, if the advance agenda is available for key project stakeholders to see, some of the stakeholders may contact the responsible person in advance to provide input. This is a good way to keep stakeholders engaged.

The third column is a time estimate for each item. While the project manager does not need to be a slave to the clock, recognition of how long team members are in meetings and how many items are accomplished goes a long way. People are more likely to attend a meeting if they are sure it will end on time.

PROJECT MEETING MINUTES TEMPLATE The second step in the PDCA process—"do"—means to conduct the meeting and to capture minutes as the meeting is conducted. Many project teams rotate the role of minutes taker so each team member feels equal. A template for taking project minutes is shown in Exhibit 5.12.

Issues Management

The project minutes mirror the agenda to the extent that both refer to the same meeting. The top part of the minutes form is logistics, just as in the agenda. From that point

---

PROJECT MEETING MINUTES TEMPLATE

Project Team _____ Date _____ Time _____

Members present:

_____

_____

Decisions Made:

_____

Issues Log:

Resolved Issues _____

New Issues _____

Action Item	Person Responsible	Completion Date

Meeting Evaluation

---

forward, however, the contents vary. The four primary types of information captured in a project meeting are:

1. Decisions made
2. New issues surfaced and old issues resolved
3. Action items agreed to
4. An evaluation of the meeting

ISSUES First, any decisions that were made should be documented. Second, any new issues that surfaced or existing issues that were resolved should be recorded. An **issue** is "a point or matter in question or in dispute, or a point or matter that is not settled and is under discussion or over which there are opposing views or disagreements."[12] An issues log is a living document that lists open issues and states when and how they are resolved. Issues logs benefit a project in at least two ways. First, when an important issue—but not one that can be solved in the immediate meeting—is introduced, the project manager can add it to the open issues and not spend time on it in the current meeting when more pressing matters need to be settled. Second, the issues log ensures that important issues are not forgotten. An issues log template is shown in Exhibit 5.13.

ACTION ITEMS The third type of project information is action items. Each of these is a task that one or more members of the project team agree to perform by a specific date. These are recorded, and the project manager reminds the team at the end of each meeting what each member agreed to do. The final item to be recorded on the project meeting minutes is an evaluation of both good points from the project meeting that the team would like to repeat or at least adapt and poor points from the meeting that the team would like to avoid in the future. An experienced team can collect these points in a minute or two; the time they save in future meetings often pays great dividends. An easy way to capture these evaluations is a Plus-Delta template as shown in Exhibit 5.14.

When assessing the project meeting with a Plus-Delta method, a project manager can simply draw the form on a flip chart or marker board. Then, each person is asked to

EXHIBIT 5.13

PROJECT ISSUES LOG

OPEN ISSUES

NAME	DATE OPENED	ORIGINATOR	POTENTIAL IMPACT	PROGRESS

CLOSED ISSUES

NAME	DATE OPENED	ORIGINATOR	HOW RESOLVED	DATE CLOSED

EXHIBIT 5.14

PROJECT MEETING PLUS-DELTA EVALUATION TEMPLATE

+	$\triangle$

offer their opinion on at least one thing that either was good (+) that he would like to see repeated or one thing that was poor (Δ) that kept the team back somehow and he would like to see overcome in future meetings. The key to making this work for the project manager is how she responds to any deltas. If the project manager responds defensively, the team members may not want to offer further suggestions. On the other hand, if project team members feel their suggestions are seriously considered, they try to make improvement suggestions and future meetings will be better.

Finally, the "act" part of the PDCA cycle for project meetings is for every team member to complete the action items they promised and for the project manager to communicate with the team members to make sure nothing is holding them back from their commitments. Wise project managers keep active but informal contact with team members between meetings to ensure action items are completed on time. When all steps of the PDCA cycle are applied to project meetings, the meetings improve; the team members gain satisfaction; and the project makes better progress.

5.6 Communications Needs of Global and Virtual Project Teams

As organizations change more rapidly, more projects are started with team members from various parts of the larger organization, from various organizations, and even from various parts of the world. These project teams certainly have the advantage of utilizing talent from a wide pool of resources. Project team members often enjoy greater autonomy and stimulation on these teams.

Virtual Teams

These advantages, however, come with added challenges. Since the team is not all co-located, the project manager relies even more on persuasion than usual to accomplish work. In contemporary project management, project managers use less onerous command and control than they might have a few years ago. This trend is even truer with global and virtual teams. A **virtual team** is "a group of persons with a shared objective who fulfill their roles with little or no time spent meeting face to face."[13] When project teams operate in a virtual mode, many of the following characteristics are present:

- Team members are physically dispersed.
- Time boundaries are crossed.
- Communication technologies are used.
- Cultural, organizational, age, gender, and functional diversity is present.[14]

Cultural Differences

Cultural patterns differ in various parts of the world so project team members need to be more sensitive to how their actions are interpreted. For example, in some cultures looking a person in the eye signifies you are paying close attention, while in other parts of the world people may look slightly downward in deference to authority. In those cultures, looking a person in the eye might be considered a challenge. When people do not have face-to-face contact, they do not have the opportunity to see and learn from a person's body language.

Project managers working with global and virtual project teams need to be especially mindful of the increased need for communications using methods other than face to

---

EXHIBIT 5.15

INCREASED CHALLENGES FOR VIRTUAL AND GLOBAL PROJECT TEAMS

PROJECT MANAGEMENT NEED	INCREASED CHALLENGES
1. Initiate project	1. More unique project needs
2. Understand stakeholders	2. More difficult to understand
3. Build relationships	3. Needs more time
4. Determine communications needs and methods	4. More unique needs, more reliance on electronic means
5. Establish change control	5. More facilitating than directing
6. Manage the meeting process	6. Less nonverbal clues, interest may wander
7. Control issues	7. With less group interaction, harder to identify

---

EXHIBIT 5.16

COUNTRIES AND PROJECT COMMUNICATION PREFERENCES

COUNTRY GROUP	PREFERENCES
1. Japan, Taiwan, and Brazil	1. Face-to-face, analytical at milestones
2. Hungary and India	2. Written status reports, fixed intervals
3. The Netherlands and Germany	3. Detailed progress reports, fixed intervals
4. Australia, United States, Canada, New Zealand, United Kingdom, and Sweden	4. Continuous phone updates, with written backup

Source: Adapted from Ralf Mueller and J. Rodney Turner, "Cultural Differences in Project Owner-Project Manager Communications," *Innovations Project Management Research 2004* (Newtown Square, PA: Project Management Institute, 2004): 412–414.

---

face. The various methods regarding charter development described in Chapter 4, along with stakeholder analysis and communications planning in this chapter, are even more critical on virtual and global teams. The more unusual a team is, the more critical charters and communications vehicles become. Exhibit 5.15 lists some of the extra communications challenges posed by virtual and global project teams. Note that each project management need has a specific increased challenge—for example, the third need, relationship building, needs more time since people do not have the advantage of full face-to-face communication. Project managers and teams can enhance stakeholder satisfaction by learning the cultural ethics and values of all their stakeholders, working hard to establish trust, and ensuring that they use fast and reliable information systems.

Countries and Project Communication Preferences

It is helpful if the project team members can meet each other face to face even one time. While this can be very expensive, it may be much less expensive than not performing well on the project. Sometimes, the core project team is assembled to write and approve the project charter. The core team members then know each other and are inclined to give each other the benefit of doubt if there is a misunderstanding. Another method that is frequently used is to confirm meetings and calls with quick meeting minutes or e-mail follow-ups. By documenting decisions, it is easier to remember what happened and to uncover lessons learned when the project is complete.

While abundant differences occur between people from various countries, the method and timing of project communications are of interest here. For example, Mueller and Turner studied how cultural differences impact preferred modes of project management communication.[15] They examined how collectivism versus individualism, along with the extent individuals in various cultures accept unequal power and ambiguity, impact project communications preferences. The results show that country preferences can be shown in four categories with common preferences on frequency and type of communications for each group, as shown in Exhibit 5.16.

5.7 Communications Technologies

Perhaps one of the most exciting and rapidly changing aspects of project management work is communications technologies. When the author first worked on projects in the 1970s, carbon copies were used extensively, careful printing was practiced so as to not mistake a number in a calculation, bidders on construction contracts needed to physically drive to a plans room to view plans and specifications so they could bid on upcoming projects, and people would proof contracts and letters multiple times since there were no spell checkers. In the late 1980s, on one of the first multibillion-dollar bank acquisition projects, the biggest argument among the project team was whether they could afford to buy a fax machine for their "war room" where they coordinated all of their onsite project activities! In the 1990s, databases, e-mail, and other electronic means of storing data and communicating became more widespread.

Current Technology Types

A project manager needs to determine what uses he or she has for communications technology. Project team members and other stakeholders need to be able to respond to each other wherever they are. They need to be able to work creatively together, have access to project documentation, and yet protect confidentiality and version control. When a project has team members and other stakeholders from multiple organizations, they need to ensure that the communications systems are compatible. One important consideration to keep in mind is that communications technology should make the project easier—not harder. Do not select the most current technology for its own sake. Select whatever technology will help get the job done. Reliable communications technologies that enable effective information sharing are essential. A project with multiple geographically dispersed, technologically savvy team members working on complex, interdependent tasks that require rapid decision making might require different communications technologies than a co-located project team working on a simple, routine project. Exhibit 5.17 lists some of the current communications technologies that global and virtual project teams use. With the pace of change, some of these technologies will soon merge into each other, become obsolete, or morph into more powerful technologies.

A project example of communications technology use is shown in Exhibit 5.18.

EXHIBIT 5.17

COMMUNICATIONS TECHNOLOGIES USED BY PROJECTS

COMMUNICATION TECHNOLOGY	EXAMPLES
Automated workflow	Automator
Blog	Twitter
Bulletin board	
Calendaring system	Windows Live Calendar, Google Calendar
Database	Oracle
Desktop videoconference	
Electronic blackboard	
E-mail	Gmail, Hotmail
Fax	
Forums	http://www.pmforum.org/
Groupware	Lotus Notes, Microsoft Exchange

(Continued)

EXHIBIT 5.17

COMMUNICATIONS TECHNOLOGIES USED BY PROJECTS (CONTINUED)

Instant messaging	MSN Messenger, Yahoo Messenger, AIM, Google Talk
Internet	
Intranet	
Shared database	Sharepoint
Shared document repository	
Shared white board	
Social network	Linkedin, Qzone, Friendster, Orkut, VK, Badoo, Mixi
Telephone/Teleconference	
Voice mail	
Voice over Internet protocol (VOIP)	Skype, Vonage
Web-based project management software	MS Project Server, Primavera, Copper Project, eRoom
Wiki	

Source: John Nagy, HSR Business to Business, Inc.

EXHIBIT 5.18

COMMUNICATIONS TECHNOLOGY PROJECT EXAMPLE

Sheetrock® brand dust control joint compound, produced by USG, is the only joint compound that dramatically reduces airborne dust because its unique formulation causes the dust to fall straight to the floor.

(Continued)

EXHIBIT 5.18

COMMUNICATIONS TECHNOLOGY PROJECT EXAMPLE (CONTINUED)

USG SHEETROCK BRAND DUST CONTROL JOINT COMPOUND PRELIMINARY COMMUNICATIONS PLAN

1   Public Relations Word-of-Mouth Mktg.

   1.1   PUBLIC RELATIONS

      1.1.1   "Try It" Media Kit

      1.1.2   Video Release

      1.1.3   Consumer Media

      1.1.4   Matte Release

      1.1.5   Trade Relations

      1.1.6   Trade Show Media

   1.2   WORD-OF-MOUTH

      1.2.1   Advisory Group

2   Online Media, Web Site

   2.1   CONTRACTOR BANNERS

      2.1.1   Series Creative

      2.1.2   Rich Media Creative

      2.1.3   Media Placement

      2.1.4   Hispanic Placement

   2.2   DIY BANNERS

      2.2.1   Series Creative

      2.2.2   Rich Media Creative

      2.2.3   Media Placement

   2.3   SEARCH ENGINE

      2.3.1   Key Word Buy

   2.4   WEB SITES

      2.4.1   Contractor Site

      2.4.2   DIY Site

3   Trade Advertising

   3.1   GENERAL CONTRACTOR

      3.1.1   Blast Creative

      3.1.2   Media Placement

      3.1.3   Hispanic Placement

      3.1.4   Tradeshow Ad

      3.1.5   Conversion

   3.2   DRYWALL TRADE PUBS

      3.2.1   Series Creative

      3.2.2   Media Placement

4   Sales Support, Point-of-Sale

   4.1   POINT-OF-SALE

      4.1.1   Counter Trial Display

      4.1.2   Counter Brochure

      4.1.3   Drywall Package

      4.1.4   Cross-Sell

      4.1.5   NASCAR Sweepstakes

   4.2   SALES SUPPORT

      4.2.1   Retailer Brochure Ad

      4.2.2   Sales Aid

      4.2.3   Specialty Retailer Direct

      4.2.4   Mail

      4.2.5   NASCAR Rewards

USG Corporation is a Fortune 500 manufacturer and distributor of high-performance building systems. Headquartered in Chicago, the company serves the residential and nonresidential construction markets, repair and remodel construction markets, and industrial processes. USG's wall, ceiling, flooring, and roofing products provide leading-edge building solutions for its customers.

HSR Business to Business Inc. is the largest independently owned business-to-business marketing communications agency in the United States. HSR's fully integrated marketing communications offering includes strategy, advertising, interactive, public relations, and relationship marketing.

Source: John Nagy, HSR Business to Business, Inc. Reprinted with permission.

Summary

This is the first chapter on project planning. After completing project initiation by writing and ratifying a charter, a project team turns to planning. Planning is iterative on projects. While there is a logical order to planning, many times information that is developed while planning one function causes a project team to modify earlier planning. Nevertheless, it makes sense to start planning by identifying the stakeholders. Once the stakeholders are identified, the project team can plan communications and determine project scope. Once scope is planned, schedule, cost, human and other resources, risk, and quality can be planned.

Projects frequently have many diverse stakeholders. Some stakeholders do not know exactly what they want, and different stakeholders sometimes want different things. The project manager and sponsor need to build effective working relationships with the project team and stakeholders. When good relationships are built and maintained, the project team can enjoy the trust that is so helpful in successfully completing the project.

Armed with the stakeholder analysis, along with the milestone schedule, acceptance criteria, and major risks from the project charter, a project team is ready to create a communications plan. One important component of the communications plan is the communications matrix. This is the document that answers the questions, Who needs to know something about the project? What does each need to know? When do they need to know it? What format is easiest for them to receive and understand the information? and Who is responsible for sending it? Other important aspects of a project communications plan include capturing and using

lessons learned, managing and improving meetings, and managing issues.

Many project teams work as virtual teams at least part of the time. Some project teams have members who are in various parts of the world. Virtual and global teams share heightened communications challenges since they often cannot physically meet. Global project management teams have the additional challenge of working with different cultures where methods of communicating may vary considerably. These added challenges reinforce the need for understanding stakeholders well and effectively planning project communications. Communications technology is changing rapidly, and many applications can work well for virtual and global project teams. The project manager needs to carefully select the technologies used so they help and do not pose added challenges.

Key Terms from the *PMBOK® Guide*

project management plan, 115
plan communications, 115
communications management plan, 115

identify stakeholders, 116
issue, 128
virtual team, 130

Chapter Review Questions

1. When do relationship building and detailed project planning occur?
2. Once a project plan is formally approved, it can only be updated by formally approved changes. True or false?
3. Which of the following is a potential complication to project success as far as stakeholders are concerned?
   a. There may be multiple users with different wants and needs.
   b. The customer may not understand each user's needs.
   c. Users may not fully understand what they want because they do not understand the alternatives.
   d. Many stakeholders in addition to the users of a project's outcome may have an interest in the project.
   e. All of the above.

4. There are always more internal than external stakeholders. True or false?
5. It is important to consider both financial and emotional interests that potential stakeholders may have. True or false?
6. Sponsors are especially useful in helping to sort out conflicting priorities. True or false?
7. What are the six Cs of project communications?
8. What are three types of project communications timing schedules?
9. Why do project teams need to keep themselves up to date?
10. What are the potential advantages of keeping a lessons learned knowledge database?
11. What are four types of information discussed at a project review meeting?

Discussion Questions

1. What does it mean to say project management planning is iterative?
2. List and describe the three aspects that should be considered when prioritizing stakeholders.
3. List and describe four ways a project manager can encourage open communications.
4. List the items that go into a project team meeting agenda and tell the purpose of each.
5. List the items that go into project team meeting minutes and tell the purpose of each.
6. Describe in your own words the planning and communications tasks MS Project will help you perform.

PMBOK® Guide Questions

1. A "formal, approved document that defines how the project is monitored, executed, and controlled" is the:
   a. project management plan
   b. plan communications
   c. milestone schedule
   d. prioritization matrix
2. Only after _____ is/are determined can the project team plan other aspects of the project, such as schedule, budget, and risks.
   a. plan communications
   b. communications management plan
   c. stakeholders
   d. scope
3. A new grocery store is being erected, which will demolish a neighborhood basketball court. A neighborhood kid who liked to play basketball there should be considered as a/an

   _____.
   a. internal stakeholder
   b. external stakeholder
   c. customer
   d. subject matter expert
4. According to Bourne and Walker, three things to take into account when prioritizing stakeholders are:
   a. proximity, competition, and urgency
   b. competition, scope, and power
   c. power, proximity, and urgency
   d. scope, plan communications, and competition
5. Betty, a project manager, sent out agendas before an upcoming meeting to everyone involved. During the meeting, she made sure there was always someone taking minutes. After the meeting, Betty followed up with the team members to check on their progress. Which of the four PDCA cycle steps did Betty not do?
   a. Plan
   b. Do
   c. Check
   d. Act

Example Project

Develop a stakeholder analysis for your example project. Identify as many stakeholders as you can using Exhibit 5.3. List stakeholders by name and title where possible. Then prioritize the listed stakeholders as shown in Exhibit 5.4. Be specific regarding each stakeholder's interests. Recognize that some stakeholders may have an interest in multiple aspects of the project process or results.

Describe the activities you are using to build relationships both within your core team and with other stakeholders. Create a project decision-making guide for your project like Exhibit 5.7. List specific examples of decisions to the extent you can.

Develop a communications matrix for your project like Exhibit 5.9. Be sure to use considerations in Exhibit 5.8 for ideas regarding purpose, structures, methods, and timing for each communications need. Describe the communications technologies (as listed in Exhibit 5.17) you will use. Use mostly familiar methods, but also use at least one method that is new to your team.

Document a project meeting with an advance agenda, meeting minutes, issues log, and Plus-Delta form of evaluation like Exhibits 5.11 through 5.14.

References

A Guide to the Project Management Body of Knowledge (PMBOK® Guide) 4th ed. (Newtown Square, PA: Project Management Institute, 2008).

Anantatmula, Vittal and Michael Thomas, "Managing Global Projects: A Structured Approach for Better Performance," *Project Management Journal* 41 (2) (April 2010): 60–72.

Assudani, Rashmi and Timothy J. Kloppenborg, "Managing Stakeholders for Project Management Success: An Emergent Model of Stakeholders," *Journal of General Management* 35 (3) (Spring 2010): 67–80.

Badiru, Adedeji B., *Triple C Model of Project Management: Communication, Cooperation, and Coordination* (Boca Raton, FL: CRC Press, 2008).

Bannan, Karen J., "All About Them: Customer Needs Should Drive Every Step of a Project," *PMNetwork* 20 (6) (June 2006): 58–64.

Bannan, Karen J., "Just the Facts," *PMNetwork* 19 (1) (January 2005): 54–59.

Bourne, Lynda and Derek H. T. Walker, "Visualizing Stakeholder Influence: Two Australian Examples," *Project Management Journal* 37 (1) (March 2006): 5–21.

Chicchio, Francois, "Project Team Performance: A Study in Electronic Task and Coordination Communication," *Project Management Journal* 38 (1) (March 2007): 97–109.

Daft, Richard L. *Management* 9th ed. (Mason, OH: South-Western Cengage Learning, 2010).

Englund, Randall L. and Alfonso Bucero, *Project Sponsorship: Achieving Management Commitment for Project Success* (Jossey-Bass, San Francisco, 2006).

Fleming, John H. and Jim Asplund, *Human Sigma* (New York: Gallup Press, 2007).

Goodpasture, John C., *Project Management the Agile Way: Making It Work in the Enterprise* (Fort Lauderdale, FL: J. Ross Publishing, 2010).

Hass, Kathleen B., *From Analyst to Leader: Elevating the Role of the Business Analyst* (Vienna, VA: Management Concepts, 2008).

Herzog, Valerie Lynn, "Trust Building on Corporate Project Teams," *Project Management Journal* 32 (1) (March 2001): 28–35.

Hollinsworth, Chauncey, "PMPs on FB? OMG!" *PMNetwork* 24 (3) (March 2010): 41–46.

Horine, Gregory M., *Absolute Beginner's Guide to Project Management* (Indianapolis, IN: Que Publishing, 2005).

Jiang, James J., Edward Chen, and Gary Klein, "The Importance of Building a Foundation for User Involvement in Information System Projects," *Project Management Journal* 33 (1) (March 2002): 20–26.

Kloppenborg, Timothy J. and Joseph A. Petrick, "Leadership in Project Life Cycles and Team Character Development," *Project Management Journal* 30 (2) (June 1999): 8–13.

Kloppenborg, Timothy J. and Joseph A. Petrick, "Meeting Management and Group Character Development," *Journal of Managerial Issues* (Summer 1999).

Mentrup, Lois, "Social Network," *PMNetwork* 20 (8) (August 2006): 26–31.

Montoya, Mitzi M., Anne P. Massey, Yu-Ting Caisy Hung, and C. Brad Crisp, "Can You Hear Me Now? Communication in Virtual Product Development Teams," *Journal of Product Innovation Management* 26 (2009): 139–155.

Montoya, Mitzi M., Anne P. Massey, and Vijay Khatri, "Connecting IT Services Operations to Services Marketing Practices," *Journal of Management Information Systems* 26 (4) (Spring 2010): 65–85.

Morris, Peter W. G. and Irene C. A. Loch, "Knowledge Creation in Project-Based Learning," *Innovations Project Management Research 2004* (Newtown Square, PA: Project Management Institute, 2004): 243–260.

Mueller, Ralf and J. Rodney Turner, "Cultural Differences in Project Owner-Project Manager Communications," *Innovations Project Management Research 2004* (Newtown Square, PA: Project Management Institute, 2004): 403–418.

Patanakul, Peerasit, Bookiart Iewwongcharien, and Dragan Milosevic, "An Empirical Study of the Use of Project Management Tools and Techniques Across Project Life-Cycle and their Impact on Project Success," *Journal of General Management* 35 (3) (Spring 2010): 41–65.

Paul, Lauren Gibbons, "It's Your Move," *PMNetwork* 19 (4) (April 2005): 34–38.

Reed, April H. and Linda V. Knight, "Effect of a Virtual Project Team Environment on Communication-related Project Risk," *International Journal of Project Management* 28 (5) (July 2010): 422–427.

Schlenkrich, Lara and Christopher Upfold, "A Guideline for Virtual Team Managers: The Key to Effective Social Interaction and Communication," *The*

Electronic Journal Information Systems Evaluation 12 (1) (2009): 109–118.

The Standard for Program Management, 2nd ed. (Newtown Square, PA: Project Management Institute, 2008).

Thomas, Dominic M. and Robert P. Bostrom, "Vital Signs for Virtual Teams: An Empirically Developed Trigger Model for Technology Adaptation Interventions," *MIS Quarterly* 34 (1) (March 2010): 114–142.

Thomas, Janice, Connie L. Delisle, and Kam Jugdev, *Selling Project Management to Senior Executives: Framing the Moves that Matter* (Newtown Square, PA: Project Management Institute, 2002).

Young R. Ralph, Steven M. Brady and Dennis C. Nagle, Jr. *How to Save a Failing Project: Chaos to Control* (Vienna, VA: Management Concepts, 2009).

Endnotes

1. *PMBOK® Guide* 443.
2. *PMBOK® Guide* 440.
3. *PMBOK® Guide* 429.
4. *PMBOK® Guide* 436.
5. Bourne, Lynda and Derek H. T. Walker, "Visualizing Stakeholder Influence: Two Australian Examples," *Project Management Journal* 37 (1) (March 2006): 5–21.
6. Adapted from Valerie Lynn Herzog, "Trust Building on Corporate Project Teams," *Project Management Journal* 32 (1) (March 2001): 33–34; and Timothy J. Kloppenborg and Joseph A. Petrick, "Leadership in Project Life Cycles and Team Character Development," *Project Management Journal* 30 (2) (June 1999): 11.
7. Adapted from John H. Fleming and Jim Asplund, *Human Sigma* (New York: Gallup Press, 2007): 161.
8. Adapted from John H. Fleming and Jim Asplund, *Human Sigma* (New York: Gallup Press, 2007): 97.

9. Badiru, Adedeji B., *Triple C Model of Project Management: Communication, Cooperation, and Coordination* (Boca Raton, FL: CRC Press, 2008): 29.
10. Adapted from Gregory M. Horine, *Absolute Beginner's Guide to Project Management* (Indianapolis, IN: Que Publishing, 2005): 218.
11. Daft, Richard L. *Management* 9th ed. (Mason, OH: South-Western Cengage Learning, 2010): 631.
12. *PMBOK® Guide* 437.
13. *PMBOK® Guide* 452.
14. Adapted from Lara Schlenkrich and Christopher Upfold, "A Guideline for Virtual Team Managers: The Key to Effective Social Interaction and Communication," *The Electronic Journal Information Systems Evaluation* 12 (1) (2009): 110.
15. Mueller, Ralf and J. Rodney Turner, "Cultural Differences in Project Owner-Project Manager Communications," *Innovations Project Management Research 2004* (Newtown Square, PA: Project Management Institute, 2004): 403–418.

PROJECT MANAGEMENT *IN ACTION*

Using Appreciative Inquiry to Understand Stakeholders

On projects that have many stakeholders with varied and uncertain needs and desires, it can be challenging to surface and make sense of the many hidden objectives. One tool that is helpful on some of these complex projects is Appreciative Inquiry (AI).

What Is Appreciative Inquiry?

The principles: Appreciative inquiry is a positive philosophy for change wherein whole systems convene to inquire for change (Cooperrider & Srivastva, 1987). AI recognizes the power of the whole and builds on conversational learning that emerges out of the whole. It operates on the belief that human systems move in the direction of their shared image and idea of the future, and that change is based on intentional and positive inquiry into what has worked best in the past. In this sense, AI suggests that human organizing and change is a relational process of inquiry that is grounded in affirmation and appreciation (Whitney & Trosten-Bloom, 2003). Typically, the process works its way through the four phases of Discovery, Dream, Design, and Delivery (Conklin, 2009).

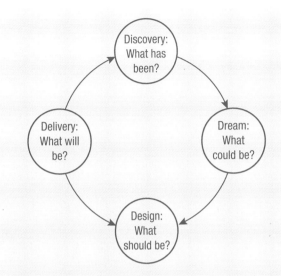

Source: (Adapted from Conklin, 2009)

Implications of AI on Defining Project Scope

One of the success parameters of project management depends upon identifying key stakeholders and eliciting their true wants and needs to determine project scope. This is critical because it lays out clear goals and boundaries of project scope. However, eliciting accurate responses may be difficult, especially since most projects may be planned and conducted in an atmosphere of uncertainty.

Appreciative inquiry is a tool that may assist project stakeholders to navigate through their inquiries via positive conversations. For example, a typical process may look like this:

Discovery (What has been?): This phase inquires into and discovers the positive capacity of the group, organization, or community. People are encouraged to use stories to describe their strengths, assets, peak experiences, and successes to understand the unique conditions that made their moments of excellence possible. In this step, stakeholders reflect on the past to recollect instances when they believed they could clearly articulate their true needs and wants; and when their needs and wants were folded into the project scope. As they discuss, they start generating a dense web of understanding—an understanding and an appreciation of all their capacities that make moments of excellence possible.

Dreaming (What could be?): Building on the moments of excellence of the participants, this phase encourages the participants to imagine what would happen if their moments of excellence were to become a norm. Participants dream for the ideal conditions and

build hope and possibility of an ideal future. As people share their stories, the focus of the process now shifts to dreaming a perfect, desirable state for the stakeholders. Through this journey, the goal should be to enable the participants to build positive energy around their strengths and also to dream about the direction in which they feel comfortable moving.

Designing (What should be?): This phase creates design principles that will help the participants realize their dream. Participants are encouraged to stretch their imagination to move the system from where it currently is to where the participants want it to be. At this stage, the participants should be encouraged to imagine a perfect world without any constraints.

Delivery (What will be?): In this phase, participants are encouraged to think of the various subsystems that should take the responsibility of the design phase to "sustain the design from the dream that it discovered" (Cooperrider et al., 2003, pg. 182). The various stakeholders are encouraged to decide what they will be committing themselves to.

Key Outcome

At the conclusion of the process, stakeholders have elicited a clear and more transparent understanding of their true needs and wants—some of which may be beneath the surface and difficult to articulate without going through a process like this. Stakeholders also have a better understanding of how their needs and wants link to and lead them to a future state. Finally, in order to sustain their dream, their commitment to sustain it is clearly articulated.

References

Conklin, T. A., "Creating Classrooms of Preference: An Exercise in Appreciative Inquiry," *Journal of Management Education* 33 (6) (2009): 772–792.

Cooperrider, D. L. and S. Srivastva, "Appreciative Inquiry in Organizational Life." In W. Pasmore and R. Woodman (eds), *Research in Organization Change and Development* (Greenwich, CT: JAI Press, 1987): 1, 129–169.

Cooperrider, D. L. D. Whitney, and J. M. Stavros, *Appreciative Inquiry Handbook* (Bedford Heights, OH: Lakeshore, 2003).

Whitney, D. and A. Trosten-Bloom, *The Power of Appreciative Inquiry* (San Francisco: Berrett-Koehler, 2003).

Source: Rashmi Assudani, Xavier University.

CHAPTER 6

Scope Planning

After completing this chapter, you should be able to:

- Describe the collecting requirements and define *scope processes*.

- Create a requirements traceability matrix, project scope statement, and change request form.

- Describe what a work breakdown structure (WBS) is and explain why it is vital to project planning and control.

- Compare and contrast different methods of developing a WBS.

- Create a WBS for a project, including work packages and a numbering system for the code of accounts.

- Set up a WBS in MS Project.

Image Source/Jupiter Images

You're browsing a favorite retailer's website, and you notice the onscreen recommendations are just right for you. The site seems to know what you've bought before, what you have researched, and maybe even things that you've purchased from the retailer's brick-and-mortar stores. This great customer service is enabled by the retailer's web intelligence solution from Teradata.

Teradata is the world's largest company focused solely on enterprise data warehousing and analytic solutions. The simple web shopping scenario is just one example of how our customers use information to improve their relationship with you.

So what does this have to do with project scope management? In this example the retailer purchased a Teradata solution that included hardware, software, and a consulting project for the implementation. Teradata implemented this project based on our experience and a methodology built upon a foundation of scope management.

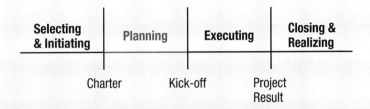

Selecting & Initiating	Planning	Executing	Closing & Realizing

Charter   Kick-off   Project Result

**PMBOK®
GUIDE TOPICS**

- Collect requirements
- Define scope
- Create WBS
- Change requests

Every successful project starts with a mutual understanding of success. This is particularly important in a contracted arrangement between a customer and a vendor, and in this case both the retailer and Teradata need to deliver the right solution, within the agreed-on business parameters. We can manage scope in various ways—ranging from traditional waterfall to agile approaches—but must manage scope to deliver the right solution in an efficient manner.

The first step in project scope management is to mutually agree what the project will deliver. In our example, the retailer needed to integrate data from their web analytics software, an in-house customer relationship system, and other sources. They also had requirements for reports and the technical integration with their IT infrastructure. The Teradata team elicited requirements in a way that uncovered what the customer really needed. An effective team must have the right mix of technical experience, business knowledge, and communications skills to get a good scope definition.

Projects often use a statement of work (SOW) or similar document to outline the high-level scope. In a Teradata project this is part of our customer contract. We then elaborate more detailed requirements in a traceability matrix. This ensures all requirements tie "end to end" from the contract through project testing and customer acceptance. This is a key scope management practice and a useful communications tool to help all stakeholders understand the scope in detail. The time spent up-front in requirements management pays dividends during project testing and customer acceptance, where discovering unknown requirements is much more time consuming and expensive.

Teradata follows traditional project management practice to develop a work breakdown structure (WBS) as the basis for a detailed project schedule and resource plan. We typically use Microsoft Project as a scheduling tool; a plan based on the WBS makes it easy to track and communicate the status of each deliverable.

Finally, the entire set of requirements is managed under change control. This is an important process, because the team must balance control and flexibility. In our projects, both Teradata and the customer want to deliver a solution that yields business value. We also must meet (or agree to change) the project cost and schedule parameters. For instance, the retailer might decide they also want to consider another source of information or to get additional reports. Our project manager facilitates an analysis of the technical, schedule, and cost impact—then all parties reach a mutual agreement on how to proceed.

This simple example illustrates how the Teradata project methodology builds upon a foundation of scope management to deliver exactly what the customer needs in the most efficient manner. An effective scope management approach fosters open communications and sound decision making to ensure all parties get the business value expected from the project.

Mike Van Horn, Teradata

6.1 Introduction to Scope Planning

Once all of the stakeholders for a project have been identified, the project team members collect project requirements, define the project's scope, and create a work breakdown structure (WBS). These are the scope planning processes that will be covered in this chapter. When planning scope, it is also wise to plan for changes. While this is not technically part of scope planning, it will also be covered in this chapter.

The flow of scope planning is illustrated in Exhibit 6.1. The boxes represent the project work processes involved, and the documents shown before and after the boxes represent major inputs needed to perform the processes as well as major outputs created by the work processes. For example, the first process, "collect requirements," uses the project charter and stakeholder register (discussed in Chapters 4 and 5, respectively) as inputs and creates a requirements matrix as a primary output.

The **product scope** is "the features and functions that characterize a product, service, or result."[1] The project team also needs to determine the **project scope** or "the work that must be performed to deliver a product, service, or result with the specified features and functions."[2] Together, the product scope (the outputs the team will deliver to its customers) and the project scope (the work they need to perform to create the project's

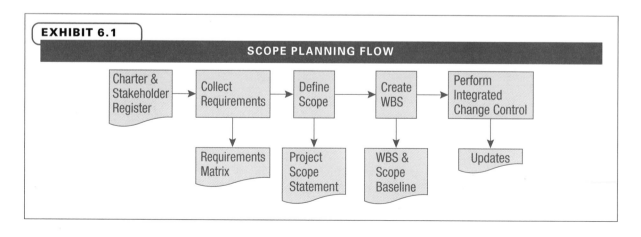

EXHIBIT 6.1

SCOPE PLANNING FLOW

Charter & Stakeholder Register → Collect Requirements → Define Scope → Create WBS → Perform Integrated Change Control

Collect Requirements → Requirements Matrix

Define Scope → Project Scope Statement

Create WBS → WBS & Scope Baseline

Perform Integrated Change Control → Updates

outputs) form the total scope. In other words, the project team members determine what they will do to ensure they have identified and organized all of the project work so they can use it as the basis of all other planning and then as the basis for executing and controlling the project work.

6.2 Collect Requirements

Collecting requirements is "the process of defining and documenting stakeholders' needs to meet the project objectives."[3] The first step in collecting requirements is to ensure that the project team is absolutely clear on the project objectives. This could be accomplished by reviewing the project charter—particularly the "why" section that justifies the project. The project team members then may describe in more depth what each believes the expected project benefits are and/or what problems the project is attempting to overcome. On simple projects, this may take just a few minutes. On complex projects, a project manager may choose to use idea generation, grouping, and/or cause-and-effect techniques to make sure that everyone on the project team understands why the project is being conducted. Understanding broad project objectives will help in making more detailed decisions later. This also reinforces the project's importance and may help motivate team members and other stakeholders during challenging times. It is especially useful with multifunctional, virtual, and global project teams. Finally, if the project needs to be replanned at some point because of changes, a clear understanding of the project's objectives helps with the gap analysis of where the team started and where it wants to go.

Gather Stakeholder Input

The second step is to gather input from the various project stakeholders. When a project manager and team listen closely to both internal and external customers, they understand better both what their needs are and what risks and issues may confront them during the project. Successful project managers know that for a project outcome to be useful to the project's customers, the customers need to be able to use the output to better serve their own customers in turn. In other words, project managers need to consider both their customers' needs and their customers' customers' needs.

The methods of developing deep understanding of customers and their needs vary extensively from one industry to another. For example, in new product development projects, teams often use voice of the customer (VOC) techniques to elicit the benefits and features the customers want out of the project expressed in the customer's language. Teams using VOC try to understand the customer by not only asking questions, but also by placing themselves in the customer's situation. If a project team is designing a new system that is to be used in the field, team members may interview multiple customer representatives regarding their perceptions of what the new system should do. For example, if one representative is a mechanic, the team member should get down in the mud with the mechanic and hand the mechanic repair tools to see from the mechanic's point of view how the new system will be used.

Once captured, these customer wants and needs are then stated in operational terms that the people performing the project work can use to plan their work. If the customer wants blue food coloring in a food item, the project team developing the item needs to know the precise desired shade of blue, the tolerance for color variation, and how the blue color may interact with other ingredients.

The project manager wants to understand how a project's success will be determined from the customer's perspective. The best way to gain this understanding (and to begin building a strong relationship with customers) is to directly ask customers. The project leaders can ask the customer(s) to specify how they will judge the quality of the project.

On an information systems project, the team may use a joint application design (JAD) session to elicit customer requirements. This is often a facilitated session in which users of the software state what their preferences are regarding how the software should work. The project manager and team often send the users their understanding of the project objectives and deliverables in advance so the users are better prepared to discuss their needs. Only one group of users is normally in this meeting at a time, while the project manager and the technical workers are in the session the entire time. Each possible feature of the system should be discussed. If the system is large and complicated, the amount of time that can be spent per item may be restricted. Users often wish to talk in depth about how they want to use the system, and developers often want a detailed discussion about how they plan to create the feature. To avoid sinking into too much detail, the project manger can ask the users to start with only a high-level description of their reason for the requested feature and then guide the discussion with the following five questions:

1. What do we not understand about the request?
2. What is the business reason for the request?
3. What is the impact of not providing this feature?
4. What action items need to be accomplished if we do this?
5. What impact will this have on other parts of the project or elsewhere?

On some types of projects, the customers can give their ideas using one of the techniques above, and the project team can be confident that the customers' wants and needs have been captured. On other projects, once the customers' viewpoint is captured, it makes sense to create a model or prototype of some sort so the customers can decide if their wishes have been fully and accurately captured. Often, this extra step helps the customers to be more fully vested in the project and creates a strong working relationship that is helpful when difficulties arise during project execution.

It is helpful to list requirements and their supporting information in a requirements matrix such as that shown in Exhibit 6.2. When requirements are complete each needs to be:

- Traceable back to the business reason for it
- Identified with the stakeholder(s) who need it

EXHIBIT 6.2

REQUIREMENTS MATRIX

BUSINESS NEED	REQUIREMENTS	STAKEHOLDER(S)	PRIORITY

- Clear so everyone understands it the same way
- Measurable so its value and completion can be verified
- Prioritized according to value, cost, time risk, or mandate so tradeoff decisions can be made if needed

6.3 Define Scope

Define scope is "the process of developing a detailed description of the project and product."[4] Essentially, the project scope statement includes three things regarding the total scope. First, the team needs to determine both what they will deliver to the project stakeholders at the end of the project and what they need to deliver along the way to ensure they will be successful in the end. These are the deliverables—the product scope. For example, if a final project deliverable is a new computer program, intermediate deliverables may include an outline of what will be included and a prototype. Second, the team should decide what work needs to be accomplished to create the deliverables This is the project work statement—the project scope. Third, the team needs to determine what will limit or influence the project work—such as exclusions, constraints, and assumptions.

Reasons to Define Scope

Scope definition is an important part of project planning because all other planning is based upon the project scope. While the requirements collected represent the customers' statement of what they need, the defined scope is the project team's response—asking the customer, "If we provide this, will it solve your problem?" It is impossible to estimate how much a project will cost, how many (and what type of) workers will be needed, how long a project will take, what risks are involved, or what quality standards will be invoked without first understanding what work the project includes.

Scope definition also is vital in preventing scope creep. Scope creep happens for two common reasons. First, if the scope is not clearly defined and agreed upon, it is easy to add to the project without realizing that more time and money will be required. Second, sometimes when a project is going well, a customer is so excited that he or she asks an innocent-sounding question: "Can the project output also do ...?" The person performing the project work is often flattered and agrees without understanding the implications. In contemporary business, pleasing the customer is desirable. However, the best time to gain customer understanding is when the project team is defining the scope—not while working to implement it.

How to Define Scope

Scope definition can vary greatly from one project to another. On some types of projects, such as a small, routine construction project, it may be quite simple to determine what project outputs will be created and what work is involved in creating them. On other projects, such as one large company acquiring another, it may be very difficult to determine the total amount of work that needs to be accomplished. Regardless of how easy or difficult it may be to define scope and in spite of industry-specific methods that may be helpful in doing so, all project teams need to complete each part of this process.

LIST DELIVERABLES AND ACCEPTANCE CRITERIA The first step is to list project deliverables. The requirements elicited from the customer often lead to some of the final deliverables. Project teams need to understand that there are often multiple deliverables. For example, if a project entails constructing a house, the homeowners probably want not only the house but also documentation on systems within it, perhaps an explanation (training) on how to use certain items such as an innovative thermostat, and a warranty guaranteeing a properly functioning house. The project team also needs to list intermediate deliverables—those things that need to be developed for the project to progress. Some of these were probably listed in the charter, but others may not yet be identified. The project team then needs to determine the acceptance criteria for each deliverable.

ESTABLISH PROJECT BOUNDARIES   The second step in defining scope is to establish the project boundaries. Think of the project boundaries as the sidelines on an athletic field. By understanding what is in play and what is not, athletes know clearly when to play and when to stop. Likewise, project team members need to know when to play and when to stop. The first part of the boundary definition is to decide which features and work elements are included (in scope) and which are excluded (out of scope). Users collectively often request far more work than a project can deliver. Therefore, the team needs to decide what is included and what is not. Sometimes, the sponsor makes the larger scope decisions, but the project manager and team still have many detailed scope decisions to make.

Expectations need to be managed regarding any project. The project team members need to understand the constraints imposed upon the project. If the work must be delivered by a certain date or if only limited resources are available, the project may be constrained and the team should be careful to only promise what it can deliver. In planning, people make assumptions about dates and times, such as that a shipment of required materials will arrive by the date the supplier promised. These assumptions should be stated. If an assumption proves to be false, it frequently increases the project risk and may also limit the project scope.

CREATE A PROJECT WORK STATEMENT   The final step is to create a project work statement. This sentence or two describes the work that needs to be accomplished to create the project deliverables. Remember the total scope entails both the product scope (deliverables) and project scope (work).

A project scope statement guides the project team during subsequent planning and execution. On some very small projects, a well-developed charter could double as a scope statement. On most projects, a scope statement needs to be developed prior to development of the work breakdown structure. An example scope statement for the Alternative Breaks project is shown in Exhibit 6.3.

6.4 Work Breakdown Structure (WBS)

A tool that is used on virtually all projects is the work breakdown structure. To understand this tool, we first define it, tell why it is important, show several common formats to use when constructing one, and demonstrate the steps required to construct a WBS.

What Is the WBS?

The work breakdown structure or WBS is a tool that project teams use to progressively divide the deliverables of a project into smaller and smaller pieces. The project team members start by identifying the major deliverables to be created and keep asking "What are the components of this deliverable?" The WBS is *not* a list of work activities, an organizational chart, or a schedule. Other tools that follow are used for those purposes. The WBS *is* a framework that is used as a basis for further planning, execution, and control.

EXHIBIT 6.3

SCOPE STATEMENT

ALTERNATIVE BREAKS PROJECT SCOPE STATEMENT

Project work statement (project scope): This project will educate groups of 12 students on social justice issues, send them to perform direct service on the issues, and provide reflective opportunities throughout the process.

Key deliverables with acceptance criteria (product scope):

KEY DELIVERABLES	ACCEPTANCE CRITERIA
Project plan	Secured housing, Agreement with organization
Fund raising	Adequate money
Education	Syllabus
Reorientation	Digital archives
Trip itself	Return safely, pre and post evaluation

Exclusions: No alcohol, drugs, or romances; ratio number of trips to student population.

Constraints: Van only holds 12 people—11 students and one faculty or staff; number of highly qualified site leaders.

Assumptions: Service builds active citizens; international trips add more value than expense; a trip is better with a staff or faculty member.

Source: Chris Bridges.

Classically, and still today on large projects, the WBS is created after the scope is defined. In contemporary project management, particularly on small and middle-sized projects, the WBS may be created concurrently with the scope statement.

The WBS is normally developed by listing deliverables—first major deliverables and then progressively smaller ones until the team feels that every deliverable has been identified. Managers of smaller projects sometimes perform another process concurrent with WBS development: defining activities and milestones. **Define activity** is "the process of identifying the specific actions to be performed to produce the project deliverables."[5] Many people find that work activities can be easily defined once the various deliverables are itemized. To clearly distinguish between the work processes of WBS development and activity development, WBS development is covered in this chapter and activity development is covered as part of project scheduling in the next chapter. Developing the WBS and defining the activities form an example of how two separate work processes are sometimes performed together (especially on small or simple projects) and sometimes separately (especially on large or complex projects).

Why Use a WBS?

The reasons for using a WBS are many. It is widely considered to be one of the most essential project management tools. Planning projects requires discipline and visibility. A WBS can be used as a pictorial representation of project deliverables. By using a systematic process for creating a WBS, project team members can ensure that they remember all deliverables that need to be created. Deliverables that are not planned, but need to be, often add to schedule delays and budget overruns.

The WBS is the basis for all subsequent planning of such important functions as schedule, resources, cost, quality, and risk. It serves as an outline for integrating these various functions. The WBS is easily modified and can thus handle the changes that often happen on projects. The impact of these changes is then shown in the schedule, budget, and other control documents. If a problem occurs during project execution, the WBS is helpful in understanding exactly where and why the problem occurred. This helps to manage the quality of the project deliverables and keep all the other facets of the project on schedule while the isolated problem is fixed.

The WBS is also helpful in project communications. Typically many stakeholders help develop the WBS, and this effort helps them understand the project. Software such as Microsoft Project enables a WBS to be shown in its entirety to people who need to understand the details, but it also allows project details to be hidden so that others can see the big picture.

Framing a house is a major deliverable in a house project.

AP Photo/Matt York

WBS Formats

There are various formats for constructing a WBS, but they all have the same purpose. The overall project is considered the first level, as shown in Exhibit 6.4. In this example, a WBS for a house is presented in the indented outline format.

The second level in this example depicts major deliverables from the house project, namely the house in its framed state, when it is wired, and when it is drywalled. This second level is indented one tab.

A WBS usually has one or more intermediate levels, which generally represent items that need to be created in order to produce the final deliverables, such as drafts, prototypes, designs, and so on. These are frequently called interim deliverables. All levels of the WBS with at least one level below are considered summary levels. The completion of summary level elements is based upon completion of all levels underneath. For example, in Exhibit 6.4, the house would not be framed until the framing contractor, wood, and assembled frame interim deliverables were complete.

Exhibit 6.4 used the indented outline format for WBS method, but other methods are sometimes used. One other method is the hierarchical or "org chart" (short for *organizational chart,* which it resembles) method. A third method is called free format because the facilitator is free to draw it in any manner. The same house project shown in Exhibit 6.4 in

---

EXHIBIT 6.4

HOUSE WBS IN INDENTED OUTLINE FORMAT

HOUSE
- Framed House
  - Framing Contractor
  - Wood
  - Assembled Frame
- Wired House
  - Wiring Contractor
  - Wiring
  - Installed Wiring
- Drywalled House
  - Drywall Contractor
  - Drywall
  - Hung Drywall

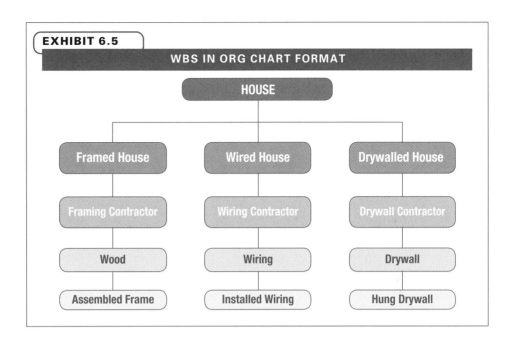

EXHIBIT 6.5

WBS IN ORG CHART FORMAT

indented outline format is shown in Exhibit 6.5 in org chart format and in Exhibit 6.6 in free format.

Both of these methods allow a team to use a marker board or flip chart and have plenty of room to add additional elements as people think of them. The WBS method using indented outlines can easily be imported into MS Project. The other methods are generally easier to use for developing ideas. Teams using the org chart or free format methods to develop their WBS generally translate it into the indented outline format for input into software.

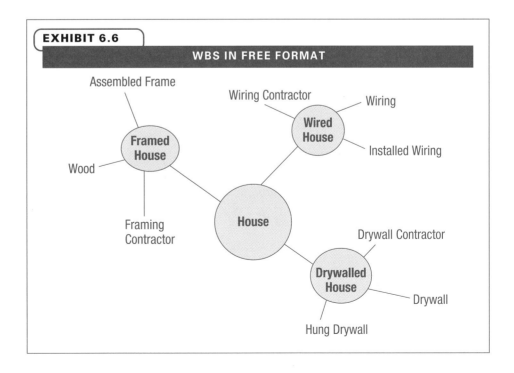

EXHIBIT 6.6

WBS IN FREE FORMAT

Work Packages

The house example above has only three levels as follows:

1. The first level, or project title level
2. One intermediate level, or summary level
3. The lowest level, or work package level

In a WBS, an element at the lowest level is called a **work package,** which is "a deliverable or project work component at the lowest level of each branch of a WBS."[6] Work packages are the fruit harvested from dividing the project work into smaller pieces. They are the basis for all subsequent planning and control activities. Exhibit 6.7 shows a WBS in org chart format with work packages in solid boxes.

One frequently asked question when breaking the deliverables into work packages is how small is small enough. The answer is, "it depends." In Exhibit 6.7, work packages occur at levels 3, 4, and 5. The work package is the point from which:

- Work activities are defined
- The schedule is formed
- Resources are assigned
- Many of the control features are developed

Work packages need to be detailed enough to facilitate further planning and control. If they are too detailed, the burden of tracking details increases. The project manager needs to feel confident that the work to create the deliverable can be assigned to one person who can estimate the schedule and cost and can be held responsible for its completion. If the work is well understood, a single deliverable is to be produced, it is clear how the deliverable will be judged for quality and completeness, and the assigned worker has proven reliable in the past, the level may not have to be too detailed. On the other hand, if the deliverable and how it will be judged are poorly understood and the assigned worker has yet to be proven reliable, a more detailed level may make sense.

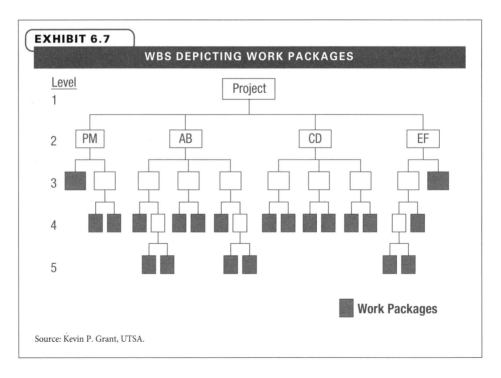

EXHIBIT 6.7

WBS DEPICTING WORK PACKAGES

Source: Kevin P. Grant, UTSA.

EXHIBIT 6.8

WORK PACKAGE DETAIL

Project: Expansion to Full Scale Production			Work Package: Test Assembly Hardware	
Description: Plan, conduct, evaluate, and report results of tests to ensure proper function of the assembly hardware.			**Deliverable(s):** Test results summary. **Input(s):** Assembly hardware prototype	
Activities		**Resource**	**Expected Duration**	**Cost**
Prepare test plan		Production Analyst	8 h	$ 720
Conduct test		Production Analyst	16 h	1440
Evaluate test results		Production Analyst	6 h	540
Prepare test results summary		Production Analyst	8 h	720
				$ 3420

Source: Kevin P. Grant, UTSA.

For ease of reading, work packages and other components on a WBS are usually stated in very few words. A **WBS component** is "an entry in the WBS that can be at any level."[7] Enough words should be used so the same name is not used more than once. However, because the names are typically short, there is still the potential to get confused by exactly what is included in a particular work package. Therefore, WBS components are often defined further by creating a WBS dictionary. A **WBS dictionary** is "a document that describes each component in the WBS. For each component, the WBS dictionary includes a brief scope description, defined deliverable(s), a list of associated activities, and sometimes other information."[8] An example of a WBS dictionary entry with detailed information for a work package is shown in Exhibit 6.8. Note that some of this additional information such as activities, resource assignments, effort, and cost will be described in subsequent chapters.

How to Construct a WBS

When a project team needs to construct a WBS, it needs to include in its planning team a subject matter expert (SME) who understands how each portion of the work will be accomplished. Teams approach this in two ways. Some teams include only the core team members and plan the WBS as far as they can. At that point, different core team members are assigned to assemble the SMEs they need to plan the remaining details. Other teams invite the SMEs to the WBS planning meeting right from the start and utilize their input right away. The choice of how to include SMEs often is determined by the size and complexity of the project and by the cultural norms of the company.

EXHIBIT 6.9

STEPS IN WBS CONSTRUCTION

1. Identify major deliverables.
2. Divide into smaller deliverables.
3. Continue until deliverables are the right size.
4. Review.

Source: Lei Fu.

The planning team uses a top-down approach in creating the WBS. This is easy to start when the type of project is familiar and at least some members of the planning team are likely to understand the general flow of work. If the project is similar to others performed, either a template or the WBS from a previous project can be used as a starting point, with the team then asking what else this project needs and what items from the template or previous project can be skipped. Templates and previous examples can save teams a great deal of time, but they must be used with caution because each project is different.

Sometimes, however, a project is so different from previous work that the team finds it useful to jump-start the WBS construction by brainstorming a list of project deliverables just to understand the overall structure of the project. However, once the overall structure is understood, the team proceeds with the typical top-down approach for the remainder of the WBS construction. The steps in WBS construction are shown in Exhibit 6.9.

IDENTIFY MAJOR DELIVERABLES The team defines the project product by reviewing the project planning completed so far. The team members review the project charter, requirements matrix, and scope statement so they can state what the project's major deliverables will be. Remember that while many projects may have a primary deliverable such as a house, almost all projects have additional deliverables dealing with documentation and customer enablement. These could include training, service, or other means of helping the customer use the project's products effectively.

One of the first decisions to be made is how to organize the second level of the WBS. (Remember the first level is the overall project.) Three methods are shown in Exhibit 6.10. One method is by project phase, with the second level being the signing of a contract, building the foundation, and framing the house. Alternatively, the second level can be organized by design components, such as kitchen, bedrooms, and bathrooms. Finally, the second level can be organized by work function. A house project organized this way might have carpentry, plumbing, and electrical as second-level elements.

EXHIBIT 6.10

WBS ORGANIZATION EXAMPLES

PROJECT PHASE	DESIGN COMPONENTS/ DELIVERABLES	WORK FUNCTION/ SUBPROJECT
Project Management	Project Management	Project Management
Contract	Kitchen	Carpentry
Foundation	Bedrooms	Plumbing
Framed House	Bathrooms	Electrical
...	...	...

Organizing by project phase has the advantage of using the milestones in the project charter as an organizing principle. It also facilitates rolling wave planning. **Rolling wave planning** is "a form of progressive elaboration planning where the work to be accomplished in the near term is planned in detail … while the work far in the future is planned at a relatively high level … the detailed planning for work to be performed … in the near future is done as work is being completed during the current time period."[9] If the planners of the project in Exhibit 6.10 used rolling wave planning, the work associated with the contract would be planned in detail immediately, and work for the foundation and framing might only be planned at a high level at first with more detail worked out as the project team worked on the contract. Rolling wave planning allows a team to get a quick start on a project—especially one where details of later phases may depend on the results of work performed during early phases. Rolling wave planning helps a project team avoid either of two extremes. One extreme is to never start doing anything because the plan is not yet complete, which is also known as analysis paralysis. The opposite extreme is not planning at all because of fear that planning will take too long; this is known as ready, fire, aim.

Organizing by either phase or design components help to focus communications on project deliverables and their interactions. Organizing by work function allows the functions to focus on their specific activities, but often does not promote cross-functional discussion. Handoffs of work from one group to another are not always as smooth. Therefore, if a project manager decides to organize the WBS by work function, extra care needs to be taken in establishing inter-functional communications.

Note that one additional second-level item is shown on all three methods—that of project management. This includes the work of planning and managing the effort and includes preparing documents, attending meetings, integrating diverse portions of the project, handling communications, and so on. Since much of the work involved in project management is level of effort, this section may not be decomposed. If the work of managing the project is left out, it is more likely that the project will not be completed on time and within the budget.

DIVIDE INTO SMALLER DELIVERABLES Once the major deliverables have been defined, it is time to break them into smaller deliverables or components. The team members can use the top-down approach, asking what all the components of each major deliverable are. Alternatively, the team members may use a bottom-up approach by brainstorming a list of both interim and final deliverables that they feel need to be created. Each deliverable can be written on an individual Post-it Note. These deliverables are then assembled on a large work space where team members group the smaller deliverables either under the major deliverables that have been previously identified or into additional related groups that are then headed by major deliverables.

CONTINUE UNTIL DELIVERABLES ARE THE RIGHT SIZE At this point, the WBS has been formed and can be reviewed for completeness. Once it is determined to be complete, the team can ask if the deliverables at the lowest level need to be divided again to be at the proper size for further planning and control as described above. For example, in the new car development project in Exhibit 6.11, level-two components, such as product design, are at too high of level. Therefore, at least one further level is included. If some of those components, such as product goals, are still too broad, yet another level would need to be developed.

REVIEW At this point, several things should be considered to ensure that the WBS is structured properly. One consideration with WBS construction is the parent–child

> ┌─────────────────┐
> │ **EXHIBIT 6.11** │
> └─────────────────┘
>
> **PARTIAL WBS OF CAR DEVELOPMENT PROJECT**
>
> Car Development Project
>   Project Management
>   Product Design
>   Product Goals
>   Concept Design
>   Modeling Design
>   Vehicle Integration
>   Engineering Feasibility
>   Detailed Engineering Design
>   Performance Development
>   Regulatory Certification
>   Process Development
>   Prototype
>   Production Materials Procurement
>   General Materials Procurement
>   Trial Manufacture

concept. The higher level is considered the parent and the lower-level elements are considered children. For example, in Exhibits 6.4 through 6.6, "Framed House" is a parent to the children: "framing contractor," "wood," and "assembled frame." "Framed House," in turn, is a child to "HOUSE." The framed house component is not complete until all of its children components are complete. The team asks if, once these elements are complete, the framing is complete. In an effort to simplify the WBS, where only one child element for a parent exists, you would not break it down. In fact, a good rule of thumb is to have somewhere between three and nine child elements for each parent. The fewer levels a WBS has, the easier it is to understand.

Each component in the WBS needs to have a unique name. If two elements have the same name, it is confusing. Therefore, two similar components may be "*draft* report" and "*final* report," instead of merely calling each "report." The team also assigns a unique number to each component. In one common numbering system, the number for a child item starts with the number assigned to its parent and adds a digit. An example of a WBS with components numbered is shown in Exhibit 6.12. Note that level one, the project title, is assigned number 0.

Different organizations sometimes develop their own unique variations of project planning and control techniques. Exhibit 6.13 describes the manner in which a large, complex organization (the U.S. Central Intelligence Agency) combines stakeholder analysis with WBS.

6.5 Establish Change Control

A **baseline** is "the approved plan for a project plus or minus approved changes."[10] The project team looks at the scope statement and WBS to ensure completeness and seeks to validate the scope by consulting with the sponsor, customers, and/or other stakeholders. Simultaneously, the project team can be planning other aspects of the project such as schedule, resources, budget, risks, and quality. Once all of these plans are complete and

EXHIBIT 6.12

LIBRARY PROJECT WBS WITH COMPONENTS NUMBERED

LIBRARY PROJECT

1. **Project Management**
   1.1 KEY STAKEHOLDERS
   1.2 KEY PARTICIPANTS
   1.3 OPERATING METHODS
   1.4 COMMUNICATIONS PLAN
   1.5 PROGRESS CONTROL
2. **Facility Needs**
   2.1 VISION STATEMENT
   2.2 STAKEHOLDER INPUT
   2.3 OPTIONS
   2.4 ACADEMIC PLAN
3. **Building Proposal**
   3.1 RECOMMENDED SIZE AND SCOPE
   3.2 SITING
   3.3 COST RATIONALE
4. **Building Approval**
   4.1 VP OF FINANCE
   4.2 PRESIDENT
   4.3 BOARD
5. **Staff Education**
   5.1 LITERATURE REVIEW
   5.2 LIBRARY VISITS
   5.3 SUPPLIER, INPUT, PROCESS, OUTPUT, CUSTOMER ANALYSIS
   5.4 TRAINING
6. **Fundraising**
   6.1 POTENTIAL DONOR LIST
   6.2 RELATIONSHIP BUILDING WITH POTENTIAL DONORS
   6.3 EDUCATION OF POTENTIAL DONORS
   6.4 DONATIONS
   6.5 FOLLOW-UP WITH DONORS
7. **Building Documents**
   7.1 FACILITY AND SITE SPECIFICATIONS
   7.2 BUILDING APPROVAL
   7.3 SCHEMATIC DESIGNS
   7.4 DEVELOPMENT PLANS
   7.5 CONTRACT DOCUMENTS
8. **Building Construction**
   8.1 ARCHITECT
   8.2 CONTRACTORS
   8.3 CONSTRUCTION
   8.4 FURNISHINGS

EXHIBIT 6.12

LIBRARY PROJECT WBS WITH COMPONENTS NUMBERED (CONTINUED)

9. **Building Acceptance**

    9.1 BUILDING AND GROUNDS ACCEPTANCE

    9.2 BUILDING OCCUPANCY

    9.3 BUILDING DEDICATION

    9.4 WARRANTY CORRECTIONS

---

any impacts to scope have been accounted for, it is time to baseline the scope statement and the entire project plan. This is discussed in more detail at the end of the planning stage.

Most projects are planned and conducted in an atmosphere of uncertainty. Projects are planned making assumptions based upon the best information available to the project team, but many things can change during the course of a project. Therefore, project teams deal with change by establishing and using a **change control system,** which is "a collection of formally documented procedures that define how project deliverables and documentation will be controlled, changed, and approved."[11] Uncontrolled change is known as scope creep. Sometimes, the effects of scope creep are so bad that a well-started project can run into serious trouble.

The critical portion of a change control system is the method of documenting changes. Each potential change to a project is normally documented by some sort of

---

EXHIBIT 6.13

STAKEHOLDER ANALYSIS AND WBS AT THE CIA

At the CIA where I created and run our agency-wide project management training and certification program, I come in contact with large numbers of dedicated project managers. With enrollment averaging about 2,500 students per year, I encounter a workforce with a broad spectrum of experiences, skills, and expectations. One of the more prevalent expectations is associated with stakeholder analysis and communication; employees invariably feel that they pretty much know most or all they need to know in this area and may even begrudge somewhat the three days associated with our Project Communications Management course. What they discover, what we lead them to discover, is the shortcomings in their appreciation for and knowledge about project communications. Using a five-point Likert scale, we have every student perform a self-assessment of their communications proficiency prior to and after the class. To the students' surprise, proficiency increases average a full point; student feedback virtually always includes statements to the effect that they didn't realize just how much more effective they can be in project management by investing more in the project communications area.

The organizational chart plays a central role in how the CIA approaches the analysis of stakeholders. Employees learn through classroom exercises to use the organizational chart as a roadmap for identifying the stakeholders. As they march through the branches in this chart, they make conscious decisions about whether the function represented by the title or box on the chart or whether the individual performing that function is a stakeholder. Once they have identified the stakeholders and performed the associated stakeholder analysis, they then turn to the WBS to help with the planning and implementation of the communications tasks that follow. In fact, communications for the types of projects undertaken at the CIA has taken on such importance that we advocate it be placed at the first level of WBS decomposition alongside equally important components such as project management. For projects of sufficient size, a full-time leader is often assigned to the communications component; the scope of their duties includes communications within the project as well as communications outside the project.

Source: Michael O'Brochta, PMP, director, PPMC Program, CIA.

EXHIBIT 6.14

CHANGE REQUEST FORM

Date: Originator: Project #:

Description of Change:

Why needed:

Impact on project scope:
Impact on deadline dates:
Impact on budget:
Impact on quality:
Impact on risk:
Impact on team:

Date approved:

Project manager   Sponsor   Customer

_____   _____   _____

---

change request, which is a written "request to expand or reduce the project scope, modify policies, processes, plans, or procedure, modify costs or budgets, or revise schedules."[12]

This means every change to a project needs to be formally proposed. The potential change is then either accepted or not. If it is accepted, the project plans are changed to reflect the impact of the change. Most people quickly understand the need to document major changes, but some resist the effort it takes to document small changes. The impact of many small changes is like the old saying "killed by a thousand small cuts." Many small changes individually have small impacts on a project, but collectively they have a major impact. Project managers need to create an expectation that all changes be formally documented using a simple change request form so all team members will document proposed changes. A simple change request form is shown in Exhibit 6.14.

Change request forms typically include several sections. The top section lists basic information to track the change request to the project and to the person who submitted it. The second section contains two simple statements describing the change and why the change is needed. The third section details the impact expected from the potential change. This can vary in length from a simple check and comment section, as in Exhibit 6.14, to an extremely involved description of potential impact on complex system projects such as designing an aircraft. In complex projects, small changes can sometimes have catastrophic impacts. Finally, there should be a space for the change to be approved. Regardless of the complexity and format, the most important consideration is that potential changes must be submitted and documented whether they are approved or not.

As a practical matter, many people resist documentation. While change control is vital, project managers may sometimes use alternative forms of documentation such as very simple forms for minor changes. If a change is actually a different method of performing an activity and the same people will do the work in the same time period with the same deliverables, perhaps a formal change request is not needed. While a project manager may balance the behavioral issues of securing a change request with the benefits, when in doubt, he or she should require the documented request and approval. While change control is introduced in this chapter dealing with scope, change control is also vital for schedule, budget, resources, and quality. Lack of control in any project aspect can lead to trouble.

6.6 Using MS Project for Work Breakdown Structures (WBS)

The WBS is a building block for the remaining detailed project planning tools. This is the place where the value of software to automate detailed work becomes apparent. Our coverage of MS Project in this chapter describes how to set up a WBS in MS Project.

Set Up the WBS

Setting up the WBS has five steps, as follows:

1. Understand WBS definitions and displays.
2. Enter summaries.
3. Create the outline for your WBS.
4. Insert row number column.
5. Hide (or show) the desired amount of detail.

STEP 1: UNDERSTAND WBS DEFINITIONS AND DISPLAYS MS Project refers to WBS elements as summary tasks or summaries. Summaries are displayed:

- In tables as an outline, with summary tasks in bold. MS Project uses only the indented outline format to display a WBS.
- In a Gantt view with different graphic shapes (there are several Gantt views).

Exhibit 6.15 shows a Gantt view of a WBS with the entry table on the left and the Gantt chart graphic on the right. At this time the Gantt graphic is of little value—there is no underlying detail with duration values that drive a summary duration longer than one day.

STEP 2: ENTER WBS ELEMENTS (SUMMARIES) Enter the summaries in the Task Name column cells as shown in Exhibit 6.16. WBS elements can be added with an insert function as follows:

1. Click on the Id field to select the row below where the new row will be. Selecting more than one row will result in that number of blank rows being inserted.
2. On the Task tab, Insert group, click Insert Task.
3. In the Task Name field, enter the name of the added WBS element.
4. Enter any additional summary(s).

STEP 3: CREATE THE OUTLINE FOR YOUR WBS Set up the outline structure using the Indent and Outdent controls shown in Exhibit 6.17 (these are two separate controls, appearing as the Task tab green arrows).

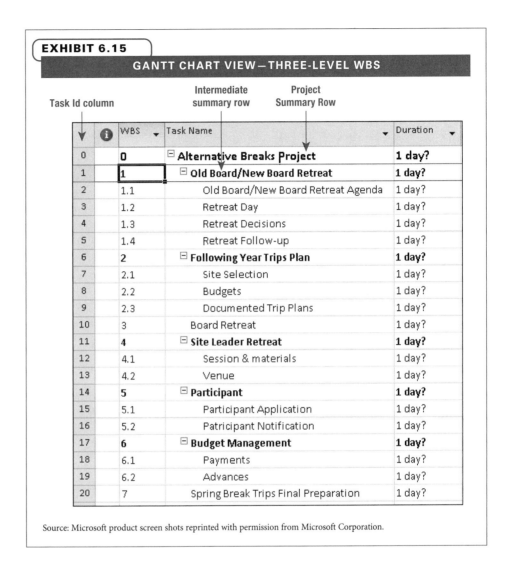

EXHIBIT 6.15

GANTT CHART VIEW—THREE-LEVEL WBS

	ⓘ	WBS ▾	Task Name ▾	Duration ▾
0		0	⊟ **Alternative Breaks Project**	**1 day?**
1		1	⊟ **Old Board/New Board Retreat**	**1 day?**
2		1.1	Old Board/New Board Retreat Agenda	1 day?
3		1.2	Retreat Day	1 day?
4		1.3	Retreat Decisions	1 day?
5		1.4	Retreat Follow-up	1 day?
6		2	⊟ **Following Year Trips Plan**	**1 day?**
7		2.1	Site Selection	1 day?
8		2.2	Budgets	1 day?
9		2.3	Documented Trip Plans	1 day?
10		3	Board Retreat	1 day?
11		4	⊟ **Site Leader Retreat**	**1 day?**
12		4.1	Session & materials	1 day?
13		4.2	Venue	1 day?
14		5	⊟ **Participant**	**1 day?**
15		5.1	Participant Application	1 day?
16		5.2	Patricipant Notification	1 day?
17		6	⊟ **Budget Management**	**1 day?**
18		6.1	Payments	1 day?
19		6.2	Advances	1 day?
20		7	Spring Break Trips Final Preparation	1 day?

Labels: Task Id column, Intermediate summary row, Project Summary Row

Source: Microsoft product screen shots reprinted with permission from Microsoft Corporation.

1. Click the Task Name field of the row to be indented.
2. On the Task tab, Schedule group, click Indent Task. Indenting a summary row will also indent its lower-level items. Multiple rows under a summary row can be indented at the same time by selecting all of them before clicking the Indent control.
3. To decrease an indent level with the Outdent control: On the Task tab, Schedule group, click Outdent Task. Any lower-level items will also be outdented.

STEP 4: INSERT WBS ROW NUMBER COLUMN MS Project will automatically number all of the summaries in your WBS if you merely insert a WBS column to the left of the Task Name column. Right-click the Task Name heading, click Insert Column, and click WBS, as shown in Exhibit 6.18. The result will appear as Exhibit 6.19.

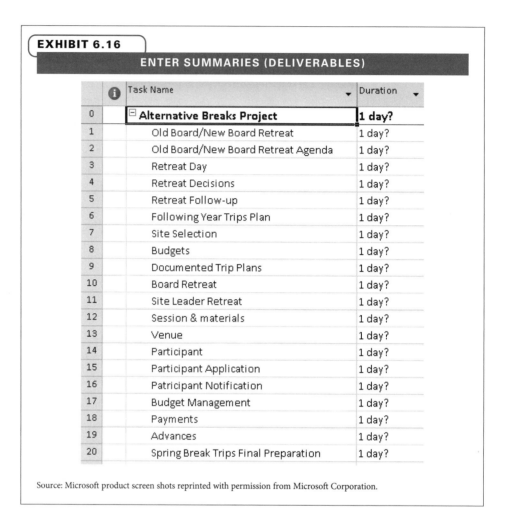

Source: Microsoft product screen shots reprinted with permission from Microsoft Corporation.

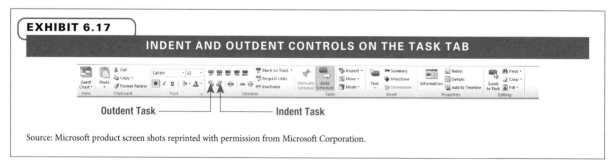

Source: Microsoft product screen shots reprinted with permission from Microsoft Corporation.

STEP 5: HIDE (OR SHOW) UNDERLYING DETAIL Some stakeholders will not want to see lower levels of WBS detail. To display the appropriate level detail, complete one or both of the following steps:

- Click Hide Subtasks (minus sign in box before the task name) to hide underlying detail, or
- Click Show Subtasks (plus sign in box) to show underlying detail.

EXHIBIT 6.18

READY TO INSERT SELECTED WBS COLUMN

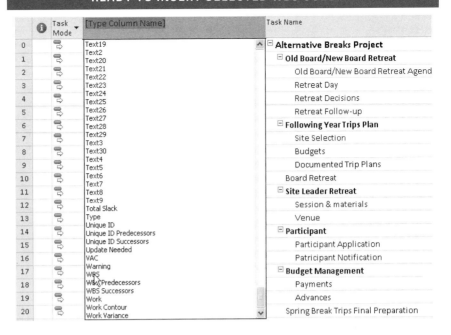

		[Type Column Name]		Task Name
0		Text19		⊟ **Alternative Breaks Project**
1		Text2		⊟ **Old Board/New Board Retreat**
2		Text20		Old Board/New Board Retreat Agend
3		Text21		Retreat Day
4		Text22		Retreat Decisions
5		Text23		Retreat Follow-up
6		Text24		
7		Text25		⊟ **Following Year Trips Plan**
8		Text26		Site Selection
9		Text27		Budgets
10		Text28		Documented Trip Plans
11		Text29		Board Retreat
12		Text3		⊟ **Site Leader Retreat**
13		Text30		Session & materials
14		Text4		Venue
15		Text5		⊟ **Participant**
16		Text6		Participant Application
17		Text7		Patricipant Notification
18		Text8		⊟ **Budget Management**
19		Text9		Payments
20		Total Slack		Advances

(dropdown list continues: Type, Unique ID, Unique ID Predecessors, Unique ID Successors, Update Needed, VAC, Warning, WBS, WBS Predecessors, WBS Successors, Work, Work Contour, Work Variance)

Spring Break Trips Final Preparation

Source: Microsoft product screen shots reprinted with permission from Microsoft Corporation.

EXHIBIT 6.19

WBS COLUMN INSERTED

		WBS	Task Name	Duration
0		0	⊟ **Alternative Breaks Project**	**1 day?**
1		1	⊟ **Old Board/New Board Retreat**	1 day?
2		1.1	Old Board/New Board Retreat Agenda	1 day?
3		1.2	Retreat Day	1 day?
4		1.3	Retreat Decisions	1 day?
5		1.4	Retreat Follow-up	1 day?
6		2	⊟ **Following Year Trips Plan**	**1 day?**
7		2.1	Site Selection	1 day?
8		2.2	Budgets	1 day?
9		2.3	Documented Trip Plans	1 day?
10		3	Board Retreat	1 day?
11		4	⊟ **Site Leader Retreat**	**1 day?**
12		4.1	Session & materials	1 day?
13		4.2	Venue	1 day?
14		5	⊟ **Participant**	**1 day?**
15		5.1	Participant Application	1 day?
16		5.2	Patricipant Notification	1 day?
17		6	⊟ **Budget Management**	**1 day?**
18		6.1	Payments	1 day?
19		6.2	Advances	1 day?
20		7	Spring Break Trips Final Preparation	1 day?

Source: Microsoft product screen shots reprinted with permission from Microsoft Corporation.

EXHIBIT 6.20

HIDE OR SHOW UNDERLYING DETAIL

ⓘ	WBS ▾	Task Name ▾	Duration ▾
0	0	⊟ **Alternative Breaks Project**	**1 day?**
1	1	⊞ **Old Board/New Board Retreat**	**1 day?**
6	2	⊟ **Following Year Trips Plan**	**1 day?**
7	2.1	Site Selection	1 day?
8	2.2	Budgets	1 day?
9	2.3	Documented Trip Plans	1 day?
10	3	Board Retreat	1 day?
11	4	⊞ **Site Leader Retreat**	**1 day?**
14	5	⊟ **Participant**	**1 day?**
15	5.1	Participant Application	1 day?
16	5.2	Patricipant Notification	1 day?
17	6	⊟ **Budget Management**	**1 day?**
18	6.1	Payments	1 day?
19	6.2	Advances	1 day?
20	7	Spring Break Trips Final Preparation	1 day?

Source: Microsoft product screen shots reprinted with permission from Microsoft Corporation.

In Exhibit 6.20, the underlying detail for the Board Retreats and Site Leader Retreat WBS elements is hidden.

Summary

Once a project is formally approved by a sponsor ratifying its charter, it is time for detailed planning. While project planning is iterative, normally the first steps are to identify stakeholders, plan communications, and determine what will be created on the project. Project teams start this process by asking customers what end-of-project deliverables they want. From the customers' response, the planning team can determine both what interim deliverables need to be created and what work needs to be performed to create all of the deliverables. Just as important as determining what will be produced during the project is determining what will *not* be produced. These boundaries of what will and will not be included constitute the project's scope.

Once the scope is defined, it can be organized into a work breakdown structure (WBS). A WBS is used to progressively decompose the project into smaller and smaller pieces until each can be assigned to one person for planning and control. The WBS serves as a basis for determining the project schedule, budget, personnel assignments, quality requirements, and risks. As those other functions are planned, items are commonly identified that should be added to the WBS.

Some teams create their WBS by hand using the org chart or free format methods, while others directly type their WBS into project scheduling software such as Microsoft Project.

Key Terms from the *PMBOK® Guide*

product scope, 142
project scope, 142

define scope, 145
define activity, 147

work package, 150
WBS component, 151
WBS dictionary, 151
Rolling wave planning, 153

baseline, 154
change control system, 156
change request, 157

Chapter Review Questions

1. What is the first step in developing the project scope management plan?
2. What areas of a project can scope creep affect?
3. A _____ is used to formally document changes made to the project.
4. List the two types of deliverables.
5. For a construction project, the house is the _____ deliverable, and reports and how-to instruction sheets are _____ deliverables.
6. What are the two main areas that need to be addressed in defining project requirements?
7. What does the acronym WBS stand for?
8. What are several uses of a WBS?
9. The lowest level of the WBS is known as a _____ .
10. List three methods that can be used to organize a WBS.
11. List several items the scope management plan includes.
12. Why is scope definition important?
13. What items are typically included in a work package description?
14. What can the project team plan after the scope is determined?
15. What is uncontrolled change known as?
16. Why do project teams use change control systems?

Discussion Questions

1. What is the difference between product scope and project scope?
2. Describe the roles various executives, managers, and associates play in scope planning.
3. List the major sections that a change request form should include. Tell why each is important.
4. Describe how to facilitate a JAD session and tell what you expect to learn from it.
5. List and describe the six steps of the scope definition process.
6. List and explain the purpose of each section of a project scope statement.
7. Compare and contrast the three formats of constructing a WBS: indented outline, org chart, and free format.
8. Tell why work packages are important for planning and control.

Exercises

1. Create a scope statement for a project in which you plan an event on your campus.
2. Construct a WBS in indented outline format for a project in which you plan an event on your campus. Be sure to number each row.

PMBOK® Guide Questions

1. A framework used to divide deliverables of a project into smaller and smaller pieces is the:
   a. organizational chart
   b. project schedule
   c. project work statement
   d. work breakdown structure
2. Defining activity is related to product scope in that:
   a. it is the process of identifying the actions that will produce product deliverables
   b. it coordinates who is doing what for whom
   c. it produces a milestone schedule
   d. it is the process of deciding how much each activity will cost
3. Which of the following is **not** a common WBS organizational format?
   a. cross-functional work
   b. design component/deliverable
   c. project phase
   d. work function/subproject

4. Which of the following is true for a work package?
   a. It requires the work of the entire project team.
   b. It is the responsibility of the project manager.
   c. It is the most detailed level of the WBS.
   d. It is the responsibility of the sponsor.

5. In addition to the project team, who needs to be included in the construction of the WBS?
   a. subject matter expert (SME)
   b. sponsor
   c. internal stakeholders
   d. external stakeholders

Example Project

For your example project, create the following:

1. Scope management plan to direct your efforts.
2. Customer needs worksheet to identify customer desires.
3. Project scope statement including each of the sections in Exhibit 6.3. (Be sure to state specifically what items are included and what items are excluded.)

4. Change request form. (Determine what level of changes you as an individual can make without further approval, what changes you as a student team can make, and what changes your sponsor needs to approve.)
5. WBS first using either the free format or the org chart format.
6. WBS in MS Project.

References

A Guide to the Project Management Body of Knowledge (PMBOK® Guide), 4th ed. (Newtown Square, PA: Project Management Institute, 2008).

Bartholomew, Doug, "Prescription for Better Projects," *Baseline* (November 2006): 55–58.

Caudle, Gerrie, *Streamlining Business Requirements: The XCellR8™ Approach* (Vienna, VA: Management Concepts, Inc., 2009).

Dobson, Michael S., *The Triple Constraints in Project Management* (Vienna, VA: Management Concepts, Inc., 2004).

Garvey, William, "Essentials of Validation Project Management," *Pharmaceutical Technology* (December 2005): 68–76.

Hass, Kathleen B., Don Wessels and Kevin Brennan, *Getting It Right: Business Requirement Analysis Tools and Techniques Structures* (Vienna, VA: Management Concepts, Inc., 2008).

Haugan, Gregory T., *Effective Work Breakdown Structures* (Vienna, VA: Management Concepts, Inc., 2002).

Howard, Dale and Gary Chefetz, *What's New Study Guide Microsoft Project 2010* (New York: Chefetz LLC dba MSProjectExperts, 2010).

Means, Jan and Terry Adams, *Facilitating the Project Life-cycle* (San Francisco: Jossey-Bass, 2005).

Miller, Dennis P. *Building a Project Work Breakdown Structure: Visualizing Objectives, Deliverables, Activities, and Schedules* (Boca Raton, FL: CRC Press, 2009).

Milosevic, Dragan Z., *Project Management Toolbox: Tools and Techniques for the Practicing Project Manager* (New York: John Wiley & Sons, 2003).

Mulcahy, Rita, *PMP Exam Prep: Rita's Course in a Book for Passing the PMP Exam*, 5th ed. (RMC Publications, Inc. 2005).

Project Management Institute Practice Standard for Work Breakdown Structures, 2nd. ed. (Newtown Square, PA: Project Management Institute, 2006).

Rad, Parviz and Vittal Anantatmula, *Project Planning Techniques* (Vienna, VA: Management Concepts, Inc., 2005).

Turk, Wayne, "Scope Creep Horror: It's Scarier than Movie Monsters," *Defense AT&L* (March–April 2010): 53–55.

Verzuh, Eric, *The Fast Forward MBA in Project Management*, 2nd ed. (Hoboken, NJ: John Wiley & Sons, 2005).

Warner, Paul and Paul Cassar, "Putting Together a Work Breakdown Structure," in David I. Cleland, *Field Guide to Project Management*, 2nd ed. (Hoboken, NJ: John Wiley & Sons, 2004).

Endnotes

1. *PMBOK® Guide* 442.
2. *PMBOK® Guide* 444.
3. *PMBOK® Guide* 429.
4. *PMBOK® Guide* 432.
5. Ibid.
6. *PMBOK® Guide* 453.
7. *PMBOK® Guide* 452.
8. *PMBOK® Guide* 453.
9. *PMBOK® Guide* 447.
10. *PMBOK® Guide* 427.
11. *PMBOK® Guide* 428.
12. Ibid.

PROJECT MANAGEMENT *IN ACTION*

Development of Inventory System Project

A private company that took over management responsibilities for a residential facility discovered that there was very little inventory control over needed supplies. It launched a project to develop a workable inventory system. The work breakdown structure is shown in Exhibit 6.21.

EXHIBIT 6.21

INVENTORY SYSTEM WORK BREAKDOWN STRUCTURE

DEVELOPMENT OF INVENTORY SYSTEM PROJECT

1. **Project Management**
   1.1 CHARTER
   1.2 COMMUNICATION PLAN
   1.3 WORK BREAKDOWN STRUCTURE
   1.4 RESPONSIBILITY MATRIX
   1.5 SCHEDULE
   1.6 PROGRESS REPORTS
2. **Systems Analysis and Problem Definition**
   2.1 INITIAL ASSESSMENT
       2.1.1 Individual Unit Assessments
           2.1.1.1 *Kitchen*
           2.1.1.2 *Laundry*
           2.1.1.3 *Maintenance*
           2.1.1.4 *Office Supplies and Furniture*
           2.1.1.5 *Commissary*
           2.1.1.6 *Administration Room*
           2.1.1.7 *Intake*
           2.1.1.8 *Pods*
       2.1.2 Intra-Unit Relationship Assessments
       2.1.3 Understanding of Current Inventory Flow
   2.2 PROBLEM AREA IDENTIFICATION
       2.2.1 Within Existing Computer Systems
       2.2.2 Policies and Procedures
           2.2.2.1 *Unorganized and Unaccounted for Material Flow*
           2.2.2.2 *Delivery Policy*
           2.2.2.3 *Keys and Access Policy*
           2.2.2.4 *Reorder Point Policy*
       2.2.3 Security
       2.2.4 Approval Process for Acquisition of Goods
       2.2.5 Evaluation of Policy
   2.3 STAFFING AND HUMAN RESOURCES PRACTICES
   2.4 STORAGE SPACE

EXHIBIT 6.21

INVENTORY SYSTEM WORK BREAKDOWN STRUCTURE (CONTINUED)

3. Recommendation Identification

    3.1 DECISION CRITERIA TO EVALUATE RECOMMENDATIONS

    3.2 ALTERNATIVE SOLUTIONS

        3.2.1 Alternative Identification

        3.2.2 Alternative Evaluation

        3.2.3 Alternative Prioritization

    3.3 FINAL RECOMMENDATIONS

CHAPTER 7

Scheduling Projects

CHAPTER OBJECTIVES

After completing this chapter, you should be able to:

- Describe five ways in which a project's schedule is limited and how to deal with each.

- Describe potential problems in estimating time accurately and how to overcome them.

- Use the activity on node (AON) method to develop a project schedule.

- Identify the critical path using both the two-pass and enumeration methods, and identify all float.

- Depict a project schedule on a Gantt chart both by hand and using MS Project 2010, showing the critical path and all float.

Andersen Ross/Stockbyte/Getty Images

The projects I'm regularly involved in these days are for web-based software implementations. I help clients with initial adoption and use of our commercially-available applications. The cost and scope of these projects is fairly straightforward. Scheduling, however, is not!

Several problems make creating and managing implementation schedules a challenge. First, decision makers who buy our software and see its value seldom lead implementations themselves, and they may be slow to designate project leaders. Once they do, there are often gaps in communicating project objectives, timelines, and measures of success. For example, when I ask project managers how and when they expect to measure initial adoption and use, they'll say "tomorrow," without realizing that such a schedule is unrealistic and far different from the expectations set with project sponsors.

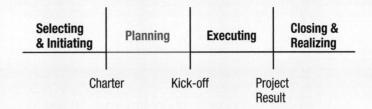

Selecting & Initiating	Planning	Executing	Closing & Realizing

Charter   Kick-off   Project Result

**PMBOK®
GUIDE TOPICS**

- Define activities
- Sequence activities
- Estimate activity durations
- Develop schedule

Second, a key success factor is populating the central repository with adequate quality content to justify the software's use. There are two different approaches clients can take when scoping this work effort: The first is schedule-driven and the second is more scope-driven, as follows.

1. Harvest, prepare, and load whatever content is readily available for quick deployment and usage.
2. Define complete content requirements prior to initial launch.

One risk using the second approach is that content development projects often have schedules with long durations, even when adequately resourced. The result: Months later, software has still not been adopted due to lack of content. Sadly, this is all too common in our industry, which is why we place great importance on a well-defined schedule and resource plan for content development.

Another critical success factor is users who have learned, retained, and mastered the skills of working with the software. This should be easy but it's not. Our products are often purchased expressly for people who are severely overburdened and pressed for time, since improved efficiency is a major benefit. Unfortunately, I see many people attend training and then forget everything they've learned because other pressing priorities prevent them from spending the time needed to practice and master new skills. As a result, training investments go to waste because learning is not retained. Consequently, implementations fail to achieve their ultimate objective—adoption and utilization.

One solution that has worked well for our customers is establishing a scope that *can* be completed in a schedule of four to eight weeks, despite the challenges I've described. We schedule a project kickoff meeting to identify a project leader, tasks, and timeline. Team members are educated on goals, critical success factors, and typical issues and challenges. Once gaining consensus on an action plan, I communicate it to both the project leader and sponsor to ensure alignment. Then the team and I meet regularly to monitor progress. If there are issues, we develop plans to resolve them and follow up at subsequent meetings.

Establishing scope that can be accomplished in a 30- to 60-day schedule helps our clients get started using their web-based applications faster. By using them, people get more motivated and committed to achieving their ultimate benefits. Therefore, customers are more likely to allocate adequate resources and time to subsequent project phases that address the full scope of their content and training requirements, no matter how many months or years that may take. Project planning for the future becomes more realistic, improving the odds of success. Meanwhile, clients are achieving return on their software investments. So it's no surprise that delivering real business benefits in the shortest possible timeframe continues to drive our scheduling approach.

Carol A. Abbott, training specialist, Sant-Kadient

7.1 Introduction to Project Time Management

A first draft of a project schedule can be constructed once the work breakdown structure (WBS) has been constructed. As is true of other project planning areas, planning for time is iterative. A project manager and team usually develop as much of the schedule as they can based upon the information in the WBS. The communication plan, requirements matrix, and scope statement are often either complete or at least in draft form at this point. Once a project is scheduled, the budget can be formulated, resource needs can be identified and resources assigned, risks can be identified and plans developed to deal with the identified risks, and a quality management plan can be created. In many projects, these are not all treated as discrete activities, and some of them may be performed together. However, for clarity, each of these planning processes will be described individually.

The building blocks of a project schedule are activities. An **activity** is "a component of work performed during the course of a project."[1] For activities to be useful as schedule building blocks, they should have the following characteristics:

- Clear starting and ending points
- Tangible output that can be verified
- Scope small enough to understand and control without micromanaging
- Labor, other costs, and schedule that can be estimated and controlled
- A single person who can be held accountable for each activity (even if more than one person does the work, one person should be responsible)[2]

Since activities represent work that needs to be performed, they should be listed in a verb–noun format, such as "prepare budget," "build frame," "test code," "transmit information," "analyze data," and "develop plan." Each activity should be clearly differentiated from other activities, so it is often helpful to write the activities in verb–adjective–noun format, such as "write draft report" and "write final report," to prevent confusion.

The Project Management Institute (PMI) has divided project time management into the following six work processes. Each will be briefly introduced here.

1. **Define activities**—the process of identifying the specific actions that need to be performed to produce project deliverables

2. **Sequence activities**—the process of identifying and documenting dependencies among schedule activities
3. **Estimate activity resources**—the process of estimating the type and quantities of material, people, equipment, or supplies required to perform each activity
4. **Estimate activity durations**—the process of approximating the number of work periods needed to complete individual activities with estimated resources
5. **Develop schedule**—the process of analyzing activity sequences, durations, resource requirements, and schedule constraints to create the project schedule
6. **Control schedule**—the process of monitoring the status of the project update progress and managing changes to the schedule baseline[3]

Defining activities, sequencing activities, estimating activity durations, and part of developing schedules will be covered in this chapter. Estimating activity resources and the remainder of developing schedules will be discussed in Chapter 8 (Resourcing Projects). Chapter 14 (Determining Project Progress and Results) will focus on controlling the schedule.

7.2 Purposes of a Project Schedule

Projects are undertaken to accomplish important business purposes, and people often want to be able to use the project results as quickly as possible. Many specific questions such as the following can be answered by having a complete and workable schedule:

- When will the project be complete?
- What is the earliest date a particular activity can start, and when will it end?
- What activity must begin before which other activities can take place?
- What would happen if a delivery of material was one week late?
- Can a key worker take a week of vacation the first week of March?
- If one worker is assigned to do two activities, which one must go first?
- How many hours do we need from each worker next week or month?
- Which worker or other resource is a bottleneck, limiting the speed of our project?
- What will the impact be if the client wants to add another module?
- If I am willing to spend an extra $10,000, how much faster can the project be completed?
- Are all of the activities completed that should be by now?

7.3 Historical Development of Project Schedules

Understanding how project scheduling developed to its current state is very helpful. Throughout history, projects have been performed, but many early projects such as great cathedrals in Europe took decades or longer to complete. As competition drove the need for more rapid project completion, systematic methods were developed for scheduling projects.

In the 1950s, two project scheduling methods were developed: program evaluation and review technique (PERT) and critical path method. The **critical path method (CPM)** is formally defined as "a schedule network analysis technique used to determine the amount of scheduling flexibility (the amount of float) on various logical network paths in the project schedule network, and to determine the minimum total project duration."[4] Both CPM and PERT were founded on the concepts still in place today of identifying activities, determining their logical order, and estimating the duration for each. Networks representing the activities were developed and the schedule calculated. Each of the techniques also boasted a capability the other did not possess.

PERT was developed in the Navy's Special Program Office because the Navy was developing the Polaris Weapons System. This system was extremely large and complex. To complete it as quickly as possible, many activities needed to be worked on simultaneously. Furthermore, many aspects of the Polaris used unproven technology. There was considerable uncertainty regarding how long some of the new technology would take to develop. Given the extreme complexity and uncertainty, PERT enabled project managers to not only estimate the most likely amount of time needed to complete a project, but also the level of confidence in completing it in a particular time. This has proven to be especially useful in research and development projects involving individual activities that are hard to estimate precisely. How uncertainty in project schedules is handled by PERT will be discussed more in Section 7.9.

CPM was developed in the Engineering Services Division of DuPont. DuPont needed to plan very large projects when it built and refurbished enormous plants. Planners using CPM estimated the time for each individual work activity using a single time estimate. The focus was on understanding the longest sequence of activities, which determined how long the project would take. CPM enabled project managers to ask what-if questions such as "If the project needs to be finished three weeks early, which activities should be speeded up and how much will it cost?" This proved to be especially useful in the construction industry where delays such as rain often necessitate the acceleration of a project.

PERT and CPM originally used a method for displaying the work activities called activity on arrow (AOA) or arrow diagramming method (ADM), in which schedule activities are represented by arrows and connected at points called nodes. Because it is often confusing to draw an accurate AOA network, this method is rarely used today. The more common method used today is called activity on node (AON) or the **precedence diagramming method (PDM)**. AON or PDM is "a schedule network diagramming technique in which the scheduled activities are represented by boxes or nodes. Schedule activities are graphically linked by one or more logical relationships to show the sequence in which the activities are performed."[5] A small project schedule is shown in Exhibit 7.1 with work activities A through D connected by arrows showing logical relationships (A must be complete before B and C can begin and both B and C must finish before D can begin).

Originally, the only relationship shown using AON was a finish-to-start relationship where the first activity must be complete before the next one can begin. While this is still the most common, other relationships can be shown with the AON, such as where one activity must start before the next one can start, or one activity must be complete two days before the next one can start. Most modern project scheduling software makes use of AON representation of the project schedule. This book will focus on these methods since the software most people use requires this understanding.

The basic logic of these techniques still serves as the backbone of many project schedules today. However, other advances have added to scheduling capability. One is that since computers are so much more powerful and easier to use, many additional features have been added to project schedules. Another trend is that with many organizations operating in a "lean" mode, resource limitations rather than just the logical order of activities are a major determinant of many project schedules.

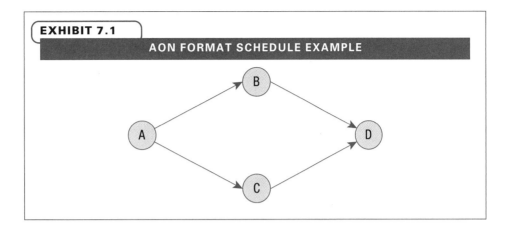

EXHIBIT 7.1

AON FORMAT SCHEDULE EXAMPLE

7.4 How Project Schedules Are Limited and Created

One way to understand project schedules and how they are constructed is to understand that five factors may limit how fast a project can be completed. The first factor is the logical order in which activities need to be completed. For example, one needs to dig a hole before cement can be poured in it. This is covered in the section on sequencing activities. The second factor is how long each individual activity will take. This is discussed in the section on estimating activity duration. It includes methods for estimating durations, problems with estimates, and remedies to those problems. The third factor is how many key resources are available at specific points in the project. For example, if six rooms were available to be painted at the same time, and fewer than six painters were available, progress would be slowed. This is discussed in Chapter 8 in the section on resource availability. The fourth factor is imposed dates. For example, a project working on a government contract may not be able to start until the government's new fiscal year, which starts on October 1. Chapter 8 also has a section on imposed dates. The fifth and final factor is cash flow. Projects may not start until money is approved, but progress may also be slowed until enough revenue arrives to cover expenses. This is covered in Chapter 9.

Recognizing that project schedules are limited by logical order, activity duration, resource availability, imposed dates, and cash flow restrictions, creating a realistic schedule is an iterative process. A common method of developing the schedule is to first identify all of the activities and then determine the logical order by creating a network diagram. Once the order is determined, resources are assigned to each activity and an estimate of the time required for that activity is made. If the assigned resource is not available when the activity is scheduled, then an adjustment of some type may need to be made. The schedule can be computed with all of this information. Next, it is time to compare the emerging schedule with any imposed dates and cash flow estimates. Any inconsistencies may cause the team to adjust the schedule. Other factors often need to be considered, such as quality demands and risk factors. When all of these have been planned, the final schedule can be prepared and approved.

The pressure to complete a project as quickly as possible is often great. The sponsor or customer may try to dictate a schedule before anyone knows whether it is feasible or not. A project manager should initially resist this pressure. The project manager must first understand what makes sense in terms of a schedule before she is in a position to know whether to accept a sponsor's suggestions or to argue about why it may be impractical. A project manager has the ethical responsibility to determine a schedule that is possible to achieve, persuade all stakeholders that the schedule makes sense, and then see to it that the project is delivered according to that agreed upon schedule.

The remainder of this chapter and the other planning chapters describe in detail how to plan each of these, culminating in an approved schedule and project plan that all stakeholders believe is reasonable. The project manager is then be accountable to deliver the project on schedule. That project delivery is the essence of the final four chapters of this book.

7.5 Define Activities

The first process in developing a project schedule is to define all of the work activities. The last row of a WBS represents the work packages—lowest-level deliverables. Now is the time to ask, "What work activities must be completed to create each of the project deliverables?" Exhibit 7.2 shows a WBS with the deliverables identified by numbers 1 through 8, and Exhibit 7.3 shows the same project with the activities required to create the deliverables listed. Notice that each row in both exhibits has a unique number and that the number of each activity shows the deliverable it helps to create. For example, activity 3.2, contact local bands, is needed for deliverable 3, entertainment.

As teams define activities, they want to be especially careful not to omit any. It is a good idea to have someone on your project team play "devil's advocate" to challenge the team to identify additional activities. It is better to identify activities that do not need to be accomplished than to forget activities that will need to be added later. The team may think all of the activities have been identified; however, when the next process is performed—activity sequencing—it may become obvious that some activities have been forgotten. Another activity can always be added later. Remember the schedule will not be approved until all of the related planning is in place. It is better to discover a missing activity in the later stages of planning than after the schedule is approved. Activities that need to be added after the final schedule is approved will add time and money to the project, perhaps driving it over budget and causing it to fall behind schedule. It is

---

EXHIBIT 7.2

WORK BREAKDOWN STRUCTURE WITH DELIVERABLES ONLY

COLLEGE FUNDRAISER PROJECT
1. Location
2. Information
3. Entertainment
4. Safety
5. Parking
6. Food
7. Sanitation
8. Volunteers

EXHIBIT 7.3

WORK BREAKDOWN STRUCTURE WITH ACTIVITY LIST ADDED

COLLEGE FUNDRAISER PROJECT

1. **Location**
   1.1 CONTACT UNIVERSITY FOR PERMISSION
   1.2 SCHEDULE APPROPRIATE TIME FOR THE EVENT
   1.3 OBTAIN PERMIT
   1.4 DETERMINE IDEAL LOCATION TO MEET CAPACITY
   1.5 DETERMINE ALTERNATIVE LOCATION IN CASE OF INCLEMENT WEATHER

2. **Information**
   2.1 PROVIDE TEAM INFORMATION
   2.2 PRODUCE PRE-EVENT ADVERTISEMENTS
   2.3 DISPLAY WELCOME SIGNS AT ALL ENTRANCES
   2.4 SET UP SIGN-IN TABLE
   2.5 DISPLAY SIGNS WITH RULES

3. **Entertainment**
   3.1 FIND INFORMATION ABOUT LOCAL NOISE ORDINANCES
   3.2 CONTACT LOCAL BANDS
   3.3 NOTIFY LOCAL COMMUNITIES OF THE EVENT
   3.4 SET UP STAGE, SPEAKERS, FUN BOOTHS

4. **Safety**
   4.1 DETERMINE LIGHTING NEEDS
   4.2 CONTACT LOCAL FIRE DEPARTMENT (EMS)
   4.3 CONTACT LOCAL POLICE DEPARTMENT
   4.4 OBTAIN PERMISSION TO USE WALKIE-TALKIES FOR COMMUNICATION DURING EVENT
   4.5 COORDINATE FIRST AID BOOTH

5. **Parking**
   5.1 FIND ADEQUATE LOTS TO ACCOMMODATE CAPACITY
   5.2 COORDINATE SHUTTLE SERVICE FROM LOTS TO SITE (IF APPLICABLE)
   5.3 ARRANGE FOR PARKING ATTENDANTS
   5.4 HAVE SPECIAL PLACES RESERVED FOR HANDICAPPED

6. **Food**
   6.1 CONTACT FOOD/BEVERAGE VENDORS FOR CONCESSIONS
   6.2 MAKE GOODIE BAGS FOR CHILDREN
   6.3 ORDER SUFFICIENT WATER

7. **Sanitation**
   7.1 PROVIDE TRASH RECEPTACLES
   7.2 CONTACT LOCAL WASTE MANAGEMENT COMPANY FOR DUMPSTERS
   7.3 PROVIDE ADEQUATE NUMBER OF PORTA-JOHNS AND DETERMINE APPROPRIATE LOCATION
   7.4 COORDINATE POST-EVENT CLEAN-UP
   7.5 PURCHASE PAPER PRODUCTS AND SOAP
   7.6 ARRANGE ON-SITE GARBAGE COLLECTION AT FREQUENT INTERVALS

EXHIBIT 7.3

**WORK BREAKDOWN STRUCTURE WITH
ACTIVITY LIST ADDED (CONTINUED)**

8.   **Volunteers**

   8.1   RECRUIT VOLUNTEERS

   8.2   PRODUCE A MASTER VOLUNTEER ASSIGNMENT LIST

   8.3   MAKE NAMETAGS FOR ALL VOLUNTEERS

---

better to take extra time up front in order to make the activity list as comprehensive as possible.

If the project being planned is similar to previous projects, the team can look at those projects both for defining activities and for other planning that follows. Some organizations have templates or checklists for certain types of projects that can be used as a starting point in defining activities. Regardless of the starting point, team members need to keep asking how this project is different from previous ones. Often, a new project includes a few unique activities that need to be included.

In addition to the activity list, the project milestones should be listed. A milestone is an important point in a project schedule that the project sponsor and manager want to use as a checkpoint. A few major milestones are often identified in the project charter, but quite commonly more milestones are identified during project schedule planning. Common milestones include completion of a major deliverable, completion of a critical activity, and the time just before a large amount of money needs to be committed to the project. A team may also decide to put a milestone at a merging point in the project schedule where multiple activities need to be complete before progress can continue. The common denominator in each of these decisions is to identify a few key points in the life of a project where management can determine if the project is progressing the way they want. A milestone list is shown in Exhibit 7.4. Note that the line numbers assigned to the milestones are one greater than the line numbers of the activities that must be completed for each milestone. For example, the milestone "Information needs finalized" (item 2.6) represents the point in time that all of the information-related activities (items 2.1 through 2.5) are completed. For clarity, items 2.1 through 2.5 have been imported from Exhibit 7.3 and set in a lighter font. Notice also that the verb choice on the milestones is past tense, such as "confirmed," "finalized," and so on. This indicates that the activities leading up to each milestone must be complete.

7.6 Sequence Activities

Once the activities have been identified, it is time to determine the logical order in which they can be accomplished. A common method of determining this sequence is to put each defined activity on a Post-it Note and to display them on a large work space (white board, several flip chart sheets on a wall, etc.). The activities that are expected to be accomplished early in the project can be placed on the left portion of the work surface, those activities expected to be accomplished midway in the project near the middle, and those expected to be last on the right. Then, one person can serve as a facilitator asking, "What activity or activities can be started right away and do not depend on any others?" Once one or more of these initial activities have been identified, the facilitator

EXHIBIT 7.4

WORK BREAKDOWN STRUCTURE WITH MILESTONE LIST

COLLEGE FUNDRAISER PROJECT

1. **Location**
   - 1.6 LOCATION CONFIRMED
2. **Information**
   - 2.1 PROVIDE TEAM INFORMATION
   - 2.2 PRODUCE PRE-EVENT ADVERTISEMENTS
   - 2.3 DISPLAY WELCOME SIGNS AT ALL ENTRANCES
   - 2.4 SET UP SIGN-IN TABLE
   - 2.5 DISPLAY SIGNS WITH RULES
   - 2.6 INFORMATION NEEDS FINALIZED
3. **Entertainment**
   - 3.5 BAND CONTRACT SIGNED
   - 3.6 ENTERTAINMENT ARRANGED
4. **Safety**
   - 4.6 SAFETY REQUIREMENTS COMPLETED
5. **Parking**
   - 5.5 ALL PARKING NEEDS ARRANGED
6. **Food**
   - 6.4 FOOD AND BEVERAGES READIED
7. **Sanitation**
   - 7.7 ALL SANITATION NEEDS IN PLACE
8. **Volunteers**
   - 8.4 VOLUNTEERS PREPARED

Javier Larrea/PhotoLibrary

Arranging adhesive notes on a wall allows team members to arrange project tasks in predecessor-successor relationships.

EXHIBIT 7.5

ACTIVITY LIST FOR PRODUCT UPGRADE PROJECT

- Determine product features
- Acquire prototype materials
- Produce prototype
- Design marketing campaign
- Design graphics
- Conduct marketing
- Perform sales calls

---

asks, "What activity or activities can we start now?" The initial activity is called a **predecessor activity,** which is "the scheduled activity that determines when the logical successor activity can begin or end."[6] The following activity is called a **successor activity,** which is "the schedule activity that follows a predecessor activity, as determined by their logical relationship."[7] The facilitator then places the successor activity after its predecessor and draws an arrow to show the relationship. The team continues with this analysis until all activities have been placed on the work surface with arrows showing the predecessor–successor relationships. At that time, the team should mentally go through the network to ensure that no "dead-ends" are present where the chain of arrows from the project start to end is broken.

Exhibits 7.5 and 7.6 illustrate sequencing activities with the simple example of upgrading a product. The activities are identified in Exhibit 7.5, and their sequence is shown in Exhibit 7.6. The first activity is to determine the product features. As soon as that is done, two other activities can be performed.

This product upgrade example illustrates the basic logic of showing predecessor–successor dependency relationships. Dependencies can be either mandatory (such as "the hole must be dug before concrete can be poured into it") or discretionary (such as "past experience tells us it is better to delay designing product graphics until the marketing plan is complete"). The team needs to include all of the mandatory dependencies and use its judgment on which discretionary dependencies to include. Most teams include no more dependencies than necessary since more dependencies give the project manager fewer choices as the project progresses.

Leads and Lags

Exhibit 7.6 shows the most common type of logical dependency, **finish-to-start (FS),** which is "the logical relationship where initiation of work of the successor activity depends on completion of work of the predecessor activity."[8] That means, in this example, that the marketing plan must be completely designed before the graphics design starts. However, maybe the graphics design could start five work days before the marketing campaign design is complete. This could be modeled as a **lead,** which is "a modification of a logical relationship that allows an acceleration of the successor activity."[9] With this lead of five work days, the arrow connecting design marketing campaign and design graphics would still represent a finish-to-start relationship, only with a five-day overlap during which time people could work on both activities. Leads are helpful if a project needs to be completed quickly since they show how a successor activity can be overlapped with its predecessor instead of waiting until the predecessor is completely finished.

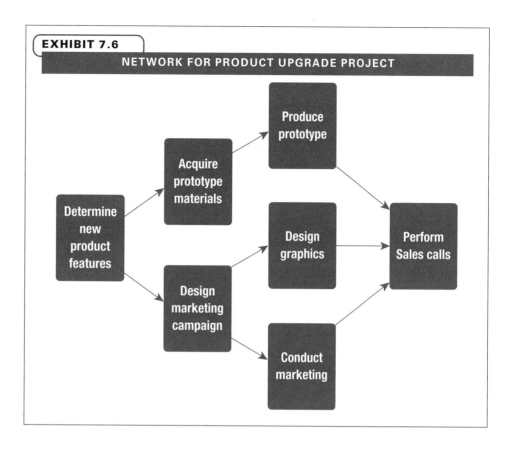

EXHIBIT 7.6

NETWORK FOR PRODUCT UPGRADE PROJECT

Perhaps in the example, the sales people are more effective if the design graphics are completed 10 days before they start performing sales calls so they have extra time to better understand the graphics. This could be shown by a **lag,** "a modification of a logical relationship that directs a delay in the successor activity."[10] In this example, the arrow connecting design graphics and perform sales calls would still represent a finish-to-start relationship, only with a 10-day gap during which no one could work on either activity.

Alternative Dependencies

Other types of relationships exist besides finish-to-start, including the following:

- **Finish-to-finish (FF)** is "the logical relationship where completion of work of the successor activity cannot finish until the completion of work of the predecessor activity."[11] For example, perhaps the graphics could be designed while the marketing campaign is being designed, but could not be completed until the marketing campaign is completed.
- **Start-to-start (SS)** is "the logical relationship where initiation of the successor schedule activity depends on the initiation of the predecessor schedule activity."[12] For example, perhaps the graphics design could not start until the design marketing campaign started.
- **Start-to-finish (SF)** is "the logical relationship where completion of the successor schedule activity is dependent on the initiation of the predecessor schedule activity."[13]

This is the least used relationship. An example is for a project to replace an old system where the new capability must be started before the old one is completely discontinued.

7.7 Estimate Activity Duration

Once the activities have been defined and sequenced, both estimating activity resources and estimating activity durations can take place. **Duration** is "the total number of work periods (not including holidays or other non-work time) required to complete a schedule activity, usually expressed as workdays or workweeks."[14]

It makes sense to identify the people who will work on each activity as soon as possible since they often have the most knowledge about how to actually do the work and how long it will take. Also, the length of time to perform an activity is often dependent upon who will do that work. We discuss resource assignments in Chapter 8.

When estimating how long activities are expected to take, each activity should be evaluated independently. All assumptions and constraints made when estimating should be documented since if one of these changes, it could change the estimate. For the first estimate of each activity, a normal level of labor and equipment and a normal work week should be assumed. If overtime is planned right from the start, the project manager is unlikely to have much flexibility if the schedule needs to be accelerated. For each activity, the output to be created and the skill level required to perform the work should be identified. Any predetermined completion date can be disregarded at this point. Negotiation with a customer or supplier may be necessary, but the project manager needs to understand what is reasonable under normal circumstances before entering those negotiations. When a past project is being used as a guide, the actual time it took to perform the activities should be used, not the time that was initially estimated.

Exhibit 7.7 is a continuation of the product upgrade example with the times estimated for individual activities. Note that the estimated times in this example are in work days. It is important to keep time estimates in the same unit of measure, be it hours, days, weeks, or another measure. Exhibit 7.8 includes suggestions for creating realistic time estimates.

EXHIBIT 7.7

ACTIVITY DURATION ESTIMATE EXAMPLE

TIME ESTIMATE IN WORK DAYS	ACTIVITY NAME
5	Determine new product features
20	Acquire prototype materials
10	Produce prototype
10	Design marketing campaign
10	Design graphics
30	Conduct marketing
25	Perform sales calls

EXHIBIT 7.8

SUGGESTIONS FOR CREATING REALISTIC TIME ESTIMATES

1. Verify all time estimations with the people doing the work. Or, even better, have the people doing the work provide the initial estimates of the activity completion time.
2. Estimate times of completion of work without initial reference to a calendar. Just consider how long you believe each activity will take under normal working conditions.
3. Make sure all time units are identical: work days, work weeks, months (consider time off for company holidays), or another measure.
4. Some people tend to estimate optimistically. Keep in mind the following time constraints:

   - Unexpected meetings
   - Inaccuracy in work instructions
   - Learning curves
   - Interruptions
   - Competing priorities
   - Emergencies and illness
   - Vacation
   - Rework
   - Resources or information not available on time

5. Contrary to point 4, some people estimate pessimistically in order to look good when they bring their project or activities in under budget and under schedule. Try to develop an understanding of the estimator's experience along with their optimistic or pessimistic tendencies and try to encourage balance in estimates.
6. Don't initially worry about *who* is going to do the work and don't worry about the mandatory deadline. Figure out a realistic estimate first, and then figure out what to cut later.
7. When using the actual time from a previous project, adjust the estimate up or down based upon size, familiarity, and complexity differences.

Problems and Remedies in Duration Estimating

Many factors can impact the accuracy of activity duration estimates. A list of potential problems, remedies for those problems, and the chapter in which each is discussed is shown in Exhibit 7.9. These techniques are not mutually exclusive. Many organizations use several of them; however, few organizations use them all. It is important for business students to be aware of these techniques and their potential benefits since each is used by some companies. Many companies customize the mechanics of how they use these techniques.

Learning Curves

The concept behind learning curves is simple: The more times a person performs an activity, the better and faster he or she becomes. The reason this concept is sometimes applied to activity duration estimating is that the rate of improvement can be studied and predicted. Therefore, on types of projects where certain activities are performed many times, a project planner can predict how long it will take each time to perform the activity. The rate of improvement can vary widely depending on many factors, such as:

- How much the culture of the organization stresses continual improvement
- How much skill is involved in the activity
- How complex that activity is
- How much of the activity is dependent on the worker versus dictated by the pace of a machine

EXHIBIT 7.9

ACTIVITY DURATION ESTIMATING PROBLEMS AND REMEDIES

POTENTIAL ACTIVITY DURATION ESTIMATING PROBLEM	REMEDY	CHAPTER
Omissions	Refining scope and WBS	6
	Checklists, templates, devil's advocate	7
	Lessons learned	15
General uncertainty in estimate	Rolling wave planning	6
	Reverse phase schedule	8
	Learning curve	7
	Identify and reduce sources of uncertainty	10, 11
	Manage schedule aggressively	14
Special cause variation	Risk analysis	4, 10
	Resolve risk events	14
Common cause variation	PERT	7
	Monte Carlo	7
	Project buffer	8
Merging (multiple predecessors)	Milestones	4, 7
	Reverse phase schedule	8
	Feeding buffer	8
	Manage float	14
Queuing	Staggering project start dates	2
	Resource leveling	8
	Resource buffer	8
Multi-tasking	Prioritizing projects	2
	Carefully authorize start of non-critical activities	8, 14
Student syndrome (starting late)	Float	7
	Critical path meetings	14
Not reporting early completion of rework	Project culture	3
	Project communications	5
	Contract incentives	11
	Project leadership	13
	Progress reporting	14

Source: Adapted from Larry Leach, "Schedule and Cost Buffer Sizing: How to Account for the Bias Between Project Performance and Your Model," *Project Management Journal* 34 (2) (June 2003): 44.

EXHIBIT 7.10

LEARNING CURVE TABLE				
ACTIVITY	60%	70%	80%	90%
1	100	100	100	100
2	60	70	80	90
4	36	49	64	81
8	21.6	34.3	51.2	72.9

The amount of time necessary to perform an activity is calculated based upon a rate of improvement that occurs every time the number of repetitions doubles. For example, if the learning rate is 80 percent and the first time the activity was performed (by producing the first unit) it took 100 minutes, then after doubling the volume, the second unit would require 80 minutes. To double the repetitions again, the fourth unit would require 64 minutes. The time estimates for each time the activity is performed can be found in learning curve tables such as the one shown in Exhibit 7.10. Notice that the rate of learning is very important since more rapid learning leads to much faster performance times for succeeding times an activity is performed.

For consumers, one result when an industry has a steep learning curve is rapidly declining prices. People expect prices to decline for new electronics and other consumer items. As a project manager, you need to make sure to also plan for the amount of learning that may take place. Further, as a project manager, you need to create and sustain the environment that encourages and expects rapid learning so you can become ever more competitive.

7.8 Develop Project Schedules

You need to complete all of the scheduling processes discussed up to this point even if you use Microsoft Project or another scheduling tool. At this point, you have defined, sequenced, and estimated the duration for all the schedule activities. Now is the time to use all of this information to develop a project schedule. Once the schedule is developed based upon this information, resource needs and availability and cash flow constraints often extend the proposed schedule, while imposed date constraints often suggest the need for schedule compression.

The first major task in developing the project schedule is to identify the **critical path,** which is "the sequence of activities that determines the duration of the project ... the longest path through the project."[15] Because it is the longest sequence of activities, the critical path determines the earliest possible end date of the project. Any time change to an activity on the critical path changes the end date of the entire project. If the project manager changes an activity on the critical path to start at a later date, then the whole project will end at a later date. If the amount of work for an activity on the critical path is increased, then the whole project will end at a later date. If, on the other hand, an activity on the critical path is performed faster than planned, the entire project could be completed sooner. The critical path gets its name not because it is the most critical in terms of cost, technical risk, or any other factor, but because it is most critical in terms of time. Since virtually everyone wants their projects completed at the promised time, the critical path gets a great deal of attention.

The two methods for determining the critical path are the two-pass and enumeration methods. Each uses the same activity identification, duration estimate, and activity sequencing data but processes the data in a different manner. While both determine the critical path, each also determines other useful information.

Two-Pass Method

The two-pass method is used to determine the amount of slack each activity has. To perform this method, two logical passes should be made through the network. The first pass is called the forward pass. The **forward pass** is "the calculation of the early start and early finish dates for the uncompleted portions of all network activities."[16] On the forward pass, the project team starts at the beginning of the project and asks how soon each activity can begin and end. If the project is being scheduled with software, actual calendar dates are used. Often, when calculating the schedule by hand, a team starts at date zero. In other words, the first activity can begin after zero days. To envision this, consider Exhibit 7.11, where all of the previously determined information has been displayed.

A legend is shown in the lower right corner of Exhibit 7.11. This explains each bit of information that is displayed for each activity. For example, the first activity name is

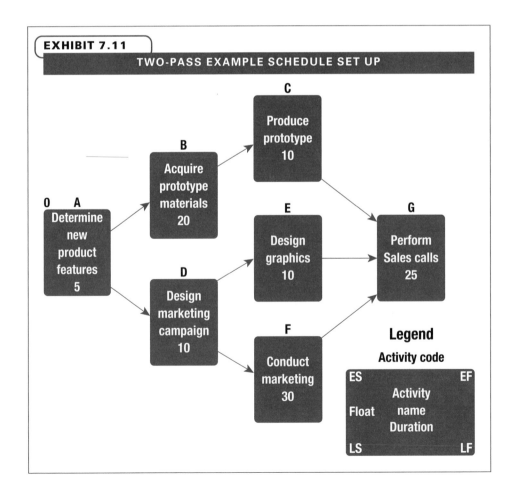

EXHIBIT 7.11

TWO-PASS EXAMPLE SCHEDULE SET UP

Legend

Activity code

ES		EF
	Activity	
Float	name	
	Duration	
LS		LF

"Determine new product features." The estimated duration for this activity is five days. This activity is coded with the letter A. The four corners of each block display four important times for each activity:

- **Early start date (ES)**—"the earliest possible point in time on which uncompleted portions of a schedule activity can start, based upon the schedule network logic, the data date, and any schedule constraints."[17]
- **Early finish date (EF)**—"the earliest possible point in time on which uncompleted portions of a schedule activity can finish, based upon the schedule network logic, the data date, and any schedule constraints."[18]
- **Late start date (LS)**—"the latest possible point in time that a schedule activity may begin, based upon the schedule network logic ... without violating a schedule constraint or delaying the project completion date."[19]
- **Late finish date (LF)**—"the latest possible point in time that a schedule activity may be completed, based upon the schedule network logic ... without violating a schedule constraint or delaying the project completion date."[20]

"Determine new product features," for example, has an early start time of zero since it can begin as soon as the project is authorized.

FIRST OR FORWARD PASS The first pass is then used to calculate the early finish, which is the early start plus the estimated duration (ES + Duration = EF). In this case, $0 + 5 = 5$ means the activity "Determine new product features" can be completed after five days. Each activity that is a successor can start as soon as its predecessor activity is complete. Therefore, the next two activities can each start after five days. To calculate the early finish for each of these activities, add its duration to the early start of 5, for early completion times of 25 and 15, respectively. The difficult part of calculating the first pass comes when an activity has more than one predecessor. For example, "Perform sales calls" cannot begin until *all three preceding activities* ("Produce prototypes," "Design graphics," and "Conduct marketing") are complete. Therefore, its early start is 45. This is true even though "Produce prototypes" and "Design graphics" have earlier finish times, because "Conduct marketing" cannot be completed until day 45. The later time is always taken. The results of the first pass are shown in Exhibit 7.12. Note that the earliest the entire project can be completed is 70 work days.

SECOND OR BACKWARD PASS The second pass is sometimes called the backward pass. The **backward pass** is "the calculation of late finish dates and late start dates for the uncompleted portions of all schedule activities."[21] When performing the backward pass, teams start at the end and work backward asking, "How late can each activity be finished and started?" Unless there is an imposed date, the late finish for the last activity during planning is the same as the early finish date. In our example, we know the earliest we can finish the entire project is 70 days, so we will use that as the late finish date for the last activity. If the activity "Perform sales calls" must end no later than 70 and it takes 25 days, then it must start no later than day 45. In other words, calculate the late start by subtracting the duration from the late finish (LF – duration = LS). The confusing part of calculating the second pass is when there is more than one successor. In Exhibit 7.13, one place this occurs at the first activity, "Determine new product features," since two activities are immediate successors. Enough time must be left for all of the successors, so whichever one must start soonest dictates the late finish date of the predecessor. In this example, "Design marketing campaign" must start no later than after day 5; therefore, five days is the late finish for the first activity.

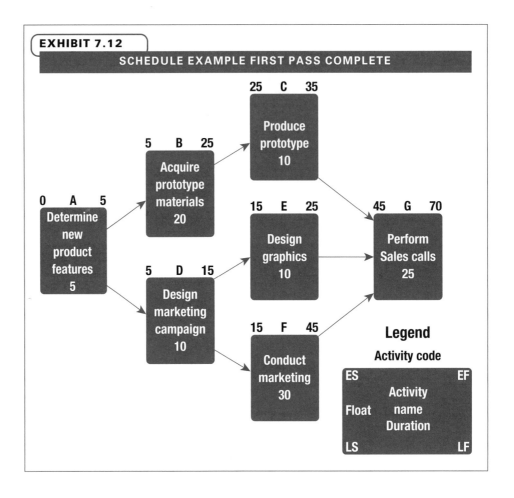

EXHIBIT 7.12

SCHEDULE EXAMPLE FIRST PASS COMPLETE

FLOAT AND THE CRITICAL PATH Once both passes are complete, the early and late start dates for every activity and the amount of time the entire project will take to complete are known. However, the team also wants to know the critical path. This is calculated easily by first determining each activity's float (sometimes float is called slack). Float can be **total float,** which is "the total amount of time a schedule activity may be delayed from its early start date without delaying the project finish date"[22] or **free float,** which is "the amount of time a schedule activity can be delayed without delaying the early start of any immediately following schedule activities."[23] A project manager wants to know how much float each activity has in order to determine where to spend her time and attention. Activities with a great deal of float can be scheduled in a flexible manner and do not cause a manager much concern. Activities with no float or very little float, on the other hand, need to be scheduled very carefully.

Float is calculated by the equation Float = Late start – Early start (Float = LS – ES). The critical path is the sequence of activities from start to finish in the network that have no float. In Exhibit 7.14, activities A, D, F, and G have no float and, therefore, create the critical path. It is typical to mark the critical path in red or in boldface to call attention to it. Activities B, C, and E each have float and are not on the critical path. If activity B is delayed, it will delay the start of activity C; therefore, activity B has total float. While activity B can be delayed up to 10 days without delaying the entire project, any delay to activity B would delay the start of activity C. On the other hand, activities C and E can be delayed

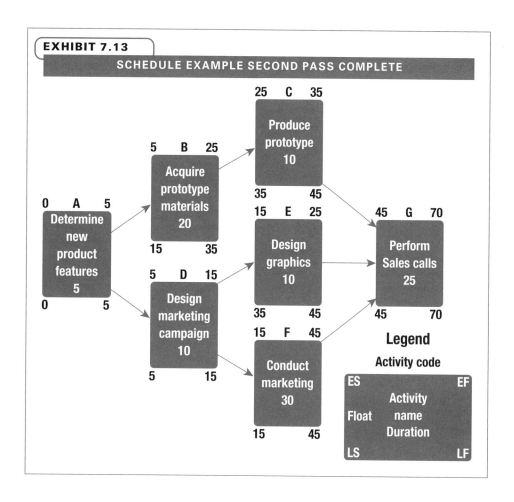

EXHIBIT 7.13

SCHEDULE EXAMPLE SECOND PASS COMPLETE

by 10 and 20 days, respectively, without causing any other activity to be delayed. Therefore, their float is free float—impacting neither the overall project nor any activity in it.

Project managers carefully monitor the critical path activities. They also closely watch activities with little float—think of these as "near-critical" activities. A project with many activities that have little float is not very stable. Even small delays on near-critical activities can change the critical path. Project managers can sometimes "borrow" resources from an activity with plenty of float to use first on an activity that is either already critical or nearly critical. Chapter 8 discusses resource scheduling in detail.

Enumeration Method

The second method of determining the critical path is the enumeration method. To complete this, a person lists or enumerates all of the paths through the network. The advantage of this method is that since all of the paths are identified and timed, if a team needs to compress the project schedule, they will know both the critical path and the other paths that may be nearly critical (or those with very little float). It is imperative to keep track of both critical and near-critical paths when compressing a schedule. In Exhibit 7.15, three paths are identified and the total duration for each is calculated. ADFG is the critical path with an expected duration of 70 days, just as was determined with the two-pass method. Now, however, we also know that path ABCG is expected to take 60 days (10 less than the critical path), and path ADEG is expected to take 50 days (20 less than the critical path).

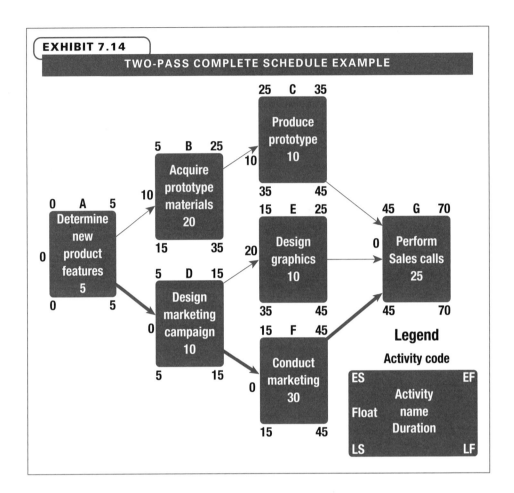

EXHIBIT 7.14

TWO-PASS COMPLETE SCHEDULE EXAMPLE

7.9 Uncertainty in Project Schedules

On some projects, it is easy to estimate durations of activities with confidence. On others, so many uncertainties exist that managers have far less confidence in their ability to accurately estimate. However, project managers still need to tell sponsors and clients how long they believe a project will take and then be held accountable for meeting those dates. One common strategy for handling this potential problem is to construct the best schedule possible and then manage the project very closely. A different strategy is to estimate a range of possible times each individual activity may take and then see what impact that has on the entire schedule. PERT and Monte Carlo are two methods sometimes used for this approach.

Program Evaluation and Review Technique

Program evaluation and review technique was developed during the 1950s to better understand how variability in the individual activity durations impacts the entire project schedule. To use PERT, a project team starts by sequencing the activities into a network as described above. However, instead of creating one estimate for the time to complete each activity, they would create three estimates: optimistic, most likely, and pessimistic. For example, the first activity, "Determine new product features," will most likely take five days, but it could take as little as four days if everything works well and as long as

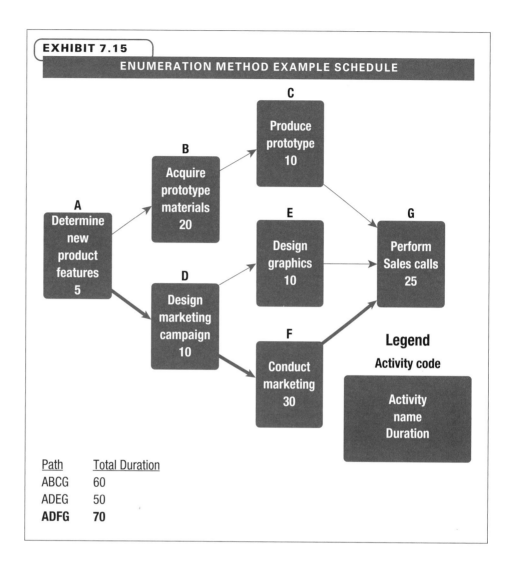

EXHIBIT 7.15

ENUMERATION METHOD EXAMPLE SCHEDULE

Path	Total Duration
ABCG	60
ADEG	50
ADFG	**70**

12 days if a variety of things interfere. The person scheduling the project then calculates the estimated time to perform each activity as shown in Exhibit 7.16 using the following equation:

$$\text{Estimated time} = \frac{\text{Optimistic} + 4(\text{Most likely}) + \text{Pessimistic}}{6}$$

Therefore, for the first activity, the estimated time $= \dfrac{4 + 4(5) + 12}{6} = 6$

The primary advantage of PERT is that it helps everyone realize how much uncertainty exists in the project schedule. When people use single time estimates, sometimes there is a tendency to believe that the estimates foretell exactly what will happen. On many projects, a great deal of uncertainty exists, and PERT helps to make this visible. In addition to making the overall uncertainty more visible, calculations often show that the expected time is actually longer than the most likely time. That is because if many things go very well on an activity, generally only a little time can be saved, but if many things go terribly wrong, a great deal of time can be lost.

EXHIBIT 7.16

PERT TIME ESTIMATE EXAMPLE

ACTIVITY	OPTIMISTIC	MOST LIKELY	PESSIMISTIC	EXPECTED
Determine new product features	4	5	12	6
Acquire prototype materials	16	20	30	21
Produce prototype	8	10	12	10
Design marketing campaign	9	10	14	10.5
Design graphics	6	10	20	11
Conduct marketing	28	30	50	33
Perform sales calls	20	25	30	25

However, using PERT involves difficulties. First, it is often hard enough to create *one* estimate of how long an activity will take, so it takes even more effort (and therefore money) to create *three* estimates. Second, there is no guarantee on how good any of the three estimates are. Third, PERT can underestimate the risk of a schedule running long because it does not accurately address when two or more activities both need to be accomplished before a third one can begin.[24]

Since PERT highlights uncertainty in project duration, its logic is useful to project managers. However, since it has some problems, only a few project managers actually use it to fully calculate and monitor project schedules. Some project managers informally use three time estimates for a few key activities on the critical path to get a sense for the amount of uncertainty and to better understand the activities that need close monitoring. Other project managers who want to understand the potential variation use Monte Carlo simulation. Students of project management need to be aware that both PERT and Monte Carlo simulations are sometimes used to help understand uncertainty in project schedules.

Monte Carlo Simulation

Monte Carlo analysis is "a technique that computes, or iterates, the project cost or project schedule many times using input values selected at random from probability distributions of possible costs or durations, to calculate a distribution of possible total project costs or completion dates."[25] Monte Carlo is more flexible than PERT in that an entire range of possible time estimates can be used for any activity. The project schedule is calculated many times (perhaps 1,000 or more), and each time the estimate for a particular activity is generated based upon the likelihood of that time as determined by the project manager. For example, suppose a project manager estimated that for a particular activity there was a 10 percent chance of taking five days, a 30 percent chance of taking six days, a 40 percent chance of taking seven days, and the remaining 20 percent chance of taking eight days. Then for each 100 times the computer generated a project schedule, when it came to that activity, 10 times it would choose five days, 30 times it would choose six days, 40 times it would choose seven days, and 20 times it would choose eight days. The output from the computer would include a distribution of how often the project would be expected to take each possible length of time. Many other possible outputs can also be generated from Monte Carlo simulations.

One advantage of Monte Carlo analysis is the flexibility it provides. This allows more realistic estimates. Another advantage is the extent of information it can provide regarding individual activities, the overall project, and different paths through the project that may become critical.

A disadvantage of Monte Carlo is the amount of time necessary to estimate not just a most likely duration for each activity, but an entire range of possible outcomes. Another disadvantage is that special software and skill are necessary to effectively use Monte Carlo. This disadvantage is not as large as it once was because more software is being developed and most students are learning at least the fundamentals of simulation in statistics or operations classes.

A project manager needs to decide when some of the more specialized techniques are worth the extra effort for a project. The old saying that a person should spend $100 to save $1,000, but should not spend $1,000 to save $100 applies. If the savings on a project from using techniques such as learning curves, PERT, or Monte Carlo are significant, project managers should consider using one of them. If not, they should create the best estimates possible without the specialized techniques, incorporate risk management by carefully identifying and planning for specific risks as discussed in Chapter 10, and manage the project schedule very carefully as discussed in Chapter 14.

These specialized techniques are sometimes used in research and development (R&D) projects. However, some R&D projects do not need this level of sophistication. Exhibit 7.17 shows an actual R&D project schedule used by D. D. Williamson of Louisville, Kentucky, when a Chinese customer asked it to develop a new product somewhat different than any it had previously developed. Once D. D. Williamson decided to take the job, it developed and communicated the project schedule to all stakeholders both in its company and the customer's company within the first week.

Australian researchers have discovered that two primary causes of late delivery of IT projects are variance in time to complete individual work activities and multiple dependencies for some activities. Suggestions for overcoming these two problems are shown in Exhibit 7.18.

EXHIBIT 7.17

NEW PRODUCT DEVELOPMENT SCHEDULE IN CHINA EXAMPLE

Week one—Request is received from the customer for a product that is darker than anything we have in our current offering. Our sales manager forwards the request to our VP sales and our R&D department. A quick review of the potential price versus cost of materials is completed by the VP sales (with finance input), and the product is deemed saleable at an acceptable margin.

Week two—A trial cook in our "baby cooker" is conducted by our R&D department. Within two attempts, a product that is within the customer requested specs is produced. An additional trial is conducted to quickly check repeatability. The trial product is express shipped to the customer and to our China facility for comparison purposes.

Week three—The formulation and related instructions for cooking are communicated to our China operations with a "red sheet" process. China has anticipated the receipt of this red sheet, and is able to schedule time in production within a week.

Week four—The initial red sheet production is successful and passes the specification tests in China and in Louisville.

Week five—Customer confirms purchase order and the first shipment is sent. The product contributes significantly to the revenues and profitability of the China facility. Success!

Key factors—Strong communication between all the players and a clear understanding of the customer expectations up front.

Source: Elaine Gravatte, D. D. Williamson.

EXHIBIT 7.18

INITIATIVES TO IMPROVE ON-TIME SCHEDULE DELIVERY

CAUSE OF LATE DELIVERY	INITIATIVE	EXPLANATION
Activity variance	Increase activity transparency	Allows for better planning
	Increase user participation	Ensures that the product delivered meets the user needs
	Reduce project size	Ensures that estimates for tasks are more accurate
	Manage expectations, e.g., set realistic goals by drawing from "outside views"	Mitigates optimism bias and misrepresentation
	Use packaged software	Provides a standard within which to develop the system
Activity dependence	De-scope	Reduces the number of dependencies
	Improve requirements definition	Ensures that there is no confusion over what is to be developed and when
	Reduce activity coupling	If activity links are reduced then dependencies exert less influence
	Stage projects (incremental development or iterative development)	Reduces delay bias by minimizing multitasking, merging, queuing (i.e., reduces the dependencies)

Source: Vlasic, Anthony and Li Liu, "Why Information Systems Projects Are Always Late," *Proceedings Project Management Institute Research and Education Conference 2010* (Oxon Hill, MD, July 2010).

7.10 Show the Project Schedule on a Gantt Chart

The discussion in this chapter so far has been how to determine the project schedule. While this is necessary, it can be confusing to show people a network diagram. A much easier to understand tool for communicating a project schedule is a Gantt or bar chart. A **Gantt chart** is "a graphic display of schedule related information."[26]

The Gantt chart is a horizontal bar chart showing each activity's early start and finish. The simplest Gantt charts show a bar for each activity stretched out over a time line. The units of time are the units the project team used in creating the schedule, whether that is hours, days, weeks, or another measure A Gantt chart is shown in Exhibit 7.19. It is easy to understand when each activity should be performed. However, the basic Gantt chart does not show other useful information such as critical path, predecessor–successor relationships, late start and finish dates, and so forth. These can all be easily displayed on a Gantt chart that is developed using scheduling software such as Microsoft Project. The instructions for using MS Project to create and print Gantt charts are covered in the following section.

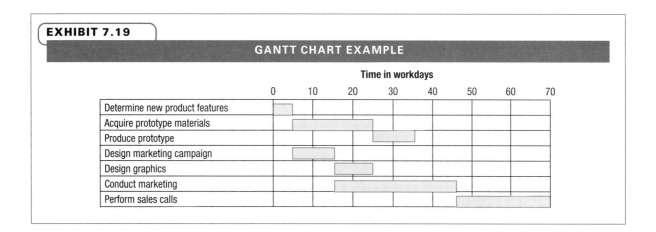

EXHIBIT 7.19

GANTT CHART EXAMPLE

7.11 Using Microsoft Project for Critical Path Schedules

Remember that five different things can limit how fast a project can be completed: the logical order of the activities, the duration of each activity, the number of key resources available when needed, any imposed dates, and cash flow. It is helpful to use MS Project to construct schedules by considering each of these limitations in order. That is, first the logical order is determined, and then duration estimates are applied. It is often helpful to confirm the logical order first because if people also apply the estimated durations right away, MS Project generates dates that may not please some decision makers. You may secure approval of a more realistic schedule if you allow people to first concentrate on the order of work and then on how long each activity takes.

This section begins with setting up the project schedule. Then logical order and activity duration estimates are included in the section on building the network diagram. Finally, this section covers understanding the critical path and displaying and printing the emerging schedule. Resource limits and imposed dates are shown in Chapter 8 and cash flow is shown in Chapter 9.

Set Up the Project Schedule

Setting up the project schedule includes defining your organization's holidays, turning off the change highlighting function, and understanding data types.

DEFINE YOUR ORGANIZATION'S HOLIDAYS MS Project has a calendar system to define working and nonworking time: a default project calendar and a resource calendar for each resource. To avoid unrealistic schedules, you must define holidays in the project calendar and resource vacations in resource calendars. The default project calendar has all days, except Saturday and Sunday, defined as eight-hour working days. The working hours during the day are 8:00 to 12:00 and 1:00 to 5:00. No holidays are defined. Holidays are blocked out by defining holidays as nonworking days. All project calendar content is copied into all resource calendars. Resource calendars are used to block out vacation days and other resource-specific nonworking days. Resource calendars are then used to determine when a resource assignment can be scheduled. If there is no resource assignment, then the project calendar is used to determine scheduling.

Use the following steps to change a working day to nonworking, as shown in Exhibit 7.20. The legend explains the day shading:

1. On the Project tab, click Change Working Time.
2. In the For Calendar: box, enter Standard (Project Calendar) if not displayed.
3. Move to the month and year using the scroll bar to the right of the calendar display.
4. Click on the day to change.
5. Click the Exceptions tab, then click an empty row.
6. Enter a description in the Name column.
7. Click another cell in the same row to review the results.
8. Repeat these steps until the organizational holidays are defined.
9. Deleting a row restores the previous definition.
10. Click OK.

EXHIBIT 7.20

STANDARD CALENDAR WITH TWO HOLIDAYS (1/3 AND 1/17) PLUS A HALF DAY (1/26) AND A WORKING SATURDAY (1/22)

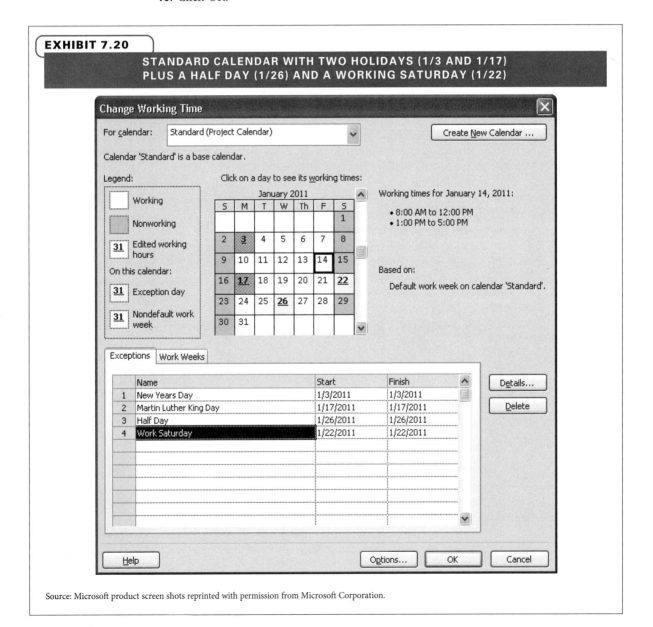

Source: Microsoft product screen shots reprinted with permission from Microsoft Corporation.

To change the working time for a day, as shown in Exhibit 7.21:

1. Select the day, enter a description, and then click Details …
2. Click Working Time and modify the From: and To: values.
3. Click OK twice.

To change a nonworking day to working:

1. Select the day and click Details…
2. Click Nonworking and click OK twice.

TURN OFF CHANGE HIGHLIGHTING MS Project automatically shows the impact of any changes you make to a project schedule. While this is useful when managing an on-going project, it can be distracting when making additions and changes to a preliminary schedule. It can be helpful to turn this function off until the project schedule is baselined (described in Chapter 11). You will then want to see the impact of all changes as shown in Exhibit 7.22.

1. Click the Task tab.
2. On the Format tab, Text Styles, Item to Change, enter Changed Cells.
3. In Background Color, enter White.
4. Click OK.

To restore the highlighting, in Background Color enter Aqua Lighter 80%.

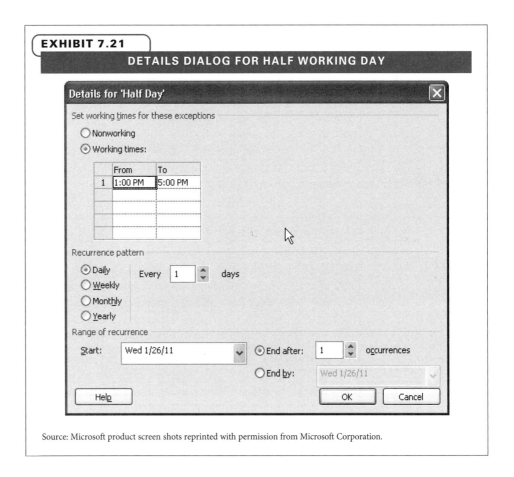

EXHIBIT 7.21

DETAILS DIALOG FOR HALF WORKING DAY

Source: Microsoft product screen shots reprinted with permission from Microsoft Corporation.

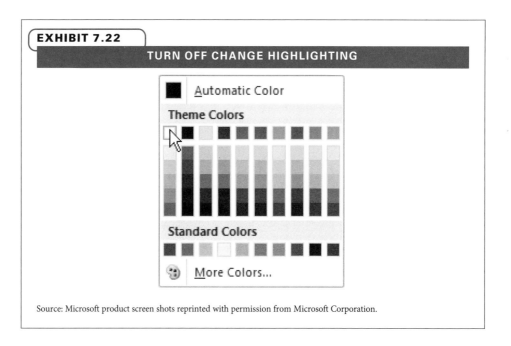

UNDERSTANDING TYPES OF PROJECT DATA MS Project works with three types of data: task, resource, and assignment.

Task Data Included in this category are two kinds of information using the same display fields and formats: WBS data and task data. MS Project refers to individual work activities as tasks and WBS elements as summary rows. MS Project marks these differently. WBS text is bolded, while task data are not. A WBS graphic is a black bar with a diamond shape hanging down from each end. The default for a critical path task is a red bar, and a blue bar is used for a noncritical path task. Neither has a diamond on the end. In this book, critical tasks will be shown in color, and noncritical tasks will be muted grey.

Some WBS element fields contain roll-up data that summarize lower-level elements. For example, the duration value in a WBS element is the number of working days in the standard calendar bounded by the start and finish dates for that element. A Gantt chart with WBS and task data is shown in Exhibit 7.23.

Resource Data While a resource is often a person, sometimes a critical machine is also defined as a resource. Each resource is described with information required for control. This should be done before the resource is assigned to a task in order to avoid the default max units value (an unlikely resource availability of 100 percent). Resource data are used by MS Project to determine assignment load, work, and cost. The resource name field is used to identify the resource wherever assignment information is displayed.

Assignment Data Assignment units, work, and cost data are calculated or set when a resource is assigned to a task. The task duration, work values, and cost values are also calculated at the time of the assignment. Assignment data are also calculated when a resource's work, units, or duration values are changed. Assignment data may be viewed in both the Task Usage view and the Resource Usage view, as well as in several forms. A time-phased display is part of these views.

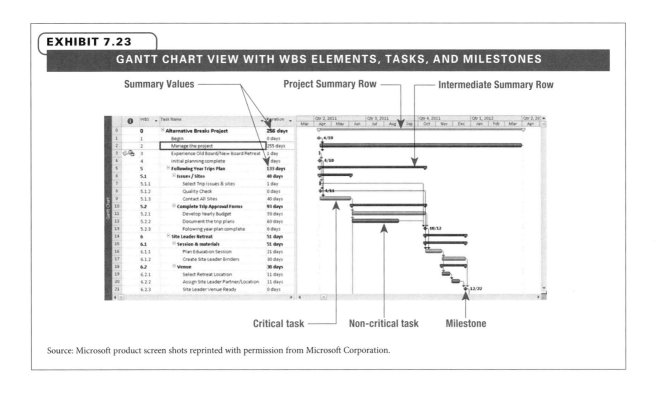

EXHIBIT 7.23

GANTT CHART VIEW WITH WBS ELEMENTS, TASKS, AND MILESTONES

Source: Microsoft product screen shots reprinted with permission from Microsoft Corporation.

Build the Logical Network Diagram

These instructions build upon those in Chapter 4 for initiating a project and Chapter 6 for setting up a WBS. The six steps to create a realistic logical network diagram in MS Project are as follows:

1. Enter tasks and milestones.
2. Understand task dependencies.
3. Define dependencies using a task table and mouse.
4. Define or delete a dependency series.
5. Understand network diagram presentation.
6. Verify the accuracy of the network diagram.

STEP 1: ENTER TASKS AND MILESTONES Tasks can be added with an insert function as follows:

1. Click on the Id field to select the row below where the new row will be.
2. On the Task tab, Insert group, click Insert Task.
3. In the Task Name field, enter the desired name of the added task.
4. Selecting more than one row results in that number of blank rows being inserted.
5. Enter any additional task(s) as above.
6. Inserted rows assume the summary level of the row above the insert location.

STEP 2: UNDERSTAND TASK DEPENDENCIES A task dependency definition includes both a logical link type (finish-to-start, start-to-start, finish-to-finish, or start-to-finish) and any associated lead or lag value. The default link type is finish-to-start. The default lead or lag value is zero days. Both of these defaults were used in the product-upgrade example earlier in this chapter. Task dependencies may be established and viewed graphically in the Network Diagram view and in several Gantt views (Detail Gantt, Gantt Chart, Leveling Gantt, and Tracking Gantt).

STEP 3: DEFINE DEPENDENCIES USING A TASK TABLE AND MOUSE Dependencies can easily be defined using the following four steps.

1. Click on the Id (task name) field to select the predecessor task row.
2. Press and hold Ctl while selecting the successor task.
3. On the Task tab, Schedule group, click on Link Tasks.
4. Delete a dependency definition by again selecting both tasks, and then on the Task tab, Schedule group, clicking on Unlink Tasks.

STEP 4: DEFINE OR DELETE A DEPENDENCY SERIES A series of dependencies can be easily defined by the following three steps.

1. Select (by dragging) all of the tasks to be linked in a series.
2. On the Task tab, Schedule group, click on Link Tasks.
3. Delete the links in a set of tasks by selecting the tasks, and on the Task tab, Schedule group, clicking on Unlink Tasks.

STEP 5: UNDERSTAND NETWORK DIAGRAM PRESENTATION The project network diagram is presented in the conventional Network Diagram view. This view shows all tasks, milestones, and WBS elements (summaries) as described in the following steps and shown in Exhibit 7.24.

1. On the Task tab, View group, click the arrow and then enter Network Diagram.
2. On the File tab, click Print, then choose appropriate settings and click the Print control.

Because of the space required by this format, it is best to print the view on a large paper size. The logical links can also be seen in Gantt Chart view as link lines connecting Gantt bars, as shown in Exhibit 7.23.

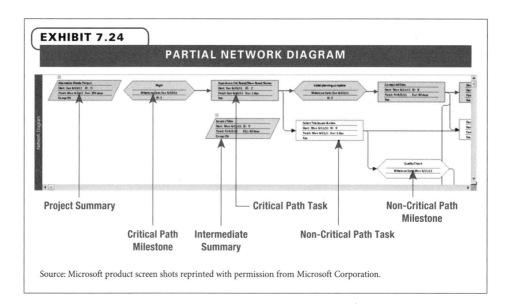

EXHIBIT 7.24

PARTIAL NETWORK DIAGRAM

Project Summary

Critical Path Task

Non-Critical Path Milestone

Critical Path Milestone

Intermediate Summary

Non-Critical Path Task

Source: Microsoft product screen shots reprinted with permission from Microsoft Corporation.

STEP 6: VERIFY THE ACCURACY OF THE NETWORK DIAGRAM The following steps are useful when verifying the accuracy of the network diagram.

1. Print the network diagram.
2. Find all tasks with no predecessor and justify each.
3. Find all tasks with no successor and justify each.
4. Verify the logic (work flow).
5. Look for opportunities to do activities in parallel or to at least overlap activities.
6. Justify or repair any gaps in the critical path.

Network diagrams will be easier to understand if all logical links are between tasks and not between tasks and summary bars.

Understand the Critical Path

Once the logic of the network is confirmed, it is time to develop and understand the critical path. This is accomplished by first assigning duration estimates and then by instructing MS Project to identify the critical path.

ASSIGN DURATION ESTIMATES The first principle to keep in mind is to use the same unit of time for each task. Mixing up hours, days, or weeks will probably create confusion. If days are used, they should always be used. The default time unit is days, so these instructions use days. The second principle is to only assign duration estimates to tasks and milestones. Milestones consume zero time; they reflect a moment in time when something is complete. MS Project calculates the duration for WBS summaries based upon the durations selected for the tasks that comprise each summary.

To assign the duration to a task, click the Duration cell of the task and enter the duration value. If days are being used, an adjustment can be made up or down with the arrows. A number can also be deleted and then another number typed in the cell. If a milestone needs to be shown, zero duration should be assigned to it. To create a milestone, enter zero in the Duration cell of the milestone.

IDENTIFY THE CRITICAL PATH In most graphical task views, MS Project marks Gantt bars of critical path tasks and network diagram task nodes in red. But, as shipped, MS Project does not display the critical path marking on the Gantt Chart graphical view. This marking is easily added. To do so, click the Task tab and then on the Format tab, Bar Styles group, click Critical Tasks. Then click OK.

If you want to monitor near-critical paths, adjust the value of the "Tasks are critical if slack is less than or equal to" setting on the Tools/Options dialog box (Tools/Options/ Calculation tab).

Display and Print Schedules with MS Project

In the contemporary work environment, many people are accustomed to e-mailing work associates a file and having the associate open the file to read it. This works very well with word processing and spreadsheets. Often, it does not work with project scheduling software, however, because in many organizations only a few people have copies of the software. Therefore, it is useful to be able to create an output that can be saved as a PDF or printed and easily read.

A Microsoft Project schedule example is shown in Exhibit 7.23. Several things can be noted in this example. First, the critical path is clearly highlighted. Second, calendar dates are used, and the weekends are shown in grey with no work scheduled. Third, the activities are listed in a WBS with WBS code shown in the left-most column. The overall project and each summary level are shown by a black bar with diamonds on the ends.

Using page setup, timescale, and a bit of editing, it is easy to create a schedule people can understand. As an older reviewer of project schedules, your author adheres to the 40-40 rule of schedule displays. More than 40 lines per page should not be shown if anyone who needs to read it is over 40 years old! Some people even insist on no more than 35 rows per page. This will help keep your sponsor and clients happy.

Summary

Project schedules are created by listing all of the activities that need to be performed. This information should be derived from the work packages at the lowest level of the work breakdown structure. Each work package may require one or more activities to be completed to create the required deliverable. Each activity needs to be defined in enough detail that it can be assigned to one person who can accurately determine how it will be accomplished and by whom, estimate how long it will take and how much it will cost, and then be held accountable to ensure it is accomplished.

Once all of the activities have been defined, they need to be sequenced—that is, the team must determine which activities must go first (predecessors) and which activities depend on others to be accomplished before they can start (successors). Many people find that determining these relationships is easiest with Post-it Notes and a large work space.

A person on the planning team needs to estimate how long each activity will take. This is greatly dependent on who will do the work, which is discussed in the next chapter. Care should be taken when creating the estimates since some people tend to be optimistic and

many things can interfere with the ability to work on a specific activity. Other people tend to pessimistically pad their estimates to make sure they can finish early and look good.

The three time management processes described above—activity definition, activity sequencing, and activity duration estimating—need to be accomplished even if scheduling software will be used. The next step is schedule development. Some teams use Post-it Notes to develop this schedule manually by making two logical passes through the network to determine both the earliest and latest any activity can be started and ended. However, this requires tedious calculations and is greatly simplified by use of software such as MS Project.

Schedule development is an iterative process. Once an initial schedule is developed, it needs to be compared to resource limits, imposed dates, and cash flow. Often, a sponsor or customer wants the project sooner than the original schedule suggests. In these cases, many approaches may be considered to expedite the schedule. These schedule adjustments will be considered in Chapters 8 and 9.

Key Terms from the *PMBOK® Guide*

activity, 170
Define activities, 170
Sequence activities, 171
Estimate activity resources, 171
Estimate activity durations, 171
Develop schedule, 171
Control schedule, 171
critical path method (CPM), 171
precedence diagramming method (PDM), 172
predecessor activity, 178
successor activity, 178
finish-to-start (FS), 178
lead, 178
lag, 179
Finish-to-finish (FF), 179

Start-to-start (SS), 179
Start-to-finish (SF), 179
Duration, 180
critical path, 183
forward pass, 184
Early start date (ES), 185
Early finish date (EF), 185
Late start date (LS), 185
Late finish date (LF), 185
backward pass, 185
total float, 186
free float, 186
Monte Carlo analysis, 190
Gantt chart, 192

Chapter Review Questions

1. Before a project schedule can be created, a(n) _____ must first be made.
2. List four network-based methods that can be used to create a project schedule.
3. List and discuss four of the potential limitations for project schedules.
4. A(n) _____ is a significant event in the life-span of a project.
5. A lead is a change in the logical relationship that results in the _____ of the successor activity.
6. If a painted wall must dry for four hours before work can continue, the result is a delay in the successor activity. The wait for the paint to dry is an example of a(n) _____.
7. A professor cannot grade his students' exams until the students have completed taking the test. What kind of relationship is this?
   a. Start-to-start relationship
   b. Start-to-finish
   c. Finish-to-finish
8. When determining an activity's duration, project managers typically include weekends, evening, and holidays in the duration time. True or false?
9. When calculating a project's duration, it is best to consider the time it will take to complete each activity individually. True or false?
10. One potential problem that can occur with activity duration estimating is having omissions. List three potential remedies for this problem.
11. According to the learning curve, performing an activity frequently results in it taking a(n) _____ amount of time to complete the same activity in the future.
12. What two methods can be used to determine the critical path of a schedule?
13. If an activity on the critical path falls behind schedule, what effect will this have on the entire project?
14. The enumeration method focuses only on one critical path. True or false?
15. A Gantt chart shows each activity's _____ and _____.
16. What is a lag in a project schedule?

Discussion Questions

1. List the main characteristics of a schedule activity. Why is each important?
2. Describe the difference between an activity resource estimate and an activity duration estimate.
3. Explain the 40-40 rule.
4. Describe four ways in which a project's schedule is limited and how to deal with each limitation.
5. Describe how a WBS and a schedule work together.
6. List at least four potential problems in creating accurate duration estimates for activities. Describe at least two methods for dealing with each potential problem.

Exercises

1. Label the box below to create a two-pass schedule legend.

2. If the learning rate is 60 percent and the first time the activity was performed took 200 minutes, the second time performing the activity should take _____ minutes and the fourth time should take _____ minutes.
3. In the example below, label which activities are predecessors and which activities are successors.

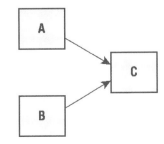

4. Create a logical network using the activities listed below.
   Planting a Flower Bed
   • Purchase flowers, potting soil, and tools.
   • Water flowers.
   • Prepare soiling by weeding and adding fertilizer.
   • Plant flowers.
   • Dig hole.

5. Calculate early start, early finish, late start, late finish, and float for each of the activities in the network below. The duration of each activity is given.

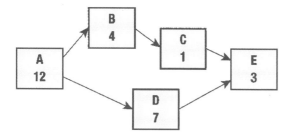

6. Identify the critical path for the network in Exercise 5. How long should the project take?

7. Given the information on the CD for Problem 07.07, create the project schedule network. Then, using the two-pass method, calculate and show the early and late starts and float for each activity and the critical path.

8. Given the information on the CD for Problem 07.08, create the project schedule network. Then, using the enumeration method, calculate and show all of the paths through the network. Show how long each path will take. Identify the critical path.

9. Using the data on the CD for Problem 07.09, schedule the problem in MS Project. Display and print the schedule in a Gantt chart showing the critical path and the predecessors.

10. Using the data on the CD for Problem 07.10, schedule the problem in MS Project. Display and print the schedule in a Gantt chart showing the critical path and the predecessors.

11. Using the information on the CD for Problem 07.07, input the data into MS Project. Display and print the schedule in Gantt chart format as shown in Exhibit 7.19.

12. Using the information on the CD for Problem 07.08, input the data into MS Project. Display and print the schedule in Gantt chart format as shown in Exhibit 7.19.

PMBOK® Guide Questions

1. The Midlands Company is eager to develop a project schedule. They have already completed drafts of the scope statement and communications plan. What else do they need before they are ready to proceed?
   a. cost estimates
   b. nothing; they are ready to proceed
   c. requirements matrix
   d. time estimates

2. Which of the following relate to an activity?
   a. It is a component of work performed during a project.
   b. It has clear starting and ending points.
   c. Regardless of the number of people working on it, only one should be held accountable.
   d. All of the above.

3. Which of the following is *not* one of PMI's six work processes?
   a. estimate personnel requirements
   b. develop schedule
   c. sequence activities
   d. estimate activity durations

4. Another name for activity on node (AON), the most commonly used project diagramming model, is:
   a. arrow diagramming method (ADM)
   b. precedence diagramming method (PDM)
   c. activity on arrow (AOA)
   d. none of the above

5. Nick has the time, money, and physical resources to finish his project. However, there is only one trained engineer assigned to the project team, and Nick needs at least three. Which of the five limiting factors will influence Nick's project schedule?
   a. logical order of activities
   b. imposed dates
   c. cash flow
   d. key resources available

Example Project

Take the WBS you have already developed. Define all of the activities that will be necessary to create each deliverable in your WBS. Create a schedule for your sample project. First, create the schedule by hand using Post-it Notes and then put the information into MS Project. Create a printed copy of the schedule on a

Gantt chart with no more than 40 lines per page. Do not use more pages than necessary. Sponsors do not like to flip pages. Be sure to include all of the summary rows (including the first row for the project title) and any key milestones. Make sure the critical path is easy to see.

References

A Guide to the Project Management Body of Knowledge (PMBOK® Guide). 4th ed. (Newtown Square, PA: Project Management Institute, 2008).

Douglas, Edward E. III, "Schedule Constructability Review," *AACE International Transactions* (2008) PS.16.1–PS.16.6.

Gray, Neal S., "Secrets to Creating the Elusive 'Accurate Estimate,'" *PM Network,* 15 (8) (August 2001): 54–57.

Haugan, Gregory T., *Project Planning and Scheduling* (Vienna, VA: Management Concepts, Inc., 2002).

Hulett, David T., "Project Schedule Risk Analysis: Monte Carlo Simulation or PERT?" *PM Network* 14 (2) (February 2000): 43–47.

Hulett, David T., "Project Schedule Risk Assessment," *Project Management Journal* 26 (1) (March 1995): 21–31.

Kelley, J. F., "Critical Path Planning and Scheduling: Mathematical Basis," *Operations Research* 9 (3) (1961): 296–320.

Leach, Larry, "Schedule and Cost Buffer Sizing: How to Account for the Bias Between Project Performance and Your Model," *Project Management Journal* 34 (2) (June 2003): 34–47.

Lukas, Joseph A., "Top Ten Scheduling Mistakes and How to Prevent Them," *AACE International Transactions* (2009): PS.10.1–PS.10.11.

Macomber, Hal, "The Last Planner System*—Roles, Reliability, and Reform," http://www.leanproject.com/lps_roles_reliability_reform.html, accessed December 22, 2006.

Malcolm, D. G. et al., "Applications of a Technique for R and D Program Evaluation (PERT)," *Operations Research* 1 (5) (1959): 646–669.

McGary, Rudd, *Passing the PMP Exam: How to Take It and Pass It* (Upper Saddle River, NJ: Prentice Hall PTR, 2006).

Moder, J. J., C. R. Phillips, and E. W. Davis, *Project Management with CPM, PERT, and Precedence Diagramming,* 3rd ed. (New York: Van Nostrand Reinhold, 1983).

Moder, Joseph J., "Network Techniques in Project Management," in David I. Cleland and William R. King, eds., *Project Management Handbook,* 2nd ed. (New York: Van Nostrand Reinhold, 1998): 324–373.

Mulcahy, Rita, *PMP Exam Prep: Rita's Course in a Book for Passing the PMP Exam,* 5th ed. (RMC Publications, Inc., 2005).

Salem, O., J. Solomon, A. Genaidy, and M. Luegrring, "Site Implementation and Assessment of Lean Construction Techniques," *Lean Construction Journal* 2 (2) (October 2005): 1–21.

Vlasic, Anthony and Li Liu, "Why Information Systems Projects Are Always Late," *Proceedings Project Management Institute Research and Education Conference 2010* (Oxon Hill, MD, July 2010).

Waterworth, Christopher J., "Relearning the Learning Curve: A Review of the Derivation and Applications of Learning-Curve Theory," *Project Management Journal* 31 (1) (March 2000): 24–31.

Webster, Francis W. Jr., "They Wrote the Book: The Early Literature of Modern Project Management," *PM Network* 13 (8) (August 1999): 59–62.

Endnotes

1. *PMBOK® Guide* 426.
2. Adapted from Gregory T. Haugan, *Project Planning and Scheduling* (Vienna, VA: Management Concepts, Inc., 2002): 52.
3. Adapted from *PMBOK® Guide* 129.
4. *PMBOK® Guide* 431.
5. *PMBOK® Guide* 441.
6. Ibid.

7. *PMBOK® Guide* 450.

8. *PMBOK® Guide* 435.

9. *PMBOK® Guide* 437.

10. *PMBOK® Guide* 437.

11. Ibid.

12. *PMBOK® Guide* 450.

13. Ibid.

14. *PMBOK® Guide* 433.

15. *PMBOK® Guide* 431.

16. *PMBOK® Guide* 435.

17. *PMBOK® Guide* 433.

18. Ibid.

19. *PMBOK® Guide* 437.

20. Ibid.

21. *PMBOK® Guide* 427.

22. *PMBOK® Guide* 451.

23. *PMBOK® Guide* 435.

24. David T. Hulett, "Project Schedule Risk Assessment," *Project Management Journal* 26 (1) (March 1995): 21–31; and David T. Hulett, "Project Schedule Risk Analysis: Monte Carlo Simulation or PERT?" *PM Network* 14 (2) (February 2000): 43–47.

25. *PMBOK® Guide* 438.

26. *PMBOK® Guide* 436.

PROJECT MANAGEMENT *IN ACTION*

Project Schedule Emphasizing Critical Path Activities

A social service agency that is expanding developed a leadership development project so they could increase the capacity of their employees. Several things can be noted from the partial schedule shown in Exhibit 7.25. First, the top row shows the summary for the entire project. Second, intermediate summaries are shown. None of these summaries are collapsed, but they could be to show more of the project at a glance. Critical ac-

tivities are shown in color. A person can read the dates at the top of the page. The activities are all connected with arrows showing their predecessor relationships. Again, some people prefer to include this and others prefer to keep the Gantt charts as simple and clean as possible. Project managers can show or hide as much detail as their sponsors and other stakeholders wish.

EXHIBIT 7.25

LEADERSHIP DEVELOPMENT PROJECT SCHEDULE

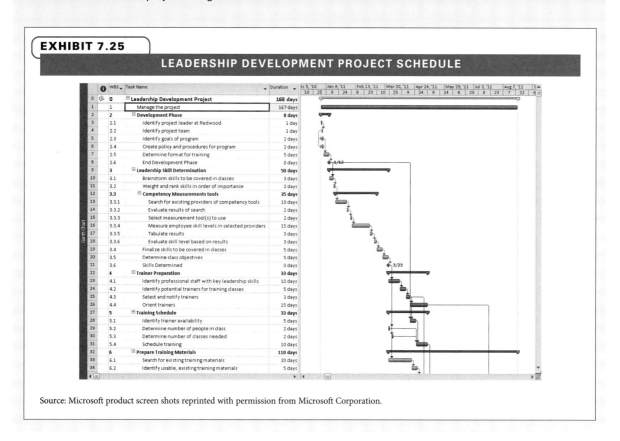

Source: Microsoft product screen shots reprinted with permission from Microsoft Corporation.

CHAPTER **8**

Resourcing Projects

CHAPTER OBJECTIVES

After completing this chapter, you should be able to:

- Identify resource needs for a project by creating a RACI chart.

- Assign a resource to each activity in a project schedule using project scheduling software.

- Show resource assignments on a MS Project schedule and identify any resource conflicts.

- Describe methods of resolving resource conflicts.

- Resource level a project using MS Project both with deadlines imposed on the project and with resource limitations.

- Compress a project schedule using crashing and fast tracking, and describe the advantages and disadvantages of both.

B. Busco/Photographer's Choice/Getty Images

How does a more than fifty-five-year-old prepress company transform its business from that of a manufacturer to a service provider? Schawk, Inc. was founded in 1953 in the basement of a Chicago home by entrepreneur Clarence W. Schawk. The product being manufactured was printing plates. More than fifty years and fifty acquisitions later, Schawk, with offices all over the world, is recognized as a global leader in brand point management.

How did we get here? Essentially Schawk capitalized on its knowledge and skills in streamlining processes and managing color. Today, one of the key challenges for product manufacturers is bringing new and/or modified products to market quickly, accurately, and consistently. This is especially challenging in high-growth, emerging markets where additional challenges, such as counterfeiting and trademark infringement, cost manufacturers

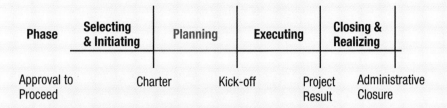

Phase	Selecting & Initiating	Planning	Executing	Closing & Realizing

Approval to Proceed   Charter   Kick-off   Project Result   Administrative Closure

PMBOK® GUIDE TOPICS

- Estimate activity resources
- Develop schedule
- Develop human resources plan

10 to 15 percent of their revenue. Being agile enough to respond to evolving consumer demand while demand is high can be key to achieving category leadership and maximizing sales. Being first to market can confer long-lasting benefits to the brands seen as "the original." Ultimately, bringing products to market that help brands win at the shelf—where the consumers votes with their wallets—delivers measurable, long-lasting benefits to brand owners.

Many of the world's largest and most respected organizations struggle immensely with managing projects globally. While their products and marketing strategies may be innovative, their go-to-market processes are often linear, time-consuming, and very inefficient. Their progress toward achieving strategic business goals through the launch of new brands and products is thwarted by many factors, including "silo-ization" and heterogeneous cultures, languages, government regulations, and time zones. In a global world, this multidimensional set of requirements and an ever-expanding scale make project management a daunting task.

Schawk has adapted by integrating our strategic, creative, and executional capabilities, which are supported by BLUE, our primary brand management technology product. BLUE enables global companies to unite their stakeholders (internal and external), projects, and processes into a single, streamlined workflow management system regardless of geographic boundaries. While workflows are unique to each company, they often combine on-, near-, and off-site project teams around the world.

Increasingly, companies outsource their non-core competencies such as internal design and production departments to Schawk, because that is a core competency of ours and we can manage these functions more efficiently. This allows the client's project manager to manage a single Schawk point of contact, allowing him or her to spend more time focusing on higher-value strategic issues and less time on tactical tasks.

All of these options help global companies speed new products to market. We identify and help remove process bottlenecks, offer online collaborative project management tools, and provide knowledgable human talent to deliver what we call brand point management. Brand point management helps companies create compelling and consistent brand experiences across brand touchpoints.

Patti A. Soldavini, director, Corporate Marketing, Schawk, Inc.

How do you decide who you need to work on your project? How do you know when you need each worker? How do you secure the services of those people? How do you make sure each worker has a steady amount of work to do, but not an overwhelming amount at any time? How do you make sure your project schedule is realistic, considering who will do the work?

These and many other related questions are answered when you correctly resource a project. Resources include people (human resources) along with machines, space, and other things you need to get the project done. In this chapter, we will primarily discuss human resources.

8.1 Abilities Needed when Resourcing Projects

Project managers need two types of abilities to correctly resource a project. The first type of skill needed is technical. Various techniques can be used to estimate resource demands, create a staffing management plan, assign one or more persons to each activity, identify when a person is assigned too much work at a point in time, schedule a project with limited numbers of key people and other resources, and compress (speed up) a project schedule.

The second type of skill needed is behavioral. As you might guess, many behavioral issues are involved in completing project resourcing tasks such as:

- Selecting the right people
- Identifying exactly what each person needs to accomplish
- Ensuring each person either has the capability needed or developing that person to be capable
- Dealing with difficult individual work schedules
- Getting people to work overtime when there are conflicts
- Making honest and open estimates of the amount of work required to complete an activity
- Assembling an effective team
- Dealing with people from diverse backgrounds
- Deciding where each person will work
- Deciding how a team that is geographically split can work in an effective virtual manner

The Science and Art of Resourcing Projects

The science and art of project resourcing are to perform the technical and behavioral aspects together in a manner that reinforces both. A resource-based schedule that is technically brilliant, but has little acceptance from those who must do the work, has little value. Likewise, an effective project team whose members have impractical resource assignments is still likely to straggle. If one needs to choose between the two, a motivated team with poor assignments is more likely to be successful than an unmotivated team with good assignments. However, when both are done well, the project has wonderful prospects.

This chapter covers both technical and behavioral aspects of determining and securing effective human resources for a project. While each specific skill and behavioral consideration is introduced separately, keep in mind that people are inclined to support what they have helped to plan. Therefore, when possible, identify your key people as soon as possible and get them engaged in the planning.

Considerations when Resourcing Projects

As we cover the specific skills and behavioral aspects of resourcing projects, the following ideas should be kept in mind:

- If some of the key people on a project do not have the skills to participate, managers should help them develop those skills.
- Projects always have tradeoffs; with regard to resources, time versus human resources versus other costs versus scope should be considered. Which of these takes precedence on the project you are planning?
- Project managers need to understand resource limitations to prevent overpromising. Often, after activities are tentatively scheduled as discussed in the previous chapter, it appears that the project can be completed by a particular date. However, the schedule may be unrealistic if enough resources are not available at key points in time.
- People are often a large portion of total project cost. This is especially true when a project requires special knowledge.

Activity- versus Resource-Dominated Schedules

All project schedules are based in part on the individual activities (both the estimates of how long each activity will take and their logical order, as discussed in Chapter 7) and in part on the number of human resources who are available when needed (the topic of this chapter). However, in some circumstances, the schedule is based more on the activities and in others it is based more on the resource limits. Exhibit 8.1 lists situations where schedules are based more on activities or more on resources.

EXHIBIT 8.1

ACTIVITY- VS. RESOURCE-DOMINATED SCHEDULE BASIS COMPARISON		
	MORE ON ACTIVITY	MORE ON RESOURCE
Time in project when scope is determined	Early	Late
Confidence in duration estimates	Great	Little
Rate of resource learning	Small	Extensive
Specialization of resources	Commodity	Unique
Availability of resources	Easily available	Tight availability
Firmness of activity predecessors (order)	Absolute	Optional
Concurrency of activities	Little	Significant

8.2 Estimate Resource Needs

The first process in resourcing a project is to estimate how many resources of each type and skill or knowledge level are needed. The PMBOK task **estimate activity resources** is "the process of estimating the types and quantities of resources required to perform each scheduled activity."[1] This can be accomplished at either a detailed or an overview level. When a project team determines a detailed list of activities that must be performed, it makes sense to ask what type of person (by specific knowledge or skill) is needed to perform each of the activities. However, when a project team does not identify individual activities, they still need to determine how many resources and what knowledge and skill each needs to complete the project. If the team uses rolling wave planning, they probably develop detailed resource requirements for the early part of the project for which they have identified specific activities, and less detailed requirements for later project phases for which the activity detail is not yet as specific.

When estimating resource needs, the team needs to make sure they have considered support needs as well such as information systems and human resources. Some types of workers have specific constraints placed upon how they are hired, scheduled, and released. These constraints need to be considered. Co-located teams and highly skilled resources often require more detailed resource planning. Many issues may be involved in securing specific knowledge or skills. When estimating resource needs, it is wise to include time to communicate between activities as well as time to perform activities. "Handoffs" occur when one person or group passes work on to another group. Handoffs can require more time and careful communication.

8.3 Create a Staffing Management Plan

A project **staffing management plan** is "the document that describes when and how human resource requirements will be met."[2] The staffing management plan addresses how to identify potential internal and/or external human resources for the project; determine the availability of each; and decide how to handle timing issues with regard to building up, developing, rewarding, and releasing the project team.

Identify Potential Resources

Identifying people who might work on a project differs significantly from one organization to another. Many organizations are staffed in a very lean manner and have few people from which to choose. In a small organization, one particular person may often be the logical choice for certain types of work on a project. However, in larger organizations and in situations where outside resources may be hired, identifying potential people becomes a bigger issue. Some high-priority projects have many resources available; many other projects have more limited choices on who is available. Whatever the situation, a project manager needs to understand who is potentially available to work on her project.

A project manager keeps in mind the estimated resources needed when identifying the people who could potentially work on the project. In some organizations, this list of potential people may have been developed for all project managers to use. In many organizations, a project manager needs to develop it. This information can include factors such as:

- Work functions (may include job titles and range of responsibilities)
- Professional discipline (may include degrees and professional certifications)
- Skill level (may include experience and performance ratings)
- Physical location (may include willingness to relocate and travel)
- Organizational/administrative unit (may include costs and contractual issues)[3]

EXHIBIT 8.2

IT COMPANY IDENTIFYING RESOURCES

A large consumer goods corporation sent out a bid to different IT vendors for developing a data warehouse. The client wanted a fixed-bid quote and was price conscious. The resourcing plan for the vendor that won the bid was a staffing mix of onsite resources (at the client site in North America) and offshore resources (from the vendor's back office in India). The roles requiring extensive client interaction were retained onsite, such as project management, requirements analysis, and technical architecture. The onsite–offshore liaison interacted with the back office development team to ensure success of the project.

Source: Rachana Thariani, PMP®.

Once this information is identified for the most likely pool of people, a project manager can compare the available people to the estimated resource needs to identify both gaps in specific skills that are needed and gaps in the number of people available versus those needed. If it is clear that more and/or different people are needed, then the project manager needs to look elsewhere for people. That could mean looking in other departments or divisions of the company or it could mean looking outside the organization. A project manager, perhaps with help from the sponsor, continues the identification of potential resources until an adequate number and mix of potential people have been identified.

Key people should be identified as early as possible. The project core team is ideally identified and assigned soon enough to participate in chartering the project. Beyond the core team, it is still helpful to get key subject matter experts (SMEs) on board very early if possible, not only to help plan the project, but also to help develop the project culture and get it off to a quick start. People are more likely to be enthusiastic about performing work they helped to plan, and this motivation often comes in handy during difficult stretches later in a project.

When possible, create options for people—try not to assign people who are unwilling participants. Experienced project managers understand that the better they take care of people who work with them on one project, the easier it is to recruit capable and enthusiastic people for their next project.

Make opportunities equally available to qualified candidates. First of all, project managers need to do this both from a legal and an ethical perspective. Successful project managers also find many advantages in having diverse teams. Different perspectives should be considered in making decisions and may help avoid major risks that a single perspective would not have uncovered. More creative approaches are undertaken. More stakeholders are effectively managed since different project team members sometimes relate better to particular stakeholders. An example of how a consulting company identifies resources is shown in Exhibit 8.2.

Determine Resource Availability

Once the potential resources have been identified and compared to the estimated resource needs, it is necessary to discover if the identified people are available and to secure their commitment. This is necessary even for internal projects because multiple projects often choose resources from the same resource pool. A schedule is preliminary until needed resources are committed to the project.

In terms of resource availability, full- and part-time resources as well as internal and external resources may be available. External resources may be more expensive. If the new project is of higher priority than an existing project, resources that were already committed may be freed up. Regarding ability to commit at a very detailed level, some

Building a committed staff is a crucial step in resourcing projects.

people have individual calendars with specific vacation or other unavailable times. Exhibit 8.3 shows how a consulting company determines resource availability.

Decide Timing Issues when Resourcing Projects

Projects, because of their temporary nature and unique outputs, have timing issues unlike those of ongoing operations. Early in the project, one timing issue is when to bring people on board. Bringing them on before they are needed can be costly. However, if the project manager takes a chance with an important resource and that person is not available, the schedule will probably be delayed. The general solution to the first timing issue is to assign key players as quickly as possible. This helps establish good project planning, effective project culture, and early project progress. Of course, a project manager may need to negotiate not just for who will be assigned to his project, but when they will be assigned.

As members are brought on board, timing issues involve getting the team functioning effectively. Team development is covered in Chapter 13 (Leading and Managing Project

---

EXHIBIT 8.3

MANAGING RESOURCE AVAILABILITY

Under pressure to complete the next phase of a new product being developed, a product development team urgently needed talented manpower. The existing team consisted of mostly technical talent (engineers, designers, and technicians). A review was performed by the product development team to find potential resources. Potential sources included:

- Existing staff
  - Within their department
  - Within their company but outside their department
- Staff misfit but talented
- Staff burned out and in need of a fresh challenge
- Temporary staff
- External supplier and customer staff

To the team's frustration, requests for additional staff were declined. To their surprise, upon further investigation, multiple opportunities developed:

- Product development staff working on separate projects had some idle time. Staff members thought to be dedicated to only a specific project were available for part-time support due to gaps in their schedule.
- Product development staff disinterested or "burned out" with their current project were eager for a different challenge.
- Underemployed staff members (at large) were found to be eager to step up to the plate. Existing projects did not keep them fully challenged.
- Some of the work required for completion of the next project phase was highly technical, requiring advanced knowledge, computer hardware, and very costly analysis software. To the team's delight, dedicated supplier staff was available to help with development. Advanced computer hardware and software, otherwise unreachable by the core team, were available if potential sales would justify the time investment. A balance was struck where the manufacturer and supplier effectively met each other's needs for mutual benefit. The product development team could overcome their technical hurdles, while the supplier could grow the business through new sales.

Source: Jeff Flynn, ILSCO Corporation.

EXHIBIT 8.4

RESOURCE TRADEOFFS

Often times in an IT project, especially when it is a fixed price (the vendor company assumes the risk of not meeting contractual terms), a balancing act has to be performed when staffing projects. IT consulting companies typically staff projects with a mix of senior resources and junior resources that shadow the senior ones on a project. Additionally, considerations such as costs of resources (some highly skilled resources may prove to be very expensive) are very important in making staffing decisions. IT consulting companies often make tradeoffs—clients want projects done in the cheapest way with the best resources, and this is practically impossible to achieve every time!

Source: Rachana Thariani. PMP®.

Teams). Team development issues include interpersonal relationships among those assigned—especially if they have different relationships in other work. Training needs and clarity of roles and responsibilities should be established. Suggestions for bringing new team members on a project and integrating them into a functional team include interviewing them to understand their desires and abilities, developing a plan to groom them, and mutually setting expectations with them.

As a project progresses, one timing issue may be how to keep the team motivated and on schedule. This issue is addressed in Chapter 13.

Near the end of a project, timing issues include rewarding, recognizing, and releasing project team members. How are they rewarded? Under what circumstances are they released from the project, and what provision is made for them to be assigned to new work and/or promoted? These issues are addressed in Chapter 15.

The staffing management plan deals with these three issues: how the project planners identify potential people for the project, how they determine which people are available and secure their services, and how to deal with timing issues of building up and then releasing the project workforce. Exhibit 8.4 shows how resource tradeoff issues are confronted by a consulting company.

8.4 Project Team Composition Issues

Project teams are often composed of people from many sources—both within and outside a parent company. Several of these issues, such as who will be on the project and where each will be physically located, are best considered when selecting team members. These issues are introduced here, and the management of teams with these compositions is discussed in Chapter 13.

Cross-Functional Teams

Projects often require cross-functional teams since the work of many projects requires input from multiple disciplines. When people from different backgrounds work together, misunderstandings often arise. An engineer may be predisposed to look at an issue one way, while an accountant may look at the same issue a different way. This may be due to education, experience, and/or personality. A project manager may feel sometimes that she is a translator between various functions that are working on the project. It is very useful for project managers to develop an ability to understand and speak effectively with various technical experts. The project manager is not the expert, but she must understand the experts, be able to communicate with the experts, and have the experts trust her judgment.

Co-Located Teams

Another team issue is where everyone physically sits. Teams are co-located if the members are assigned work spaces near each other. Project managers and teams can often take advantage of many modern methods for communicating from anywhere on the planet. These methods are used often, especially for larger decisions. However, many minor decisions are made every day on projects. Many times, a person might not feel that something is important enough to create a formal document or make a phone call. That same person might ask the person sitting in the next desk or a person he runs into in the hall. Sometimes a person does not want to interrupt her thought process, but would casually ask a person right next to herself a question. Co-location helps to create these opportunities for easy communications. On some projects, members of a supplier company and/or representatives from the customer may have a desk in the project work space.

Virtual Teams

Virtual teams are also common and represent the opposite approach. Members of virtual teams do not meet face to face very often. Sometimes a project requires the expertise of many far-flung people, and it is impractical to have them all work in the same area. These teams require many forms of communications. Many people report that if they have met another person face to face even once, they feel they can relate better to that person. Therefore, even for far-flung teams, it is fairly common to bring people together once for a chartering session or a project kickoff session. Of course, some project managers travel frequently to allow for regularly scheduled face-to-face contact with important team members, customers, and suppliers.

Outsourcing

Many project managers are faced with the prospect of not finding the necessary talent within their organization. When that is the case, project managers often need to hire expertise from one or more other organizations. This is discussed in Chapter 12. The author remembers one project where he worked for a European consulting firm that was hired to establish project management discipline at the IT headquarters of a large accounting firm. The accounting firm had fired its own internal consultants and replaced them with those of the European company, yet it decided to keep one of its own consultants from each of its Boston and New York offices on the team for political reasons. This was an awkward arrangement for everyone, but this type of situation occurs fairly often. Outsourcing can allow a project to bring in talent from anywhere in the world, but it can also lead to some tense situations.

8.5 Assign a Resource to Each Activity

Once you have identified the workers you want, sometimes you will be able to easily get them. This is especially true if your project is a high priority for your organization and if you have already developed a reputation as a project manager with whom many people want to work. However, a project manager is unlikely either to initially secure all the people he needs or to secure all the necessary highly qualified resources. He can expect to negotiate for the desired people and to bring some up to speed.

Hopefully, the core team was assigned during the initiating stage and participated in chartering the project. Now is the time to ensure that the core team is complete and without undue overlaps. It is also the time to assign workers to each activity. On small projects, most of these assignments may be to core team members. On larger projects, many other individuals may be involved as subject matter experts. It is also helpful to specify exactly what each person is responsible for and what authority that person has.

Show Resource Responsibilities on RACI Chart

A **responsibility assignment matrix** (RAM) is "a structure that relates the project organizational breakdown structure to the work breakdown structure to help ensure that each component of the project's scope of work is assigned to a person or team."[4] A common type of RAM is a RACI chart. RACI stands for Responsible, Approve, Consult, and Inform. The first column on a RACI chart is usually the work breakdown structure (WBS) coding of work packages with corresponding project activities. The second column includes the names of the project activities that correspond to the WBS. The remaining columns each represent a person who is involved with the project. A partial RACI chart example is shown in Exhibit 8.5.

In Exhibit 8.5, many activities have more than one person who has some involvement. For example, for the activity "finalize skills to be covered," the executive director has final approval, the directors need to be consulted, the project leader has primary responsibility to ensure that the activity is completed, and the project team needs to be informed. In a RACI chart, only one person should have primary responsibility for any activity. If more than one person has responsibility, it is too easy for them to blame each other if something goes wrong.

EXHIBIT 8.5

PARTIAL RACI CHART EXAMPLE

WBS	ACTIVITY	Executive Director	Directors	Project Leader	Project Team
1	**Develop Leadership Program**				
1.1	**Project Development**				
1.1.1	Identify project leader	A	R	I	
1.1.2	Identify project team	A	R	C	I
1.1.3	Identify goals of program	A	C	R	C
1.1.4	Create policy and procedures	A	C	R	
1.1.5	Determine format for training		C	R	
1.2	**Leadership Skills**				
1.2.1	Brainstorm skills to be covered	C	C	R	C
1.2.2	Rank skills in order of importance	A	C	R	C
1.2.3	Finalize skills to be covered	A	C	R	I
1.2.4	Determine class objectives	A	C	R	I
1.3	**Positions in Needing Training**				
1.3.1	Interview top management	C	C	R	
1.3.2	Evaluate organization chart	C	C	R	
1.3.3	Select staff positions for focus	C	C	R	I

RACI Key: (R) Responsible, (A) Approve, (C) Consult, (I) Inform

RACI charts are extremely useful for assigning activities to project core team members, subject matter experts, and the project manager. They are also useful in managing project communications. They go further than the original communications plan in that they identify every project activity and specify the exact involvement of each stakeholder.

Show Resource Assignments on Gantt Chart

Once it has been decided who will perform each activity, it is an easy matter to show the assignments on a project schedule. For example, the responsible person for each activity for a portion of the Alternative Breaks project is listed right next to the activity in the Gantt chart schedule in Exhibit 8.6. Showing the responsibilities directly on the schedule is a simple, visual way to communicate responsibilities. For simplicity's sake, each person has been assigned to work on most activities 75 percent of their time. In some projects, some people will spend 75 percent of their time for the duration of a specific activity, while other activities may require only a small fraction of their time across the activity's duration. Generally people are available for work on a project less than 100 percent of their time for many reasons (such as those described in Exhibit 7.8). Nevertheless, this demonstrates how to keep track of all of the time a person spends working on a project. Directions for how to construct each of the exhibits regarding resources in MS Project are given in Section 8.9.

Summarize Resource Responsibilities by Time Period with Histogram

Once it is clear who is responsible for each activity, it is time to understand how the multiple demands add up on each worker. Are any of the workers overloaded? To answer this question, the demands for each worker at each time period should be added. Exhibit 8.7 shows the responsibilities for the project leader (Patrick) for the various activities.

When looking at overloaded workers, it is easiest to consider each worker individually. For this example, the person in question is the project leader. Remember, we assigned the project leader to work on each activity 75 percent of his time so that we could see how the total demands add up. In the example in Exhibit 8.7, the project leader is grossly overloaded at several points. In fact, through most of the schedule, the project leader is scheduled to work 150 percent of his available time!

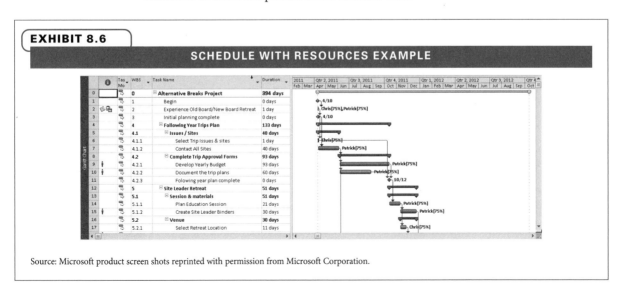

EXHIBIT 8.6

SCHEDULE WITH RESOURCES EXAMPLE

Source: Microsoft product screen shots reprinted with permission from Microsoft Corporation.

EXHIBIT 8.7

RESPONSIBILITY HISTOGRAM EXAMPLE

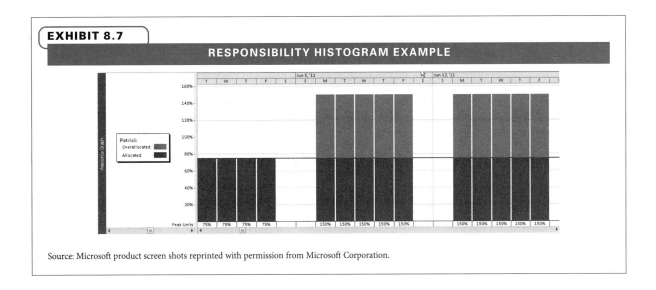

Source: Microsoft product screen shots reprinted with permission from Microsoft Corporation.

8.6 Dealing with Resource Overloads

Once it is obvious that a particular person has been overloaded at a given point in time, it is helpful to identify exactly which activities are involved. One easy way to do that is to compare the resource histogram, such as the one in Exhibit 8.7, to the Gantt chart schedule, shown in Exhibit 8.6. It is helpful to view both charts together using the same time scale, as shown in Exhibit 8.8.

Clearly, the project leader is scheduled to perform several activities at the same time and is overloaded much of the time. The worst overload starts on Monday, June 6, when the project leader has two activities to perform simultaneously. Project scheduling software helps to deal with resource overloads by pinpointing when the overloads occur for each worker and by identifying which activities that worker is assigned to perform. How should this be resolved? Software greatly assists in identifying and understanding the problem, but it takes management decisions to solve the problem.

EXHIBIT 8.8

PARTIAL SCHEDULE AND RESOURCE HISTOGRAM EXAMPLE

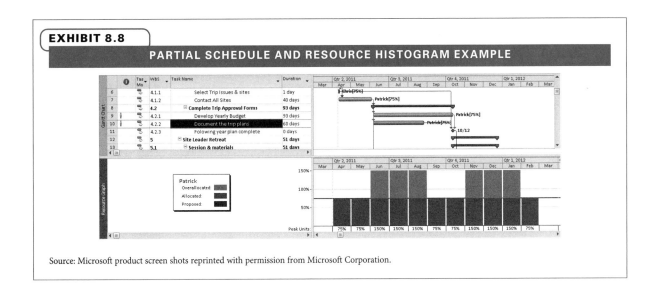

Source: Microsoft product screen shots reprinted with permission from Microsoft Corporation.

Methods of Resolving Resource Overloads

Once a project manager understands who is overloaded and what activities are involved, she can employ many possible methods to rework the project schedule so the worker is not too overloaded. Some of these methods are as follows:

- Assign certain activities to other workers. In our example, perhaps "identify goals of program" could be handled by the directors, and perhaps "document the trip plans" could be handled by Tori. This new schedule is shown in Exhibit 8.9. Note the project leader is still overallocated, but only for three months starting in November. While this is an improvement, perhaps other means should also be used.

- Sometimes an activity can be split into two activities, with the first part being performed as scheduled and the last part delayed. This is probably not a good strategy in our example project because it would probably only delay the overload rather than resolve it. This is often not an attractive strategy since many activities when split take more total time. It often takes a person a little time to remember where they left off when they resume work.

- Another method of resolving the overloads is to reorder the activities. This may include questioning the logic that was used when creating the schedule. One means of reordering activities, fast tracking, is covered in Section 8.7 on compressing schedules.

- Sometimes when people understand how badly overloaded a resource is, they decide they need to acquire or borrow additional resources.

- If a resource is impossibly overloaded, perhaps the project scope needs to be reduced or the schedule needs to be extended.

- If there is a severe overload and one of these strategies needs to be employed, it usually makes sense to inform the sponsor. The project manager needs to understand who is overloaded, when the overload occurs, and what activities cause the overload. Good project managers will then be able to determine possible courses of action. However, it may be up to the sponsor to make the final decision on how to resolve the overload.

- It is often helpful to resource level the overloaded person's schedule as described below.

Resource leveling is "any form of schedule network analysis in which scheduling decisions ... are driven by resource constraints."[5] The most common form of resource

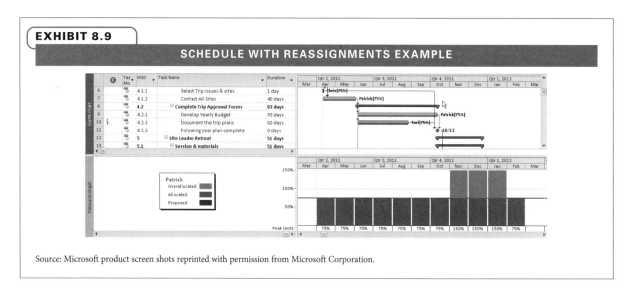

EXHIBIT 8.9

SCHEDULE WITH REASSIGNMENTS EXAMPLE

Source: Microsoft product screen shots reprinted with permission from Microsoft Corporation.

leveling is when activities are delayed so the person does not need to perform as many activities at the same time. Normally, noncritical activities are delayed by an amount no more than their slack in the hope that the overloads can be resolved without extending the project schedule. However, if none of the alternatives discussed above is feasible and delaying the noncritical activities within their slack is not sufficient, the project schedule will slip. Essentially, this delay reduces peak demand and smoothes the period-to-period resource usage. An example follows, starting with Exhibit 8.10.

In this example, Jane has been assigned all of the activities. They will require 40 percent, 55 percent, or 75 percent of her time as marked. During the middle part of the schedule, Jane has too many activities to perform at the same time. Therefore, any activities scheduled at that time that are not critical should be considered for delay. The easiest way to understand the work demands and be able to adjust the schedule within the limits of their available work time starts with creating a critical path schedule, as shown in the bottom portion of Exhibit 8.10. It is helpful to clearly mark the critical path and to "front load" the schedule—that is, to show every activity starting as soon as the activities that precede it are complete. Then, a resource histogram can be built for each person who may be overloaded. Start by putting the critical path activities on the bottom, because those activities need to be completed as scheduled or the entire project will be late. In our example, those are activities 1, 3, 6, and 7. Next, add all of the non-critical path activities above at the earliest time they can be scheduled. In our example these are 2, 4, and 5. With the 75 percent line showing Jane's maximum available time, it is easy to see that she cannot complete everything as scheduled.

The first conflict is activities 2 and 3. Since activity 3 is on the critical path, activity 2 should be compromised. If Jane waited until there was no conflict to schedule activity 2, however, the project would be delayed. Notice that activity 2 is currently scheduled for 40 percent of Jane's time for three working days, for a total of 1.2 days of work. If Jane can work on activity 2 for 20 percent of her time during the six days she is working the other 55 percent on activity 3, she would complete both after six work days. Activities 4 and 5 would both then be delayed until activity 2 is complete. This partially leveled schedule is shown in Exhibit 8.11. Notice that Jane has time to finish activity 4 without delaying activity 7 (and, therefore, the critical path). Part of activity 5 could be worked after activity 4 and before activity 7 without overloading Jane, but a portion of activity 5 would still force an overload situation.

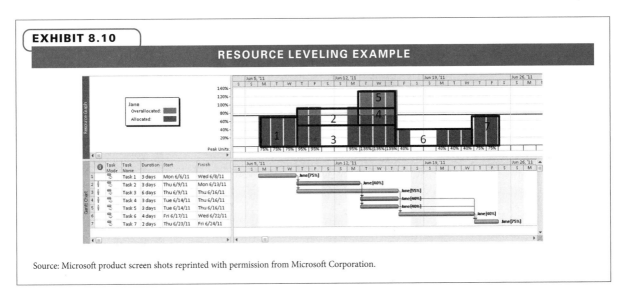

EXHIBIT 8.10

RESOURCE LEVELING EXAMPLE

Source: Microsoft product screen shots reprinted with permission from Microsoft Corporation.

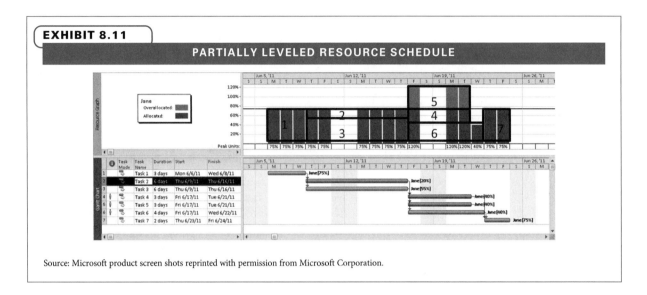

EXHIBIT 8.11

PARTIALLY LEVELED RESOURCE SCHEDULE

Source: Microsoft product screen shots reprinted with permission from Microsoft Corporation.

If the noncritical activities must be completed at the rate of effort shown in the original schedule, some of them may need to be assigned to another worker. Resource leveling can be as much art as science. The combination of the critical path schedule and resource histogram allows a project manager to understand who is overloaded, at what time, and by what specific activities. Then, the project manager seeks to move some of the noncritical activities within their slack to level the demand for that worker. If enough leveling can be done, the project can proceed as scheduled. If not, some activities must be accomplished by other means, the schedule will slip, or perhaps the scope will need to be reduced.

8.7 Compress the Project Schedule

Now that the project manager knows how long the project schedule is expected to take, he can compare it with what the sponsor or customer wants. If the expected time is too long, he will need to reduce the critical path (remember that because the critical path is the longest, it dictates the total project duration).

Actions to Reduce the Critical Path

A variety of actions can be taken to reduce the critical path as follows:

- Reduce the project scope and/or quality.
- Overlap sequential activities using finish-to-finish (FF), start-to-start (SS), or start-to-finish (SF) relationships.
- Partially overlap sequential activities by using time leads.
- Increase the number of work hours per day or work days per week.
- Schedule activities that are normally in sequence at the same time.
- Shorten the duration of critical activities.
- Shorten activities by assigning more resources.
- Shorten activities that cost the least to speed up.

The first item, reducing scope and/or quality, normally requires permission from the sponsor and/or customer. Scope reductions are fairly common. Sometimes, the original scope includes features that are nice to have but are not essential, which people are willing to give up when they understand the schedule impact. Quality reductions are far less common and are discussed in Chapter 11.

The next two items, time leads and alternative dependencies, are discussed in Chapter 7. The last five items, on the other hand, apply to two other techniques used to compress schedules, namely crashing and fast tracking. **Crashing** is "a specific type of project schedule compression technique performed by taking action to decrease the total project duration after analyzing a number of alternatives to determine how to get the maximum schedule duration compression for the least additional cost."[6] **Fast tracking** is "a specific project schedule compression technique that changes network logic to … perform schedule activities in parallel."[7]

One simple way to understand the differences between crashing and fast tracking is to determine what is given up in return for the faster schedule. Crashing almost always costs more money to speed up the schedule. Fast tracking almost always increases the risk to speed up the schedule. Both make management more difficult since either more activities take place at the same time and/or more activities have workers on overtime. Let us turn to the specifics of each.

Crashing

When crashing a project schedule, certain activities are performed at a faster-than-normal pace. This often requires overtime pay, but could also require extra charges for expedited deliveries, more expensive machinery, or other methods. When deciding which activities to speed up, two questions must be asked. First, which activities are on the critical path? Since the critical path determines how long the project takes, speeding up any activity not on the critical path makes no difference. Second, which critical path activity costs the least on a per-day basis to speed up? There is no sense in paying more than necessary. We will use the project in Exhibit 8.12 to illustrate crashing.

Note the enumeration method was used to identify each path and its duration. Path ABEG at 25 days is the critical path. This example is in days, but it works equally well with weeks or any other unit of time. Also note that three small tables of information are included in Exhibit 8.12 to help us keep track of times and costs as we make the crashing decisions. The first table is the list of the paths with the time each is expected to take. Remember, we only want to crash activities on the critical path. Every time we reduce the length of an activity, we record the impact on the affected path(s).

The second information table lists each activity along with the normal time and cost (the expected time and cost if this activity is not crashed), the crash cost and time (the fastest the activity could be accomplished and the total cost incurred if it is crashed), and the crash cost per unit of time (in this example, per day). The activities that are on the critical path are identified by a triangle symbol. Two activities, A and C, have the same crash time as normal time. This means they cannot be crashed and are crossed out. We need the information in this table to identify which critical path activities cost the least to speed up.

We use the third small table to keep track of how long the project is, which activity(ies) we choose to speed up, and how much it costs. Using the normal time for all activities, the project is expected to take 25 days. We crash activities one day at a time. Note that path ADFG requires 24 days—only one day less than the critical path.

Activities A, B, E, and F are on the critical path. Activity A cannot be crashed. Some activities are impractical to speed up, even for extra cost. Activity B at $50 is the least expensive of the choices, so that is the one to crash first. Note that activity F only costs $25 to speed up, but it is not on the critical path so it is not chosen. Once we speed up B by one day, the resulting information is placed into the tables, as shown in Exhibit 8.13.

In the first table, path ABEG has been reduced to 24 days since B is now being crashed. In the second table, activity B is now shown as seven days since it has been crashed one day. In the third table, the duration is now 24 days, B is crashed, the incremental cost is

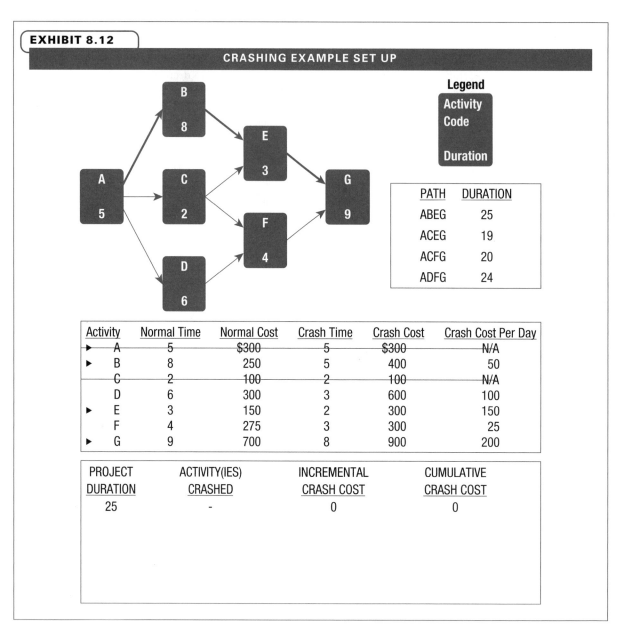

EXHIBIT 8.12

CRASHING EXAMPLE SET UP

PATH	DURATION
ABEG	25
ACEG	19
ACFG	20
ADFG	24

Activity	Normal Time	Normal Cost	Crash Time	Crash Cost	Crash Cost Per Day
A	5	$300	5	$300	N/A
B	8	250	5	400	50
C	2	100	2	100	N/A
D	6	300	3	600	100
E	3	150	2	300	150
F	4	275	3	300	25
G	9	700	8	900	200

PROJECT DURATION	ACTIVITY(IES) CRASHED	INCREMENTAL CRASH COST	CUMULATIVE CRASH COST
25	-	0	0

$50, and so is the cumulative cost because that is the only activity crashed so far. Now there are two critical paths of 24 days each. The activities on the second critical path, ADFG, are identified by a circular symbol. To further crash the project, both paths need to be shortened. This could be accomplished by crashing one activity on each critical path, such as B or E on the first path and D or F on the second path. It could also be accomplished by crashing one activity that is on both paths, such as activity G. The least expensive of these alternatives is B and F for a total cost of $75. The results of this are shown in Exhibit 8.14.

After two rounds, both critical paths are 23 days. Note that path ACFG is also reduced, as F is on it and F was crashed. Since F cannot be crashed any further, a line is drawn through it. The cumulative cost of crashing the project two days is $125. Exhibit 8.15 shows the choices of continuing to crash activities until it is no longer worthwhile. That

EXHIBIT 8.13

CRASHING EXAMPLE AFTER ONE ROUND

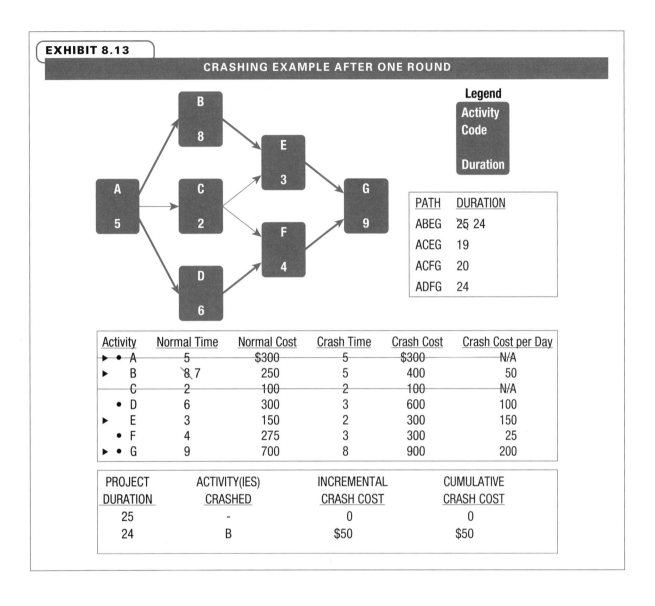

PATH	DURATION
ABEG	25 24
ACEG	19
ACFG	20
ADFG	24

Activity	Normal Time	Normal Cost	Crash Time	Crash Cost	Crash Cost per Day
▶ • A	5	$300	5	$300	N/A
▶ B	8 7	250	5	400	50
C	2	100	2	100	N/A
• D	6	300	3	600	100
▶ E	3	150	2	300	150
• F	4	275	3	300	25
▶ • G	9	700	8	900	200

PROJECT DURATION	ACTIVITY(IES) CRASHED	INCREMENTAL CRASH COST	CUMULATIVE CRASH COST
25	-	0	0
24	B	$50	$50

is called an "all-crash" schedule. Note that even in that circumstance activity D is not reduced the full amount possible since reducing it further would not make a difference in the length of the overall project.

Many questions can be answered with this information, such as the following:

- How fast can the project be completed?
- To crash the project one day, what activity would be crashed, and what would it cost?
- To crash the project two days, what activities would be crashed, and what would it cost in total?
- If there is a bonus of $125 per day for finishing early, what activities would be crashed, and how fast would the project be completed?
- If there is a bonus of $225 per day for finishing early, what activities would be crashed, and how fast would the project be completed?

EXHIBIT 8.14

CRASHING EXAMPLE AFTER TWO ROUNDS

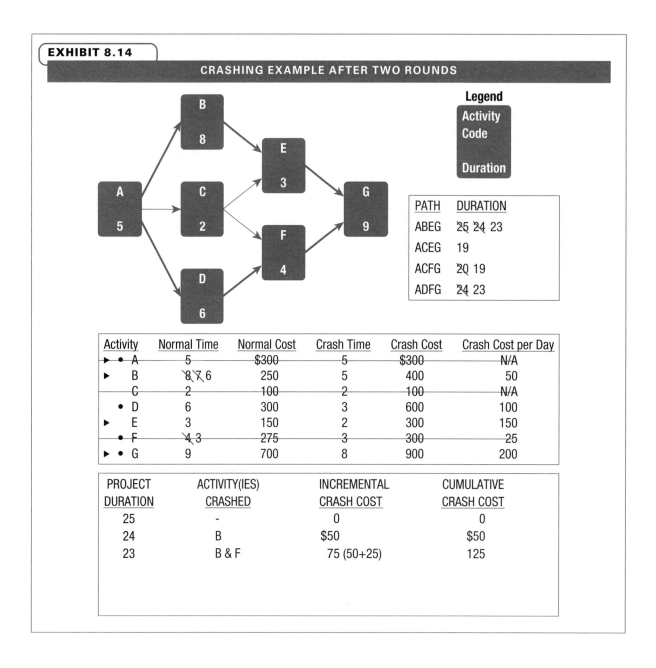

Legend

Activity Code

Duration

PATH	DURATION
ABEG	25 24 23
ACEG	19
ACFG	20 19
ADFG	24 23

Activity	Normal Time	Normal Cost	Crash Time	Crash Cost	Crash Cost per Day
► • A	5	$300	5	$300	N/A
► B	8 7 6	250	5	400	50
C	2	100	2	100	N/A
• D	6	300	3	600	100
► E	3	150	2	300	150
• F	4 3	275	3	300	25
► • G	9	700	8	900	200

PROJECT DURATION	ACTIVITY(IES) CRASHED	INCREMENTAL CRASH COST	CUMULATIVE CRASH COST
25	-	0	0
24	B	$50	$50
23	B & F	75 (50+25)	125

Fast Tracking

Fast tracking occurs when activities that are normally performed in series (one after the other) are performed at the same time. In Exhibit 8.16, fast tracking could potentially be accomplished at several points. For example, while A is being done, B could also be performed. This certainly can speed things up as more things can be done at the same time. There is a risk, however. For example, if activity A is to design a part and activity B is to order material for the part, the normal routine would be to wait until the part is designed to be sure to order the correct materials. By performing both at the same time, there is a risk that the design will call for different materials than expected and the materials will need to be reordered. One strategy to gain benefits of fast tracking while

EXHIBIT 8.15

CRASHING EXAMPLE IN "ALL-CRASH" MODE

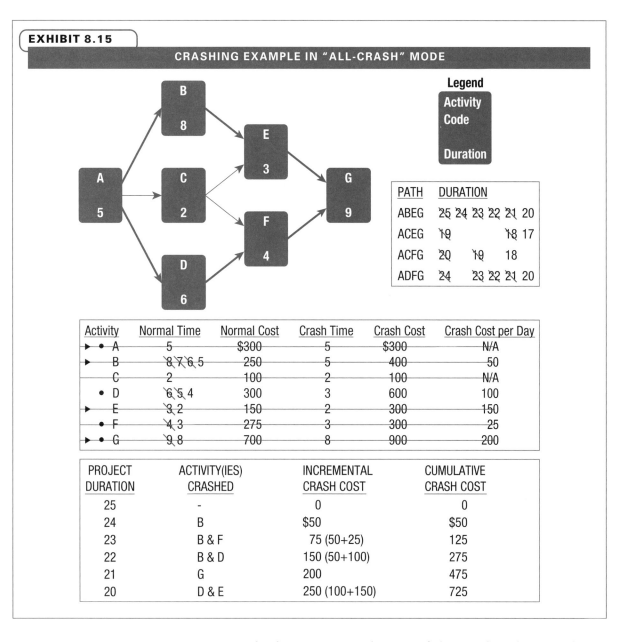

Legend

Activity
Code

Duration

PATH	DURATION
ABEG	25 24 23 22 21 20
ACEG	19 18 17
ACFG	20 19 18
ADFG	24 23 22 21 20

Activity	Normal Time	Normal Cost	Crash Time	Crash Cost	Crash Cost per Day
► • A	5	$300	5	$300	N/A
► B	8 7 6 5	250	5	400	50
C	2	100	2	100	N/A
• D	6 5 4	300	3	600	100
► E	3 2	150	2	300	150
• F	4 3	275	3	300	25
► • G	9 8	700	8	900	200

PROJECT DURATION	ACTIVITY(IES) CRASHED	INCREMENTAL CRASH COST	CUMULATIVE CRASH COST
25	-	0	0
24	B	$50	$50
23	B & F	75 (50+25)	125
22	B & D	150 (50+100)	275
21	G	200	475
20	D & E	250 (100+150)	725

attempting to control risk is to use a combination of alternate dependencies with time leads and lags to only partially overlap activities, as described in Chapter 7. Partial activity overlaps entail less risk than full overlaps. Another strategy is to only overlap a few activities so you can manage them closely. One would ordinarily look for long-duration activities on the critical path for this overlapping.

8.8 Alternative Scheduling Methods

Several alternative approaches are used in certain industries or certain situations to create project schedules, including critical chain, reverse phase, agile, auto/manual, and rolling wave scheduling. These approaches are not mutually exclusive—a person can use some of the logic from more than one of these methods on the same project.

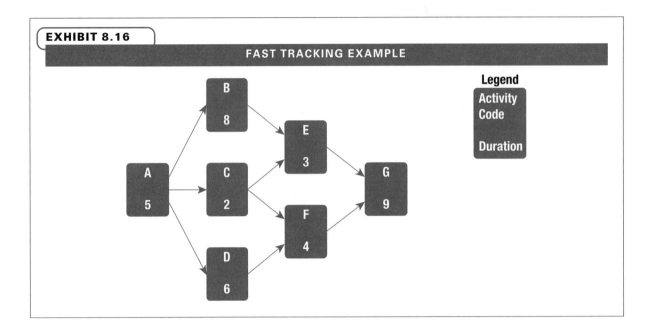

EXHIBIT 8.16

FAST TRACKING EXAMPLE

Legend

Activity
Code

Duration

Critical Chain Project Management (CCPM)

There are several problems with scheduling projects in many organizations that traditional critical path scheduling, even with resource leveling, does not always address satisfactorily. Some of these problems are as follows:

- Many people make conservative duration estimates. Often, people are punished for completing work late, so they give themselves plenty of time in their estimates.
- Durations of some activities vary greatly. The part of this variation that is due to specific possible events taking place can be managed by risk management techniques as discussed in Chapter 10. The other part of the variation, known as common cause or random variation, sometimes is just difficult to accurately estimate.
- Many project workers tend to use all of the time available to them. Instead of finishing early and getting the work to the next person, they keep fine-tuning their work and turn it in on time.
- To keep multiple projects moving, many workers are asked to multitask. Up to a point, multitasking is helpful in keeping multiple projects moving and keeping the workers stimulated. However, many people are asked to multitask far beyond that point; by not focusing on a limited number of things, they sometimes cannot give adequate attention to any.

One approach to address problems such as these is called critical chain project management (CCPM). CCPM is also sometimes known as the critical chain method. The **critical chain method** is "a schedule network analysis technique that modifies the project schedule to account for limited resources."[8] Simply put, rather than calculate the critical path based upon predecessor–successor relationships alone, it also incorporates calculations on resource availability. Once the resource that is most in demand is identified, efforts are made to keep that resource appropriately busy on critical chain activities (those critical both because of the predecessor–successor relationships and because of resource shortages) but not overloaded. Other components of the CCPM system include the following:

- Avoiding multitasking
- Estimating aggressively how quickly each activity can be completed

- Putting a feeding buffer of time directly in front of critical chain activities to ensure they will not be delayed
- Putting the time normally reserved for the uncertainty in each individual activity at the end of the project as a total project buffer that the project manager can use as needed
- Finishing activities early if possible and passing the work on to the next worker

The critical chain method has been a topic of much discussion during the last decade. Proponents say it is a major innovation that helps to overcome some of project management's most difficult scheduling and resourcing problems. Detractors say it is another approach that may work in certain circumstances. However, it requires a great deal of reeducation and communication on everyone's part to make it successful, and when resources are reallocated from the buffer to a task in trouble more work may be created. Project management students need to be aware of this approach that some organizations use.

Reverse Phase Schedules

Another alternative scheduling method that is sometimes used in the construction industry is called a reverse phase schedule. The reverse phase schedule is developed by the people closest to the work (often either the hands-on workers or the forepersons who directly supervise work) by starting with the final project deliverables and continually asking what needs to be completed prior to starting work on this deliverable. As each activity is defined, its order is established and the person proposing it verifies that their company has the worker(s) to complete the activity as shown in the tentative schedule.

Using this method, the team systematically works from the end of the project toward the beginning. This is also a good practice to help ensure that both all of the project deliverables and the list of activities are complete because by working backward missing deliverables and activities tend to be easier to identify.

Agile Project Planning

The fundamental ideas behind agile project planning are to use a collaborative approach with workers and other stakeholders heavily involved in planning; to recognize that while it may be difficult to scope the entire project at the outset, stakeholders do want to have an idea of total cost, schedule, and functionality before approving a project; and to understand that while uncontrolled change is bad, too strenuous of change control often means valid emergent stakeholder wishes are not met. These ideas permeate the contemporary project management approach of this book and are explained in more detail in the Project Management in Action example at the conclusion of this chapter.

Auto/Manual Scheduling

Microsoft Project 2010 includes a new feature called manual scheduling to enable users to more closely emulate MS Excel. This may be comforting for users who are more familiar with Excel than Project. When people are chartering a project and want to show the few milestones without committing to dates, manual scheduling may be a good starting point. Also, for projects with few predecessor–successor relationships, manual scheduling may sometimes be useful. However, for the vast majority of projects, the ability of MS Project to plan and track activities based upon logical relationships is very useful and suggests manual scheduling is not enough.

Rolling Wave Planning

The idea behind rolling wave planning is to plan the first part of the project in as much detail as needed and to plan later portions only at a high level. This allows the project team to focus on the near term without ignoring the longer term. It means the project team needs to plan progressively more detail as information becomes available. Rolling wave planning is illustrated near the end of Chapter 9 by showing a dummy activity for a late project phase.

8.9 Using MS Project for Resource Allocation

Up to this point, a project manager has created a file with a project in MS Project, created the WBS for the project, defined the predecessor–successor relationships among the tasks, entered the expected duration for each task, and shown the critical path in red. This covers the first two ways in which a project schedule may be constrained—namely the logical order of tasks and the expected duration of each. Now we consider the third way in which a schedule may be constrained—the number of key resources available when needed. For the final constraints on schedules, cash flow will be covered in Chapter 9 and imposed dates will be covered in Chapter 11. Using MS Project to understand resource limitations includes four steps:

1. Define resources.
2. Assign resources.
3. Identify overallocated resources.
4. Deal with overallocations.

We can perform the first three steps very well with MS Project alone, but need to consider managerial options as well as options MS Project can identify to deal with the overallocations.

Step 1: Defining Resources

For a resource to be available to a project, it must be described in Microsoft Project's database. A resource may be a single unit, such as a person, or a resource may be a pool of like units, such as five welding machines. Resources may include people, buildings, materials, facilities, or supplies—anything necessary for the completion of a task.

If possible, resource information should be entered in advance of the time of assignment to a task. If entered at the time of assignment, only minimal information is supplied, and the resource detail information must be completed later.

While many fields can be used for defining resources, at a minimum, the Resource Name and Max Units fields need definition. If costs are to be modeled, then the Std. Rate, Ovt. Rate, Cost/Use, and Accrue At values must also be defined. See Exhibit 8.17. Steps in defining resources include:

1. On the View tab, Resource Views group, click Resource Sheet.
2. In the first blank row, enter the resource name in the Resource Name cell.
3. In the Initials cell, enter the initials of the resource.
4. Click the Max Units cell and enter the resource's maximum availability.

Max Units defines the availability of a resource for project work. The default is 100 percent, but individual resources are not 100 percent available even if they are working full time on a project. Availability will be something less than eight hours if that is the normal working day. The unavailability includes general tasks required of employees. It can also include ongoing process work such as a part-time help desk role. For example, a

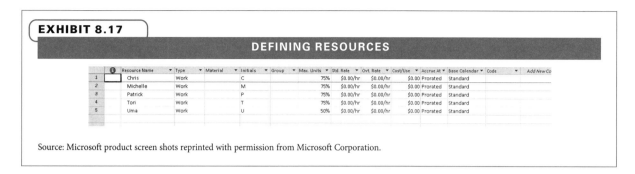

EXHIBIT 8.17

			Resource Name	Type	Material	Initials	Group	Max. Units	Std. Rate	Ovt. Rate	Cost/Use	Accrue At	Base Calendar	Code	Add New Co
1			Chris	Work		C		75%	$0.00/hr	$0.00/hr	$0.00	Prorated	Standard		
2			Michelle	Work		M		75%	$0.00/hr	$0.00/hr	$0.00	Prorated	Standard		
3			Patrick	Work		P		75%	$0.00/hr	$0.00/hr	$0.00	Prorated	Standard		
4			Tori	Work		T		75%	$0.00/hr	$0.00/hr	$0.00	Prorated	Standard		
5			Uma	Work		U		50%	$0.00/hr	$0.00/hr	$0.00	Prorated	Standard		

Source: Microsoft product screen shots reprinted with permission from Microsoft Corporation.

person assigned primarily to one project may be available about six hours per day (or 75 percent) for that project. If so, 75 percent would be the Max Units for that resource. Note in Exhibit 8.17 that Chris is available up to 75 percent of his time for the project, while Uma is only available 50 percent of her time.

Things to consider when determining each resource's Max Units value are as follows:

- Determine what is considered project work.
- Determine what is not considered project work (100 percent Max Units).
- Organizational holidays are accounted for in the Standard (MS Project) calendar.
- Vacation days are accounted for in each resource calendar.

CALENDARS If a different project calendar is needed because one or more resources are working different days or shifts, or are subject to a different holiday schedule, the Base Calendar field is used to specify that different project calendar.

Resource calendars are used to block out vacation days and other resource-specific nonworking days. Resource calendars inherit project-wide working day definitions from the standard (MS Project) calendar at the time the resource is first defined. Resource calendars are used by MS Project to determine when a resource assignment can be scheduled. If a task has no resource assignment, then the project calendar is used to determine task scheduling.

Setting Up a Resource Calendar

1. Double click a resource row to activate the Task Information dialog for the resource whose calendar needs revision.
2. On the General tab, click Change Working time … (see Exhibit 8.18).
3. Confirm the correct resource is chosen. The resource name is near the top of the dialog.
4. Make revisions in the manner described in Chapter 6.

Step 2: Assigning Resources

During resource assignment, a project manager allocates one or more resources to an activity. Microsoft Project then generates assignment information based on activity information, resource information, switch settings, and possible data overrides. Assigning a resource to an activity with no existing resource assignments (using default settings) includes the following steps and is illustrated in Exhibit 8.19.

1. On the Task tab, View group, click Gantt Chart.
2. Right click in the Start column header, click Insert Column and enter Work to add the Work column.
3. On the view tab, in the Split View group, click on Details.

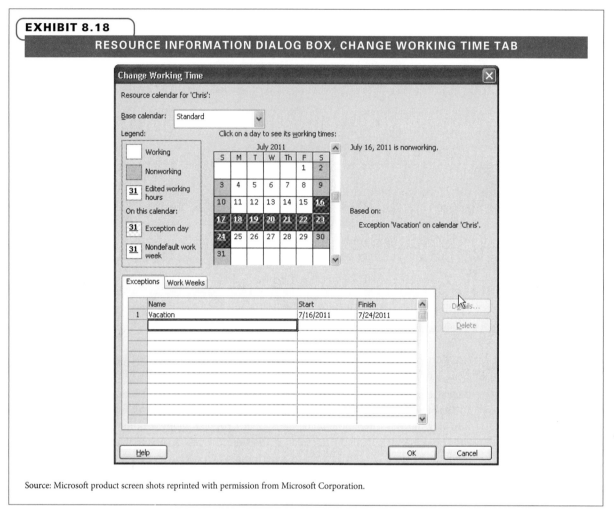

4. Right click the form in the lower pane and select Resources and Predecessors (if not already present).
5. In the upper pane, click the activity row needing a resource assignment.
6. Click the next blank row in the Resource Name column in the lower pane's form.
7. Enter the resource name from the drop-down list.
8. Repeat steps 6 and 7 to add additional resources to the assignment list.
9. Enter a units value if the Max Units value is not correct for any assignment.
10. Click the OK button. No assignment is made until the OK button is clicked.
11. Note that Work is calculated and the activity duration value did not change.

Verify that the assignment work and task work values reconcile with the estimated duration value.

The following data are necessary for creating assignments:

- Duration is the number of time units between the activity start and end. The default display value is in days. Each day spans eight work hours, plus one nonworking hour after four hours have passed.
- Units represent the availability of a resource for work each day. This value is the same as the resource Max Units value unless it is overridden.
- Work (assignment) is calculated by multiplying the Duration value (converted to hours) by the Units value.

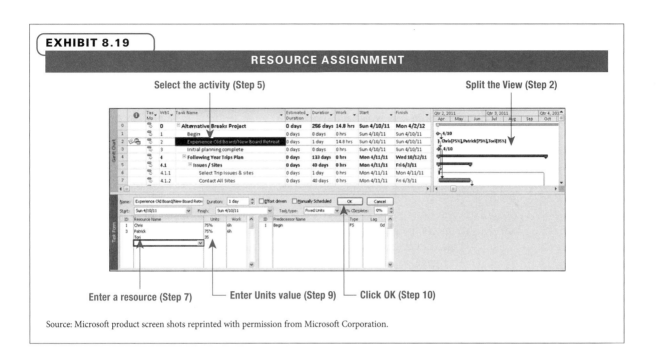

Source: Microsoft product screen shots reprinted with permission from Microsoft Corporation.

- Task type is a switch that determines which of three values (duration, units, and work) changes when one of the other two is modified. The switch settings are Fixed Units (default), Fixed Duration, and Fixed Work.

BASIC ASSIGNMENT CALCULATION WITH FIXED UNITS SELECTED (DEFAULT SETTINGS)
When an assignment is made, MS Project uses the Duration and Units values to calculate the number of hours a resource will work on the activity. The activity Duration and Work fields may be adjusted. The Work field value in an activity row (Task Usage view) is the sum of all of the assignment Work field values. The Work field value in a resource row (Resource Usage view) is the sum of all of the resource assignment work values.

- Activity with no prior resource assignments—MS Project uses the Duration and Units values to calculate the assignment work value and sums the assignment Work values into the activity Work field. The assignment of a 100 percent available resource (Units = 100%) to a two-day-duration activity (eight-hour days) results in sixteen hours of resource work across the two-day duration. An assignment of two 75 percent available resources (Units = 75%) results in twenty-four hours of work assigned across the two-day duration.
- Activity with one or more resources already assigned—when yet another resource(s) is added, MS Project holds the activity Duration value constant and adjusts the activity Work value. The addition of a 100 percent available resource (Units = 100%) to a two-day duration activity that has a 100 percent available resource already assigned results in thirty-two hours of activity work across the two-day duration activity, with each resource assigned sixteen hours of assignment work.
- Removal of resources works in reverse of the above. Removal of the resource from an activity with one resource assigned results in zero task work. Removal of one resource from an activity with two resources assigned results in the activity duration held constant, work calculated for the remaining resource assignment, and the activity work value the same as the assignment value.

MODIFYING AN ASSIGNMENT After an assignment is made, MS Project maintains a relationship among the Duration, Units, and Work values. With the Fixed Units as the Task Type:

1. Change the duration and MS Project changes the assignment work and task work values.
2. Change the task work and MS Project changes the duration and assignment work value(s).
3. Change an assignment units value and MS Project holds the assignment work value constant and changes the task duration.

Tips include the following:

- If you don't like MS Project adjusting the Duration value as you add and remove resources assignments, an alternative is to switch the Task Type setting to Fixed Work. On the File tab, Options, Schedule page, enter Fixed Duration. Also on the same page, on the Scheduling Options for this Project field, enter All New Projects.
- When trying different resource assignments on an activity, it is easy to lose the original duration value, so save your original estimated duration value in a user-defined Duration or Work field. On the Task tab, click Gantt Chart, right click the Duration column heading, click Insert column and enter Duration1. Then right click the Duration1 heading, click Field Settings, and enter Estimated Duration in the Title box to name the column.

Step 3: Finding Overallocated Resources

A resource overallocation usually occurs when a resource is assigned to two or more activities whose start and finish dates overlap, if only for a very small duration. An overallocation can also occur if an assignment Units value is greater than the resource's Max Units value.

MS Project has a good set of tools to help find and understand each overallocation. Once understood, you can make a management decision about an appropriate solution. Most solutions cannot be automatically implemented. There is an MS Project feature (Level Resources) that resolves most overallocations by delaying the start of all but one of the conflicting activity assignments. This may produce an unacceptably lengthened schedule, so consider this as just one of many solution options. The Gantt Chart Indicators field will display a red stick figure symbol if an assigned resource is overallocated.

RESOURCE ALLOCATION VIEW With slight modification, the Resource Allocation view is very helpful. The Show in menu checkbox makes this view available in the View menu. The Detail Gantt marks the critical path (bold red) and graphically displays free slack following each activity, which shows how much the activity can be delayed before creating a new, longer critical path.

1. On the Task tab, View group, Gantt Chart drop-down menu, click More Views ...
2. On the More Views dialog, scroll the Views display, enter Resource Allocation, and click Edit.
3. On the View Definition dialog, click the Details Pane drop-down menu and enter Detail Gantt.
4. On the View Definition dialog, click Show in menu.
5. Click OK, then click Apply.
6. In the upper pane, right click the Work column header and enter Insert Column.
7. Enter Max Units, then click Enter.
8. Add the activity Work column in the lower pane's table to the left of the Leveling Delay column (as above).

EXHIBIT 8.20

VIEW DEFINITION DIALOG BOX

View Definition in 'AB Project Schedule 3 Resourced...

Name: Resource Allocation

Views displayed:

Primary View: Resource Usage

Details Pane: Detail Gantt

☑ Show in menu

Help   OK   Cancel

Source: Microsoft product screen shots reprinted with permission from Microsoft Corporation.

9. Hide the assignment rows in the upper pane's table: right click in the Resource Name field header to select all rows. On the View tab, Data group, Outline, enter Hide Subtasks.

The results of these steps can be seen in Exhibit 8.20.

The Resource Allocation view is a combination view with the Resource Usage view in the upper pane and the Detail Gantt view in the lower pane. The time scale in the upper pane is synchronized with the Gantt graphic in the lower pane. Adjusting the zoom affects both panes.

The Gantt bars in the lower pane represent the duration of the work hours displayed in the upper pane. Selecting a resource in the upper pane's table displays the assignments of that resource in the lower pane. Selecting a resource assignment in the upper pane displays information about that assignment in the lower pane.

Resource data displayed in red in the upper pane's table mark that resource as overallocated. In addition, if a yellow diamond with an exclamation mark is displayed in that resource's Indicator field, the overallocation is probably more serious.

Project uses the resource Max Units value and a basis value (the default is day-by-day). If a resource is momentarily overloaded, the resource is marked overallocated. If the resource has enough time in one day to complete all assignments, the yellow diamond does not display. If not enough time is available, then the yellow diamond is displayed.

In a task view, a red stick figure is displayed. In Exhibit 8.21, both Chris and Patrick are marked as overallocated. The total assignment hours are displayed in the upper pane. The Gantt bars in the lower pane represent each assignment.

A straightforward method of finding overallocated resources is as follows:

1. Set the timescale to the start of the schedule.
2. Slowly scroll the timescale toward the end of the schedule.
3. Analyze each instance of cell values displayed in red for cause and severity.

Step 4: Dealing with Overallocations

Once overallocations have been identified, there are many possible things a project manager can do. The point to remember at this time is that MS Project is a tool only. It is

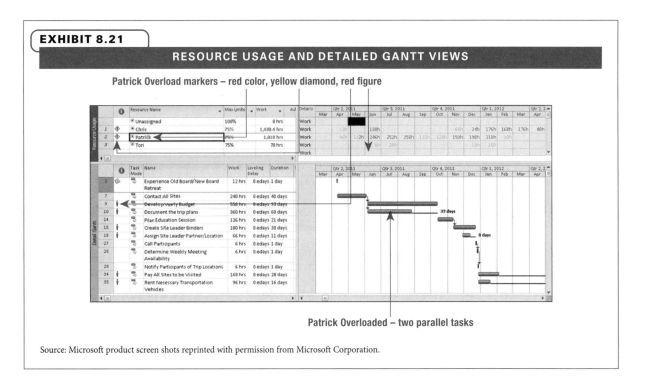

EXHIBIT 8.21

RESOURCE USAGE AND DETAILED GANTT VIEWS

Source: Microsoft product screen shots reprinted with permission from Microsoft Corporation.

very helpful in identifying overallocations, but the project manager is responsible for deciding what to do once the overallocation is found. Below are a few choices.

- Keep MS Project's resource leveling function set to Manual (Resource Leveling dialog box).
- Protect the schedule's critical path.
- Replace an overallocated resource with one that has time for the assignment.
- Reduce the Units assignment, extending the activity duration.
- De-scope the activity(ies).
- If some assigned resources are performing little work, remove them.
- Use the Leveling Delay task field to delay the start of one of the conflicting activities; the duration value is in the elapsed duration form, in which all calendar days are included, not just working days. Continue adding delay until the delay creates a new critical path.
- Check the Network Diagram for accuracy—correcting errors may remove the conflict.
- Ignore the overload if the resource impact is temporary.

Tips include the following:

- Note the project finish date, work, and cost values.
- Be aware of resource vacation days and organizational holidays.
- If changing assignments, note the duration and work values for the task.
- If swapping resources and there is a mix of units values among assigned resources, it may be easier to remove all resource assignments and then reassign them.
- Try Level Now (Resource Leveling dialog box, Tools menu); if the plan is suitable, then go forward (delay is imposed).
- Work from beginning to end. One fix may break something else.

Summary

Resourcing projects goes hand in hand with scheduling (Chapter 7) and budgeting (Chapter 9). To ensure that adequate human and other resources are assigned to a project, first the project manager needs to look at the listed activities and estimate the resources needed to perform each. Potential resources need to be identified, and their availability needs to be confirmed. The project manager may need to negotiate to secure the services of the needed people. Usually, some people assigned to the project are ready to go, while others need training and/or mentoring. Project teams sometimes need to rely on co-located and/or outsourced team members.

Several tools are useful in identifying and scheduling people. Resource assignments are often posted directly on a Gantt chart schedule. RACI charts are matrices that depict work activities on the vertical scale (often in the form of a WBS) and the various people who are involved on the horizontal scale. Work responsibilities are shown by code in the cells. Once workers have been assigned, responsibility histograms can be developed for each worker to determine whether he or she is overloaded at any point.

The combination of the critical path schedule with resource assignments and the resource histogram allows project planners to determine who is overloaded, at what time, and by what activities. Resource leveling is the method of using this information to reduce the peak demands for workers by postponing some of the noncritical activities within the amount of available slack. Sometimes this solves the problem. If not, some work might be assigned to a different person, the schedule might be delayed, the project scope might be reduced, and/or other methods might be employed. Often, the sponsor will want to be involved in making these decisions.

Once the project schedule is established and resources are assigned, it sometimes appears that the hoped-for completion date is not attainable. In these cases, it is common to look for methods of accelerating (or compressing) the project schedule. One frequently used method is crashing, in which a decision is made to pay extra money (often in the form of overtime pay) to speed up certain activities on the critical path. Another frequently used method is fast tracking, whereby activities that are normally conducted in sequence are either overlapped or performed in parallel. Fast tracking can lead to faster schedules. However, the risk is increased because the activity that normally is a successor depends on the output of its predecessor, and if that output is not as expected, the successor activity may need to be reworked.

Several alternative methods of scheduling can be used by themselves or combined with traditional scheduling and resourcing. These methods include critical chain, reverse phase, agile, auto/manual, and rolling wave scheduling. Experienced project managers attempt to use the best ideas from several of these alternative approaches.

Project scheduling software such as Microsoft Project is extremely useful when determining the resources for a project. This software helps pinpoint exactly when each worker is needed, for what activity, and where there are overloads. Despite the power of these scheduling systems, they do not make all of the decisions for a project. The project manager needs to understand the output of the software and may be able to ask a number of what-if questions. Ultimately, the project manager needs to make the decisions—often in conjunction with the sponsor.

Key Terms from the *PMBOK® Guide*

estimate activity resources, 211
staffing management plan, 211
responsibility assignment matrix, 216
Resource leveling, 219

Crashing, 222
Fast tracking, 222
critical chain method, 227

Chapter Review Questions

1. A project manager needs two types of skills, _____ and _____, to successfully resource a project.

2. To help ensure project support, it is important to involve workers in the _____ phase of the project.

3. What does a staffing management plan include?
4. A(n) _____ is a tool that is used to show resource assignments.
5. The first column of a RACI chart contains the _____. The second column contains the _____, and the remaining columns contain the _____.
6. It is best to only have one person assigned primary responsibility for an activity. True or false?
7. A(n) _____ is often used to show resource assignments.
8. Using a(n) _____ can help a project manager identify if workers are overloaded.
9. _____ is any form of schedule network analysis in which scheduling decisions are driven by resource constraints.
10. With resource leveling, _____ activities are often delayed first.
11. When performing resource leveling, it is helpful for the project manager to consult both the _____ and the _____.
12. Critical chain project management is a technique which uses both the predecessor–successor relationship and _____ and to calculate the project's critical path.
13. To reduce the total project duration, activities that are on the noncritical paths must be reduced. True or false?
14. _____ and _____ are two techniques that are used to compress project schedules.
15. When crashing a project, what two criteria are considered when deciding which activities to speed up?
16. List four common assignments that are given to workers on RACI charts.

Discussion Questions

1. Identify three examples of when a project manager uses technical skills and three examples of when a manager uses behavioral skills.
2. Describe the importance of activity resource estimating.
3. List at least four factors that a project manager should consider when identifying individuals to work on a project. Why is each important?
4. Why is it important to identify key members of a project early on?
5. Describe a potential timing issue that can occur early in a project and a potential timing issue that can occur at the end of a project. How would you address each of these issues in your project?
6. Describe two ways that a project manager can resolve resource overloads. Under what circumstances should each be used?
7. List three common problems that can occur when traditional critical path scheduling is used. How would you address each?
8. Give an example of what is given up in a project when it is crashed and when it is fast tracked.
9. Describe several instances in which a project schedule is limited mostly by activities. Describe several instances in which a project schedule is limited mostly by resources.
10. Explain how a project can be fast tracked.
11. Describe how to perform resource leveling.
12. Describe problems with traditional project scheduling techniques that encourage some organizations to use critical chain project management.
13. What considerations must a project manager keep in mind when identifying potential workers for a project?
14. Describe components of a critical chain project management system.
15. How are fast tracking and crashing different? How are they similar?

Exercises

1. A certain project has three activities on its critical path. Activity A's normal completion time is five days. It can be crashed to three days at a cost of $500. Activity B's normal completion time is six days, and it can be crashed to four days at a cost of $50. Activity C's normal completion time is eight days. It can be crashed to three days at a cost of $1,000. Which activity should the project manager crash and by how many days? How much will it cost?
2. Using the data on the CD for Problem 08.02, create the project schedule using normal times.

Determine the order in which you would crash the project one day, two days, and so on until it is in an all-crash mode. Identify how much it would cost for each day you crash the schedule.

3. Using the data on the CD for Problem 08.03, create the project schedule using normal times. Determine the order in which you would crash the project one day, two days, and so on until it is in an all-crash mode. Identify how much it would cost for each day you crash the schedule.

4. Using the data on the CD for Problem 08.04, create the project schedule in MS Project. Be sure to use both the predecessor relationships and the resource assignments. Use a split screen to show both the Gantt chart with critical path and resource assignments with overloads.

5. Using the data on the CD for Problem 08.05, create the project schedule in MS Project. Be sure to use both the predecessor relationships and the resource assignments. Use a split screen to show both the Gantt chart with critical path and resource assignments with overloads.

PMBOK® Guide Questions

1. Resources can refer to:
   a. people
   b. machines
   c. space
   d. all of the above

2. A(n) _____ addresses logistics regarding human resource requirements.
   a. critical chain method
   b. staffing management plan
   c. estimate activity resources
   d. project charter

3. Estimating activity resources is the "process of estimating the _____ and _____ of resources required to perform each scheduled activity."
   a. types; quantities
   b. costs; quantities
   c. types; costs
   d. none of the above

4. Key participants are ideally identified early enough to help:
   a. charter the project
   b. create a RACI chart
   c. debate the critical chain method
   d. write the work breakdown structure

5. What are the three "r" activities that take place near the end of a project, regarding team members?
   a. reevaluating, releasing, and recognizing
   b. rewarding, recognizing, and releasing
   c. releasing, rewarding, and reevaluating
   d. reevaluating, rewarding, and recognizing

Example Project

For your example project, create the following:

1. Staffing management plan
2. RACI chart
3. Schedule with resource assignments
4. Histogram of demands on each key participant's time
5. Plan for resolving resource overloads

References

A Guide to the Project Management Body of Knowledge (PMBOK® Guide), 4th ed. (Newtown Square, PA: Project Management Institute, 2008).

Brown, David, "Top 10 Steps to Schedule Management," *Electrical Construction and Maintenance* (March 2008): C22–C28.

Gagnon, Michel, "A Method of Integrating Personnel into the Project Schedule," *Proceedings, PMI Research Conference 2006* (Montreal, July 2006).

Globerson, Shlomo, "*PMBOK®* and the Critical Chain," *PM Network* 14 (5) (May 2000): 63–67.

Grant, Kevin P. and Michael R. Baumann, "Leveraging Project Team Expertise for Better Project Solutions,"

Proceedings, PMI Research Conference 2006 (Montreal, July 2006).

Hartman, Francis and Rafi Ashrafi, "Development of the SMART™ Project Planning Framework," *International Journal of Project Management* 22 (2004): 499–510.

Haugan, Gregory T., *Project Planning and Scheduling* (Vienna, VA: Management Concepts, Inc., 2002).

Horng, Shwu-Min, "A Stage-Based Human Resource Allocation Procedure for Project Management with Multiple Objectives," *Proceedings, PMI Research Conference 2006* (Montreal, July 2006).

Howard, Dale and Gary Chefetz, *What's New Study Guide Microsoft Project 2010*, (New York: Chefetz LLC dba MSProjectExperts, 2010).

Leach, Larry P., "Critical Chain Project Management Improves Project Performance," *Project Management Journal* 30 (2) (June 1999): 39–51.

Milosevic, Dragan Z., *Project Management Toolbox: Tools and Techniques for the Practicing Project Manager* (New York: John Wiley & Sons, 2003).

Piney, Crispin, "Critical Path or Critical Chain: Combining the Best of Both," *PM Network* 14 (12) (December 2000): 51–55.

"PMI Code of Ethics and Professional Conduct," *PMI Today* (December 2006): 12–13.

Rad, Parviz and Vittal Anantatmula, *Project Planning Techniques* (Vienna, VA: Management Concepts, Inc., 2005).

Raz, Tzvi, Robert Barnes, and Dov Dvir, "A Critical Look at Critical Chain Project Management," *Project Management Journal* 34 (4) (December 2003): 24–32.

Smith, Preston G, "Concurrent Product-Development Teams," in David I. Cleland, ed., *Field Guide to Project Management*, 2nd ed. (Hoboken, NJ: John Wiley & Sons, 2004).

Trietsch, Dan, "Why a Critical Path by Any Other Name Would Smell Less Sweet?" *Project Management Journal* 36 (1) (March 2005): 27–36.

Wheatley, Malcolm, "You Can't Always Get What You Want," *PM Network* 19 (12) (December 2005): 41–44.

http://www.ambysoft.com/essays/agileProjectPlanning.html, accessed August 3, 2010.

http://www.youtube.com/watch?v=IExA5fuWFgg, accessed August 3, 2010.

http://jbep.blogspot.com/2010/01/rolling-wave-planning-or-sliding.html, accessed August 3, 2010.

http://www.brighthub.com/office/project-management/articles/8717.aspx, accessed August 3, 2010.

http://office.microsoft.com/en-us/project-help/fast-track-tasks-to-shorten-your-project-schedule-HA010036399.aspx, accessed August 3, 2010.

http://en.wikipedia.org/wiki/Critical_Chain_Project_Management, accessed August 3, 2010.

Endnotes

1. *PMBOK® Guide* 434.
2. *PMBOK® Guide* 449.
3. Adapted from Parviz Rad and Vittal Anantatmula, *Project Planning Techniques* (Vienna, VA: Management Concepts, Inc., 2005): 68–72.
4. *PMBOK® Guide* 446.
5. Ibid.
6. *PMBOK® Guide* 431.
7. *PMBOK® Guide* 435.
8. *PMBOK® Guide* 431.
9. Ken Schwaber and Mike Beedle, *Agile Software Development with Scrum* (Prentice Hall, 2001).

PROJECT MANAGEMENT *IN ACTION*

Managing Software Development with Agile Methods and Scrum

The *Scrum* or rugby formation approach was first described by Takeuchi and Nonaka[9] as a holistic approach to managing new product development projects. They described this holistic approach as having six characteristics: built-in instability, self-organizing project teams, overlapping development phases, "multilearning" (across multiple levels and across multiple functions), subtle control, and organizational transfer of learning. The Scrum process was described for use in agile software development by Ken Schwaber and Mike Beedle. Exhibit 8.22 illustrates the *Scrum* process.

In practice, many agile methods and variations are utilized, but they all share a basis in iterative development, extensive verbal communication, team interaction, and the reduction of resource-intensive intermediate products. Agile software development methods attempt to minimize risk via short time boxes called iterations or *Sprints.* Typically, the time boxes are from one to a maximum of four weeks and usually include numerous subtasks. This is not completely inconsistent with the *PMBOK*®-recommended eighty-hour task rule. Each Sprint is frequently like a software development project in and of itself and includes planning, requirements analysis, design, coding, testing, and documentation. Some iterations may generate new products or capa-

bilities, but most are integrated into larger groups to be released as new products. Scalability is one of the benefits of the approach, and another is the opportunity to reevaluate priorities in an incremental fashion. This technique, therefore, can be used effectively for software maintenance and enhancements, as well as new product development.

Scrum is facilitated by a *ScrumMaster* who organizes the project like any good project manager. This person has the primary task of removing impediments to the ability of the team to deliver the Sprint goal and project objectives. The ScrumMaster is not necessarily the leader of the team in the traditional formal sense (as the teams are self-organizing), but acts as a productivity buffer between the team and any destabilizing influences. This encourages the emergence of informal leadership and team cohesiveness. Scrum includes the following elements, which define the process:

- A dynamic backlog of prioritized work to be accomplished
- The use of short iterations or Sprints
- A brief daily meeting or Scrum session during which progress is explained, upcoming work is described, and impediments are identified and if possible immediately resolved

---

EXHIBIT 8.22

SCRUM APPROACH TO NEW PRODUCT DEVELOPMENT PROJECTS

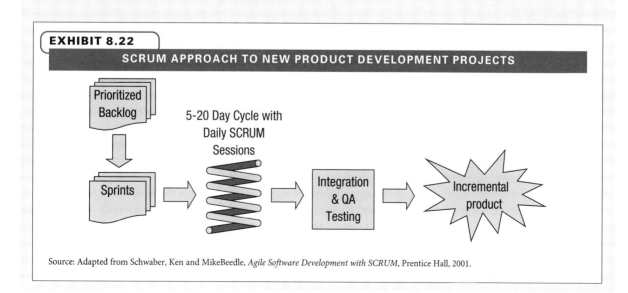

Source: Adapted from Schwaber, Ken and MikeBeedle, *Agile Software Development with SCRUM*, Prentice Hall, 2001.

- A brief planning session during which the prioritized backlog of items for the Sprint is identified and further defined by the team
- A brief retrospective during which all team members reflect about the past Sprint and any design or other influences on future Sprints or objectives

This approach keeps everyone on the team engaged and focused. It works very well when everyone is co-located to facilitate verbal communications, but has been shown to work well in virtual teams or geographically dispersed teams as well. The emphasis on verbal communications has proven to be particularly useful for international teams where written communications alone may not be clearly understood. The use of video conferencing and virtual development environments is also beneficial in these situations.

Agile software development teams include all resources necessary to accomplish the tasks and finish the software product. This includes designers, architects, analysts, testers, technical writers, managers, and customers (the people who define the final product).

The primary metric for progress in this environment is working software based on the scope as identified in the Sprints. Schedules and other resources are based on accomplishing the Sprints and removing impediments. With their preference for verbal communications, agile methods produce very little written documentation relative to other methods. That is not to say that the team produces no documentation, as it is important to have requirements, design, and other aspects of the software product documented to facilitate maintenance and support and in some cases to meet industry regulatory compliance requirements. This reduced emphasis on documentation has resulted in criticism of agile methods as undisciplined or, as some have called it, "cowboy coding." As a rule, this does not seem to be the case in practice because, if properly implemented, the requirements are documented in the prioritized backlog; the design is documented in the Sprints and Scrum sessions; and the testing, user, and technical documents complete the documentation set. It is important to note that the use of a scribe during Scrum sessions, planning, or retrospective sessions is vital to capture what is transpiring, since the sessions tend to be short and intense by nature.

Many companies have now embraced the agile methods to reduce development time, foster innovation, and reduce development risk. One example is a Seattle-based company that has utilized Scrum to shorten development cycle time and improve quality for software deliveries to its clients. It uses Sprints to group similar requirements and provide a two-week window of work for its developers. Daily Scrum sessions help it stay focused and deal immediately with impediments. This works ideally in that it keeps task scope to a minimum for the developers, and everyone on the team is aware of what is transpiring throughout the development process. This has shortened development time and led to more rapid release of products and enhancements to the clients, thus reducing development costs and improving margins.

Another example is an Ohio company that utilizes agile methods and Scrum for software development for clients in the highly regulated pharmaceutical, bio-tech, and medical device industries. A recent software system developed to be used in manufacturing data acquisition and control for products requiring complete traceability, including raw materials and processes, was designed and development in five months to beta delivery. The software will ultimately track and control all of the company's production when fully implemented. The system was put into a pilot manufacturing line. It was working within 30 minutes of software installation, and processed product through the pilot production facility the same day without a glitch. The system was delivered essentially bug free. This was unheard of previously using traditional development methods and would have taken a year or more to get to beta delivery, with many more issues. The company accounts for this success due to the use of the agile process, Scrum, and thorough quality testing. The requirements in this regulated environment were developed in a traditional manner; however, once the requirements were approved by the client management, the Scrum approach was used, which represented a departure from the traditional waterfall approach. Each module of the system was developed separately using the Scrum approach by focusing on developing a few design elements at a time rather than trying to focus on the entire system design at once. In this way, the development team could focus and accomplish a few things at a time and leave the big picture design and architecture to the ScrumMaster and development management. Use of this approach exceeded all expectations. Since the beta delivery six months ago, the system has operated in the pilot plant and is now being updated with three minor bug fixes and seven enhancements prior to being validated and placed into the production environment in 2007.

Source: Warren A. Opfer, CCP, PMP®.

CHAPTER 9

Budgeting Projects

CHAPTER OBJECTIVES

After completing this chapter, you should be able to:

- Define project cost terms and tell how each is used in estimating project cost.

- Compare and contrast analogous, parametric, and bottom-up methods of estimating cost.

- Describe issues in project cost estimating and how to deal with each.

- Create a time phased, bottom-up budget for a project.

- Show both summary and bottom-up project budget information with cumulative costs using MS Project.

Jupiterimages/Comstock/Jupiterimages

I sold escalators and elevators for my first job out of business school. As part of my training, before I was sent to the field, I would look over the estimates made by the sales staff. This served to double-check their math so the company had confidence in their estimates. It also served to teach me many of the little nuances that more experienced estimators used. I had my training manuals, lists of standards, main methods of calculation, and so forth, but learning from others' experience instead of making all my own mistakes helped.

One of the last parts in my training was to spend eight weeks at the Denver branch to get seasoned a little bit. Construction was booming in Denver during the late 1970s. In fact, some days I needed to bid more

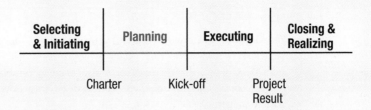

Selecting & Initiating	Planning	Executing	Closing & Realizing

Charter   Kick-off   Project
                                          Result

PMBOK®
GUIDE **TOPICS:**

- Estimate cost
- Determine budget
- Control cost

than one job. The first part of putting together a bid was to go the office where the requests for proposals, plans, specifications, and the like were stored. Then, armed with that information, I would put together an estimate. Finally, the actual bidding took place—usually over the phone. The problem was that creating a detailed estimate would generally take at least half a day. If that was my only duty (it was not), I would still have had a hard time when multiple jobs were let for bid on the same day. Something had to give.

Every morning around 10 A.M., I met the construction superintendent for coffee. We would discuss each bid that was due. What other job was it like? How was it bigger or smaller than a recently completed job? What features did it include more or less than a previous job? Did we make money on that job? We used these questions to compare an upcoming job to other recently completed jobs. We would also ask, "What do we think our competition will bid?" By the end of the conversation, we had determined our strategy for bidding the job. If we won the bid, we would complete a detailed cost estimate to see if we were close.

After my training, I was transferred to Kansas City. Kansas City had less construction than Denver. I had enough time to perform detailed cost estimates before I submitted bids. Therefore, we were more certain that if we got the bid, we would have a good chance of making money.

I worked for the same company in both cities. However, we used two very different methods of estimating cost. Both made sense where they were used. In Denver, if we wanted to bid every job (and you cannot win the job if you do not bid on it), we needed a fast method. In Kansas City, we had the time to develop detailed cost estimates, and so we took the time. There are many methods of estimating project costs and each has its place.

9.1 Introduction to Project Budgeting

This chapter starts with estimating project costs. Once the overall cost is estimated, the next step is to develop the budget by aggregating the costs and determining the project's cash flow needs. Project managers also need to establish a system to report and control project costs. The final chapter section deals with how to use Microsoft Project to aid in cost management activities.

Cost and schedule are closely related. Sometimes, the two move in the same direction. For example, when a schedule calls for materials to be delivered, or for workers to perform, money needs to be available to pay for the materials or workers. Sometimes, they move in opposite directions. For example, if a project needs to be completed earlier than planned, more money will probably need to be found to pay for overtime.

Cost planning entails developing a cost management plan for your project. The **cost management plan** is "the document that sets out the format and establishes the activities and criteria for planning, structuring, and controlling the project costs."[1] On small projects, this can be as simple as ensuring accurate estimates are made, securing the funding, and developing cost reporting procedures to ensure that the money is spent correctly. On large projects, each of these processes can be significantly more involved; in addition, developing and using accurate cash flow estimates become critical.

A project cost management plan needs to be consistent with the methods of the parent organization. In many organizations, project managers are provided with specific guidance on setting up their cost management plan. The plan provides guidance to the project manager and other stakeholders in order to serve several purposes:

- First and most fundamentally, it shows how to develop and share relevant, accurate, and timely information that the project manager, sponsor, and other stakeholders can use to make intelligent and ethical decisions.
- It provides feedback, thereby showing how the project's success is linked to the business objectives for which it was undertaken.
- It provides information at a detailed level for those who need details and at appropriate summary levels for those who need that.
- It helps all project stakeholders focus appropriately on schedule and performance as well as cost.[2]

9.2 Estimate Cost

Estimate cost is "the process of developing an approximation of the cost of the resources needed to complete project activities."[3] Cost estimating is linked very closely with scope, schedule, and resource planning. To understand cost well, a project manager needs to understand what the work of the project includes, what schedule demands exist, and what people and other resources can be used. As more of this detail becomes known, the cost estimates can be more precise.

The first principle in dealing with project costs is for the project manager to never lie to himself. Many times, in dealing with project costs, the project manager will need to negotiate with sponsors, customers, and other stakeholders. If he does not understand what the project costs really are, he is just trading meaningless numbers. That is neither an effective nor an ethical method of establishing and committing to sensible budgets.

The second principle in dealing with project costs is for the project manager to never lie to anyone else. Since sponsors, customers, and other stakeholders can often dictate, it is sometimes tempting to shade the truth to secure funding that appears to be necessary. This is wrong on two fundamental counts. First, it is ethically wrong. Second, as a practical matter, a project manager's reputation goes a long way for good or for bad.

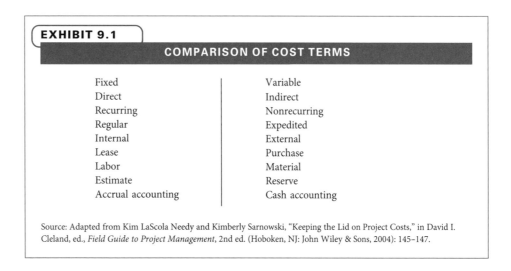

EXHIBIT 9.1

COMPARISON OF COST TERMS

Fixed	Variable
Direct	Indirect
Recurring	Nonrecurring
Regular	Expedited
Internal	External
Lease	Purchase
Labor	Material
Estimate	Reserve
Accrual accounting	Cash accounting

Source: Adapted from Kim LaScola Needy and Kimberly Sarnowski, "Keeping the Lid on Project Costs," in David I. Cleland, ed., *Field Guide to Project Management*, 2nd ed. (Hoboken, NJ: John Wiley & Sons, 2004): 145–147.

People are more inclined to work with project managers who are viewed as being honest and trustworthy.

To estimate project costs accurately, the project manager must understand the various types of cost, the timing and accuracy of cost estimates, the different methods that can be employed to estimate costs, and a variety of cost estimating issues.

Types of Cost

Costs can be better understood by considering various types of classifications such as those shown in Exhibit 9.1.

FIXED VERSUS VARIABLE COSTS   Cost can first be classified as either being fixed or variable. Fixed costs are those that remain the same regardless of the size or volume of work. For example, if you need to buy a computer for your project, the cost is the same regardless of how much you use it. Variable costs are those that vary directly with volume of use. For example, if you were building a cement wall, the cost of the cement would vary directly with the size of the wall. To understand the importance of fixed versus variable costs, a project manager ideally structures costs and the impact of changes on those costs. When a project manager understands how big a project is likely to be, she will try to determine how to complete all of the project work for the least cost. On many projects, there are choices of how to perform certain activities. Some of these choices reflect a high-fixed-cost and low-variable-cost alternative such as buying an expensive machine that can make parts with low variable costs versus a more manual process of inexpensive machines but high labor costs. These choices require both some fixed and some variable costs. Ideally, the cost curve for the expected project volume appears as shown in Exhibit 9.2. This reflects the lowest possible total cost at the size the project is expected to be. That is good. Unfortunately, problems may occur if the volume of the project work is substantially larger or smaller than first expected. If the volume drops a little bit, the total costs may drop very little. If the volume expands a little, the costs may go up significantly. Therefore, when considering fixed and variable cost choices, it is important to understand the project scope.

DIRECT VERSUS INDIRECT COSTS   A second classification divides project costs into direct and indirect costs. Direct costs are those that only occur because of the project and are often classified as either direct labor or other direct costs. For example, direct

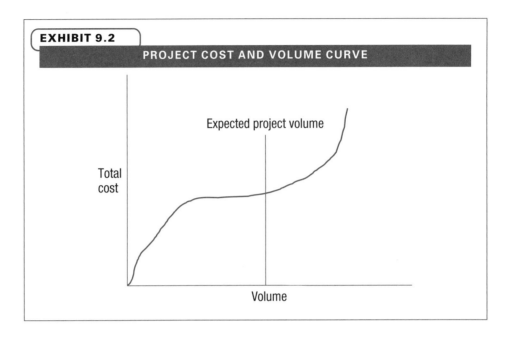

labor includes workers who are hired specifically to work on the project and who will be either assigned to a new project or released when the project is complete. Other direct costs may include such items as materials, travel, consultants, subcontracts, purchased parts, and computer time.

Indirect costs are those that are necessary to keep the organization running, but are not associated with one specific project. The salaries of the company executives and the cost of company buildings, utilities, insurance, and clerical assistance are examples. These costs are allocated among all of the projects and other work that benefit from them. The methods of allocating these costs have evolved in recent years thanks to activity-based costing, as described in the cost estimating issues section. Exhibit 9.3 shows both direct and indirect costs for a work package.

RECURRING VERSUS NONRECURRING COSTS The third cost comparison is recurring versus nonrecurring costs. Recurring costs are those that repeat as the project work continues, such as the cost of writing code or laying bricks. Nonrecurring costs are those that happen only once during a project, such as developing a design that, once approved, guides the project team. Nonrecurring costs tend to occur during project planning and closing, while recurring costs tend to occur during project execution.

REGULAR VERSUS EXPEDITED COSTS A fourth way of looking at project costs is as being either regular or expedited. Regular costs are preferred and occur when progress can be made by normal work hours and purchasing agreements. Expedited costs occur when the project must be conducted faster than normal and overtime for workers and/or extra charges for more rapid delivery from suppliers are necessary. The comparison of these costs shows why it is vital to understand schedule pressures and resource demands as costs are estimated.

OTHER COST CLASSIFICATIONS The next several cost comparisons require little explanation. They are helpful to understand both in structuring the cost estimates and as checklists to help remember items that may be forgotten. One comparison is costs

EXHIBIT 9.3

DIRECT AND INDIRECT COSTS IN A WORK PACKAGE

Project: Accounts Payable Refinement	Work Package: Install Module 1	
Description: Install accounts payable refinement application and related hardware.	**Deliverable(s):** Installed and functioning accounts payable module.	
Cost Categories	**Quantity**	**Total**
Direct Labor		
Programmer	120 hrs @ $ 75/hr	9,000
Systems Analyst	40 hrs @ $ 100/hr	4,000
Systems Architect	20 hrs @ $ 120/hr	2,400
Other Direct		
Hardware		20,000
Software		8,400
Consultant Services		12,000
Direct Overhead (.6 * DL)		**9,240**
	Total	**65,040**

Source: Kevin P. Grant, University of Texas, San Antonio. Adapted with permission.

internal to the parent organization versus those external to it. Major external cost items such as equipment can be either leased or purchased. Direct cost items are often labor or materials.

Estimate versus reserve costs form the next comparison. The **estimate** is "a quantified assessment of the likely amount. ... It should always include an indication of accuracy."[4] The **reserve** is "a provision in the project management plan to mitigate cost and/or schedule risk. Often used with a modifier (e.g. management reserve, contingency reserve) to provide further detail on what types of risk are meant to be mitigated."[5]

Just as uncertainty exists when estimating how long an activity will take, there is uncertainty regarding how much an activity will cost. Some activities are easy to estimate with precision. Other less familiar activities have many uncertainties, and estimating their cost is more like guessing. If one were to estimate conservatively on each uncertain activity, the total estimate for the project would likely be too high to be approved. To overcome this problem, project managers are encouraged to estimate at least a bit more aggressively. That means some activities will run over their estimates, while others will cost less. Project managers frequently add a reserve to cover the activities that run over their aggressive estimates.

Yet another comparison is between two methods of accounting for costs rather than categories of costs. In accrual accounting, transactions are recorded for the time period in which the expense occurred. This helps project managers understand when invoices are submitted for costs incurred. On the other hand, cash accounting records transactions when money is spent; this helps project managers understand the cash flow on their projects. Of the two, cash accounting is used more often on projects.[6]

Accuracy and Timing of Cost Estimates

Project managers need to understand when cost estimates should be developed, how accurate they need to be, and how they will be used. During project initiation, many project managers need to develop cost estimates to have their project charters approved. At this point, very little detail is understood regarding the project, so the estimates are only approximate. However, as the scope becomes well defined in the work breakdown structure (WBS), schedules are planned, and specific resources are assigned, the project manager knows much more and can estimate more precisely. Many organizations have specific names and guidance for their estimates and these vary widely. Normally, estimates should be documented and the level of confidence in the estimate should be described. Exhibit 9.4 shows several points regarding different types of project cost estimates.

ORDER OF MAGNITUDE ESTIMATES Several things should be noted from these comparisons. First, estimates go by several different names. For example, order of magnitude estimates that are often used to seek initial charter approval are also sometimes called "ball park," "conceptual," "initial," or "level-one" estimates. These early estimates are often created during the project initiating stage when very little detail is known about the project. At this point, a very rough order of magnitude estimate that could underestimate the project by as much as 100 percent (that is, the final cost could be double the initial estimate) may be the only possible estimate. There is no way to really know how accurate an estimate is until the project has been completed, but with less detailed knowledge concerning the project in the initiating stage, there is likely to be a larger margin of error. Order of magnitude cost estimates and the parallel high-level looks at each of the other planning areas can quickly give enough information to decide whether to approve the project charter and begin to invest time and money into detailed planning.

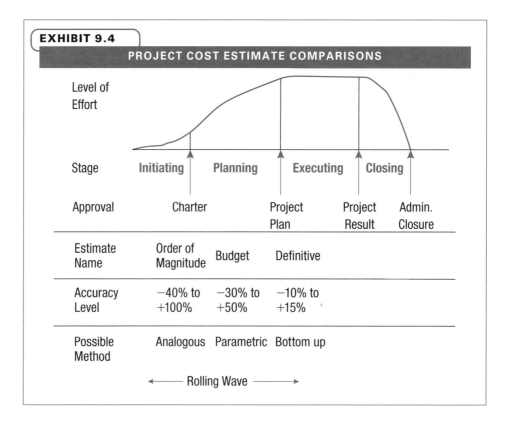

EXHIBIT 9.4

PROJECT COST ESTIMATE COMPARISONS

Stage	Initiating	Planning	Executing	Closing
Approval	Charter		Project Plan	Project Result	Admin. Closure
Estimate Name	Order of Magnitude	Budget	Definitive	
Accuracy Level	−40% to +100%	−30% to +50%	−10% to +15%	
Possible Method	Analogous	Parametric	Bottom up	

←——— Rolling Wave ———→

BUDGET AND DEFINITIVE ESTIMATES Once a project manager enters into the more detailed planning stage, it is generally possible to create a more accurate cost estimate. This is the same thought that goes into creating a more detailed project schedule, resource estimates, risk profiles, quality plans, and communications plans. Depending on the complexity and size of their projects and organizational norms, some project managers can proceed directly to definitive cost estimates at this point. Others may still need to look at one or more intermediate levels of detail before they have enough detailed knowledge to create cost estimates with accuracy. At the end of project planning, cost estimates should have a small enough margin of error that they can be used to create a project budget, show cash flow needs, and be used as a basis for controlling the project. Most project organizations want an accuracy level of no more than plus or minus 10 to 15 percent, and some require considerably better, such as plus or minus 5 percent.

Especially on complex projects such as research and development of major new products, project managers may use rolling wave planning to estimate costs. They do this by creating a definitive estimate for the first stage of the project (and committing to it) and an order of magnitude estimate for the remainder of the project. As the work on the first stage proceeds, the project manager then creates a definitive estimate for the second stage and reevaluates the order of magnitude estimate for the remainder of the project. At each stage, the project manager has more information than at the preceding stage and can create more accurate estimates.

Methods of Estimating Costs

Many methods can be used for estimating project costs. Most of the methods are variations of one of the following techniques. While these methods can sometimes also be used to estimate project scope or duration, in this chapter, the discussion centers on using them to estimate project cost. Exhibit 9.4 indicates that as more details of a project are known as planning progresses, more detailed estimating methods may be used. However, Exhibit 9.5

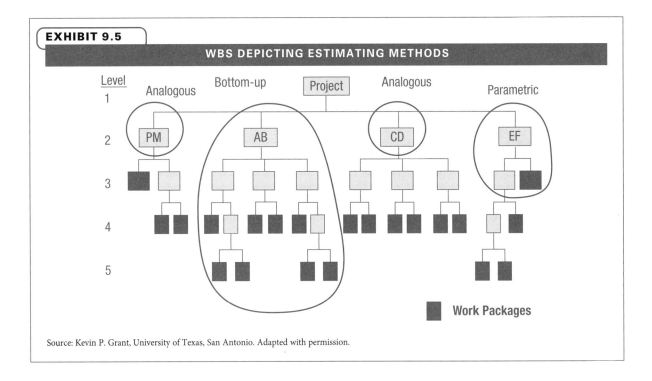

EXHIBIT 9.5

WBS DEPICTING ESTIMATING METHODS

Source: Kevin P. Grant, University of Texas, San Antonio. Adapted with permission.

shows that even at the end of project planning, a project manager may sometimes use a combination of cost estimating methods. If the organization has accurate enough analogous and parametric estimating methods and capable estimators, sometimes portions of a project can be estimated by those methods instead of the more detailed (and time-consuming) bottom-up methods. The method used should account for the extent of complexity, risk, interdependencies, work force specialization, and site-specific issues of the project.[7]

ANALOGOUS ESTIMATING **Analogous estimating** is "an estimating technique that uses parameters such as scope, cost, budget, or duration, or measures of scale such as size, weight, or complexity, from a previous similar activity as the basis for estimating the same parameter or measure for a future activity."[8] Analogous estimating was the method used in Denver in this chapter's opening vignette. To create a bid for a project—in this case, the installation of elevators—a similar project was considered as the starting point. Immediately, questions were asked regarding how this job compared in size and complexity with the previous job. Several things need to be in place for analogous estimates to be effective. First, the organization needs to have experience in performing similar projects and know how much each of those projects actually cost (not just what they were estimated to cost). Second, at least on a big picture basis, the estimator needs to know how the proposed project differs from the previous project. Third, the estimator needs to have experience with the methods by which the project will be performed. In the example, sales and construction people jointly discussed how much the project would cost.

PARAMETRIC ESTIMATING **Parametric estimating** is "an estimating technique that uses a statistical relationship between historical data and other variables to calculate project costs."[9] A bit more information is needed to complete a parametric cost estimate. Exhibit 9.5 shows this graphically by suggesting that another level of detail in the WBS might be used. In the chapter opener example of estimating the cost of elevator installation projects, parametric estimates might involve finding a bit more information regarding the project. For example, one might want to know how tall the elevator was, how fast it needed to travel, how large the platform would be, the trim level, the complexity of the controls, and the like. Each of those factors would have an impact on the elevator installation cost. For example, the cost per foot traveled might be calculated (this would cover the cost of providing and installing guide rails, wiring, etc.). Another cost might be associated with speed because faster elevators require bigger motors, more stability, stronger brakes, and so on.

BOTTOM-UP ESTIMATING **Bottom-up estimating** is "a method of estimating a component of work. The work is decomposed into more detail. An estimate is prepared of what is needed to meet the requirements of each of the lower, more detailed pieces of work, and these estimates are then aggregated into a total quantity for the project."[10] For a bottom-up estimate, the WBS needs to be broken down to the most

© Andia/Alamy

Parametric estimating can be used to determine the impact of variables on project costs.

detailed level and the specifications need to be very clear. In the elevator example, bottom-up estimates were created in Kansas City. Details to be estimated included exactly how many buttons the control panel had, exactly what kind of light fixtures were mounted in the ceiling, what kind of finish was requested, and so on. The cost was estimated for each item. For example, for the process of installing the guide rail, first there was a small amount of time, such as one hour, to set up or get everything in place to do this step. Then, it took a certain fraction of an hour of labor to secure each foot of the rail into position. A material charge was incurred for the guide rails themselves and the fasteners that held them in place. The cost of supervision was charged for the foreperson who ensured the work was scheduled and performed properly. Finally, overhead costs (indirect costs) were allocated to each dollar of fixed costs.

Bottom-up estimating is the most detailed, time-consuming, and potentially accurate way to estimate. Most projects use this method eventually to serve as a basis for estimating cash flow needs and for controlling the project. One important caution on bottom-up estimating is to ensure that every item is included. If a portion of the project is left out, that portion is underestimated by 100 percent! Exhibit 9.6 summarizes differences in cost estimating methods.

Project Cost Estimating Issues

Regardless of what method is used to estimate project costs, several issues need to be considered. Some of these issues are pertinent to all projects; others only pertain to certain projects. These issues are shown in Exhibit 9.7.

SUPPORTING DETAIL Supporting detail for project cost estimates includes describing the scope, method used to create the estimate, assumptions, constraints, and range of possible outcomes. The project scope tends to be the least well defined at the project outset and becomes increasingly well defined throughout project planning. Each estimate

---

EXHIBIT 9.6

COST ESTIMATING METHOD COMPARISON

	ANALOGOUS	PARAMETRIC	BOTTOM-UP
Amount of Information Required	Least	Middle	Most
Amount of Time Required	Least	Middle	Most
Accuracy Obtained	Lowest	Middle	Highest

EXHIBIT 9.7

ISSUES IN PROJECT COST ESTIMATING

Supporting detail
Causes of variation
Vendor bid analysis
Value engineering
Activity-based costing
Life cycle costing
Time value of money
International currency fluctuations

should state exactly what scope it involves. Version control is critical for this. The method used might be analogous, parametric, or bottom-up. The name of the method and exactly how the method is used should be described.

When creating an estimate, many assumptions and constraints are often used. Assumptions should be outlined because two different people coming from two different backgrounds may assume that two different things will happen. Even if everyone involved with planning a project assumes the same thing, it still may not happen. Assumptions that are not true often cause more work or other problems for a project. As more detail becomes known, a project manager may review assumptions with an eye toward uncovering assumptions that have now proven to be false. When this happens, the project manager can investigate any impact this may have on the project budget (and schedule and scope). Examples of assumptions that may arise when estimating the cost of direct labor might include the following:

- Workers will be paid at the prevailing wage rate of $14 per hour.
- Workers are already familiar in general with the technology being used on the project.
- Workers will be paid for 40 hours per week whether there is always that much work for them or not.
- Overtime will never be authorized.
- The project schedule can be delayed if the only alternative is to pay overtime.

Constraints are also important to bring to the surface since they often dictate the methods available for performing the project work. Examples of constraints include:

- Only in-house workers will be used.
- No extra space will be provided.
- No extra budget will be allowed.
- The current version of the XYZ software will be incorporated into the design.

The range of possible outcomes should always be stated with any project cost estimate. If the range is not stated, people may lock onto the first number they hear. If the actual project costs could be 100 percent higher than the order of magnitude estimate, the project manager had better state that loud and clear or she may find herself continually explaining why she is grossly over budget. In fact, many estimators resist giving an order of magnitude estimate because they fear they will be held to it. A natural tension exists between executives and managers who try to effectively manage their departments by establishing budgets as soon as possible and project managers who try to provide budget estimates as late as possible (once they know more about the project).

CAUSES OF VARIATION There are many causes of variation in project costs. On routine projects using proven technology and an experienced and well-known project team, the causes may be relatively few and easy to categorize. On other projects where some of these factors are not true, more causes of uncertainty in project costs may exist, and some of those may be from unknown sources. Statisticians classify variation as coming from either normal or special causes, as shown in Exhibit 9.8.

Variation occurs in all work processes. The more routine a process is and the more work is driven by machines, the less variation occurs. Projects, however, tend to have novel work and high human interaction, so there are many opportunities for variation. Normal variation comes from many small causes that are inherent in a work process. For instance, the variation in the productivity of a programmer writing code could be from phone calls, instant messages, and in-person interruptions that occur each day. Special cause variation, on the other hand, is when something out of the ordinary occurs. For

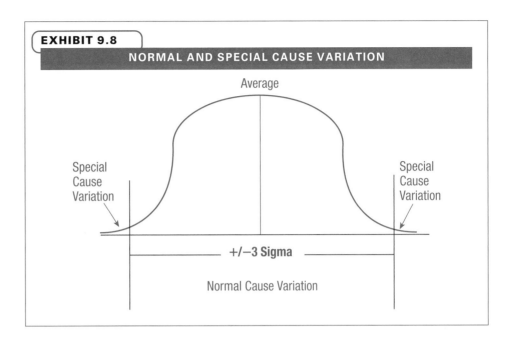

EXHIBIT 9.8

NORMAL AND SPECIAL CAUSE VARIATION

Average

Special
Cause
Variation

Special
Cause
Variation

+/−3 Sigma

Normal Cause Variation

example, a lightning strike could cause such a large power surge that it overwhelms the normal protectors and destroys some of the computers. Most causes of variation are of the normal variety, and improving work methods (as discussed in Chapter 11) can help to reduce this type of variation. Special causes, however, are handled more as risks as discussed in Chapter 10. Both types of variation add to project costs and need to be considered.

VENDOR BID ANALYSIS On some projects, most or all of the cost is internal to the parent organization. On other projects, a substantial portion of the budget goes to securing services and supplies from vendors. Vendor bid analysis is used to determine whether the price being asked by the vendors appears to be reasonable. If several vendors compete for the work, it is reasonable to believe that the lowest responsible offer is fair. In the absence of competition, however, other methods may be needed to ensure a fair price. On some items, prices are determined in the marketplace and reported in business papers and websites for anyone to read. On specialized services and products, one often must negotiate with a vendor. In the absence of any other method, for an expensive item, a project manager may need to develop a "should cost estimate." That is, try to determine how much effort the vendor may need to expend and add a fair profit margin to arrive at the price you believe the vendor should charge.

VALUE ENGINEERING **Value engineering** is "an approach used to optimize project life cycle costs, save time, increase profits, improve quality, expand market share, solve problems, and/or use resources more effectively."[11] Value engineering can be a very powerful method of double-checking all of the chosen methods for accomplishing work and the features of the project deliverable. Frequently, stakeholders find a feature that was in the specifications costs more money to create than they wish to pay. In a project to update an older church, the liturgical committee proposed many controls for special lighting that would only be used on special occasions. The general contractor suggested simplifying the controls, while retaining all of the new lights, at a savings of $100,000! While the liturgical committee was disappointed, the church council readily agreed.

Value engineering is so common in some industries that a separate stage is incorporated late in the project planning to ensure that time is spent in this effort to reduce project cost and/or time and to improve project quality and/or usefulness.

ACTIVITY-BASED COSTING Another issue project managers need to understand when estimating costs is what type of accounting system the organization uses. Historically, most companies used functional-based accounting systems. When using these systems, overhead (indirect) costs are assigned to a cost pool, which is allocated to direct costs based most frequently on volume. When direct costs were a large percentage of total costs, this made sense. In more contemporary times, indirect costs form a much larger percentage of total costs, so careful allocation of them is necessary both for selecting the projects that truly will contribute the most profit and for ensuring a focus on controlling the highest costs. Activity-based costing is another accounting approach, by which indirect costs are allocated to fixed costs based upon four different types of drivers. The cost drivers are number of units produced (frequently, the only method used in functional-based accounting), number of batches run, number of product variations, and amount of facility utilized. Activity-based costing requires more involved methods for allocating indirect costs, but yields more accurate cost information. Project managers need to understand how costs are allocated in their organization so they can accurately estimate the amount of indirect costs that will be assigned to their projects.

LIFE CYCLE COSTING Life cycle costing is another concept project managers need to understand when estimating their project costs. Many project selection decisions are made based upon the total costs of both creating the project and of using the result of the project during its useful life. This total cost is called the life cycle cost. Many times, tradeoff decisions are considered that might involve spending more during the project to create a product that costs less to operate during its useful life. In an age when environmental concerns are appropriately being considered more heavily, to calculate total life cycle costs, a project manager may also need to consider disposition costs of the product after its useful life is complete. This can entail designing more recyclable parts (even at a higher cost) into the product.

TIME VALUE OF MONEY AND INTERNATIONAL CURRENCY FLUCTUATIONS When considering costs in the future, project managers need to understand how to calculate the time value of money. One dollar today is presumably worth more than one dollar next year. Discounting the value of future revenue and cost streams to account for this enables better project decisions. Project managers need to discount future dollars by the appropriate factor. Often, the finance department at a company tells the project manager what rate to use. The rate depends upon the underlying inflation rate plus the cost of capital. On international projects, it can also depend upon international currency fluctuations.

9.3 Determine Budget

Once the project costs have been estimated, it is time to establish the project budget. **Budgeting** is "the process of aggregating the estimated costs of individual activities or work packages to establish an authorized cost baseline."[12] To develop the budget, the project manager starts by aggregating all of the various costs. Once those are totaled, it is time to determine how much money is required for reserve funds. Finally, the project manager must understand cash flow—both in terms of funding and requirements for costs.

Aggregating Costs

When the entire project costs, both direct and indirect, have been added up, the result is a **cost performance baseline**, which is "a specific version of a time-phased budget used to compare actual expenditures to planned expenditures to determine if preventive or corrective action is needed to meet the project objectives."[13] This cost baseline forms an integral part of the project management plan. The cost baseline can only be changed by going through a formal change management process, described in Chapter 14.

The work packages that are identified when creating a WBS not only take time, but they also cost money. The project budget can be aggregated from the work packages. Exhibit 9.9 shows how six work packages appear on a Gantt chart with the cost of each work package listed on a monthly basis. The total cost for the month is shown and the cumulative cost for the project below that. Finally, a graph appears at the bottom that shows the cumulative cost of the project at each point in time. This represents the time-phased project budget. This will be used as the project progresses for control purposes. Note the cumulative cost curve approximates an "S" shape with slow expenditures (and progress) early in the project, rapid in the middle, and slow late in the project. This

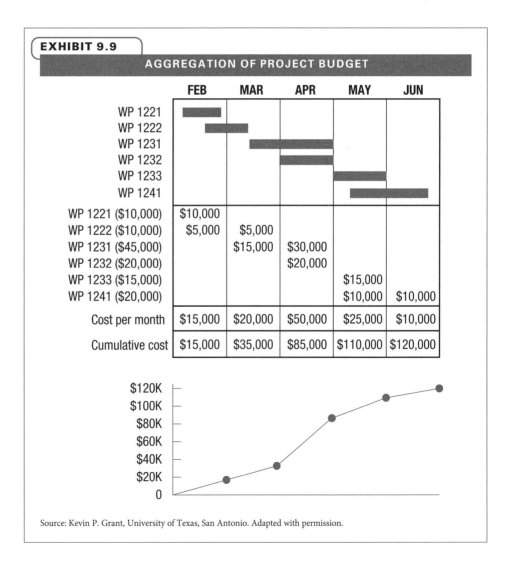

EXHIBIT 9.9

AGGREGATION OF PROJECT BUDGET

	FEB	MAR	APR	MAY	JUN
WP 1221 ($10,000)	$10,000				
WP 1222 ($10,000)	$5,000	$5,000			
WP 1231 ($45,000)		$15,000	$30,000		
WP 1232 ($20,000)			$20,000		
WP 1233 ($15,000)				$15,000	
WP 1241 ($20,000)				$10,000	$10,000
Cost per month	$15,000	$20,000	$50,000	$25,000	$10,000
Cumulative cost	$15,000	$35,000	$85,000	$110,000	$120,000

Source: Kevin P. Grant, University of Texas, San Antonio. Adapted with permission.

EXHIBIT 9.10			
ESTIMATING COSTS OF PROJECT VARIATION			
HOW VARIATION IS UNDERSTOOD	KNOWN KNOWNS	KNOWN UNKNOWNS	UNKNOWN UNKNOWNS
How It Is Discovered	Scope definition Create WBS	Risk identification	Situation occurs
Stage When It Is Usually Uncovered	Initiating or planning	Initiating or planning	Executing
Method of Estimating Costs	Estimate directly	Contingency reserves	Management reserves

is common as projects often require much planning early and have a variety of activities to finish at the end.

Analyzing Reserve Needs

Another view of project cost variation is to consider how well it is understood and how each type is handled. This is displayed in Exhibit 9.10.

Variation in project costs (and schedules) can be partially explained by the presence of certain events. These events are classified as known knowns, known unknowns, or unknown unknowns depending on the extent to which they are understood and predicted. Known knowns are discovered during planning and can be estimated directly. An example could be that when a construction crew takes soil samples, they discover that extra pilings are required to stabilize the new building, and they add the cost into the project estimate to cover that expense.

Known unknowns are events discovered during risk identification that may or may not occur. An example could be snowstorms that cause traffic problems for three days at a critical time, preventing workers from getting to their jobs. In the next chapter on risk, methods for calculating this cost are shown. It will appear as contingency reserves.

Finally, sometimes things that are totally unexpected happen that cause an increase in cost and/or schedule. For example, perhaps a very dependable supplier goes out of business due to the sudden death of the owner. These unknown unknowns (commonly called *unk unks* by people who have felt burned by them) also need to be covered in the project budget. The money used to cover them is frequently called a management reserve.

The amount placed into contingency reserve is calculated during risk analysis. The amount placed into management reserve is determined by how much uncertainty management feels exists in the project. Typical ranges are from 5 percent of project costs for a well-understood, routine project to 30 percent or more of project costs for poorly understood, unusual projects. These costs are not to be used to overcome poor estimating or project execution.

Once the cost baseline is determined and both contingency and management reserves have been added, it is time to determine if sufficient funds are available. On many potential projects, a funding limit exists. The project sponsor for internal projects and the customer for external projects need to be very clear if the necessary funds exceed the limit of what is available. If enough funds are not available, this is the time to look hard at all of the estimates, schedule, and scope to determine what changes need to be made before the project management plan is accepted. It does no good for anyone to deliberately start a project with insufficient funds.

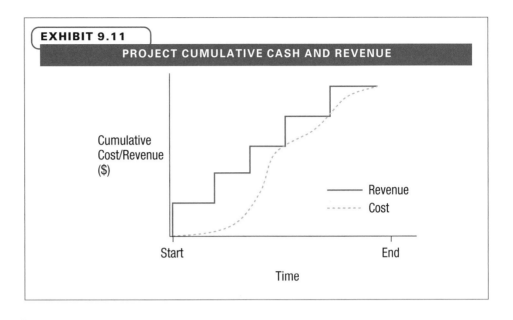

EXHIBIT 9.11

PROJECT CUMULATIVE CASH AND REVENUE

Cumulative Cost/Revenue ($)

—— Revenue
----- Cost

Start   End

Time

Determining Cash Flow

Projects require cash to keep moving. Suppliers and workers need to be paid in a timely fashion. The difficulty that sometimes occurs is that the project's customer may not pay for the work until it is completed—often months after project bills need to be paid. Therefore, the timing of cash coming in and going out for a project is just as important as the amount of money required.

Just as the demands on individual workers can be applied to individual activities in the project schedule to determine where overloads may occur, expenses can be applied to individual activities in the schedule to see when cash is needed. Revenue can also be tracked to interim deliverables in the project schedule to show when revenue can be expected. If a project is internal to a company, the timing of cash availability is also important to understand. While workers may work every day and suppliers may deliver frequently, cash may be supplied through organizational budgets only on a periodic basis. A project manager needs to ensure that the cumulative amount of cash coming into the project either from internal budgeting or from customer payments meets or exceeds the demands for paying cash out. This cash flow is shown in Exhibit 9.11 where incoming cash is in large increments, yet outgoing cash is almost continuous. The cumulative revenue at project completion minus the cumulative cost at project completion equals the profit (or surplus) generated by the project.

9.4 Establishing Cost Control

The approved project budget with contingency and/or management reserves serves as a baseline for project control. The budget shows both how much progress is expected and how much funding is required at each point in time. These are used for establishing project control. **Controlling cost** is "the process of monitoring the status of the project to update the project budget and manage changes to the project baseline." Cost control is discussed in Chapter 14.

When establishing cost control, a typical measuring point is a milestone. Major milestones are often identified in the milestone schedule in the project charter, and additional milestones may be identified in constructing the project schedule. Project managers can use the cash flow projections they have made to determine how much funding they expect to need to reach each milestone. This can then be used for determining how well the project is progressing. The sponsor and project manager often jointly determine how many milestones to use. They want enough milestones to keep track of progress, but not so many that they become an administrative burden. Microsoft Project and other software can be used to automate the cost reporting.

9.5 Using MS Project for Project Budgets

MS Project supports both bottom-up and summary level cost modeling. Bottom-up cost modeling is primarily based on the cost of each resource assignment. Assignment costs are totaled in the related activity's Cost field. The resulting activity costs are summarized in the parent WBS levels.

Summary level cost modeling consists of a summary level estimate for all the effort represented by that level, with no underlying detail entered. This can be helpful when the detail is not known, but the schedule must provide an overview of the entire estimated time and cost schedule.

Develop Bottom-Up Project Budget

To develop a bottom-up project budget, a project manager needs to understand four things: assignment costs, activity costs, project total costs, and the different perspectives from which to view costs.

ASSIGNMENT COSTS The following data are used to compute each assignment's cost value:

- Assignment work hours—calculated when the work assignment is made (Assignment units × Resource calendar hours per each day of the activity duration)
- Resource standard rate
- Resource overtime rate (only if modeling overtime)

An assignment cost value is the total number of assignment hours times the standard rate. Each resource has a standard cost rate, and some resources may have an overtime cost rate as well. These can be assigned when defining the resource as described in Chapter 8, or assigned later as shown in Exhibit 9.12.

ACTIVITY COSTS The activity cost value is the sum of all assignment cost values plus any activity fixed cost value as shown in Exhibit 9.13, which displays the Task Usage view in the top pane (with the Cost column inserted) and the Resource Work form in the lower pane.

EXHIBIT 9.12

ASSIGN COST RATES

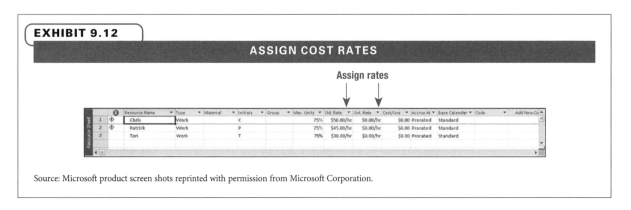

Source: Microsoft product screen shots reprinted with permission from Microsoft Corporation.

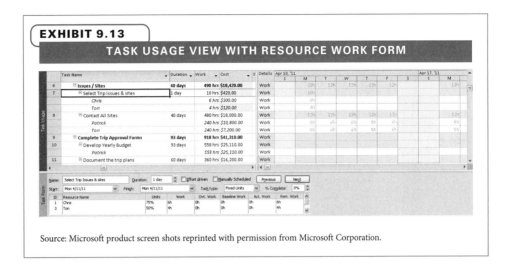

EXHIBIT 9.13

TASK USAGE VIEW WITH RESOURCE WORK FORM

Source: Microsoft product screen shots reprinted with permission from Microsoft Corporation.

In Exhibit 9.13, the first row and row 9 are summaries. Rows 7, 8, 10, and 11 are activities. The unnumbered rows are assignments. Row 7 is the activity "Select Trip Issues & Sites." Both Chris and Tori are scheduled to work one day on that activity. Remembering the rates of $50 per hour for Chris and $45 per hour for Tori, it is possible to see how the cost is totaled. The assignment Units and Work values for some of the "Select Trip Issues & Sites" activity are shown in the lower pane. To generate the Task Usage view with Resource Work form:

1. On the Task tab, View group, enter Task Usage.
2. On the View tab, Split View group, click Details.
3. On the View tab, Split View group, enter Task Form (if not already displayed).
4. Right click in the form in the lower page and enter "Work."
5. In the upper pane, expose the Start column and right click in the Start column header to add a column. Enter "Cost" when prompted.

VARIOUS PERSPECTIVES The preceding discussion has been from the view of the WBS perspective. Cost data may also be viewed from a resource perspective, using the Resource Usage view. In this view, assignment costs are summarized at the resource level.

In Exhibit 9.14, the most indented rows are activities. The "Unassigned" set represents activities with no assigned resources. Resources with no show/hide control have no assignments. The zoom scale is set to month over weeks.

Develop Summary Project Budget

Early in planning, sometimes detail is not yet known for later project phases. However, stakeholders still want an ongoing projection of the completion date and cost. A solution is to add a dummy activity under each phase summary for which not enough information to plan in detail is known yet. Estimate both the phase duration and the phase cost. Put the duration estimate in the dummy activity's Duration field. Put the cost estimate in the dummy activity's Cost field. Remember to remove each dummy activity when detail is added.

In Exhibit 9.15, the "Process Improvement" row has a dummy activity, "Assessment & Process changes." No resources are assigned to it.

EXHIBIT 9.14

RESOURCE USAGE VIEW

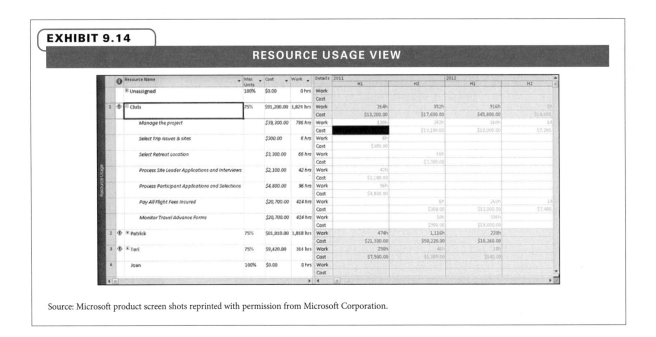

Source: Microsoft product screen shots reprinted with permission from Microsoft Corporation.

EXHIBIT 9.15

DUMMY ACTIVITY FOR LATE PHASE

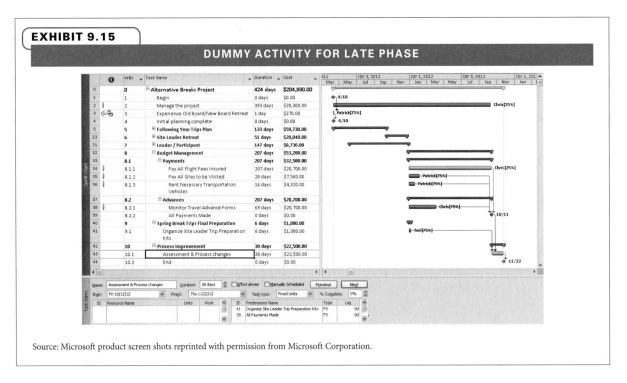

Source: Microsoft product screen shots reprinted with permission from Microsoft Corporation.

Summary

The cost management plan outlines how to structure and control project costs. On a small project, it can be very simple. On a large, complex project, it may need more structure. It guides the project manager during the project.

Cost estimating can be challenging because some activities may have a great deal of variation. Many methods are available to assist in cost estimating. Use a simple method if it will suffice, and more rigor if necessary. Generally as project planning identifies more specifics, more detailed and accurate cost estimates can be made.

Cost budgeting includes aggregating individual costs, analyzing needs for cost reserves where uncertainty exists, and determining cash inflow and outflow.

Establishing cost controls includes establishing cost reporting systems. MS Project can assist in developing either bottom-up project budgets or summary project budgets.

Key Terms from the *PMBOK® Guide*

cost management plan, 244
Estimate cost, 244
estimate, 247
reserve, 247
Analogous estimating, 250
Parametric estimating, 250

Bottom-up estimating, 250
Value engineering, 253
Budgeting, 254
cost performance baseline, 255
Controlling cost, 257

Chapter Review Questions

1. Cost estimating is closely linked with _____ and _____.
2. It is better to begin cost negotiations with project stakeholders before conducting a cost estimate. True or false?
3. _____ costs do not depend on the size of the project.
4. For a cake baker, ingredients such as flour and eggs are examples of _____ costs, while the oven is an example of a(n) _____ cost.
5. The salary of a vice president of an organization is an example of a(n) _____ cost, while the salary of an electrician hired to work on a construction project is an example of a (n) _____ cost.
6. Recurring costs typically occur during the _____ phase of a project.
7. _____ is a method in which transactions are recorded when the expense is actually incurred.
8. _____ is a method of accounting in which transactions are recorded when the money is actually spent.

9. _____ estimates are often created during the beginning of the project and likely to be less accurate than later estimates.
10. Which cost estimating technique requires an organization to use a larger amount of information —analogous estimating or parametric estimating?
11. Which of the following cost estimating techniques requires the most time to perform? Which requires the least?
    a. Analogous estimating
    b. Bottom-up estimating
    c. Parametric estimating
12. It is possible to completely avoid variation in a project. True or false?
13. _____ is used to determine whether a vendor's bid is reasonable.
14. It is important that project managers calculate the _____ of money when considering costs in the future.
15. For routine projects, _____ percent is a typical amount of money to be put into contingency reserves. For an unusual project, _____ percent is a typical amount to be put into contingency reserves.

Discussion Questions

1. Explain the importance of creating a cost management plan.
2. What is cost estimating?
3. Why is it important for project managers to understand the fixed and variable costs of a project?

4. Describe the difference between direct and indirect project costs.
5. During which phase(s) of a project do nonrecurring costs typically occur? Give an example of a nonrecurring cost.

6. Why do project managers prefer to use regular project costs?

7. List three things that must be in place in order for an analogous estimate to be effective.

8. Why is it important for assumptions to be listed in the cost estimate?

9. What is a cost baseline, and what types of costs does it include?

10. What is activity-based costing, and what impact does it have on project budgeting?

Exercises

1. A baker has a contract to bake three dozen chocolate chip cookies for a customer's party. Create a bottom-up estimate that includes both items needed for the project and the cost. According to your estimate, how much should the baker charge for the cookies?

2. Using the data for Problem 09.02 on the CD, create a time-phased budget for the project. Show how much the daily and cumulative costs for the project are just as the monthly and cumulative costs are shown in Exhibit 9.9.

3. Using the data for Problem 09.03 on the CD, create a time-phased budget for the project. Show how much the daily and cumulative costs for the project are just as the monthly and cumulative costs are shown in Exhibit 9.9.

PMBOK® *Guide* Questions

1. _____ costs are those necessary to keep an organization running, but are not associated with one specific project.
   a. direct
   b. variable
   c. indirect
   d. fixed

2. An estimate cost should always include _____.
   a. unknown unknowns
   b. value engineering
   c. analogous estimating
   d. indication of accuracy

3. Bringing in a consultant to assess productivity and optimize project life cycle costs would be an example of _____.
   a. vendor bid analysis
   b. "should cost estimation"
   c. value engineering
   d. activity-based costing

4. _____ is "the process of aggregating the estimated costs of individual activities or work packages to establish an authorized cost baseline."
   a. determine cash flow
   b. estimate cost
   c. determine budget
   d. value engineering

5. A(n) _____ is used to compare actual project spending with planned expenditures to determine if corrective action is needed.
   a. cost performance baseline
   b. project budget
   c. known known
   d. contingency reserve

Example Project

Create a time-phased budget for your example project using bottom-up estimating. To the extent your sponsor supplies rates for workers, use those. Approximate rates for ones you cannot get. Ask your sponsor how they treat indirect costs. Be sure to include direct labor costs for yourself and your teammates. Budget your costs at the starting salary you expect to receive when you graduate (or your current salary if you are employed). Divide your annual salary by 2,080 hours and add 20 percent for fringe. State all assumptions and constraints you have used when creating your budget. State how confident you are in your estimates and what would make you more confident. Give examples of known knowns and known unknowns on your project. Tell how you have budgeted for both of them as well as how you have budgeted for unknown unknowns.

References

A Guide to the Project Management Body of Knowledge (PMBOK® Guide), 4th ed. (Newtown Square, PA: Project Management Institute, 2008).

Cimino, John, "Feel the Cash Flow," *PM Network* 17 (9) (September 2003): 56–62.

Good, Gordon K., "Project Development and Cost Estimating: A Business Perspective," *AACE International Transactions* (2009)" TCM.01.01–TCM 01.14.

Goodpasture, John C., *Project Management the Agile Way: Making It Work in the Enterprise* (Fort Lauderdale, FL: J. Ross Publishing, 2010).

Gray, Neil, "Secrets to the Elusive Accurate Estimate," *PM Network* 15 (8) (August 2001): 54–57.

Hansen, Don R. and Maryanne M. Mowen, *Managerial Accounting*, 9th ed. (Mason, OH: Cengage South-Western, 2010).

Horine, Gregory M., *Absolute Beginner's Guide to Project Management* (Indianapolis, IN: Que Publishing, 2005).

Jackson, Lynne, "Hit the Mark," *PM Network* 17 (7) (July 2003): 37–40.

Kinsella, Steven M., "Activity-Based Costing: Does It Warrant Inclusion in *A Guide to the Project Management Body of Knowledge (PMBOK® Guide)?*" *Project Management Journal* 33 (2) (June 2002): 49–56.

Kwak, Young Hoon and Rudy J. Watson, "Conceptual Estimating Tool for Technology Driven Projects: Exploring Parametric Estimating Techniques," *Technovation* 25 (12) (2005): 1430–1436.

Milosevic, Dragan Z., *Project Management Toolbox: Tools and Techniques for the Practicing Project Manager* (New York: John Wiley & Sons, 2003).

Needy, Kim LaScola and Kimberly Sarnowski, "Keeping the Lid on Project Costs," in David I. Cleland, ed., *Field Guide to Project Management*, 2nd ed. (Hoboken, NJ: John Wiley & Sons, 2004).

Rad, Parviz F., *Project Estimating and Cost Management* (Vienna, VA: Management Concepts, Inc., 2002).

Rad, Parviz F. and Vittal S. Anantatmula, *Project Planning Techniques* (Vienna, VA: Management Concepts, Inc., 2005).

Tichacek, Robert L., "Effective Cost Management: Back to Basics," *Cost Engineering* 48 (3) (March 2006): 27–33.

Todd, Greg, "Five Considerations to Improve Project Estimates," *Information Management* (November/December 2009): 45–47.

Uppal, Kul B., "Cost Estimating, Project Performance and Life Cycle," *AACE International Transactions* (2009): TCM .03.01–TCM .03.09.

Westney, Richard E., "Risk Management: Maximizing the Probability of Success," in Joan Knutson, ed., *Project Management for Business Professionals: A Comprehensive Guide* (Hoboken, NJ: John Wiley & Sons, 2001).

Endnotes

1. *PMBOK® Guide* 430.
2. Adapted from Kim LaScola Needy and Kimberly Sarnowski, "Keeping the Lid on Project Costs," in David I. Cleland, ed., *Field Guide to Project Management*, 2nd ed. (Hoboken, NJ: John Wiley & Sons, 2004): 150.
3. *PMBOK® Guide* 434.
4. *Ibid.*
5. *PMBOK® Guide* 445.
6. Frank Toney, "Accounting and Financial Management: Finding the Project's Bottom Line," in Joan Knutson, ed., *Project Management for Business Professionals: A Comprehensive Guide* (Hoboken, NJ: John Wiley & Sons, 2001): 107.
7. Todd, Greg, "Five Considerations to Improve Project Estimates," *Information Management* (November/December 2009): 47.
8. *PMBOK® Guide* 427.
9. *PMBOK® Guide* 439.
10. *PMBOK® Guide* 427.
11. *PMBOK® Guide* 452.
12. *PMBOK® Guide* 432.
13. *PMBOK® Guide* 430.

PROJECT MANAGEMENT *IN ACTION*
The Value of Budget Optimization

At a major midwestern electric utility, budgeting for the ongoing capital expansion of the electric power system represents a process at the core of the organization's strategy and operations. During extensive annual planning efforts, a three-year capital project portfolio is developed for implementation and budgeted. The budgeting process is used to ensure that available capital is carefully scrutinized by management and applied judiciously to those projects providing the greatest strategic value on a schedule minimizing overall risk. Maintaining the forecasted budget and completing projects as planned ensures the integrity of the electrical system and the financial strength of the business.

The budgeting process itself is actually conducted year-round as planners, engineers, project managers, and financial experts endeavor to balance multiple competing objectives into a rational, achievable, and ongoing capital spending plan. There is little margin for error. Annual spending for major capital projects is typically over $250 million, representing approximately 500 projects to be completed across a five-state area. Underbudgeting means that projects potentially critical to the reliability of the electrical network may not be completed. Overbudgeting could result in investment dollars not yielding a return and reducing earnings.

As with any enterprise, the electric utility capital budget is restricted by annual spending targets necessary to maintain prudent financial ratios. In the case of capital spending, one key element involves maintaining a targeted debt-to-equity ratio. For this reason, judgments need to be made about the cost versus the value of projects considered for investment and the risks associated with potentially postponing projects to maintain favorable financial ratios.

To enable this entire process to work continuously and effectively, the utility adopted a project portfolio optimization process to create, analyze, and refine the budget for the project portfolio. This process involves executive management in creating a strategic value and risk scoring methodology that is applied during the planning phase for each project. The method assigns a value and risk score based on each individual project's forecasted impact in five critical strategic areas: financial, reliability, customer, regulatory, and system operations. A computer-based mathematical algorithm is used to optimize all possible spending portfolios to maximize value and minimize risk at specified budget levels. Within hours, the utility can analyze multiple optimized budget scenarios at various annual spending levels involving thousands of projects and nearly $1 billion of investment.

This methodology has several key benefits for the electric utility that can be applied to any organization attempting to make budgeting decisions for complex project portfolios.

- **Budget strategy well understood and communicated through the organization**—The process starts with an annual review by executive management of the strategy categories to which value and risk assessments will be applied. These categories and relative importance weightings can be adjusted to match the organization's current strategic emphasis. These categories and their relative weightings are published, communicated, and used throughout the organization.
- **Budget optimized for strategic objectives**—The scores of value and risk for each project are applied to the strategy categories and optimized to provide maximum value and minimum risk for the capital spending available. Computer software allows instant scenario changes and what-if options to be analyzed. The outcome provides management with consistent and well-understood decision-making information.
- **Consistent organizational strategy ensured**—Projects are submitted for budget consideration in the capital portfolio from throughout the utility's five-state operating area. There is a diverse array of business and financial reasons for each project to be evaluated. The use of a single enterprise-wide tool allows all projects to be analyzed on an equal basis, providing assurance that the organizational strategy is universally applied.
- **Risk thresholds and tolerance understood**—Postponing projects to conserve capital brings with it certain risks. The budget optimization process provides detailed risk analysis information on all deferred projects. Widespread communication of these risks and expert analysis of the consequences

and probability allow management to make calculated and carefully considered decisions. Importantly, management gains recognition of its own risk tolerance and risk threshold levels as a result.

- **Planning horizon and purchasing power expanded**— The most significant result of the budget optimization process is the certainty with which implementation (the project execution phase) of the budget plan can be approached. The high levels of up-front management scrutiny leave little doubt about executive support for the plan going forward. This enables the planning horizon to be significantly expanded into future years and brings with it an enormous level of labor and material purchasing power in the market.

- **Project Dynamics Accounted For**—Although the three-year budget plan is updated annually, there are still elements of uncertainty associated with implementation of a large project portfolio. These changes might be items such as significant shifts in public policy or regulations, fundamental changes to the business model, unexpected weather events, and so on. These midstream shifts can be dealt with readily, if needed, by changing project scoring criteria, reoptimizing the project mix, and reevaluating the resulting information for options going forward.

Source: Paul R. Kling, PE, PMP, director of project management and controls, Duke Energy.

CHAPTER **10**

Project Risk Planning

CHAPTER OBJECTIVES

After completing this chapter, you should be able to:

- Describe how to plan for risk management, identify risks, analyze risks, and create response plans for identified risks.

- Identify and classify risks for a project and populate a risk register.

- Describe various risk assessment techniques and tell when each is appropriate to use.

- Prioritize each risk on a project using an appropriate assessment technique and develop and defend at least one strategy for each of the high-priority risks.

- Compare and contrast the various strategies for dealing with risks.

Logan Mock-Bunting/Getty Images News/Getty Images

The Texas Medical Center (TMC) is composed of 49 not-for-profit institutions that are dedicated to the highest standards of patient care, research, and education. These institutions include 13 renowned hospitals and two specialty institutions, two medical schools, four nursing schools, and schools of dentistry, public health, pharmacy, and virtually all health-related careers. People come from all walks of life and from all over the world to have access to the best health care anywhere. Member institutions specialize in every imaginable aspect of health care, including care for children and cancer patients, heart care, organ transplantation, terminal illness, mental health, and wellness and prevention.

Currently 11 major construction projects are underway, including the Texas Children's Hospital's 407,000-square-foot Neurological Research Institute and 720,000-square-foot Maternity Center, along with a 12-story,

266

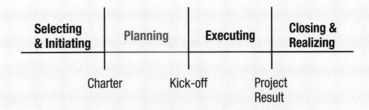

Selecting & Initiating	Planning	Executing	Closing & Realizing

Charter   Kick-off   Project Result

PMBOK® GUIDE TOPICS

- Plan risk management
- Identify risks
- Perform qualitative risk analysis
- Perform quantitative risk analysis
- Plan risk responses

27,000-square-foot concrete-frame addition to the M. D. Anderson Cancer Center of the University of Texas Medical Center. Collectively these major projects will add facilities that will be staffed by up to 27,000 additional employees. When complete, TMC will have 40 million square feet of occupied space. If you consider downtown business space, by itself it forms the seventh largest downtown business district in the United States.

With hurricane season approaching, TMC held a conference for over 100 contractors to review how to prepare for a potential hurricane. Contractors must have a plan in place detailing how they are going to secure their construction sites and keep materials from becoming airborne missiles in the event of a hurricane. Conference attendees were given a handout describing TMC's hurricane guidelines. These guidelines call for storm preparations to be completed 24 hours before tropical storm winds are predicted to hit land. Examples of storm preparations include dismantling scaffolds and privacy screens, securing giant cranes, emptying and weighting down dumpsters, photographing all buildings and assets, and unblocking all streets for emergency access.

While project managers cannot prevent hurricanes, through careful risk planning, actions can be taken to greatly mitigate the impact.

Rhonda Wendler, Texas Medical Center News

Imagine you are asked to plan for risks on two different projects. One is a major construction project at TMC with hurricane season approaching. The other is planning a small fund-raising event for charity. Would you handle the risks on these two projects the same way? Would you invest the same level of time and energy into planning these two projects? The answers are yes and no. Yes, you would approach the risks in the same way. But you would not spend the same amount of time planning for risk on both projects. You would spend considerably more time and money on risk management planning for the major construction project that is vulnerable to a hurricane than for the small fund-raiser project. Just as in other types of project planning, there is an approach to planning for risks that all projects follow; however, the depth of planning depends greatly on the potential risks of the project. In other words, a smart project manager gladly spends $100 in risk planning to save $1,000 in expected consequences, but does not gladly spend $1,000 to save $100.

The purpose of risk management is to reduce the overall project risk to a level that is acceptable to the project sponsor and other stakeholders. The methods that project managers use in risk management start with identifying as many risks as possible. Once the risks are identified, each risk is analyzed so that the project team can concentrate their attention on the most critical risks. Analysis always consists of a qualitative or judgmental approach and sometimes also includes a quantitative approach. In the final risk management process, the project team decides how to respond to each potential risk. Once all of the risk management planning has initially been accomplished, the response plans are incorporated into the overall project management plan. Changes may need to be made to the schedule, budget, scope, or communication plans to account for certain risks. These risk management planning processes are covered in this chapter. Risk management also includes monitoring and controlling the risks according to plan. These are covered, along with ongoing risk planning, in Chapter 14, Determining Project Progress and Results.

10.1 Plan Risk Management

Planning risk management is "the process of defining how to conduct risk management activities for a project."[1] To plan for project risks, a project manager must first understand the project's objectives. A project manager develops this understanding initially by realizing what project success in general is and then by understanding the specific priorities of the most important project stakeholders, as discussed in Chapter 5. Much research has been done on general project success. Exhibit 10.1 summarizes current research results.

The first set of general project success measures is meeting agreements. This includes meeting the technical requirements while not going over the cost and schedule agreements. The second set of project success measures focuses on the project's customers. Specifically, did the project result meet the customers' needs, was the project result used by the customers, and did it enhance the customers' satisfaction? The third set of success measures deals with the future of the parent organization. The specific measures in this area vary, but essentially they ask whether the project helped the performing organization. The **performing organization** is "the enterprise whose personnel are most directly involved in doing the work of the project."[2] Typical measures here include market share, new markets and/or technologies, and commercial success of the project output. The final set of project success measures deals with the project team. Did they become better and more dedicated employees?

EXHIBIT 10.1

PROJECT SUCCESS MEASURES

- **Meeting Agreements**
  Cost, schedule, and specifications met
- **Customer's Success**
  Needs met, deliverables used, customer satisfied
- **Performing Organization's Success**
  Market share, new products, new technology
- **Project Team's Success**
  Loyalty, development, satisfaction

EXHIBIT 10.2

SPECIFIC PROJECT STAKEHOLDER PRIORITIES

	IMPROVE	KEEP	SACRIFICE
Scope		X	
Quality		X	
Time			≤1 month to save $5,000
Cost	Want to save		
Contribution to Organization		X	
Contribution to Society		X	

Source: Adapted from Timothy J. Kloppenborg and Joseph A. Petrick, *Managing Project Quality* (Vienna, VA: Management Concepts, Inc., 2002), 46.

The specific priorities of the project's most important stakeholders can be summarized in a table such as Exhibit 10.2. A project manager and team need to understand not only what the project plans call for but also what area(s) the most important stakeholders would like to improve and what area(s) they are willing to sacrifice to enable those improvements. For example, consider a project that calls for building a four-bedroom house of 2,800 square feet. Perhaps the homeowner (the most important stakeholder) insists on keeping the size at 2,800 square feet and insists on the normal quality (no leaks, square walls, etc.), but would like to improve on the cost (pay less money). To improve on the cost objective, one of the other objectives probably needs to be sacrificed. Perhaps the homeowner would be willing to move in a month late if the savings were $5,000.

Once the project team understands the project success measures and priorities, attention is turned to understanding the project risks. All projects have some risk, and the more unique a project is, the more sources of risk may be present. It is impossible to remove all sources of risk. It is undesirable to even try to remove all risk because that means the organization is not trying anything new. A risk is anything that may impact the project team's ability to achieve the general project success measures and the specific project stakeholder priorities. This impact can be a negative one, in which something poses a **threat** or "a condition or situation unfavorable to the project … a risk that will have a negative impact on a project objective if it occurs."[3] The impact, on the other hand, could be positive, in which something poses an **opportunity** or "a condition or situation favorable to the project … a risk that will have a positive impact on a project objective if it occurs."[4]

Wise project managers strive to develop a **risk management plan,** which is "the document describing how project risk management will be structured and performed on a project,"[5] and have it in place before risk events occur. By documenting risk information in a proactive manner, a project manager can eliminate or reduce the impact of some threats and capitalize on some opportunities. The risk management plan is also useful for communicating with the various project stakeholders and for later analysis to determine what worked well and may be good practice to use on future projects, and what went poorly and should be avoided on future projects.

EXHIBIT 10.3

RISK MANAGEMENT PLAN GUIDANCE FOR AN IT CONSULTING COMPANY

Risk management includes guidance on how to perform three risk management activities:

1. Decide what level of risk premium to charge for the project. The team must rate factors such as project size, complexity, technology, and type. The combined ratings dictate that a risk premium of 0, 10, or 20 percent be added to the estimated project cost or, for very risky projects, that executive approval is mandated.
2. Mitigate risk external to the firm through contract clauses and risk internal to the firm through agreements.
3. Manage the risk very carefully through specifically designed weekly conference call meetings and reports.

Source: Rachana Thariani, PMP®.

Some risk management plans include all of the topics in this chapter. Others are smaller. For example, a risk management plan template for an IT consulting company is shown in Exhibit 10.3.

Roles and Responsibilities

It is good practice to encourage wide participation in risk management activities. One reason is that everyone has a different perspective. The more perspectives that are considered, the more likely important risks will be uncovered early. Another good reason is that people often resist when they are told what to do, but work with great enthusiasm if they participated in the planning. This is very true in project risk management. The surest way to get the various project stakeholders to buy into a risk management approach is to involve them right from the beginning in risk management planning. Potential critics can be turned into allies if their concerns are included.

The risk management plan should define who has responsibility for each risk management activity. On small projects, this is often the project manager or a core team member for most activities. On larger projects, the plan can be more elaborate, with subject matter experts involved at many points.

Categories and Definitions

Most projects have many types of possible risks. Therefore, it is helpful to look at risks in a systematic manner so as to consider as many types of risks as possible. One way to look at risk is by considering when it occurs in the project life cycle. For example:

- Certain types of risks, such as a customer not agreeing on the price, may occur during project initiation.
- Others, such as not finding a capable supplier, may occur during project planning.
- Risks such as delivery difficulties from a supplier may occur during project execution.
- Risks such as the project deliverable not actually working properly may even appear near the project conclusion.

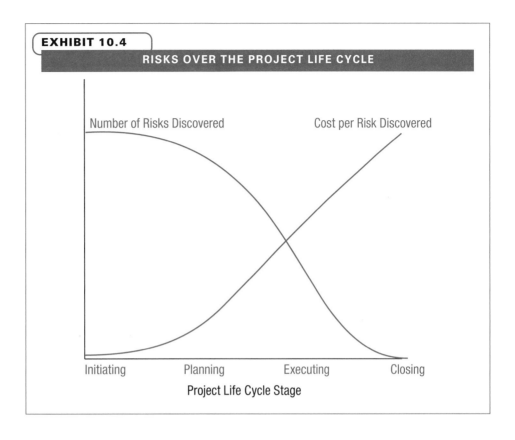

EXHIBIT 10.4

RISKS OVER THE PROJECT LIFE CYCLE

Number of Risks Discovered

Cost per Risk Discovered

Initiating   Planning   Executing   Closing

Project Life Cycle Stage

The number and costs of project risks over a project life cycle are graphed in Exhibit 10.4. More project risks are typically uncovered early in the life of a project. However, the cost per risk discovered early is often less since there is time to make changes in plans. Risks discovered late in a project can be very expensive. Experienced project managers work hard to uncover risks as early in the project as feasible. Usually, at least some risks are uncovered during project chartering. On small, simple projects this may be the biggest risk identification push, but on other projects, a great deal of time and effort may also be expended during project planning.

In addition to being categorized by when they might occur in a project, risks can also be categorized by what project objective they may impact, such as cost, schedule, scope, and/or quality. Risks can also be classified as external to the performing organization or internal to it. Many organizations have developed lists of risks for certain types of projects they routinely perform. Additionally, many writers have created general lists of risk factors for certain types of projects. For example, Exhibit 10.5 shows a few typical international construction project risks, and Exhibit 10.6 shows common risks for information systems projects.

Yet another method of classifying project risk is by what is known about each. Something that is a "known known" can be planned and managed with certainty. Therefore, it is not a risk. An example is that cement will harden. The next level is "known unknowns," which are risks that can be identified and may or may not happen. These risks should be identified, and a contingency reserve needs to be established to pay for them. An example on a long construction project is that bad weather will probably happen at some points, but no one knows exactly when or how bad it will be. The final level is for

EXHIBIT 10.5	
INTERNATIONAL CONSTRUCTION PROJECT RISK FACTORS	
FACTOR GROUP	**SPECIFIC FACTORS**
Technical	Poor scope definition; project complexity; design changes; lack of qualified equipment, personnel, or materials; poor workmanship
Financial	Inaccurate cost budgets, inflation, lack of funds, subcontractor failure, interest rate fluctuations, inflation, currency fluctuations
Safety	Poor safety awareness, lack of safety resources, reckless operation, poor site conditions
Environmental	Harmful gases, solid and liquid wastes, dust, noises, exposure to contaminated materials
Legal	Environmental clearance, land acquisition, permits, local law changes
Political	Government refuses to honor agreements, environmental groups block completion, acts of terrorism, kidnapping
Acts of God	Earthquake, rain and flood, soil collapse

Source: Adapted from Mark Ingebretsen, "Never a Sure Thing," *PM Network* 16 (1) (January 2002): 31; Prasanta Kumar Dey, "Process Re-engineering for Effective Implementation of Projects," *International Journal of Project Management* 17 (3) (1999): 156; and Patrick X. W. Zou, Guomin Zhang, and Jiayuan Wang, "Understanding the Key Risks in Construction Projects in China," *International Journal of Project Management* 25 (6) (2007): 603.

the true uncertainties. These are called "unknown unknowns" (or "unk unks" by people who must deal with them). Since they cannot even be envisioned, it is hard to know how much reserve time and money is needed to cover them. They are usually covered by a management reserve, and the amount of this reserve is often negotiated based upon the confidence level the project manager and key stakeholders have regarding how well they understand the project. An example could be a 100-year flood that covers a construction site that everyone thought was on high enough ground to stay dry—an event so rare it is expected to happen only once a century.

10.2 Identify Risks

Once the risk management planning is in place, it is time to begin identifying specific risks. **Identifying risks** is "the process of determining which risks might affect the project and documenting their characteristics."[6] Project managers are ultimately responsible for identifying all risks, but often they rely upon subject matter experts to take a lead in identifying certain technical risks.

Information Gathering

A large part of the risk identification process is gathering information. The categories and definitions described above can be a good starting point in this information gathering. The project manager either needs to act as a facilitator or get another person to serve as facilitator for information gathering. This is essentially a brainstorming activity, during which time the question "what could go wrong?" is repeatedly asked of everyone who is present. It is helpful to use Post-it notes and write one risk per note to prepare for further processing the risks during risk analysis.

EXHIBIT 10.6

INFORMATION SYSTEMS PROJECT RISK FACTORS

Risks Associated with Roles and Responsibilities
1. Corporate management does not monitor the project.
2. Corporate management loses interest in the project.
3. Project has a weak or lacking champion in senior management.
4. The champion does not inquire frequently.
5. Corporate leadership is lacking.
6. Corporate environment is unstable; competitive pressures radically alter user requirements.
7. Corporate management does not make decisions at critical junctures.
8. Change in ownership or senior management causes mismatch between corporate needs and project objectives.
9. Unethical behavior occurs.
10. Project has no business value and is used as a diversionary tactic to avoid facing real needs.

Risks Associated with Scope and Requirements
1. Project changes are managed poorly.
2. Goals are unclear.
3. Deliverables are unclear.
4. No general agreement on goals exists among management, IS staff, and users.
5. The requirements are misunderstood. Requirements are not thoroughly defined before starting.
6. Lines of communication within the project team are unclear.
7. Project is not broken into manageable "chunks."
8. Project managers do not understand user needs.
9. Planners ignore the obvious.
10. Frozen requirements are lacking.

Risks Associated with Operations
1. Budgeting entire project at the outset is required, leading to underfunding later in the project.
2. The budget for a development effort is set before the scope and requirements are defined.
3. Artificial deadlines are set.
4. Excessive schedule pressure exists to meet a real or imagined need.
5. Bad estimation occurs. Effective tools or structured techniques to properly estimate scope of work are lacking.
6. Project preempted by higher priority project.
7. Personnel fail to manage end-user expectations.
8. Cooperation from users is lacking.
9. Planners fail to identify all stakeholders.
10. Adequate user involvement is lacking.

Source: Adapted from Timothy J. Kloppenborg and Debbie Tesch, "Using a Project Leadership Framework to Avoid and Mitigate Information Technology Project Risks," in Dennis P. Slevin, David I. Cleland, and Jeffrey K. Pinto, eds., *Innovations: Project Management Research 2004* (Newtown Square, PA: Project Management Institute, 2004).

Classic rules for brainstorming are used. For example, every idea is treated as a useful idea. The risks will be assessed next. If one suggested risk does not prove to be important, it does not hurt to keep it on the list. Also, sometimes a risk that is obviously not important—or is even humorous—may cause another person to think of an additional risk they would not have considered otherwise. For example, in a brainstorming session with students meant to identify good health habits, one student suggested "drink more beer." While this may be enjoyable, the health benefit may be dubious. However, that suggestion prompted another student to say "drink more water," which was deemed to be useful.

While it is helpful to have as many stakeholders together as possible to "piggy-back" on each other's ideas, with the information technology available today, much of the same interaction can be achieved by global and virtual teams. It just takes a bit more careful planning. Variations and extensions of possible risks can help a team to identify additional risks.

Several other techniques are also used in risk identification. Sometimes, team members interview stakeholders. Other times a strengths, weaknesses, opportunities, and threats (SWOT) analysis is used to identify risks. **SWOT analysis** is "an information gathering technique used to examine the project from perspectives of each project's strengths, weaknesses, opportunities, and threats to increase the breadth of risks considered."[7] Remember, risks can be both threats to overcome and opportunities to exploit. Yet another method of identifying risks is the **Delphi technique,** which is "an information gathering technique used as a way to reach a consensus of experts on a subject ... Responses are summarized and recirculated for further comment."[8] Finally, a team can use a structured review to identify risks.

Reviews

A project manager and team can review a variety of project and other documents to uncover possible risks. Exhibit 10.7 lists some of the documents a project manager may use and typical questions he or she would ask for each. Project teams can often identify risks from each type of review shown. Balance must be given to the extent of the reviews and the amount of useful information regarding risks expected to result. As with the brainstorming mentioned previously, it is better to identify many possible risks and later determine that some of them are not major, rather than to *not* identify what *does* turn out to be a big risk.

EXHIBIT 10.7	
PROJECT RISK REVIEWS	
TYPE OF REVIEW	QUESTION
Charter	Is there clarity and common understanding in each section?
Stakeholder register	What could upset any of them?
Communication plan	Where could poor communications cause trouble?
Assumptions	Can you verify that each assumption is correct?
Constraints	How does each constraint make the project more difficult?
WBS	What risks can you find going through the WBS item by item?
Schedule	What milestones and other merge points might be troublesome?
Resource demands	At what points are certain people overloaded?
Touchpoints	What difficulties may arise when some project work is handed off from one person to another?
Literature	What problems and opportunities have been published concerning similar projects?
Previous projects	What projects and opportunities have similar projects in your own organization experienced?
Peers	Can your peers identify any additional risks?
Senior management	Can senior management identify any additional risks?

Understanding Relationships

Project managers can also seek to identify risks by learning the cause-and-effect relationships of risk events. One useful technique is a flow chart that shows how people, money, data, or materials flow from one person or location to another. This is essentially what the team does when it reviews the project schedule, provided it looks at the arrows that show which activities must precede others.

A second method of understanding risk relationships is to ask why a certain risk event may happen. This can be accomplished through **root cause analysis,** which is "an analytical technique used to determine the basic underlying reason that causes a variance or defect or risk. A root cause may underlie more than one variance or defect or risk."[9] A simple approach to root cause analysis is to simply consider each risk one at a time and ask "Why might this happen?" At this point, since many potential risks have probably been identified, project teams do not spend a large amount of time on any single risk. If necessary, the project team can perform more detailed root cause analysis of the few risks that have been designated as major risks during risk analysis.

One more type of relationship project managers like to understand is **triggers,** or "indications that a risk has occurred or is about to occur."[10] A trigger can be specific to an individual risk, such as when a key supplier stops returning phone calls, which may jeopardize their delivery of materials. Triggers can also be general indications of problems for the project as a whole, as shown in Exhibit 10.8.

Risk Register

The primary output of risk identification is the risk register. When complete, the **risk register** is "the document containing the results of the qualitative risk analysis, quantitative risk analysis, and risk response planning. The risk register details all identified risks, including description, category, cause, probability of occurring, impact(s) on objectives, proposed responses, owners, and current status."[11] At this point (the end of risk identification), the risk register includes only the risk categories, identified risks, potential causes, and potential responses. The other items are developed during the remainder of risk planning. An example of a partial risk register is shown in Exhibit 10.9.

The risk register is a living document. As a risk is identified, it is added. More information regarding a risk can be added as it is discovered. As risks are handled, they can be removed because they are no longer of the same level of concern. On smaller projects, a spreadsheet works fine for a risk register. On larger, more complex projects, some organizations use databases.

EXHIBIT 10.8

TRIGGERS FOR A PROJECT AS A WHOLE

- Project manager displays lack of self-esteem.
- Team members do not show enthusiasm for project.
- Project was started with inadequate time for planning.
- Communications are overly general, with little focus.
- Reports yield little information about true project status.
- Little effort has been given to risk management.

Source: Adapted from Peter Fretty, "Why Do Projects Really Fail?" *PM Network* 20 (3) (March 2006): 47.

EXHIBIT 10.9

PARTIAL RISK REGISTER

CATEGORY	RISK	POTENTIAL CAUSE(S)	POTENTIAL RESPONSE(S)
Meeting agreements	Cost overrun	Budget entire project from outset	Budget project one phase at a time
			Add enough contingency funds
			Clearly communicate budget risks
	Schedule overrun	Handle project changes poorly	Establish simple change control process
			Determine in advance changes sponsor wants to approve
			Agree to track progress
Customer success	Fail to meet customer's needs	Ignore real project requirements in favor of new technology	Validate business case with customer
			Conduct feasibility studies
			Pilot new technology
	Fail to satisfy customers	Fail to meet user expectations	Ask user to be part of leadership team
			Put all agreements in writing
			Hold design review sessions with user

Note that at this point both the cause and response columns are listed as potential. Once risks are identified, it is fairly common to at least start speculating on potential causes and courses of action. In fact, on small projects, risk identification and analysis are often performed together. However, especially on larger projects, many teams do not go into great depth studying risks until they prioritize them during analysis. That way, they only need to analyze the big risks.

10.3 Risk Analysis

If a project team is serious about risk identification, they probably uncover quite a few risks. Next, the team needs to decide which risks are major and need to be managed carefully, as opposed to those minor risks that can be handled more casually. The project team should determine how well they understand each risk and whether they have the necessary reliable data. Ultimately, they must be able to report the major risks to decision makers.

Perform Qualitative Risk Analysis

Performing qualitative risk analysis is "the process of prioritizing risks for further analysis or action by assessing and combining their probability and impact."[12] All project teams usually perform this task. If they understand enough about the risks at this point, they proceed directly to risk response planning for the major risks. If not, they use more quantitative techniques to help them understand the risks better.

DIFFERENTIATING BETWEEN MAJOR AND MINOR RISKS The primary questions project teams use in qualitative risk analysis are "how likely is this risk to happen?" and

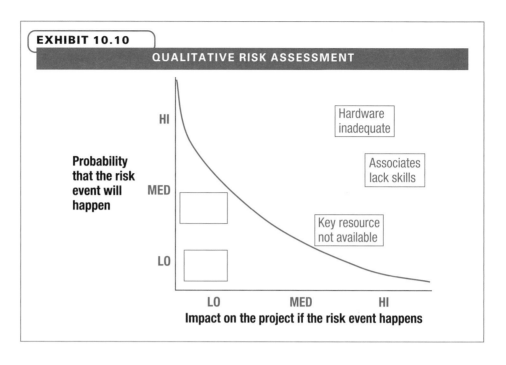

EXHIBIT 10.10

QUALITATIVE RISK ASSESSMENT

Probability that the risk event will happen

HI

MED

LO

Hardware inadequate

Associates lack skills

Key resource not available

LO   MED   HI

Impact on the project if the risk event happens

"if it does happen, how big will the impact be?" This was shown in Exhibit 4.8 (see page 96) and is repeated in Exhibit 10.10. Note that for each dimension—probability and impact—a simple scale of high, medium, and low is used. Some teams prefer to use a numerical scale of 1 to 3, 1 to 5, or 1 to 10. The scale does not matter as long as it is applied consistently and is easy for everyone to understand. Note also the curved line. This line separates the major risks that need either further analysis and/or specific contingency plans from those more minor risks that can just be listed and informally monitored. Without making a distinction like this, project teams may be tempted to either ignore all risks or to make contingency plans for all risks. Ignoring all risks almost guarantees the project has problems. Making contingency plans for even minor risks is a terrible waste of time and draws focus away from the really big risks.

Project teams sometimes also ask, for each risk, when is it likely to occur in the project. This can be useful because those risks that are likely to occur earlier often need to be assigned a higher priority. Teams also sometimes ask how easy it is to notice and correctly interpret the trigger. Risks with triggers that are difficult to notice or interpret often are assigned a higher priority.

CAUSE-AND-EFFECT RELATIONSHIPS One additional type of qualitative risk analysis is to determine cause-and-effect relationships. This is part of root cause analysis, which was described in the previous section on understanding relationships. While effects are often more visible, it is often easier to change the effect by changing the underlying cause. For example, assume that a construction worker is not laying stones evenly for a patio (the effect); perhaps the easiest way to ensure that future stones are placed evenly is to understand why the worker is having problems. The cause may turn out to be inconsistent stone size, incorrectly prepared ground, the cement for holding the stones having bigger gravel than normal, or an improperly functioning level. Once the causes are understood, they can serve as triggers to identify that a risk event may be about to happen. This knowledge is useful when developing responses to risks.

Teams should assess potential risks and predict possible outcomes involved in a project.

CAUSE-AND-EFFECT DIAGRAM A tool that is useful in this analysis is the cause-and-effect diagram. Many project teams use this diagram to identify possible causes for a risk event. An example is shown in Exhibit 10.11.

The cause-and-effect diagram is also known as the fishbone diagram because the many lines make it look like the skeleton of a dead fish. To construct the cause-and-effect diagram, the project team first lists the risk as the effect in a box at the head of the fish. In this example, it is late delivery. The more specifically the risk is stated, the more likely the team can uncover its real causes. The next step is to name the big bones. In this case, there are four big bones named *people, machines, methods,* and *materials*. There can be any number of big bones, and they can be named whatever makes sense to the team constructing the diagram. Team members are then encouraged to keep asking the question "why?" For example, why could people be a cause? Because they are not trained properly or because they are overallocated are the two reasons shown. Often, a team proposes many possible reasons. The team continues to break down the reasons—that is, asking why until it no longer makes sense to ask why. Cause-and-effect diagrams are frequently much fuller than this small example, with dozens of potential causes. Once the team can no longer think of possible causes, they need to determine which of the many

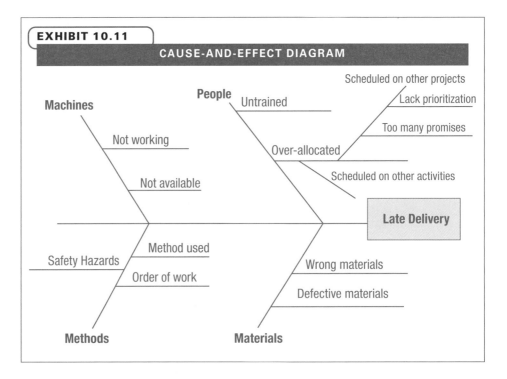

EXHIBIT 10.11

CAUSE-AND-EFFECT DIAGRAM

possible causes are true causes. This can be accomplished by first selecting a few likely causes and then testing them.

Perform Quantitative Risk Analysis

Performing quantitative risk analysis is "the process of numerically analyzing the effect of identified risks on overall project objectives."[13] While all projects use qualitative risk analysis, quantitative risk analysis is only used when necessary. Bigger, more complex, riskier, and more expensive projects often can benefit from the additional rigor of these more structured techniques. Quantitative risk analysis is often used when being able to predict with confidence what the probability is of completing a project on time, on budget, and with the agreed upon scope and/or the agreed upon quality is critical. Some of the more frequently used quantitative techniques are shown in Exhibit 10.12. Criteria to help select a suitable quantitative risk technique include the following:

- The methodology should utilize the explicit knowledge of the project team members.
- The methodology should allow quick response.
- The methodology should help determine project cost and schedule contingency.
- The methodology should help foster clear communication.
- The methodology should be easy to use and understand.[14]

Risk Register Updates

The probability of each risk occurring and the impact if it does happen are added to the register for each risk. The priority for each risk is also listed. Some organizations use a "Top 10" list to call particular attention to the highest priority risks. In addition, some organizations choose to place higher priority on risks that are likely to happen soon. Some organizations want to call attention to risks that are difficult to detect—that is, risks with obscure triggers. Any of these means of calling attention to certain risks are also listed in the risk register. If the project team performed any quantitative risk analysis, the results are also documented in the risk register.

10.4 Plan Risk Responses

Once risks have been identified and analyzed, the project team decides how they will handle each risk. **Planning risk responses** is "the process of developing options and

---

EXHIBIT 10.12

COMMON QUANTITATIVE RISK ANALYSIS TECHNIQUES	
Decision Tree	Breaks a complex problem down by mapping alternatives and states of nature to calculate expected monetary value of decisions.
Failure Modes and Effects Analysis (FMEA)	Used primarily in product development projects. Quantifies severity, occurrence, and detection for each risk to aid in deciding on controls.
Fault Tree Analysis	Tree diagram; depicts patterns of events and calculates probability of project failure.
Financial Engineering	Calculates net present value (NPV) of current project (or approach) in comparison to NPV of abandoning approach or project.
Simulation or Monte Carlo Simulation	Selects values of controllable inputs and randomly generates values of probabilistic inputs to calculate probability of outputs.
Tornado Diagram	Sensitivity analysis chart with the most critical variables shown on top.

actions to enhance opportunities and reduce threats to project objectives."[15] This is often a creative time for project teams as they decide how they will respond to each major risk. Sometimes a team develops multiple strategies for a single risk because they do not believe one strategy will reduce the threat or exploit the opportunity as much as the stakeholders would like. The team may decide that it is not worth the effort to completely eliminate a threat. In those cases, the goal is to reduce the threat to a level that the sponsor and other stakeholders deem acceptable.

Strategies for Responding to Risks

Because so many possible strategies can be developed for dealing with project risks, it helps to classify the strategies. Common risk strategies are shown in Exhibit 10.13.

AVOID RISK Many people prefer to avoid a risk if possible, and sometimes that is the best strategy. Sometimes, a project plan can be altered to avoid a risk by deleting the risky section. For example, if the organizers of a parade are told by the local police that traffic patterns on one section of their route are very difficult to control, perhaps they may alter the route. Project risk response strategy decisions often must be made with a

---

EXHIBIT 10.13

COMMON PROJECT RISK STRATEGIES

STRATEGY	TYPE OF RISK	EXAMPLES
Avoid	Threat	1. Change project plan and/or scope 2. Improve project communications 3. Decide not to perform project
Transfer	Threat	1. Insurance 2. Fixed-price contract 3. Hire expert
Mitigate	Threat	1. Lower probability and/or impact of threat 2. Build in redundancy 3. Use more reliable methods
Accept	Threat and opportunity	1. Deal with it if and when it happens 2. Establish triggers and update frequently 3. Establish time and/or cost contingencies
Research	Threat and opportunity	1. Get more and/or better information 2. Verify assumptions 3. Use prototype
Exploit	Opportunity	1. Assign talented resources to project 2. Give more emphasis to project
Share	Opportunity	1. Allocate partial ownership to third party 2. Form joint venture
Enhance	Opportunity	1. Increase probability and/or positive impact 2. Identify and maximize key drivers 3. Add more resources

Source: Adapted from *A Guide to the Project Management Body of Knowledge (PMBOK® Guide)* (Newtown Square, PA: Project Management Institute, 2008): 261–263; Paul S. Royer, *Project Risk Management: A Proactive Approach* (Vienna, VA: Management Concepts, Inc., 2002): 35; and Eric Verzuh, *The Fast Forward MBA in Project Management*, 2nd ed. (Hoboken, NJ: John Wiley & Sons, 2005): 100–103.

thorough understanding of the priorities key stakeholders have of cost, schedule, scope, and quality. In this example, if no powerful stakeholder had a strong interest in the exact route, the change might be easily made. However, project managers need to understand that every decision they make regarding risk response strategies may impact something else. Another avoidance strategy is to ensure communications are good, especially concerning risky issues. Many risks can be more easily addressed with prompt and accurate information. The ultimate avoidance strategy is to not perform the project at all. This choice is sometimes made when the risks posed by the project are deemed unacceptably large given the potential benefits. Before a decision is made not to perform a project at all, normally each of the other strategies is considered.

TRANSFER RISK Sometimes, a decision is made to transfer some or all of a project risk to another organization. One common means to do so is through insurance. Project insurance works like any other type of insurance: a premium is paid so another organization will assume a level of risk. Higher premiums need to be paid for more risk to be assumed (think of lower deductibles). Therefore, using insurance as a risk transfer strategy is a two-part decision: Do we transfer risk, and, if so, how much risk do we transfer? The answer generally is "enough so the overall risk is acceptable to key stakeholders."

A second transfer strategy deals with the type of contract used. An owner wishing to transfer risk to a developer will want to use a fixed-price contract. The developer who accepts the risk would insist on a higher price to cover her uncertainty. A developer who wishes to transfer risk to an owner would prefer a cost-plus contract under which she is compensated for her cost plus a certain amount of profit. The owner, in turn, would prefer to drive for a low cost in such an arrangement because he is assuming the risk. Other types of contracts can be written so that both parties share the project risk.

A third risk transfer strategy is to hire an expert to perform in the area of the risk and to hold that person accountable. None of the transfer strategies eliminate risk; they just force someone else to assume it.

MITIGATE RISK Mitigation strategies are those in which an effort is made to lower risk. In general, this means either reducing the probability of a risk event happening and/or reducing the impact if it does happen. For example, in Exhibit 10.10, one of the major risks is that a key resource may not be available. To reduce the probability of that happening, perhaps the person could be hired well in advance of the project and protected from work on competing projects. To reduce the impact if this person was not available after all, perhaps the project team would like to use the second mitigation strategy and build in redundancy. They could train another team member to do the work of the key resource. Redundancy is a way of life in systems projects such as developing an aircraft. However, the simple answer is not to continue to build in more and more redundancy, because the aircraft would eventually become so heavy it could fly and so expensive no one could afford it. Therefore, a third mitigation strategy is often utilized: Use more reliable methods. If the primary way of performing a key activity is highly reliable, there is less need for other mitigation strategies.

ACCEPT RISK A fourth risk response strategy is to accept the risk. This is often used for the risks deemed to be minor. The project team deals with them if and when they happen. If the risks deemed to be minor really are, most of them will not happen, and when they do, most will not cause major disruptions. However, some risks a team chooses to accept can have an unfortunate impact on the project if left untended. Therefore, project teams often define a trigger for one of these accepted risks. The trigger marks the dividing point where, instead of just watching for the risk, the team starts to deal with it. For fruit and vegetable growers in California, the trigger may be a weather report predicting cold temperatures. Armed with that knowledge, the growers enact strategies to protect their crops to the extent possible and cost effective. The growers are willing to accept the risk of cold weather once in awhile because they make enough money at other times to compensate. If they were in a climate with more cold weather, they may choose not to grow sensitive crops during the cold season. One other acceptance strategy is to put contingencies of time and/or money into the project plan to cover the risks that transpire. Each of these acceptance strategies can also be used to take advantage of opportunities. Establishing triggers to notify the team when an opportunity is present, dealing with it as it happens, and having a little extra time and money to alter the project plans to reap the potential benefits all make sense. An example could be when a company develops a new style of hat, a celebrity wears it on TV, and the demand then takes off. By using more money to advertise to the unexpected audience, the company may generate many additional sales.

RESEARCH RISK The best way to handle a risk may sometimes be to learn more about it. The first research strategy, therefore, is to secure better and/or more information so the project team understands what they are dealing with. Projects often are conducted in a rapidly changing environment in which decisions need to be made quickly, often based upon imperfect and incomplete information. It is unusual to be able to gather and verify all the information desired; however, sometimes it is useful to improve the information available. Another research strategy is to verify assumptions that have been made. Assumptions that prove to be false become risks. Yet another research strategy is to perform the project on a small scale first to see if it works. This can include constructing a prototype, test marketing a new product, running new software in one department first, and so on. Project teams can often learn a great deal from trying their ideas on a small scale first. These research strategies work well for both reducing threats and capitalizing on opportunities.

EXPLOIT OPPORTUNITY One strategy that is aimed exclusively at opportunities is exploitation. A project manager may identify triggers that, if reached, will allow her to go to her sponsor to request that the project become a higher priority. If the organization wants to exploit opportunities, they can assign more or better resources to the project, remove barriers, and give it more visibility in management reviews.

SHARE OPPORTUNITY One additional exploitation strategy deals with the results of the project. Perhaps the project team is able to develop a new product or service so revolutionary that the parent organization is not capable of fully exploiting it. In a case like this, the parent organization may spin off a nimble subsidiary, form a joint venture with another firm, or sell the rights to the product.

ENHANCE OPPORTUNITY Essentially, a project team wants to either maximize the probability that an opportunity will occur and/or maximize the impact if it does. The project manager wants to identify key drivers of these positive impacts and develop strategies to capitalize upon them. Certainly, adding more or better resources is one way of enhancing opportunities.

Risk Register Updates

The project manager sees that the risk register is updated with the results of the response planning. For each risk, this means the response strategy is noted. It also means that a single person is assigned as the "owner" of each risk. That person is responsible for understanding the trigger and for implementing the strategy. Finally, any changes that need to be made to the project schedule, budget, resource assignments, and communications plan should be included.

Summary

All projects have some risks. More unique projects have more unknowns and, therefore, more risks. A project manager needs to use an appropriate level of detail in risk planning—enough to plan for major risks, yet not so much that a great deal of time is spent on minor risks.

Risk management planning starts with understanding what constitutes success for the upcoming project. This may require understanding the tradeoff decisions that key stakeholders are willing to make. Risk management planning is part of the overall project management plan and may be performed concurrently with other project planning.

Identifying risks includes gathering information on potential risks. This can be accomplished by having the project core team and selected subject matter experts brainstorm all of the possible risks. Many times, a core team can review documents such as the project charter, communication plan, or schedule to help identify risks. The core team can look outside project documentation for reviews of literature by peers. Once risks have been identified, the core team creates the risk register with each risk categorized. Sometimes, a team also lists potential causes for each risk and potential responses at this time.

The next major activity is to analyze the risks. At a minimum, this involves determining which are major risks—at least from the standpoints of how likely each risk event is and how big of an impact it will have if it happens. Sometimes, more sophisticated analysis is performed to identify the root causes of risks, to identify the triggers that signify the risk event is about to happen, or to consider more complex relationships among risks.

Risk response planning involves determining in advance how to respond to each major risk. Minor risks are handled by simply being aware of their potential and dealing with them if and when they occur. Eight types of risk response strategies that can be applied to major risks are avoid, transfer, mitigate, accept, research, exploit, share, and enhance. A project manager may decide to use multiple strategies on a large and critical risk. Armed with proper risk planning, a project manager is confident to begin even a risky project.

Key Terms from the *PMBOK® Guide*

Planning risk management, 268
performing organization, 268
threat, 269
opportunity, 269
risk management plan, 269
Identifying risks, 272
SWOT analysis, 274

Delphi technique, 274
root cause analysis, 275
triggers, 275
risk register, 275
Performing qualitative risk analysis, 276
Performing quantitative risk analysis, 279
Planning risk responses, 279

Chapter Review Questions

1. _____ is an uncertain event or condition that, if it occurs, has a positive or negative effect on a project's objectives.

2. A negative impact is known as a(n) _____, while a positive impact is known as a(n) _____.

3. To reduce the impact of threats and capitalize on opportunities, a project manager should create a _____.

4. A project manager should solely handle the responsibility of identifying potential risks for the project. True or false?

5. Most risks are typically uncovered in the _____ stage of the project.

6. The cost per risk discovered is typically highest in the _____ stage of the project.

7. _____ is the process of determining which risks might affect the project and documenting their characteristics.

8. When a project manager is gathering information about risks, it is best if she sets a limit on the number of risks that will be considered. True or false?

9. It is often helpful if a project manager reviews previous projects to help identify potential risks. True or false?

10. _____ is an analytical technique used to determine the basic underlying causes of a risk.

11. A key supplier for your project has not been returning your calls or responding to your e-mails. This is an example of a(n) _____, which indicates that a risk is likely to occur.

12. Every risk, no matter how minor or major it is projected to be, should have a contingency plan created to address it. True or false?

13. A qualitative risk assessment typically categorizes the probability and impact of the risk as _____, _____, or _____.

14. A(n) _____ is a tool that is useful for analyzing the cause-and-effect relationship of risks.

15. Quantitative risk analysis is used on all projects. True or false?

16. In the risk register, only one person should be assigned as the "owner" of each identified risk. True or false?

Discussion Questions

1. What is the purpose of risk management?
2. List and describe the three different categories of project success measures.
3. List six examples of project stakeholder priorities. Describe tradeoffs that may need to be made between them.
4. Why is it helpful to have a high level of participation in risk management activities?
5. List three methods that can be used for categorizing project risks. For a fund-raising project, give examples of risk using each categorizing method.

6. List some helpful questions that a project manager could ask when reviewing the project charter and the WBS.
7. List the various types of information that are often contained in the risk register.
8. List and briefly explain the eight common risk strategies that are used. Describe how you might use two or three of them together on a project.
9. List and describe at least three common quantitative risk analysis techniques. Describe circumstances in which you would find each useful.
10. What are the two types of risk analysis?

Exercises

1. For a project in which you are planning a campus event with a well-known speaker, identify and quantify risks and develop contingency plans for the major risks.
2. For the same campus event project, perform a literature review to identify risks.

3. Engage another student team to perform a peer review of project risks for your project; you perform a peer review for theirs.
4. For one of the risks identified in Exercises 1 through 3 above, construct a cause-and-effect diagram to determine possible root causes.

Determine which of the possible root causes are probable. Describe how you would test each probable root cause to determine if it really is a root cause.

5. For the risks identified in Exercises 1 through 3 above, identify triggers that indicate each risk may be about to happen.

6. Brainstorm and group at least 12 risk factors (as shown in Exhibits 10.5 and 10.6) for risks in one of the following types of projects:
   • Research and development projects
   • Organizational change projects
   • Quality improvement projects

PMBOK® *Guide* Questions

1. A SWOT analysis is an information gathering tool that examines strengths, weaknesses, _____, and threats to a project.
   a. opportunities
   b. options
   c. origins
   d. organizations
2. The _____ is an iterative document containing the results of qualitative and quantitative risk analysis as well as risk response planning.
   a. root cause analysis
   b. risk register
   c. risk management plan
   d. cause and effect diagram
3. While all projects use _____ risk analysis, _____ risk analysis is only used when necessary.

   a. quantitative, qualitative
   b. quantitative, opportunity
   c. opportunity, qualitative
   d. qualitative, quantitative
4. A team lists all the possible threats they can think of to an upcoming project on individual sticky notes during _____.
   a. plan risk responses
   b. mitigate risk
   c. identify risk
   d. risk register updates
5. Avoid risk, mitigate risk, accept risk, and _____ are all strategies for responding to risks.
   a. undo risk
   b. prevent risk
   c. transfer risk
   d. identify risks

Example Project

Create a risk register for your example project. Categorize each risk, list potential causes, and list potential responses for each cause, as shown in Exhibit 10.9.

Describe what each project success measure (from Exhibit 10.1) looks like on your example project. Identify at least three risks to each success measure, determine which are major risks, and for each major risk develop one or more contingency plans. Identify whether the contingency plan is an avoidance plan (reducing the probability of the risk event), a miti-

gation plan (reducing the impact of the event), or both.

Facilitate a discussion with the sponsor and other key stakeholders of your project. Have them determine the relative importance of their priorities and document them, as shown in Exhibit 10.2.

Perform a risk review for your example project. Use at least three types of review, as shown in Exhibit 10.7. Which of these types gave you the most useful information? Why?

References

A Guide to the Project Management Body of Knowledge (PMBOK® Guide), 4th ed. (Newtown Square, PA: Project Management Institute, 2008).

Brassard, Michael et al., *The Problem Solving Memory Jogger™: Seven Steps to Improved Processes* (Salem, NH: GOAL/QPC, 2000).

Evans, James R. and William M. Lindsay, *An Introduction to Six Sigma and Process Improvement* (Mason, OH: Thomson South-Western, 2005).

Fairley, Richard E. and Mary Jane Willshire, "Why the Vasa Sank: 10 Problems and Some Antidotes for Software Projects," *IEEE Transactions on Software* (March/April 2003): 18–25.

Jiang, James J., Edward Chen, and Gary Klein, "The Importance of Building a Foundation for User Involvement in Information System Projects," *Project Management Journal* 33 (1) (March 2002): 20–26.

Jiang, James J. and Gary Klein, "Software Project Risks and Development Focus," *Project Management Journal* 32 (1) (March 2001): 4–9.

Jiang, James J., Gary Klein, and T. Selwyn Ellis, "A Measure of Software Development Risk," *Project Management Journal* 33 (3) (September 2002): 30–41.

Kloppenborg, Timothy J. and Joseph A. Petrick, *Managing Project Quality* (Vienna, VA: Management Concepts, Inc., 2002).

Kloppenborg, Timothy J., Arthur Shriberg, and Jayashree Venkatraman, *Project Leadership* (Vienna, VA: Management Concepts, Inc., 2003).

Kloppenborg, Timothy J. and Deborah Tesch, "Using a Project Leadership Framework to Avoid and Mitigate Information Technology Project Risks," in Dennis P. Slevin, David I. Cleland, and Jeffrey K. Pinto, eds., *Innovations: Project Management Research 2004* (Newtown Square, PA: Project Management Institute, 2004).

Kloppenborg, Timothy J., Deborah Tesch, and Ravi Chinta, "Demographic Determinants of Project Success," *Proceedings, PMI Research and Education Conference 2010* (Washington, DC, July 2010).

McCray, Gordon E., Russell L. Purvis, and Coleen G. McCray, "Project Management Under Uncertainty: The Impact of Heuristics and Biases," *Project Management Journal* 33 (1) (March 2002): 49–57.

Means, Jay and Tammy Adams, *Facilitating the Project Life-cycle* (San Francisco: Jossey-Bass, 2005).

Merritt, Guy M. and Preston G. Smith, "Techniques for Managing Project Risk," in David I. Cleland, ed., *Field Guide to Project Management*, 2nd ed. (Hoboken, NJ: John Wiley & Sons, 2004).

Milosevic, Dragan Z., *Project Management Toolbox: Tools and Techniques for the Practicing Project Manager* (New York: John Wiley & Sons, 2003).

Mulcahy, Rita, *PMP Exam Prep: Rita's Course in a Book for Passing the PMP Exam*, 5th ed. (RMC Publications, Inc., 2005).

Royer, Paul S., *Project Risk Management: A Proactive Approach* (Vienna, VA: Management Concepts, Inc., 2002).

Schmidt, Roy, Kalle Lyytinen, Mark Keil, and Paul Cule, "Identifying Software Project Risks: An International Delphi Study," *Journal of Management Information Systems* 17 (4) (Spring 2001): 5–36.

Verzuh, Eric, *The Fast Forward MBA in Project Management*, 2nd ed. (Hoboken, NJ: John Wiley & Sons, 2005).

Zou, Patrick X. W., Guomin Zhang, and Jiayuan Wang, "Understanding the Key Risks in Construction Projects in China," *International Journal of Project Management* 25 (6) (2007): 601–614.

http://international.fhwa.dot.gov/riskassess/risk_hcm06_04.cfm, accessed August 17, 2010.

http://leadershipchamps.wordpress.com/2009/06/14/find-how-sensitive-is-your-project-against-variables-tornado-diagram/, accessed August 17, 2010.

Endnotes

1. *PMBOK® Guide* 440.
2. Timothy J. Kloppenborg, Debbie Tesch, and Ravi Chinta, "Demographic Determinants of Project Success," *Proceedings, PMI Research and Education Conference 2010* (Washington, DC, July 2010).
3. *PMBOK® Guide* 440.
4. *PMBOK® Guide* 451.
5. *PMBOK® Guide* 439.
6. *PMBOK® Guide* 447.
7. *PMBOK® Guide* 436.
8. *PMBOK® Guide* 450.
9. *PMBOK® Guide* 432.
10. *PMBOK® Guide* 447.
11. *PMBOK® Guide* 452.
12. *PMBOK® Guide* 447.
13. *PMBOK® Guide* 289.
14. *PMBOK® Guide* 294.
15. http://international.fhwa.dot.gov/riskassess/ risk_hcm06_04.cfm, accessed August 17, 2010.
16. *PMBOK® Guide* 440.
17. Software Engineering Institute, Carnegie Mellon University, http://www.sei.cmu.edu/risk/main. html.

PROJECT MANAGEMENT *IN ACTION*

Risk Management on a Satellite Development Project

Introduction

Proactive risk management is definitely one of the key advantages in implementing and using standardized project management practices today. We always have the balancing act of managing the triple constraint of cost, time, and scope, and on top of that, we need to effectively assure project quality and that we have enough resources to do the job. In this age, we are continuously asked to optimize our performance and "be more efficient"; often, this is because we simply have too much work and not enough people to do it. So, in practice, we work with risks every day—from the risk of not spending enough time planning to the risk of not having enough supplies, or even the risk of not running a thorough enough risk management program.

Some time ago, I worked on a satellite development project that involved a lot of research technologies. There were many unknowns, with variables in the manufacture of components, integration of systems, working with subcontractors, tests, and other areas that made the project full of risk. Additionally, we were on a tight timeline for production and had only limited budget reserves available to handle cost overruns. Thus, we needed a practical way to manage and deal with the risks of the project. By systematically working with the risks of the project, we were better able to prepare responses to the risks if and when they occurred.

Planning

For our project, it was essential to have an integrated system and mechanism for risk management. Thus, at the outset of the project, during the planning phase, we developed our risk management plan and established with the team the process for dealing with not only risk but also any subsequent changes that could occur with the project as a result of the risk. This was done during a day-long clinic where we exclusively worked on developing this risk plan, as we knew our project was high risk and we wanted to make sure we could work with the plan. We developed criteria for evaluating probabilities of occurrence and impact for the risk and also for prioritizing risks. Furthermore, we researched and compared our

methods to industry standards for risk management such as those from SEI®.[16]

Execution

Once we had a solid approach for risk management in this project, we then went forward with the processes of identifying our project risks, analyzing the risks, developing potential responses for the risks, and deciding upon next steps for the risks. Our approach to all this was an integrated one, using a risk management database tool we developed as its cornerstone. This tool allowed for anyone in the project team to view the risks, enter new risks, and provide input for potential risk responses. An example of a similar type of tool is shown in Exhibit 10.14, where each risk is logged as a record in the database. The database allowed the team to have a single repository for recording and logging all the risks for the project, which was critically important because the risks in satellite development were constantly changing.

Every other month, the project team would hold a risk management review, in which each risk would be discussed and any decisions on actions would be made. Typically, we would meet and review the risks logged in the database in this group setting, and the risk's assigned owner would talk about the background of the risk, things that occurred since the risk was first logged (or since the last risk review), and what he or she felt the next steps needed to be. Project team members brought up other areas of the project that might have been impacted by the risk or new risks that resulted from the occurrence of the risk, or provided potential ideas for deferring, transferring, mitigating, or accepting the risk. The team also determined whether the risk decision needed to be elevated.

Another reason we held risk management reviews was to make sure that the team was up to date with the overall project's risks. Based on the criteria we defined in developing the risk management plan, the database tool provided us a prioritized report of all the project's risks. That risk report was used by the group to make decisions about the project and look at mitigation strategies for the project as a whole. The risk management review provided us with an avenue through which we could work together to resolve the

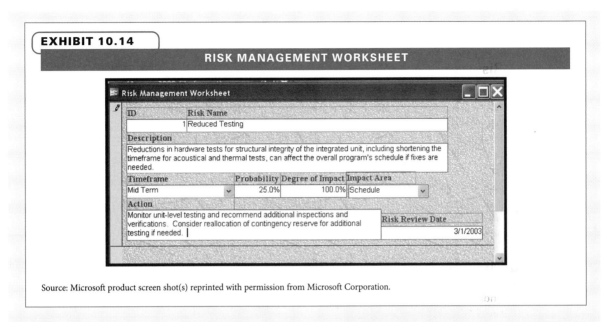

EXHIBIT 10.14

RISK MANAGEMENT WORKSHEET

Risk Management Worksheet

ID	Risk Name
1	Reduced Testing

Description

Reductions in hardware tests for structural integrity of the integrated unit, including shortening the timeframe for acoustical and thermal tests, can affect the overall program's schedule if fixes are needed.

Timeframe	Probability	Degree of Impact	Impact Area
Mid Term	25.0%	100.0%	Schedule

Action

Monitor unit-level testing and recommend additional inspections and verifications. Consider reallocation of contingency reserve for additional testing if needed.

Risk Review Date
3/1/2003

Source: Microsoft product screen shot(s) reprinted with permission from Microsoft Corporation.

high-priority risks of the project. Often, the high-priority risks were related to overall project drivers, and it was essential to be as proactive as possible in managing those risks. Moreover, by examining and analyzing the project risks in this manner, potential risks for other related projects, in this case other satellite development projects, were also identified.

The level of risk management necessary for a project can vary greatly. On the satellite development project, it was necessary to have a comprehensive program to address risk because there were many unknowns. We performed all our duties with the notion of understanding risk, and thus the risk management program addressed both the daily needs of logging and updating risks and the long-term strategic needs of understanding risk implications. However, for a smaller or more well-defined project, having such a detailed level of risk management may be unwieldy and difficult to manage. The key is finding the appropriate level for the project at hand.

Source: Lydia Lavigne, PMP, Ball Aerospace Co. Reprinted with permission.

CHAPTER 11

Project Quality Planning and Project Kick-off

After completing this chapter, you should be able to:

- Describe the major contributions to contemporary project quality made by each of the quality gurus and by TQM, ISO, and Six Sigma.

- Define each core project quality concept and explain why each is vital in planning and managing projects.

- Describe each of the project quality tools and tell when to use each.

- Explain what may be included in a project quality management plan.

- Compile a complete project management plan, use it to kick off the project, and then baseline and communicate the plan.

© Creatas Images/Jupiterimages

It was my desire to get rid of quality problems in our company. I have been running Advanex Inc. (formerly Kato Spring Works Co., Ltd.) for 20 years. Our company has produced precision components in Japan for over 60 years. We now have 20 factories in eight countries. My dream is to make this company the number one precision components manufacturer in the world. Since I took over the management of the company, I have been trying to create a quality company that not only consistently produces quality products but also consistently offers quality services to our customers. Our major business is to manufacture custom-made precision components to meet customers' specifications. However, it was not easy to get rid of quality problems, and my improvement efforts are ongoing. Our quality level has continued to improve and our people are very motivated.

One day, I read the book called *The Secret* by Rhonda Byrne. When I reached the part of this book explaining about the secret of the "Law of

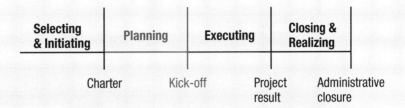

Selecting & Initiating	Planning	Executing	Closing & Realizing

Charter   Kick-off   Project result   Administrative closure

**PMBOK®
GUIDE TOPICS**

- Plan quality
- Perform quality assurance
- Perform quality control
- Develop project management plan

Attraction," I was shocked by how it was described clearly in this book. The message is, when you focus your thoughts on something, you are summoning that thing with great power. If you focus on the negative, you will attract that negative.

Some days later, I thought this might be a great idea to apply to our quality problems. We had been trying hard to reduce rejects. This was the same as saying, "I don't want to produce bad parts," and having the law of attraction interpret it as "I want to produce bad parts!" I now realized what we needed to do. We needed to focus on good-quality products and happy customers. I tried hard to talk to our people about this but almost nobody understood. However, I requested our people change the graph of "rejection rate improvement chart" to "good-parts rate improvement chart." We then studied and interviewed the people who were always making good-quality products to discover their effective habits. We then created posters showing "effective habits of people who are making quality products all the time."

We translated the simple and effective methods of consistently achieving quality into the native language spoken at each of our factories around the world. The Vietnamese and English versions are displayed in Exhibit 11.1. On every project we:

- Keep our focus on happy customers (stakeholders)
- Seek to understand, control, and improve our work processes
- Practice fact-based management by gathering and communicating important information
- Empower our workers to consistently perform well both individually and collaboratively

Our good-parts rate has been improving continuously. Now we are becoming a high-quality company that is producing good-quality products and offering good-quality services all the time. I am getting close to my dream.

Yuichi Kato, C.E.O.—Advanex Inc.

Perhaps the best way to understand the contemporary approach to project management is to learn how the contemporary approach to project quality management developed. Many people have influenced the modern approaches to quality, and their various contributions have largely been meshed together to give project managers a full understanding of project quality demands, processes, and tools. With this understanding, project

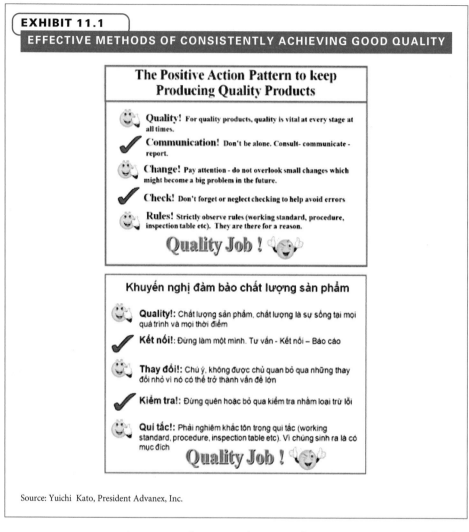

EXHIBIT 11.1

EFFECTIVE METHODS OF CONSISTENTLY ACHIEVING GOOD QUALITY

The Positive Action Pattern to keep Producing Quality Products

Quality! For quality products, quality is vital at every stage at all times.

Communication! Don't be alone. Consult- communicate - report.

Change! Pay attention - do not overlook small changes which might become a big problem in the future.

Check! Don't forget or neglect checking to help avoid errors

Rules! Strictly observe rules (working standard, procedure, inspection table etc). They are there for a reason.

Quality Job !

Khuyến nghị đảm bảo chất lượng sản phẩm

Quality!: Chất lượng sản phẩm, chất lượng là sự sống tại mọi quá trình và mọi thời điểm

Kết nối!: Đừng làm một mình. Tư vấn - Kết nối – Báo cáo

Thay đổi!: Chú ý, không được chủ quan bỏ qua những thay đổi nhỏ vì nó có thể trở thành vấn đề lớn

Kiểm tra!: Đừng quên hoặc bỏ qua kiểm tra nhằm loại trừ lỗi

Qui tắc!: Phải nghiêm khắc tôn trọng qui tắc (working standard, procedure, inspection table etc). Vì chúng sinh ra là có mục đích

Quality Job !

Source: Yuichi Kato, President Advanex, Inc.

managers are ready to perform project quality management—all the necessary work to ensure that project deliverables satisfy their intended purpose. This chapter includes the first part of project quality management, namely **planning quality**, which is "the process of identifying quality requirements and/or standards for the project and product, and documenting how the project will demonstrate compliance."[1] The remaining parts of quality management are covered in Chapter 14.

This is the final chapter dealing with project planning. Quality planning is often performed simultaneously with other aspects of project planning. Once the various aspects of planning are complete, the project manager leads the team in sorting out any inconsistencies. The team then takes the completed project plan to the sponsor and other stakeholders for approval. Once the plan is accepted, it is communicated widely and the project execution formally begins. Completing and approving the overall project management plan in this manner demonstrates how contemporary project management is integrative, iterative, and collaborative.

11.1 Development of Contemporary Quality Concepts

The contemporary approach to quality management has evolved first from the teachings of several quality "gurus" from the 1950s through the 1980s and then through various frameworks popularized during the last 20 years.

Quality Gurus

Arguably the most influential thought leader in quality was W. Edwards Deming. While Deming wrote and spoke widely regarding quality for 50 years, one concise way to summarize his ideas is his four-part Profound Knowledge System, shown in Exhibit 11.2. Deming started as a statistician, and initially preached that understanding variation was essential to improving quality. By the time he had fully developed this system, he also stated that it is important to understand how companies operate as systems; that managers need insight in order to accurately predict the future; and that leaders need to understand individual motivations.

Joseph Juran, who was a contemporary of Deming, also wrote and lectured prolifically for decades. Juran is perhaps best known for his Quality Trilogy of quality planning, quality control, and quality improvement, as shown in Exhibit 11.3. The *PMBOK® Guide* coverage of quality largely mirrors Juran's approach. Juran offered large amounts of specific guidance regarding how to plan, control, and improve quality.

Many other pioneers in quality, particularly Japanese and American, have added to the body of quality concepts and tools. Several of the most influential, and their contributions that apply specifically to project quality, are shown in Exhibit 11.4. Most of these thought leaders have teamed up with multiple partners.

Much of the work of these pioneers and many others has been incorporated into three popular frameworks that many organizations use to define and organize their quality initiatives. These frameworks are Total Quality Management (TQM), the International Organization for Standardization (ISO), and Six Sigma.

Total Quality Management/Malcolm Baldrige

TQM came into vogue during the late 1980s when it was becoming more widely apparent that the old way of trying to catch quality problems by inspection was not adequate. Many early advocates of TQM used slightly different ways of describing it. What the

---

EXHIBIT 11.2

DEMING'S PROFOUND KNOWLEDGE SYSTEM	
Systems	Interactions occur among parts of a system and parts cannot be managed in isolation.
Variation	Managers need to understand common and special causes of variation and then work to reduce both.
Knowledge	Managers need to learn from the past and understand cause-and-effect relationships to predict future behavior.
Psychology	Leaders need to understand what motivates each individual and how different people and groups interact.

Source: Adapted from James R. Evans and William M. Lindsay, *The Management and Control of Quality*, 8th ed. (Mason, OH: Cengage Learning South-Western, 2011): 94–99.

EXHIBIT 11.3

JURAN'S QUALITY TRILOGY

Quality Planning	Identify all customers and their needs, develop requirements based upon those needs, and develop the methods to satisfy those requirements.
Quality Control	Determine what to control, establish measurement systems, establish standards, compare performance to standards, and act on differences.
Quality Improvement	Select and support improvement projects, prove causes, select and implement solutions, and maintain control of improved processes.

Source: Adapted from James R. Evans and William M. Lindsay, *The Management and Control of Quality*, 8th ed. (Mason, OH: Cengage Learning South-Western, 2011): 104–106.

various descriptions had in common was implied by the first word in the name: *total*. Most serious practitioners included several components in their TQM system. In the United States, many government, business, consulting, and academic specialists in quality worked together to develop a common means of describing total quality management. This description forms the key areas of the Malcolm Baldrige National Quality Award. While the key areas remain constant, the specific criteria for judging are adjusted slightly every two years to reflect current times and state-of-the-art understanding. The current key areas and specific criteria are shown in Exhibit 11.5.

EXHIBIT 11.4

OTHER PROJECT QUALITY PIONEERS

THOUGHT LEADER	ADDITIONAL KEY PROJECT QUALITY CONTRIBUTIONS
Clifton	High-quality organizations encourage individuals to develop their strengths.
Crosby	Quality is meeting requirements, not exceeding them.
	The burden of quality falls on those who do the work.
	Quality costs least when work is done correctly the first time.
	Quality improves more by preventing defects rather than fixing them.
Harrington	Business processes can be improved using a systematic method.
Ishikawa	Quality outputs start with understanding customers and their desires.
	Work to identify and remove root causes, not just symptoms. All workers at all levels must engage to improve quality. Most quality problems can be solved by using simple tools.
Senge	Team learning is necessary to improve quality.
Shiba	Societal networking accelerates quality improvement.
	When continual improvement is not enough, breakthrough is needed.
Taguchi	Reducing variation saves money.
	Project deliverables will be better with a focus on improving methods.
Zeithaml	Services pose different challenges from manufacturing when improving quality.

EXHIBIT 11.5

MALCOLM BALDRIGE NATIONAL QUALITY AWARD KEY AREAS AND SPECIFIC CRITERIA

KEY AREA	SPECIFIC CRITERIA
1. Leadership	Senior leaders personal actions
	Organization governance system
	Fulfill responsibilities and support key communities
2. Strategic Planning	Develop strategic objectives and action plans
	Deploy strategic objectives and action plans
	Measure progress
3. Customer Focus	Engage customers
	Build customer-focused culture
	Listen to voice of customer and use this information to improve
4. Measurement, Analysis, and Knowledge Management	Select, gather, analyze, manage, and improve data, information, and knowledge assets
	Manage information technology
	Reviews and uses reviews for performance improvement
5. Workforce Focus	Engage, manage, and develop workforce
	Assess workforce capability and capacity
	Build workforce environment conductive to high performance
6. Process Management	Design work systems
	Designs, manages, and improves key processes
	Readiness for emergencies
Results	Performance and improvement in all six key areas
	Performance levels relative to competitors

Source: Adapted from Baldrige National Quality Program, "Criteria for Performance Excellence," http://www.nist.gov/baldrige/publications/upload/2009_2010_Business_Nonprofit_Criteria.pdf, accessed August 19, 2010.

ISO 9001:2008

While the Baldrige Award is a framework developed in the United States, ISO represents a framework developed in Europe. The International Organization for Standardization has developed many technical standards since 1947. ISO 9001 is the quality management standard, and the 2008 designation is the latest revision of the standard. When the standards first appeared, they focused largely on documenting work processes. However, over the years the standards have evolved, and the current five quality management areas with specific requirements are shown in Exhibit 11.6. Notice that they contain many of the same ideas as the current Baldrige Award key areas and specific responsibilities.

Six Sigma

Sigma stands for *standard deviation*—a statistical term for the amount of variation in data. Six Sigma quality literally means quality problems are measured in parts per million opportunities. Many projects have few routine activities and many unusual activities, so the rigor of the statistics in Six Sigma is not always applicable. However, the ideas behind Six Sigma provide a meaningful framework for project quality. As of this

---

EXHIBIT 11.6

ISO 9001:2008 AREAS AND SPECIFIC RESPONSIBILITIES

AREA	SPECIFIC REQUIREMENT
General	Develop quality management system (QMS)
	Document QMS system including manual and records
Management	Focus on customers
	Develop and support quality policy and objectives
	Allocate QMS responsibility and authority
Resources	Provide competent resources
	Provide needed infrastructure
	Provide suitable work environment
Realization	Control customer-related processes
	Control product design and development
	Control purchasing and production
	Control monitoring and measuring equipment
Remedial	Carry out monitoring and measuring activities
	Identify and control nonconforming product
	Collect and analyze quality management data
	Make improvements and take remedial action

Source: Adapted from International Organization for Standardization, "Quality Management Principles," http://www.iso.org/iso/iso_catalogue/management_standards/iso_9000_iso_14000/qmp.htm, accessed August 18, 2010; and "ISO 9001 2008 Translated Into Plain English," http://www.praxiom.com/iso-9001.htm, accessed August 19, 2010.

---

writing, Six Sigma is a popular approach to quality as Motorola, General Electric, and many other companies have promoted its usage. General Electric in particular expanded the focus of Six Sigma to include many service processes that people had previously said were too difficult to measure.

DMAIC METHODOLOGY Six Sigma uses a disciplined process called the define, measure, analyze, improve, and control (DMAIC) process to plan and manage improvement projects. The DMAIC methodology is a 15-step process broken up into five project phases: define, measure, analyze, improve, and control, as shown in Exhibit 11.7. The DMAIC process is illustrated to show objectives within each of the five key stages. It is shown as a continuous, circular flow because DMAIC is typically used as a method of implementing continuous improvement and thus can be practiced repeatedly within a process to further improve the process performance.

SIX SIGMA THEMES A simple, consolidated description of the primary Six Sigma themes is shown in Exhibit 11.8.

11.2 Core Project Quality Concepts

Each of the quality gurus and frameworks provides input into the contemporary understanding of project quality. As stated in Chapter 1, *A Guide to the Project Management Body of Knowledge (PMBOK® Guide)* uses a simple definition of project quality: "the

EXHIBIT 11.7

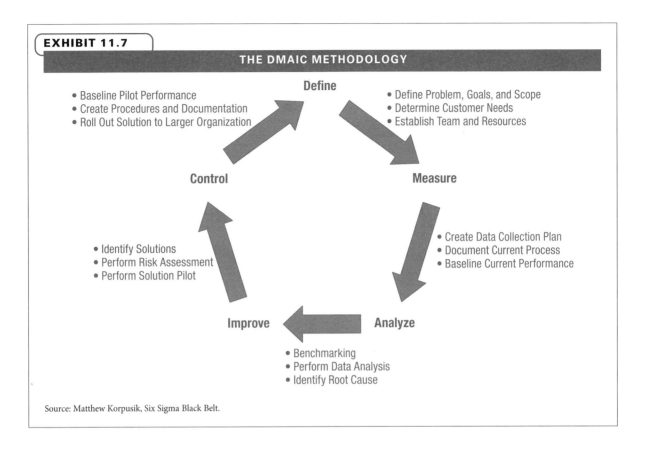

THE DMAIC METHODOLOGY

Define

- Baseline Pilot Performance
- Create Procedures and Documentation
- Roll Out Solution to Larger Organization

- Define Problem, Goals, and Scope
- Determine Customer Needs
- Establish Team and Resources

Control

Measure

- Create Data Collection Plan
- Document Current Process
- Baseline Current Performance

- Identify Solutions
- Perform Risk Assessment
- Perform Solution Pilot

Improve

Analyze

- Benchmarking
- Perform Data Analysis
- Identify Root Cause

Source: Matthew Korpusik, Six Sigma Black Belt.

EXHIBIT 11.8

SIX SIGMA THEMES

THEME	BRIEF DESCRIPTION
Customer Focus	Relentless focus on customers and their needs is a strong driver of good quality.
Fact-Driven Management	Develop appropriate metrics in a top-down fashion and rigorously analyze them statistically.
Process Management and Improvement	Understand, control, and improve key business and operational processes to reduce cost and time.
Goal Setting	Determine objectively what needs to be improved and then set stretch goals for that improvement.
Project Management Roles	Develop executive sponsors and process experts (black belts), collaborate with suppliers and customers, and deploy project.
DMAIC Process	Carefully apply the define, measure, analyze, improve, and control (DMAIC) process.

Source: Adapted from James R. Evans and William M. Lindsay, *An Introduction to Six Sigma & Process Improvement*, lst ed. (Mason, OH: Thomson South-Western, 2005): 13–16; and Steve Neuendorf, *Six Sigma for Project Managers* (Vienna, VA: Management Concepts, Inc., 2004): 24–34.

degree to which a set of inherent characteristics fulfills requirements."[2] However, to fully understand both the meaning of this definition and how to achieve it, one needs to understand the four contemporary core project quality concepts that have evolved from the sources above. The four core project quality concepts are:

1. Stakeholder satisfaction
2. Process management
3. Fact-based management
4. Empowered performance

Stakeholder Satisfaction

Stakeholder satisfaction consists of identifying all stakeholders, using a structured process to determine relevant quality standards, and understanding the ultimate quality goals with respect to stakeholders. External stakeholders for projects can include customers, suppliers, the public, and other groups. Internal stakeholders include shareholders and workers at all levels and all functions within the organization. It often makes sense for leaders to identify key stakeholders for partnering opportunities.

DEVELOPING QUALITY STANDARDS BASED UPON STAKEHOLDER REQUIREMENTS The decision process for developing relevant quality standards on a project consists of the following steps:

1. Identify all stakeholders.
2. Prioritize among the stakeholders.
3. Understand the prioritized stakeholders' requirements.
4. Develop standards to ensure the requirements are met.
5. Make tradeoff decisions.

STAKEHOLDER ANALYSIS A stakeholder analysis allows a project manager to identify all parties involved in a project. Once all stakeholders are identified, their position, influence on the project, and the level of change they need to undergo as a result of the project can be determined. These determinations allow the project manager to understand who can be leveraged to champion the project and who may need a focused effort in order to sell them on the project's value. A stakeholder analysis example is shown in Exhibit 11.9.

Stakeholders actively participate in the process of developing quality standards. Therefore, they make judgments about the quality of a process based on what they see. Thus, stakeholders judge the quality both of project work processes and of deliverables. When making tradeoff decisions, the project manager often facilitates the process, and the stakeholders actually make the decisions. Stakeholders frequently need to be reminded that the relative importance of cost, schedule, scope, and quality can be very helpful in determining sensible standards.

STAKEHOLDER SATISFACTION SAYINGS When satisfying stakeholders, it is helpful to remember a few sayings. One is the old carpenters' advice of "measure twice, cut once." This careful planning tends to yield less variation, less cost, and faster delivery—all of which satisfy stakeholders. Another saying is "meet requirements, but exceed expectations." Contractually, a project must meet the agreed upon specifications, but if stakeholders see excellent work processes and experience clear communications, their expectations will be exceeded and they will be even happier. This point regarding meeting requirements while exceeding expectations comes from two sources. Good project management practice is to meet requirements without spending extra money or time. Good quality practice is to not only satisfy but also to delight customers. The third saying is "a smart project manager develops capable customers." That means the customer is able to

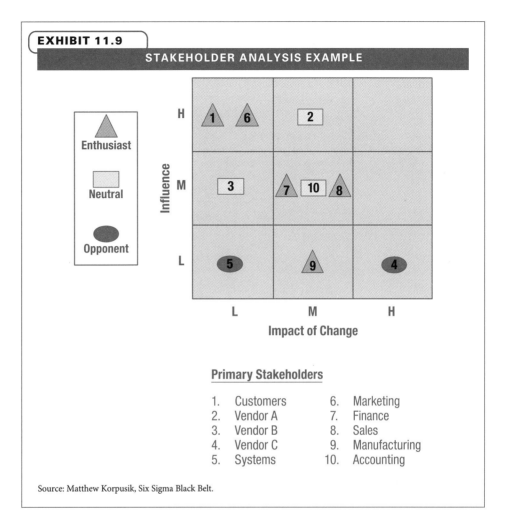

EXHIBIT 11.9

STAKEHOLDER ANALYSIS EXAMPLE

Primary Stakeholders

1. Customers
2. Vendor A
3. Vendor B
4. Vendor C
5. Systems
6. Marketing
7. Finance
8. Sales
9. Manufacturing
10. Accounting

Source: Matthew Korpusik, Six Sigma Black Belt.

use the project deliverables to do his or her job better. This often results in opportunities for additional revenue streams by partnering, training, and supporting the customer.

Process Management

A **process** is "a set of interrelated actions and activities performed to achieve a pre-specified product, result, or service. Each process is characterized by its inputs, the tools and techniques that can be applied, and the resulting outputs."[3] The second contemporary project quality core concept deals with managing processes. To effectively manage project processes, project managers need to understand, control, and improve them.

PROCESS UNDERSTANDING WITH A SIPOC MODEL   The first part of understanding a project is to demonstrate that all work flows from suppliers, through the project, to customers. A useful way to envision this is a tool called a supplier-input-process-output-customer (SIPOC) model, as shown in Exhibit 11.10.

In Exhibit 11.10, the process boundaries are clearly defined from when the newly hired employee starts work until the employee's elections are recorded by HR/payroll. This prevents future scope creep from occurring by eliminating previous or later steps in the process. The SIPOC above also begins to identify key stakeholders who both provide inputs into the process (suppliers) and receive benefits from the process (customers). Notice that the same parties may be both suppliers and customers to the same process.

EXHIBIT 11.10

NEW HIRE BENEFITS ENROLLMENT SIPOC EXAMPLE

Suppliers	**Input**	**Process**	**Output**	**Customers**
New Hires	Social Security #		New Elections	New Hire
HR	Date of Hire		Pay Deduction	New Hire's Family
Payroll	Enrollment Elections		Insurance Cards	Insurance Co.
Insurance Co.	Employee Handbook			

Process flow:
- New Hire Starts Work
- New Hire Receives Handbook
- New Hire Chooses Elections
- Elections are Recorded by HR/Payroll

Source: Matthew Korpusik, Six Sigma Black Belt.

One way to interpret the SIPOC is to think backward from the project's customers. As described previously in the stakeholder satisfaction section, it is helpful for a project manager to identify all of the customers for his or her project and the outputs each desires. Since that is usually a far-reaching list, prioritization decisions need to be made. At that point, the project manager can work with the project core team to define the work processes necessary to create those outputs. Then they can identify the inputs they need in order to accomplish those activities and determine who will supply them.

Once the supplier–customer view is understood, it is time to determine whether the process is capable of creating the project deliverables. This discussion should be initiated when the project charter is developed. As people discuss the milestone schedule, risks, and constraints, if there are serious doubts, they should be raised. On some small projects, that may be enough to determine if the proposed methods of creating the project deliverables will work. On others, much more detailed analysis of schedule, resources, and risks may yield further insight. When considering if a project process is capable, the project manager needs to understand the conditions in which the project may operate and ensure that the methods can be flexible enough to handle various contingencies that might develop.

Experienced project managers understand that it is far better to design quality into their processes than to find problems with inspection. In the first place, it costs more to make junk and then remake good outputs. Secondly, having to rework anything aggravates time pressure that already exists on many projects. Finally, even the best inspectors do not find every mistake. If poor quality exists in project processes, some of the mistakes are likely to reach the customers.

PROCESS CONTROL The second aspect of process management is process control. **Control** is "comparing actual performance with planned performance, analyzing

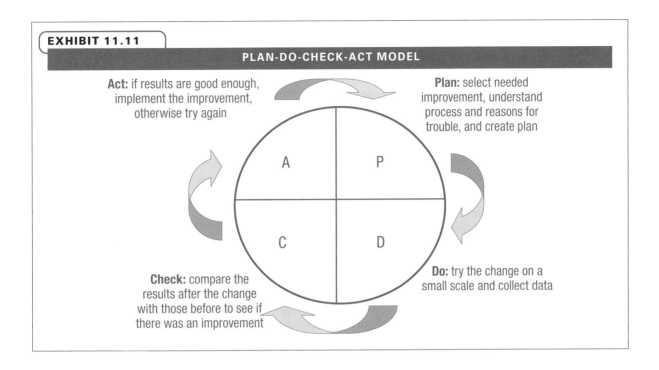

EXHIBIT 11.11

PLAN-DO-CHECK-ACT MODEL

Act: if results are good enough, implement the improvement, otherwise try again

Plan: select needed improvement, understand process and reasons for trouble, and create plan

A P

C D

Check: compare the results after the change with those before to see if there was an improvement

Do: try the change on a small scale and collect data

variances, assessing trends to effect process improvements, evaluating possible alternatives, and recommending appropriate corrective action as needed."[4] The purpose of process control is to be able to have confidence that outputs are predictable. Process control is covered in Chapter 14. If the outputs are not predictable—or if they are predictable but not satisfactory—then a project manager needs to use the third aspect of process management: process improvement.

Even with good inspectors, some mistakes will reach customers if poor quality exists in project processes.

PROCESS IMPROVEMENT WITH A PDCA MODEL

Processes can be improved in either a continuous or a breakthrough fashion. All project core team members and subject matter experts should be thinking of little ways they can improve at any time. Slow and steady improvement is a good foundation. However, sometimes substantial improvement is necessary and a breakthrough is in order. Regardless of the size of improvement desired, many models exist to guide the effort. Improvement models such as DMAIC are usually based upon the plan-do-check-act (PDCA) improvement cycle, as displayed in Exhibit 11.11.

When project managers are considering process improvements, they often involve suppliers and/or customers in a partnering arrangement. Often, they need to forecast changes in their work environment, technology, or customer desires. Organizations that take a balanced view of long-term improvement and short-term results create a culture where project process improvement can thrive. Organizations that focus almost exclusively on short-term results make it hard for project managers to devote much energy to process improvement.

Fact-Based Management

One challenge many project managers face is making decisions based upon facts. Facts are what actually happened. Making decisions using facts sounds like a sensible thing to do, yet it is difficult because:

- Opinions get in the way.
- It is hard to know what data need to be collected.
- Projects often operate with so much time pressure that decisions need to be made quickly.

FOUR ASPECTS OF FACT-BASED MANAGEMENT Fact-based management includes four key ideas: understanding variation, deciding what to measure, working correctly with data, and using the resulting information appropriately.

UNDERSTANDING VARIATION Project decision makers need to understand the difference between two types of variation. A **common cause** is "a source of variation that is inherent in a system and predictable. On a control chart, it appears as the part of the random process variation … [that] would be considered normal or not unusual, and is indicated by a random pattern of points within the control limits."[5] On the other hand, a **special cause** is "a source of variation that is not inherent in the system, is not predictable, and is intermittent. It can be assigned to a defect. … On a control chart, points outside the control limits, or non-random patterns within the control limits indicate it."[6] It is important to determine when there is variation on a project whether it is within the range of what can be expected for that particular work activity or deliverable (common cause) or whether something unusual is happening (special cause). If the variation is due to a common cause, but the results are still not acceptable, some change needs to be made to the system—the way in which the work is accomplished. However, if the change is due to a particular cause, then the way to improve is to change that particular cause and not the entire system. Many quality proponents estimate that a large majority of variation is due to common causes, yet many managers are quick to try to find a person or issue to blame (special cause). The problem is often compounded when a cause is really part of the system, yet individuals are blamed. The problem does not go away, and people become fearful. Management by facts requires an understanding that variation can be due to either common or special causes, a determination to discover which type, and the resolve to act appropriately upon that discovery.

DETERMINING WHAT TO MEASURE A second aspect of fact-based management is the determination of what to measure. A project manager wants to avoid the extreme of not measuring anything since he or she is in a hurry and there is not enough time, and the other extreme of measuring many things just to be sure. As project managers become more experienced, they develop an understanding of how many data are useful to collect and when they need to move into action regardless of the data they have. If a good charter was created, a milestone schedule with acceptance criteria for each milestone was developed. These can be useful measures. Project teams often can seek useful measures when they study lessons learned from previous projects. Many lessons either state what worked well and should be repeated on future projects or what worked poorly and should be avoided on future projects. Both often provide ideas for useful measures. The project manager and sponsor should agree on what measures will be taken, when they will be taken, and under what circumstances. While many sponsors can be quite busy, the more specific this agreement becomes, the more useful the data collected are likely to be.

WORKING CORRECTLY WITH DATA A third aspect of management by facts is how the identified data are collected, handled, and stored. Data are simple representations of facts that are collected using a measurement process.[7] Generally, the person(s) closest to the situation are best for collecting data. Efforts should be made to ensure they are complete, without errors, and timely. Many project teams either use templates from their organization or create their own forms for collecting data. When more than one person is involved, efforts should be made to be consistent. Once the data are collected, they should be analyzed. A great deal can be learned by using simple tools to look for patterns and trends in data. On larger, more complex projects and sophisticated Six Sigma projects, more detailed statistical analysis is often used. The analysis should turn the raw data into information useful to decision makers.

USING THE RESULTING INFORMATION APPROPRIATELY The final aspect of making fact-based decisions is how the information is used. Information is derived from data and understood in the context of the project.[8] Project communications plans often spell out how the information is disseminated. The best project cultures encourage truth and transparency in communication—even when it is inconvenient. People are encouraged to use information to challenge opinions and decisions. Making decisions based upon facts often requires courage. It also requires judgment because challenges that are of a factual nature are helpful, yet if the challenges become personal and are not fact based, they can be destructive.

Empowered Performance

The fourth and final core project quality concept is empowered performance. The goal of empowered performance is to have capable and willing workers at every level and every function within a company. Corporate leaders set the stage for this by developing the organizational culture. Project sponsors and managers, in turn, develop the project culture. Remember from Chapter 1 that organizational culture includes the formal and informal practices utilized, along with the values shared by members of an organization. Part of an empowered performance culture is setting an expectation for managers to allow and encourage their associates to take appropriate risks and to treat risk events as learning opportunities, not as a time to punish. Part of it is training and equipping workers so they are willing to take risks. Part is getting managers to let go of some decision-making authority so those lower in the organization can make some decisions. Yet another aspect of empowered performance is helping to develop specialists who can aid anyone in the organization. An example is a person trained as a Black Belt in a Six Sigma organization, who becomes an expert in guiding process improvement projects.

RECOGNIZE INDIVIDUALITY One essential understanding in creating capable and willing workers is that everyone is an individual. Leaders at all levels can promote inclusiveness and recognize that diversity is not only accepted, but also very helpful as projects develop. Project managers often have one-on-one conversations with new core team members and subject matter experts. An appropriate question to ask is: "I know you want to help the project succeed, but what else do you want to get out of this work assignment?" If the worker wants visibility, new friends, a chance to work with new technology, travel, or whatever, the project manager can help the worker and the project by trying to provide that. Different workers have different talents, and the best project managers carefully match individuals to tasks.

CAPITALIZE ON INDIVIDUAL STRENGTHS Outstanding project managers not only want to recruit and develop a unique team, they also want to capitalize on each person's unique strengths. Each person has unique talents, and the best opportunity for each person to improve and feel validated is to use their unique talents. When a person feels his boss understands him and works to create opportunities for him to do both what he most wants to do and what he has the potential to be best at, he achieves at the highest possible level.

EMPHASIZE INDIVIDUAL RESPONSIBILITIES   Empowered performance requires that people understand and accept their responsibilities. Much of the responsibility falls upon the project manager and core team. However, subject matter experts (SMEs) are responsible for their individual activities. Functional managers, who are the technical supervisors of the SMEs, are responsible for the methods of work chosen. Project sponsors share a high-level responsibility for project completion with project managers. Customer representatives are responsible for understanding the impact of directives they may give a project manager. Ultimately, everyone must understand what they need to do, realize how it fits in the bigger picture, and then commit to both completing their work correctly and accepting the consequences of their decisions. The more a project manager can help workers understand how their portion of work is critical to the entire project, the more committed most workers become.

USE APPROPRIATE COLLABORATION   Finally, appropriate collaboration is a key to developing empowered performance. This is true both within and beyond the organizational boundaries. A great deal of project work is performed by cross-functional teams. Cross-functional teams are most effective when individual, team, and organizational learning flourishes. One effective method of encouraging this learning in projects is to develop lessons learned at the completion of project milestones and at project closure. These lessons then need to be shared openly with other project teams. Collaboration

---

EXHIBIT 11.12

VINTAGE AIRCRAFT SHIPPING PROJECT

Global Shipping Company (GSC) was approached by an individual who was interested in selling and shipping an antique $1 million 1942 Staggered-Wing Beech aircraft from Cincinnati to a buyer in Australia. Since the aircraft was fragile, a plan needed to be developed for moving it as economically as possible while avoiding damage.

One challenge was handling the entire project in-house using only the company's staff, equipment, and resources, and the other was to devising a custom solution for moving this unusual piece of cargo.

GSC has an organizational culture that encourages cross-training, collaboration among departments, risk-taking, and designing creative approaches to problem solving while minimizing cost. Because of the size and fragility of the aircraft, a strategy was devised to dismantle it and ship via containerized ocean freight. The project was broken down into five distinct segments: pick up, dismantling, packing, loading, and shipping.

To pick up the entire aircraft, the equipment, permits, and escorts had to be arranged to get the aircraft intact from the airport and move it to the warehouse down a major street on the back of a flatbed truck. In order to fit in a standard ocean container, the aircraft had to be dismantled—under the supervision of the FAA—and documented to meet FAA regulations. To avoid damage, each piece had to be individually packaged. Different types of cloth and foam had to be tested and selected in order to prevent scratching the aircraft. Due to the height restrictions, the warehouse personnel had to design and build a custom

gurney to allow the body of the plane to be wheeled into the container and secured. Once packaged, the individual pieces were then loaded, blocked, and braced into the container to prevent damage while in transit; then the aircraft was shipped. The dismantling, documentation, and packing process was designed in a way that the new owner of the aircraft could replicate it in order to move the plane for air shows and events.

The project's success was achieved by having the courage to take on the project in the first place, the ability to use the company's resources creatively and efficiently, and the ability to adapt the plan when unexpected events occurred. The result was a project that was successfully completed, meeting all FAA standards, exceeding stakeholder expectations, and developing a shipping process that can be replicated.

Source: Danny McKee, Global shipping Company.

and learning really accelerate when people share outside of their parent organization. Of course, some things cannot be shared, but a surprising number of things can be shared. When the recipients of those lessons reciprocate, the first team learns. This type of external sharing can be through conferences, company exchanges, or other means. An example of a unique project challenge that needed empowered performance to be successful is the vintage aircraft shipping project in Exhibit 11.12.

Summary of Core Concepts

A summary of project quality core concepts is shown in Exhibit 11.13.

EXHIBIT 11.13

PROJECT QUALITY CORE CONCEPTS	
CONCEPT	SPECIFIC GUIDANCE
Stakeholder Satisfaction	Identify all internal and external stakeholders.
	Prioritize among the stakeholders.
	Understand the prioritized stakeholders' requirements.
	Develop standards to ensure the requirements are met.
	Make tradeoff decisions.
	Realize that stakeholders will judge quality both of project work processes and deliverables.
	Measure twice, cut once. (Plan and check the plan.)
	Meet requirements, but exceed expectations.
	Develop capable customers.
Process Improvement	Learn about process with the supplier-input-process-output-customer model.
	Realize that designing a quality process is far better than merely trying to find mistakes.
	Ensure project processes are capable and flexible.
	Control project processes to make them predictable.
	Improve project processes using a model based upon the plan-do-check-act concept.
Fact-Based Management	Understand the difference between common and special causes of variation.
	Select a few key well-defined items to measure.
	Carefully collect the data and use analysis techniques appropriate to the project to turn it into useful information.
	Encourage truthful, transparent, and challenging communication when making project decisions.
Empowered Performance	Develop capable and willing workers at every level and every function within a company.
	Develop a risk-taking project culture.
	Understand each person is an individual.
	To the extent possible, let everyone do what they will enjoy doing and what their strengths support.
	Ensure everyone understands and accepts their responsibilities.
	Share lessons learned and other information as widely as possible.

11.3 Project Quality Management Plan

The **quality management plan** "describes how the project management team will implement the performing organization's quality policy."[9] Therefore, a logical place to start is by understanding what a quality policy is and how it governs the actions of a project manager and team. The remainder of this section discusses the components of a project quality management plan. In addition to the quality policy, most project quality management plans describe which quality standards the project will use and how the project team will implement them. The quality management plan may include a description of the quality baseline by which the project will be judged, along with methods for quality assurance and control.

The quality management plan is a portion of the overall project management plan. On many small, simple projects, the quality planning is performed concurrently with other planning, and the quality plan is seamlessly incorporated into the project plan. On some large, complex, or unusual projects, the quality planning is handled separately, and the plan, while a portion of the overall project plan, appears as an additional document.

A project quality management plan should describe how to identify some or all of the following:

- The project's overall quality objectives
- Key project deliverables and the standards to evaluate each
- Deliverable completeness and correctness criteria from the customer's viewpoint
- Quality control activities
- Critical project work processes and standards to review each
- Stakeholder expectations for project processes
- Quality assurance activities
- Quality roles and responsibilities
- Quality tools
- Quality reporting plan[10]

Quality Policy

The top management of an organization normally writes a concise statement to guide their company's quality efforts. This policy reflects top management's principles of achieving quality and the benefits they hope to achieve with good quality. Project managers normally first consider using the quality policy of their parent company—if it is a good fit. If not, or if the project is a partnership between organizations, the project manager may need to combine and/or supplement the quality policies. However, the project's quality policy should never violate the intent of the quality policies of either the parent company or of a major customer.

A study of quality policies using an Internet search found that they vary widely. Some are less than 20 words, while others are over 200 words. The content and style can be quite different. The frequency of terms that interest project managers is shown in Exhibit 11.14.

Several interesting patterns can easily be found. First, virtually every policy includes a reference to customers. The vast majority state that customers are the reason for their existence. Next, most quality policies include satisfying requirements, but very few include exceeding requirements. This means that, for most companies, quality is measured by how well requirements are met, not exceeded. A large majority of policies mention both products and services—a reminder to project managers that services and information are frequently needed along with products to satisfy a customer's needs. A large majority of firms explicitly include improving processes, products, services, or communications.

> ### EXHIBIT 11.14
>
> | TERMS IN CORPORATE QUALITY POLICIES | |
> | --- | --- |
> | TERM | PERCENT OF POLICIES |
> | Customer | **96** |
> | Satisfy requirements | **78** |
> | Exceed requirements | **26** |
> | Product | **74** |
> | Service | **67** |
> | Improve | **67** |
> | Project stage (e.g., design) | **44** |
> | Time/responsive | **41** |
> | Value/cost | **<20** |
> | Comply with standard | **<20** |
> | Prevent mistakes | **<20** |
> | Commitment | **<20** |
> | Excellence | **<20** |
> | Measure | **<20** |
> | Partner/stakeholder | **<20** |

The next tier of responses deals specifically with project process or results. Almost half of the policies (44%) specifically state something about their quality success being tied to the quality of the processes by which they make their products and services (i.e., stages in the project life cycle). Many of those specifically state that decisions made during the design stage are critical. Forty-one percent of the quality policies specifically mention time-based competition as an important aspect of quality.

The lowest tier lists many other words that appeared in more than one but fewer than 20 percent of the policies. That does not mean decision makers necessarily feel these terms are unimportant—just that they are not as important as the ones explicitly mentioned. Remember, many of these policies are very short and only include a few key thoughts. They are meant to set direction, not plan detail.

If the project is quite large and/or complex, sometimes a quality policy is written specifically for the project. An example is shown in Exhibit 11.15.

Quality Baseline

The project work should be clearly defined by this point, in a scope statement and/or a work breakdown structure. Appropriate quality standards are selected for the materials and other inputs, work activities, documentation, and project deliverables. These standards might be industry norms, customer-specific standards, or government regulations. The project manager is ultimately responsible for selecting appropriate standards and developing additional standards that may be needed. However, project managers normally take their cues from functional managers and subject matter experts for many standards dealing with methods and from customers on standards dealing with documentation and deliverables.

EXHIBIT 11.15

TRAM PROJECT QUALITY POLICY

The Edinburgh Tram project will deliver a new tram network for the City of Edinburgh.

The project will adopt a quality management system which conforms to the principles and requirements of BS EN ISO 9001:2000 Quality Management Systems.

tie recognises that the achievement of the objectives set for the Edinburgh Tram project requires that the project is underpinned by a systematic approach with a "right first time" attitude. The management team:

- shall promote a positive culture through leadership and communication,
- use effective communication within the team as a primary enabler of quality,
- shall put in place suitable management arrangements for the effective execution of the Edinburgh Tram project,
- is committed to continual improvement of its management arrangements throughout the project life cycle,
- set quality objectives which shall be monitored and reviewed for effectiveness and suitability,
- will deliver a tram network that is fit for purpose, meeting the technical requirements of the project's stakeholders and being delivered to time and cost.

It is recognised that everyone involved with the Edinburgh Tram project is responsible for the quality of the delivery. Quality must be considered as a core value that is to taken into account by Edinburgh Tram project staff and suppliers in all their project related activities.

This policy shall be communicated to Edinburgh Tram project staff and suppliers.

This policy shall be reviewed annually for continuing suitability.

Source: http://www.tie.ltd.uk/policy_docs/del.hsqe.103.pdf, accessed August 19, 2010.

The quality baseline reflects the agreed upon quality objectives. It can include metrics that define exactly what will be measured, how each will be measured, and the target value of each.

Quality Assurance

Performing quality assurance (QA) is "the process of auditing the quality requirements and the results from quality control measurements to ensure appropriate quality standards and operational definitions are used."[11] This is a broad set of management activities designed to give key stakeholders confidence that sensible methods and capable people are working on the project. This hopefully yields good project deliverables and documentation. Quality assurance is one way to simultaneously improve quality and manage stakeholder relations.

Perhaps quality assurance is best understood by considering two of its primary methods: the quality audit and process improvement. A quality audit is used to determine what methods are being used (hopefully the methods determined in the quality baseline) and whether they are effective. For audits to be effective, people need to be convinced that the real purpose is to improve work methods and not to punish individuals.

Process improvement can follow an improvement model such as the DMAIC method shown in Exhibit 11.7 or the PDCA model shown in Exhibit 11.11. Process improvement is used to improve both quality and productivity. Process improvement can be of a continuous nature, in which many incremental improvements are made over time, or of a breakthrough nature, in which a substantial change is planned and implemented at once.

Quality Control

Performing quality control (QC) is "the process of monitoring and recording results of executing the quality activities to assess performance and recommend necessary changes."[12] This detailed set of technical activities tests whether specific project deliverables meet their quality standards. Quality control may include inspection of inputs, activities, and deliverables. It includes a reporting system. Outputs of quality control are recommendations that may include the following:

- **Preventive actions**—"documented direction to perform an activity that can reduce the probability of negative consequences associated with project risks."[13]
- **Corrective actions**—"documented direction for executing the project work to bring expected future performance of the project work in line with the project management plan."[14]
- **Defect repair**—"formally documented identification of a defect in a project component with a recommendation to either repair the defect or replace the component."[15]
- **Validated deliverables**—components or products "that have been completed and checked for correctness by the Perform Quality Control process."[16]

11.4 Project Quality Tools

Literally hundreds of tools have been developed to help organizations manage the quality of their processes. Many of these tools are slight variations of each other and have multiple names. Many of the quality tools can be applied specifically to managing project quality. Exhibit 11.16 lists some of the more frequently used and more important project quality tools with brief descriptions. Since many of these tools can also be used on projects for areas in addition to quality, the chapter in which each first appears is also listed. The project quality tools are shown in the stage of the DMAIC improvement cycle where they might be most frequently used, although many of them can be used in multiple stages.

11.5 Complete Project Management Plan

Chapters 5 through 11 have all dealt with aspects of project planning. On small, simple projects, the various portions of this planning may be combined to a large extent. On larger, more complex projects, specific methods are often used to plan the various project aspects separately, such as cost, schedule, resources, communications, risk, and quality. If they have not been planned together, they need to be compiled into a unified project management plan. Conflicts need to be resolved. A configuration management system need to be selected or developed. Finally, the project manager should apply a sanity test to all project plans.

Resolve Conflicts

Sometimes, when all parts of the plan come together, it becomes obvious that the overall plan is impractical. If this occurs, the key stakeholders may need to determine their priorities and tradeoffs. What do they really most want and need from the project? Are all of the quality standards truly mandatory, or can one of them be relaxed a bit? Is the imposed deadline really critical or, seeing the impact it poses for costs and risks, can it be relaxed a bit? Is the budget a true maximum, or can it be adjusted to secure the

EXHIBIT 11.16				
		PROJECT QUALITY TOOLS		
DMAIC PHASE	**PROJECT QUALITY TOOL**	**BRIEF DESCRIPTION**	**CHAPTER INTRODUCED**	**WHY USE THIS TOOL?**
Define	Charter	High-level agreement to start project	4	Sets expectations, scope, identifies resources needed for project kick-off
	Stakeholder Analysis	Identifying and prioritizing needs of persons interested in project	5	Identifies all of the parties that are affected by the planned project and what their position regarding the project is
	Communication Plan	Living document to guide communications	5	Needed to ensure all stakeholders are aware of the project's progress and set communication intervals
	Voice of the Customer (VOC)	Using customer desires when designing product	6	Needed to develop and translate customer CTQs. Can also be done for internal business partners, vendors, etc.
	Supplier-Input-Process-Output-Customer (SIPOC)	Structured approach to learning supplier–customer desires	11	Provides a high-level view of the process and stakeholders. Can help with scoping and boundaries
Measure	Critical to Quality (CTQ)	Characteristics vital to customer satisfaction	6	This identifies what process qualities the project should focus on to most improve the customers' experience
	Metrics (Operational Definition)	Crisp definition of what and how to measure specific performance	6	Clear and specific definition about what data is needed, from where, for what time period, and who is responsible
	Flow Chart (Process Map)	Shows order of activities or information travel	11	Visually illustrates the steps and decision points within the current process to identify timing, pain points, responsibilities, and bottlenecks
	Data Collection Plan (Define Measures)	Determining what and how to measure	11	Defines where data is stored, how much data is needed, and what other supporting data is needed to find root cause
Analyze	Histogram	Vertical bar graph showing process average, spread, and shape	8	To view the performance and tendencies of the current process
	Pareto Chart	Vertical bar chart focusing on key problems	11	Helps identify and rank key reasons/categories for defects
	Root Cause Analysis	Technique to determine underlying reason for problem	10	Key to understanding what is causing defects to provide direction on what should be focused on for improvements

(continued)

EXHIBIT 11.16				
PROJECT QUALITY TOOLS (CONTINUED)				
DMAIC PHASE	**PROJECT QUALITY TOOL**	**BRIEF DESCRIPTION**	**CHAPTER INTRODUCED**	**WHY USE THIS TOOL?**
	Run Chart (trend chart)	Line graph showing variation over time	11	Shows process performance over time, and can also show major shifts in performance due to changes within the process
	Failure Mode and Effect Analysis (FEMA)	Understanding potential causes of failure	11	Identifies and prioritizes risks within the current process, suggests abatements, and adjusts prioritized scores after abatements are in place
Improve	Brainstorming	Quickly generating many ideas	6	Can help identify current process gaps/issues, potential roadblocks, or potential solutions
	Cause and Effect (Fishbone) Diagram	Exploring many possible causes of problem	10	Helps identify many possible causes of problems
	Pilot	Testing potential project solution on small scale	11	Important to ensure that any improvements are properly tested and any results meet the project's goals
Control	Control Chart	Understanding variation over time	9	Shows how much variation is in a process over time
	Dashboards (Scorecards)	Few measures that summarize performance	11	Use to baseline existing performance and performance after changes have been made to measure improvement
	Lessons Learned	Knowledge from experience captured and shared	4	Documents any issues encountered and best practices for future projects to consider
All Phases	Project Review	Assess project progress and problems for continuation	10	Necessary to ensure the project stays on schedule/budget during milestones and to discuss anything required of the project sponsors or stakeholders
	Change Management	Structured approach to overcome resistance	11	Needed to gain and maintain buy-in and acceptance of any changes

desired features? These questions and others like them have probably been asked all along, but now they take on added urgency because once the project plan is approved it may be more difficult to make these changes.

Establish Configuration Management

Project planning can be hard work. Once the plan is in place, it still takes hard work to control the project. One last part of planning is to create a configuration management system to aid in that control. A **configuration management system** is "a collection of formally documented procedures used to … identify and document functional and physical characteristics of a product, result, service or component; control any changes; record and report each change; and support the audit … to verify conformance to requirements."[17]

Apply Sanity Tests to All Project Plans

A common saying is appropriate to consider here: "can't see the forest for the trees." This means that sometimes a person is so concerned with details that they forget the big picture. During the first project stage (initiating), the primary deliverable the team created was a charter. The charter is a high-level look at a project, so seeing the big picture was easy. During the more detailed planning stage, however, the team looked in great detail at scope, resources, cost, communications, risks, and quality. Now they need to step back a bit and ask if these all work well together. The project manager and core team should apply a sanity test to their project plans by asking one another questions to be sure that the plan makes sense. Some of these questions could be as follows:

- Does the critical path look reasonable?
- Do the milestones look achievable?
- Are some resources overallocated?
- Does everyone understand what they are supposed to do?
- Do we really understand our customers?
- Are the customers' desires likely to change?
- How well do we understand the standards we will be judged against?
- Are the methods for completing our work really sensible?
- Are we confident we can gather and analyze the data we need to control this?

11.6 Kick Off Project

Project kick-off meetings are conducted for many reasons. First, everyone should express their legitimate needs and desires and should strive to understand the desires of all the other stakeholders. If the leader charged with accomplishing the project does not have the full authority to direct all of the project work activities, she needs to use her influence to get everyone excited about the project, to feel pride in their participation, to feel they share in the risks and rewards the project offers, and to be motivated to self-manage as much as possible. Many people may have helped with some parts of the project planning. This is their chance to see how all the parts fit together. Since many projects fail because of "touch points" where one worker hands off work to another, it is critical for all parties to understand these potential trouble spots. Kick-off meetings are also helpful in convincing all the project stakeholders that the project leaders (sponsor, project manager, and core team) will be good stewards of the customer's and the parent organization's assets. Answering any remaining questions and overcoming lingering concerns helps to accomplish this. Finally, all interested parties (outside customers, top management, functional managers, frontline workers, and any others) should be eager to commit to the project and get on with the work!

Preconditions to Meeting Success

Several preconditions that must be met for project kick-off meetings to be successful are as follows:

- The sponsor and project manager need to set clear direction during the planning.
- The core team needs to commit to the project first—it is hard for them to convince others if they do not believe themselves.
- An atmosphere of trust and relationship building should be set by all.
- Project leaders need to practice active listening to uncover potential problems.
- As many people as possible should be included in parts of the planning to enhance chances so they will buy in to the resulting project plan.

EXHIBIT 11.17

IS&T PROJECT LAUNCH ASSESSMENT AGENDA

Purpose: The Project Manager is to illustrate to an executive audience the chartered IS&T project's readiness to successfully launch. Upon conclusion of the Project Manager's presentation, the executive audience will determine and document the actions required for the project to launch.

Prerequisite: The Project Manager is required to complete the Project Deliverable Review and receive documented approval from the Project Deliverable Review Board in order to proceed to the Project Launch Assessment.

Standard Participants
- Core Group (CG) (CIO and IS&T Director)
- PMO Manager
- Project Manager
- Functional Manager
- PMO Consult
- Quality Consult
- Security Consult (Optional)
- Test Coordinator
- Sponsor

Required Documents: The Project Manager is required to present the PLA materials online. If a paper copy is needed, it should be printed double-sided.

- Project Charter
- PMO Risk Forms
- Project Financial Worksheet
- Master Test Plan
- Progress Report – PDR

Project Launch Assessment Agenda: The Project Manager is required to present all of the listed deliverables in the provided order, focusing on specifically the identified components and content specified.

1. Project Charter—Discuss Business Need, Purpose, Logical Scope: In-Scope, Out-of-Scope, and Assumptions.
2. Master Test Plan—Discuss Sections 1.3—Test Levels, Objectives, and Deliverables; 3—Test Timeline and Key Events; and 5—Define System Characteristics, Relative Importance, and Subsystems.
3. Privacy and Security—Discuss the Security and HIPAA Template For PMO Projects.
4. Risk Forms—Discuss all populated and scored forms created to date.
5. Project Financial Worksheet—Discuss populated spreadsheet.
6. Progress Report (PDR)—Speak to the current status of all actions provided for each deliverable.

Source: Nancy D'Quila, PMP.

Meeting Activities

The formality of a kick-off meeting can vary considerably depending on the size and type of project. Typical activities that might be included in the kick-off meeting are the following:

- The sponsor and project manager describing the importance of the project
- The customer(s) describing their acceptance standards, sense of urgency, and budget concerns
- The project manager outlining the project goals
- The project manager and the core team describing work expectations
- The project manager unfolding the project plan and its current status (if work has commenced)
- The core team explaining the communications, risk, and quality plans
- Everyone asking questions and making suggestions
- The project manager authorizing appropriate changes to the project plan
- Everyone concurring with the overall plan and to his or her individual action items

On small, simple projects, the charter presentation and signing can take the place of a kick-off meeting. However, on many projects, the team needs to perform much more detailed planning after the charter is signed. Project kick-off meetings are vital for communications and commitment on these projects. Exhibit 11.17 is an example of how the information systems and technology division of a major health care company kicks off a project.

11.7 Baseline and Communicate Project Management Plan

Once the project plan is complete and accepted by the stakeholders, the plan is baselined. A baseline is the approved plan. Many project plans are developed iteratively as more information comes to light. A project plan is considered to be in draft form until enough information is available for the key stakeholders to commit to all of the details and baseline the plan. At that point, it becomes official, and any changes in the future need to be formally approved and documented.

This is a time of great joy, because this marks the transition between planning and executing the project. In reality, on many projects, some activities that are on the critical path or nearly critical paths are started before the official project kick-off. Planning also continues in the form of replanning to adjust to changing circumstances. However, the majority of planning is done, and the majority of executing is just starting.

The project management plan needs to be communicated in accordance with the communications plan requirements. Hopefully, many of the key stakeholders are able to attend the kickoff meeting. Regardless of who is present, proper communication needs to be sent to all stakeholders.

11.8 Using MS Project for Project Baselines

MS Project can be used as a tool to automate and communicate many facets of a project. However, those involved in the project should be sure that they are ready to use it effectively. Before a baseline is created with MS Project, the following should be verified:

- QA and QC activities are included.
- Risk response plan activities (or duration compensation) are included.
- Performance posting activities are included.
- All "hard" date constraints are incorporated.
- A realistic start date is chosen.
- Resource overloads are addressed.
- Organizational holidays are entered.
- Resource vacations are entered.
- Resource allocations are realistic.
- A management reserve is in the schedule.
- A contingency reserve is in the schedule.
- Time and cost tradeoffs are applied to the schedule.

Baseline the Project Plan

Microsoft Project supports three sets of activity metrics, each set having five fields. The sets are used for cross-comparison purposes to better understand impacts, such as progress or requested change. The sets and their field names are shown in Exhibit 11.18.

The first column is often referred to as the scheduled values. These values are based on current project information. They are recalculated if an input to MS Project's calculation algorithm changes. Inputs include estimated duration, work, and cost. Progress information

---

EXHIBIT 11.18

MS PROJECT ACTIVITY METRICS

CURRENT SCHEDULE (SCHEDULED)	PLANNED SCHEDULE (BASELINE)	WHAT ACTUALLY HAPPENED (ACTUAL)
Duration	Baseline duration	Actual duration
Start	Baseline start	Actual start
Finish	Baseline finish	Actual finish
Work	Baseline work	Actual work
Cost	Baseline cost	Actual cost

---

such as actual start, actual finish, actual duration, actual cost, and actual work causes recalculation. Changing information such as resource assignments, constraints, working time, lead-lag values, and the project start date can also cause a recalculation of the scheduled values.

MS Project's baseline is a set of five activity metrics, sometimes called the planned values. The five are the activity baseline start, activity baseline finish, activity baseline duration, activity baseline cost, and activity baseline work. These values, together with project quality and scope targets, are what the stakeholders agreed to, approved, and expect as key measures of project success. Collectively, these values and targets, along with the risk and communications plans, form the project management plan.

The project manager can use MS Project to compare the baseline with actual schedule, work, and cost variance values and display these graphically and in tables. This comparison can be used to predict future impacts to time and cost targets. With this understanding, project managers can take action to reduce or eliminate undesirable future impacts. This is a powerful capability for the project manager.

First Time Baseline

Once key stakeholders agree to the project plan, the baseline is created by:

1. On the Project tab, Schedule group, click Set Baseline, then click Set Baseline …
2. The defaults should be accepted as shown in Exhibit 11.19; click OK.

Subsequent Baselines

For any number of reasons, it may not be useful to continue to manage to the present baseline. Reasons to change the baseline might include changes to the project scope, project delay or restart, unavailability of planned resources, slower cash flow than planned, occurrence of risk events, and quality problems. Remember, any change to the project baseline must be officially designated as an approved change. If a change has been approved, then the changed material must be re-baselined, as well as the WBS parents of the new or changed material (step 3 below):

1. Select the changed or added activities, milestones, and WBS elements.
2. On the Project tab, Schedule group, click Set Baseline, then click Set Baseline …
3. Click Selected tasks, then click To all summary tasks
4. Click OK.

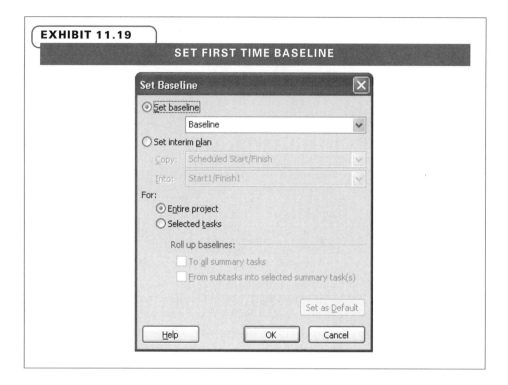

EXHIBIT 11.19

SET FIRST TIME BASELINE

Summary

Quality planning is an interesting place to end the planning portion of our work. Deming, Juran, and many other people have contributed to the modern approaches to quality. The Malcolm Baldrige Award, ISO certification, and Six Sigma each present a framework with many good points. The contemporary approach to project quality draws upon all of these sources.

The first concept in contemporary project quality management is stakeholder satisfaction. It is critical to understand project stakeholders, prioritize their needs, manage toward those needs, keep the relationships strong, and always strive to help ensure that the customer is capable of using the project deliverables. The second concept is process management. This includes understanding both continual and breakthrough forms of improvement, seeking the root cause of problems, and using an appropriate model such as DMAIC to guide improvement efforts. The third concept is fact-based management. This entails understanding variation, making good decisions regarding what to measure, capturing and analyzing data correctly, and using the information in an open and honest decision-making manner. The final concept is empowered performance. Project managers want to have capable and willing workers throughout their project and should treat each person as an individual, ensure people accept responsibility, and strive to get more done through collaboration.

When project managers perform quality management planning, the first thing they need to do is either adopt the quality policy of their parent organization or supplement it. The policy should broadly guide their efforts. The quality plan should include the quality baseline defining performance expectations. It should also include instructions for how the quality assurance and quality control will be handled.

Many quality tools have been developed over the years, and quite a few of them work very well on projects. Many of these tools can be used in additional project management activities.

Once the quality management plan and all of the other subsidiary plans have been developed, it is time to iron out any inconsistencies between the various plans. The overall project plan needs to make sense. Quality, cost, schedule, human resources, risk, and communications may have been planned somewhat independently on a large project, and now is the time to make sure they all work well together.

The project core team usually asks themselves a number of questions concerning the practicality of the overall plan and then holds a kick-off meeting with all of the project stakeholders. Hopefully, the outcome of the meeting is commitments and excitement all around. Now, the project officially moves into execution. While some of the project activities may already be under way (or even complete), the approval of the project plan signals the change from primarily planning to primarily execution. Ongoing planning and replannig still occur, but managing the performance of project activities and communicating with various stakeholders consume much of the project manager's time from this point forward.

Key Terms from the *PMBOK® Guide*

planning quality, 292

process, 299

Control, 300

common cause, 302

special cause, 302

quality management plan, 306

perform quality assurance (QA), 308

perform quality control (QC), 309

Preventive actions, 309

Corrective actions, 309

Defect repair, 309

Validated deliverables, 309

configuration management system, 311

Chapter Review Questions

1. Within Exhibit 11.16, what tools could be helpful during project kick-off?
2. Define quality assurance and the primary methods that can be used to achieve it.
3. Define quality control and the primary methods that can be used to achieve it.
4. What are the definitions of common and special cause of variation?
5. Identify activities that should be in place prior to officially kicking off a project.
6. Identify and describe the steps within the PDCA model.
7. _____ is the process of identifying which quality standards are relevant to the project and how to satisfy them.
8. _____ was a very influential thought leader in the area of quality who created the Profound Knowledge System.
9. _____ is best known for creating the Quality Trilogy.
10. Many leaders in the area of quality come from the countries of _____ and _____.
11. The acronym TQM stands for _____.
12. The Baldrige Award was developed in _____, while ISO 9001:2008 was developed in _____.

13. The ISO 9001 principle of _____ involves understanding both current and future customer needs and striving to exceed these needs.
14. _____ is a statistical term that indicates the amount of variation in a set of data.
15. _____ is the degree to which a set of inherent characteristics fulfills a requirement.
16. External stakeholders can include _____, _____, and the _____.
17. The goal of _____ is to create capable workers at every level of the organization.
18. The two types of variation are _____ and _____.
19. Processes can be improved by either a(n) _____ or _____ manner.
20. The four core project quality concepts are _____, _____, _____, and _____.
21. The _____ describes how the project management team will perform the performing organization's quality policy.
22. The term "customer" appears in the vast majority of corporate quality policies. True or false?
23. A review of corporate quality policies revealed that most are very similar in terms of length and content. True or false?

Discussion Questions

1. Name the previously discussed quality gurus and describe the quality concepts they are credited with developing.
2. Give some examples of common and special variation within business practices. Which of these causes of variation can be addressed through continuous improvement?
3. Identify any similarities and differences in the approaches between TQM, ISO, and Six Sigma.

What strengths and weaknesses are inherent in each of these approaches?

4. Based on your experience, have you seen companies integrate quality within their project planning processes? If so, how have they integrated it? Is quality typically addressed in one area of the overall project plan or continuously throughout the plan?

5. Describe the four parts of W. Deming's Profound Knowledge System.

6. Describe the three areas covered in Juran's Quality Trilogy.

7. Discuss four core values of the Malcolm Baldrige Award.

8. Discuss the underlying themes of Six Sigma. Which do you feel is most important and why?

9. Describe the process of achieving stakeholder satisfaction.

10. Why is it important to consider stakeholder satisfaction?

11. Explain the difference between common cause and special cause.

12. Discuss the four areas of fact-based decision making.

13. Discuss the four areas of the plan-do-check-act model.

14. Describe the four outputs of quality control.

15. List the project quality tools you expect to use on your project. Tell where you plan to use each tool and why it is important.

16. Describe the main components of the SIPOC model.

Exercises

1. Create a SIPOC for an everyday activity (i.e., paying bills, parallel parking, or making cookies).

2. Identify key quality project plan steps that you feel should be included within a typical overall project plan. Be sure to include quality items throughout the project plan life cycle.

3. Create a SIPOC model for a project where your university is modernizing its student center to include space for on-campus, student-run businesses. Be sure to include all relevant stakeholder groups. Describe how you would use this information to design quality into your project.

4. Improve a work process using either the DMAIC or the PDCA model to guide your actions. What project quality tools did you use, and why did you select each?

5. Identify the quality policy for a local company. Speculate how the policy focuses the efforts on a project in that company. Find a project manager at that company and ask his or her opinion of the quality policy's impact.

PMBOK® *Guide* Questions

1. Learning from the past and understanding cause-and-effect relationships to predict future behavior pertain to which part of Deming's Profound Knowledge System?
   a. systems
   b. variation
   c. knowledge
   d. psychology

2. All of the following are popular frameworks for quality *except*:
   a. TQM
   b. Six Sigma
   c. ISO
   d. DMAIC

3. Which of the following describes Six Sigma?
   a. Its name stands for *standard deviation*.
   b. It measures quality problems in parts per million.
   c. It is used extensively by companies such as General Electric.
   d. All of the above.

4. All of the following are areas of the International Organization for Standardization (ISO)'s quality management *except*:
   a. reaction
   b. management
   c. realization
   d. remediation

5. A _____ is characterized by its inputs, tools, techniques, and outputs.
   a. control
   b. common cause
   c. process
   d. special cause

Example Project

Talk with your sponsor to determine if the organization for which you are planning your example project has a quality policy. If it does, determine whether you will adopt it as is or ask to augment it. Tell why you wish to either accept or modify it.

With your sponsor, determine the quality baseline for your project. What standards will you use?

Perform a stakeholder analysis. After completing the tool, are there any stakeholders that you didn't think of before? Are there any who are opponents? What actions could you take to try to change those who are opponents into enthusiasts?

Create a SIPOC for your project. What did you learn that surprised you? How will your project plan be different because of what you learned?

Create an agenda for a kick-off meeting for your project. Conduct the kick-off meeting and capture minutes for it. Tell what went as you expected and what went differently than you expected.

Baseline your project management plan with the activity baseline start, activity baseline finish, activity baseline duration, activity baseline cost, and activity baseline work shown in MS Project. Also show in your project management plan the agreed upon quality and scope targets, risk, and communications plans.

Pick one work process related to your example project. Use the DMAIC model to improve the process. Perform the define and measure steps. Tell what you learned. Identify what project quality tools you expect to use on the remaining steps and tell why you will use them.

References

A Guide to the Project Management Body of Knowledge (PMBOK® Guide), 4th ed. (Newtown Square, PA: Project Management Institute, 2008).

Baldrige National Quality Program, "Criteria for Performance Excellence," http://www.nist.gov/baldrige/publications/upload/2009_2010_Business_Nonprofit_Criteria.pdf, accessed August 19, 2010.

Brassard, Michael and Diane Ritter, *The Memory Jogger™ II: A Pocket Guide of Tools for Continuous Improvement & Effective Planning* (Salem, NH: GOAL/QPC, 1994).

Buckingham, Marcus and Donald O. Clifton, *Now, Discover Your Strengths* (New York: The Free Press, 2001).

Byrne, Rhonda. *The Secret.* (New York: Attria Books, 2006).

Crawford, Lynn and Jeanne Dorie, "Quality First," *PM Network* 20 (5) (May 2006): 42–47.

Evans, James R. and William M. Lindsay, *An Introduction to Six Sigma & Process Improvement*, 1st ed. (Mason, OH: Thomson South-Western, 2005).

Evans, James R. and William M. Lindsay, *The Management and Control of Quality*, 8th ed. (Mason, OH: Cengage Learning South-Western, 2011).

Hoffman, William, "Steering Quality," *PM Network* 16 (5) (May 2002): 26–32.

International Organization for Standardization, "Quality Management Principles," http://www.iso.org/iso/iso_catalogue/management_standards/iso_9000_iso_14000/qmp.htm, accessed August 18, 2010.

Juran, Joseph M., *A History of Managing for Quality: The Evolution, Trends, and Future Directions of Managing for Quality* (Madison, WI: ASQC Quality Press, 1995).

Kloppenborg, Timothy J. and Joseph A. Petrick, *Managing Project Quality* (Vienna, VA: Management Concepts, Inc., 2002).

Kwak, Young Hoon, John J. Wetter, and Frank T. Anbari, "Business Process Best Practices: Project Management or Six Sigma?" *Proceedings, PM1 Research Conference 2006: New Directions in Project Management* (Montreal, Canada, 2006).

Milosevic, Dragan Z., *Project Management Toolbox: Tools and Techniques for the Practicing Project Manager* (New York: John Wiley & Sons, 2003).

Mulcahy, Rita, *PMP Exam Prep: Rita's Course in a Book for Passing the PMP Exam*, 5th ed. (RMC Publications, Inc., 2005).

Neuendorf, Steve, *Six Sigma for Project Managers* (Vienna, VA: Management Concepts, Inc., 2004).

PMI Code of Ethics and Professional Responsibility, http://www.pmi.org/PDF/ap_pmicodeofethics.pdf, accessed August 20, 2010.

Rose, Kenneth H., *Project Quality Management: Why, What and How* (Boca Raton, FL: Ross Publishing, Inc., 2005).

Shiba, Shoji and David Walden, *Breakthrough Management* (New Delhi, India: Confederation of Indian Industry, 2006).

Stevens, James D., Timothy J. Kloppenborg, and Charles R. Glagola, *Quality Performance*

Measurements of the EPC Process: The Blueprint (Austin, TX: Construction Industry Institute, 1994).

Wagner, Rodd and James K. Harter, *12: The Elements of Great Managing* (New York: Gallup Press, 2006).

Zhang, Weiyong and Xiaobo Xu, "Six Sigma and Information Systems Project Management: A Revised Theoretical Model," *Project Management Journal* 39 (3) (2008): 59–74.

Zeithaml, Valarie, A. Parasuraman, and Leonard L. Berry, *Delivering Service Quality: Balancing Cus-tomer Perceptions and Expectations* (New York: The Free Press, 1990).

"ISO 9001 2008 Translated Into Plain English," http://www.praxiom.com/iso-9001.htm, accessed August 19, 2010.

http://www.pma.doit.wisc.edu/plan/3-2/print.html, accessed August 19, 2010.

http://www.tie.ltd.uk/policy_docs/del.hsqe.103.pdf, accessed August 19, 2010.

Endnotes

1. *PMBOK® Guide* 440.
2. *PMBOK® Guide* 445.
3. *PMBOK® Guide* 37.
4. *PMBOK® Guide* 430.
5. *PMBOK® Guide* 429.
6. *PMBOK® Guide* 449.
7. James R. Evans and William M. Lindsay, *The Management and Control of Quality*, 8th ed. (Mason, OH: Thomson South-Western, 2011): 364.
8. Ibid.
9. *PMBOK® Guide* 445.
10. Adapted from http://www.pma.doit.wisc.edu/plan/3-2/print.html, accessed August 19, 2010.
11. *PMBOK® Guide* 440.
12. Ibid.
13. *PMBOK® Guide* 83.
14. Ibid.
15. Ibid.
16. *PMBOK® Guide* 124.
17. *PMBOK® Guide* 429.

PROJECT MANAGEMENT *IN ACTION*

Affinity and Relationship Diagrams for Project Kick-off

"Eat a hearty breakfast," they say. "It will give you a good start to the day."

"Dig a deep hole, add fertilizer and water," they say. "It will give your plant a good start on life."

A good start—it's as important for your projects as it is for your plants or your day. After all the planning you've done on your project, you want to have a good start for the actual project execution. A well-planned and executed project kick-off meeting is a critical event to help ensure overall project success.

Making sure that all stakeholders are involved or have bought into the project at the beginning is important. Giving each of one an opportunity to express his or her needs or desires, while hearing the needs or desires of others, lays a good foundation for the future activities and ultimate successful outcome of the project.

One way to start the kick-off meeting uses an affinity diagram, which is a quality tool that helps to make visible and organize individual thinking around a particular topic. In so doing, it potentially and hopefully builds a shared understanding of a topic—in this case, the value and/or intent of the project.

Over the past years, while working with a variety of diverse organizations, I have used this approach to begin project kick-off meetings, as well as many other introduction-type meetings.

The technique is a simple one: The leader asks each stakeholder present to print on one Post-it Note a sentence answering the question "Why is this project important?" or "Why are we doing this project?"

Once all the notes have been created, they are read one at a time and posted. Similar notes are then grouped (generally by the leader with the help of the

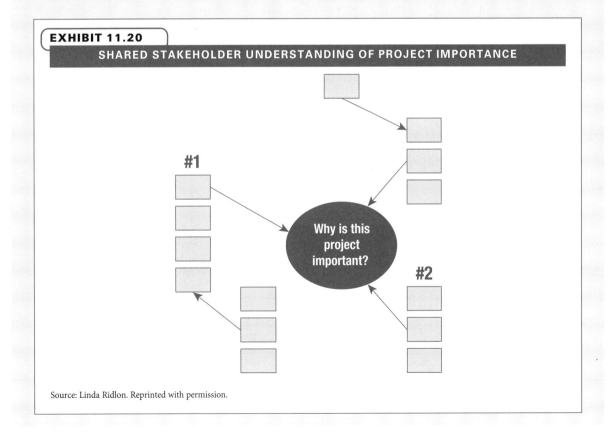

EXHIBIT 11.20

SHARED STAKEHOLDER UNDERSTANDING OF PROJECT IMPORTANCE

#1

Why is this project important?

#2

Source: Linda Ridlon. Reprinted with permission.

other participants) according to their affinity, or connection to one another. Each group of notes is then titled (with a label printed in red) to reflect the common theme of that group of labels. Labels that do not seem to be related to others, and therefore do not fit into a group, are left to stand by themselves.

When all labels have been reviewed, and grouped and titled where appropriate, the next step enables relationships between the groups to be discovered and displayed. The groups of labels with red titles and the ungrouped labels are organized on the page, and the participants look for causal or influence relationships and draw relationship arrows between the labels accordingly. If desired, voting can also be done to determine the agreed-upon priorities among the groupings (see Exhibit 11.20).

The resulting diagram (a very simple interrelationship diagraph or relationship diagram) serves several purposes, as follows:

- It makes visible the individual and collective thinking regarding the importance or intent of the project.
- It illustrates the simple use of a quality tool, which can be helpful in a variety of situations where the diverse thinking of each participant is solicited and organized into a coherent whole.
- It demonstrates a technique encouraging equality of participation, particularly helpful for those folks who

may be less verbal or who may feel intimidated by others in the group.
- It frequently serves as a tangible expression of commitment or buy-in (particularly if there is much affinity or strong relationships between the individual statements of purpose).
- It can be used as a foundation or blueprint document for the future. If questions come up about the project's importance or purpose, this diagram can show "here's what we all put together at the start of the project."
- If there, by chance, is not good agreement and/or shared understanding regarding the project's importance or purpose, it will help to alert the project leader and sponsor to potential problems that may well need to be addressed before going further.

Consider helping your project get off to a good start with an initial activity at the project kick-off meeting that stresses inclusiveness, models the group participation that will be needed throughout, and results in a visible depiction of both the individual perspectives and the shared understanding the stakeholders have regarding the importance of the project. People, plants, and projects all benefit from that initial nurturing that enables a good start.

Source: Linda Ridlon

PART 3

PERFORMING PROJECTS

organize / plan / perform

Chapter 12
Project Supply Chain Management

Chapter 13
Leading and Managing Project Teams

Chapter 14
Determining Project Progress and Results

Chapter 15
Finishing the Project and Realizing the Benefits

CHAPTER 12

Project Supply Chain Management

CHAPTER OBJECTIVES

After completing this chapter, you should be able to:

- Identify the role of supply chain management in project management and its importance for ensuring project success.

- Describe how to plan, conduct, administer, and close project procurements.

- Describe the various formats for supply contracts and when each type is appropriate.

- Explain how to utilize the contemporary approach to project partnering and collaboration.

Fuse/Jupiter Images

This story was born when I encountered an unexpected challenge that threatened to derail another project. The solution to the previous project took on a life of its own and became a significant independent project called Super Absorbent Polymer Turf (SAPTURF). The problem related to synthetic turf systems and the extreme heat generated on the surface of these systems, 50 to 60 degrees above the ambient temperature, which is unpleasant and even dangerous for people participating in activities on the turf.

I chose a large multinational based in Europe to partner with on the next step in the commercialization of SAPTURF. The firm uses a major American university as their contract research and product development department. I also set up trials at the University of Cincinnati to provide a control during the testing.

I chose this international partner to work with due to the fact that they are the market leaders and have sophisticated business minds in leadership

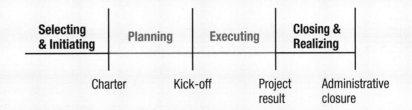

Selecting & Initiating	Planning	Executing	Closing & Realizing

Charter Kick-off Project result Administrative closure

**PMBOK®
GUIDE TOPICS**

- Plan procurements
- Conduct procurements
- Administer procurements

roles. I still control all of the intellectual property (IP) and have entered into an agreement to further test my technology in order to calibrate the value. This approach is a bit risky as opposed to an immediate license arrangement. However, I feel the trials will drive great value and at the same time shift all product development costs over to my partner. At the end of the trial period a license agreement will be executed with the appropriate values assigned to up front payment, annual minimums, and royalties. This license may be with any firm; the only contractual provision is that my commercialization partner gets the opportunity to match any offer from another firm.

The SAPTURF project required a strong team in order to move forward. Successful commercialization of IP is a long shot, so room for project management error is slim. I realized I would need to carefully build a team and organize a plan that would compensate for lack of in-house resources. Lack of in-house resources sounds like a problem from a project management perspective, but in many cases it is an advantage! I was free to look for the best resources to meet the specific and unique project challenges, including the following:

- **Need 1**—Significant and skilled legal resources were crucial in order to protect and advance the entrepreneur's (my) interest. Few entrepreneurs can afford to have top legal talent in house.

    SAPTURF project solution—Talented and accomplished corporate lawyer John Gierl of Katz, Teller, Brant, and Hild was invited to join the SAPTURF team and be compensated on a percentage-of-yield basis.
- **Need 2**—Technical validation was very important. The potential end users are busy people and only have so much time to evaluate the products' credibility.

    SAPTURF team solution—Well-known polymer scientist Dr. Ray Berard, who owns 30-plus patents and has been recognized for his work with Titleist golf balls and as chief technical officer of Interface Foundation, has enhanced our scientific credibility. Ray also joined the team on a percentage basis.

- **Need 3**—Small enterprises can hardly afford the technical capability and physical plant required to do R&D and prototyping.

  SAPTURF team solution—We identified a capable resource that has a product that can be a component of our finished product. A division of German giant BASF was invited to join the team, and their top technical and sales personnel have been involved in the project on a daily basis.

- **Need 4**—There existed a critical need for an organized system of communication and documentation with a team of independent players. Without such a tool effective project management, using contract and success-based participants, would be all impossible.

  SAPTURF team solution—I chose to use a hosted project management tool, "Basecamp," to provide the collaborative communication tool for the SAPTURF project. It has the essential functionality and user friendliness required, and can be used in conjunction with more sophisticated project management tools when necessary.

  Chris Tetrault, owner and founder, SAPTURF

The transition from project planning into project execution is not straightforward. The most visible portion of the transition occurs when the project stakeholders accept the project plan and a project kick-off is conducted. However, a certain amount of project execution often takes place prior to the formal kick-off, and most projects require additional planning. In this text, we use the topic of supply chain management to help transition into execution because planning and execution topics under the umbrella of project supply chain management are most easily understood if covered together.

12.1 Introduction to Project Supply Chain Management

As the opening case illustrates, almost no serious projects are completed from scratch by in-house personnel anymore. At the beginning of this chapter, let's first ask a trivial question: Can you provide a project example that is fully completed by the project organization itself, without using any products or services from outside suppliers? Most likely the answer is no. In fact, outsourcing part of project tasks has been a well-established practice in various industries for quite a long time. In many cases, companies have to rely on external suppliers for acquiring many of the unique resources projects they need. In this chapter, we consider the inter-organizational purchasing-related issues (hereafter referred to as supply chain management) in the context of project management.

A supply chain consists of all parties involved, directly or indirectly, in fulfilling a customer request. In project management, this request can be made by the project team in order to acquire some specific product or service required for completing various stages of the project. The request also can be made by the customer whom the project team serves. As a result, supply chain operations require managerial processes that span across functional areas within individual organizations and link trading partners and customers

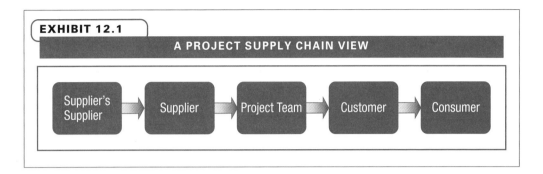

across organizational boundaries. In recent years, the topic of supply chain management has evolved into a systematic approach for managing all material and information flows across supply chain partners. With its broader coverage and profound impact, project supply chain management has become a challenge to many business firms. Because the ultimate goal of serving project customers hinges on the systematic performance of various partners (including suppliers, transporters, etc.), supply chain management becomes a critical project management activity. However, many companies normally have been concerned with purchasing and procurement, where the goal was to obtain necessary goods and services at the lowest possible price. This stays in line with the budget limitation of project management reality. In this chapter, we cover not only traditional procurement and contractual management topics, but also supplier partnership and collaboration issues.

In this chapter, we define project supply chain management as a system approach to managing the entire flows of physical products, information, and funds from suppliers and producers, through resellers, and finally the project organization for creating customer satisfaction. A sample project supply chain is shown in Exhibit 12.1.

As Exhibit 12.1 shows, the traditional purchasing perspective is only concerned with the relationship between the project team and its supplier(s)—those who supply the project organization directly. At its most extensive, supply chain management involves strategic and operational issues concerned with all organizational partners involved in projects. Doubtless, all supply chain parties need to work together to complete the project faster, better, and/or cheaper. They all need to remember the tradeoffs determined by the key project stakeholders for better achieving project outcomes.

In traditional project procurement management literature, *purchasing, supply management,* and *procurement* are usually used interchangeably to refer to the integration of related functions to purchase or acquire the needed materials and services for the project team. Thus, procurement management is not only concerned with the standard steps in the purchasing process such as recognizing needs, translating needs into commercially equivalent descriptions, and searching for suppliers. Further responsibilities of a project supply chain may also include receiving, inspection, storage, in- and outbound transportation, and disposal. Project procurement management can also be extended to cover various stages of the supply chain for providing the necessary goods or services (e.g., the supplier's supplier). Though supply chain management (SCM) and project management (PM) are traditionally separate business areas, we find that integrating SCM into PM can significantly enhance the effectiveness of project management. This chapter starts by explaining the traditional project purchasing functions. As single-layer buyer–seller relationships have been extensively studied in the project management literature, we go beyond that and further discuss how to manage multilayer project supply chains.

SCM Components

In particular, this chapter focuses on the following project supply chain management components:

- Make-or-buy decisions—While many companies implement project activities in house today, some other organizations conduct relatively little of their own project work, preferring to have it carried out by outside contractors or specialists. This is especially typical in industries such as construction, equipment manufacturing, and so on.
- Contract management—We introduce the contact types and compare their advantages and disadvantages in case a buy decision is warranted.
- Collaboration and cooperation—As different firms take care of their own interests, it is essential to coordinate their project activities to ensure the deliverables are produced as scheduled.
- System integration concerning the tradeoffs among project goals such as time, cost, and quality.

SCM Factors

We also need to mention that the importance of SCM to general project management depends on a number of factors. Generally, supply chain management is more important to projects where a large portion of the work is being subcontracted and more company collaboration is needed. Other factors include the following:

- The value of the outsourced products or services relative to the total value of the project
- The timing of the work being purchased
- The capability of the project team
- The role of the outsourced work in the entire project
- The number of suppliers required
- The structure of the procurement supply chain (the number of stages in the supply chain and the nature of the intercompany relationship)

We also discuss the fundamentals of project procurement management. The last section of the chapter covers the additional aspects of project supply chain management.

As noted earlier, it is fairly common for a significant part of the value of a project to come from various external suppliers. It is also increasingly common for some organizations to even exist as coordinators of activities, without having their own capability of offering the project deliverables. In the meantime, not only do large companies outsource project tasks, but many small businesses are also doing so. In fact, small firms tend to rely more on outside resources as they may not have the special capability of in-house execution for certain project activities.

SCM Decisions

We start this section by discussing some of the major supply chain management decisions:

- Distribution network configuration
- Inventory control in a supply chain
- Logistics
- Supply contracts

- Distribution strategies
- Supply chain integration and strategic partnering
- Outsourcing and procurement strategies
- Product design
- Information technology and decision-support systems

In practice, these decisions often involve quantitative analysis. As can be seen, all of these decisions can play an important role in managing a complex project. The implication is that project managers must be aware of these methodologies for ensuring project completion in a timely and economic way.

Project Procurement Management Processes

Project procurement management includes the following four processes. The first three are described here, and closing procurements is covered in Chapter 15, Finishing the Project.

1. Plan procurements
2. Conduct procurements
3. Administer procurements
4. Close procurements

12.2 Plan Procurements

The PMBOK® process **plan procurement** is "the process of documenting project purchasing decisions, specifying the approach, and identifying potential sellers."[1] It identifies those project needs that can be met by acquiring products or services from outside suppliers, determines what to purchase or acquire, and determines when and how to do so. On some projects, a portion of the services or materials may be sourced from another company; on other projects, the bulk or even all of the work may be performed by an external company. A client company needs to plan for purchasing and acquisition whether it is for part or all of a project. The needs of the parent organization should be considered as well as those of the project when deciding how to acquire necessary items because it may be better for the parent organization to buy an item rather than to rent it for the current project and then rent it again for a future project.

To effectively plan for purchasing and acquisition of materials and services, a project team typically finishes most of the project planning so they understand what the true project needs are. At a minimum, the project team requires a **project scope statement**, which is "the narrative description of the project scope, including major deliverables, project assumptions, project constraints, and a description of work that provides a documented basis for making project decisions and for confirming or developing a common understanding of scope among the stakeholders."[2] Once the requirements are identified, a project manager should be able to determine whether or not to buy, what to buy, and the quantity to buy.

Outputs of Planning

One primary output of this planning is a **procurement management plan,** which is "the document that describes how procurement processes from developing procurement documentation through contract closure will be managed."[3] The procurement management plan can include guidance for types of contracts to be used, risk management issues, and how to select potential suppliers. This plan guides the client company's efforts through all activities dealing with the acquisition of all the necessary materials and services to complete the project. Another major output is the **procurement statements of work**, which "describes the procurement item in sufficient detail to allow prospective sellers to determine if they are capable of providing the products, services, or results."[4] This document should ensure that both the contractor and client companies understand the work that is being requested in the same clear manner, for example, offering information such as specifications, quantity desired, quality levels, performance data, work requirements, and other requirements. Together, these documents prepare the client company to plan contracting.

Make or Buy Decisions

Project procurement can be considered from the view of the buyer–seller interface. This interface exists at all levels of any project supply chain and between businesses internal to and external to the project organization. Depending on the application areas, the seller can be called a supplier, supplier's supplier, or contractor. Depending on the buyer's position in the project acquisition cycle, the buyer can be called a customer, a service requestor, or a purchaser. The seller can be viewed during the contract life cycle first as a bidder and then as the contracted supplier or vendor.

For any products or services needed in a project, during the purchase planning phase, the project team determines which project needs can best be met by purchasing or acquiring products and services from an outside provider and which project needs can be accomplished by the project team during project execution. Buying from an outside supplier to meet project needs is already a well-established practice. For example, many firms tend to outsource their information technology requirements, accounting work, legal functions, logistics, and so on. This practice is an indication of the growing magnitude of job specialization and outsourcing of project tasks.

REASONS TO BUY OR SELL However, this make-or-buy decision is by no means a trivial one. In fact, it involves a number of intricate issues such as a project organization's competitive analysis and demand analysis. The project team also needs to evaluate the advantages and disadvantages of outsourcing from the viewpoint of time, cost, and performance control. The analysis should also include both direct and indirect costs so that the final decision is based on equal comparisons. The project personnel evaluate alternative suppliers and provide current, accurate, and complete data that are relevant to the buy alternative. Exhibit 12.2 lists a variety of considerations for make-or-buy decisions.

Most firms begin conducting a strategic outsourcing analysis by identifying their major strengths and then building on them. A firm's competitive advantage is often

EXHIBIT 12.2	
REASONS TO MAKE OR BUY	
REASONS TO MAKE	**REASONS TO BUY**
1. Lower production cost	1. Frees project team to deal with other important activities
2. More control over quality and time	2. Ability to utilize specialized suppliers
3. Lack of suitable suppliers	3. Flexibility in procurement
4. Obtain a customized item	4. Inadequate managerial or technical resources
5. Utilize project team's expertise and time	5. Inadequate capacity
6. Protect proprietary design or knowledge	6. Small volume requirements

defined as lower cost, product differentiation (better quality), and/or responsiveness (fast delivery). To project teams, these are of different levels of importance, depending on the wishes of the customer and the progress the project is making at the moment. Project time–cost analysis often helps generate insights about making efficient procurement decisions. For example, a noncritical activity may be outsourced with a focus on minimizing cost but not necessarily receiving the fastest delivery. However, during different stages of a project, a noncritical task can become a critical task, which raises the importance of timing. Factors like this can hold quite different implications for a make-or-buy decision in difference phases of project execution. While make-or-buy investigations usually begin with a cost analysis, various qualitative factors frequently portend more far-reaching consequences than does the cost analysis. A thorough investigation is clearly complicated by the dynamics and uncertainties of various project activities.

OUTSOURCING ISSUES While outsourcing has gained in popularity in the real world, there are potential issues related to the downsides of outsourcing. Some of these are relatively important with regard to the goal of projects.

- Loss of time control for completing project activities
- Lack of cost control for outsourced activities
- Gradual loss of special skills for doing some specific activities
- Loss of project focus and a potential conflict of interest
- Ineffective management as a result of complicated business interactions
- Loss of confidentiality and double outsourcing when a third party is used

The concepts and techniques of project supply chain management possess strategic importance because of these potential issues related to outsourcing. Purchasing can contribute to the achievement of benefits such as higher product quality, shorter lead times, and lower costs. Project procurement strategies can differ from corporate procurement strategies because of constraints, availability of critical resources, and specific project requirements. After making the make-or-buy decision, the project team proceeds to the next step of project outsourcing for selecting the right supplier and negotiating the contract.

The outputs of procurement planning also include documents and criteria for selecting a supplier, if a buy decision has been made. When multiple suppliers are available, selection standards such as total cost of ownership and risk also need to be developed.

When a buy decision is made, the client company is attempting to create a situation in which prospective contractor companies have the capability and motivation to provide useful and complete proposals that are easy to evaluate and determine which best suits the client company's needs. The client company typically uses **procurement documents**, which are "those documents utilized in bid and proposal activities to solicit proposals from prospective sellers, which include buyer's invitation for bid (IFB), request for information (RFI), request for quotation (RFQ), request for proposal (RFP)."[5] The client company creates evaluation criteria to define how they will evaluate and rank the proposals. Armed with these documents, the client company is now prepared to conduct the procurement.

12.3 Conduct Procurements

The second project procurement management process is to **conduct procurements**, which is "the process of obtaining seller responses, selecting a seller, and awarding a contract."[6] Client firms need to decide which potential contractor companies they wish to solicit and then make sure those companies know about the potential project. Sometimes, firms develop a qualified sellers list and only allow listed companies to submit a proposal on the upcoming project. Other times, they advertise widely in hopes of attracting new contractors' interest. In either event, a formal request is normally sent out with hopes that competent firms will compete for the right to perform the project.

Sources for Potential Suppliers

Based on the nature of what is being requested in early procurement stages, the project team usually starts the selection process by establishing a robust list of potential suppliers. The following information sources are frequently used to identify these potential suppliers:

- Supplier websites
- Supplier information files
- Supplier catalogs
- Trade journals
- Phone directories
- Sales personnel
- Trade shows
- Professional organizations and conferences

Information for Potential Suppliers

Exhibit 12.3 is an example of information sent to potential suppliers who may wish to qualify for work on an exciting new project.

Once potential contractors submit bids or proposals, the client company applies previously defined selection criteria to select one or more sellers who are qualified to perform the work and are acceptable as sellers. On some projects in which the services or materials are commodities, the selection decision is made mostly or entirely on price. On other projects, the client chooses the contractor on the basis of life cycle cost—that is, the cost to both purchase the item and use it for all of its useful life. On still other projects, price is one of multiple considerations. On more complex projects, the client company may very well decide that one company is more capable than another on technical, managerial, financial, or experiential grounds. The evaluation criteria developed during the plan procurement process described previously should guide this decision. For example, a study in Singapore found that when a client selects a design-build contractor (one who supervises both the design and construction for a project with many other companies involved), quite a few factors should be considered, as shown in Exhibit 12.4.

Approaches Used When Evaluating Prospective Suppliers

After developing a comprehensive list of potential suppliers, the project team needs to evaluate each prospective supplier individually. The approaches and analyses can include:

- Supplier surveys that provide sufficient knowledge of the supplier to make a decision to include or exclude the firm from further consideration
- Financial condition analysis that reveals whether a supplier is clearly incapable of performing satisfactorily
- Third-party evaluators such as Dun and Bradstreet that can be hired for obtaining relevant information

EXHIBIT 12.3

REQUEST FOR SUPPLIER INFORMATION REGARDING QUALIFICATION

CINCINNATI FINANCIAL CORPORATION

Tower #3 Expansion

Request for Information

Cincinnati Financial Corporation is expanding its corporate headquarters in Fairfield, Ohio. Messer Construction, acting as the design/builder, is requesting prequalification of all subcontractors. The expansion project consists of a three-story, 700-car underground parking garage supporting a seven-story office tower above. The tower will be 416,000 square feet with a parking garage of 274,500 square feet below. The building will tie into the existing facility at each floor. The building structure is to be a concrete frame on drilled pier foundations: the exterior skin is to be similar to the existing office towers on site with precast concrete and glass perimeter. The interior finishes are to be similar to the existing tower with access floor and under floor air distribution anticipated throughout the office building. The prequalification criteria used are as follows:

- Previous and similar construction experience—evaluation of previous projects of similar size and scope with references.
- Commitment to safety and a safe work environment—EMR, incident rates, frequency, and severity rates will be evaluated based upon past experience. Commitment to quality, schedule, and cost control—past experience with references.
- Available resources—quantity of trade workers and depth of resources.
- Local business partners—local companies within 100 miles are preferred.
- Economic inclusion—minority and disadvantaged business participation percentage. Participation and commitment to programs such as "Careers Under Construction."
- Business relationship with Cincinnati Financial Corporation.
- Bonding capacity and rate—both total and available capacity along with bonding rates.

Source: Tom Keckeis, President, Messer Construction Company. Reprinted with permission.

EXHIBIT 12.4

FACTORS TO CONSIDER WHEN SELECTING A DESIGN-BUILD CONTRACTOR

TASK PERFORMANCE FACTOR	CONTEXTUAL PERFORMANCE FACTOR	PRICE FACTOR	NETWORK FACTOR
General mental ability	Conscientiousness	Low fees	Prior relationship
Job knowledge	Initiative		Ongoing relationship
Task proficiency	Social skills		Reputation
Job experience	Controllability		Future relationship
	Commitment		

Source: Adapted from Yean Yng Ling, George Ofori, and Sui Pheng Low, "Evaluation and Selection of Consultants for Design-Build Projects," *Project Management Journal* 34 (1) (March 2003): 13.

- Facility visits to allow the project team to obtain first-hand information concerning the adequacy of the firm's technological capabilities, manufacturing or distribution capabilities, and managerial orientation
- Quality ability analysis that examines the potential supplier's quality capability
- Delivery ability analysis that estimates the supplier's capability to deliver the required product or services on time; backup solutions can also be considered

The analyses given above should not necessarily be limited to potential first-tier suppliers. In some cases where second- or even third-tier suppliers are involved, the project team needs to evaluate all these suppliers as well. This proactive screening process usually generates a handful of potential suppliers with good standing. If the organization has a list of current qualified sellers, it can be the basis for new projects.

Supplier Selection

After one or more potential suppliers have passed the evaluation process, the selection process must begin. The project team now invites potential suppliers to submit bids or proposals. Procurement documents are used to solicit proposals from various vendors. The most common procurement document is the request for proposal (RFP). The RFP can be a foundation for the future working relationship between the buyer and the supplier. In fact, the proposal prepared by the vendor often becomes a part of the final contract, as an addendum or exhibit, between the supplier and the vendor. A request for proposal usually includes the following items:

- Purchasing overview
- Basic supplier requirements
- Technical requirements
- Managerial requirements
- Pricing information
- Appendices

The basic supplier selection decision is a classical decision tree problem. This is a choice between alternatives under uncertainty. The outcome is concerned with both price and performance, including delivery time. Does the decision maker wish to trade a higher price against supply assurance under all circumstances? The difficulty in quantifying all consequences reinforces the need for sound judgment in key decisions.

Evaluation criteria are used to rate proposals and other supplier characteristics. The criteria can be objective or subjective, and they are often provided in the RFP. Typically, the most important evaluation criterion is price. Other important ones include the vendor's technical capability, reputation, and so on. Exhibit 12.5 shows factors in addition to price that can be used in assessing suppliers.

The project team selects one or more sellers who are both qualified and acceptable as sellers. Many tools and techniques, including the following, can be used in the seller selection decision process.

- Weighting system
- Independent estimates
- Screening system
- Seller rating system

EXHIBIT 12.5

FACTORS USED IN ASSESSING POTENTIAL SUPPLIERS

- Replenishment lead time: This is the lead time between placing an order and receiving the order, which can be translated into the required responsiveness for purchasing.
- On-time performance: This affects the variability of the lead time.
- Supply flexibility: Supply flexibility is the amount of variation in order quantity that a supplier can tolerate without letting other performance factors deteriorate.
- Delivery frequency and minimum lot size, which affects the size of each replenishment lot ordered by a firm.
- Supply quality: A worsening of supply quality increases the variability of the supply of components available to the firm.
- Inbound transportation cost: The total cost of using a supplier includes the inbound transportation cost of bringing materials in from the supplier.
- Information coordination capability affects the ability of a firm to match supply and demand.
- Design collaboration capability.
- Exchange rates, taxes, and duties can be quite significant for a firm with a global manufacturing and supply base.
- Supplier viability is the likelihood that the supplier will be around to fulfill the promises it makes. This consideration can be especially important if the supplier is providing mission-critical products for which it would be difficult to find a replacement. If a supplier has two key people who can each perform the necessary work, the second worker is sometimes considered to be "truck insurance" in case the first worker gets run over by a truck.

- Expert judgment
- Proposal evaluation techniques

The goal of selecting suppliers is to award a contract to each selected seller. A contract is a legal relationship between parties, and it is subject to remedy in the court system. The contract can be in the form of a complex document or a simple purchase order. A **contract** is "a mutually binding agreement that obligates the seller to provide the specified product/service and obligates the buyer to pay for it."[7] As such, a contract binds both the seller and buyer. The seller must deliver what is promised, and the buyer must pay. The project organization can be a seller in dealing with the project owner or customer and a buyer in a more prevalent procurement setting. In many project management scenarios, the project manager must be aware of how a wide range of contracts is developed and executed. In *A Guide to the Project Management Body of Knowledge (PMBOK® Guide)*, procurement management is discussed on the basis of the buyer–seller relationship. The underlying assumption is that the buyer is internal to the project team while the seller is external to the team. This can be easily extended to the situation where the team is, in fact, the supplier of project deliverables.

A procurement contract is awarded to each selected seller. The contract can be in the form of simple purchase order or a complex document. The major components in a contract document generally include the following:

- Statement of work of deliverables
- Schedule baseline
- Period of performance
- Roles and responsibility
- Pricing
- Payment terms
- Place of delivery
- Limitation of liability
- Incentives
- Penalties

EXHIBIT 12.6

TYPES OF CONTRACTS

CONTRACT TYPE	COST RISK ABSORBED BY	APPROPRIATE WHEN
Firm-fixed-price	Seller	Costs are well known
Fixed-price-incentive-fee	Mostly seller	Costs are well known and buyer wants to maximize some performance aspect
Cost-plus-incentive-fee	Mostly buyer	Costs are not well known and buyer wants to maximize some performance aspect
Cost-plus-fixed-fee	Buyer	Costs not well known
Time and material	Buyer	Cost rates known, volumes are unknown

12.4 Contract Types

Different types of contracts can be used as tools in planning acquisitions specified in the make-or-buy decision. Contracts differ by type with regard to how the risk is distributed and how the project is performed. The five most common types of project procurement contracts are shown in Exhibit 12.6.

Fixed-Price Contracts

Fixed-price contracts are "a category of contracts with a fixed total price for a defined product or service to be provided … may also incorporate financial incentives"[8] The most common variations of fixed-price contracts are firm-fixed-price and fixed-price-incentive-fee. Those are the types covered in this book.

FIRM-FIXED-PRICE (FFP) CONTRACTS **Firm-fixed-price contracts** are "a type of fixed-price contract where the buyer pays the seller a set amount as defined in the contract, regardless of the seller's cost."[9] Any cost increase due to adverse performance is the responsibility of the seller, who is obligated to complete the effort. A simple form of a firm-fixed-price contract is a procurement order for a specified item to be delivered by a certain date for a specified price, such as a truckload of mulch delivered on the job site of 3110 Elm Street on May 15 for $300.

FIXED-PRICE-INCENTIVE-FEE (FPIF) CONTRACTS On the other hand, **fixed-price-incentive-fee contracts** are "a type of contract where the buyer pays the seller a set amount as defined by the contract, and the seller can earn an additional amount if the seller meets defined performance criteria."[10] An example is a contract for rebuilding a bridge for a fixed price of $1,250,000 with an incentive of an extra $3,000 for every day it is complete before the scheduled date of September 15. The buyer would like to have use of the bridge sooner, and the seller would like to earn a higher fee, so both have an incentive to finish the project early. Performance incentives can also include bonuses for better quality, more features, or anything else that the buyer wishes to maximize and is willing to pay for.

Fixed-price contracts provide low risk for the buyer, since the buyer does not pay more than the fixed price regardless of how much the project actually costs the seller. Consequently, a seller bidding on a fixed-price project must develop accurate and complete cost estimates and include sufficient contingency costs. Certainly, overpricing should be avoided, as a competing contractor with a lower price might be selected.

In case the seller does not have a clear understanding about the project scope, the next type of contract should be considered as an alternative.

Cost-Reimbursable Contracts

Cost-reimbursable contracts are "a category of contracts involving payment to the seller for the all legitimate costs incurred for completed work, plus a fee typically representing the seller's profit."[11] The two variations of commonly used cost-reimbursement contracts are cost-plus-fixed-fee and cost-plus-incentive-fee.

COST-PLUS-FIXED-FEE (CPFF) CONTRACT A **cost-plus-fixed-fee contract** is "a type of cost-reimbursable contract where the buyer reimburses the seller for the seller's allowable costs (allowable costs are defined by the contract) plus a fixed amount of profit (fee)."[12]

COST-PLUS-INCENTIVE-FEE (CPIF) CONTRACT A **cost-plus-incentive-fee contract** is "a type of cost-reimbursable contract where the buyer reimburses the seller for the seller's allowable costs (allowable costs are defined by the contract) and the seller earns a profit if it meets defined performance criteria."[13] These criteria can be for schedule, cost, and/or performance. An example of a schedule criteria is a contract for constructing a college dormitory that calls for completion by August 15 so it is ready for the fall semester. A cost criteria example is the buyer of a small house negotiating a total project cost of $150,000. A performance criteria example is when an auto company enters a contract with a supplier to develop a battery that can get 55 miles per gallon in a 3,000-pound car. In each of these cases, the contract can call for the seller to receive a bonus if it does better than the agreed-upon target and/or a penalty if it does worse. Both the buyer and the seller can benefit if performance criteria are met.

Time and Material (T&M) Contracts

Time and material contracts are "a type of contract that is a hybrid ... containing aspects of both cost-reimbursement and fixed-price contracts."[14] In this type of contract, the unit rate for each hour of labor or pound of material is set in the contract as in a fixed-price contract. However, the amount of work is not set, so the value of the contract can grow like a cost-reimbursement contract. The seller simply charges for what is done to produce the product or service in the contract. This can be problematic if the time scheduled for production is greatly underestimated.

In choosing the right type of contract, the nature of the outsourced project activity plays an important role. The requirements that a buyer imposes on a seller, along with other planning considerations such as the degree of market competition and degree of risk, also determine which type of contract is used. The following items are frequently considered when selecting the right type of contract:

- Overall degree of cost and schedule risk
- Type and complexity of requirements
- Extent of price competition
- Cost and price analysis
- Urgency of the requirements
- Performance period
- Contractor's responsibility
- Contractor's accounting system
- Extent of subcontracting

One of the important factors to know is the degree of risk for the seller and the buyer that each type of contract contains. Each of the contract types has risk attached to it. When considering different contracts, it must be clear who assumes the most risk—the buyer or the seller. Under normal conditions, the greatest risk to the buyer is the cost-plus-fixed-fee contract. The contract with the greatest risk to the seller is the firm-fixed-price contract. Generally, the buyer and seller negotiate details of the contract that offer risks and benefits that both parties can accept.

One risk management technique that is rapidly becoming popular for insuring large projects is the use of wrap-ups. A wrap-up, or owner-controlled insurance program (OCIP), is a single insurance policy providing coverage for all project participants, including the owner and all contractors and subcontractors. An OCIP can potentially reduce an owner's total project cost by 1 to 2 percent compared to traditional fragmented programs. Its major advantages include broader coverage, volume discounts, and reduced claims due to comprehensive loss control programs. The type and complexity of the agreements may also necessitate assistance from legal specialists, buyers, and contracting experts.

12.5 Administer Procurements

The PMBOK® process **administer procurements** is the "process of managing procurement relationships, monitoring contract performance, and making changes and corrections as needed."[15] Both buyers and sellers administer contracts to make sure that the obligations set forth in the contract are met and to make sure neither has any legal liability. Both must perform according to the contract terms. The seller creates performance reports and the buyer reviews these reports to ensure that the performance of the seller satisfies the obligations of the contract.

12.6 Improving Project Supply Chains

Project supply chain performance can be improved by careful and innovative use of partnering, third-party involvement, lean purchasing, sourcing, logistics, and information.

Project Partnering and Collaboration

Companies are constantly in need of outsourcing or contracting significant segments of project work to other companies. The trend for the future suggests that more and more projects will involve working with people from different organizations. Research also finds that through strategic partnering, companies are more likely to access advanced technology, share risks, and improve project-based performance and relative competitiveness. This section extends the previous discussion of project procurement and contracting by focusing specifically on issues surrounding working with different suppliers to complete a project. The term *partnering* is used to describe this process. Partnering is a method for transforming contractual arrangements into a cohesive, collaborative project team with a single set of goals and established procedures for resolving disputes in a timely and cost-efficient manner. The single set of goals takes care of the customer requirements and the entire project instead of each individual organization. Exhibit 12.7 presents an excellent example of project partnering and collaboration in the international airport industry.

SOURCES OF CONFLICT DURING PROJECT PURCHASING
In the procurement and purchase environment, conflicts are inevitable. For example, many people envision the purchasing process as a type of zero-sum game, meaning what one party loses is what the other

---

EXHIBIT 12.7

JORGE CHÁVEZ INTERNATIONAL AIRPORT, LIMA, PERU

The location of Lima in the center of the south cone and on the west coast of South America presents an extended area of attraction, making the airport into a natural international hub. The proximity of Jorge Chávez International Airport (JCIA) to Port Callao, the principal port of Peru, offers the possibility of developing an sea/air plan in favor of external commerce.

LIMA AIRPORT PARTNERS

On November 15, 2000 the Fraport-Bechtel-Cosapi Consortium won the international public tender for the concession of the JCIA. With an equity contribution of $30 million, the consortium founded Lima Airport Partners (LAP), which began operations on February 14, 2001. The three consortium partners each have impressive track records. Fraport AG operates the Frankfurt Airport, considered one of the largest in continental Europe. Fraport also provides other airport services such as handling and other commercial services. Fraport participates in more than 50 projects around the world. Bechtel is a private construction company founded in 1898. It has participated in more than 1000 projects in 67 countries, of which 80 have been airport projects. Cosapi is a local construction company founded in 1960 with projects in South America. Currently, LAP's shareholders are Fraport AG, the International Finance Corporation (IFC) and the Fund for Investment in Infrastructure, Utilities and Natural Resources, managed by AC Capitales SAFI S.A.

LAP's objectives are to improve both facilities and operation of JCIA. The improved facilities will be transferred to the State of Peru. The concession term is 30 years with an option for a 10 year extension.

Source: Patricia Quiroz, Professor of Pontificia Universidad Catolica del Peru.

---

party gains. (The most common type of conflict is this: Lower price means cost reduction for the buyer, but it also means revenue loss to the seller.) In fact, many types of interest conflicts arise among different companies. For example, delays in construction are common and expensive, and litigation related to design and construction is rising at an exponential rate. Obvious conflicts of interest predispose owners and contractors to be suspicious of one another's motives and actions. Suspicion and mistrust prevent effective problem solving throughout the process. In taking care of each party's own interests, mistakes and problems are often hidden. When conflicts emerge, they often create costly delays as well as questionable responses simply because the information transferred may be distorted many times before it reaches the decision maker. The consequences, however, are totally avoidable from the very beginning.

RESOLVING PROJECT PURCHASING CONFLICTS One approach to resolving conflict is to use project partnering as an effective way to engage both the project owner and contractors. Project partnering naturally developed as people began to realize that the traditional win/lose adversarial relationship between owner and contractor degenerates into a costly lose/lose situation for all the parties involved. The systematic project supply chain management view goes beyond this traditional view to increase the baseline of trust and collaboration.

Five core sharing requirements for effective project partnerships are shown in Exhibit 12.8.

MUTUAL GOALS IN PROJECT PARTNERSHIPS Some common goals warrant a more supportive relationship. For example, both the buyer and seller would like to complete the project on time and safely. Both parties would prefer to avoid costly and time-consuming litigation. On the other hand, once the specified project can be finished on a faster and cheaper basis, either party is in a better position of getting better operational rewards. Some of the many advantages for establishing a project partnership are shown in Exhibit 12.9.

For example, Procter & Gamble (P&G) started using the Web to share information and streamline purchasing a few years ago. Ford used 900 virtual work spaces to design

---

EXHIBIT 12.8

SHARING REQUIREMENTS FOR EFFECTIVE PROJECT PARTNERSHIPS

1. Shared responsibilities—Suppliers and customers share responsibility for outcomes and quality.
2. Shared resources—Suppliers and customers jointly make resource decisions.
3. Shared information—Suppliers and customers openly share information with each other, recognizing that appropriate information power occurs when all parties can utilize all important information.
4. Shared rights—Everyone holds the right to disagree, and project managers use dialog to influence others instead of coercion.
5. Shared risks—Everyone shares the project rewards and risks.

Source: Adapted from Jack Ricchiuto *Collaborative Creativity: Unleashing the Power of Shared Thinking*. Akron, OH: Oakhill Press (1996): 101–102.

EXHIBIT 12.9

ADVANTAGES OF PROJECT PARTNERSHIPS

ADVANTAGES TO BOTH PARTIES	ADVANTAGES TO CLIENTS	ADVANTAGES TO VENDORS
Shared motivation	More effectively managed risks	Clearly stated expected outcome
Flexibility	Reduced up-front project cost	Greater potential profit
Reduced administration of frequent bids	Potential of lower cost	More dependable stream of work
Improved project execution	Ability to focus on core capabilities	Opportunity to prove oneself
Ability to explore new technologies		
Improved communication		
Ability to make better decisions		
Improved resource utilization		

Source: Adapted from Tom Chaudhuri and Leigh Hardy, "Successful Management of Vendors in IT Projects," *PM Network* 15 (6) (June 2001): 48; and HeZhang and Peter C. Flynn, "Effectiveness of Alliances Between Operating Companies and Engineering Companies," *Project Management Journal* 34 (3) (September 2003): 49.

---

cars and hold meetings. In one project, Ford used digital conference rooms from eRoom to manage the formation of the auto industry e-marketplace Covisint. Lawyers from law firms and three automakers shared virtual rooms to haggle over contracts.

EFFECTIVE PROJECT PARTNERING APPROACHES Many differences exist between the way traditional project procurement unfolds and the way contemporary project procurement takes place in a partnering mode. Exhibit 12.10 lists some of the requirements of effective project partnering.

Many large Japanese manufacturers have found a middle ground between purchasing from few suppliers and vertical integration. These manufacturers are often financial supporters of suppliers through ownership or loans. The supplier then becomes part of a company coalition known as a *keiretsu*. Members of the keiretsu are assured long-term relationships and are therefore expected to function as partners, providing technical expertise and stable quality production to the manufacturer. Members of the keiretsu can also have suppliers farther down the chain, making second- and even third-tier

---

EXHIBIT 12.10

EFFECTIVE PROJECT PARTNERING APPROACHES

Organization-Wide Willingness to:

- Use long-term perspective
- Share power with partner
- Trust partner
- Adapt to partner
- Go beyond contractual obligations

Mutual Commitment to:

- Quality
- Continuous improvement
- Clearly understand partner
- Ongoing relationship with partner

Effective Methods:

- Openly share information
- Develop contractual relationships
- Develop interpersonal relationships
- Resolve conflict

---

suppliers part of the coalition. Most partners value their membership and work hard to do their part. In the rare instance in which a partner consistently takes advantage of the situation, the partner is eventually dropped.

Companies can use different purchasing modes for specific purchasing items when dealing with large projects. For example, one major Chinese petroleum company used five purchasing models for multiple projects, which include purchasing mechanisms for strategic materials, full competitive products, limited resource products, nonstandard products, and existing long-term collaboration suppliers. Third-party inspection companies were hired to conduct onsite assessment and quality approval for the incoming materials of multiple projects at the same time. The integrated onsite warehousing management system streamlined the management process, reduced unnecessary inventory to almost zero, and minimized the total investment of the projects.

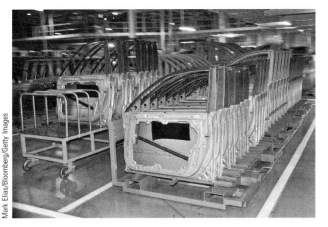

Mark Elias/Bloomberg/Getty Images

Many large Japanese manufacturers have built partnerships with their suppliers through ownership or loans.

SECURING COMMITMENT TO PARTNERING

When developing a project supply chain partnership, a project manager may want to consider contractors with a mutual interest and expertise in partnership. At the beginning, the owner needs to get the commitment of the top management of all firms involved. All the benefits of the partnership and how the partnership would work need to be described in detail. Team building is an effective approach for involving all the key players from different firms. Separate training sessions and workshops are offered to promote a collaborative spirit. One of the major goals of the team-building sessions is to establish a "we" as opposed to an "us and them" attitude among the different participants. A second objective of the sessions is to establish a mechanism in advance designed to ensure that this collaborative spirit is able to withstand the problems and setbacks that will invariably occur on the project. Some of the most significant mechanisms are as follows:

- Problem resolution—Solving problems at the lowest level of organizations and having an agreed-upon escalation procedure
- Continuous improvement—Endless waste elimination and cost reduction
- Joint assessment—Reviewing the partnering process jointly
- Persistent leadership—Displaying a collaborative response consistently

More and more project organizations are pursuing partnering relationships with each other. Project partnering represents a proactive way for handling many of the challenges associated with working with different organizations. The process usually starts with some agreed-upon procedures and provisions for dealing with various problems and issues before they actually happen. One way is to design a special contract with specific incentives and penalties. On the other hand, partnering is not just about relationship contracting. For example, although many companies may wish to develop company-wide policies and procedures for interfirm conflict resolution, this method is less effective since each project and each company is different. The partnering approach has to be dynamic to unite a wide variety of suppliers and contractors for some common goals that everyone cares about. Although the project purchasing relationship has been moved from short-term arrangements based on contracts to long-term relationships based on trust, this change is by no means universally applicable.

Partnering fosters a strong desire to contain costs when changes are necessary and leads to a team approach in resolving any financial and time consequences. In the next section, we discuss the integrated project supply chain management approach.

Partnering seeks to recast relations between actors in projects by promoting the use of collaborative, more open relationships. The integrated supply chain perspective further shifts traditional channel arrangements from loosely linked groups of independent businesses that buy and sell products or services to each other toward a managerially coordinated initiative to increase customer satisfaction, overall efficiency, continuous improvement, and competitiveness. For example, in the construction industry, the construction supply chain (CSC) consists of all the construction partners such as client, designer, general contractor, subcontractor, supplier, and consultant. In fact, the CSC itself represents a concept of systematic coordination of relevant business activities within the supply chain.

Third Parties

In general, third parties can increase the supply chain performance effectively if they are able to aggregate supply chain assets or flows to a higher level than a firm can by itself. Third parties can use various mechanisms to grow the supply chain performance (e.g., reducing delivery time and cost), such as the following:

- Capacity aggregation
- Inventory aggregation
- Transportation aggregation by transportation intermediaries and storage intermediaries
- Warehousing aggregation
- Information aggregation
- Receivables aggregation

- Relationship aggregation
- Lower costs and higher quality

Lean Purchasing

Lean purchasing refers primarily to a manufacturing context and implementation of just-in-time (JIT) tools and techniques to ensure every step in the supply process adds value while various costs are kept at the minimum level. By reducing ordering cost for placing orders (e.g., the fixed part of the shipping cost), project organizations can use JIT for eliminating waste in ordering time and cost, which eventually results in timely completion of projects and customer satisfaction.

Doubtlessly, integrating SCM into project management helps project managers create win/win situations for all parties involved in the project supply chain as they become more efficient and effective. The specific supply chain techniques can help project managers make better tradeoffs between project cost and time so as to create better customer satisfaction.

Sourcing

Sourcing encompasses all processes required for a firm to purchase goods from suppliers. Effective sourcing decisions thus have a significant impact on project performance. Good project sourcing decisions can improve project performance by aggregating orders, making procurement transactions more efficient, achieving design collaboration with suppliers, facilitating coordinated forecasting and planning with suppliers, and improving customer satisfaction.

Logistics

Logistics, in contrast to supply chain management, is the work required to move and position inventory throughout a supply chain. Supply chains use a combination of the following modes of transportation:

- Air
- Package carrier
- Truck
- Rail
- Water
- Pipeline
- Intermodal (the use of more than one mode of transport)

The transportation cost a supply chain incurs is closely linked to the degree of responsiveness the supply chain aims to provide. Thus, decision makers must consider the tradeoff between responsiveness and transportation cost when making the relevant logistics decisions. Moreover, the necessity of shipping speed needs to be considered, as noncritical project activities tend to have some slack.

Information

On the other hand, information is also key to the success of project supply chain management because it enables management to make decisions over a broad scope that crosses both functions and firms. For instance, information sharing in many cases can allow the project supply chain to shorten the delivery time and, at the same time, offer better-quality products or services to meet the dynamic demand of a project. Information must have the following characteristics to be useful when making supply chain decisions:

- Information must be accurate.
- Information must be accessible in a timely manner.
- Information must be of the right kind.

Information is a key ingredient not just at each stage of the project supply chain, but also within each phase of supply chain decision making. This is where IT comes into play. IT consists of the hardware, software, and people throughout a project supply chain that gather, analyze, and execute upon information. In today's business world, IT-based information management is crucial to the performance of project supply chains simply because it provides the basis of decision making, which has profound impacts for every aspect of project management.

Summary

More and more companies are seeking cooperative relationships with each other to compete in today's demanding marketplace. Project supply chain management represents a set of proactive responses to many challenges created by people from different organizations working together on one-time projects. By identifying the project needs and wants, project organizations start with assessing the need to outsource part of the project work. Contracting is commonly used to specify and manage supplier–buyer relationships.

Purchasing details such as scope, deliverables, and quality expectations are legally enforced in the contract. As such, project teams take great care in selecting a specific and attainable contract to meet customer delivery expectations and internal profitability goals. However, project supply chain management is not just about contracting. Partnering and coordination of purchasing across all supplier stages allow a firm to maximize economies of scale in purchasing and also to reduce transaction costs.

Key Terms from the *PMBOK*® *Guide*

plan procurement, 329
project scope statement, 329
procurement management plan, 329
procurement statements of work, 330
procurement documents, 331
conduct procurements, 331
contract, 335
Fixed-price contracts, 336

Firm-fixed-price contracts, 336
fixed-price-incentive-fee contracts, 336
Cost-reimbursable contracts, 337
cost-plus-fixed-fee contract, 337
cost-plus-incentive-fee contract, 337
Time and material contracts, 337
administer procurements, 338

Chapter Review Questions

1. Most organizations have the ability to fully complete a project by themselves. True or false?
2. Small businesses typically do not outsource project work. True or false?
3. _____ is the first step in the project procurement process.
4. In supply chain management, the seller can also be called a(n) _____ or _____.

5. In supply chain management, which of the following terms can be used to mean "buyer"?
   a. Service requester
   b. Vendor
   c. Customer
   d. Both a and c
6. List three functional areas that are frequently outsourced by business organizations.

7. Project teams need to evaluate the advantages and disadvantages of outsourcing from the three viewpoints of _____, _____, and _____.

8. Which of the following areas can be considered a competitive advantage for a firm?
   a. Ability to deliver the product faster
   b. Ability to offer the product at a lower cost
   c. Ability to offer the product in a higher quality
   d. All of the above are areas of competitive advantage

9. After an organization has developed a list of potential suppliers, the organization should evaluate each supplier individually. True or false?

10. What does the acronym *RFP* stand for?

11. A(n) _____ is a mutually binding agreement that obligates the seller to provide the specified product or service and obligates the buyer to pay for the product or service.

12. In a time and material contract, the seller assumes the greatest level of risk. True or false?

13. A(n) _____ contract is a good contract to use if it is necessary for both parties to share the risk.

14. In a(n) _____ contract, the seller assumes the greatest level of risk.

15. A(n) _____ is a single insurance policy that is used to provide coverage for all project participants.

16. _____ is a method for transforming contractual arrangements into a cohesive, collaborative project team with a single set of goals and established procedures for resolving disputes.

Discussion Questions

1. What is the ultimate goal of supply chain management?

2. Describe the project procurement management process.

3. List three reasons why an organization might choose to make the product or service in house, and list three reasons why an organization would buy or outsource the work.

4. When outsourcing a noncritical activity, which of the three competitive advantages would be most important in the selection of a supplier?

5. What are three potential downsides to outsourcing?

6. List four potential information sources that organizations can use to identify potential suppliers.

7. Describe two methods that can be used to evaluate potential suppliers.

8. Describe what items a request for proposal typically contains.

9. What items should a project team consider when selecting the proper type of contract to use?

10. Describe three differences between a partnering relationship and a traditional practice.

11. Discuss some of the advantages of establishing a long-term partnership.

12. Why should a project team and contractors want to enter a partnering arrangement with each other?

13. How can a project manager influence supplier expectations and perceptions?

14. Enter "project partnering" in an Internet search engine and browse different websites containing information on partnering. Who appears to be interested in partnering? To what kind of projects is partnering being applied? Does partnering mean the same thing to different people?

15. What is the relationship between project supply chain management and traditional procurement? Discuss under what circumstances project supply chain management is more effective in managing projects, and explain why.

PMBOK® *Guide* Questions

1. Project procurement management includes all of the following *except:*
   a. plan procurements
   b. conduct procurements
   c. price procurements
   d. close procurements

2. To plan for purchasing and acquisition of materials, a project team needs a list of major

deliverables, project assumptions and constraints, and a description of work. These are all summed up in the _____.
a. project scope statement
b. procurement documents
c. cost-reimbursable contracts
d. procurement statement of work

3. Two major outputs of the planning stage for purchasing and acquisition of materials are:
a. fixed-price contracts and procurement management plan
b. procurement management plan and procurement statements of work
c. procurement scope statement and procurement statements of work

d. procurement management plan and procurement scope statement

4. Which of the following is a downside to outsourcing?
a. ability to utilize specialized suppliers
b. small volume requirements
c. increased confidentiality
d. loss of time control

5. The client company typically uses _____ to solicit proposals from prospective sellers.
a. procurement documents
b. time and material contracts
c. procurement scope statements
d. cost-reimbursable contracts

Exercises

Find a story in your local newspaper about a project that is about to start. For that project, answer each of the following questions and justify your answers:

1. Using the ideas in Exhibit 12.2, speculate what activities, supplies, or services could be contracted out.
2. Create a request for information for one portion of the project work that could be contracted out.
3. Using ideas from Exhibits 12.4 and 12.5, determine criteria you would use to select sellers for the portion of contract work under consideration.

4. Determine what type of contract you would use for this work and tell why.
5. Describe the extent to which any partnering makes sense for this project. What are the challenges and benefits to this partnering? What would prevent any further partnering?

Example Project

Using the ideas in Exhibit 12.2, determine what activities, supplies, or services needed on your example project could be contracted out. Create a request for information for one portion of the project work that could be contracted out. Using ideas from Exhibits 12.4 and 12.5, determine criteria you would use to select sellers for the portion of contract work under consideration. Determine what type of contract you would use for this work and tell why. Describe the extent to which you are partnering on your example project. Describe the extent to which any other person or group may be partnering on the project. What are the challenges and benefits to any partnering that is occurring? What is preventing any further partnering?

References

A Guide to the Project Management Body of Knowledge (PMBOK® Guide) (Newtown Square, PA: Project Management Institute, 2008).

Alderman, N. and C. Ivory, "Partnering in Major Contracts: Paradox and Metaphor," *International Journal of Project Management* 25 (2007): 386–393.

Benton, W. C., *Purchasing and Supply Management* (McGraw-Hill, 2007).

Bowersox, D. J., D. J. Closs, and M. B. Cooper, *Supply Chain Logistics Management*, 3rd ed. (McGraw-Hill, 2010).

Bozarth, Cecil C. and Robert B. Handfield, *Introduction to Operations and Supply Chain Management*, 2nd ed.) (Upper Saddle River, NJ: Pearson Prentice Hall, 2008).

Burt, D. N., D. W. Dobler, and S. L. Starling, *World Class Supply Management: The Key to Supply Chain Management* (McGraw-Hill, 2003).

Chaudhuri, Tom and Leigh Hardy, "Successful Management of Vendors in IT Projects," *PM Network* 15 (6) (June 2001): 45–48.

Chen, Wei Tong and Tung-Tsan Chen, "Critical Success Factors for Construction Partnering in Taiwan," *International Journal of Project Management* 25 (5) (July 2007): 475–484.

Chopra, S. and P. Meindl, *Supply Chain Management: Strategy, Planning and Operations*, 4th ed. (Prentice Hall, 2009).

Fleming, Q. W., *Project Procurement Management: Contractor, Subcontracting, Teaming* (Tustin, CA: FMC Press, 2003).

Haried, Peter and K. Ramamurthy, "Evaluating the Success in International Sourcing of Information Technology Projects: The Need for a Relational Client-Vendor Approach," *Project Management Journal* 40 (3) (September 2009): 56–71.

Leenders, M. R., P. F. Johnson, A. E. Flynn, and H. E. Fearon, *Purchasing and Supply Management: With 50 Supply Chain Cases*, 13th ed. (McGraw-Hill, 2006).

Ling, Yean Yng, George Ofori, and Sui Pheng Low, "Evaluation and Selection of Consultants for Design-Build Projects," *Project Management Journal* 34 (1) (March 2003): 12–22.

Love, Peter E. D., Mistry, Dina, Davis, Peter R, "Price Competitive Alliance Projects: Identification of Success Factors for Public Clients." *Journal of Construction Engineering & Management* 136 (9) (2010): 947–956.

Lu, S. K. and H. Yan, "An Empirical Study on Incentives of Strategic Partnering in China: Views from Construction Companies," *International Journal of Project Management* 25 (2007): 241–249.

Martinsuo, Miia and Tuomas Ahola, "Supplier Integration in Complex Delivery Projects: Comparison Between Different Buyer–Supplier Relationships." *International Journal of Project Management* 28 (2) (2010): 107–116.

Mueller, Eric, "Multiplicity," *PMNetwork* 19 (8) (August 2005): 28–32.

Simchi-Levi et al., *Designing & Managing the Supply Chain* (McGraw-Hill, 2009).

Wang, Fang, "Standardization of Modes of Project Purchase Management," *Journal of Sinopec Management Institute* 10 (3) (2008): 72–74.

Zhang, He and Peter C. Flynn, "Effectiveness of Alliances Between Operating Companies and Engineering Companies," *Project Management Journal* 34 (3) (September 2003): 48–52.

Endnotes

1. *PMBOK® Guide* 440.
2. *PMBOK® Guide* 444.
3. *PMBOK® Guide* 441.
4. *PMBOK® Guide* 325.
5. *PMBOK® Guide* 441.
6. *PMBOK® Guide* 429.
7. Ibid.
8. *PMBOK® Guide* 322.
9. *PMBOK® Guide* 435.
10. Ibid.
11. *PMBOK® Guide* 323.
12. *PMBOK® Guide* 431.
13. Ibid.
14. *PMBOK® Guide* 451.
15. *PMBOK® Guide* 427.
16. Larry Huston and Nabil Sakkab, "Connect and Develop: Inside Procter & Gamble's New Model for Innovation," *Harvard Business Review* 84 (3) (March 2006): 58–66.

PROJECT MANAGEMENT *IN ACTION*

Implications for Project Management in a Networked Organization Model

What Is a Networked Organization?

Simply put, a networked organization is one in which you identify the core competencies that are unique to your company or organization and focus on building and retaining this competitive advantage. You then build alliances with best-in-class companies, service providers, and even unique individuals who provide services and capabilities for your company in the areas outside of your designated core competencies.

This is an "open" organizational model in which a company focuses on its core unique equity and operates as a central hub to continuously connect and exploit the best alliances it needs to be very successful in its business model(s). Alliances are based on unique special skills or capabilities and can come from government, universities, service provider companies, and even peer companies.

This new business model drives speed and greater value since you are no longer constrained by your existing capacity and you can leverage resources outside your own company.

An Example—Procter & Gamble's Connect and Develop Strategy

Procter & Gamble (P&G) recognized in 2000 that it would not be able to maintain the levels of top-line growth of sales and profit that its business goals demanded by continuing to do new product innovation with its own research and development employees. The strategy was not to replace the capabilities of these 7,500 researchers and support staff but to better leverage them. P&G's CEO, A. G. Lafley, established a goal that 50 percent of P&G's new products would come *"from our own labs* and the other half *would come through them."* P&G discovered that for every P&G researcher there were 200 scientists or engineers elsewhere in the world who were just as good—a total of 1.5 million people whose talents it could potentially utilize. Therefore, P&G created an open innovation model called "Connect & Develop" in which its research and development (R&D) organization was now defined as 7,500 people inside plus 1.5 million outside. The model is working at P&G as described in a recent *Harvard Business Review* article.[16]

Impact on Managing Projects with Alliance Partners

P&G's R&D Connect & Develop is a prime example of a networked organization. P&G has taken this approach and expanded it through much of the company, establishing strategic alliances for everything from contract manufacturing, to PC desktop support, to running its global buildings and real estate, to running and supporting the computer data centers used to run the operations of the company worldwide.

The challenge that this new organizational model introduces at a scale not seen before is that, "in a world where many of your operations and business processes are run by a significant number of external business partners, many if not most projects will need to be staffed with people from not only your company but with people from *multiple* organizations. How should we address these new types of projects from a project management perspective?"

Key Learning from P&G's Networked Organization Project Management

1. You need to adopt an industry standard project management methodology so you and all your alliance partners can speak a common language and use a common framework and methodology. Since 2003, P&G has adopted and is broadly using the Project Management Institute (PMI) methodology.

   The key message here is, in projects that involve one or more alliance partner organizations, your project management approach needs to become more formal, documented, and rigorous. This does not mean bureaucratic! It does, however, mean that shortcuts that existed when everyone was from the same company and culture and knew how to work together need to be replaced by simple but more formal rules of the game.

2. As you build mastery in your own organization's project management capability, you will need to also adopt an industry-standard certification process for qualifying your people. At P&G, project management is one of our core competencies, with four levels of proficiency: basic, proficient, advanced, and master. P&G provides the training required for basic and proficient levels of project management, but all advanced- and master-level training is done exclusively with industry standard training offerings.

3. The five major topics within the PMI methodology in which these new types of alliance partner projects force new and different approaches are:

- Monitoring and controlling
- Communication
- Risk
- Human resources
- Procurement

A top-line identification of the types of required changes for projects with one or more alliance partners is discussed in the following sections.

Monitoring and Controlling

- First of all, it must be clear who the project manager is. You only have *one* project manager per project! At P&G, the project manager in nearly every project (with only rare exceptions) is a P&G person with the right level of skill and experience in project management.
- You need to have very simple and clear expectations on how schedule, costs, quality of tasks, and risks are accounted for and tracked across all organizations whose people who are on the project and how often (daily, weekly, or monthly).

Communication

- Again, you need to be clear regarding what people in each organization need to be communicated to, on what topics, how often, at what level of detail, and using what media.
- Methods for accessing information between scheduled communications need to be known and available.

Risk

- Define, document, and communicate your risk management plan (methodology, roles and responsibilities, budgeting, and timing).
- Define and follow a process for risk identification.
- Define and follow an approach for risk analysis and response (avoid, mitigate, accept, or transfer).

Human Resources

- Identify the specific role and responsibility for each project team member.
- Acquire a level of mastery in talking with alliance partners and suppliers about what skills you need and how they are measured so that, as you assemble the team from various organizations, you know how to get the skills you require.
- Politics!—It is inevitable that with multiple organizations involved in staffing and executing a project, the goals and objectives and what is rewarded within each organization will play out in either explicit or implicit behavior. Your project manager needs to have a level of savvy and experience to be effective at dealing with this level of political activity.

Procurement

- You need to be explicit in identifying a framework of the different types or categories of projects you expect to be involved in with your alliance partner(s) and lay out guidelines on when you use which approach or type of engagement.

In P&G's relationship with one of its strategic alliances, different types of projects have been classified in a basic framework that lets P&G people and people from the alliance organization know when to use which type of project.

PROJECT TYPE	WHEN TO USE
Staff Augmentation	When there is need of a particular resource on a project for a short period of time
Time and Materials	Where there is a high risk associated with the project, coming from technical unknowns or simply unclear or changing requirements
Fixed Price Project	When there are clear project requirements and both parties agree that the level of risk identified in the project enables a fixed-bid approach
Flexible Resource Pool	Used primarily for change requests for existing applications
Generic Service Request (GSR)	Used for small, simple projects, usually no longer than one effort month, and involving only the alliance partner and no other vendors
Rough Order of Magnitude	Used to obtain an estimate of the cost required to execute a project; this is the only deliverable for this type of engagement

Source: Laurence J. Laning, chief enterprise I.T. architect, Procter & Gamble Co. Reprinted with permission.

CHAPTER 13

Leading and Managing Project Teams

CHAPTER OBJECTIVES

After completing this chapter, you should be able to:

- Describe stages of team development and strategies to move teams through the project life cycle.

- Describe characteristics of a high-performing project team and assess your individual and team capability to describe how your team can improve.

- Explain how to utilize the project team relationship and process ground rules to improve.

- Describe methods of project team decision making and the circumstances when each is likely to be most effective.

- Describe types of project manager power and when each is appropriate.

- Describe typical sources of project conflict along with the steps in a conflict resolution process, styles of handling conflict, and steps in a negotiation process.

© John-Francis Bourke/Corbis

Gallup Consulting is a global research-based consultancy, specializing in employee and customer management. Our goal is to take the discoveries made within the academic disciplines of behavioral economics and apply them to management and business problems. Every organization has an enormous, but largely untapped, potential for breakthrough improvements in productivity through leveraging how human nature drives business performance. This unrealized potential represents an internal economy with its own set of rules and dynamics—an emotional economy—that can be measured and managed to improve business performance.

Our consulting work is managed as a series of projects with each client. At the start of each client engagement, project leaders gather the high-level information required to identify the client's problems and possible remedies, while understanding any constraints that will affect project success over the long term. The resulting project charter is a

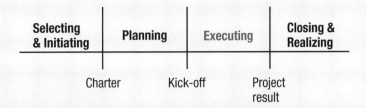

Selecting & Initiating	Planning	Executing	Closing & Realizing

Charter   Kick-off   Project result

**PMBOK®
GUIDE TOPICS**

- Acquire project team
- Develop project team
- Manage project team
- Manage stakeholder expectations

business case for the project and a description of how Gallup will add value to the client's organization. Codifying the commitments in this way also helps in enumerating the various roles and responsibilities of the members of the project team.

Staffing a team is critical to project success. Our research shows that there are three keys to being an effective project leader:

1. Knowing and investing in your own strengths and the strengths of your project team.
2. Getting people with the right talents on your team.
3. Satisfying the four basic needs of those who follow your leadership: trust, compassion, stability, and hope.

By "strength," I mean an ability to provide consistent, near-perfect performance in a specific activity. The first step to building a strength is to identify your greatest talents—the ways in which you most naturally think, feel, or behave as a unique individual. Talents are inherent predispositions that exist deep within us, like a natural tendency to assume command or an instinctive sense of the feelings of other people. Strengths are created when your naturally powerful talents are combined with more learnable skills, such as how to put together a project budget. Gallup has researched this topic for more than 35 years, studying more than 6 million people in the process, and we have found that individuals and organizations have much more potential for growth and productivity in areas of great talent than areas of weakness.

A strengths-based approach improves team cohesion and generates better results. We have found that high-performing teams are more likely to match individuals' talents to assigned tasks and emphasize individual strengths versus seniority in making personnel decisions. High-performing teams also have leaders who meet the core emotional needs of trust, compassion, hope, and stability. Those who lead with Futuristic strengths meet these core needs in different ways than those who lead with Belief; what is important is that they are addressed authentically.

Finally, we have found that while each team member has his or her own unique strengths, the most successful and cohesive teams possess a broader array of strengths. One way to think about this is to consider how team members contribute to the most basic operations of a flourishing team. A tool like the Clifton StrengthsFinder® is useful for helping team members identify the ways they can best contribute to the team's goals. Our research shows that the 34 StrengthsFinder themes naturally cluster into these four groups:

1. Executing—making things happen
2. Influencing—reaching a broader audience
3. Relationship building—holding the team together
4. Strategic thinking—focusing on all the possibilities

Individual team members may have themes from more than one of these categories, but it is not important that each individual be well-rounded. Rather, it is the team that needs contributions from all four of these categories. Team leaders should therefore staff their teams accordingly.

Jim Asplund, Gallup Consulting

At this point in a project, all of the original planning is complete. There is often a need for replanning some portions that require change and a need to plan the later sections of some projects if they were only planned at a rough level earlier. Also at this point, suppliers to the project and customers of the project have normally been engaged. Of primary concern now is the need to perform according to the plans that were so diligently created. The hard work of planning will prove to be worthwhile if the plans are used. The plans often evolve through the change control process, but they still direct project performance.

An experienced project manager envisions project performance as two related activities. First, people must perform their roles in completing work activities according to the plan. Performance by people is the topic of this chapter. Second, data must be collected and used to determine the project progress and results. Data collection and determining project progress as measured in schedule, cost, quality, and risk terms are the subject of Chapter 14. While determining progress and results is conducted largely in parallel with people performing the project, the two are covered in separate chapters to emphasize exactly what needs to be done in each.

"Management is the attainment of organizational goals in an effective and efficient manner through planning, organizing, leading, and controlling organizational resources."[1] The first 11 chapters and part of Chapter 12 of this book deal primarily with planning and organizing. Chapter 14 deals mostly with controlling, and this chapter deals mostly with leading. "Leadership is the influencing process of leaders and followers to achieve organizational objectives through change."[2] While certain aspects of both management and leadership are necessary in dealing with project teams, in the contemporary approach to projects, the project manager works collaboratively with the project team to the extent possible while continually pushing to reach project goals.

This chapter starts with acquiring the project team up to the point that team members have been successfully brought on board to the project. The second section deals with various activities needed to develop the project team's capability. The third section includes several considerations for the project manager when ensuring the performance of the project team. The fourth section describes how to manage stakeholder expectations. Finally, when dealing with both team members and stakeholders, conflict sometimes occurs. The last section discusses project conflict and resolution.

13.1 Acquiring the Project Team

Acquiring the project team is "the process of confirming human resource availability and obtaining the team necessary to complete project assignments."[3] Chances are the core team has already been assembled, as it is very helpful to have the core team together for planning—and even earlier, for chartering a project. However, on some projects, some core team members may be added later due to transfers and other causes. Also, on many large projects, many subject matter experts (SMEs) may be added at this point. This section deals with the timing of assigning a project team member (preassignment), securing the needed and desired team members (negotiation), and successfully adding them to the project team (on-boarding).

Preassignment of Project Team Members

Generally, it is helpful to a project to assign both core team members and subject matter experts as early as possible. One reason is that people often do not like to be told what they must do, but are often enthusiastic when they help create a plan. Therefore, it is good for motivation to include the implementers in planning. A second reason is that when the people who will actually perform the work help to plan it, many more details may be considered and the resulting plans are often more realistic. Yet another reason to assign project team members early is to be sure they will be available when needed. For external projects, it is common to list specific workers who will be assigned to a project team in the proposal. If the project is secured, it is helpful to bring them onto the project as quickly as possible.

The downside to bringing SMEs on board before they need to complete project activities is that they cost money. For a highly paid expert, this can be substantial and impractical. Another problem with bringing people on board early is that they may first be committed to finishing work on a previous project. Regardless of how early you bring a person on a project, it is very helpful to keep communications open with both that person and his or her boss so they understand when the person is needed. This is especially critical if the project has a very tight deadline and/or if your organization is using critical chain project management.

Negotiation for Project Team Members

Depending on the norms of the organization, a project manager may need to negotiate with the functional manager and/or a worker directly to secure his or her services for a project. The functional manager (perhaps called a department head or line manager) has the responsibility of running his or her department. For example, the head of accounting is responsible for how accounting is performed. She wants to keep all of her workers busy, but not too busy, and wants all of her workers to progress in their capability. The functional manager may see this project as a good opportunity for some on-the-job training to help a newer employee gain experience. The project manager, on the other hand, wants the "best" resource for his or her project. The best resource may already be busy. Wise project managers often develop good relationships with functional managers so it is easier to negotiate for a good worker. Each manager may look at the situation from the perspective of his or her own department or project and have different ideas of who is the appropriate person to work on the project. A project manager cannot expect to have the best resource from every department (unless perhaps the project is the highest priority project for the company). The functional manager may sometimes need to agree to a different resource than he or she prefers. In short, most projects have a combination of experienced and inexperienced resources. If a project manager finds all functional managers are only offering inexperienced people, he should probably go to his sponsor for help.

> **EXHIBIT 13.1**
>
> **TATRO, INC., STRATEGY FOR RECRUITING PROJECT TEAM MEMBERS**
>
> Tatro, Inc., is a designer and builder of high-end landscape projects. Its strategy is to retain its core strengths of securing contracts, designing exceptional landscapes, and managing projects with demanding clients. It subcontracts most other work, but wants to be very careful that the work is done as well as possible. Tatro understands it needs to have self-motivated workers who are very presentable to discriminating clients. Tatro primarily relies on recommendations to identify potential workers. To screen potential workers, Tatro performs extensive background checks. It examines previous work performed by the worker, talks to previous clients, and attempts to ensure the worker's finances will allow him or her to be stable.
>
> At that point, it attempts to recruit these proven workers. Chris Tetrault, president of Tatro, Inc., states that he uses a combination of four strategies to recruit, as follows:
>
> 1. Pay well.
> 2. Pay quickly.
> 3. Provide signature projects for the workers to showcase their skills.
> 4. Try to get them to like me.
>
> Source: Chris Tetrault, President, Tatro, Inc. Reprinted with permission.

In many organizations, project managers also need to persuade workers to work on their project. For experienced project managers, reputation goes a long way. A project manager can earn a reputation of being a good boss by caring for team members, helping people develop, and assisting them in securing interesting work and promotions at the end of a project. Many workers campaign hard to work for a great project manager and avoid a poor project manager as much as they can. When negotiating with a potential team member, a project manager wants to sell the person on the project. Of course, strong technical skills are important for subject matter experts and are helpful for core team members. However, especially for core team members, it may be more critical to be an excellent generalist. Many core team members need to deal with a variety of issues beyond their discipline, and focus on making tradeoffs that key stakeholders demand and on finishing the project.

Sometimes, it is necessary to recruit project team members from outside of the parent organization. Tatro, Inc., uses this strategy, as described in Exhibit 13.1.

On-Boarding Project Team Members

The ideal time to on-board team members, and even a few subject matter experts, is when the charter is being written. When that is not possible, the first thing a project manager might do is e-mail the charter and the minutes from the last couple of project meetings to the new member. Once the person has read them, the project manager can have a one-on-one discussion with the new member. There are several purposes to this discussion. The first is to ensure that the new person both understands the project at a high level and is enthusiastic about being part of it. The second is to learn about the person's personal motives. The most effective and happy workers are those who understand how their personal goals and project goals are aligned. What does the worker most want to get out of the project? Does he or she want to experience the joy of working on something new, travel, training, new coworkers, and so on? What unique strengths does he or she already bring to the project, and what strengths does he or she want to further develop? At this point, the project manager can accomplish the third purpose of the talk, which is to assign the new worker to specific activities and develop a plan for personal

---

EXHIBIT 13.2

ACQUIRING AND ON-BOARDING RESOURCES AT ATOS-ORIGIN

Resources are the most important assets of a consulting company. It becomes very important to nurture them, utilize them effectively, and at the same time make money for the company. At Atos-Origin (a leading IT consulting company), a structured process is followed to manage resources. Resource skills, credentials, and travel preferences; the business unit to which the resource belongs; a summary of projects worked on; and so forth are maintained in a searchable database. Utilization (amount of time a resource is used on projects) is tracked on at least a weekly basis. Resource availability (amount of time each resource is idle or is available for client projects) is also tracked and published to a large group of managers to keep in mind for upcoming assignments.

A central resource manager is responsible for tracking and managing resource utilization. If any member of the management team has an open requirement, the resource manager is first notified of the requirement, so that work can begin on tracking the right person for the role. Resource managers from each business unit meet regularly to discuss staff availability and open positions.

Weekly meetings are held with senior management teams to understand the open staffing requirements. As a first fit, internal available resources are aligned (based on the skills required, time frame of the project, and whether the role aligns with a person's career preferences) with open positions. Since Atos-Origin is a global organization, this helps the company to increase utilization of the individual resource and of the group as a whole. If existing resources are not available or do not fit into the assignment, a requisition to hire new resources is completed and the job is posted for recruitment.

Atos-Origin considers three different type of external hires: full-time employees (the preferred option), hourly employees (work on an hourly basis; the option used when the project is for a short period of time or when the right resource does not want to accept a full-time offer), and subcontractors (contracting with other companies; the option used sometimes to mitigate resource risks).

The new resource who is hired is on-boarded to the company in a structured fashion, and the same process for managing the person's utilization and availability is followed. This structured process has helped reduce attrition, increased internal transfer of resources, helped individual resource growth, and increased the company's profitability.

Source: Rachana Thariani, PMP, Atos-Origin.

---

improvement. Exhibit 13.2 illustrates how one consulting company that has many projects acquires and on-boards resources.

13.2 Developing the Project Team

Developing the project team is "the process of improving the competencies, team interaction, and the overall team environment to enhance project performance."[4] Developing a highly effective project team requires the following six activities from the project manager. Note these six activities build upon each other and are, therefore, somewhat overlapping.

1. Understand stages of project team development.
2. Understand characteristics of high-performing project teams.
3. Assess individual member capability.
4. Assess project team capability.
5. Build both individual and team capability.
6. Establish team ground rules.

Stages of Project Team Development

Project teams typically go through a predictable set of stages as they work together. By effectively using project tools and developing trust and understanding within their teams, project managers can greatly diminish some of the negative aspects of project team development stages. However, most teams still spend at least some time in most stages. While almost all teams go through these stages, just as one child may spend more time in a particular stage of human development, some project teams spend more time in certain stages of team development. Some teams get "stalled" in an early stage and do not progress. Some get further along and then have a setback. Setbacks for project teams can come from losing or gaining core team members or subject matter experts, changes in project requirements, quality problems with project deliverables, or other reasons. The good news for a team that suffers a setback is that because they worked through the team development stages once, they can probably work through the stages more quickly and easily the second time. The bad news is that they do need to work their way through.

Each stage of team development has its own challenges. For a project manager to successfully help a team develop, he or she should be aware of how team members feel and what behaviors they frequently attempt at each stage. Armed with that understanding, he or she can develop strategies to promote the needs of the parent organization, the project, and the team members. Quite a few of these strategies can be implemented by developing and using some of the project management tools that are described throughout this book. For example, when a team works together to create a good project charter, they rapidly work through the project norming stage and often begin to develop the openness, understanding, and trust that help make their storming stage faster and easier. All of the information regarding the issues, behaviors, and strategies that are often associated with each stage is displayed in Exhibit 13.3.

Understanding the stages of development that project teams typically progress through is a basis for project managers' continued goal attainment and project team development. For example, if a project manager of a new team wants to help his or her team progress through the stages without too much trouble, he or she can look at the top and bottom rows of Exhibit 13.3. New members often feel a combination of excitement about being picked for the new team and concern that the work may be difficult. The project manager can help the new team develop team operating methods very early—when they construct the project charter. Having the team decide how they will work together helps establish workable methods and simultaneously helps the team members start to know and trust each other. Once the initial forming is over, it is common for teams to "storm"—that is, to feel more stress as they begin to understand how big and difficult the project appears upon closer scrutiny. Some of the team members may want to perform the project, yet may resist committing fully. A project manager may work with the team to help ensure that everyone understands and accepts their respective roles. Further, when each team member understands the other members' roles, they can see how the project will be accomplished. The project manager can continue to encourage all team members to actively participate and to refine the team operating methods into ground rules if necessary. Once a project team weathers the storming period, the members often are relieved because they start to really believe they will be successful. Continued team building can help a team to refine its ability to perform. As team members are encouraged to collaborate and build capability, the team moves to a higher level, which is often called the performing stage. Not every team reaches this level. However, it is very satisfying for the teams that do and is a wonderful situation for capturing learnings to help improve other project teams. Finally, project teams disband when the project is over. If the project has been successful, team members often feel both excited about facing new challenges and sad about leaving such a satisfying experience and such good friends. Project managers should use celebration, rewards, and appropriate follow-on work to guide the team through this last stretch.

EXHIBIT 13.3

PROJECT TEAM PROGRESSION THROUGH DEVELOPMENT STAGES					
	FORMING	STORMING	NORMING	PERFORMING	ADJOURNING
Team member relationship issues	Feel excitement, yet skepticism	Feel resistance, yet longing to commit to project	Feel part of team and believe project will succeed	Feel close to teammates and understand teammates	Feel strong attachment to team and feel loss when team disbands
Team members attempt to	Understand expectations, activities needed, and power structures	Jockey for power, ask many questions, and establish dubious goals	Accept team members, hold open discussions, and establish team norms	Improve self, prevent and solve problems, and expand beyond official role	Complete project on high note, maintain relationships with teammates, and seek next challenge
PM strategies to promote organization needs	Develop business case and acceptance criteria in charter	Develop stakeholder analysis, communication plan, budget, and quality plan	Manage tradeoffs per stakeholder desires, include sponsor in talks, and conduct audit	Share applied learnings with organization and report progress to stakeholders	Secure customer acceptance of deliverables, honestly appraise team members, and provide ongoing support to users
PM strategies to promote project needs	Develop scope overview, milestone schedule, risks, and learnings in charter	Develop scope statement, WBS, schedule, and risk register	Add SMEs as needed, authorize work, and improve work processes	Monitor and control project according to plan and update plans as needed	Test project deliverables and secure team member endorsement of them
PM strategies to promote teammember needs	Develop team operating methods and commitment in charter, and help members build relationships	Clarify each member's role, encourage all to participate, and determine team ground rules	Personalize each member's role, collaborate when possible, and assess and build members and team capability	Capture applied learnings and improve meeting and time management	Celebrate success, reward team members, and help team members secure follow-on work

Source: Adapted from Barbara J. Streibel, Peter R. Sholtes, and Brian L. Joiner, *The Team Handbook*, 3rd ed. (Madison, WI: Oriel Incorporated, 2005): 6–8.

Characteristics of High-Performing Project Teams

Once a project manager understands the typical stages of team development, it is time to understand the characteristics of high-performing project teams. These characteristics, which are an elaborate expansion of the performing column in Exhibit 13.3, reflect the ideals toward which a project manager tries to guide his or her team. This chain of high-performing project team characteristics is shown in Exhibit 13.4. Remember, this is the ideal. Many project teams perform well and exhibit some, but not all, of these characteristics. Nevertheless, a conscientious project manager keeps these characteristics in mind and strives to help his team develop each one.

The characteristics of high-performing project teams start with the personal values of individual team members. While a project manager can and should strive to improve upon these values, it is far easier if team members are recruited with a good start on the following values:

- High need for achievement
- Understanding and acceptance of personal responsibility

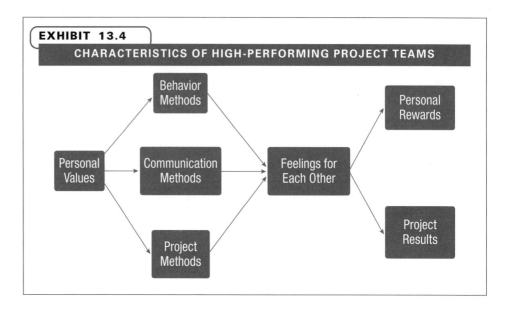

EXHIBIT 13.4

CHARACTERISTICS OF HIGH-PERFORMING PROJECT TEAMS

- Commitment to self-development and self-directed behavior
- Ability to put project needs before their own needs within reason
- Willingness to consider alternative views and to change
- Personal commitment to the project

The personal values can be enhanced by utilizing the following effective team behavior methods:

- Team members are selected to have the right skill mix.
- Team members help each other.
- Team members demonstrate a constant focus on improvement.
- Team members use effective time and meeting management.
- Team members strive for innovation with a minimum of formal procedures.
- Team members capture, share, and use lessons learned.

The personal values can be further improved by practicing the following beneficial communications methods:

- Information is freely and widely shared within and beyond the team.
- All important topics are openly discussed.
- Conflict over approaches is valued but personal conflict is discouraged.
- Potential problems are proactively reported.
- Teams conduct frequent debriefings and reflect to collectively learn.
- Barriers to communication are overcome.

Project managers can certainly use some of the following project management methods to further the team development:

- Agree on common goals and objectives for the project.
- Jointly plan the project.
- Use the charter to guide joint decision making.
- Work together to accomplish activities.
- Proactively identify and solve problems.
- Hold each other mutually accountable with individualized feedback.

Using effective team, communications, and project management methods leads to development of the following appropriate feelings that team members can begin to hold toward one another:

- Recognizing how interdependent they are
- Being flexible on how each contributes to the project
- Being willing to share risks with teammates
- Understanding, appreciating, liking, and trusting each other
- Sharing in strong project leadership

This chain leads to two favorable outcomes. The first set of outcomes is personal rewards that each team member is likely to receive such as the following:

- Enjoyment of their work
- High spirit and team morale
- Pride in being part of the team
- Satisfaction in project accomplishments

The other set of favorable outcomes is the following strong project results:

- Persevering despite challenges
- Producing high-quality results
- Consistently meeting or exceeding stakeholder expectations.[5]

Assessing Individual Member Capability

Great team synergy can help a team's capability be better than the individual members' capabilities. Likewise, poor team synergy can produce a team with less capability than the individuals on the team would suggest. However, more often, individual team members with high capability can be effectively developed into a strong team. So, what capabilities should project team members possess? Five types of useful project team member capabilities are as follows:

1. Activity-specific knowledge and skills
2. Personal planning and control
3. Personal learning
4. Organizational understanding
5. Interpersonal skills and sensitivity

The first type is activity-specific capability. If a team member is responsible for a specific function such as managing the construction of a stone wall, he or she should understand in detail what needs to be accomplished to create a desirable stone wall. If she personally builds the wall, she also needs the skills to do so. A second desirable capability is personal planning and control such as setting personal goals, accomplishing work as planned, and time management. Third, project team members should desire to continually improve and invest effort in their personal improvement.

These first three capabilities are necessary for a person to be a strong individual performer. However, the last two capabilities really help a person become a valuable team player. While all five are useful, if a project manager wants to develop a strong project team, the last two capabilities may be more important. Too many teams have not achieved the expected success because team members were content to just be individual performers.

The fourth useful capability is understanding the organizational structure, culture, and roles and using that knowledge to help the project manager get things done. This involves knowing the informal methods and networks within the parent organization. If the project is being performed for a client, it can also include knowing how things work within the client's organization. The last useful team member capability is interpersonal skills and sensitivity. This includes skills such as active listening, effective speaking, and conflict management. It also includes sensitivity to others who have different personalities or backgrounds.

Assessing Project Team Capability

When assessing project team capability, the project manager should remember that his or her responsibilities are to simultaneously support the parent organization, the project, and the project team. These three are intertwined in many ways. While much has been written concerning teams, Exhibit 13.5 summarizes the success factors of project teams. Note that the right-hand column states the related chapter number and specific topic where this book gives guidance to help achieve each success factor. Many practices of good project management (and good organizational management practices) help a project team to excel, just as many team success factors help a project team deliver good project and organizational results.

For example, the project charter covered in Chapter 4 is helpful in achieving many of the project team success factors. The entire project charter is a basis for more detailed project planning and for understanding project objectives. Working together to develop, sign, and distribute the charter greatly aids in communications and commitment. Specific sections of the charter also help teams develop successfully. The team operating methods section helps guide team member behaviors as they resolve conflicts, the applied learnings help create a stimulating work environment, and the acceptance criteria help team members understand when they satisfy project stakeholders.

Following is a brief description of why each project team success factor listed in Exhibit 13.5 is useful.

1. Project teams with strong leadership are more likely to be successful. Leadership can occur at every level within a project team. Each member performs better by understanding both his or her own role and those of all of the other executives, managers, and associates that are part of the team. Part of project team leadership is the project culture nurtured by the sponsor and project manager.

2. Effective team leadership can lead to mutual trust, respect, and credibility among all parties.

3. This, in turn, can lead to the cross-functional cooperation and support that helps guide a project through turbulent situations.

4-5. Project managers have many project tools to guide a team—charters, stakeholder analysis, communications plans, scope statements, WBSs, schedules, and kick-off meetings. Collectively done well, they help to create clarity and active support for the project. It is difficult to overestimate the impact that effective communication has on project teams. When people are not told something, they must guess. Proactive project managers realize that planning and executing effective two-way communications is a major key to their teams' success.

6-8. The next three project team success factors—skills, objectives, and behaviors—apply specifically to the team. Assembling the right quantity and variety of skills and experience for the project team can be quite challenging. This is especially true in the current work environment of careful cost control. One method that project managers can use is to staff the project with a combination of experienced and less-experienced members. It often costs less to use an inexperienced person. An expectation can be set for the more experienced person to help mentor the junior person. This helps with organizational learning as well as achiev-

EXHIBIT 13.5		
PROJECT TEAM SUCCESS FACTORS		
PROJECT TEAM SUCCESS FACTORS	**CPM CHAPTER**	**TOPIC**
1 Team leadership in setting direction and project culture	3	Project management roles, organization, and project cultures
2 Mutual trust, respect, and credibility among team members and leaders	3	Project management roles
	5	Build relationships
	13	Develop project team
3 Cross-functional cooperation, communication, and support	4	Project charter
	5	Communications planning
4 Clear project plans created by team and supported by organization	4	Project charter
	5	Stakeholder analysis
	6	Scope and WBS
	7	Activity schedule
	11	Kick off project
5 Effective communications including feedback on performance	5	Communications planning
	13	Information distribution
	14	Report progress
	15	Secure customer acceptance
6 Team skills and experience appropriate and adequate	8	Resource projects
	13	Acquire and develop project team
	14	Manage overloads and resolve resource conflicts
7 Clearly defined and pursued project and team objectives	4	Project charter
	14	Direct and manage project execution
8 Use of task and relationship behaviors to resolve conflicts and problems	4	Team operating methods
	5	Build relationships, meeting management
	10	Risk planning
9 Stimulating work environment with opportunities for improvement and learning	4	Applied learnings
	14	Process improvement
	15	Capture and share applied learnings
10 Opportunity for team and personal recognition when project satisfies stakeholders	4	Acceptance criteria
	15	Celebrate success

Source: Adapted from Hans J. Thamhain, "Team Leadership Effectiveness in Technology-Based Project Environments," *Project Management Journal* 35 (4) (December 2004): 38–39; and Roy C. Herrenkohl, *Becoming a Team: Achieving a Goal* (Mason, OH: Thomson South-Western, 2004): 9, 25.

ing the project's goals in a less costly manner. Many project teams include a section in their charter on team operating methods. This section often spells out methods of decision making, meeting management, and demonstrating respect. While working through this, an astute project manager may notice which team members help accomplish project meeting tasks and which help with team relationships. Both are necessary, and if either is lacking, the project manager may want to either help develop or recruit to ensure that those needs are met.

9-10. When the first eight project team success factors are being adequately met, the last two are often results. These last two—stimulating work and opportunity for recognition—have shown the strongest correlation to successful project performance as perceived by senior managers.[6] People work hard and enthusiastically if they find their work stimulating and believe they will be rewarded for it. Appropriate and sincere recognition can often be at least as powerful a motivation as monetary rewards. Project managers can use their creativity to reward all who are worthy.

All 10 of these project team success factors can be influenced by a project manager guiding his or her team through the various topics shown. Many of the success factors require some early work, such as the project charter, and some continuing work as the project progresses. A new project manager can ask questions to determine to what extent his project team currently displays each of these success factors. Then he will be ready to build the team's capacity upon this base.

Building Individual and Project Team Capability

Project managers have many tools at their disposal for developing individuals and teams. Many of the methods can be used together and reinforce each other. Seven methods that many project managers find useful are as follows:

1. Demonstrate personal leadership.
2. Utilize project management tools.
3. Demand situational leadership.
4. Create a desirable team identity.
5. Teach personal responsibility.
6. Develop understanding and respect.
7. Use a learning cycle.

PERSONAL LEADERSHIP A good way for project managers to build the capability of their team is to start by being an effective leader. Leading by example gives team members a model to follow. A project manager leads by balancing the demands of the parent organization, the project, and the team members. In this context, the project manager is a team member—but one who treats both herself and all of the other team members in a respectful manner. The project manager must use the highest levels of honesty and ethics. This includes never stating something that is false, but also not giving a false impression. This can cause a bit of extra work or conflict in the short term, but it is the only appropriate behavior and pays great dividends in the long run by encouraging (and even demanding) everyone else to do what is right.

PROJECT MANAGEMENT TOOLS Project managers can use project management tools to give their team focus. For example, the charter gets a team started quickly. The WBS, schedule, and other project management tools each help to focus the team in specific ways. Teams need to work toward specific goals.

SITUATIONAL LEADERSHIP Depending on the team's initial capability, a project manager may need to start as a strong individual leader, but the goal is certainly to develop multiple leaders on the project team. In fact, in a great project team, leadership is situational. That is, each member may have both a leadership role in certain circumstances and followership roles in other situations. Where a junior team member has specific knowledge, he or she should ensure that everyone understands the situation. Even a junior team member is often expected to lead in certain situations.

DESIRABLE TEAM IDENTITY Another way to build team capacity is to create a desirable team identity. Frequently, the project manager and sponsor start thinking about this even before they recruit the first team members. People want to be associated with a winner. If people believe that a project is vital to the organization and that the work is professionally stimulating, they want to be part of the team. Depending on the organization, some teams give detailed thought to the project name and "brand."

PERSONAL RESPONSIBILITY Project team members need to understand they all have three responsibilities. The first is to complete their individual work on time, on budget, and correctly. Second is to complete their joint work responsibilities with teammates on time, on budget, and correctly. Third, each team member is also responsible for improving work methods. Each needs to improve his or her personal work and to work with the team to jointly improve the project team's capabilities.

UNDERSTANDING AND RESPECT Project team members need to develop understanding of and trust in each other if they want to develop capability as a team. Understanding others starts with understanding oneself. A self-aware individual is more effective in establishing relationships by better appreciating and valuing the contributions of others and being willing to learn from them. One method of understanding both oneself and others better is to use StrengthsFinder and to realize how each individual strength can be productively applied on projects, as shown in Appendix B. As team members understand one another and develop interdependence, they are naturally more able to understand and develop interdependence beyond the project team. Since most projects have multiple stakeholders, this ability to connect at many levels and manners is vital to team development.

LEARNING CYCLE Building project team capability can be envisioned as a learning cycle in which the team uses creativity to jointly develop and consider alternative approaches while striving to learn at each point in the process. This learning cycle can be easily understood using the plan-do-check-act (PDCA) model already introduced in Chapters 5 and 11. The project team capability building cycle is shown in Exhibit 13.6.

Project team capacity building is performed in the context of planning and executing project work. Project teams can repeatedly pass through this capability building cycle as they progressively learn how to work better together to reach their project goals. Free and open communications along with a willingness to challenge each other is important because the project team may need to unlearn or give up past behaviors in favor of new approaches that might be more effective.

In the "plan" step, project teams are challenged with using lessons learned from previous projects to drive their improvement efforts. These lessons need to be compared to the emerging requirements for the project that the team learns from methods such as gathering requirements, meeting with customers, brainstorming risks, and holding design reviews.

In the "do" step, the project team then uses this knowledge to develop shared meaning and potential approaches that they may use. The team uncovers assumptions, brainstorms alternative approaches, and often develops rolling wave plans so the results of early work will give the information needed to create good plans for later work.

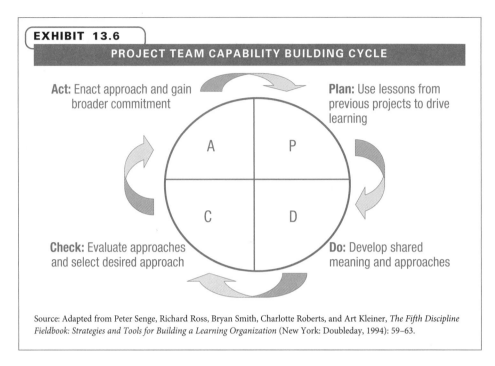

EXHIBIT 13.6

PROJECT TEAM CAPABILITY BUILDING CYCLE

Act: Enact approach and gain broader commitment

Plan: Use lessons from previous projects to drive learning

A   P

C   D

Check: Evaluate approaches and select desired approach

Do: Develop shared meaning and approaches

Source: Adapted from Peter Senge, Richard Ross, Bryan Smith, Charlotte Roberts, and Art Kleiner, *The Fifth Discipline Fieldbook: Strategies and Tools for Building a Learning Organization* (New York: Doubleday, 1994): 59–63.

In the "check" step, the project team evaluates the potential approaches and selects one. They can use techniques such as piloting new technology, creating a subject matter expert panel to make recommendations, conducting feasibility studies, and reviewing the problem with key stakeholders to obtain a clear decision.

In the "act" step, the project team finishes the planning, carries it out, and gathers data regarding it. Simultaneously, they seek acceptance beyond their team through articulating the project's business case, involving key stakeholders, proactively communicating according to plans, and not acting until enough support is in place.

The cycle then repeats. Project teams that are serious about improving their capability repeat this cycle quickly within project stages, at key milestones, and from project to project. The improved capacity of one project team can be shared with other projects through lessons learned and sharing core team members and SMEs with other projects.

Establishing Project Team Ground Rules

Project teams often create a brief set of operating principles in their charter as described in Chapter 4. For small teams performing simple projects, these principles are enough to guide their behavior. This is especially true if the company has a track record of success with teams. However, many managers understand that more specific project team ground rules can help prevent many potential problems that some teams encounter. Ground rules are acceptable behaviors adopted by a project team to improve working relationships, effectiveness, and communication. Therefore, many times the simple set of operating principles is expanded into a broader set of ground rules.

Andersen Ross/Iconica/Getty Images

Select team members with a variety of strengths to ensure balanced participation.

EXHIBIT 13.7

A DOZEN GROUND RULE TOPICS FOR PROJECT TEAMS

RELATIONSHIP TOPICS	PROCESS TOPICS
1. Encourage participation.	**1. Manage meetings.**
Consistency	Achiever
Includer	Discipline
2. Discuss openly.	**2. Establish roles.**
Communication	Arranger
Intellection	Individualization
3. Protect confidentiality.	**3. Maintain focus.**
Deliberation	Command
Relator	Focus
4. Avoid misunderstandings.	**4. Consider alternatives.**
Connectedness	Analysis
Harmony	Strategic
5. Develop trust.	**5. Use data.**
Belief	Context
Responsibility	Input
6. Handle conflict.	**6. Make decisions.**
Adaptability	Activator
Empathy	Restorative

Exhibit 13.7 lists a dozen of the most frequent topics that project teams choose to create ground rules to cover. Note the topics are classified as either dealing primarily with process issues or primarily with relationship issues. Note also that there is more than one way to implement each ground rule. Also listed in Exhibit 13.7 are two strengths from Appendix B that might be used to accomplish each ground rule—although other strengths could be applied as well.

RELATIONSHIP TOPICS The relationship topics both help the team make better decisions and help project team members feel valued. People who feel valued often work with much more enthusiasm and commitment.

Encourage Participation The first relationship topic is to encourage balanced participation. This balance can include drawing out a quiet person and asking a talkative person to let another individual speak. Balance can mean ensuring that all functions are given the opportunity to provide input. Balanced participation can also mean sharing leadership roles. The project manager certainly needs to be a leader, but each project team member can provide leadership in certain situations.

Discuss Openly and Protect Confidentiality The second relationship topic is to encourage open discussion. When some topics are "off limits" for discussion, sometimes important issues are not raised and poor decisions are made. Closely related to open discussion is protecting confidentiality. People need to be able to trust that a sensitive issue will not be repeated outside of the project team. It is very hard to work effectively together if team members are concerned that when important issues are raised, they will be shared inappropriately.

Avoid Misunderstandings   Since projects are often staffed by people from different functions and even different companies, there is a strong potential for misunderstandings to occur. Both the person stating something and the person who is listening have a responsibility to head off potential misunderstandings. Many active listening techniques are useful for this, such as repeating in your own words what was said or asking for an example.

Develop Trust   The fifth relationship topic is to develop trust. Each project team member has two responsibilities with regard to establishing trust. First, each needs to personally always be worthy of the trust of his or her teammates. This means accomplishing work as promised and always being completely truthful. Part of being truthful may be admitting in advance a concern about being able to do certain work—because of ability, knowledge, or time constraints. The second responsibility is to trust his or her teammates unless and until one proves unworthy of trust. Many people live up to or down to the expectations others have for them. By practicing the highest ethical standards and expecting team members to do so as well, most team members demonstrate their trustworthiness. Note that this does not mean naively trusting that an inexperienced person can independently figure out how to perform a complex task. Common sense must still be used with the choice of work assignments and the level of help that is given to each person.

Handle Conflict   The final relationship ground rule topic is how to handle conflict. Conflict over which approach is best can be useful because it may bring out creative discussion and lead to better methods. However, conflict that becomes personal can be destructive. Therefore, conflict over ideas is often encouraged (up to a point), while personal conflict is often settled by the individuals off the project. The project manager may get involved and/or may bring in a neutral third party if necessary. Conflict management is covered later in this chapter.

PROCESS TOPICS   Process topics include how a project team works together as they gather data, meet, and make important project decisions.

Manage Meetings   The process topic regarding meeting management is introduced in Chapter 5 in the context of improving and documenting meetings. Special applications of meeting management are covered in Chapter 11 for kick-off meetings and Chapter 14 for progress reporting meetings.

Establish Roles   The second process topic is to establish roles. People are usually assigned to a project team in the role of project manager, core team member, or subject matter expert. Within the team, however, it is often helpful to assign roles regarding items such as who plans a particular meeting, who watches the time, and who records the minutes. One important principle with roles is to try to help everyone feel valued. A person who is constantly assigned unpleasant tasks may not feel as important or as motivated to contribute. Another part of assigning roles is to assign most project team members work to do between most meetings. Each worker is then responsible for completing their assignments—although a wise project manager often informally checks up on team members.

Maintain Focus   Projects are often under terrific pressure to be completed quickly. Therefore, project managers need to consider the third process topic, which is to ensure that the team stays focused. One way to do this is to bring out the charter when people are arguing over a decision. The charter can remind the team what they are really trying to accomplish and why. Another means of maintaining focus is to return to the stakeholder analysis and the tradeoff decisions that the key stakeholders have indicated. The key with focus is to spend the most time and energy on important issues and to delegate, postpone, or ignore less important issues.

Consider Alternatives The fourth process-oriented ground rule topic is to always consider at least two alternative approaches before proceeding. It is amazing how many project teams simply agree with the first suggestion that someone makes. A team that invests as little as a couple of minutes of time can ensure that they have considered alternative approaches. Quite often, a much better idea emerges from a second or third suggestion than the first one. Also, many times a project team decides to combine the better parts of two approaches. This consideration of alternatives not only often yields a better approach, but it also often results in better commitment because more people's ideas were considered. For example, in a project to install a suite of equipment at a customer's site, a final site investigation revealed that a major piece of equipment was not functional. One answer was to expedite the shipment of a duplicate piece of equipment, while a competing alternative was to use overtime labor and consultants to refurbish the onsite equipment. Both alternatives were expensive, and neither looked very promising. However, upon further discussion, it was determined that one section of the equipment was the primary concern, so a new section could be air-freighted in and the workers onsite could install it. This hybrid alternative proved to be far less expensive and more practical than either alternative that the panicked team first considered.

Use Data The fifth process-oriented ground rule topic is to always use data when possible. Gather the facts instead of arguing over opinions. In meetings, make the data visible to everyone on the team so that all can use it to help make informed decisions. Many of the quality tools listed in Exhibit 11.16 help the project team to gather, organize, prioritize, and analyze data for making informed decisions.

Make Decisions The final process-related topic is decision making. Project decisions can be made in several different ways. Adherence to the other ground rule topics will help regardless of which decision-making method is chosen. Methods that project teams often use to make decisions include the following:

- The project manager or sponsor makes the decision.
- One or two team members make the decision.
- The project team uses consensus to make the decision.
- The project team votes to make the decision.

On some issues, the project sponsor or project manager retains the right to make a decision. Sometimes, this is because a decision needs to be made quickly or it takes higher authority. A sponsor or project manager may also ask for input from the team and then make the decision. While this is often a good idea, that person should be very careful to tell the team up front that he or she still intends to make the decision. Otherwise, the team members who provided input may feel that their ideas were not considered.

Project managers may choose to delegate a decision to one or two team members—either members of the core team or subject matter experts. This strategy works well when not enough information or time is available at the current meeting and the decision needs to be made before the following meeting. Decisions that primarily impact one or two members rather than the entire project team are ripe for delegation. Delegating to two team members has the secondary benefit of them getting to know each other better and working together. A variation on this delegation strategy is to ask the one or two team members to investigate and recommend a solution so the team can make a decision at the next meeting. Over the course of a project, most team members will probably get the chance to make certain decisions while other team members will get to make others.

Consensus is a wonderful, but time-consuming, technique. True consensus means each person actively supports the decisions—even if it is not his or her first choice. The team tells stakeholders that after discussion they understand the decision that was made is the best one for the project. To reach this true consensus, each person needs to be able to articulate what he or she believes is important in the decision and why. Creative approaches may need to be developed when none of the original ideas pleases everyone. Consensus is very helpful when significant commitment is necessary to implement the decision.

One final method that project teams might use to make decisions is to vote. This is often a poor choice since the losers of the vote may not be very enthusiastic about the decision. One of the other methods may be better. Voting can be useful, however, when it is a straw vote—that is, to test for agreement, a team may take a nonbinding vote. If most of the team agrees, then it may not take long to drive toward consensus. If many members do not agree, then delaying the decision, gathering more data, or agreeing to let one person make the decision may be in order.

13.3 Managing and Leading the Project Team

Managing and leading the project team consists of keeping tabs on what is happening, assessing human performance in comparison with plans, taking action to get the team back (or keep it) on track, motivating both individual members and the team as a whole, and continually improving the capability and satisfaction of both the project participants and the methods they use.

Managing the project team is "the process of tracking team member performance, providing feedback, resolving issues, and coordinating changes to enhance project performance."[7] When managing the project team, a project manager uses various forms of power to get team members to prioritize and commit to project work. Project managers are often called upon to either assess members' performance or to at least provide input for the performance assessments. A variety of outputs are created by managing the project team.

Project Manager Power and Leadership

Since project managers often rely on people who do not report directly to them to perform some of the project work, they need to use various forms of power to encourage people to perform. Types of power available to project managers are shown in Exhibit 13.8.

LEGITIMATE POWER Project managers often do not have the authority to tell subordinates what to do. Therefore, project managers often have less legitimate power than other managers. However, to the extent that project managers can ask team members to perform certain activities, they should do so. In contemporary project management, a project manager often has a core team to help plan and manage some of the project. These core team members are probably the people the project manager can order to perform certain activities, but he or she would be better served when possible to ask them to help plan the activities. The old axiom is true: People tend to support the things they helped to create.

REWARD AND COERCIVE POWER Reward and coercive power are opposites of each other. Rewards do not all need to cost money. In fact, stimulating work is one of the most powerful rewards. Enticing people to perform well so they can be assigned to more interesting and/or challenging work in the future helps the team member, the im-

---

EXHIBIT 13.8

TYPES OF PROJECT MANAGER POWER

TYPE OF POWER	BRIEF DESCRIPTION	WHEN USED
Legitimate	Formal authority based upon user's position	Asking people to perform within their job description
Reward	Persuading others based upon giving them something	If team members perform well and if negotiating for resources
Coercive	Punishing others for not performing	Only when needed to maintain discipline or enforce rules
Referent	Persuading others based upon personal relationship	Frequent since project managers often lack legitimate power based upon position
Expert	Persuading others based upon your own knowledge and skills	When others respect your opinions
Information	Control of information	Frequent, as a large part of a project manager,s role is to convey information
Connection	Informal based upon user's relationships with influential people	When working with project sponsors and when negotiating for resources

Source: Adapted from Robert N. Lussier and Christopher F. Achua, *Leadership: Theory, Application, Skill Development*, 4th ed. (Mason, OH: South-Western Cengage Learning, 2010): 110–117.

---

mediate project, and the organization by increasing competence. While reward power is the preferred method, there are times when a person is not performing and a threat may be necessary. This is especially true if most members of the project team are performing and one or two members are not. People who work hard value teammates who also work hard and are often upset when some members do not do their share.

REFERENT POWER Referent power is when a project team member does work for the project manager out of personal desire. Project managers sow the seeds for referent power when interviewing candidates for their project team. If the project manager takes the time to understand the personal motives of each worker, he or she can create desirable opportunities for each. Individual project managers who remember the adage "no one loves your project as much as you do" use their referent power by continuing to describe their project's purpose in ways that appeal to each individual worker's desires. Many successful project managers work hard to develop both friendships and respect with their team members. Loyalty must go both ways. If a team member believes a project manager has his best interests at heart and will advocate for him, then he is more likely to work hard for the project manager.

EXPERT POWER Generally, people want to succeed in whatever they do. Project managers can tap into this desire by using expert power. If a project manager has a reputation for success and can convince others that he or she understands enough of the project technology and politics to successfully guide the project, people will be more inclined to work hard on the project. They will be convinced that their efforts will pay off.

INFORMATION POWER   Information power is something that project managers want to use, but not in a coercive manner. While information is power, withholding or distorting information is unethical. A project manager's responsibility is to ensure that whoever needs certain information receives it in a timely manner, in a form they can understand, and with complete honesty. That does not mean sharing confidential information inappropriately. It does mean empowering the core team to distribute information promptly and accurately according to the communication plan. This gives the core team more power.

CONNECTION POWER   The very reason for having executives sponsor projects is because the sponsor frequently has more legitimate power than the project manager. Project managers can use the power of the sponsor when necessary. A project manager who frequently asks the sponsor to intervene looks weak. On the other hand, a project manager who does not ask for the sponsor's help when it is really needed lacks judgment. Project managers can create many champions for their project by continuing to expand their contacts with important people and by continuing to talk about the importance of their project.

Assessing Performance of Individuals and Project Teams

The second aspect of leading and managing project teams is assessing the performance of both individuals and the project team. Goals of performance assessments include administrative uses such as rewards and promotions and developmental uses such as determining areas for improvement. In many organizations, a large percentage of people dread performance assessments. Many people do not enjoy giving honest feedback—particularly about shortcomings. Also, many people do not like to receive constructive feedback. However, to both reward and improve performance, honest assessments are needed. Performance assessment can be both informal and formal. Project managers often perform informal assessments by observing, asking questions, and providing suggestions. This improves performance if it is done regularly, as timely and specific feedback is most effective.

Formal performance assessments are often the primary responsibility of the direct manager. In many organizations, this is a functional manager. However, because many project team members spend significant time on a project, the project manager is often asked to provide input for the formal performance assessment. The ideal situation for this input is when the team member helped participate in the project planning and is judged by how his or her work corresponds to the planned work. Many project team members may work on several projects during the course of the formal assessment period (often one year). When that is the case, the projects where they spent the greatest time would ideally count the most toward their performance rating. On some large projects, a project manager may seek input from other team members regarding the team member's performance.

Project Team Leadership and Management Outcomes

A variety of outcomes may result from managing the project team, such as the following:

- Morale changes
- "Quarter-mile stones" to "inch stones"
- Staff changes
- Training needs
- Discipline
- Role clarification
- Issues
- Lessons learned

MORALE CHANGES Many projects have periods that are difficult, when work demands are high and milestones to celebrate are few. At these times, the project manager needs to remember that how he or she wields power, communicates, appraises progress, and generally manages can enhance or detract from the morale of all involved. Continuing to reinforce the project's purpose, encouraging and supporting workers, and trying very hard to understand their concerns can go a long way to boosting morale.

"QUARTER-MILE STONES" TO "INCH STONES" When constructing the project charter, the team developed a list of milestones that could be used to measure progress. On some projects, that is enough detail against which performance can be measured. On other projects, however, more detail is needed. Perhaps this greater detail could be considered as "quarter-mile stones"—giving the ability to check progress a bit more frequently. When assessing the performance of individual workers, if one individual worker consistently does not perform well, the project manager may decide that more detailed oversight is necessary. This could result in "yard, foot, or inch stones," depending on the level of oversight deemed necessary. Hopefully, for most projects and most workers, this additional oversight is not necessary. It takes time and effort that could be spent on other things. However, a wise project manager is not going to let a project get derailed because of one worker who is not performing well.

STAFF CHANGES As a result of poor appraisals, insufficient progress, conflict, necessary reassignments, or other causes, some staff may need to be changed on a project. When this occurs, wise project managers treat everyone with respect and recognize that the changes are happening. When new people are added, they are on-boarded with project information and introductions.

TRAINING NEEDS In the course of appraisals, training needs are sometimes discovered. Project managers should keep the immediate project needs along with the training needs in mind as they approve the scheduling of training.

DISCIPLINE Performance on some projects is so poor that workers need to be disciplined. While coercive power is often considered a last resort, it should be used at times. Project managers must ensure that the need for the discipline is explained clearly, specific behaviors or lack of progress are documented, and specific improvement strategies are developed to reduce the chance that further discipline will be needed.

ROLE CLARIFICATION Sometimes, progress may be lacking because of misunderstandings in responsibilities. In those cases, the project manager and all impacted workers can clarify roles by detailing who is responsible for each work activity.

ISSUES AND LESSONS LEARNED Many project managers keep issue logs. These serve as living documents of issues that arise in the course of managing the project team. As issues are raised, they are added to the log. As they are resolved, they are deleted. The resolved issues sometimes make good lessons learned if they can help future project teams avoid problems. These lessons can be documented and stored for easy retrieval in a lessons-learned knowledge base.

13.4 Managing Stakeholder Expectations

Managing stakeholder expectations is "the process of communicating and working with stakeholders to meet their needs and addressing issues as they occur."[8] This process can be visualized as shown in Exhibit 13.9.

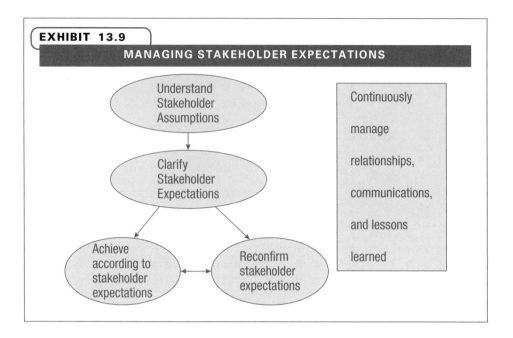

The vertical box in Exhibit 13.9 shows three things a project manager must manage throughout the process of managing stakeholder expectations: relationships, communications, and lessons learned. The project manager and project team must build trust with all project stakeholders through honest and ethical behavior. They need to continually manage effective two-way communications with all stakeholders as described in the communications plan. This includes a true willingness to have stakeholders ask probing questions, because that is an effective way for some stakeholders to develop confidence in the project manager. Finally, they should use lessons learned from previous projects and previous phases of the current project. Armed with trusting relationships, effective communications, and methods that overcome some problems from previous projects, the team is prepared to go through the various portions of managing stakeholder expectations.

The first part—understanding stakeholder assumptions—was performed while creating the charter (Chapter 4), stakeholder register (Chapter 5), and requirements matrix (Chapter 6). Different stakeholders may hold very different assumptions concerning the project at the outset, and these assumptions form the basis of their expectations. Therefore, the project manager clarifies the assumptions, challenges some of them, and uses them in project planning.

These clarified assumptions are then stated as expectations regarding project deliverables, features of the product, timelines, costs, quality measures, and generally how the project manager and team will act. The stakeholders then have a chance to agree or challenge the expectations that are then documented.

During project execution, the team works toward satisfying the expectations. This achievement is composed of work between project meetings to complete assigned activities and to quickly resolve problems that have surfaced. Concurrent with the achievement of expectations is the continual reconfirmation of expectations. One method that project teams can use to reconfirm expectations is to share planning documents, such as schedules, with stakeholders. The team tells the stakeholders that this is their understanding of what they have been asked to do. It is what they expect to achieve and be judged against. Some stakeholders may identify further expectations when they see everything spelled out. Project managers often hold informal conversations with various stakeholders to ensure that they fully understand and agree with all of the planning details. Finally, as project teams report progress to stakeholders, additional expectations emerge. When additional expectations emerge, they need to be considered in terms of the project's formal change control process, and if accepted, become additional project activities to be performed.

13.5 Managing Project Conflicts

Projects create unique outputs, have diverse stakeholders, often have team members from various functions and even different companies, and frequently operate in a matrix environment. All of these factors, along with time pressure, contribute to potential conflicts. Many project management initiating and planning tools exist at least partly to reduce destructive aspects of conflict. There are various ways to view conflict, along with various styles and approaches for dealing with it. This section also introduces a project conflict resolution process model.

Project charters are meant to help the project core team, project manager, and sponsor understand many aspects of the project at a high level and head off potential conflict between those individuals. Several components included in charters such as assumptions, risks, roles, responsibilities, and acceptance criteria are examples of potential sources of conflict. Stakeholder analysis and communications planning can identify needs and desires of many others who will be impacted by either the process of performing the project or a deliverable of the project. These tools help to identify and deal with potential sources of conflict among the broader stakeholders. The more detailed planning tools such as the WBS, schedule, and budget help to identify other conflict sources.

Sources of Project Conflict

Some conflict on projects is useful; other conflict is destructive. Conflict over ideas on how to proceed with a project can lead to more creative approaches. Conflict over how to complete a project with a tight schedule can also be positive. Competition for ideas on how to best handle a project activity has the potential for generating more innovative and successful approaches and can be highly stimulating work. However, when conflict becomes personal, it can often become negative. These types of conflict need to be handled with care. A few typical sources of project conflict are shown in Exhibit 13.10. Generally, it is better to deal with conflict on projects promptly—or even proactively. Conflicts do not get better with time! This is especially true for projects with significant pressure to stay on schedule or on budget (in other words, many projects).

Virtually all studies determine that relationship conflict can be detrimental to project team success. When people spend time and emotional energy arguing, they have less energy to work on the project. Also, when people have personal conflicts to the point where they really do not like each other, they often feel less committed to the project and to their team.

Task conflict is a bit more complicated. A certain amount of task conflict can encourage people to consider alternative approaches and to better justify decisions. Up to that point, task conflict can be useful. However, beyond a certain point, when people spend a great deal of time arguing over task-type issues, it still takes away from the project team's progress and camaraderie. The timing of task conflict can also make a difference on whether it helps or hurts the project. The best times to discuss different options are during the initiating stage, when high-level approaches are being decided, and during the planning stage, when more detailed decisions are being made. However, once the plans

---

EXHIBIT 13.10

TYPICAL SOURCES OF PROJECT CONFLICT

Relationship Sources	Task Sources
Roles and responsibilities	Stakeholder expectations
Lack of commitment	Unique project demands
Communications failure	Money and other resources
Different personalities	Technical approach
Stakeholder relationships	Priorities
Personal motives of participants	Differing goals of stakeholders
Energy and motivation	Task interdependencies
Next project assignment	Schedule
Individual rewards	Risks

---

are made, a project team needs to be a bit more careful because prolonged discussions during the executing periods of the project can lead to schedule slippage and cost overruns.

Conflict Resolution Process and Styles

Once a project manager realizes a conflict exists, if it is a task conflict, he or she tries to utilize it to develop a better solution. If it is a relationship conflict, he or she tries to resolve it before it escalates. A project manager can use the six-step project conflict resolution process, making sure to pay attention both to the tasks and relationships needed at each step.

Six-Step Project Conflict Resolution Process

1. Understand the conflict.
2. Agree on conflict resolution goals.
3. Identify causes of the conflict.
4. Identify potential solutions for the conflict.
5. Pick the desired conflict solution.
6. Implement the chosen solution.

First, what are the signs of the conflict? Is it specific to a certain stage in the project? Does each party in the conflict understand it the same way? If not, ask clarifying questions, summarize how the other person has stated the problem, and confirm that you have a common understanding.

Next, ensure that all parties agree on what a successful conflict resolution would be. While there are often conflicting goals on projects, all stakeholders typically want useful deliverables on time and on budget. Use the project goals as a basis for what the solution needs to cover.

Many conflicts have multiple causes, such as those shown in Exhibit 13.10. Identify potential causes and then verify which cause(s) are actually contributing to the conflict.

The next step is to identify potential solutions to the conflict. This is clearly a time where creativity and trust are helpful.

The fifth step is deciding how to resolve the conflict. There are five general styles for resolving project conflict, as depicted in Exhibit 13.11.

EXHIBIT 13.11

STYLES OF HANDLING PROJECT CONFLICT

STYLE	CONCERN FOR SELF	CONCERN FOR OTHERS	WHEN APPROPRIATE FOR PROJECTS
Forcing/Competing	High	Low	Only when quick decision is necessary, we are sure we are right, and buy-in from others is not needed
Withdrawing/ Avoiding	Low	Low	Only when conflict is minor, there is no chance to win, or it is helpful to secure needed information or let tempers cool
Smoothing/ Accommodating	Low	High	Only when we know we are wrong, it is more important to other party, or we are after something bigger later
Compromising	Medium	Medium	Only when an agreement is unlikely, both sides have equal power, and each is willing to get part of what they want without taking more time
Collaborating/ Problem Solving	High	High	Whenever there is enough time, trust can be established, the issue is important to both sides, and buy-in is needed

Source: Adapted from Richard L. Daft, *Management*, 9th ed. (Mason, OH: Southwestern Cengage Learning, 2010): 519–520. Ramon J. Aldag and Loren W. Kuzuhara, *Mastering Management Skills: A Manager's Toolkit* (Mason, OH: Thomson South-Western, 2005): 416–419; and *PMBOK® Guide* 240.

The collaborative style is preferred for important decisions that require both parties to actively support the final decision. However, collaboration requires both parties to develop trust in each other and frequently takes longer than the other styles. Therefore, each style has its place in dealing with project conflicts.

The final step is to implement the chosen solution. For a major conflict, this could be almost like a mini–project plan with activities identified and responsibility assigned. It is vital to include communication of the solution to all concerned parties.

Negotiation

Project managers are generally held accountable for more performance than they have responsibility to direct people to perform. Because of this, project managers must negotiate. As stated earlier in this chapter, they often need to negotiate with functional managers for the particular people they wish to have work on the project. Project managers often need to negotiate with customers concerning schedule, budget, scope, and a myriad of details. They often need to negotiate with sponsors, suppliers, SMEs, and core team members.

Nobody loves a project as much as the project manager does. However, a project manager must remember that negotiations will be smoother if she realizes that everyone she negotiates with has their own set of issues and goals.

Many of the project management tools discussed thus far in this book, such as charters, stakeholder analysis, communication plans, schedules, budgets, and change control, make negotiations easier. Several of the soft skills discussed in this book, such as involving your team in planning, treating everyone with respect, keeping communications open, and establishing trust, also simplify negotiations. The issues project managers need to negotiate can greatly vary in size and complexity. For example, many very small

NEGOTIATION PROCESS	
STEP	EXPLANATION
1. Prepare for negotiation	Know what you want and who you will negotiate with.
2. Know your walk-away point	Determine in advance the minimum you need from the negotiation.
3. Clarify both parties' interests	Learn what the other party really wants and share your true interests to determine a common goal.
4. Consider multiple options	Brainstorm multiple approaches—even approaches that only solve part of the issue.
5. Work toward a common goal	Keep the common goal in mind: seek and share information, make concessions, and search for possible settlements.
6. Clarify and confirm agreements	Agree on key points, summarize, and record all agreements.

Source: Adapted from Ramon J. Aldag and Loren W. Kuzuhara, *Mastering Management Skills: A Manager's Toolkit* (Mason, OH: Thomson South-Western, 2005): 129–132; and Timothy T. Baldwin, William H. Bommer, and Robert S. Rubin, *Developing Management Skills: What Great Managers Know and Do* (Boston: McGraw-Hill, 2008): 307–318.

issues can involve day-to-day scheduling issues. On the other hand, the entire set of project deliverables with accompanying schedule and budget are often negotiated.

Regardless of the negotiation size or complexity, the six-step process shown in Exhibit 13.12 can serve as a guide.

The negotiation process is based on the project manager and the other party attempting in good faith to reach a solution that benefits both—in other words, a win-win solution. Project managers need to be vigilant, however, because not every one they must negotiate with takes that same attitude. Smart project managers recognize that their reputation is based on how they act in all situations. Therefore, even when negotiating against someone who plays hardball, it is still wise to stay ethical and keep emotions in check.

Step 1 involves advance fact finding to determine what is needed from the negotiation. This may include checking with the sponsor and/or other stakeholders and determining the impact that various settlements may have on the project. It also includes seeking to understand both what the other party is likely to want and how he or she will act during the negotiations.

Step 2 is for the project manager to understand the bottom line. What is the minimum acceptable result? Just as when buying a car, a project manager needs to understand when to walk away. This can vary a great deal depending on how much power each party has. Project managers need to understand that if they have the power and take advantage of their negotiation partner, that partner may not work with them on a future project. Therefore, the goal is not to always drive the hardest bargain, but to drive a fair bargain.

Step 3 is for the project manager to understand the underlying needs of the other party and to share his or her own needs. This is not a 10-second political sound bite that says "take it or leave it." This is developing a real understanding of each other's needs. Once both parties understand what the other really needs, various creative solutions can be developed. This is the essence of Step 4.

Step 5 consists of the process and strategies of the negotiation itself. It is very helpful to keep in mind the ultimate goal while focusing on the many details of information sharing, trading of concessions, and exploring possible solutions. Step 6 is actually a reminder to reach an agreement and then to document that agreement.

Summary

While the project core team is ideally assembled early in the project to participate in chartering and planning the project, SMEs are commonly assigned as needed. Project managers often try to secure the services of these important people as early in the project as possible. This often involves negotiating with the functional managers to whom the SMEs report. When new project team members arrive, whether they are core team members or SMEs, they need to be on-boarded; that is, they need to understand the project and start to develop working relationships with their new team members. Experienced project managers ensure that the new members understand project goals but also share their personal goals so that both can simultaneously be achieved.

Teams progress through typical stages of development. High-performing project teams share a number of characteristics. Project managers can use understanding of these stages and characteristics to guide their team to better performance. They do this by assessing individual and team capabilities and developing strategies to improve both. The project team often develops team operating principles in the charter. Many teams expand upon these with more specific team ground rules. The ground rules are tailored to the unique needs of the project situation, but generally include both rules for improving relationships among team members as well as improving the process of how the team works.

The project manager must monitor and control the human side of his project. This involves utilizing appropriate forms of power in managing the project team to obtain desired results. Project teams also need to manage stakeholder expectations through understanding their expectations, delivering on those expectations, and communicating effectively. Projects are ripe for many kinds of conflict. Constructive conflict over ideas often yields better approaches, but destructive conflict that gets personal needs to be headed off when possible and dealt with when it occurs. Many good project management practices and techniques are helpful in channeling conflict in constructive directions. Project managers also need to utilize many general conflict reduction techniques within the project team, but also with and between various stakeholders.

Key Terms from the *PMBOK*® *Guide*

acquire project team, 353
develop project team, 355

manage project team, 368
manage stakeholder expectations, 371

Chapter Review Questions

1. _____ is a set of interrelated actions and activities performed to achieve a specified set of products, results, or services.
2. The potential downside to bringing in project workers too early in the project is:
   a. They may still be working on other projects.
   b. It is unethical to take them on the team before they are needed.
   c. It is costly.
   d. Both a and c.
3. Typically, project managers need to negotiate with _____ within the organization for the project to go successfully.
4. It is often necessary for project managers to persuade workers to be a part of the project team. True or false?
5. The best time to on-board core team members is during the _____ phase.

6. The five stages of team development are
   _____, _____, _____, _____, and
   _____.

7. During the _____ stage, team members often feel close to their fellow teammates and have a good understanding of how to work together.

8. During the _____ stage, it is common for teammates to feel resistance and jockey for power.

9. During the_____ stage, there is a great deal of excitement for the project, but there is also a high level of skepticism.

10. During all five stages of team development, it is important that the project manager keep in mind the needs of what three groups?

11. Acme Company produces widgets. It used to take the company eight inputs to produce one widget. Now, Acme can produce one widget with only six inputs. Acme Company has improved its _____.

12. _____ are a list of acceptable and unacceptable behaviors adopted by a project team to improve working relationships, effectiveness, and communications.

13. _____ power is the ability to persuade others based upon the project manager's personal knowledge and skills.

14. _____ power should be used by a project manager when she is asking her team members to perform a task within their job description.

15. _____ power should only be used in instances where it is necessary to maintain discipline.

16. A project manager is responsible for assessing the performance of both individual team members and the project team as a whole. True or false?

17. In order to manage stakeholders, a project manager needs to understand the stakeholders' assumptions. This is often achieved when the _____ is created.

18. Conflict can be both useful and destructive for a project. True or false?

19. Which of the following steps is not part of the six-step project conflict resolution process?
    a. Identify causes of conflict.
    b. Identify potential solutions.
    c. Determine which teammate was in the wrong.
    d. Understand the conflict.

20. Which of the following styles for handling conflict have a *low* concern for self?
    a. Avoiding
    b. Compromising
    c. Accommodating
    d. None of the above
    e. Both a and c

21. The collaborating style for handling conflict has a(n) _____ concern for self and a(n) _____ concern for others.

Discussion Questions

1. Describe how to use project documents to help a team progress through the stages of development.

2. Describe, in your own words, what a high-performing project team can do.

3. Differentiate between types of conflict and how you would handle each.

4. Pick the four ground rule topics for project teams that you believe are the most important. Tell why you believe each is so critical, explain how they are related to each other, and give at least two specific suggestions for each.

5. Describe, in your own words, what you believe are the four most important characteristics of high-performing project teams. Tell why you believe each is so critical, explain how they are related to each other, and give at least two specific suggestions for each.

6. Assess your individual capability for project team work. Tell why you feel you are strong in certain capabilities and give strategies for improving in areas where you feel you need to develop.

7. Describe each method of decision making a project team may use. Using examples, tell when each is most appropriate.

8. Using examples, describe how a project manager can use active listening. Why is this useful?

9. Describe two activities that an experienced project manager should expect to occur during the project execution phase.

10. List and give an example of the three sets of needs that a project manager must promote during the project execution phase.

11. Why is it important for project managers to have one-on-one discussions with their core team members?
12. How can a project manager promote the team members' needs during the forming phase?
13. How can a project manager promote the needs of the organization during the norming phase?
14. How can a project manager be an effective leader?
15. Describe the three responsibilities of project team members.
16. List the various methods that project teams can use to make decision.
17. You are a project manager leading an IT development project. Halfway through your project, you realize that you need to hire an additional worker in order to complete the project on time. You are organizing a meeting with project sponsors to discuss the situation. Which type of power(s) would be best to use in this situation and why?
18. List several characteristics of a project that can often result in creating conflict.
19. Give an example of when conflict would be beneficial to a project and an example of when conflict would be harmful to a project.
20. When would it be appropriate to use the compromising style of conflict management?

PMBOK® Guide Questions

1. The process of influencing leaders and followers to achieve organizational objectives through change is _____.
   a. management
   b. leadership
   c. control
   d. acquisition
2. The ideal time to on-board team members (and a few subject matterexperts) is _____
   a. After the project kick-off
   b. Immediately before the execution phase of the project
   c. When the charter is being written
   d. Any of the above
3. Assessing both individual member capability and project team capability are crucial aspects of _____.
   a. Developing a project team
   b. Acquiring a project team
   c. Managing a project team
   d. Managing stakeholder expectations
4. Not all project teams reach the _____ stage.
   a. storming
   b. forming
   c. norming
   d. performing
5. Project team capacity building is performed in the context of _____ and _____ project work
   a. planning; executing
   b. planning; evaluating
   c. executing; evaluating
   d. none of the above

Example Project

Assess your project team's capability. Develop a strategy to improve your team's capability.

As a team, audit one of the other project teams in your class and have them audit your team. Develop an improvement strategy for that team based on the audit results.

Identify what you have done to manage stakeholder expectations and how you know the current level of satisfaction that your stakeholders feel.

References

A Guide to the Project Management Body of Knowledge (PMBOK® Guide), 4th ed. (Newtown Square, PA: Project Management Institute, 2008).

Aldag, Ramon J. and Loren W. Kuzuhara, *Mastering Management Skills: A Manager's Toolkit*, 1st ed. (Mason, OH: Thomson South-Western, 2005).

Baldwin, Timothy T., William H. Bommer, and Robert S. Rubin, *Developing Management Skills: What Great Managers Know and Do* (Boston: McGraw-Hill, 2008).

Chen, Hua Chen and Hong Tau Lee. "Performance Evaluation Model for Project Managers Using Managerial Practices," *International Journal of Project Management* 25 (6) (2007): 543–551.

Daft, Richard L. *Management*, 9th ed. (Mason, OH: Cengage South-Western, 2010).

De Dreu, Carsten K. W. and Laurie R. Weingart, "Task Versus Relationship Conflict, Team Performance, and Team Member Satisfaction: A Meta-Analysis," *Journal of Applied Psychology* 88 (4) (2003): 741–749.

Fleming, John H. and Jim Asplund, *Human Sigma* (New York: Gallup Press, 2007).

Herrenkohl, Roy C., *Becoming a Team: Achieving a Goal*, 1st ed. (Mason, OH: Thomson South-Western, 2004).

Jehn, Karen A. and Elizabeth A. Mannix, "The Dynamic Nature of Conflict: A Longitudinal Study of Intragroup Conflict and Group Performance," *Academy of Management Journal AA* (2) (2001): 238–251.

Kloppenborg, Timothy J., Arthur Shriberg, and Jayashree Venkatraman, *Project Leadership* (Vienna, VA: Management Concepts, Inc., 2003).

Lee-Kelley, Liz and Tim Sankey, "Global Virtual Teams for Value Creation and Project Success," *International Journal of Project Management* 26 (1) (2008): 51–62.

Loo, Robert, "Journaling: A Learning Tool for Project Management Training and Team Building," *Project Management Journal* 33 (4) (December 2002): 61–66.

Lussier, Robert N. and Christopher F. Achua, *Leadership: Theory, Application, Skill Development*, 4th ed. (Mason, OH: South-Western Cengage learning, 2010).

Melkonian, Tessa and Thierry Picq, "Opening the Black Box of Collective Competence in Extreme Projects: Lessons from the French Special Forces," *Project Management Journal* 41 (3) (June 2010): 79–90.

Opfer, Warren, "Building a High-Performance Project Team," in David I. Cleland, ed., *Field Guide to Project Management*, 2nd ed. (Hoboken, NJ: John Wiley & Sons, 2004): 325–342.

Pellerin, Charles J, *How NASA Builds Teams: Mission Critical Soft Skills for Scientists, Engineers, and Project Teams* (Hoboken, NJ: John Wiley & Sons, 2009).

PM1 Code of Ethics and Professional Responsibility, http://www.pmi.org/PDF/ap_pmicodeofethics.pdf, accessed August 20, 2010.

Rath, T. and B. Conchie, *Strengths Based Leadership: Great Leaders, Teams, and Why People Follow* (New York: Gallup Press, 2008).

Senge, Peter, Richard Ross, Bryan Smith, Charlotte Roberts, and Art Kleiner, *The Fifth Discipline Fieldbook: Strategies and Tools for Building a Learning Organization* (New York: Doubleday, 1994).

Sense, Andrew J., "Learning Generators: Project Teams Re-Conceptualized," *Project Management Journal* 34 (3) (September 2003): 4–12.

Sotirou, Dean and Dennis Wittmer, "Influence Methods of Project Managers: Perceptions of Team Members and Project Managers," *Project Management Journal* 32 (3) (September 2001): 12–20.

Streibel, Barbara J., Peter R. Sholtes, and Brian L. Joiner, *The Team Handbook*, 3rd ed. (Madison, WI: Oriel Incorporated, 2005).

Thamhain, Hans J., "Team Leadership Effectiveness in Technology-Based Project Environments," *Project Management Journal* 35 (4) (December 2004): 35–46.

Thamhain, Hans J. "Influences of Environment and Leadership on Team Performance in Complex Project Environments," *Proceedings, Project Management Institute Research and Education Conference 2010*.

Wagner, Rodd and Gale Muller, *Power of 2: How to Make the Most of Your Partnerships at Work and in Life* (New York: Gallup Press, 2009).

Endnotes

1. Richard L. Daft, *Management*, 9th ed. (Mason, OH: Southwestern Cengage Learning, 2010): 5.
2. Robert N. Lussier and Christopher F. Achua, *Leadership: Theory, Application, Skill Development*, 4th ed. (Mason, OH: South-Western Cengage learning, 2010): 6.
3. *PMBOK® Guide* 426.
4. Adapted from Roy C. Herrenkohl, *Becoming a Team: Achieving a Goal* (Mason, OH: Thomson Southwestern, 2004): 185 and 216–217; Warren Opfer, "Building a High-Performance Project Team," in David I. Cleland, ed., *Field Guide to*

Project Management, 2nd ed. (Hoboken, NJ: John Wiley & Sons, 2004): 326–327; and Tessa Melkonian and Thierry Picq, "Opening the Black Box of Collective Competence in Extreme Projects: Lessons from the French Special Forces," Project Management Journal 41 (3) (June 2010): 79–90.

5. *PMBOK® Guide* 433.
6. Hans J. Thamhain, "Team Leadership Effectiveness in Technology-Based Project Environments," *Project Management Journal* 35 (4) (December 2004): 39.
7. *PMBOK® Guide* 437.
8. *PMBOK® Guide* 438.

PROJECT MANAGEMENT *IN ACTION*

Centralizing Planning and Control in a Large Company After many Acquisitions

The restaurant chain where I have consulted was founded over 50 years ago. Through internal growth and external mergers and acquisitions this company has become a Fortune 500 company with thousands of retail stores plus manufacturing facilities and a distribution network. The company recently decided to centralize merchandizing, retail operations control, advertising, and sales planning for the enterprise. This was a significant change!

Human resources (HR) and other support organizations needed to improve their performance to support this massive change. Cycle times were too long, service quality was lower than expected, and internal customers of each operation frequently complained about corporate functions. HR started its transformation by creating a process improvement team to lead toward a process-driven structure with work drivers identified to establish staffing levels. A new HR vice president had a vision for the operation, and her leadership was critical to make anything happen. Other corporate operations are waiting to see the impact of the project on results.

Up to this point, process engineering had only been applied to manufacturing and distribution operations. The culture for process engineering, project management, and change management was generally immature in the company and especially in the corporate functions. This was declared to be the biggest change to our HR function in 35 years. A vice president was assigned to make the HR transition happen. Rather than doing organizational changes the common way—Get in a room, draw some boxes, and announce the change—this VP wanted to do something differently and better.

The project manager assigned to this project immediately interviewed the various management members of the HR organization and the retail operations transition team. He created a project charter to define the scope, objectives, problem statement, outcomes expected, benefits, team members, and inputs for this project. This project manager interviewed all senior staff members for their insights. A communications plan was drafted because this change directly touched several hundred persons and indirectly many tens of thousands. The company is a very large distributed organization with many global operations. Therefore, a great deal of collaboration was required to create the buy-in needed to convince the operational leaders of the need for any specific change designed. A conference was held for all HR leaders to begin developing this needed buy-in.

In preparation for the conference, the project manager created the following high-level WBS:

1. Planning the HR Transformation
2. Initiating the Project
3. Planning the Workshops
4. Stakeholder Analysis
5. Communications Plan
6. Planning the Project
7. Executing the Plan
8. Holding the Workshops
9. Identifying Opportunities for Improvements
10. Obtaining the VOC (Voice of Customer)
11. Creating the Foundational Communications
12. Initial Launch
13. Executing the Implementation Plan
14. Sustaining the Transformation

A schedule was created that reflected all the WBS elements needed to perform this massive organizational change initiative, driven by process analysis and by meeting all the relevant PMI PMBOK® guidelines for project management good practices. This project schedule covered the elements of a plan to gather Voice of the Customer information and perform workshops for the identified Centers of Excellence:

1. The business processing center
2. Total reward systems
3. Administration systems
4. Workforce planning systems
5. Talent management systems
6. Systems and data management
7. Training and development

The project schedule included all the communications needed to create synergy toward an agreed upon solution. At the end of the first conference, we had a core team meeting of five leaders. The job of the core team was to define a vision for the organization, a mission statement for the operation, and an elevator speech that defined the project's objectives and could be repeated in less than 45 seconds to a novice on the topic. This team's efforts gave us great clarity regarding what we were trying to accomplish.

Next, we brought in over 100 HR professionals from around the company for a series of COE (Centers of Excellence) workshops. An agenda and handouts were created to drive the workshops. During the workshops artifacts were created to define the "as is" and "to be" process states. These models were built in Supplier, Input, Process, Output, Customer (SIPOC) and organization deployment process maps. In addition, we created organization structures to support the future-state process maps. Once we designed structures, we built job description documents and measurement plans for the new and old processes. The processes modeled impacted all HR operations from the individual stores to zones to regions to corporate. We needed to know where the work would be accomplished. We started the detailed organization chart reviews. We needed to know where the work was done, and by how many persons, today. Then we could start to estimate how many resources might be needed in a future state by location and by element of work.

We evolved a framework of principles to drive the project forward, which included:

- Streamline every process using the lean Six Sigma tools.
- Focus on quality, speed, and cost while delivering improved value.
- Take transactions out to a service center where a lower cost is achieved.
- Drive all outside agreements toward negotiated service level agreements.
- Consider multiple alternatives for the sourcing of needed services.
- Improve the client-facing organization.
- Build Centers of Excellence that deliver improved value.
- Push employee support closer to them while leveraging consolidated service center capabilities.

Monthly HR leader conference calls, weekly status reports, preliminary design sessions, corporate staff design sessions, and follow-up conferences for leaders were all part of the high-touch, high-communications approach to this project. We expect the many automation initiatives, headcount reductions, vendor outsourcing efforts, and in-sourcing of transactions to a wholly owned service center to deliver millions of dollars of cost reductions across the company. We promoted lean and improvement ideas continually to the leadership. We have collected field-based best practices and have moved into a phase to validate these practices. Once validated, these best practices will be rolled out to all operations. We communicate by posting everything to a SharePoint site for all to see. We also use e-mail communications and have many one-on-one telephone calls.

We are now presenting the new design for implementation and are getting buy-in. We continue to involve others and to learn what will meet their needs—and so far we are spot on with high acceptance. At one time, we thought all regions were different, and they are, but their processes and structures are nearly 80 percent the same. We have reached agreement that one common process is acceptable to all regions asked. This is a major breakthrough. We also have had concessions from labor relations regarding its role and from those regions that were already down the road on a couple key position implementations.

The team concepts that were applicable to this project were as follows:

- Recognize the Forming, Storming, Norming, and Performing stages.
- Create a strong vision to rally the team.
- Ask the customers of the process for requirements.
- Have consistent sponsorship of the project.
- Respect, empower, and engage everyone in a change initiative.
- Respect differences and leverage the value of diversity.
- You cannot over communicate—so communicate.
- Make everything an open book.

Source: William Charles (Charlie) Slaven, PMP.

CHAPTER 14

Determining Project Progress and Results

CHAPTER OBJECTIVES

After completing this chapter, you should be able to:

- Develop and demonstrate use of a change control system.

- Demonstrate how to monitor and control project risks with various resolution strategies.

- Create and present a project progress report.

- Describe project quality control terms and tools, including how and when to use each.

- Calculate current project schedule and budget progress, and predict future progress, using earned value analysis.

- Document project progress using MS Project.

© Mike Kemp/Rubberball/Corbis

The fundamental reason for determining project progress and results comes down to one thing—*presenting actionable, decision-making information to project leaders.*

A major U.S. electric utility company is continuously faced with the daunting task of managing over 1,200 simultaneous projects in all phases of planning, execution, and completion over a geographic area consisting of five states. These projects are supported by over 40 departments within the utility and hundreds of external contractors and equipment suppliers. Over 85 percent of these projects take place over multiple years. There are over 15,000 activities tracked for active projects every month. Today, many of these projects are related to SmartGrid efforts to fundamentally change the way the electric utility system delivers power to homes, schools, and businesses.

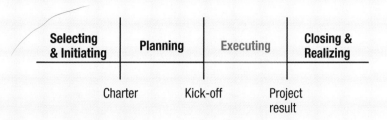

Selecting & Initiating	Planning	Executing	Closing & Realizing

Charter · Kick-off · Project result

PMBOK®
GUIDE TOPICS

- Direct and manage project execution

- Monitor and control project work

- Perform integrated change control

- Monitor and control risks

- Distribute information

- Report performance

- Perform quality assurance

- Perform quality control

- Control scope

- Control schedule

- Control cost

This utility regularly sets the standard for its industry each year by completing over 90 percent of its projects on time and utilizing its annual project budget within just a few percentage points. How is this accomplished?

By identifying and collecting just the right amount of financial, scheduling, resource, and risk management data, and by focusing intently on turning raw data into actionable information for the groups leading and supporting the projects, the utility's project controls staff is able to continuously find and highlight the information that requires leadership attention and project team action.

With the large number of projects being managed, the focus on individual projects decreases and management of the entire group of projects as a portfolio becomes paramount. The actionable information presented highlights significant issues for individual projects, but more importantly is able to forecast trends over the entire portfolio and extended spans of time, helping turn earned-value statistics into meaningful strategies.

Presenting valuable decision-making data to the multiple resource and leadership groups required to support a project provides the critical linkage between the feedback of raw data and the ability to successfully control a single project or an entire multi-year portfolio. Project data collection and management presents the opportunity to simultaneously manage an organization's "profit, people, and planet" objectives in an optimal way.

As you move forward with this chapter and your own projects, consider the use and impact of the project information that needs to be collected. What are the key factors for your project—financial, environmental, resource management, scheduling, risk identification, stakeholder management, or others? Who needs the project progress data, and exactly what do they need to know to make good decisions and successfully achieve organizational objectives?

Identifying, collecting, managing and presenting data that allow you to control critical aspects of your projects is a fundamental element of project success.

Paul Kling, director—project management and controls,
Power Delivery Engineering, Duke Energy

The word *determine* has multiple meanings. While each offers a slightly different perspective, collectively, they help a project manager understand what she needs to do to ensure that her project is progressing adequately and will yield the intended results in the end. *Determine* can mean:

- To give direction to or decide the course of
- To be the cause of, to influence, or to regulate
- To limit in scope
- To reach a decision
- To come to a conclusion or resolution[1]

Project managers, in the course of planning, give direction to a project. Many projects also require replanning due to any number of causes. Project managers sometimes can only influence how work is accomplished (when people do not report to them), but they may be able to regulate or demand the work to be accomplished at a particular time or in a particular manner. To be successful in influencing and regulating project work, the project manager needs to consider the stakeholder priorities and communications needs, as discovered in Chapter 5, and use those to design the monitoring and control mechanisms described in this chapter. Many stakeholders on projects attempt to persuade the project manager and team to deliver more scope, but one important role of the project manager is to jealously guard the agreed upon scope. Many times during a project, decisions need to be made. The project manager needs to do one of the following:

- Personally make these decisions
- Be part of a group that makes them
- Delegate them to others
- Facilitate the process by which the decision is made

Project managers frequently need to follow up to ensure that decisions are made and then carried out. Finally, the project manager is responsible for making sure that the project is satisfactorily completed.

14.1 Project Balanced Scorecard Approach

To successfully accomplish all five aspects of project determination, a project manager can think in terms of a balanced scorecard approach to her project. The concept behind a balanced scorecard is that an organization needs to be evaluated along customer, internal business, financial, and growth and innovation perspectives. If one considers a project as a temporary organization, the same aspects make sense to monitor and control a project. Exhibit 14.1 shows a project balanced scorecard approach to project determination.

When a project manager seeks to monitor and control a project, the different aspects are often interrelated and their impacts on each other need to be considered. For example, a proposed change may impact the scope, quality, schedule, and/or cost. However, to understand project control, each aspect must first be considered individually. This chapter begins with the project manager controlling internal project issues. The next major section of this chapter deals with the customer-related issue of quality. The final sections deal with the financial issues of scope, schedule, and cost. The project manager can utilize a number of tools to manage schedule overloads and conflicts as well as to reprioritize the work. Earned value and project scheduling software such as MS Project can prove to be useful for this. Growth and innovation issues of participant development are covered in Chapter 13, and knowledge management are covered in Chapter 15.

EXHIBIT 14.1

BALANCED SCORECARD APPROACH TO PROJECT DETERMINATION

INTERNAL PROJECT	CUSTOMER	FINANCIAL
Direct and manage project execution	Perform quality assurance	Control scope
Monitor and control project work	Perform quality control	Control schedule
Perform integrated change control		Control costs
Monitor and control risks		
Report performance		
Distribute information		

Source: Adapted from Kevin Devine, Timothy J. Kloppenborg, and Priscilla O'Clock, "Project Measurement and Success: A Balanced Scorecard Approach," *Journal of Healthcare Finance* 36 (4) (2010): 38–50.

14.2 Internal Project Issues

While all aspects of a project are important and interrelated when determining progress and results, a logical starting place is the project work that needs to be accomplished. Closely related are the risks that may impede the work and reporting performance. Collectively, these form the project's internal issues. These issues can be envisioned as the project's nerve center. Problems in any of them travel to all other project areas just as nerves in a body carry information throughout. When dealing with this project nerve center, project managers direct and manage project execution; monitor and control the project work; perform integrated change control; monitor and control project risks; report project performance; and distribute information.

Direct and Manage Project Execution

Directing and managing project execution is "the process of performing the work defined in the project management plan to achieve the project's objectives."[2] When project managers authorize project work, they should empower others to the extent possible, yet control them to the extent necessary. It should be clear who is allowed to authorize each portion of work to commence. The project management plan identifies work to be accomplished, but the project manager or his or her appointee must tell someone when it is time to perform the work. Often, spending limits are intertwined with work authorization (i.e., "Please perform this activity and do not spend more than $X on it. Report back to me for approval if you need to spend more.").

The work to be performed can come from one of several sources. The primary source is the work package level of the work breakdown structure. However, approved corrective actions, preventive actions, and defect repairs may also trigger work to be authorized.

When directing project work, tradeoffs are often present both between the project and other work and within the project itself. Organizations often have many projects and a variety of other work that must all be accomplished. Some work is of higher priority than other work. A project manager needs to understand where her work fits in the priority. If her project is relatively low in priority, she may have trouble getting people to perform their activities very quickly. In a case like that, the project manager and sponsor should have open communications so the sponsor can either help the project manager secure the resources needed and/or understand that the project could be late through no fault of the project manager. As the project progresses, are there changing priorities

---

EXHIBIT 14.2

PROJECT TRADEOFF DECISIONS AT TATRO, INC.

Tatro, Inc. is a company that describes itself as a designer, builder, and caretaker of fine landscaping. It has both commercial and private (homeowner) clients. Landscaping projects for private homes often are well over $100,000. Homeowners who contract for landscaping projects of this magnitude are ultra-successful people who will not change their mind once they decide they want something special. These clients tend to focus closely on the process of a project. They wish to have polite, skilled workers with no interruptions. The reason they wish to have the project completed is to create a "wow factor." Therefore, they will rarely compromise at all on either scope or quality, but they will often compromise on the necessary cost and schedule.

Source: Chris Tetrault, president, Tatro, Inc. Reprinted with permission.

---

that impact project priorities? Remember, any proposed change to the project scope, quality, schedule, or budget needs to be processed through the integrated change control system described later in this chapter.

Projects are undertaken with scope goals and with constraints on cost, schedule, and quality. Exhibit 14.2 gives an example of Tatro, Inc., dealing with project tradeoffs.

Well-developed project charters, effective stakeholder management, and clear communications all help the project manager make sensible tradeoff decisions. Sometimes, an owner representative works closely with the project manager to make these decisions. A recent study identified the skills an owner representative can use when working closely with a project manager to effectively make these tradeoff decisions. These results are shown in Exhibit 14.3.

EXHIBIT 14.3

USEFUL OWNER REPRESENTATIVE SKILLS IN PROJECT TRADEOFF DECISION MAKING

Partnership	Building trust
	Improving relations
	Collaborating
	Creating alliances
	Assuring quality
Management	Planning
	Managing change
	Aligning resources
Leadership	Communicating
	Team building
Technical	Project management
	Knowledge of criteria

Source: Adapted from Denis R. Petersen and E. Lile Murphree, Jr., "The Impact of Owner Representatives in a Design-Build Construction Environment," *Project Management Journal* 35 (3) (September 2004): 35–36.

Monitor and Control Project Work

As stated in Chapter 1, **monitoring and controlling project work** includes "the processes required to track, review, and regulate the progress to meet the performance objectives of the project plan."[3] To **monitor** means to "collect project performance data with respect to a plan, produce performance measures, and report and disseminate performance information."[4] As stated in Chapter 11, **control** means "comparing actual performance with planned performance, analyzing variances, assessing trends to effect process improvements, evaluating possible alternatives, and recommending appropriate corrective action when needed."[5] A **variance** is "a quantifiable deviation, departure, or divergence away from a known baseline or expected value."[6] What all of this means is that a smart project manager keeps an eye on many things that can indicate how well the project is doing and is prepared to act if necessary to get the project back on track. The most difficult part of monitoring and controlling is figuring out what metrics to keep, what to measure, and how to report the results to various decision makers as necessary.

Monitoring and controlling are not the kinds of work that is done once and is finished. Monitoring and controlling activities occur in parallel with project execution. Monitoring and controlling are actually a continuous, overarching part of an entire project's life cycle, from project initiation through project closing. Since the purpose of monitoring and controlling project work is to be able to take corrective action, these activities need to be timely. In fact, the reverse of an old adage is in order. Instead of shooting the messenger when there is bad news, reward the messenger if the message is delivered quickly enough to bring the project back into control quickly and at low cost.

To the extent possible, letting workers self-control their work adds to their enthusiasm. However, the project manager is ultimately accountable for all of the project results and needs to develop a sense for how much control is necessary given the work and the person performing it.

TYPES OF PROJECT CONTROL While this section deals with monitoring and controlling project work, the remainder of this chapter deals with monitoring and controlling each of the other project management knowledge areas. Two types of control are used extensively on projects. Both compare actual performance against the project plan. One type is steering control, in which the work is compared to the plan on a continual basis to see if progress is equal to, better than, or worse than the project plan. Adjustments can be made as often as necessary. The second type of control is go/no go control. Go/no go control requires a project manager to receive approval to continue. This can be conducted at milestones (such as those developed in the project charter) or when someone needs to determine if a key deliverable is acceptable or not. If it is acceptable, the project continues as planned. If not, either the work needs to be redone or the project could even be cancelled. For both types of control, resulting change requests can include corrective actions, preventive actions, or defect repair.

The results of monitoring and controlling project work, schedule, budget, risks, or anything else can range from minor to major depending on how close the actual progress is to the plan. This can be seen in Exhibit 14.4.

Depending on the extent to which actual progress performance varies from planned performance, the results of monitoring and controlling activities can suggest anything from modifying the charter to transferring project deliverables as planned.

- If the actual progress is very different than the original intent, perhaps the project charter needs to be revisited to ensure that the project still makes sense.
- If progress is somewhat different than planned but the charter is still a good guide, perhaps the project plan needs to be adjusted.

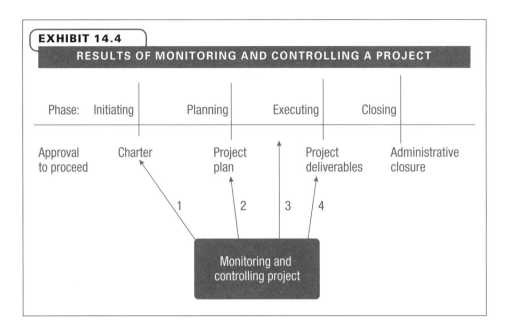

EXHIBIT 14.4

RESULTS OF MONITORING AND CONTROLLING A PROJECT

Phase: Initiating   Planning   Executing   Closing

Approval   Charter   Project   Project   Administrative
to proceed   plan   deliverables closure

1   2   3   4

Monitoring and
controlling project

- If the project plan is still a useful guide, perhaps minor adjustments need to be made in day-to-day instructions within the project executing stage.
- Finally, if the results indicate the customer is ready to accept the project deliverables, perhaps it is time to proceed into the project closing stage.

PERFORM INTEGRATED CHANGE CONTROL   George and John are new project managers fresh out of college. Both are approached by internal customers of their projects (managers of departments where the project deliverables will be used). Their customers tell them what a fantastic job each is doing. The customers then say, "This is great! Could you add these couple of little improvements to it? Then it would be even more valuable to me." George, wanting to please his customer, says, "Yes, we can add that little bit." John's immediate answer is "Let's see what impact that might have on the schedule, budget, quality, and project team. I will be happy to consider it, but want to be sure to deliver the project results we promised on time and on budget." George, in his eagerness to please, made a classic mistake. Many great projects have been derailed because someone stroked the ego of a project manager who then agreed to changes without understanding their impact.

Performing integrated change control is "the process of reviewing all change requests, approving changes, and managing changes to deliverables, organizational process assets, project documents, and project management plan."[7] **Change control** includes "identifying, documenting, approving or rejecting, and controlling changes to the project baselines."[8] Change control includes considering the impact of any change, deciding whether to agree to the change, and then documenting and managing that change. Proposed changes are documented in a change request such as the one shown in Exhibit 6.14.

The decision to approve the proposed change then needs to be made by the correct person or group. Generally, if the change requires a change in the project charter (or contract for an external project), then the sponsor and/or customer decide. If the change does not rise to that level, often a project manager is empowered to make the decision. Some organizations use a **change control board** which is "a formally constituted group of stakeholders responsible for reviewing, evaluating, approving, delaying, or rejecting changes to the project."[9] The change control board is often composed of the project manager, sponsor, core team, and perhaps other key stakeholders. Since some changes have far-reaching impacts, it is often wise to include people with different knowledge and skills on the change review board.

Change is a reality on virtually all projects. While we cannot predict or plan what changes will occur, we can plan for how we will deal with those changes. Some projects are easier than others to plan, especially the later parts of the project. If the planning team can plan most details at the outset, change control may be the primary method they use for handling change. On other projects, where it is difficult to plan the later part in detail until results from the early parts of the project are known, change control is still used, but it is not enough. What is also used in these cases is rolling wave planning, described in Chapter 6. The early parts of the project are planned in detail and the later parts are planned in less detail until later when additional detail is added. Often, a detailed plan for the following section of the project is required before being allowed to proceed.

Monitoring and Controlling Project Risk

During project planning, the project team normally develops a risk management plan that is used to guide risk monitoring and controlling activities. They also normally create a risk register to record each identified risk, its priority, potential causes, and potential responses. The risk management plan and risk register are used to monitor and control project risks and to resolve them when they occur.

Monitoring and controlling risk is "the process of implementing risk response plans, tracking identified risks, monitoring residual risks, identifying new risks, and evaluating risk processes throughout the project."[10] On some projects, the majority of risk events that materialize are ones that the project team has previously identified. Efforts needed on these risks largely include tracking the identified risks, executing the response plans, and evaluating their effectiveness. Project managers know it is wise to consider multiple responses to a given risk. This is true both because some risks cannot be fully handled with just one strategy and because the first strategy may not be the best strategy.

On other projects, however, many unanticipated risks may materialize. This could be partly because risk planning was not complete and sound. However, it could be at least partly due to events that would have been so unlikely that the team could not have been expected to plan for them. In either event, specific contingency plans may not be in place to deal with these risks. Identifying these new risks is vital—and the sooner the better. Two categories of project management methods can help to deal with previously unidentified risks. First, the project team in planning may recognize that unknown risks may surface, and they may add contingency time, budget, and/or other resources to cover these unknowns. Good project practice suggests a need for this. The amount of cost and budget reserves that are included can vary extensively based upon the customer's perception of risk and the type of project that is involved. Competitive pressures often dictate a lower limit on reserves than project managers may prefer.

The second category of project management methods includes a number of good practices that project managers often utilize anyway. These practices can be classified according to whether the project team has full, partial, or no control over the events, as shown in Exhibit 14.5. Note especially the second column, which deals with risks partially within a project manager's control. A project manager cannot completely control many situations, but by using good leadership and ethics, the project manager can certainly help create a situation where others want to help the project.

RISK EVENT RESOLUTION STRATEGIES

RISKS WITHIN PROJECT CONTROL	RISKS PARTIALLY WITHIN PROJECT CONTROL	RISKS OUTSIDE PROJECT CONTROL
Understand and control WBS	Establish limits to customer expectations	Understand project context and environment
Closely monitor and control activity progress	Build relationships by understanding project from client's perspective	Actively monitor project environment
Closely manage all project changes	Use honesty in managing client expectations	Understand willingness or reluctance of stakeholders to agree to changes
Document all change requests	Work with client to reprioritize cost, schedule, scope, and/or quality	
Increase overtime to stay on schedule	Carefully escalate problems	
Isolate problems and reschedule other activities	Build team commitment and enthusiasm	
Research challenging issues early		

Source: Adapted from Hazel Taylor, "Risk Management and Problem Resolution Strategies for IT Projects: Prescription and Practice," *Project Management Journal* 37 (5) (December 2006): 55–60.

Distribute Information

Distributing information is "the process of making relevant information available to project stakeholders as planned."[11] To successfully distribute the right project information to the right stakeholders, in the right format, at the right time, several things must happen. First, all of this needs to be in the project communications plan, as described in Chapter 5. Then, while the project is underway, the project manager and team need to determine any additional information needs not already uncovered, establish an information retrieval and distribution system, collect information on executed work and work in progress, and then report progress to all stakeholders.

DETERMINE PROJECT INFORMATION NEEDS Some stakeholder information needs were identified during communications planning such as authorization to proceed, direction setting, status reporting, and approval of outputs. Other information needs arise during project execution. All need to be handled accurately, promptly, and in a manner that balances effectiveness with cost and effort.

- Communicate accurately—Accurate communications means not only being factually honest, but also presenting information in a manner that people are likely to interpret correctly.
- Communicate promptly—"Promptly" means providing the information soon enough so that it is useful to the recipient.
- Communicate effectively—Effectiveness is the extent to which the receiver opens, understands, and acts appropriately upon the communication.

It is very easy to just copy everyone on an e-mail, but that is not convenient or effective for some people. Face-to-face communication tends to be most effective, telephone less so, and e-mail and formal reports even less. It is in the project manager's best interest to communicate effectively since the information provided allows stakeholders to make decisions, remain motivated, and believe that the project is in control.

ESTABLISH INFORMATION RETRIEVAL AND DISTRIBUTION SYSTEM Project information can be retrieved from many different sources. It can also be distributed via many systems. Project management software such as MS Project is frequently used for schedule information and sometimes for cost and human resource information. Many methods of communicating, such as those in Exhibit 5.17, are used by project managers. In this information age, project managers need to keep three things in mind with communications.

1. Target the communications. More is not better when people are already overloaded.
2. Many methods are available, and the choices change rapidly. Use new methods as they help, but do not discard proven methods just for the sake of change.
3. Projects often have many stakeholders who need specific information. Use your communications plan and always keep asking if there is any other stakeholder in need of upward, downward, or sideways communications.

Tatro, Inc., uses a hosted project management page on its website that clients can access with a password to witness project progress from anywhere in the world on a 24/7 basis. It displays photos that show actual progress for the client to view.

One specific skill that project managers can use to retrieve information is active listening. Active listening requires focus on what the person is saying. The active listener can ask clarifying questions and paraphrase to ensure that he or she understands exactly what is meant. Making eye contact and using eager body language encourages the speaker to continue. An effort to simultaneously understand both the meaning of the message and the emotions the communicator is feeling helps the receiver to understand the full message. Recognizing that many speakers are not especially skilled and paying more attention to their message than their style of delivery also helps. A project manager often can successfully end the conversation by orally confirming what he or she just heard and by following up with an e-mail for documentation.

COLLECT INFORMATION ON EXECUTED WORK AND WORK IN PROGRESS Project managers gather data on the work they have authorized so they can understand the progress they are making. This information is necessary for scheduling additional work, for understanding how they are doing with respect to the schedule, and for quality purposes. A project manager may try to gather data to answer the following typical questions:

- How well is this particular activity proceeding in terms of time and budget?
- How well is the entire project proceeding in terms of time and budget?
- How much more money will need to be spent to finish?
- To what extent does the quality of this work meet requirements?
- How many hours of human resource time have we used to complete this activity compared to how much we estimated?
- What methods that we have used are worth repeating?
- What methods that we have used need to be improved before we do that type of work again?
- What evidence supports the answers to the above questions?

REPORT PERFORMANCE **Reporting performance** is "the process of collecting and distributing performance information, including status reporting, progress measurements and forecasting."[12] Performance reporting includes meetings, reports, feedback received, and documentation. Performance can be reported either at fixed time intervals or at key project milestones. Detailed progress can be reported frequently within the project team and to functional managers who control resources—perhaps weekly or even daily on a project with critical time pressure. One military officer preferred daily "stand-up" meetings with no refreshments so people would report quickly as they were not very comfortable. More general progress may be reported on a less frequent basis to sponsors, senior management, and clients—perhaps semiweekly or monthly. If regular reports and meetings already exist within the parent organization that can serve for performance reporting vehicles for a project, by all means use them. On the other hand, if your project needs additional or different meetings and reports, then develop and use those as well.

Progress reporting within the project team and to functional managers who control resources is often done in the form of meetings. The emphasis should be on specifics. Each team member can report for each deliverable for which he is responsible: the target date, current status, and what other work or information on which progress depends. Once all of the deliverables have been reported, the project team can update the risk register and issues log. Recommended changes that are within the project manager's discretion are either approved or rejected and then documented. Recommended changes beyond the project manager's discretion are formally sent to the sponsor or change control board for consideration. Approved changes become part of the project plan with activities, responsibilities, and timing assigned. Finally, progress reporting meetings are a great time to capture lessons learned and to eat free food!

Reporting performance to sponsors, management, and clients can be in the form of either meetings or reports. Think in terms of three time horizons, as shown in Exhibit 14.6. It is often helpful to establish an agenda for progress report meetings based upon what sponsors wish to know concerning each of these three time horizons.

1. Past time period—The first time horizon is the immediate past period between your last report and now. When looking back like this, it is important to be able to state what the plan called for to be accomplished during that time and what was actually accomplished. Any variance or difference between the approved plan and actual performance, along with reasons for the variance, should also be part of the retrospective portion of performance reporting.
2. Current time period—The second time horizon is from now until the next performance report is due. What work is to be accomplished in this time period (current plan)? What risks and issues are foreseen? Finally, what changes need to be approved?

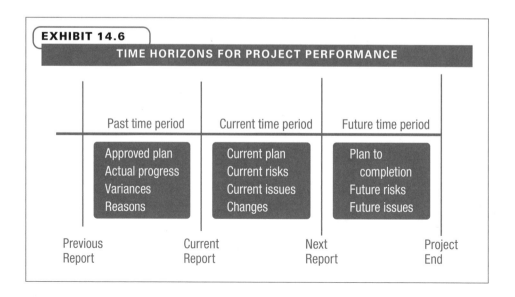

EXHIBIT 14.6

TIME HORIZONS FOR PROJECT PERFORMANCE

Past time period	Current time period	Future time period
Approved plan Actual progress Variances Reasons	Current plan Current risks Current issues Changes	Plan to completion Future risks Future issues

| Previous
Report | Current
Report | Next
Report | Project
End |

3. Future time period—The third time horizon is after the next reporting period. Remember the concept of rolling wave planning—the plan for the later part of the project might still be evolving, but what is known about it right now? Sponsors especially want to know what future risks and issues are envisioned because they may be able to head some problems off before they grow.

14.3 Customer Issues

The second major perspective included in a balanced scorecard approach to project control is the customer. Customers want the deliverables of the project. They want the results to be useful (quality).

Perform Quality Assurance

As previously defined in Chapter 11, **performing quality assurance** is "the process of auditing the quality requirements and the results of quality control measurements to ensure appropriate quality standards and operational definitions are used."[13] This implies that a project manager both ensures that work is performed correctly and that key stakeholders are convinced that the work is performed correctly. Project stakeholders form their opinions regarding quality of a project both by how the work is performed and by how the deliverables meet standards. Many activities that form this broad interpretation of quality assurance are related to other project management processes. For example, to convince customers that you are performing work correctly, some customer relationship–building activities also fit in the manage stakeholder expectations process. For another example, to perform the work correctly, some of the building human capability activities can also fit in the process of developing a project team.

Two areas that are specific to project quality assurance are conducting quality audits and improving project processes.

AUDITS A project quality audit is a review of documented procedures and actual practice. For an audit to be successful, the intent must be to improve the manner in which work is accomplished and not to punish people. With this in mind, an audit can begin with a review of the official documentation of how a process should be performed. The auditors then often interview the workers and have them explain (or better yet, demonstrate) how they perform the work. Records are investigated to see if the documentation is complete and current. At this point, the auditors have the following three sets of data:

1. Documentation of how the work is supposed to be done (the standards either developed or adopted in quality planning)
2. Descriptions of how the work is actually done
3. Documentation to verify how the work was completed

If discrepancies are found among these three, the auditors can recommend that workers perform work more consistently with the standards, that workers document their work better, and/or that some of the standards be improved. Project quality audits can be a fruitful source of lessons learned. These lessons should be shared so that other project teams can benefit. Remember, project quality audits, as part of quality assurance, are meant to help deliver good quality results and convince stakeholders that everything is OK because proper procedures are being used.

PROCESS IMPROVEMENT A process is a set of interrelated actions and activities performed to achieve a specified set of products, results, or services. Processes can be measured for both efficiency and effectiveness. Efficiency is the ratio of outputs to inputs.

A more efficient process uses fewer inputs to create the same number of outputs. This could equate to less work hours or less money spent to create the same project deliverable. Effectiveness is the extent to which a process is creating the desired deliverables. A more effective process is one that creates higher-quality deliverables and that better pleases the stakeholders. Process improvement can deal with both efficiency and effectiveness.

There are many avenues for improving project processes. One is to interpret the results of quality control measurements with an eye toward process improvement. These quality control measurements can often be used in the context of a seven-step or DMAIC process improvement model such as the one shown in Exhibit 3.10. Feedback from customers, suppliers, work associates, and other stakeholders can often lead to suggestions for improving processes. These suggestions might pinpoint opportunities to improve both the inputs into a process and the actions within the process.

Another useful method of process improvement is benchmarking. Benchmarking is a structured consideration of how another organization performs a process with an eye toward determining how to improve one's own performance. It is not directly copying the methods. Benchmarking consists of the following steps:

1. Determine a process that needs dramatic improvement.
2. Identify another organization that performs that process very well.
3. Make a deal with that organization to learn from them (they might require payment or the sharing of one of the observer's best practices with them).
4. Determine what needs to be observed and what questions need to be asked.
5. Make a site visit to observe and question the other organization.
6. Decide which observed methods will help the organization.
7. Adapt the methods to fit the organization's culture and situation.
8. Try the new methods on a small scale.
9. Evaluate the results.
10. If the methods are good enough, adopt them.

Perform Quality Control

Quality assurance deals with using correct policies and convincing stakeholders that the project team is capable of producing good output. Quality control (the current subject), on the other hand, deals with comparing specific project measurements with stakeholders' standards. The purposes of quality control on projects are to reduce the number of defects and inefficiencies, as well as to improve the project process and outputs. Quality control consists of:

- Monitoring the project to ensure that everything is proceeding according to plan
- Identifying when things are different enough from the plan to warrant preventive or corrective actions
- Repairing defects
- Determining and eliminating root causes of problems
- Providing specific measurements for quality assurance
- Providing recommendations for corrective and preventive actions
- Implementing approved changes as directed by the project's integrated change control system.

MONITOR THE PROJECT QUALITY Project managers using quality control focus on project inputs, processes, and outputs. When considering inputs, a project manager wants to ensure that workers assigned are capable of doing their work. They also work with

Project managers monitor work quality and verify deliverables at each stage of the project to minimize rework.

suppliers to ensure that the materials, information, and other inputs provided meet the required specifications and work satisfactorily. When considering the project processes, the manager wants to minimize rework because it wastes time and money, which are in short supply on most projects. Rework also often has negative impacts on both worker morale and stakeholder relations because it is very discouraging to make and/or receive junk, even if it is fixed eventually. When considering outputs, a project manager may first use internal inspection to ensure the deliverables work before they are sent to the customer. External inspection may also be required to prove to the customer that the deliverables are correct.

While the specifics vary greatly from project to project, there are some useful general lessons regarding the timing and types of project inspections, including the following:

- Inspect before a critical or expensive process to make sure the inputs are good before spending a large amount of money or time on them.
- Process steps where one worker hands off work to another worker are good places for both workers to inspect.
- Milestones identified in the project charter provide good inspection points.
- As practiced in software development, think of inspection in terms of units (individual components), integration (how components work together), and the system (how the deliverable as a whole performs).

QUALITY CONTROL TERMS Many terms with specific meanings are used in project quality control. Exhibit 14.7 shows pairs of terms that are sometimes confused, and the differences between each pair are described in the following paragraphs. While few projects repeat processes enough times to formally use statistical quality control, the concepts are still quite useful in making good decisions.

Prevention Versus Inspection Prevention is keeping errors out of a process, while inspection is trying to find errors so they do not reach the customer. Preventing a problem in the first place is preferred over trying to use an inspection to find it. Prevention is a cheaper method. Inspection does not guarantee that a problem is found. Inspection should be practiced, but every effort should be made to prevent problems from happening in the first place.

EXHIBIT 14.7

PAIRS OF PROJECT QUALITY CONTROL TERMS

TERM:	SOMETIMES CONFUSED WITH:
Prevention	Inspection
Sample	Population
Attribute	Variable
Precision	Accuracy
Tolerance	Control limit
Capable	In-control
Special cause	Common cause
Preventive action	Corrective action

Sample Versus Population   A population is all of the possible items in a set, such as all the students in a class. It is often costly, difficult, or even impossible to inspect an entire population. When that is the situation, a sample or subset is inspected. Three students, picked randomly, would be a sample. The key is to use a big enough sample to be representative of the population, but a small enough sample that it is cost and time effective.

Attribute Versus Variable   An attribute is determined with a yes-or-no test, while a variable is something that can be measured. Either one may be chosen. For example, if one of the goals of a project was to teach all of the people in a client's company, an attribute for each employee might be, "Did that person pass the test?" A variable might be, "How many questions did each employee score correctly?" Attributes are usually quicker (and cheaper) to observe, but may not yield as much detailed information. Project managers make a tradeoff between more information and more cost when they decide if they will count or measure.

Precision Versus Accuracy   A process is precise when the outputs are consistently very similar, such as shooting three shots at a target that all land in a cluster near each other. A process is accurate when, on the average, it produces what the customer wants, such as three shots that triangulate on the target. Ideally a process is both precise and accurate.

Tolerance Versus Control Limit   A tolerance limit is what the customer will accept and is sometimes called the voice of the customer. This could be if the customer wants a 1-inch bolt, perhaps they are willing to accept bolts ranging from a lower tolerance limit of 0.99 inches to an upper tolerance limit of 1.01 inches. A control limit reflects what the process can consistently deliver when things are behaving normally and is sometimes called the voice of the process. The upper and lower control limits are often statistically calculated to be three standard deviations above or below the process average.

Capable Versus In Control   A process is determined to be in control when the outputs are all within the control limits. A process is considered capable when control limits are within the tolerance limits so that customers can remain satisfied with project performance even when the performance is outside of its tolerance. Project managers try to ensure that their processes are both in control and capable of consistently delivering acceptable quality.

Special Versus Common Cause   Special causes are statistically unlikely events that usually mean something is different than normal. Common causes are normal or random variations that are considered part of operating the system at its current capability. Special causes are identified by individual points outside of the control limits or unusual patterns within the limits. Common causes need systematic change for improvement—perhaps new methods or better training or tools that would allow workers to more consistently produce excellent quality. Special causes, on the other hand, require specific interventions that include identifying the root causes and making changes so those same root causes do not happen again.

Preventive Versus Corrective Action   Preventive action is a proactive approach of making a change because a problem may occur otherwise. Corrective action is a reactive approach of making a change to fix a problem that has occurred.

QUALITY CONTROL TOOLS   A variety of quality control tools can be used effectively on projects. Some of the most common tools and their primary uses on projects are shown in Exhibit 14.8.

The following discussion presents a small example of a project process that is used to demonstrate the project quality control tools. A straightforward presentation of each tool is demonstrated. Multiple variations exist for some of the tools, and an interested student can find more detailed examples and instruction in a statistics or quality textbook.

EXHIBIT 14.8

PROJECT QUALITY CONTROL TOOLS

TOOL	DESCRIPTION AND USE
Flow chart	A visual model used to show inputs, flow of work, and outputs and to identify possible data collection points for process improvement
Check sheet	A simple, structured form used to gather and organize data for analysis
Pareto chart	A vertical bar graph used to identify and plot problems or defects in descending order of frequency or cost
Cause and effect diagram	A visual outline, often resembling a fish skeleton, used to identify and organize possible causes of a stated outcome.
Histogram	A vertical bar chart used to show the average, extent of variation, and shape of measurements recorded for a process variable
Run chart	A special type of scatter diagram in which one variable is time, used to see how the other variable changes over time
Control chart	A run chart with process average and control limits used to distinguish between common and special causes of variation

Flow Chart A flow chart is a tool that project managers use as they begin to control quality. Flow charts can be used to show any level of detail from the overall flow of an entire project (such as a network diagram of the project schedule) down to very specific details of a critical process. Flow charts show clearly where a process starts and ends. Each step in the process is shown by a box. Arrows show the direction in which information, money, or physical things flow. Exhibit 14.9 is a flow chart of the process of estimating project cost.

This is a high-level flow chart of the process. Perhaps the project team looks at this and realizes labor cost estimates are unreliable. They might decide they need more

EXHIBIT 14.9

ESTIMATING PROJECT COST FLOW CHART

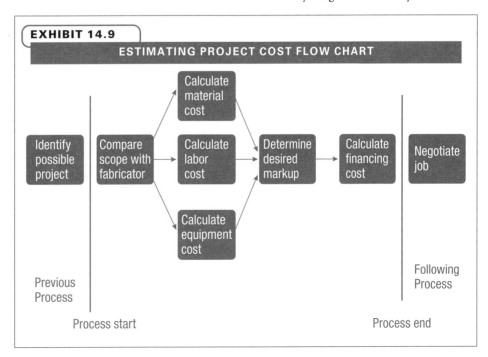

EXHIBIT 14.10

CHECK SHEET FOR LABOR COST ESTIMATING			
LABOR COST ISSUE	DOLLAR IMPACT	DATE DISCOVERED	ACTION TAKEN
Incorrect scope used			
Category of labor			
Quantity of labor			
Hourly rate			
Pace of labor learning			
Unexpected experience level			
Mathematical error			
Other (be specific)			

detailed understanding of this step. One method would be to create a more detailed flow chart of just that step. Another method is to gather some data using a check sheet such as the one shown in Exhibit 14.10.

Check Sheet   Check sheets are customized for each application. Decide exactly what data will be useful in understanding, controlling, and improving a process and create a form to collect that information. It is helpful to also collect the date or time when each event happened and notes regarding the impact or any special circumstances. When creating categories on a check sheet, it is wise to have a category entitled "other" because many times a problem comes from an unexpected source.

Pareto Chart   Once a check sheet is used, the gathered data can be displayed on an analysis tool such as the Pareto chart shown in Exhibit 14.11. The purpose of the Pareto chart is to quickly understand the primary causes of a particular problem using the 80/20 rule, where 80 percent of defects often come from only about 20 percent of all the sources.

   Note that, in this example, the error of using an incorrect scope shows the highest cost impact by far. Therefore, that is probably the first place the project team looks for improvements.

Cause and Effect Diagram   Exhibit 14.12 shows how the largest bar on the Pareto chart often becomes the head of the fish on the cause and effect diagram—the result that the project team tries to improve.

   The cause and effect diagram (also commonly known as the fishbone diagram, because it resembles a fish skeleton, and the Ishikawa diagram, after its developer) is constructed with each "big bone" representing a category of possible causes. For example, in Exhibit 14.12, one of the possible categories is "deliverable design," meaning that maybe something about the design of the project's deliverables contributed to problems with the "head of the fish"—in this case, using incorrect scope to estimate the labor cost. Once categories of possible causes are identified, the project team brainstorms ideas with the goal of identifying as many potential causes as possible. Once the team can think of no additional possible causes, they decide to test one or more possible causes to see if they actually have an impact. Testing can be done by gathering more data on the project as it is currently operating. Alternatively, a project team can test a new method and then collect data on it.

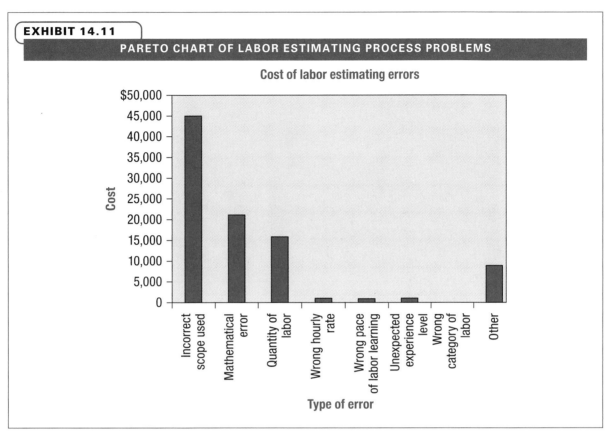

EXHIBIT 14.11

PARETO CHART OF LABOR ESTIMATING PROCESS PROBLEMS

Cost of labor estimating errors

Histogram Once the additional data are gathered, they can be analyzed using a histogram, run chart, and/or control chart. For example, if one of the potential causes of using incorrect scope is that the client demands the cost estimate within four days of job notification (this is within the timing category), perhaps the charts would appear as shown in Exhibit 14.13, Exhibit 14.14, or Exhibit 14.15.

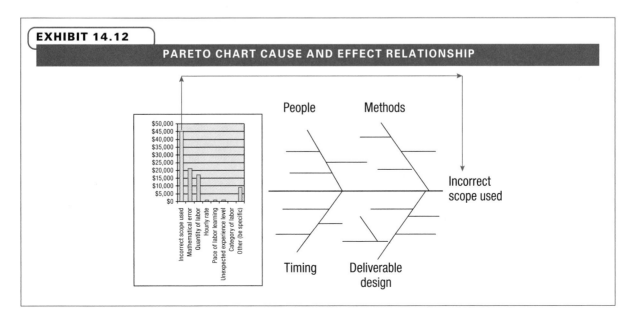

EXHIBIT 14.12

PARETO CHART CAUSE AND EFFECT RELATIONSHIP

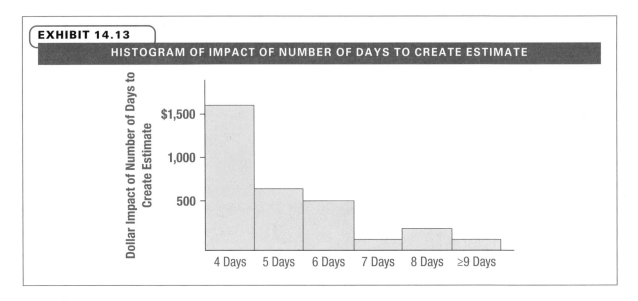

EXHIBIT 14.13

HISTOGRAM OF IMPACT OF NUMBER OF DAYS TO CREATE ESTIMATE

A project manager can interpret several things from a histogram such as the one shown in Exhibit 14.13. First, if nothing unusual is happening, a normal or bell-shaped curve might be expected. However, this histogram is highly skewed, with much more impact happening when the client demands an estimate within four days. When the client demands the estimate in four days, the impact is approximately $1,600. When comparing that to the total impact of about $15,000 for using the wrong scope, this error appears to explain only a bit more than 10 percent of the total problem. It might be

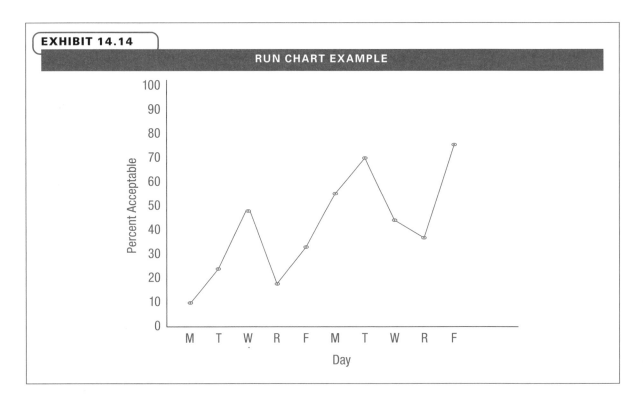

EXHIBIT 14.14

RUN CHART EXAMPLE

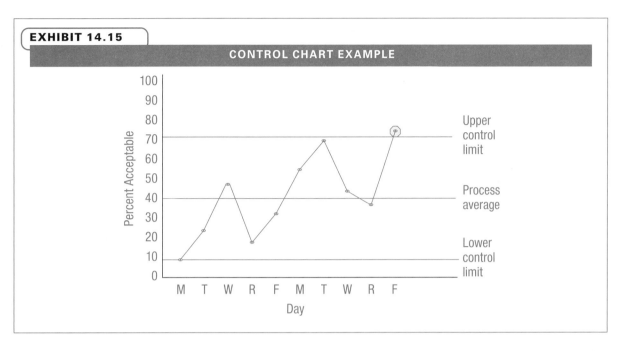

EXHIBIT 14.15

CONTROL CHART EXAMPLE

worth changing this, but most of the problem will still exist. Therefore, changing this factor alone does not solve the entire problem.

Run Chart Perhaps the project team wants to see how one specific aspect of the work process may change over time. If they collect data for two weeks on a daily basis and show them on a run chart such as the one in Exhibit 14.14, they could determine trends in how the process is changing over time.

The team could look for three types of variation. First, is there a trend either up or down? In this example, there is an upward trend. Second, is there a repeating pattern—such as a low every Monday or a high every Wednesday? In this case, it is too early to tell. Both Tuesdays are up from Mondays, and both Thursdays are low, but day of week does not seem like the major source of variation. The third type of variation is abrupt changes, such as either a single point far higher or lower than the others or all of the points suddenly being much higher or lower than previous points. The question teams ask when trying to find this variation is: "How big of a change is big enough to count?"

Control Chart Quality control charts are helpful in answering this question. Exhibit 14.15 displays the same data on a control chart with a process average and control limits shown. This chart shows the final point above the upper control limit. This means the variation is enough that it is not likely to have happened purely by chance. Something is causing the variation—some sort of special cause.

When considering any of these quality control tools, remember, it is easy to get lost in the details, but the purpose of quality control is to make sure the agreed upon scope and quality are met per the project charter.

14.4 Financial Issues

Cost control is obviously a financial issue. Cost, schedule, and scope are often so closely intertwined that they are monitored and controlled at the same time, and changes in one impact the others. Because of the close interrelationships between them, cost, schedule, and scope are envisioned here as financial issues.

Control Scope

Controlling scope is "the process of monitoring the status of the project and product scope and managing changes to the scope baseline."[14] Ideally, project managers and teams practice scope control in a proactive manner. They attempt to understand what might cause changes to either the product scope (the features of the project deliverables) or the project scope (the work that must be done to create the deliverables). Once a project team discovers something that may cause a need to change the scope, their first effort is typically to head it off. It is easiest if the stakeholders can still be satisfied and project objectives can be met by not changing the scope. However, many times it is necessary to make a scope change. A **scope change** is "any change to the project scope. A scope change almost always requires an adjustment to the project cost or schedule."[15] For this reason, proposed scope changes are processed through the integrated change control system to determine what impact each might have on other aspects of the project. Some scope changes start as proposed changes to cost or schedule, just as some changes to cost or schedule start as proposed scope changes.

Just as for any type of proposed change, to understand scope changes, one must have a scope baseline. That is, the approved scope definition and work breakdown structure must be clearly understood. Only then can the project team determine how big a proposed scope change is, what impact it will have, and how to best manage it. **Variance analysis** is "a method for resolving the total variance in a set of scope, cost, and schedule variables into specific component variances."[16] Variance analysis includes determining how large the difference is between the actual and planned scope (or schedule or budget), the reasons for the difference, and whether action is necessary to resolve it. For scope variances, the action can include updating the scope definition and work breakdown structure.

Control Schedule and Costs

Schedule and cost control are very similar in concept to control in other knowledge areas. The project manager should start with the approved cost and schedule baseline. Next, the current status of the schedule and cost should be determined. For example, Exhibit 14.16 shows the schedule for converting money market funds from one system to another. On such a fast-paced project, the project manager probably keeps track of the actual schedule progress several times every day.

If the schedule or budget has changed by at least a pre-agreed amount, changes should be formally recommended and managed through the integrated change control system to ensure that any impacts on other areas are taken into account. Cost control often has one additional consideration—that is, ensuring that no more money is spent than the amount authorized. This may force other changes on the project, such as delaying the schedule or reducing part of the project scope. While many methods exist for controlling cost and schedule, the two discussed in this chapter are earned value management and project scheduling software such as MS Project.

Very often, the project manager must work with his or her company's finance department or CFO to get the proper data on accounts payable, accounts receivable, and other information. The project may require someone skilled in financial software. If the project manager is not personally adept at using such software, someone from the finance department might be included as part of the project team either in a core team member or SME capacity.

Earned Value Management for Controlling Schedule and Costs

Earned value management is "a management methodology for integrating scope, schedule, and resources, and for objectively measuring project performance and progress. Performance is measured by determining the earned value and comparing it to the actual

EXHIBIT 14.16

MONEY MARKET CONVERSION SCHEDULE

Money Market Conversion
Conversion Week Procedures

Day	Date	Action
Monday	5:00 P.M.	Compliance gathers all negative responses received to date, creates a report and sends it to Brokerage Ops
	5:00 P.M.	Brokerage Ops receives report of negative response accounts and deletes accounts from conversion file
Friday	10:00 A.M.	Compliance gathers all negative responses received since Monday's report, creates a 2nd report and sends it to Brokerage Ops
	10:00 A.M.	Negative responses received between Friday 10:00 A.M. and end of day Saturday will be included in conversion
	12:00 P.M.	Brokerage Ops receives 2nd report of negative response accounts and deletes accounts from conversion file
	12:15 P.M. – 3:15 P.M.	Clearing Company produces WSF2 report of conversion accounts and makes it available to Compliance
	12:15 P.M. – 3:15 P.M.	Compliance reviews WSF2 report and verifies a sampling of accounts for conversion
	3:00 P.M.	Compliance calls Brokerage Ops to either OK WSF2 report or submit issues. Brokerage Ops to re-run report upon resolution
	4:00 P.M.	Final opportunity to run / rerun WSF2 report
Sunday		Clients hold Not Our Fund Company shares and receive applicable dividend through Sunday
Monday	12:00 A.M.	Not Our Fund Company holdings are redeemed and purchased into corresponding XYZ Funds according to conversion maps created Friday
Tuesday	12:00 A.M.	Conversion transactions reflected on Clearing Company system (transaction shows as a redemption of the Not Our Fund Company and a purchase of the XYZ Fund) Negative responses received between Friday 10:00 A.M. and end-of-day Saturday must be manually converted back to previous Not Our Fund Company CUSIP by Compliance (customer monthly statement will show conversion and transaction back, a call to the Rep and client required)
Friday	12:00 A.M.	Clearing Company runs a report showing any accounts holding the 3 Not Our Fund Company cusips and sends it to Compliance

Source: MichaelCassani, Fund Project Services, Inc. Reprinted with permission.

EXHIBIT 14.17

EARNED VALUE MANAGEMENT TERMS

QUESTION	TIMING	ANSWER	ACRONYM
How much work *should be* done?	Now	Planned value	**PV**
How much work *is* done?	Now	Earned value	**EV**
How much *did the* "is done" work cost?	Now	Actual cost	**AC**
How much was the total project *supposed to* cost?	**End**	Budget at completion	BAC
How much *is* the project schedule ahead or behind?	Now	Schedule variance	**SV**
How much *is* the project over or under budget?	Now	Cost variance	**CV**
How efficient is the project *so far* with its schedule?	Now	Schedule performance index	SPI
How efficient is the project *so far* with its budget?	Now	Cost performance index	CPI
How much more do we expect to spend to finish the project?	**End**	Estimate to complete	**ETC**
What do we now think the total project will cost?	**End**	Estimate at completion	EAC

---

cost."[17] Earned value allows a project team to understand their project's progress in terms of cost and schedule as well as to make predictions concerning the project's schedule and cost control until the project's conclusion. Earned value is used as a decision-making tool. The project manager can quickly assess how the project is doing according to the baseline plan and whether the project will end without major cost and/or schedule impacts. The earned value data allow a project manager to decide on the status of his or her project at a given point in time.

When interpreting earned value management, cost and schedule must be considered independently. A project can be either ahead or behind the planned schedule and either over or under the planned budget. Secondly, all earned value terms deal with one of two time frames. Each represents either current status as of the last date that project data were gathered or a prediction for the end of the project. Exhibit 14.17 lists 12 questions and answers that introduce all of the earned value management terms.

Exhibit 14.18 demonstrates how to calculate each of the earned value management terms.

CURRENTLY KNOWN VALUES In this example, the first several items are provided.

$$PV = \$250,000, \ EV = \$200,000, \ AC = \$400,000, \ and \ BAC = \$750,000$$

Each of these terms also has a formal definition.

Planned value (PV) is "the authorized budget assigned to the scheduled work to be accomplished."[18] In our example, we expected to spend $250,000 for the work we planned to have accomplished by now.

Earned value (EV) is "the value of completed work expressed in terms of approved budget assigned to that work."[19] In our example, the work that has been completed is worth $200,000.

Actual cost (AC) is the "total costs actually incurred and recorded in accomplishing work performed during a given time period."[20] In our example, we actually owe $400,000 for the work that has been completed.

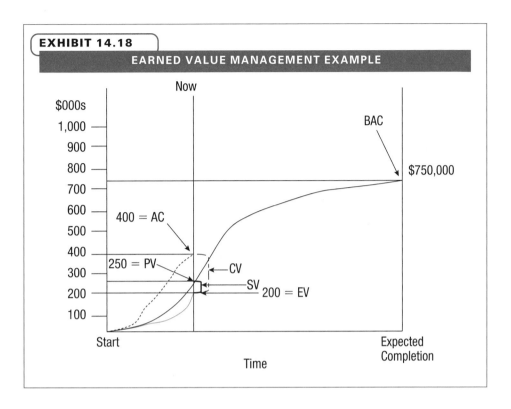

Budget at completion (BAC) is "the sum of all budgets established for the work to be performed on a project.... The total planned value of the project."[21] In this example, our approved budget for the entire project is $750,000. Now that we know these four pieces of information, we can calculate answers to all of the remaining questions listed in Exhibit 14.17.

VARIANCES **Schedule variance (SV)** is "a measure of schedule performance on a project. It is ... EV minus PV."[22] In our example it is calculated as $200,000 − $250,000 = −$50,000. We know we are behind schedule because the variation is negative (unfavorable).

$$SV = EV − PV$$

Cost variance (CV) is "a measure of cost performance on a project. It is ... EV − AC."[23] In our example, it is calculated as $200,000 − $400,000 = −$200,000.

$$CV = EV − AC$$

We know we are over budget because the variation is negative (unfavorable). The two variances help us understand in dollar terms how poorly or well we are performing on cost and schedule. In this example, we are performing poorly in terms of both cost and schedule. These are commonly used indicators. However, some people prefer to use efficiency measures to understand in percentage terms how well or poorly the project is performing.

INDEXES **Schedule performance index (SPI)** is "a measure of schedule efficiency on a project. It is ... EV divided by PV."[24] In our example, it is calculated by $200,000/$250,000 = 80%.

$$SPI = EV/PV$$

We know our project is behind schedule because we only accomplished 80 percent of what we planned. With performance indexes, 100 percent means right on schedule, less than 100 percent means less efficient than planned, and over 100 percent means more efficient than planned.

Cost performance index (CPI) is "a measure of cost efficiency on a project. It is ... EV divided by AC."[25] In our example, it is calculated by $200,000/$400,000 = 50%.

$$\textbf{CPI} = \textbf{EV/AC}$$

We know our project is over budget because we have only received $0.50 worth of results for every dollar we have spent.

Now that we understand how we have performed so far (rather poorly in our example), it is time to forecast how we will perform for the remainder of the project. The simplest way to estimate future performance is to predict that past performance will continue. The following calculations are based upon that assumption. There are projects, however, that may have unusual circumstances in the early stages that are not likely to be repeated later. In those instances, the project manager and sponsor need to use judgment to determine how much to modify their forecasts in hopes that performance will improve.

ESTIMATES **Estimate to complete (ETC)** is "the expected cost needed to complete all the remaining work for ... the project."[26] In our example, if we predict that our future performance will have the same efficiency as our past performance, it is calculated by (BAC– EV)/ CPI = ($750,000 − $200,000)/50% = $1,100,000.

$$\textbf{ETC} = \textbf{(BAC} − \textbf{EV)/CPI}$$

Unless we improve upon our efficiency, we can expect to pay more for the remaining project work than we originally expected to pay for the entire project!

Estimate at completion (EAC) is "the expected total cost of ... the project when the defined scope of work will be completed. Typically it is based upon AC plus ETC."[27] In our example, it is calculated by $400,000 + $1,100,000 = $1,500,000.

$$\textbf{EAC} = \textbf{AC} + \textbf{ETC}$$

Because our cost efficiency is only half of our plan (as we learned from our CPI), unless we become more efficient, we can expect to pay double our original estimate!

In earned value management, each term helps project managers understand a bit more about their project's performance. Collectively, the earned value management terms give project managers great added insight for monitoring and controlling project cost and schedule. In addition to earned value management, many project managers use scheduling software to help control their projects.

14.5 Using MS Project to Monitor and Control Projects

MS Project and other software are primarily helpful in monitoring and controlling the project schedule, cost, and resources. Some companies prefer to use other software for parts of this—particularly cost control. In using MS Project for project control, it is helpful to understand the following three items:

1. What makes a schedule useful
2. How MS Project recalculates the schedule based upon reported actuals
3. The current and future impacts of time and cost variances

Once these three items are understood, the project manager is prepared to define the performance update process that will be used and to update the MS Project schedule in a step-by-step fashion.

What Makes a Schedule Useful?

A project manager must provide useful status reports, produce accurate assignment dates, take timely corrective actions, and make other necessary management decisions. This is difficult or impossible to do well without a sufficiently useful schedule.

To be sufficiently useful, three sets of data must exist for comparison purposes. Each set includes dates, duration, work, and cost. Approved changes (scope, risk response activities, corrective action within contingency, management reserve limits, etc.) must be included. The three sets are as follows:

1. The Baseline set (Baseline Start, Baseline Finish, Baseline Duration, Baseline Work, and Baseline Cost)—This set is a copy of the stakeholder-approved scheduled values (as discussed in Chapter 11). This baseline information is sometimes called the planned schedule.
2. Past actual time and cost results, or the Actual set (Actual Start, Actual Finish, Actual Duration, Actual Work, and Actual Cost)—This set, sometimes called performance data, is what actually happens as reported by the resources assigned to activities.
3. Future estimated time and costs, or the Scheduled set (Start, Finish, Duration, Work, and Cost fields)—These values are used or calculated by MS Project. They are continuously recalculated as activities and estimates are entered, as the project network is defined, as resources are assigned and balanced, and as actuals are entered.

How MS Project Recalculates the Schedule Based on Reported Actuals

As actual data are entered into an activity's Actual fields, MS Project copies those data into the activity's Scheduled fields, replacing the estimated values. MS Project then recalculates the schedule for future activities based on a combination of what actually happened and the estimates of the remaining activities.

Current and Future Impacts of Time and Cost Variance

With the three sets of data, comparisons can now be made between any two of the sets. This is useful in understanding future impacts of various issues, such as:

- Time and cost performance variances from baseline
- Critical path changes
- Resource allocation issues
- Emerging risks
- Remaining contingency and management reserves
- The impacts of proposed changes

Define the Performance Update Process

The performance update process is defined by stating who needs to report, what is in each report, when each report needs to be filed, and how each report is submitted.

WHO REPORTS? All team members and suppliers assigned to activities that were scheduled during the past reporting period need to report. Also, any resource wanting to change the estimate of a soon-to-be-starting activity must report the new estimate.

WHAT IS REPORTED?   Actual Start, Actual Finish, Actual Duration Complete, and Estimated Remaining Duration are reported. Estimated Remaining Duration is one of the two most important values collected, the other being Actual Finish. The sooner the project manager learns of variances from estimates, the sooner he or she can take corrective action.

WHEN TO REPORT?   Publish the day of the week (Status Date or As of Date) for reporting, as well as the frequency. The Status Date is usually driven by the date of the stakeholder review meeting and the time needed to make adjustments before that meeting. The best available data are needed for that meeting.

HOW TO REPORT?   Team members on active activities need a request for performance data. The project manager provides each team member the list of their current assignments together with any previously reported Actuals—Start, Completed Duration, and Remaining Duration—for those assignments.

The time that performance data are entered is also a good time to make necessary modifications such as approved changes, risk response activities, revised estimates, rolling wave detail, resource balancing, corrective action, and so forth.

Steps to Update the Project Schedule

The process of updating the project schedule includes six steps. Each step is described below and several screen shots from Microsoft Project are displayed to demonstrate.

STEP 1: ACQUIRE THE PERFORMANCE DATA   These are duration-based data. For each resource assignment, collect the date when the assignment started, how much duration is now completed, how much duration remains, and the actual finish date (if finished).

STEP 2: SET THE STATUS DATE (AS OF)   With the status date entered, Microsoft Project can assist with the posting of performance data.

1. On the Project tab, in the Properties group, click Project Information.
2. In Status date, enter the status date for the concluding status period as shown in Exhibit 14.19.
3. Click OK.

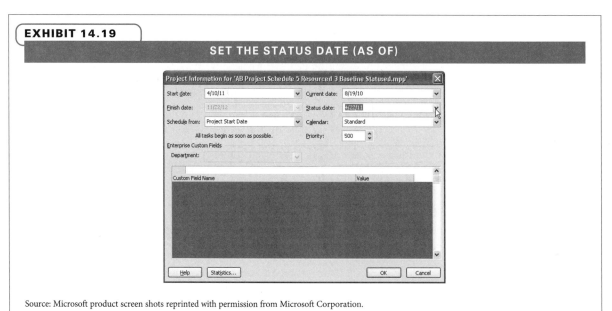

EXHIBIT 14.19

SET THE STATUS DATE (AS OF)

Source: Microsoft product screen shots reprinted with permission from Microsoft Corporation.

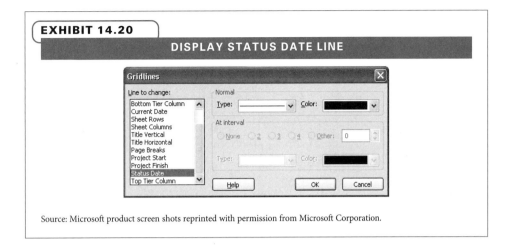

EXHIBIT 14.20

DISPLAY STATUS DATE LINE

Source: Microsoft product screen shots reprinted with permission from Microsoft Corporation.

STEP 3: DISPLAY THE STATUS DATE LINE ON THE GANTT CHART

1. On the Format tab, in the Format group, click Gridlines and enter Gridlines …
2. In Line to change: enter Status Date, as shown in Exhibit 14.20.
3. In Type: select the solid line.
4. In Color: select Darker Orange.
5. Click OK.

STEP 4: ENTER THE DURATION-BASED PERFORMANCE DATA
Exhibit 14.21 shows a project schedule with resourced activities A through F. The upper pane displays the Gantt Chart view. Next to each activity name is the performance report from the assigned resource(s)—a user-defined text field modified for the purposes of this text. The Status date is end of day on Thursday, June 9th (vertical line). The lower pane displays the Task Usage view with the Scheduled and Actual Work rows in the timescale.

Resource Rl reports Activity A performance was as scheduled through the end of day on Thursday.

1. Click Activity A.
2. On the Task tab, in the Schedule group, click Mark on Track.
3. Notice the black progress bar in the Gantt bar through the end of day on Thursday (status date).

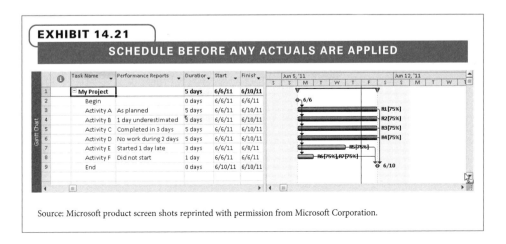

EXHIBIT 14.21

SCHEDULE BEFORE ANY ACTUALS ARE APPLIED

Source: Microsoft product screen shots reprinted with permission from Microsoft Corporation.

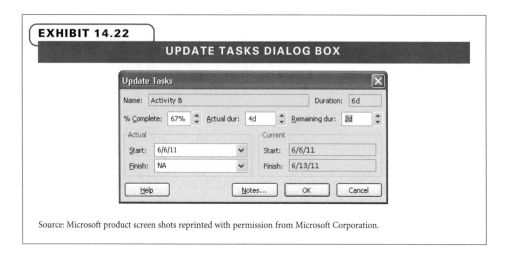

EXHIBIT 14.22

UPDATE TASKS DIALOG BOX

Source: Microsoft product screen shots reprinted with permission from Microsoft Corporation.

Resource R2 reports Activity B performance as scheduled, but the estimated remaining duration is two days instead of one.

1. Click Activity B.
2. On the Task tab, in the Schedule group, click the Mark on Track drop-down and then click Update Tasks.
3. In the Update Tasks dialog, in Actual dur: enter "4d" and for Remaining dur: enter "2d," as shown in Exhibit 14.22.
4. Click OK.
5. Notice Activity B's duration is now six days and extends through the end of day Monday, as shown in Exhibit 14.23.

Resource R3 reports that Activity C finished two days early.

1. Click on Activity C.
2. On the Task tab, in the Schedule group, click the Mark on Track drop-down and then click Update Tasks.

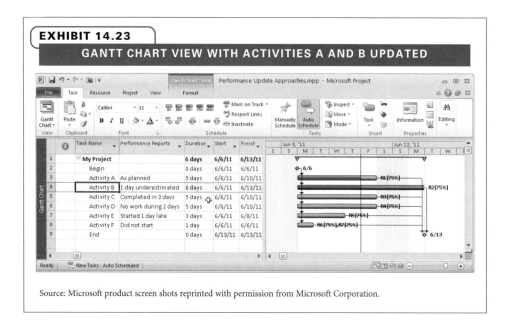

EXHIBIT 14.23

GANTT CHART VIEW WITH ACTIVITIES A AND B UPDATED

Source: Microsoft product screen shots reprinted with permission from Microsoft Corporation.

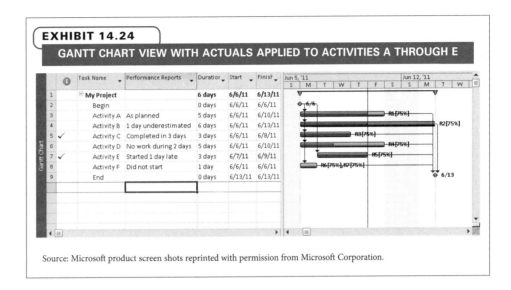

EXHIBIT 14.24

GANTT CHART VIEW WITH ACTUALS APPLIED TO ACTIVITIES A THROUGH E

Source: Microsoft product screen shots reprinted with permission from Microsoft Corporation.

3. In the Update Tasks dialog, in Actual dur: enter "3d" and in Remaining Dur: enter "0d."

4. Click OK.

5. Notice in Exhibit 14.24 that Activity C's duration is now three days and the activity is marked complete (check mark in the Indicators column.

Resource R4 reports that no work was done for two of the four days on Activity D.

1. Click on Activity D.

2. On the Task tab, in the Schedule group, click the Mark on Track drop-down and then click Update Tasks.

3. In the Update Tasks dialog, in Actual dur: enter "2d" and in Remaining Dur: enter "3d."

4. Click OK.

5. Notice that Activity D still has work scheduled for Wednesday and Thursday.

Resource R5 reports that Activity E started one day late.

1. Click on Activity E.

2. On the Task tab, in the Schedule group, click the Mark on Track drop-down and then click Update Tasks.

3. In the Update Tasks dialog, enter "6/7/11" in Start:, enter "3d" in Actual dur:, and enter "0d" in Remaining Dur:.

4. Click OK.

5. Notice that Activity E is marked as complete.

Resources R6 and R7 report that no work was done on Activity F.

STEP 5: RESCHEDULE REMAINING WORK Activities D and F have work that is still scheduled for dates prior to the Status date. This work must be moved to start no earlier than the day following the Status date.

1. Click on Activity D.

2. On the Project tab, Status group, click on Update Project.

3. In the Update Project dialog, click Reschedule uncompleted work to start after:.

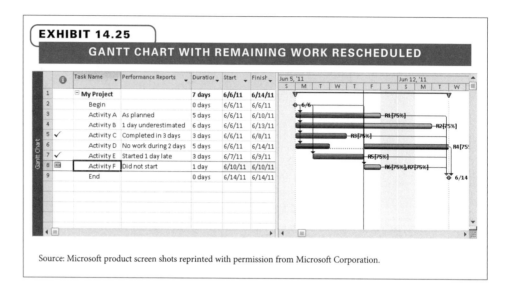

EXHIBIT 14.25

GANTT CHART WITH REMAINING WORK RESCHEDULED

Source: Microsoft product screen shots reprinted with permission from Microsoft Corporation.

4. Enter the Status Date if not already entered.
5. Click on Selected tasks.
6. Repeat these steps for Activity F.

Activity D is now split, with the completed work showing on Monday and Tuesday, and the remaining work rescheduled to resume on Friday. If a more likely date to resume work is not Friday, drag and drop the Gantt bar to resume on the likely date.

Activity F is also scheduled to resume on Friday. When all of an activity is rescheduled, a start-no-earlier constraint is applied by project. Modify that constraint to select a more likely resume date. Ignoring unfinished work that is scheduled earlier than the status date is a risky practice. This rescheduling is shown in Exhibit 14.25.

STEP 6: REVISE FUTURE ESTIMATES The most accurate estimates are often those made just before an activity has started. Therefore, it is a good practice to ask all project team members if they believe the estimates for any of their activities should be updated.

14.6 Replanning if Necessary

Sometimes it becomes necessary to replan a project. Certainly, the project manager can use the integrated change control system to understand the impact the proposed changes may have and to secure approval to make the change. The changes are then reflected in a revised plan. The schedule, cost, and resource changes can be shown on an updated MS Project schedule. Other changes can be reflected in risk register updates or issues log updates. Two questions still exist regarding replanning: "What kinds of changes might be made in response to the problems?" and "Does the approval for a change need to be escalated to higher management?"

Changes a project manager may need to recommend include reassigning activities to different workers, splitting activities so at least some work can get started, reordering activities so they may be accomplished sooner, borrowing or acquiring additional resources, reducing scope, and so on. Many of these types of change can help a project get back on track; however, make sure the appropriate stakeholders agree with the changes because many times a change that improves one aspect of a project degrades another.

Consider that people at each level in an organization have the ability to make specific decisions and are generally allowed a certain amount of time to deal with a problem before notifying a superior. Whoever makes the decision is still expected to document it appropriately. If a very minor problem occurs on a project, perhaps a team member can make the decision regarding how to handle it. A bit larger problem may fall in the domain of the project manager. Large decisions may go to the sponsor, and really critical decisions may be sent to the leadership of the parent organization. Escalation answers the question of what kinds of decisions are submitted to a higher level and how much time the lower-level person gets before raising the problem. A person who escalates minor decisions, or even major decisions very quickly, gives the impression of being weak and indecisive. However, a person who does not escalate important decisions or who takes so long to escalate them that the problem has worsened exhibits poor judgment.

Summary

For a project manager to effectively determine the desired project progress is being made and results are delivered, a multitude of things need to be monitored and controlled. Many of these are interdependent, so a project manager needs to understand how changes in one area might impact another area.

Project managers need to monitor and control the actual work of the project, or the activities. This entails observing the work as it is executed and making adjustments as needed. Any adjustments that may have a sizable impact must be processed through the project's integrated change control process. Each potential change is proposed, approved or disapproved, and documented, and the approved changes are implemented. A risk register is maintained to keep track of active risks, whether the risk events transpire, and how they are handled. New risks are added as discovered, and no-longer-relevant risks are retired.

Project managers also need to control the various aspects of the project that are subject to potential trade-offs—namely, scope, quality, cost, and schedule. When controlling these, the project manager remembers to look for variances—that is, any difference between what was planned and what has actually happened. The project manager also seeks to understand how a change in any one will impact the others. Several tools exist for helping project managers with this control. Many quality control tools are widely used when seeking to understand what the quality level is, where problems may exist, what the root causes are for problems, and how to improve the project processes so the problems do not reoccur. Sponsors and other stakeholders want to understand progress made on the project, current plans, and what might derail the project. Regular progress meetings and reports serve this purpose. Earned value management and MS Project are both quite helpful in understanding, documenting, and improving upon cost and schedule progress.

Key Terms from the *PMBOK® Guide*

Direct and manage project execution, 387
Monitor and control project work, 389
Monitor, 389
Control, 389
Variance, 389
Perform integrated change control, 390
Change control, 390
Change control board, 390
Monitor and control risk, 391
Distribute information, 392
Report performance, 393
Perform quality assurance, 395
Control scope, 404

Scope change, 404
Variance analysis, 404
Earned value management, 404
Planned value (PV), 406
Earned value (EV), 406
Actual cost (AC), 406
Budget at completion (BAC), 407
Schedule variance (SV), 407
Cost variance (CV), 407
Schedule performance index (SPI), 407
Cost performance index (CPI), 408
Estimate to complete (ETC), 408
Estimate at completion (EAC), 408

Chapter Review Questions

1. List each project control issue and where it fits in the project balanced scorecard.
2. _____ is a quantifiable deviation away from an expected value.
3. When should information regarding corrective action be given?
4. What should your initial response be if a customer asks for a change to your project?
5. A project manager normally only needs to do monitoring and controlling work once during the duration of the project. True or false?
6. List each item that should be included in progress reports for the past, current, and future time periods. Tell why each is helpful.
7. Describe project scope control.
8. _____ is the type of control in which work is continually compared to the plan in order to measure the level of progress.
9. It is best if a project manager agrees to all additions to the scope so that he or she keeps key stakeholders happy. True or false?
10. A(n) _____ is a formal group of stakeholders responsible for reviewing, evaluating, approving, and rejecting proposed changes to the project.
11. The _____ is used to guide the monitoring and controlling of risk-related activities of the project.
12. _____ deals with comparing specific project measurements with established standards.
13. Contrast each pair of quality control terms in Exhibit 14.7.
14. _____ is all the possible items in a set.
15. _____ is a visual model that shows inputs, the flow of work, and outputs.
16. The highest bar on a Pareto chart often becomes the "head of the fish" in the _____.
17. When using a control chart, a project manager notices that there is one point which falls above the project's upper control limit. This kind of variation is a(n) _____.
18. _____ is a management methodology for integrating scope, schedule, and resources and for objectively measuring project performance and progress.
19. Which of the following earned value management terms does *not* deal with timing at the end of the project?
    a. BAC
    b. PV
    c. ETC
    d. EAC
20. _____ and _____ a project's execution is the process of executing the work defined in the project management plan to achieve the project's requirements as defined in the project scope statement.
21. The primary source of work to be performed is at the _____ level.
22. _____ is the application of planned, systematic quality activities to ensure that the project employs all processes needed to meet requirements.
23. The two areas of project quality assurance are _____ and _____.
24. A project manager should use a quality audit to determine which team members need to be punished for not completing the work properly. True or false?
25. Project audits are good sources to gain lessons learned. True or false?
26. _____ is the process of making needed information available to project stakeholders in a timely manner.
27. Processes can be measured for _____ and _____.
28. What three sets of data should a project manager have after completing a project audit?

Discussion Questions

1. Using examples, explain each of the five meanings of *project determination*.
2. Using an example, describe possible changes that might occur if project progress is not as planned.
3. Describe how a project manager can determine project progress for each element in the project balanced scorecard.
4. Give specific examples of risks on a project within the team's control, partially within the team's control, and outside the team's control. Tell how you would deal with each.
5. What is the main purpose of monitoring and controlling a project?

6. Describe the purpose of using an integrated change control system.
7. What members of the project team should serve on the change control board?
8. What is the purpose of having quality control on projects?
9. List and describe the purpose of the seven project quality control tools in Exhibit 14.8.
10. Using a project example, describe each earned value term listed in Exhibit 14.17.
11. Define what makes an MS Project schedule useful and tell why.

12. Why is it important for project managers to gather data on the work that has been executed in the project?
13. Explain the difference between efficiency and effectiveness.
14. Briefly describe the 10 steps of benchmarking.
15. Describe the three time horizons for project performance reporting, what should be reported concerning each, and why.

PMBOK® Guide Questions

1. To _____ is to "collect project performance data with respect to a plan, produce performance measures, and report and disseminate performance information."
   a. control
   b. monitor
   c. budget at completion
   d. estimate to complete
2. Two types of _____ used on projects are steering and go/no go.
   a. control
   b. variance
   c. scope change
   d. cost variance
3. When a project customer comes to Juan, asking him to increase the project's scope, Juan's first step should be to _____.

   a. determine the schedule performance index
   b. determine the estimate to complete
   c. perform integrated change control
   d. none of the above
4. Of the two, _____ is cheaper and more preferable to _____.
   a. prevention; inspection
   b. precision; accuracy
   c. accuracy; precision
   d. inspection; prevention
5. The upper and lower _____ are often three standard deviations above or below the process average.
   a. control limits
   b. tolerance
   c. quality control tools
   d. earned values

Exercises

1. Use the following information to answer parts a through f. Describe what the results of each calculation mean to you as a project manager. What do you propose to do?

   $$PV = \$500,000$$
   $$EV = \$350,000$$
   $$AC = \$550,000$$
   $$BAC = \$1,200,000$$

   a. Calculate the schedule variance (SV).
   b. Calculate the cost variance (CV).
   c. Calculate the schedule performance index (SPI).
   d. Calculate the cost performance index (CPI).
   e. Calculate the estimate to complete (ETC).

   f. Calculate the estimate at completion (EAC).
2. Use the following information to answer parts a through f. Describe what the results of each calculation mean to you as a project manager. What do you propose to do?

   $$PV = \$25,000$$
   $$EV = \$30,000$$
   $$AC = \$29,000$$
   $$BAC = \$1,000,000$$

   a. Calculate the schedule variance (SV).
   b. Calculate the cost variance (CV).
   c. Calculate the schedule performance index (SPI).
   d. Calculate the cost performance index (CPI).

e. Calculate the estimate to complete (ETC).

f. Calculate the estimate at completion (EAC).

3. A project manager has just learned that the schedule performance index (SPI) for his project is 85 percent. The calculation of the cost performance index (CPI) is 107 percent. How would you describe this project both in terms of budget and schedule?

4. Document the flow of a project work process. Be sure to identify the starting and ending points.

5. Create a check sheet to gather data regarding a step in the process flow chart you constructed in Exercise 4 above.

6. For a cost savings project, you have captured data that show the following costs: delays between operations = $900; broken/missing tools = $1200; water losses = $3,700; poor seals = $1,500; other = $2,000. Construct a Pareto chart. What would your next course of action be?

7. For a productivity improvement project, you discover the most frequent cause of delays in receiving payment is incorrect invoices. Construct a fishbone diagram to identify possible reasons for this problem. What action do you recommend with the results of your fishbone diagram?

8. Using the data on the CD for Problem 14.08, construct a run chart to visualize how the number of customer complaints is changing over time. Describe what you find in terms of trends, repeating patterns, and/or outliers.

9. Using the data on the CD for Problem 14.09, construct a schedule in MS Project. Show where the project is ahead and/or behind schedule. Be specific. Which activities did the best? Which had the most problems?

10. Find a company (or other organization) that has a reputation for excellence in some aspect of project work. Benchmark their methods and determine how you can use the results to help your team improve.

11. Create a process improvement plan using the DMAIC model in Exhibit 3.10 to improve a project work process either for your own project or for another one.

Example Project

For your example project, complete the following at a minimum:

1. Document the change requests and their disposition (if you have had any changes proposed to your project).

2. Identify any changes to your risk register with new changes added and/or old ones removed.

3. Show any quality control tools you have used and explain how you interpret and act upon the results from them.

4. Show your progress updates on MS Project.

5. If you are tracking cost on your project, show the most current status of the 10 earned value management terms.

6. Create one key deliverable for your project. This should be one deliverable that your sponsor asked your team to create when you wrote the charter. Gather information regarding your process of creating the deliverable.

7. Describe tradeoff issues on your project. These can include tradeoffs between the needs of your sponsor's organization, the project, and your project team. The tradeoffs can also be within the project objectives and constraints of scope, quality, time, cost, other resources, and stakeholder satisfaction.

8. Create and document the information retrieval and distribution system for your project according to your project communications plan. Show the information you have collected.

References

A *Guide to the Project Management Body of Knowledge (PMBOK® Guide)*, 4th ed. (Newtown Square, PA: Project Management Institute, 2008).

Anbari, Frank T., "Earned Value Project Management Methods and Extensions," *Project Management Journal* 34 (4) (December 2003): 12–23.

Bauch, Garland T. and Christopher A. Chung, "A Statistical Project Control Tool for Engineering Managers," *Project Management Journal* 32 (2) (June 2001): 37–44.

Brassard, Michael and Diane Ritter, *The Memory Jogger™ II: A Pocket Guide of Tools for Continuous*

Improvement & Effective Planning (Salem, NH: GOAL/QPC, 1994).

Cerpa, Narciso and June M. Verner, "Why Did Your Project Fail?" *Communications of the ACM* 52 (12) (December 2009): 130–134.

Devine, Kevin, Timothy J. Kloppenborg, and Priscilla O'Clock, "Project Measurement and Success: A Balanced Scorecard Approach," *Journal of Health Care Finance* 36 (4) (2010): 38–50

Evans, James R. and William M. Lindsay, *The Management and Control of Quality*, 8th ed. (Mason, OH: South-Western Cengage Learning, 2010).

Howard, Dale and Gary Chefetz, *What's New Study Guide Microsoft Project 2010* (New York: Chefetz LLC dba MSProjectExperts, 2010).

Kloppenborg, Timothy J. and Joseph A. Petrick, *Managing Project Quality* (Vienna, VA: Management Concepts, Inc., 2002).

Kloppenborg, Timothy J., Arthur Shriberg, and Jayashree Venkatraman, *Project Leadership* (Vienna, VA: Management Concepts, Inc., 2003).

Means, Jay and Tammy Adams, *Facilitating the Project Life-cycle* (San Francisco: Jossey-Bass, 2005).

Meier, Steven R. "Causal Inference of the Cost Overruns and Schedule Delays of Large-Scale U.S. Federal Defense and Intelligence Acquisition Programs," *Project Management Journal* 41 (1) (March 2010): 28–39.

Mulcahy, Rita, *PMP Exam Prep: Rita's Course in a Book for Passing the PMP Exam*, 5th ed. (RMC Publications, Inc., 2005).

Norie, James and Derek H. T. Walker, "A Balanced Score-card Approach to Project Management Leadership," *Project Management Journal* 35 (4) (December 2004): 47–56.

Petersen, Denis R. and E. Lile Murphree, Jr., "The Impact of Owner Representatives in a Design-Build Construction Environment," *Project Management Journal* 35 (3) (September 2004): 27–38.

Rose, Kenneth H., *Project Quality Management: Why, What and How* (Boca Raton, FL: Ross Publishing, Inc., 2005).

Rozenes, Shai, Gad Vitner, and Stuart Spraggett, "Project Control: Literature Review," *Project Management Journal* 37 (4) (September 2006): 5–14.

Stewart, Wendy E., "Balanced Scorecard for Projects," *Project Management Journal* 32 (1) (March 2001): 38–53.

Taylor, Hazel, "Risk Management and Problem Resolution Strategies for IT Projects: Prescription and Practice," *Project Management Journal* 37 (5) (December 2006): 49–63.

Yosua, David, Karen R. J. White, and Lydia Lavigne, "Project Controls: How to Keep a Healthy Pulse on Your Projects," *2006 PMI Global Congress Proceedings* (Seattle, Washington).

Endnotes

1. Adapted from *The American Heritage Dictionary of the English Language* (1981): 359.
2. *PMBOK® Guide* 433.
3. *PMBOK® Guide* 438.
4. Ibid.
5. *PMBOK® Guide* 430.
6. *PMBOK® Guide* 542.
7. *PMBOK® Guide* 440.
8. *PMBOK® Guide* 428.
9. Ibid.
10. *PMBOK® Guide* 438.
11. *PMBOK® Guide* 433.
12. *PMBOK® Guide* 445.
13. *PMBOK® Guide* 440.
14. *PMBOK® Guide* 430
15. *PMBOK® Guide* 448.
16. *PMBOK® Guide* 452.
17. *PMBOK® Guide* 433.
18. *PMBOK® Guide* 441.
19. *PMBOK® Guide* 433.
20. *PMBOK® Guide* 426.
21. *PMBOK® Guide* 428.
22. *PMBOK® Guide* 448.
23. *PMBOK® Guide* 431.
24. *PMBOK® Guide* 448.
25. *PMBOK® Guide* 430.
26. *PMBOK® Guide* 434.
27. *PMBOK® Guide* 184, 434.

PROJECT MANAGEMENT *IN ACTION*

D. D. Williamson's Rules for Project Control

D. D. Williamson, the caramel color producer described in earlier chapters, established the following rules for monitoring and controlling its projects:

Face-to-Face Meetings—report to GOT 1/mo.

- Deadline pressures
- Sponsors report (all at one meeting, once a month)
- Using charter for high-level planning discussion

  - *Reaffirm purpose and scope*

- Initially report on all projects, eventually cut back to level 3 projects
- Sponsor needs to review database, check with Courtney, and confirm with PM before reporting back to GOT on project status.

Project Management Office—weekly updates/monitoring

- PMO will be generating inquiries for current projects
- Set up weekly (?/every two weeks) reporting from each plant, specific days to spread out work and set up routine. Frequency of reporting to be determined in chartering.
- Follow-up with phone call to clarify (if needed)
- Need to provide discipline to get people thinking ahead for next milestone. (Template for Reporting)

  - *What has happened with project*

  - Progress against milestones vs. what we have actually done

  - *What is going to happen in the next two weeks— expected actions/progress*

  - *Refer to charter*

  - *Any possible/proposed changes for the life of the project*

  - *Risks—revisit major risks (from charter) and ask for any new risks/concerns*

- Updates will begin immediately, be kept in SPDB, phone/face-to-face contact once a month
- Need to keep track of baseline (original) goals in case current plan has changes (agreed upon by sponsor/GOT) for future reference and improvement on other projects

- Microsoft Project may be needed to help monitor/ prioritize projects that have critical paths

GOT

- All GOT members talking with PM face-to-face any time they are at each plant

  - *Could cause confusion/overlap between functional link vs. location leadership*

- When Ted or S is on site they will meet with entire project team (or at *minimum* PM) to talk about all CI projects
- Dialog on measurement—keep issue of project submittal in front of Plant Manager
- What to monitor

  - *Cap-ex—we have 3 forms that are very similar... what are we missing that is keeping us from getting these projects chartered?*

  - *5 steps to improving variable expenses at each site*

  - *Have you identified a project to charter/monitor out of these 5 cost categories?*

  - *Do these projects already exist in our list of projects to select from?*

  - *Need to remove "cost reduction" measurement system (method of project identification) project from matrix and replace with actual projects— name at least one to undertake each quarter*

  - *These will then be subject to reprioritization based on its own merit*

  - *Code appropriately to indicate a cost project (color code on matrix by umbrella issues)*

  - *All other projects—update to charter template based on initial trials, remove redundancy*

  - *Eliminate "future state"*
  - *Lump assumptions with risks*
  - *Layout so that future state is at the end of the first page (for paper version) and tables fit on each page and have 2 1/2 page charter*
  - *Combine roles and responsibilities with signature block*

- Each project proposed needs to be submitted with the following, in writing for consideration of making the matrix list
  - *Descriptive title*
  - *What (scope overview) with future state (1–2 sentences)*
  - *Why, including expected savings level (1–2 sentences)*
- Reprioritization
  - *Has anything changed that would change the weight of the criteria?*
- We have a handful of newly proposed projects to rate against existing criteria that we can't/don't want to wait until next quarter to start—what can we do about it?
  - *Creativity, innovation, empowerment projects that have momentum*
  - *Need to monitor resources to avoid overcommitment*
  - *Come up with a balance for reprioritization—develop general understanding of how much will we tolerate, under what circumstances will we accept new projects in a quarter, how will we fold them back into matrix*
  - *Must not interfere with global priorities*
  - *Provide for local issues to be addressed—allow to push the envelope to help determine where the capacity is met*
  - *Experiment on a local basis to determine what issues are important and propose these issues for global consideration, if they require significant support from outside*
  - *If it requires time or resource that cannot then be utilized on other projects, this needs to be addressed by our process*

- *What is daily work and what is project work?*
- *IT—How to deal with customer requirements*
- This system is not black and white; 80% will fit nicely into classifications, 20% (gray area) will require management decisions
- Quarterly reprioritization
  - *Look at any projects that didn't get chartered/ started last quarter*
  - *Consider projects that were slated for next quarter/this year*
  - *Add any new projects to be considered*
  - *Use matrix system to prioritize for Q2 or just reprioritize to determine if any new projects have surfaced that are significant to delay Q1 projects*
  - *Should we do this once a quarter or more often? Once a quarter would allow for extreme exceptions*
  - *How do we want to set a precedent? On a rolling basis (about a month before start of next quarter), reprioritize 02 projects and only allow for new projects to be started/addressed on special cases*
  - *Determine resources needed for existing 01 projects to continue in 02*
  - *Remove 5 variable expenses and determine if a project is already proposed on matrix. Continue with 5 measurements with the expectation that one will be addressed each quarter (propose additional one for 02, quickly or it will be pushed back to Q3/skunk work)*
  - *Add new projects to matrix list*
- Need for ongoing lessons learned

Source: Elaine Gravatte, D. D. Williamson. Reprinted with permission.

CHAPTER **15**

Finishing the Project and Realizing the Benefits

© STOCK4B GmbH/Alamy

After managing a number of international projects to what I thought was successful completion, it wasn't until I was overseeing a project in Trinidad and Tobago that I fully realized the importance of recognizing the project team and celebrating its success, no matter how simple or grand.

When this particular project opportunity first arose, I had to consult a world atlas to confirm exactly where I was headed. For those of you who don't know, Trinidad and Tobago is the southernmost Caribbean Island, only 7 miles off the coast of Venezuela. The client company, Trinmar Limited, was formed as a joint venture between Texaco and Petrotrin, wholly owned by the government of the Republic of Trinidad and Tobago. Texaco had recently sold its equity share in Trinmar, leaving state-owned Petrotrin on its own to produce 35,000 to 40,000 barrels of oil per day.

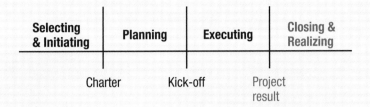

Selecting & Initiating	Planning	Executing	Closing & Realizing

Charter   Kick-off   Project result

**PMBOK®
GUIDE TOPICS**

- Verify scope
- Close procurements
- Close project or phase

Many of the rigs inherited by Trinmar were over 25 years old and declining in production. In addition to building a new organization and strategy, Trinmar faced the difficult decision of whether or not to upgrade existing rigs or invest in building new rigs. This resulted in my working with company executives to prioritize and implement the company's portfolio of projects.

Our consulting team quickly identified over 80 projects the company was considering. Working closely with the executive team, we were able to facilitate a portfolio optimization process to establish the strategic criteria and then help Trinmar evaluate, prioritize, and make final decisions regarding each project. Within 12 months, the company invested in only a few new capital projects, while focusing efforts more aggressively on monthly well output and proactive preventative maintenance measures, resulting in an overall increase in oil and gas production.

Throughout the project, we closely followed project management best practices, and project completion was no exception. Flying in from Miami to meet and discuss the final steps of the project closing process, I was greeted at the airport by the company driver offering a gift bag. Inside was a polo shirt with an embroidered company logo, along with a card.

The day was spent in a series of semi-formal meetings with company executives and the portfolio team. We presented and discussed the culmination of the periodic customer reviews that had been conducted throughout the project—customer feedback and areas for improvement, lessons learned, project results, and approval of the final project deliverables.

The evening had a much different tone, with live calypso music, an assortment of local delicacies, and drinks flowing freely from our tree-house perch. All of the company executives, along with their spouses, were joined by anyone and everyone associated with the project. Several project team members brought relatives, including cousins. Partway into the evening, the CEO stood and made an announcement, describing the project success and complimenting our partnership. He proceeded to personally recognize everyone associated with the project. Each team member received an award of accomplishment and had their picture taken with the CEO for the company newsletter. I have never seen a more positive and uplifting reaction to recognition. The celebration continued late into the evening. Before he left, the CEO pulled me aside and said, "Mr. Miller, on behalf of our company and country, we sincerely thank you for hosting us with this generous celebration".

When I arrived back at the hotel early the next morning after settling the evening's bill, I saw the gift bag and finally opened the card. "Mr. Bruce Miller cordially invites you and your guest to join us in a celebration of our project success," it read.

It was only later that I was sheepishly advised by one of my fellow consultants that he had offered to have our company sponsor the celebration, and that he'd simply not had the chance to tell me in advance. But the true impact of the celebration—reflected in the sincere joy and pride of the project team members as they received the sincere thanks of their CEO—had already proven the value of the event several times over.

Bruce Miller, PMP, managing partner, Xavier Leadership Center, Xavier University

Projects are often started with great enthusiasm. They serve as vehicles to accomplish important organizational objectives. Many things happen during the course of a project that may impact its success. Regardless of the level of success achieved by the project, going out on a strong note is good for everyone involved.

A project moves into the closing stage when its customers verify that the scope is complete and accept the project deliverables. A project can close as planned or be terminated early. In either event, closing activities include securing customer feedback and approval, planning and conducting a smooth transition of project deliverables to a client or into ongoing operations, capturing and sharing lessons learned, performing administrative closure, celebrating success, and providing ongoing support.

When purchasing a new home, buyers and a builder's representative do a "walk through" to inspect the finished product and discuss mechanical functions and features of the home.

15.1 Verify Scope

Verifying scope is "the process of formalizing acceptance of the completed project deliverables."[1] Stakeholders verify that scope is complete with interim deliverables throughout the project and with final deliverables near the end. When the stakeholders formally accept the final project deliverables, the project finishes the executing stage and proceeds into the closing and realizing stage. To illustrate, imagine you have contracted with a construction company to build a new home. Before you close on the house, you want to make sure the house has been properly finished. Therefore, the common practice is to have a "walk through" where as a customer you literally walk through the house with a representative from the building company. The representative points out features and describes how things work. You try light switches, look at the finish, and consider all of the things you wanted (and agreed to pay for) in the house. Often, a few little things are not yet finished, and these can form a "punch list" of items to

Bruce Miller

complete. If the punch list is small enough, as a customer you agree to formally take possession of the house subject to the contractor finishing the punch list items. Once you formally agree the work is complete and agree to take possession, the house becomes an accepted deliverable.

However, if there are major concerns and/or a long punch list, you may decide not to formally accept the house until certain things are complete. Most projects are like this: The customer only formally accepts the deliverables once he or she is convinced they will work as planned. At that point, the buyer provides the seller with a formal written acceptance and the project transitions from the executing stage to the closing stage.

Project managers need to ensure that all work on their project has been successfully completed. They can refer back to the charter, scope statement, WBS, schedule, and all communications plans to verify that everything they said they would do is actually done. Many organizations also use project closeout checklists that itemize typical project activities and/or deliverables. These can be used to assign responsibility to each item concerning project closeout. An example of a project closeout checklist for real estate developer Paul Hemmer Companies is shown in Exhibit 15.1.

15.2 Close Procurements

Closing procurements is "the process of completing each procurement."[2] In some organizations, particularly government organizations, a formal procurement audit is conducted on large projects. This is to ensure that tax money is spent correctly. While the formality may be less on smaller and nongovernmental projects, the concept of a procurement audit is still valid. Someone in the parent organization (often not the project manager) verifies that proper methods were used for all purchasing and that all contracts have been successfully completed. Actually closing the contracts includes verifying that all deliverables were accepted, all money has been properly distributed and accounted for, and all property has been returned.

Terminate Projects Early

Ideally, all projects continue until successful conclusion, with all deliverables meeting specifications and pleasing customers. However, this is not always the case. Sometimes, a project is terminated before its normal completion. Early termination can be by mutual agreement between the contractor and buyer, because one of the parties has defaulted (for cause), or for convenience of the buyer.

MUTUAL AGREEMENTS On some projects, by close-out, not all of the deliverables are yet completed. Remaining deliverables need to be integrated into another project, stopped altogether, or continued as a lesser project or a further phase of the finishing project. If both parties agree to stop the project before its planned completion, a negotiated settlement may take place. If some of the deliverables or documentation are not completed, the project manager may need to negotiate with the customer. Perhaps the customer would rather have most of the capability now rather than all of it later. The project team may have made a larger-than-expected breakthrough in one area and can negotiate with the customer to deliver more in that area and less in another. Ideally both parties agree what deliverables or partial deliverables go to the buyer, what compensation goes to the seller, and any outstanding issues are resolved. If agreement cannot be reached by direct negotiations, either courts or alternative dispute resolution can be used to reach a settlement. Perhaps it is in all parties' best interest to finish the project as is and part as friends.

TERMINATIONS FOR DEFAULT Terminations for default often result from a problem with the project's cost, schedule, or performance. A buyer can also decide to terminate a

EXHIBIT 15.1

PAUL HEMMER COMPANIES PROJECT CLOSEOUT CHECKLIST

Job Number: Substantial Completion Date:

Job Name: Closeout Date:

Project Team:

  Project Manager: Estimator:

  Superintendent: Sales:

  Design:

Item	Who	Target Date	Completion Date
Final Certificate of Occupancy			
Punch List Complete			
Notice of Punch List Completion			
Certificate of Substantial Completion			
Utilities Transferred to Owner			
Notice to Owner on Insurance			
Facility Manual			
As-Built Drawings			
Attach Job Files to Database			
AS400 Cost Clean Up			
Update Projects Database			
Final Retainage Billing			
Release of Subcontractor Retainage			
Complete Subcontractor Evaluations			
Team Close-Out Meeting			
Send Out Owner Survey	Paul Hemmer Jr.		
Close Job in AS400	Accounting		
Bond Release			
Estimating Feedback Cost Report			

Approved for Closeout:

_____   _____   _____

Project Manager   Superintendent   Vice President – Construction

Source: Michael Hemmer, Paul Hemmer Companies. Reprinted with permission.

project early because he or she has lost confidence in the contractor who is performing the project. Good project management practices consistently applied throughout the project can lessen the chance of early termination for cause by managing stakeholder expectations and by delivering what customers want on spec, on time, and on budget.

TERMINATIONS FOR CONVENIENCE OF BUYER Projects can also be cancelled for the convenience of the buyer. This can happen through no fault of the contractor. Sometimes, the buyer faces unexpected difficulties or changing priorities. If a customer's needs change, they might decide that the resources assigned to a project could be more profitably applied to a different project. If a customer decides to terminate a project for convenience, they invoke a contract clause. This clause normally stipulates that the contractor is reimbursed for the money they have spent up to that point and the customer takes ownership of the deliverables in whatever form they currently exist.

Project managers can pursue two avenues to possibly head off early termination. First, a project manager who has been serious about managing stakeholder relationships may be able to find other stakeholders in the customer organization or elsewhere who can provide some funds to keep the project viable—even if it has to be reduced. Second, the project manager can look internally to find ways of continuing with the project, but at lower cost.

Project managers serve as the strongest advocates for their projects throughout the project's life. Considering that most projects face many challenges, this unwavering support is often critical to project success. However, when a project is no longer needed or no longer viable, project managers owe honest and timely communication to their parent organization. Project managers need to present the facts of project progress and make recommendations for early termination if they feel it is warranted.

If a decision is made to terminate a project early, the project manager owes it to his or her team to communicate quickly and honestly. Let the team know as soon as possible and tell them exactly why the decision was made. Care must be taken to ensure that no unjust blame is placed. It is absolutely unethical to have reputations and careers suffer for a termination where the impacted party was not at fault. Once a decision is made and communicated to terminate a project early, much of the remaining work is similar to that for a project that finishes as planned.

15.3 Close Project

As stated in Chapter 1, closing a project entails finalizing all activities needed to finish the project. The remainder of this chapter details what a project team does when finishing a project on time. Customers are asked both to accept the project deliverables and to provide feedback. Lessons learned are captured and shared. Contracts are closed. Participants are reassigned and rewarded. Reports are created and archived. Success is celebrated, and the project team ensures that customers receive the ongoing support they need to successfully use the project deliverables.

A few key challenges arise at the end of projects. One is to keep the right workers engaged until project completion. Some of the final activities are administrative. Often, new projects are starting up that are more exciting.

Write Transition Plan

A project manager may decide to create a transition plan to help the customer successfully use the project deliverables. Project transition plans are a sort of charter for the customer, or an instruction manual on how the customer should use the project deliverables once the project team has completed its work.

The reason a project is performed is that some person or organization wants to be able to use the resulting deliverables. Some project deliverables are created by one group and turned over to another group. Sometimes the group performing the project also uses the results. In either case, a transition plan can ensure that all responsibilities are considered and all deliverables—whether complete or not—are given with appropriate documentation to the people who will use them. If any activities remain incomplete when the deliverables are transitioned, they should be itemized and responsibility for each should be clearly identified. For example, if a home buyer wanted to close on a house before everything is complete, a punch list of remaining items would be determined and the contractor would agree to complete them. A brief transition plan is shown in the Project Management in Action feature at the end of this chapter. A transition plan helps to ensure:

- Quality problems are avoided during the transition.
- The project deliverables transition into their service or operational role.
- The needed maintenance, upgrades, and training take place.[3]

Knowledge Management

The fourth area identified in using the balanced score card approach to controlling and improving projects is growth and innovation. While the portion of this pertaining to team development is covered in Chapter 13, the portion concerning knowledge management is covered here. Knowledge management should occur throughout the project life, but it may be most apparent as a project comes to a close. Project customers, whether internal or external to a company, can provide valuable feedback concerning both the project process and results. Ask them what they think! Exhibit 15.2 is a simple form for asking project customers for their opinions.

CAPTURE LESSONS LEARNED Lessons learned are the useful knowledge gained by a project team as they perform a project and then reflect on both the process of doing the work and the results that transpired. Lessons can include what worked well that the project team members think should be copied and/or adapted for use on future work. Lessons can also include areas for which a different method may yield better results. The project meeting Plus-Delta evaluation template shown in Exhibit 5.14 is an example of capturing lessons learned at the end of a project meeting. Lessons can also be captured at milestones and at the end of a project. On long-duration projects, it is often better to capture lessons frequently because people may not remember clearly what happened months previously. Therefore, most project managers capture lessons learned early and often. A project manager may wish to capture lessons learned first from the core project team and then from all of the stakeholders.

The first step in capturing project-end lessons learned is for the project manager to send an e-mail asking the participants to identify major project issues. Then, the actual meeting begins with each participant writing his or her top issues on a flip chart or other work space where everyone can see them. Once all participants have listed their top issues, the entire group can vote on the top five (or perhaps top 10 on a large project). Then the project manager can go through one top issue at a time by asking leading questions to determine what went wrong and how it might be avoided in future projects.

Likewise, the participants can list significant successes on the project and discuss what caused each. They can then ask what practices can be used to re-create similar successes on future projects.

Some organizations use a standard form for capturing project lessons learned such as the one shown in Exhibit 15.3.

PROJECT CUSTOMER FEEDBACK FORM

Customer:_____   Date:_____

	Rating	**Importance (Rank order 1= most important)**

1. How would you rate the quality of our deliverables?

```
|---+---+---+---|
1           5
Poor   Avg.  Excellent
```
☐

2. How well did we control schedule?

```
|---+---+---+---|
1           5
Poor   Avg.  Excellent
```
☐

3. How well did we control budget?

```
|---+---+---+---|
1           5
Poor   Avg.  Excellent
```
☐

4. How would you rate stakeholder relationships?

```
|---+---+---+---|
1           5
Poor   Avg.  Excellent
```
☐

5. How effective were our communications?

```
|---+---+---+---|
1           5
Poor   Avg.  Excellent
```
☐

6. Overall, how would you rate your satisfaction?

```
|---+---+---+---|
1           5
Poor   Avg.  Excellent
```
☐

7. How can we improve?   _____
                           _____

DISSEMINATE AND USE LESSONS LEARNED The process of capturing and discussing lessons learned is valuable learning for the participants. However, for the remainder of the organization to capitalize on those lessons, a method must be established for documenting and sharing the lessons. More organizations effectively collect lessons learned than effectively disseminate and use them. One problem is deciding how to store the lessons so all workers in a company can easily access them. Some companies have created databases, shared folders, or wikis for this purpose. Many companies that do a good job with lessons learned have one person assigned to "own" the lessons learned database. Every project team that collects lessons then sends the new lessons to this "owner,"

EXHIBIT 15.3

LESSONS LEARNED PROJECT CLOSING DOCUMENT

D.D.Williamson
World Leader in Caramel Color

PROJECT CLOSING DOCUMENT:

Project Number:
Closing Date:

As your project comes to a close, please capture continuous improvements, lessons learned and issues to consider for future projects. Please focus on the positive aspects that would help other teams in the future and you would like to see done again (+) and on things that could be changed/improved upon in the future (Δ) . These learnings will be entered into a database for future reference to help all associates.

Criteria	Plan	Actual	Learnings (+/Δ)
Outcome • Future state achieved? • Success measure (attach graph/data)			
Schedule • Milestones • Completion			
Cost (Cap Ex)			
Hours required: • Project Manager • Sponsor • Core team members • SMEs			

Risks and Countermeasures	
Anticipated	**Unanticipated**

Communication Plan Implementation	
What worked well (+)	**What did not work (Δ)**

Other Learnings	
What worked well (+)	**What did not work (Δ)**

(Continued)

who compares the new lessons with existing lessons and decides whether to modify, combine, or add the lessons. In this manner, the database only grows when unique and useful new lessons are added. Coding each lesson by type of project, stage in project life cycle, issue it concerns, and so on helps future project teams when they search for new lessons to apply. Many organizations find that it is helpful to have a limited number of

EXHIBIT 15.3

LESSONS LEARNED PROJECT CLOSING DOCUMENT (CONTINUED)

Quality Tools Used:

Open Items to Complete/Follow up:

Future Improvement Ideas:

Signature Block with Dates:

Role	Name	Signature	Date
Sponsor		_____	_____
Project Manager		_____	_____
Team Member		_____	_____
Team Member		_____	_____
Team Member		_____	_____
Subject Matter Expert		_____	_____
Other Stakeholder		_____	_____

*Post Project Close (to be captured by sponsor):
- **Recognition and celebration completed**
- **Documentation captured for personnel files (contributions, individual problems, etc.)**

Source: Elaine Gravatte, D.D. Williamson.

categories and have each lesson stored according to the category in which it best fits. The nine *PMBOK® Guide* knowledge areas can be a useful starting point when determining useful categories.

Another problem is that most people are very busy and do not seek lessons learned just for fun. One way to overcome this is for sponsors to only sign charters if lessons from other recently completed projects are included. That forces project teams to consider what lessons they can use. Some lessons learned are more effectively transferred by informal means such as conversations, unscheduled meetings, or having a project team member also serve as a team member on another project. An organization that seriously uses a lessons learned process makes continual improvements in its project management processes. The best lessons learned are only of value if they are used!

EXHIBIT 15.4

CLOSEOUT REPORT TEMPLATE

This deliverable, required for each small project, contains the project charter, the original work breakdown structure, summary of weekly progress reports, and client feedback summary.

PROJECT SUMMARY REPORT FOR PROJECT ―――――――――

TASK OR ITEM DESCRIPTION	SATISFACTORY	UNSATISFACTORY	COMMENTS
A. Project charter updated and included			
B. Original WBS included			
C. Weekly progress report summary included			
D. Client feedback summary included			

Closure of a project entails ensuring that all work has been accomplished, all resources have been reassigned, and all documentation is complete. The project manager and team can review the project charter, WBS, and schedule to make sure that everything that was promised was delivered. They can review the issues log and risk register to ensure all items on both have been addressed. They can review the communications plan to check that all documentation was created. The customer feedback and scope verification should also be reviewed to verify that the customers thought everything was accomplished.

Create the Closeout Report

Many organizations have formal procedures for closeout reports and archiving project records. The closeout report usually includes a summary status of the project that can be gleaned from progress reports. The closeout report also normally includes lessons learned. Finally, the closeout report often contains a review of the project's original justification. Did the project accomplish what it was originally approved to do? This is an important question because many projects change along the line. The exact timing, costs, and deliverables may have changed, but did the project still accomplish its goals? Finally, the project manager needs to ensure that the records are in a workable format and stored in a manner that will allow others in the organization access for lessons learned, financial audits, or other uses.

Organizations often create templates for closeout reports such as the one in Exhibit 15.4.

15.4 Post-Project Activities

Reassign Workers

Project managers owe the members of their team timely updates for their personnel records, honest recommendations and help securing their next assignments, and rapid notification of any issues. Wise project managers know it is not just ethical to treat their members well; if a project manager develops a reputation for taking good care of team members, it becomes much easier to recruit team members for future projects. Helping good workers secure follow-on work is one of the most important things a project manager must do near the end of a project. Many of these workers will be eager to work again for that project manager and will tell others of their good experience.

Celebrate Success and Reward Participants

The successful conclusion of a project should be celebrated for many reasons. Perhaps one way to understand the many reasons is to utilize a play on the very word *celebrate*.

Challenge

Energize

Limit

Exert

Believe

Recognize

Acknowledge

Transition

Ease Stress

When people are reminded of their recent accomplishments, they realize they just met a large challenge and are motivated to undertake new challenges. The team members are frequently energized to finish the last few administrative chores so they are done. By recognizing their accomplishments, they are now ready to say "the project is over; we will limit any additional work on this project." The team members exert themselves to finish the last few items. Celebrations can persuade members to believe they can do just a bit more than they might otherwise think is possible. Celebrations are excellent times to recognize and acknowledge both effort and results. Celebrations mark transition points as people leave one project and move on to another. Finally, celebrations of success ease the stress of working hard for a prolonged period of time trying to accomplish a project.

When a primary project deliverable is quite visible, such as a new building, celebrating right at the project site makes sense. People feel success partly just by observing the deliverable. When the project deliverables are less visible, project managers can still create ceremonial deliverables to demonstrate the project results. Project managers may be able to use specially packaged software, oversized checks, posters of thanks from customers, or other creative means of visualizing project results.

Provide Ongoing Support

Ultimately, a project manager wants to ensure that customers can effectively use the project deliverables. This may include providing ongoing support in the forms of training, change management, and/or other services. A transition plan can guide this support.

Project managers want to create useful project deliverables on time and on budget. They want to turn those deliverables over to capable, satisfied customers who will directly provide more project work in the future and who will enthusiastically tell others how pleased they are.

Ensure Project Benefits Are Realized

Many organizations insist that project managers follow up with customers weeks or months after the project deliverables are in use. One of the most important measures of project success is how well the customers are able to use the deliverables created by the project. When considering the full impact of the project results, project managers are encouraged to consider use by direct customers and other stakeholders (people), and also how they contribute to the other parts of the triple bottom line—profit for the parent company and sustainability of the planet.

15.5 Using MS Project for Project Closure

Just as software such as Microsoft Project 2010 can be useful in planning and managing a project, it can be useful when finishing a project and leveraging the benefits. Specifically, it is helpful to complete and archive the schedule and to capture lessons learned specific to the scheduling process.

1. Complete the schedule to maximize its future usefulness. This includes:

   - Applying performance data
   - Applying approved changes
   - Ensuring all activities are complete

2. Archive the schedule for use as a template or "starter" file.

   - Decide the data format—Microsoft Project or a longer-term format.
   - Decide which baselines to keep (there could be many if there were many approved changes)

3. Capture and publish lessons learned about the effectiveness and efficiency of the employed schedule and cost management processes, such as:

   - Frequency and method of team member performance data collection
   - Activity duration maximum and minimum limits
   - Status reporting to stakeholders
   - Communication technology employed
   - Schedule and cost estimate accuracy
   - Max Units value—maximum availability of a resource for work
   - WBS structure

Summary

Hopefully, most projects will be successfully completed. However, some projects are terminated early either because the customer is dissatisfied or wishes to invest their time and money in a different way. Regardless of whether a project was terminated early or on time, a variety of closeout procedures is required. All activities must be completed, money paid and accounted for, documentation completed and distributed, workers reassigned and rewarded, lessons learned recorded, and success celebrated. A project manager would like to end a project with team members eager to work for him or her again and satisfied customers who will either hire the project manager again or direct other potential customers her way by their enthusiastic singing of her praises.

Key Terms from the *PMBOK® Guide*

Verify scope, 424

Close procurement, 425

Chapter Review Questions

1. All projects end at their planned completion time. True or false?
2. Early termination can stem from _____ and _____.
3. If a project is terminated early, the customer is typically responsible for paying the total cost of the project. True or false?
4. If a project is terminated early, the customer typically gets to take ownership of the deliverables regardless of whether or not they are complete. True or false?
5. If a project terminates early, a project manager must communicate to the team in a manner that is both _____ and _____.

6. It is important to assign blame to individuals on the project team who might be responsible for the early termination of a project. True or false?

7. It is often difficult to keep project members engaged throughout the completion of a project. True or false?

8. A(n) _____ is a good method for collecting opinions about the project.

9. _____ is the process of formalizing acceptance of the completed project deliverables.

10. When stakeholders formally accept the project deliverables, the project moves into the _____ stage.

11. A(n) _____ contains all remaining items that need to be completed on the project.

12. On small projects, the primary time for collecting lessons learned is at the _____ of the project.

13. On large projects, a manager should make sure that lessons learned are captured at various times during the life of the project. True or false?

14. Lessons learned should contain both _____ and _____ that were experienced during the life of the project.

15. _____ is the process of completing and settling the contract, including the resolution of any open items and the closing of each subcontract.

Discussion Questions

1. Give two examples of why a project might be terminated early for cause and two examples of why a project might be terminated early for convenience.

2. How can a project manager help to prevent a project from being terminated early?

3. A project manager is in the finishing stage of his or her project. It is apparent that one of the project's deliverables will not be completed before the project is wrapped up. What options does the project manager have for this uncompleted deliverable?

4. Provide an example of how poor escalation of a project problem can create additional problems.

5. How does celebrating the completion of a project benefit the project manager?

PMBOK® Guide Questions

1. The process of formalizing acceptance of the completed project deliverables is _____.
   a. verify scope
   b. close procurements
   c. close project
   d. none of the above

2. An auditor from the parent company verifying that all contracts are completed and proper methods were used for purchasing is an example of _____.
   a. verify scope
   b. close procurements
   c. close project
   d. none of the above

3. Terminations for _____ often result from a problem with the project's cost, schedule, or performance.
   a. default

   b. convenience of the buyer
   c. mutual agreement
   d. lack of confidence

4. If a buyer decides to terminate a project early, his or her responsibilities to the contractor are laid out in the project's _____.
   a. work breakdown structure (WBS)
   b. communications plan
   c. contract clause
   d. scope statement

5. During the administrative closure of a project, the team and project manager may wish to review the _____.
   a. project charter
   b. work breakdown structure (WBS)
   c. project schedule
   d. all of the above

Exercises

1. Utilizing the ideas in Exhibit 15.3, create a project closeout checklist for a project of one of the following types:

   • Information systems

   • Research and development
   • Quality improvement
   • Organizational change

Example Project

For your example project, complete the following:

1. Capture customer feedback concerning your project using the questions from Exhibit 15.1 or other questions of your choice.
2. Capture lessons learned from your project to date using the questions from Exhibit 15.2 or other questions of your choice. Show how you will use these lessons both to improve the remainder of your project and for the next project on which you may work.
3. Create a transition plan so that the recipients of your project deliverables will be capable and enthusiastic users. Secure client acceptance of your project.

References

A Guide to the Project Management Body of Knowledge (PMBOK® Guide), 4th ed. (Newtown Square, PA: Project Management Institute, 2008).

Aldag, Ramon J. and Loren W. Kuzuhara, *Mastering Management Skills: A Manager's Toolkit*. (Mason, OH: Thomson South-Western, 2005).

Barclay, Corlane, "Knowledge Management Practices in IT Projects: An Exploratory Assessment of the State of Affairs in the Caribbean," *Proceedings, Project Management Institute Research and Education Conference 2010*.

Chiocchio, Francois, "Project Team Performance: A Study of Electronic Task and Coordination Communication," *Project Management Journal* 38 (1) (March 2007): 97–109.

Daft, Richard L., *Management*, 9th ed. (Mason, OH: South-Western Cengage Learning, 2010).

Dalton, Aaron, "Human Capital," *PMNetwork* 20 (8) (August 2006): 70–75.

Dobson, Michael S. and Ted Leemann, *Creative Project Management* (New York: McGraw-Hill Company, 2010).

Flanes, Steven W. and Ginger Levin, *People Skills for Project Managers* (Vienna, VA: Management Concepts, Inc., 2001).

Hildebrand, Carol, "Give Peace a Chance," *PMNetwork* 21 (4) (April 2007): 38–45.

Hynes, Martin D., III, "Information Management: For the Project Manager in an Information Age," in Joan Knutson, ed., *Project Management for Business Professionals: A Comprehensive Guide* (New York: John Wiley & Sons, 2001), pp. 179–199.

Kloppenborg, Timothy J. and Joseph A. Petrick, *Managing Project Quality* (Vienna, VA: Management Concepts, Inc., 2002).

Kloppenborg, Timothy J., Arthur Shriberg, and Jayashree Venkatraman, *Project Leadership* (Vienna, VA: Management Concepts, Inc., 2003).

Knutson, Joan, "Transition Plans," *PMNetwork* 18 (4) (April 2004): 64.

Logue, Ann C., "Dysfunction Junction," *PMNetwork* 20 (8) (August 2006): 76–81.

Lussier, Robert N. and Christopher F. Achua, *Leadership: Theory, Application, Skill Development*, 4th. ed. (Mason, OH: South-Western Cengage Learning, 2010).

Mayer, Margery, "Expectations Management: Reconfirming Assumptions," in Joan Knutson, ed., *Project Management for Business Professionals: A Comprehensive Guide* (New York: John Wiley & Sons, 2001), pp. 179–199.

McGary, Rudd, *Passing the PMP Exam: How to Take It and Pass It* (Upper Saddle River, NJ: Prentice Hall PTR, 2006).

Milosevic, Dragan Z., *Project Management Toolbox: Tools and Techniques for the Practicing Project Manager* (New York: John Wiley & Sons, 2003).

Mulcahy, Rita, *PMP Exam Prep: Rita's Course in a Book for Passing the PMP Exam*, 5th ed. (RMC Publications, Inc., 2005).

Nance-Nash, Sheryl, "Everybody's a Critic," *PMNetwork* 20 (10) (October 2006): 36–42.

Pritchard, Carl L., "Project Termination: The Good, the Bad and the Ugly," in David I. Cleland, ed., *Field Guide to Project Management*, 2nd ed. (Hoboken, NJ: John Wiley & Sons, 2004), pp. 503–520.

Reich, Blaize Horner, Andrew Gemino and Chris Sauer, "Modeling the Knowledge Perspective of IT Projects," *Project Management Journal* 39 (2) (2008): S4–S14.

Senge, Peter, Richard Ross, Bryan Smith, Charlotte Roberts, and Art Kleiner, *The Fifth Discipline*

Fieldbook: Strategies and Tools for Building a Learning Organization (New York: Doubleday, 1994).

Wang, Xiaojin and Lonnie Pacelli, "Pull the Plug," *PMNetwork* 20 (6) (June 2006): 38–44.

Whitten, Neil, "Celebrate," *PMNetwork* 19 (8) (August 2005): 21.

Wiewiora, Anna, Liang Chen and Bambang Trigunarsyah, "Inter- and Intra-Project Knowledge Transfer: Analysis of Knowledge Transfer Techniques," *Proceedings, Project Management Institute Research and Education Conference 2010*.

Endnotes

1. *PMBOK® Guide* 452.
2. *PMBOK® Guide* 428.
3. Dobson, Michael S. and Ted Leemann, *Creative Project Management* (New York: McGraw-Hill Company, 2010), p. 216.

PROJECT MANAGEMENT *IN ACTION*

Transition Plan for Beech Acres Knowledge Management Project

Transition Plan Summary

One of the deliverables that the student team has developed for Beech Acres (BA) is a work breakdown schedule that details the collection of information from employees and input of the information into a knowledge management (KM) system that BA has already developed. This project plan details such steps as gaining employee buy-in, assigning KM champions, and maintaining data.

Gaining Employee Buy-In

Employee buy-in will be obtained in two phases. Phase 1 involves sending out an informative e-mail to all employees that explains what KM is, how it will benefit the organization, and the plans for implementing the system. Phase 2 will involve training sessions that further reinforce what a KM system is, its benefits, and the mechanics of how it will be implemented and function at BA.

Assigning KM Champions

The KM champions will be the functional managers of different units at BA. The primary reason for this is that a program such as the implementation of a KM system should have highly visible leaders. By using management, employees will see that the organization is taking the matter seriously, which will assist in gaining employee buy-in.

Maintaining Data

Maintenance of the KM system is the responsibility of the KM librarian. The most logical choice for this position would be the IT person who created the database being assisted by the KM champions or designees from each functional area.

Related to maintaining the data is making sure that new information is continually being added to the system. This can be accomplished in one of two ways. One method would have the KM champions and their teams continually being on the lookout for information, data, processes, and so forth that belong in the KM library. The second method would be to let everyone at BA know that the KM system is a living, dynamic system where all knowledge regarding BA operations belongs. This can be reinforced through the training programs. There could be an online form that allows anyone to submit information to the system. Once filled out, any information being put into the KM library would have to be given approval by the person's functional KM champion and the KM librarian.

Employee Usage

Once the system is up and running, the employees must use the system for its intended purpose for the project to be successful. Measuring the usage of the system by employees will show Beech Acres management how successful the project was.

Source: Beech Acres Parenting Center.

PMBOK® Guide Area

The numbers in color refer to the text page where the process is defined.

PM Framework 1

Portfolio and Program Mgt 2

Projects and Strategic Planning 2

Project Life Cycle 1, 3

Organizational Influences 3

Knowledge Areas	Project Management Process Groups				
	Initiating	**Planning**	**Executing**	**Monitoring and Controlling**	**Closing**
Integration	Develop Project Charter 4	Develop Project Management Plan 5, 11	Direct and Manage Project Execution 14	Monitor and Control Project Work 14 Perform Integrated Change Control 6, 14	Close Project or Phase 15
Scope		Collect Requirements 6 Define Scope 6 Create WBS		Verify Scope 15 S.S. Control Scope 14	
Time		Define Activities 7 Sequence Activities 7 Estimate Activity Resources 8 Estimate Activity Durations 7, 8 Develop Schedule 7, 8		Control Schedule 14	
Cost		Estimate Costs 9 Determine Budget 9		Control Costs 9, 14	
Quality		Plan Quality 11	Perform Quality Assuarance 11, 14	Perform Quality Control 11, 14	
Human Resource		Develop Human Resource Plan 3, 8	Acquire Project Team 5, 13 Develop Project Team 5, 13 Manage Project Team 5, 13		
Communications	Identify Stakeholders 4, 5	Plan Communications 5	Distribute Information 14 Manage Stakeholder Expectations 5, 13	Report Performance 14	

Knowledge Areas	Project Management Process Groups				
	Initiating	Planning	Executing	Monitoring and Controlling	Closing
Risk		Plan Risk Management 10 Identify Risks 4, 10 Perform Qualitative Risk Analysis 4, 10 Perform Quantitative Risk Analysis 10 Plan Risk Responses 4, 10		Monitor and Control Risks 14	
Procurement		Plan Procurements 12	Conduct Procurements 12	Administer Procurements 12	Close Procurements 15

Source: Adapted from *A Guide to the Project Management Body of Knowledge (PMBOK® Guide), 4th ed.* (Newtown Square, PA: Project Management Institute, Inc., 2008): 43.

Strengths Themes as Used in Project Management

Theme*	Project Mgmt Version
Achievement	You must accomplish something every day. You have great stamina and internal motivation. When you finish one task, you quickly want to work on another so you can complete milestones. You manage proactively by setting plans, working to achieve them, and asking people to report progress.
Activity	You want to make decisions and start quickly. Results of early actions will provide input into following decisions and actions. You want to be judged by your actions and results. You encourage others to action and help them overcome obstacles. You create a sense of urgency and energy when needed.
Adaptability®	You live in the moment. Decisions made now create the future. You keep making progress in the face of unknowns. You balance conflicting demands of tasks and people, of various stakeholders, of risks, and of proposed changes. You understand reality, bring emotional stability, and do not need to control everything.
Analysis	You are objective, search for reasons, and want to see proof. You ask questions, research intensively, and then develop logical explanations. In ambiguous situations you simplify concepts, recognize patterns, understand limits, describe causes and effects, and establish order. You fearlessly make honest decisions based upon facts.
Arrangement	You are organized yet flexible. You have defined values and priorities. You arrange people and other resources, improving work processes to best achieve your primary objectives. You thrive on cooperation and collaboration in complex settings. You depend on honest, timely, and transparent information to make rapid adjustments.
Belief®	You possess enduring core values that guide and energize your behavior. You walk the talk as a dependable and trustworthy sounding board. You are committed to work and people, encouraging your team to display high ethics and to help others.
Command®	You take charge, directly sharing your opinions and aligning people to your goals. You challenge others and lead forcefully when necessary. You thrive in crisis, making rapid decisions and encouraging others to take risks.
Communication®	You speak and write clearly. You place high value on human interaction, talking with—not to—people. You tell stories to enliven your ideas, gain commitment, and maintain enthusiasm. You ask good questions, listen well, and help others express their feelings. You "think out loud" and encourage collaboration.
Competition®	You want to outperform everyone either individually or as a team. This invigorates you and helps you achieve your ambitions. You define, measure, and ensure progress. You select contests you believe you can win and then celebrate your successes.
Connectedness®	You believe everything happens for a reason and is part of something larger. Your thinking extends beyond your self-interests. You see no boundaries and celebrate when people find common ground around shared meaning. Your hopefulness helps you achieve personal and organizational goals.
Context®	You look back to understand the original purpose and past actions that shaped the present. You share stories to connect with people. You ask questions and take time to understand root causes. This perspective gives you confidence to decide what is enduring and what can change, inspiring confidence in followers.
Deliberation	You are a private person who identifies and analyzes risks, plans carefully, avoids problems, trusts your instincts, and makes no hasty decisions. You help others consider all factors in sensitive decisions. You have a few close friends in whom you confide. You only praise when it is well deserved.
Development	You see potential and small improvements in people. You enjoy observing, advising, encouraging, challenging, and improving inexperienced people. You encourage teams to try, fail, and try again, helping them set appropriate expectations and celebrate success. By mentoring individuals you develop effective teams.
Discipline™	The world can be chaotic, but you create predictability with plans, priorities, routines, timelines, and structures. Through your attention to detailed planning and consistent execution, you create order and deliver effective and timely results. You carefully monitor progress, adhere to uncompromising standards, and celebrate excellence.

* All theme names are trademarked by Gallup, Inc.

Theme*	Project Mgmt Version
Empathy™	You are highly instinctive and feel the emotions of others so strongly it is as if they were your own. You do not necessarily agree with others' choices, but you understand. You respect everyone's feelings and help them express them. People trust your discretion and you help resolve conflict.
Consistency™	You treat everyone the same, with clear rules based upon values. You create a predictable and calm environment. You value loyalty and routines and accurately document requirements.
Focus™	You work best when you know what is important and have a clear end goal. You define outcomes, determine priorities, set intermediate goals, follow through, make mid-course corrections, and deliver results. You concentrate deeply and are impatient with delays. You help others set goals and concentrate on critical issues.
Futurism	You are intrigued by the future and enjoy describing your conceptions of it. Your emotional yet realistic contemplations help others to understand how supporting your project helps them accomplish their goals.
Harmony®	You look for a common ground to find agreement. You value expert perspectives, perhaps merging ideas as long as you retain your basic values and shared sense of purpose. You have a calm, facilitating manner, avoid confrontation, bring practical knowledge, and strive for consensus.
Ideation®	You are energized by finding new perspectives on familiar situations. You are innovative and creative, love to brainstorm, and strive to make things better. You take calculated risks and share excitement. You create useful plans, overcoming resource limits and risks.
Inclusiveness	You feel the pain of those who are left out and understand the power of a larger team of active and unified participants in which all voices are heard. You are accepting, as you feel we are all equally important. You ensure information and decision making are widely shared.
Individualization®	You perceive differences in how people think, feel, and behave. You bring out the best in each person and foster effective, diverse teams in which everyone is encouraged to do what they do best. As a mentor and leader, you treat each person according to their unique needs and dreams.
Input®	Your curiosity enables you to be a great researcher. You enjoy being up to date and gathering and sharing information. You view whatever you collect—ideas or tangible items—as resources. You may be an expert or good at making concepts seem real.
Intellection®	You enjoy taking quiet time to read and think. While your thoughts may be focused or diverse, you often generate wisdom and clarity. You help your team make better decisions by asking great questions, giving your honest opinions, and engaging in deep conversations.
Learning	You are energized by the process of learning and considering possibilities. You excel on short project assignments and as a change agent where you need to learn quickly. As you continuously study and improve you gain confidence. You help your team improve by co-learning with them and tracking lessons learned.
Maximization	Your greatest joy is taking good performance of your own, of another individual, or of a team to a higher level. You prefer to capitalize upon raw talent. You strive for quality and excellence.
Positivity®	You always see and communicate the good. You lift others with your enthusiasm. Life and work are fun. You give people frequent praise and focus on making progress no matter the situation. Your hope for the future, good humor, and eagerness to celebrate make you a valued team member.
Relating	You enjoy being around your close friends, learning about their feelings and goals. You derive satisfaction from working hard with these friends. You honor trust and show respect.
Responsibility®	You enjoy volunteering, and when you commit, no one needs to check your progress. You have the highest ethics, usually fulfilling your many obligations, and making amends when you cannot. You are a serious, dedicated role model. You may feel overwhelmed, but you are satisfied when you complete commitments.
Restoration	You diagnose problems, determine root causes, and implement solutions. Bad news with no sugar coating motivates you, whether it concerns people or things. You can identify risks and devise contingency plans in advance.
Self-Assurance®	Your confidence inspires others. You research issues and listen to experts, but then make up your own mind and act decisively. You completely commit to critical challenges not because you have no fear, but because you know someone needs to lead and you are bold and resolute.
Significance™	You want to make a lasting difference in this world and be known for it. You dream big dreams, need affirmation, fear failure, but are comfortable with risk and public scrutiny. You champion others' needs and achievements. You want to associate with other top performers.
Strategy	You plan backward from goals to various means of accomplishing them. You see patterns where others see chaos. You research alternatives and select one—often avoiding potential problems. You see the big picture and are flexible concerning how to achieve it.
Woo™	You enjoy meeting new people and discovering common interests or other connections. The thrill of meeting a new person may be greater than developing a deep relationship. You naturally put people at ease and facilitate interchange of ideas. You ask questions and get others to support your goals.

* All theme names are trademarked by Gallup, Inc.

Glossary Terms from the *PMBOK® Guide*

A

Acceptance criteria   Criteria, including performance requirements and essential conditions, that must be met before project deliverables are accepted.

Acquire project team   The process of obtaining human resources needed to complete the project.

Activity   A component of work performed during the course of a project.

Actual cost (AC)   Total costs actually incurred and recorded in accomplishing work performed during a given time period.

Administer procurements   Process of managing procurement relationships, monitoring contract performance, and making changes and corrections as needed.

Analogous estimating   An estimating technique that uses the cost along with measures of scale such as size, weight, or complexity from a previous project to estimate cost for a similar, future project.

Assumptions   Factors that, for planning purposes, are considered to be true, real, or certain without proof or demonstration.... Project teams frequently identify, document, and validate assumptions as part of their planning process. Assumptions generally involve a degree of risk.

B

Backward pass   The calculation of late finish dates and late start dates for the uncompleted portions of all schedule activities.

Baseline   The approved time phased plan ... plus or minus approved project ... changes ... Usually used with a modifier.

Bottom-up estimating   A method of estimating project costs in which the work is decomposed into more detail. An estimate is prepared of what is required to meet the requirements of each of the lower, more detailed pieces of work, and these estimates are then aggregated into a total quantity for the project.

Budget   The approved estimate for the project or any work breakdown structure component or any schedule activity.

Budget at completion (BAC)   The sum of all budgeted values established for the work to be performed on a project.... The total planned value of the project.

Business case   Provides the information needed from a business standpoint to determine if the project is worth the investment.

C

Change control board   A formally constituted group of stakeholders responsible for reviewing, evaluating, approving, delaying, or rejecting changes to the project.

Change control system   Collection of formally documented procedures that define how project deliverables and documentation will be controlled, changed, and approved.

Change control   Identifying, documenting, approving or rejecting, and controlling changes to the project baselines.

Change request   Request to expand or reduce the project scope, modify policies, processes, plans, or procedure, modify costs or budgets, or revise schedules … Only formally documented changes are processed and only approved change requests are implemented.

Close procurement   The process of completing each procurement.

Close project   The process of finalizing all activities across all of the project process groups to formally close a project or phase.

Closing   Formalized acceptance of project outcomes and ending the project.

Co-location   An organizational placement strategy where the project team members are physically located close to one another to improve communication, working relationships, and productivity.

Common cause   A source of variation that is inherent in a system and predictable. On a control chart, it appears as the part of the random process variation … and would be considered normal or not unusual.

Communications management   Generating, collecting, disseminating, storing, and disposing of timely and appropriate project information.

Communications management plan   The document that describes: the communication needs and expectations for the project; how and in what format information will be communicated; when and where each communication will be made; and who is responsible for providing each type of communication.

Conduct procurements   The process of obtaining seller responses, selecting a seller, and awarding a contract.

Configuration management system   A collection of formally documented procedures used to … identify, document, control, and track characteristics of project deliverables.

Constraint   An applicable restriction or limitation, either internal or external to the project, that will affect the performance of the project.

Contract   A mutually binding agreement that obligates the seller to provide the specified product/service and obligates the buyer to pay for it.

Control schedule   The process of monitoring the status of the project update progress and managing changes to the schedule baseline.

Control scope   The process of monitoring the status of the project and product scope and managing changes to the scope baseline.

Control   Comparing actual performance with planned performance, analyzing variances, assessing trends to effect process improvements, evaluating possible alternatives, and recommending appropriate corrective action as needed.

Corrective actions   Documented direction for executing the project work to bring expected future performance of the project work in line with the project management plan.

Cost management   Planning, estimating, budgeting, and controlling costs.

Cost management plan   The document that sets out the format and establishes the activities and criteria for planning, structuring, and controlling the project costs.

Cost performance baseline   A specific version of a time-phased budget used to compare actual expenditures to planned expenditures to determine if preventive or corrective action is needed to meet the project objectives.

Cost performance index (CPI)   A measure of cost efficiency on a project. It is … EV divided by AC.

Cost variance (CV)   A measure of cost performance on a project. It is … $EV - AC$.

Cost-plus-fixed-fee contract   A type of cost-reimbursable contract where the buyer reimburses the seller for the seller's allowable costs (allowable costs are defined by the contract) plus a fixed amount of profit (fee).

Cost-plus-incentive-fee contract   A type of cost-reimbursable contract where the buyer reimburses the seller for the seller's allowable costs (allowable costs are defined by the contract) and the seller earns a profit if it meets defined performance criteria.

Cost-reimbursable contracts   A type of contract involving payment by the buyer to the seller for the seller's actual costs, plus a fee typically representing the seller's profit.

Crashing   A specific type of project schedule compression technique performed by taking action to decrease the total project duration after analyzing a number of alternatives to determine how to get the maximum schedule duration for the least additional cost.

Critical chain method A schedule network analysis technique that modifies the project schedule to account for limited resources. The critical chain method mixes deterministic and probabilistic approaches to schedule network analysis.

Critical path The sequence of activities that determines the duration of the project … the longest path through the project.

Critical path method (CPM) A schedule network analysis technique used to determine the amount of scheduling flexibility on various network paths in the project schedule network, and to determine the minimum total project duration.

D

Defect repair Formally documented identification of a defect in a project component with a recommendation to either repair the defect or replace the component.

Define activity The process of identifying the specific actions to be performed to produce the project deliverables.

Define scope The process of developing a detailed description of the project and product.

Deliverable Any unique and verifiable product, result, or capability to perform a service that must be produced to complete a process, phase, or project. Often … subject to approval by the project sponsor or customer.

Delphi technique An information gathering technique used as a way to reach a consensus of experts on a subject … Responses are summarized and recirculated for further comment.

Determine budget The process of aggregating the estimated costs of individual activities or work packages to establish an authorized cost baseline.

Develop project team The process of improving the competencies and interaction of team members to enhance project performance.

Develop schedule The process of analyzing activity sequences, durations, resource requirements, and schedule constraints to create the project schedule.

Direct and manage project execution The process of executing the work defined in the project management plan to achieve the project's requirements defined in the project scope statement.

Distribute information The process of making relevant information available to project stakeholders as planned.

Duration The total number of work periods (not including holidays or other non-work time) required to complete a schedule activity.

E

Early finish date (EF) The earliest possible point in time on which uncompleted portions of a schedule activity can finish, based upon the schedule network logic, the data date, and any schedule constraints.

Early start date (ES) The earliest possible point in time on which uncompleted portions of a schedule activity can start, based upon the schedule network logic, the data date, and any schedule constraints.

Earned value (EV) The value of completed work expressed in terms of approved budget assigned to that work.…

Earned value management A management methodology for integrating scope, schedule, and resources, and for objectively measuring project performance and progress.

Estimate activity durations The process of approximating the number of work periods needed to complete individual activities with estimated resources.

Estimate activity resources The process of estimating the type and quantities of material, people, equipment, or supplies required to perform each activity.

Estimate at completion (EAC) The expected total cost of … the project when the defined scope of work will be completed. It is AC plus ETC.

Estimate cost The process of developing an approximation of the cost of the resources needed to complete project activities.

Estimate to complete (ETC) The expected cost needed to complete all the remaining work for … the project.

Estimate A quantified assessment of the likely amount.… It should always include an indication of accuracy.

Executing Directs and manages people and other resources to accomplish project work.

F

Fast tracking   A specific project schedule compression technique that changes network logic to … perform schedule activities in parallel.

Finish-to-finish (FF)   The logical relationship where completion of work of the successor activity cannot finish until the completion of work of the predecessor activity.

Finish-to-start (FS)   The logical relationship where initiation of work of the successor activity depends on completion of work of the predecessor activity.

Firm-fixed-price contracts   A type of fixed-price contract where the buyer pays the seller a set amount as defined in the contract, regardless of the seller's cost.

Fixed-price contracts   A type of contract involving a fixed total price for a well-defined product.

Fixed-price-incentive-fee contracts   A type of contract where the buyer pays the seller a set amount as defined by the contract, and the seller can earn an additional amount if the seller meets defined performance criteria.

Forward pass   The calculation of the early start and early finish dates for the uncompleted portions of all network activities.

Free float   The amount of time a schedule activity can be delayed without delaying the early start of any immediately following schedule activities.

Functional manager   Someone with management authority over an organizational unit…. The manager of any group that actually makes a product or performs a service.

Functional organization   A hierarchical organization where each employee has one clear superior, staff are grouped by areas of specialization, and managed by a person with expertise in that area.

G

Gantt chart   A graphic display of schedule related information.

H

Human resources management   Acquiring, developing, and managing the project team.

I

Identify risks   The process of determining which risks might affect the project and documenting their characteristics.

Identify stakeholders   The process of identifying all people or organizations impacted by the project, and documenting relevant information regarding their interests, involvement, and impact on project success.

Initiating   Defines and authorizes a project or a project phase.

Integration management   Unifying and coordinating the other knowledge areas by creating and using tools such as charters, project plans, and change control.

Issue   A point or matter in question or in dispute, or a point or matter that is not settled and is under discussion or over which there are opposing views or disagreements.

L

Lag   A modification of a logical relationship that directs a delay in the successor activity.

Late finish date (LF)   The latest possible point in time that a schedule activity may be completed, based upon the schedule network logic … without violating a schedule constraint or delaying the project completion date.

Late start date (LS)   The latest possible point in time that a schedule activity may begin, based upon the schedule network logic … without violating a schedule constraint or delaying the project completion date.

Lead   A modification of a logical relationship that allows an acceleration of the successor activity.

Lessons learned   The learning gained from the process of performing the project.

Lessons learned knowledge base   A store of historical information and lessons learned about both the outcomes of previous project selection decisions and previous project performance.

M

Manage project team   The process of tracking team member performance, providing feedback, resolving issues, and coordinating changes to enhance project performance.

Manage stakeholder expectations The process of communicating and working with stakeholders to meet their needs and addressing issues as they occur.

Matrix organization Any organizational structure in which the project manager shares responsibility with the functional managers for assigning priorities and directing work of persons assigned to the project.

Milestone A significant point or event in the project.

Milestone schedule A summary-level schedule that identifies the major schedule milestones or significant points or events in the project.

Monitor Collect project performance data with respect to a plan, produce performance measures, and report and disseminate performance information.

Monitor and control project work The process of monitoring and controlling the processes required to initiate, plan, execute, and close a project to meet the performance objectives.

Monitor and control risk The process of implementing risk response plans, tracking identified risks, monitoring residual risks, identifying new risks, and evaluating risk processes throughout the project.

Monitoring and controlling Collects data and checks progress to determine any needed corrective actions.

Monte Carlo analysis A technique that computes, or iterates, the project cost or project schedule many times using input values selected at random from probability distributions of possible costs or durations, to calculate a distribution of possible total projects cost or completion dates.

O

Opportunity A condition or situation favorable to the project … a risk that will have a positive impact on a project objective if it occurs.

P

Parametric estimating An estimating technique that uses a statistical relationship between historical data and other variables to calculate project costs.

Perform integrated change control The process of reviewing all change requests, approving changes, and managing changes to deliverables, organizational process assets, project documents, and project management plan.

Perform qualitative risk analysis The process of prioritizing risks for further analysis or action by assessing and combining their probability and impact.

Perform quality assurance (QA) The process of auditing the quality requirements and the results from quality control measurements to ensure appropriate quality standards and operational definitions are used.

Perform quality control (QC) The process of monitoring and recording results of executing the quality activities to assess performance and recommend necessary changes.

Perform quantitative risk analysis The process of numerically analyzing the effect of identified risks on overall project objectives.

Performing organization The enterprise whose personnel are most directly involved in doing the work of the project.

Plan communications The process of determining project stakeholder information needs and defining a communications approach.

Plan procurement The process of documenting project purchasing decisions, specifying the approach, and identifying potential sellers.

Plan risk management The process of defining how to conduct risk management activities for a project.

Plan risk responses The process of developing options and actions to enhance opportunities and reduce threats to project objectives.

Planned value (PV) The authorized budget assigned to the scheduled work to be accomplished….

Planning Defines and refines objectives and plans actions to achieve objectives.

Planning quality The process of identifying quality requirements and/or standards for the project and product, and documenting how the project will demonstrate compliance.

Precedence diagramming method (PDM) A schedule network diagramming technique in which the scheduled activities are represented by boxes or nodes. Schedule activities are graphically linked by one or more logical relationships to show the sequence in which the activities are performed.

Predecessor activity   The scheduled activity that determines when the logical successor activity can begin or end.

Preventive actions   Documented direction to perform an activity that can reduce the probability of negative consequences associated with project risks.

Process   A set of interrelated actions and activities performed to achieve a specified set of products, results, or services.

Procurement documents   Those documents utilized in bid and proposal activities, which include buyer's invitation for bid, invitation for negotiations, request for information, request for quotation, request for proposal, and seller's responses.

Procurement management   Processes necessary to purchase or acquire products, services, or results from outside the project team.

Procurement management plan   The document that describes how procurement processes from developing procurement documentation through contract closure will be managed.

Procurement statements of work   Describes the procurement item in sufficient detail to allow prospective sellers to determine if they are capable of providing the products, services, or results.

Product scope   The features and functions that characterize a product, service, or result.

Project   A temporary endeavor undertaken to create a unique product, service, or result.

Project charter   A document issued by the project initiator or sponsor that formally authorizes the existence of a project, and provides the project manager with the authority to apply organizational resources to project activities.

Project life cycle   A collection of generally sequential project phases whose name and number are determined by the control needs of the organization or organizations involved in the project.

Project management   The application of knowledge, skills, tools and techniques to project activities to meet project requirements.

Project management office (PMO)   An organizational body or entity assigned various responsibilities related to the centralized and coordinated management of those projects within its domain. The responsibilities of the PMO can range from providing project management support functions to actually being responsible for the direct management of a project.

Project management plan   A formal, approved document that defines how the project is executed, monitored, and controlled. It may be summary or detailed and may be composed of one or more subsidiary management plans and other planning documents.

Project management process group   A logical grouping of the project management processes described in the PMBOK® Guide. They include initiating, planning, executing, monitoring and controlling, and closing processes. Collectively, these five process groups are required for any project, have clear dependencies, and must be performed in the same sequence on each project, independent of the application area or the specifics of the applied project life cycle.

Project management team   Members who are directly involved in project management activities.

Project manager   The person assigned by the performing organization to achieve the project objectives.

Project schedule   The planned dates for performing schedule activities and the planned dates for meeting schedule milestones.

Project scope   The work that must be performed to deliver a product, service, or result.

Project scope statement   A definition of the project … documents the characteristics and boundaries of the project and its associated products and services, as well as methods of acceptance and scope control.

Projectized organization   Any organizational structure in which the project manager has full authority to assign projects, apply resources, and direct work of persons assigned to the project.

Q

Quality   The degree to which a set of inherent characteristics fulfills requirements.

Quality management   Quality planning, assurance, and control.

Quality management plan   Describes how the project management team will perform the performing organization's quality policy.

R

Report performance   The process of collecting and distributing performance information, including status reporting, progress measurements and forecasting."

Requirements   A condition or capability that must be met … to satisfy … needs, wants, and expectations of the sponsor, customer, and other stakeholders.

Reserve   A provision in the project management plan to mitigate cost and/or schedule risk.

Resource leveling   Any form of schedule network analysis in which scheduling decisions … are driven by resource constraints.

Responsibility assignment matrix   A structure that relates the project organizational breakdown structure to the work breakdown structure to help ensure that each component of the project's scope of work is assigned to a person or team.

Risk   An uncertain event or condition that, if it occurs, has a positive or negative effect on a project's objectives.

Risk management   Risk identification, analysis, response planning, and monitoring and control.

Risk management plan   The document describing how project risk management will be structured and performed on a project.

Risk register   The document containing the results of the qualitative risk analysis, quantitative risk analysis, and risk response planning. The risk register details all identified risks, including description, category, cause, probability of occurring, impact(s) on objectives, proposed responses, owners, and current status.

Rolling wave planning   A form of progressive elaboration planning where the work to be accomplished in the near term is planned in detail … while the work far in the future is planned at a relatively high level … the detailed planning for work to be performed … in the near future is done as work is being completed during the current time period.

Root cause analysis   An analytical technique used to determine the basic underlying reason that causes a variance or defect or risk. A root cause may underlie more than one variance or defect or risk.

S

Schedule performance index (SPI)   A measure of schedule efficiency on a project. It is … EV divided by PV.

Schedule variance   A measure of schedule performance on a project. It is … EV minus PV.

Scope   The sum of all products, services, and results to be provided by the project.

Scope change   Any change to the project scope. A scope change almost always requires an adjustment to the project cost or schedule.

Scope creep   Adding features and functionality (project scope) without addressing the effects of time, costs, resources, or without customer approval.

Scope management   Determining all the work and only the work necessary for project completion.

Sequence activities   The process of identifying and documenting dependencies among schedule activities.

Special cause   A source of variation that is not inherent in the system, is not predictable, and is intermittent. It can be assigned to a defect.… On a control chart, points outside the control limits, or non-random patterns within the control limits indicate it.

Sponsor   The person or group that provides the financial resources, in cash or in kind, for the project.

Staffing management plan   The document that describes when and how human resource requirements will be met.

Stakeholders   Persons or organizations … that are actively involved in the project, or whose interests may be positively or negatively affected by … the project.

Start-to-finish (SF)   The logical relationship where completion of the successor schedule activity is dependent on the initiation of the predecessor schedule activity.

Start-to-start (SS)   The logical relationship where initiation of the successor schedule activity depends on the initiation of the predecessor schedule activity.

Statement of work   A narrative description of products or services to be provided by the project.

Successor activity   The schedule activity that follows a predecessor activity, as determined by their logical relationship.

SWOT analysis   An information gathering technique used to examine the project from perspectives of each project's strengths, weaknesses, opportunities, and threats to increase the breadth of risks considered.

T

Threat   A condition or situation unfavorable to the project ... a risk that will have a negative impact on a project objective if it occurs.

Time and material contracts   A type of contract that is a hybrid ... containing aspects of both cost-reimbursement and fixed-price contracts.

Time management   Defining, sequencing, estimating duration, and resourcing work activities as well as developing and controlling the schedule.

Total float   The total amount of time a schedule activity may be delayed from its early start date without delaying the project finish date.

Triggers   Indications that a risk has occurred or is about to occur.

V

Validated deliverables   Components or products that have been evaluated ... to ensure they comply with specific requirements.

Value engineering   A creative approach used to optimize project costs, save time, increase profits, improve quality, expand market share, solve problems, and/or use resources more effectively.

Variance   A quantifiable deviation, departure, or divergence away from a known baseline or expected value.

Variance analysis   A method for resolving the total variance in a set of scope, cost, and schedule variables into specific component variances....

Verify scope   The process of formalizing acceptance of the completed project deliverables.

Virtual team   A group of persons with a shared objective who fulfill their roles with little or no time spent meeting face to face.

W

WBS component   An entry in the WBS that can be at any level.

WBS dictionary   A document that describes each component in the WBS. For each component, the WBS dictionary includes a brief scope description, defined deliverable(s), a list of associated activities, and sometimes other information.

Work breakdown structure (WBS)   A deliverable-oriented hierarchical decomposition of the work to be executed by the project team to accomplish the project objectives and create the required deliverables. It organizes and defines the total scope of the project. Each descending layer represents an increasingly detailed definition of the project work.

Work package   A deliverable ... at the lowest level of each branch of a WBS. The work package includes the schedule activities and schedule milestones required to complete the work package deliverable.

Index

Terms from the *PMBOK® Guide* are set in **bold** in this index.

A

AC (actual cost), 406
acceptance criteria, 88–89, 91, 302
accrual accounting, 247
acquire project team, 353
action items, 128–130
active listening, 360, 366
activities, 170–171
   assignment of resources to, 214–216
   control schedule, 171
   define, 170
   develop schedule, 171
   estimate activity durations, 171
   estimate activity resources, 171
   sequence, 171
activity, 170
activity durations, estimating, 171
activity on arrow (AOA), 172
activity on node (AON), 172
activity resources, estimating, 171
activity sequencing, 171
   and project schedules, 183–187
activity-based costing, 254
actual cost (AC), 406
ADM (arrow diagramming method), 172
administer procurements, 338
Advanex Inc., 289
affinity diagram, 321–322
agile project life cycle model, 64
agile project planning, 227
agile software development methods, 239–241
"all-crash" schedule, 223
alternative logical dependencies, 179–180
analogous estimating, 250
AOA (activity on arrow), 172
appreciative inquiry, 138–139
arrow diagramming method (ADM), 172
Asplund, Jim, 352

assumptions, 89, 252
Atos Origin, 52–53
attribute vs. variable, 398
audits, 395, 425
authority, 6
auto/manual scheduling, 227

B

BAC (budget at completion), 407
background, 88, 91, 93
backward pass, 185
balanced scorecard approach, 386
Baldridge, Malcolm, 293
Ball Aerospace & Technologies Corp., 82–83
baseline, 154, 314
BCR (benefit-cost ratio), 37
Beech Acres Parenting Center, 438
Beedle, Mike, 239
benefit-cost ratio (BCR), 37
bottom-up cost modeling, 258
bottom-up estimating, 250–251
budget, definition of, 17. *See also* project budgets
budget at completion (BAC), 407
budget estimates, 90, 96, 249
Built Green Home at Suncadia, Washington, 28–29, 112–113
business case, 35, 88, 92

C

capable vs. in control, 398
CAPM (Certified Associate in Project Management), 8
cash accounting, 247
cash flow, 257
cause-and-effect diagram, 278–279, 400
CCPM (critical chain project management), 226–227
celebrate, 433
Central Intelligence Agency (CIA), 3

Certified Associate in Project Management (CAPM), 8
change control, 390
change control board, 390
change control system, 156
change request, 157–158
change request form, 157
check chart, 400
chief projects officer (CPO), 67–68
CIA (Central Intelligence Agency), 3
Cincinnati Children's Hospital Medical Center, 30
close procurements, 425–427
close project, 19
closeout checklist, 426
closeout report, 432
closing document, 430–431
closing process group, 8
closing stage, 6
CMI Homes, 112–113
collecting requirements, 143–145
co-located teams, 214
co-location, 56
commitment, 91, 98
common cause, 302
   vs. special cause, 398
communications management plan
communications management, 9
   considerations, 123–124
   cultural differences, 130–131
   definition of, 115
   global teams, 130–131
   knowledge management, 125
   matrix, 124–125
   project quality planning, 314
   purposes of, 122–123
   virtual teams, 130
communications matrix, 124–125
communications plan, 74

communications technologies, 131–134
  example, 132–134
  types of, 132
conduct procurements, 331–336
  definition of, 331
  evaluating prospective suppliers, 332–334
  information for potential suppliers, 332
  sources for potential suppliers, 332
  supplier selection, 334–335
configuration management system, 311
conflict management, 373–377
conflicts, 366
  managing, 373–377
  negotiation, 375–377
  project management plan and, 309–310
  resolution process and styles, 374–375
  sources of, 373–374
constraints, 89, 252
construction project life cycle model, 63
contingency reserve, 256, 271
contracts
  cost-plus-fixed-fee contract, 337
  cost-plus-incentive-fee contract, 337
  cost-reimbursable contracts, 337
  firm-fixed-price contracts, 336
  fixed price contracts, 336
  fixed-price-incentive-fee contacts, 336–337
  time and material contracts, 337
  types of, 336–338
control, 301, 389
control chart, 403
control schedule, 171
cost baseline, 254
cost control, 257–258, 404–408
cost estimates
  accuracy and timing of, 248
  activity-based costing, 254
  analogous estimating, 250
  bottom-up estimating, 250–251
  budget, 249
  definitive, 249
  issues, 251–254
  life cycle costing, 254
  methods of estimating costs, 249–251
  order of magnitude estimates, 248
  parametric estimating, 250
  types of, 248–249
  value engineering, 253–254
  variation, 252–253
  vendor bid analysis, 253
cost management, 9
cost management plan, 244
cost performance baseline, 255
cost performance index (CPI), 408
cost variance (CV), 407
cost-plus-fixed-fee contract, 337
cost-plus-incentive-fee contract, 337
cost-reimbursable contracts, 337
costs
  aggregating, 255–256

direct vs. indirect, 245–246
estimate vs. reserve costs, 247
fixed vs. variable, 245
internal vs. external, 246–247
other cost classifications, 246–247
recurring vs. nonrecurring, 246
regular vs. expedited, 246
types of, 245–247
CPI (cost performance index), 408
CPM (critical path method), 171–172
crashing, 221–223
criteria
  determining mandatory, 38
  evaluating projects, 39–40
  identifying potential, 38
  weighting, 38–39
critical chain method, 226–227
critical chain project management (CCPM), 226–227
critical path
  activities, 205
  crashing and, 221–222
  definition of, 183
  enumeration method and, 187
  float and, 186–187
  reducing, 220–221
  schedules, 193–200
critical path method (CPM), 171–172
cross-functional teams, 213
Crystal, 64
cultural differences, 130–131
currency fluctuations, 254
customer feedback form, 429
customer tasks, 73–74
CV (cost variance), 407

D

D. D. Williamson, 26–27, 48–51, 191, 420–421
data, 303
defect repair, 310
define activity, 147, 170
define scope, 145–146
define-measure-analyze-improve-control (DMAIC) Model, 63, 296, 297
definitive estimates, 249
deliverables
  close procurements and, 425–427
  definition of, 88
  scope verification and, 424–425
  validated, 310
  in work breakdown structure (WBS), 152–153
Deming, W. Edwards, 293
develop project team, 355, 368
develop schedule, 171
direct vs. indirect costs, 245–246
discipline, 371
DMAIC (define-measure-analyze-improve-control) Model, 63, 296, 297
DuPont, Engineering Services Division, 172

duration, 180–183
  learning curves, 181–183
  problems and remedies, 181

E

EAC (estimate at completion), 408
early finish date (EF), 185
early start date (ES), 185
earned value (EV), 406
earned value management, 404–408
  terms, 406–446
EF (early finish date), 185
effective speaking, 360
empowered performance, 303–305
enumeration method, 187
ES (early start date), 185
estimate, 247
estimate activity durations, 171
estimate activity resources, 171, 210
estimate at completion (EAC), 408
estimate cost, 244
estimate to complete (ETC), 408
estimates. *See* cost estimates
ETC (estimate to complete), 408
EV (earned value), 406
EVO, 64
evolutionary, 64
executing process group, 8
executing stage, 6
expedited vs. regular costs, 246
external vs. internal costs, 247

F

facilitator, 14, 71–72
fact-based management, 302–303
  aspects of, 302–303
fast tracking, 221, 224–225, 226
FF (finish-to-finish), 179
financial issues, 403–408
  control scope, 404
  schedule and cost control, 404
financial models, 37–38
  advantages and disadvantages, 38
  benefit-cost ratio (BCR), 37
  internal rate of return (IRR), 37
  net present value (NPV), 37
  payback period (PP), 37
finish-to-finish (FF), 179
finish-to-start (FS), 178
firm-fixed-price contracts, 336
fishbone diagram, 278–279
fixed price contracts, 336
fixed vs. variable costs, 245
fixed-price-incentive-fee contacts, 336–337
float and critical path, 186–187
flow chart, 399–400
flow-down objectives, 31
forward pass, 184, 185
FS (finish-to-start), 178
functional manager

definition of, 6
role in matrix organization, 57–59
functional organization, 54–55

G

Gallup Consulting, 350–352
Gantt charts
aggregating costs, 255
example, 193
in MS project, 158–159, 232–234
project schedules, 192
resourcing projects, 216
global teams, 130–131
Gravatte, Elaine, 17
ground rules, 364–368
Guide to the Project Management Body of Knowledge, A (PMBOK® Guide), 7–9, 19, 20, 114, 296, 335, 431, 439–440
guiding principles, 28–29

H

hard skills, 5–6
histograms, 216, 401–403
Hixson Architecture and Engineering., 61
human resources management, 9

I

identify stakeholders, 117
IFB (invitation for bid), 331
indirect vs. direct costs, 245–246
information, project supply chain management, 343–344
information distribution, 392–393
information gathering, 272–274
information systems (IS) project life cycle model, 64
initiating process group, 8
initiating stage, 6
insurance, 338
integration management, 8
internal costs vs. external costs, 246–247
internal project issues
directing and managing project execution, 387–388
distributing information, 392–393
monitoring and controlling project work, 389
monitoring and controlling risk, 391
performing integrated change control, 390–391
project control, 389–390
reporting performance, 393–395
internal rate of return (IRR), 37
International Organization for Standardization, 295
invitation for bid (IFB), 331
IRR internal rate of return (IRR), 37
IS (information systems) project life cycle model, 64
ISO 9001:2008, 295
issue, 128

issues log, 128–129, 371
issues management, 127–130

J

Juran, Joseph, 293

K

Kato, Yuichi, 289
Kennedy, John F., 29
kickoff project
meeting activities, 313–314
preconditions, 312
Kling, Paul, 385
knowledge areas
communications management, 9
cost management, 9
human resources management, 9
integration management, 8
procurement management, 9
quality management, 9
risk management, 9
scope management, 8
time management, 9
knowledge management, 125, 428
known knowns, 256, 271
known unknowns, 256, 271

L

lags, 179
late finish date (LF), 185
late start date (LS), 185
Lavigne, Lydia, 83
leadership, 362, 368–371
leads, 178
lean purchasing, 343
learning curves, 181–183
lessons learned
capturing project-end, 428
definition of, 90
disseminate and use, 429–432
instructions, 98
lessons learned knowledge base, 90
LF (late finish date), 185
life cycle costing, 254
logical dependencies, 178–180
logistics, 343
LS (late start date), 185
Lundberg, Grey, 112–113

M

make or buy decisions, 330
Malcolm Baldrige National Quality Award, 294–295
manage stakeholder expectations, 371
management reserve, 256
matrix organization, 56–59
Microsoft® (MS) Project. *See* MS Project
Midland Insurance Company, 60
milestone schedule
constructing in MS Project, 103–104

constructing project charter, 91
cost control, 257
definition of, 88
example, 94
steps in constructing, 92–95
milestones, 176, 257, 302, 371
Miller, Bruce, 424
mission statement, 30
monitor, 389
monitoring and controlling process group, 8
monitoring and controlling project work, 19
Monte Carlo analysis, 190–191
MS Project, 16
constructing **milestone schedule**, 103–104
for critical path schedules, 193–200
initialize project, 101–103
introduction to, 99–100
to monitor and control projects, 408–414
plan and measure projects, 11
for project baselines, 314–316
project budgets, 258–260
for project closure, 434
for resource allocation, 228–234
start project using, 99–104
for **work breakdown structures (WBS)**, 158–162
Mueller, Ralf, 131
mutual agreements, 425

N

negotiation, 375–377
net present value (NPV), 37
network diagrams, 172, 197–199
networked organization model, 348–349
Nonaka, Ikujiro, 239
nonrecurring vs. recurring costs, 246
Nunes, Brenda, 112–113

O

O'Brochta, Michael, 3
OCIP (owner-controlled insurance program), 338
opportunity, 269
order of magnitude estimates, 248
organizational culture
culture of parent organization, 60
culture of project, 61–62
impact on projects, 59–62
types of power in, 60
organizational structures
comparison of, 58
types of, 54–59
outsourcing, 214
owner-controlled insurance program (OCIP), 338

P

parametric estimating, 250
Pareto chart, 400, 401
partnering, 338, 340–342

payback period (PP), 37

PDCA (plan-do-check-act) model, 126, 301

PDM (precedence diagramming method), 172

performance assessments, 370

performing organization, 268

performing quality assurance, 395

personal culture, 60

PERT (program evaluation and review technique), 171–172

phased delivery, 64

plan communications, 115, 122–125

plan procurement, 329

definition of, 329

make or buy decisions, 330

outputs of planning, 329–330

outsourcing issues, 331

reasons to make or buy, 330–331

plan-do-check-act (PDCA) model, 126, 301

planned value (PV), 406

planning process group, 8

planning quality, 292

planning stage, 6

Plus-Delta method, 128–129, 428

PMBOK® Guide (A Guide to Project Management Body of Knowledge), 7–9, 19, 20, 114, 296, 335, 431, 439–440

PMI (Project Management Institute), 7–8

PMI Code of Ethics and Professional Conduct, 62

Polaris Weapons System, 172

portfolio, 32

alignment, 31–41

assessing ability to perform projects, 35

Identifying potential projects, 35–36

methods for selecting projects, 36–37

program, 32–33

projects and subprojects, 33–35

power culture, 60

Power Delivery Engineering, Duke Energy, 385

PP (payback period), 37

precedence diagramming method (PDM), 172

precedence diagramming method (PDM), 172

precision vs. accuracy, 398

predecessor activity, 178

prevention vs. inspection, 397–398

preventative vs. corrective action, 398

process, 299

process control, 301

process groups, 8

process improvement, 395

process management, 299–301

procurement audit, 425

procurement documents, 331

procurement management, 9

procurement management plan, 329

procurement statements of work, 330

product scope, 87, 142

Profound Knowledge System, 293

program, 32–33

program evaluation, 188–190

program evaluation and review technique (PERT), 171–172

project budgets, 242–265

cost control, 257–258

cost management plan, 244

determine budget, 254–257

estimate cost, 244

MS Project, 258–260

project charter

constructing, 91–98

decision matrix, 86

definition of, 16, 84

elements in, 85–91

information systems enhancement, 107–110

project title, 87

purposes of, 84–85

ratifying, 99

project classifications

application, 13

industry, 11

size, 11–12

timing of project scope clarity, 12–13

project completion, 424–438

close procurements, 425–427

close project, 427–432

post-project activities, 432–434

verify scope, 424–425

project conflicts, 373–377

negotiation for, 375–377

project management plan and, 309–310

resolution process, 374–375

sources of, 373–374

styles of handling, 374–375

project costs

estimating issues, 251–254

volume curve and, 246

project customer tradeoff matrix, 10

project determination, 386–421

balanced scorecard approach, 386

customer issues, 395–403

D. D. Williamson's rules for project control, 420–421

financial issues, 403–408

internal project issues, 387–395

replanning, 414–415

project executive-level roles, 14, 65–68

sponsor, 66–67

steering team, 65–66

project kickoff, 312–314

affinity and relationship diagrams for, 321–322

project life cycle, 6–7

definition of, 6

example, 7

models of, 62–65

stages of, 6

project life cycle,risks, 271

project management

definition of, 4

history of, 4–5

Project Management in Action

affinity and relationship diagrams for project kick off, 321–322

appreciative inquiry to understand stakeholders, 138–139

budget optimization, 264–265

D. D. Williamson, 48–51

D. D. Williamson's rules for project control, 420–421

development of inventory system project, 166–167

implications in networked organization model, 348–349

information systems enhancement project charter, 107–110

project schedule emphasizing critical path activities, 205

project teams, 382–383

risk management, 287–288

Scrum, 239–241

Skyline Chili, 24–25

transition plan for Beech Acres knowledge management plan, 438

TriHealth, 80–81

Project Management Institute (PMI), 7–8

project management office (PMO)

definition of, 14

project executive-level roles, 67–68

role in matrix organization, 58

project management plan

definition of, 115

developing, 114–116

project management process group, 8

Project Management Professionals (PMPs), 99

project management, real world examples

Atos Origin, 52–53

Built Green Home at Suncadia, Washington, 28–29, 112–113

Cincinnati Children's Hospital Medical Center, 30

D. D. Williamson, 26–27, 48–51

DuPont, Engineering Services Division, 172

Skyline Chili, 24–25

TriHealth, 80–81

U. S. Navy, Special Program Office, 172

project management team, 15

project management-level roles, 68–74

customer, 72

facilitator, 14, 71–72

functional manager, 14, 68

project managers, 14, 68–71

senior customer representative, 14

project managers

challenges, 70–71

communication channels, 70

definition of, 14

desired behaviors, 68–70
judgment calls, 71
managing stakeholder expectations, 371–372
methods for building individual and project team capability, 362–364
power and leadership, 368–370
project team development, 355–356
role in matrix organization, 57–59
project meeting agenda template, 126–127
project meeting management, 126–130
action items, 128–130
agenda template, 126–127
issues management, 127–130
minutes template, 127
plan-do-check-act (PDCA) model, 126
project meeting minutes template, 127
project procurement management. *See also* project supply chain management
processes, 329–331
project proposal, 43
project quality
definition, 295–296
tools, 309, 310–311
project quality core concepts
fact-based management, 302–303
process management, 299–301
stakeholder satisfaction, 298–299
project quality planning, 293–312
baseline and, 314
communications plan requirements and, 314
core project quality concepts, 296–305
development of contemporary quality concepts, 293–296
management plan, 306–312
tools, 309, 310–311
project risk planning, 266–289
identifying risks, 272–276
risk analysis, 276–279
risk management, 268–272
risk responses, 279–283
project risk strategies
accept risk, 281–282
avoid risk, 280–281
enhance opportunity, 282
exploit opportunity, 282
mitigate risk, 281
research risk, 282
share opportunity, 282
transfer risk, 281
project roles
associate-level, 15
executive-level, 14
management-level, 14
project schedules, 17, 168–205
construction of, 173–174
define activities for, 174–176
developing, 183–187
duration, 180–183
Gantt charts, 192

history of, 171–172
limitations of, 173–174
purposes of, 171
sequence activities for, 176–180
uncertainty in, 187–191
using MS Project for critical path schedules, 193–200
project scope, 87, 139
project scope statement, 329
project stakeholders. *See* **stakeholders**
project supply chain management, 324–350
administer procurements, 338
components of, 328
conduct procurements, 331–335
conflicts, 338–339
contracts, 336–338
decisions, 328–329
factors, 328
improving, 338–344
introduction to, 326–329
partnering, 338, 340–342
plan procurement, 329–331
project team members, 353–355
negotiation for, 353–354
on-boarding, 354–355
preassignment, 353
project teams, 350–383
acquiring, 353–355
assessing capability of, 360–362
assessing individual member capability, 359–360
characteristics of, 357–359
core team members, 74–75
development activities, 355–368
development stages, 355–356
fitting people into, 75
ground rules, 364–368
leadership and management outcomes, 370–371
managing and leading, 368–371
managing stakeholder expectations, 371–372
performance assessments of individuals and, 370
project conflicts, 373–377
roles, 74–75
subject matter experts (SME), 75
success factors, 360–362
project time management, 170–171
project title, 87
project tools, scalability of, 13
project work
description of, 5–7
statement, 146
projectized organization, 55–56
projects
benefits, 433
budgeting, 242–265
classifying, 11–13
completion, 424–438

conflict management, 373–377
culture of, 61–62
defining success and failure, 10–11
definition of, 4
goals and constraints, 9–10
Identifying potential, 35–36
methods for selecting, 36–37
vs. operations, 5
prioritizing, 40–41
resourcing, 206–241
schedules, 17, 168–205
securing, 42–43
selecting and prioritizing, 9
subprojects and, 33–35
types of, 11–13
using financial model to select, 37–38
using scoring model to select, 38–40
PV (planned value), 406

Q

qualitative risk analysis, 276–277
quality, 9
quality assurance (QA), 308–309, 395
quality baseline, 307–308
quality control (QC), 309, 396–403
monitoring, 396–397
terms, 397–398
tools, 398–403
quality gurus, 293
quality management, 9
quality management plan, 306
quality assurance (QA), 308–309
quality baseline, 307–308
quality control (QC), 309
quality policy, 306–307
tools, 309, 310–311
quality policy, 306–307
Quality Trilogy, 293–294
quantitative risk analysis, 279

R

R&D (Research and Development) project life cycle model, 63
RACI chart, 215
rapid protyping, 64
realizing stage, 6
reassignments, 432
recurring vs. nonrecurring costs, 246
regular vs. expedited costs, 246
relationship diagram, 321–322
request for information (RFI), 331
request for proposal (RFP), 331, 334
request for quotation (RFQ), 331
requirements, 87
Research and Development (R&D) project life cycle model, 63
reserve, 247
reserve needs, 256
reserve vs. estimate costs, 247
resource leveling, 218
resource needs, estimating, 171, 210

resource overloads
  dealing with, 217–218
  methods for resolving, 218–222
resources
  availability, 211–212
  overloads, 217–220
  potential, 210–211
  responsibilities, 216
resourcing projects, 206–241
  abilities needed, 208–209
  activity assignments, 214–216
  activity vs. resource-dominated schedules,
    209
  alternative scheduling methods, 225–228
  considerations, 209
  estimating resource needs, 209
  Gantt chart, 216
  project schedules, 220–225
  project team composition issues, 213–214
  resource allocation, 228–234
  resourcing overloads, 217–230
  staffing management plan, 209–213
responsibility, 6
responsibility assignment matrix (RAM),
  215
reverse phase schedules, 227
review technique, 188–190
RFI (request for information), 331
RFP (request for proposal), 331, 334
RFQ (request for quotation), 331
risk, 89
risk analysis, 276–279
  cause-and-effect diagram, 278–279
  cause-and-effect relationships, 277
  major and minor risks, 276–277
  qualitative risk analysis, 276–277
  techniques, 279
risk management, 9
  categories and definitions, 270–272
  information gathering, 272–274
  planning, 268–272
  relationships, 275
  reviews, 274
  risk register, 275–276
  roles and responsibilities, 270
  satellite development project,
    287–288
risk management plan, 269
risk register, 275–276
risk response planning, 279
risk strategies. *See* project risk strategies
risks, identifying, 272–276
role culture, 60
rolling wave planning, 227
root cause analysis, 275
run chart, 402, 403

S

Sampat, Rachana, 53
sample vs. population, 398
sanity tests, 312

SAPTURF (Super Absorbent Polymer Turf),
  324–326
satellite development project, 287–288
Schawk, Clarence W., 206
Schawk, Inc., 206–208
schedule performance index (SPI),
  407–408
schedule variance (SV), 407
schedules. *See also* project schedules
  activity vs. resource-dominated, 209
  "all-crash", 223
  auto/manual, 227
  control, 171
  cost control and, 404
  crashing, 221–223
  development of, 171
  earned value management for, 404–408
  fast tracking, 221, 224–225, 226
  reverse phase, 227
Schwaber, Ken, 239
scope, 9
scope change, 404
scope creep, 87
scope management, 8
scope overview, 87–88, 91, 92
scope planning, 140–167
  change control, 154–158
  collecting requirements, 143–145
  introduction to, 142–143
  scope definition, 145–146
  using MS Project in, 158–162
  work breakdown structure (WBS),
    146–154
scope verification, 424–425
scoring models, 38–40
  evaluating criteria, 39–40
  mandatory criteria, 38
  potential criteria, 38
  sensitivity analyses, 40
  weighting criteria, 38–39
Scrum, 64, 239–241
selecting stage, 6
sensitivity analyses, 40
sequence activities, 171
SF (start-to-finish), 179–180
sigma, 295
signatures, 91, 98
SIPOC (supplier-input-process output-
    customer) model, 299–301
six sigma, 295–296, 297
Six Sigma
  DMAIC (define-
    measure-analyze-improve-control)
    model and, 63
  milestone schedule and **acceptance cri-
    teria template**, 95
Skyline Chili, 24–25
slack, 186
SME (subject matter experts), 75, 127
soft skills, 5–6
Soldavini, Patti A., 208

sourcing, 343
SOW (statement of work), 35, 141
special cause, 302
  vs. common cause, 398
spending approvals, 90, 96
SPI (schedule performance index),
  407–408
sponsor, 14
  definition of, 66–67
sprints, 239
Sputnik, 29
SS (start-to-start), 179
stakeholder analysis, 298
stakeholder list, 90, 97
stakeholder satisfaction, 298–299
stakeholders, 4
  appreciative inquiry and, 138–139
  examples of, 117
  identify, 116–117
  input from, 143–145
  managing expectations of, 371–373
  prioritize, 117–120
  quality standards based upon, 298
  relationships with, 120–122
  satisfaction, 298–299
  satisfaction sayings, 298–299
  specific priorities, 269
  stakeholder analysis, 298
  understanding, 116–120
standard deviation, 295
start-to-finish (SF), 179
start-to-start (SS), 179
statement of work (SOW), 35, 141
steering team, 65–66
strategic analysis. *See* SWOT analysis
strategic objectives, 31
strategic planning process, 28–31
  flow-down objectives, 31
  guiding principles, 28–29
  strategic analysis, 28
  strategic objectives, 31
strengths, weaknesses, opportunities, and
    threats (SWOT). *See* SWOT analysis
StrengthsFinder, 75
subject matter experts (SME), 75, 127, 304
subprojects, 33–35
successor activity, 178
Super Absorbent Polymer Turf (SAPTURF),
  324–326
supplier-input-process output-customer
  (SIPOC) model, 299–301
SV (schedule variance), 407
SWOT analysis, 28, 42

T

Takeuchi, Hirotaka, 239
task culture, 60
team operating principles, 90
team operating principles instructions, 97
teams. *See also* project team members;
    project teams

co-located, 214
cross-functional, 213
virtual, 130, 214
Teradata, 140–142
termination
for convenience of buyer, 427
for default, 425–427
early, 425
mutual agreements, 425
Tetrault, Chris, 326
Texas Medical Center News, 267
Texas Medical Center (TMC), 266–267
third parties, 342–343
threat, 269
time and material contracts, 337
time management, 9
time value of money, 254
tolerance vs. control limit, 398
total float, 186
total quality management (TQM), 293–294
TQM (total quality management), 293–294
transition plans, 427–428
triggers, 275
TriHealth, 80–81, 85
Turner, J. Rodney, 131
two-pass method, 184–187

U

U. S. Navy, Special Program Office, 172
unk unks, 256, 272
unknown knowns, 256
unknown unknowns, 256, 272

V

validated deliverables, 310
value engineering, 253–254
variance, 389
variance analysis, 404
variation, 252–253, 302
variable vs. fixed costs, 245
vendor bid analysis, 253
verify scope, 424–425
virtual teams, 130, 214
vision, 29
VOC (voice of the customer), 143
voice of the customer (VOC), 143
volume curve and project costs, 246

W

WBS (work breakdown structure). *See*
work breakdown structure (WBS)
WBS component, 151
WBS dictionary, 151

Wendler, Rhonda, 267
work breakdown structure (WBS), 141,
142, 146–154
constructing, 151–154
definition of, 17, 146–147
formats, 148–149
in project data, 196
project teams and, 362
in project time management, 170
reasons for use, 147–148
resource responsibilities and, 215
using MS Project for, 158–162
work packages in, 150–151
work packages, 150–151
wrap ups, 338

X

Xavier University, 424
XP, 64

Z

Zozer Inc., 3